Praise for *Deep Learning for Coders with fastai and PyTorch*

If you are looking for a guide that starts at the ground floor and takes you to the cutting edge of research, this is the book for you. Don't let those PhDs have all the fun—you too can use deep learning to solve practical problems.

> —Hal Varian, Emeritus Professor, UC Berkeley;
> Chief Economist, Google

As artificial intelligence has moved into the era of deep learning, it behooves all of us to learn as much as possible about how it works. Deep Learning for Coders provides a terrific way to initiate that, even for the uninitiated, achieving the feat of simplifying what most of us would consider highly complex.

> —Eric Topol, Author, Deep Medicine;
> Professor, Scripps Research

Jeremy and Sylvain take you on an interactive—in the most literal sense as each line of code can be run in a notebook—journey through the loss valleys and performance peaks of deep learning. Peppered with thoughtful anecdotes and practical intuitions from years of developing and teaching machine learning, the book strikes the rare balance of communicating deeply technical concepts in a conversational and light-hearted way. In a faithful translation of fast.ai's award-winning online teaching philosophy, the book provides you with state-of-the-art practical tools and the real-world examples to put them to use. Whether you're a beginner or a veteran, this book will fast-track your deep learning journey and take you to new heights—and depths.

> —Sebastian Ruder, Research Scientist, Deepmind

Jeremy Howard and Sylvain Gugger have authored a bravura of a book that successfully bridges the AI domain with the rest of the world. This work is a singularly substantive and insightful yet absolutely relatable primer on deep learning for anyone who is interested in this domain: a lodestar book amongst many in this genre.

—*Anthony Chang, Chief Intelligence and Innovation Officer,*
Children's Hospital of Orange County

How can I "get" deep learning without getting bogged down? How can I quickly learn the concepts, craft, and tricks-of-the-trade using examples and code? Right here. Don't miss the new locus classicus for hands-on deep learning.

—*Oren Etzioni, Professor, University of Washington;*
CEO, Allen Institute for AI

This book is a rare gem—the product of carefully crafted and highly effective teaching, iterated and refined over several years resulting in thousands of happy students. I'm one of them. fast.ai changed my life in a wonderful way, and I'm convinced that they can do the same for you.

—*Jason Antic, Creator, DeOldify*

Deep Learning for Coders is an incredible resource. The book wastes no time and teaches how to use deep learning effectively in the first few chapters. It then covers the inner workings of ML models and frameworks in a thorough but accessible fashion, which will allow you to understand and build upon them. I wish there was a book like this when I started learning ML, it is an instant classic!

—*Emmanuel Ameisen, Author,*
Building Machine Learning Powered Applications

"Deep Learning is for everyone," as we see in Chapter 1, Section 1 of this book, and while other books may make similar claims, this book delivers on the claim. The authors have extensive knowledge of the field but are able to describe it in a way that is perfectly suited for a reader with experience in programming but not in machine learning. The book shows examples first, and only covers theory in the context of concrete examples. For most people, this is the best way to learn. The book does an impressive job of covering the key applications of deep learning in computer vision, natural language processing, and tabular data processing, but also covers key topics like data ethics that some other books miss. Altogether, this is one of the best sources for a programmer to become proficient in deep learning.

—*Peter Norvig, Director of Research, Google*

Gugger and Howard have created an ideal resource for anyone who has ever done even a little bit of coding. This book, and the fast.ai courses that go with it, simply and practically demystify deep learning using a hands-on approach, with pre-written code that you can explore and re-use. No more slogging through theorems and proofs about abstract concepts. In Chapter 1 you will build your first deep learning model, and by the end of the book you will know how to read and understand the Methods section of any deep learning paper.

—*Curtis Langlotz, Director, Center for Artificial Intelligence in Medicine and Imaging, Stanford University*

This book demystifies the blackest of black boxes: deep learning. It enables quick code experimentations with a complete python notebook. It also dives into the ethical implication of artificial intelligence, and shows how to avoid it from becoming dystopian.

—*Guillaume Chaslot, Fellow, Mozilla*

As a pianist turned OpenAI researcher, I'm often asked for advice on getting into Deep Learning, and I always point to fastai. This book manages the seemingly impossible—it's a friendly guide to a complicated subject, and yet it's full of cutting-edge gems that even advanced practitioners will love.

—*Christine Payne, Researcher, OpenAI*

An extremely hands-on, accessible book to help anyone quickly get started on their deep learning project. It's a very clear, easy to follow and honest guide to practical deep learning. Helpful for beginners to executives/managers alike. The guide I wished I had years ago!

—*Carol Reiley, Founding President and Chair, Drive.ai*

Jeremy and Sylvain's expertise in deep learning, their practical approach to ML, and their many valuable open-source contributions have made then key figures in the PyTorch community. This book, which continues the work that they and the fast.ai community are doing to make ML more accessible, will greatly benefit the entire field of AI.

—*Jerome Pesenti, Vice President of AI, Facebook*

Deep Learning is one of the most important technologies now, responsible for many amazing recent advances in AI. It used to be only for PhDs, but no longer! This book, based on a very popular fast.ai course, makes DL accessible to anyone with programming experience. This book teaches the "whole game", with excellent hands-on examples and a companion interactive site. And PhDs will also learn a lot.

—*Gregory Piatetsky-Shapiro, President, KDnuggets*

An extension of the fast.ai course that I have consistently recommended for years, this book by Jeremy and Sylvain, two of the best deep learning experts today, will take you from beginner to qualified practitioner in a matter of months. Finally, something positive has come out of 2020!

—*Louis Monier, Founder, Altavista;*
former Head of Airbnb AI Lab

We recommend this book! *Deep Learning for Coders with fastai and PyTorch* uses advanced frameworks to move quickly through concrete, real-world artificial intelligence or automation tasks. This leaves time to cover usually neglected topics, like safely taking models to production and a much-needed chapter on data ethics.

—*John Mount and Nina Zumel,*
Authors, Practical Data Science with R

This book is "for Coders" and does not require a PhD. Now, I do have a PhD and I am no coder, so why have I been asked to review this book? Well, to tell you how friggin awesome it really is!

Within a couple of pages from Chapter 1 you'll figure out how to get a state-of-the-art network able to classify cat vs. dogs in 4 lines of code and less than 1 minute of computation. Then you land Chapter 2, which takes you from model to production, showing how you can serve a webapp in no time, without any HTML or JavaScript, without owning a server.

I think of this book as an onion. A complete package that works using the best possible settings. Then, if some alterations are required, you can peel the outer layer. More tweaks? You can keep discarding shells. Even more? You can go as deep as using bare PyTorch. You'll have three independent voices accompanying you around your journey along this 600 page book, providing you guidance and individual perspective.

—*Alfredo Canziani, Professor of Computer Science, NYU*

Deep Learning for Coders with fastai and PyTorch is an approachable conversationally-driven book that uses the whole game approach to teaching deep learning concepts. The book focuses on getting your hands dirty right out of the gate with real examples and bringing the reader along with reference concepts only as needed. A practitioner may approach the world of deep learning in this book through hands-on examples in the first half, but will find themselves naturally introduced to deeper concepts as they traverse the back half of the book with no pernicious myths left unturned.

—*Josh Patterson, Patterson Consulting*

Jeremy, Sylvain, and Rachel are the absolute masters of creating accessible tools and building community around AI. This is yet another installment of the fast.ai team creating an amazing resource that will help onboard the next hundred thousand aspiring AI researchers globally. Congrats!!!

—*Joe Spisak, PyTorch Product Manager, Facebook*

Deep Learning for Coders with fastai and PyTorch
AI Applications Without a PhD

Jeremy Howard and Sylvain Gugger

Beijing · Boston · Farnham · Sebastopol · Tokyo

Deep Learning for Coders with fastai and PyTorch

by Jeremy Howard and Sylvain Gugger

Copyright © 2020 Jeremy Howard and Sylvain Gugger. All rights reserved.

Published by O'Reilly Media, Inc., 1005 Gravenstein Highway North, Sebastopol, CA 95472.

O'Reilly books may be purchased for educational, business, or sales promotional use. Online editions are also available for most titles (*http://oreilly.com*). For more information, contact our corporate/institutional sales department: 800-998-9938 or *corporate@oreilly.com*.

Acquisitions Editor: Jonathan Hassell
Development Editor: Melissa Potter
Production Editor: Christopher Faucher
Copyeditor: Rachel Head
Proofreader: Sharon Wilkey

Indexer: Sue Klefstad
Interior Designer: David Futato
Cover Designer: Karen Montgomery
Illustrator: Rebecca Demarest

July 2020:   First Edition

Revision History for the First Edition
2020-06-29:   First Release
2020-09-18:   Second Release
2020-12-18:   Third Release
2021-05-07:   Fourth Release
2021-11-05:   Fifth Release

See *http://oreilly.com/catalog/errata.csp?isbn=9781492045526* for release details.

978-1-492-04552-6

[LSI]

Table of Contents

Part II.   Understanding fastai's Applications

Part III.   Foundations of Deep Learning

Preface

Deep learning is a powerful new technology, and we believe it should be applied across many disciplines. Domain experts are the most likely to find new applications of it, and we need more people from all backgrounds to get involved and start using it.

That's why Jeremy cofounded fast.ai, to make deep learning easier to use through free online courses and software. Sylvain is a research engineer at Hugging Face. Previously he was a research scientist at fast.ai and a former mathematics and computer science teacher in a program that prepares students for entry into France's elite universities. Together, we wrote this book in the hope of putting deep learning into the hands of as many people as possible.

Who This Book Is For

If you are a complete beginner to deep learning and machine learning, you are most welcome here. Our only expectation is that you already know how to code, preferably in Python.

No Experience? No Problem!

If you don't have any experience coding, that's OK too! The first three chapters have been explicitly written in a way that will allow executives, product managers, etc. to understand the most important things they'll need to know about deep learning. When you see bits of code in the text, try to look them over to get an intuitive sense of what they're doing. We'll explain them line by line. The details of the syntax are not nearly as important as a high-level understanding of what's going on.

If you are already a confident deep learning practitioner, you will also find a lot here. In this book, we will be showing you how to achieve world-class results, including techniques from the latest research. As we will show, this doesn't require advanced mathematical training or years of study. It just requires a bit of common sense and tenacity.

What You Need to Know

As we said before, the only prerequisite is that you know how to code (a year of experience is enough), preferably in Python, and that you have at least followed a high school math course. It doesn't matter if you remember little of it right now; we will brush up on it as needed. Khan Academy (*https://www.khanacademy.org*) has great free resources online that can help.

We are not saying that deep learning doesn't use math beyond high school level, but we will teach you (or direct you to resources that will teach you) the basics you need as we cover the subjects that require them.

The book starts with the big picture and progressively digs beneath the surface, so you may need, from time to time, to put it aside and go learn some additional topic (a way of coding something or a bit of math). That is completely OK, and it's the way we intend the book to be read. Start browsing it, and consult additional resources only as needed.

Please note that Kindle or other ereader users may need to double-click images to view the full-sized versions.

Online Resources

All the code examples shown in this book are available online in the form of Jupyter notebooks (don't worry; you will learn all about what Jupyter is in Chapter 1). This is an interactive version of the book, where you can actually execute the code and experiment with it. See the book's website (*https://book.fast.ai*) for more information. The website also contains up-to-date information on setting up the various tools we present and some additional bonus chapters.

What You Will Learn

After reading this book, you will know the following:

- How to train models that achieve state-of-the-art results in
  - Computer vision, including image classification (e.g., classifying pet photos by breed) and image localization and detection (e.g., finding the animals in an image)

- Natural language processing (NLP), including document classification (e.g., movie review sentiment analysis) and language modeling

- Tabular data (e.g., sales prediction) with categorical data, continuous data, and mixed data, including time series

- Collaborative filtering (e.g., movie recommendation)

- How to turn your models into web applications

- Why and how deep learning models work, and how to use that knowledge to improve the accuracy, speed, and reliability of your models

- The latest deep learning techniques that really matter in practice

- How to read a deep learning research paper

- How to implement deep learning algorithms from scratch

- How to think about the ethical implications of your work, to help ensure that you're making the world a better place and that your work isn't misused for harm

See the table of contents for a complete list, but to give you a taste, here are some of the techniques covered (don't worry if none of these words mean anything to you yet —you'll learn them all soon):

- Affine functions and nonlinearities

- Parameters and activations

- Random initialization and transfer learning

- SGD, Momentum, Adam, and other optimizers

- Convolutions

- Batch normalization

- Dropout

- Data augmentation

- Weight decay

- ResNet and DenseNet architectures

- Image classification and regression

- Embeddings

- Recurrent neural networks (RNNs)

- Segmentation

- U-Net

- And much more!

Chapter Questionnaires

If you look at the end of each chapter, you'll find a questionnaire. That's a great place to see what we cover in each chapter, since (we hope!) by the end of each one, you'll be able to answer all the questions there. In fact, one of our reviewers (thanks, Fred!) said that he likes to read the questionnaire *first*, before reading the chapter, so he knows what to look out for.

O'Reilly Online Learning

 For more than 40 years, *O'Reilly Media* has provided technology and business training, knowledge, and insight to help companies succeed.

Our unique network of experts and innovators share their knowledge and expertise through books, articles, and our online learning platform. O'Reilly's online learning platform gives you on-demand access to live training courses, in-depth learning paths, interactive coding environments, and a vast collection of text and video from O'Reilly and 200+ other publishers. For more information, visit *http://oreilly.com*.

How to Contact Us

Please address comments and questions concerning this book to the publisher:

O'Reilly Media, Inc.
1005 Gravenstein Highway North
Sebastopol, CA 95472
800-998-9938 (in the United States or Canada)
707-829-0515 (international or local)
707-829-0104 (fax)

We have a web page for this book, where we list errata, examples, and any additional information. You can access this page at *https://oreil.ly/deep-learning-for-coders*.

Email *bookquestions@oreilly.com* to comment or ask technical questions about this book.

For news and information about our books and courses, visit *http://oreilly.com*.

Find us on Facebook: *http://facebook.com/oreilly*

Follow us on Twitter: *http://twitter.com/oreillymedia*

Watch us on YouTube: *http://www.youtube.com/oreillymedia*

Foreword

In a very short time, deep learning has become a widely useful technique, solving and automating problems in computer vision, robotics, healthcare, physics, biology, and beyond. One of the delightful things about deep learning is its relative simplicity. Powerful deep learning software has been built to make getting started fast and easy. In a few weeks, you can understand the basics and get comfortable with the techniques.

This opens up a world of creativity. You start applying it to problems that have data at hand, and you feel wonderful seeing a machine solving problems for you. However, you slowly feel yourself getting closer to a giant barrier. You built a deep learning model, but it doesn't work as well as you had hoped. This is when you enter the next stage, finding and reading state-of-the-art research on deep learning.

However, there's a voluminous body of knowledge on deep learning, with three decades of theory, techniques, and tooling behind it. As you read through some of this research, you realize that humans can explain simple things in really complicated ways. Scientists use words and mathematical notation in these papers that appear foreign, and no textbook or blog post seems to cover the necessary background that you need in accessible ways. Engineers and programmers assume you know how GPUs work and have knowledge about obscure tools.

This is when you wish you had a mentor or a friend that you could talk to. Someone who was in your shoes before, who knows the tooling and the math—someone who could guide you through the best research, state-of-the-art techniques, and advanced engineering, and make it comically simple. I was in your shoes a decade ago, when I was breaking into the field of machine learning. For years, I struggled to understand papers that had a little bit of math in them. I had good mentors around me, which helped me greatly, but it took me many years to get comfortable with machine learning and deep learning. That motivated me to coauthor PyTorch, a software framework to make deep learning accessible.

Jeremy Howard and Sylvain Gugger were also in your shoes. They wanted to learn and apply deep learning, without any previous formal training as ML scientists or engineers. Like me, Jeremy and Sylvain learned gradually over the years and eventually became experts and leaders. But unlike me, Jeremy and Sylvain selflessly put a huge amount of energy into making sure others don't have to take the painful path that they took. They built a great course called fast.ai that makes cutting-edge deep learning techniques accessible to people who know basic programming. It has graduated hundreds of thousands of eager learners who have become great practitioners.

In this book, which is another tireless product, Jeremy and Sylvain have constructed a magical journey through deep learning. They use simple words and introduce every concept. They bring cutting-edge deep learning and state-of-the-art research to you, yet make it very accessible.

You are taken through the latest advances in computer vision, dive into natural language processing, and learn some foundational math in a 500-page delightful ride. And the ride doesn't stop at fun, as they take you through shipping your ideas to production. You can treat the fast.ai community, thousands of practitioners online, as your extended family, where individuals like you are available to talk and ideate small and big solutions, whatever the problem may be.

I am very glad you've found this book, and I hope it inspires you to put deep learning to good use, regardless of the nature of the problem.

— Soumith Chintala
Cocreator of PyTorch

PART I

Deep Learning in Practice

CHAPTER 1

Your Deep Learning Journey

Hello, and thank you for letting us join you on your deep learning journey, however far along that you may be! In this chapter, we will tell you a little bit more about what to expect in this book, introduce the key concepts behind deep learning, and train our first models on different tasks. It doesn't matter if you don't come from a technical or a mathematical background (though it's OK if you do too!); we wrote this book to make deep learning accessible to as many people as possible.

Deep Learning Is for Everyone

A lot of people assume that you need all kinds of hard-to-find stuff to get great results with deep learning, but as you'll see in this book, those people are wrong. Table 1-1 lists a few things you *absolutely don't need* for world-class deep learning.

Table 1-1. What you don't need for deep learning

Myth (don't need)	Truth
Lots of math	High school math is sufficient.
Lots of data	We've seen record-breaking results with <50 items of data.
Lots of expensive computers	You can get what you need for state-of-the-art work for free.

Deep learning is a computer technique to extract and transform data—with use cases ranging from human speech recognition to animal imagery classification—by using multiple layers of neural networks. Each of these layers takes its inputs from previous layers and progressively refines them. The layers are trained by algorithms that minimize their errors and improve their accuracy. In this way, the network learns to perform a specified task. We will discuss training algorithms in detail in the next section.

Deep learning has power, flexibility, and simplicity. That's why we believe it should be applied across many disciplines. These include the social and physical sciences, the arts, medicine, finance, scientific research, and many more. To give a personal example, despite having no background in medicine, Jeremy started Enlitic, a company that uses deep learning algorithms to diagnose illness and disease. Within months of starting the company, it was announced that its algorithm could identify malignant tumors more accurately than radiologists (*https://oreil.ly/aTwdE*).

Here's a list of some of the thousands of tasks in different areas for which deep learning, or methods heavily using deep learning, is now the best in the world:

Natural language processing (NLP)
Answering questions; speech recognition; summarizing documents; classifying documents; finding names, dates, etc. in documents; searching for articles mentioning a concept

Computer vision
Satellite and drone imagery interpretation (e.g., for disaster resilience), face recognition, image captioning, reading traffic signs, locating pedestrians and vehicles in autonomous vehicles

Medicine
Finding anomalies in radiology images, including CT, MRI, and X-ray images; counting features in pathology slides; measuring features in ultrasounds; diagnosing diabetic retinopathy

Biology
Folding proteins; classifying proteins; many genomics tasks, such as tumor-normal sequencing and classifying clinically actionable genetic mutations; cell classification; analyzing protein/protein interactions

Image generation
Colorizing images, increasing image resolution, removing noise from images, converting images to art in the style of famous artists

Recommendation systems
Web search, product recommendations, home page layout

Playing games
Chess, Go, most Atari video games, and many real-time strategy games

Robotics
Handling objects that are challenging to locate (e.g., transparent, shiny, lacking texture) or hard to pick up

Other applications
Financial and logistical forecasting, text to speech, and much, much more...

What is remarkable is that deep learning has such varied applications, yet nearly all of deep learning is based on a single innovative type of model: the neural network.

But neural networks are not, in fact, completely new. In order to have a wider perspective on the field, it is worth starting with a bit of history.

Neural Networks: A Brief History

In 1943 Warren McCulloch, a neurophysiologist, and Walter Pitts, a logician, teamed up to develop a mathematical model of an artificial neuron. In their paper "A Logical Calculus of the Ideas Immanent in Nervous Activity," they declared the following:

> Because of the "all-or-none" character of nervous activity, neural events and the relations among them can be treated by means of propositional logic. It is found that the behavior of every net can be described in these terms.

McCulloch and Pitts realized that a simplified model of a real neuron could be represented using simple addition and thresholding, as shown in Figure 1-1. Pitts was self-taught, and by age 12, had received an offer to study at Cambridge University with the great Bertrand Russell. He did not take up this invitation, and indeed throughout his life did not accept any offers of advanced degrees or positions of authority. Most of his famous work was done while he was homeless. Despite his lack of an officially recognized position and increasing social isolation, his work with McCulloch was influential and was taken up by a psychologist named Frank Rosenblatt.

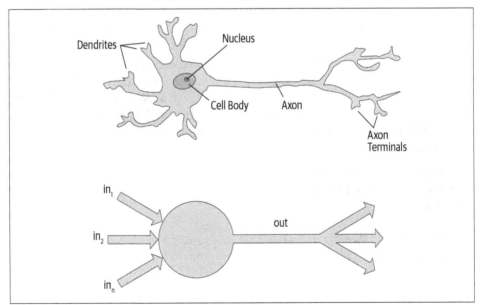

Figure 1-1. Natural and artificial neurons

Rosenblatt further developed the artificial neuron to give it the ability to learn. Even more importantly, he worked on building the first device that used these principles, the Mark I Perceptron. In "The Design of an Intelligent Automaton," Rosenblatt wrote about this work: "We are now about to witness the birth of such a machine—a machine capable of perceiving, recognizing and identifying its surroundings without any human training or control." The perceptron was built and was able to successfully recognize simple shapes.

An MIT professor named Marvin Minsky (who was a grade behind Rosenblatt at the same high school!), along with Seymour Papert, wrote a book called *Perceptrons* (MIT Press) about Rosenblatt's invention. They showed that a single layer of these devices was unable to learn some simple but critical mathematical functions (such as XOR). In the same book, they also showed that using multiple layers of the devices would allow these limitations to be addressed. Unfortunately, only the first of these insights was widely recognized. As a result, the global academic community nearly entirely gave up on neural networks for the next two decades.

Perhaps the most pivotal work in neural networks in the last 50 years was the multivolume *Parallel Distributed Processing* (PDP) by David Rumelhart, James McClelland, and the PDP Research Group, released in 1986 by MIT Press. Chapter 1 lays out a similar hope to that shown by Rosenblatt:

> People are smarter than today's computers because the brain employs a basic computational architecture that is more suited to deal with a central aspect of the natural information processing tasks that people are so good at....We will introduce a computational framework for modeling cognitive processes that seems...closer than other frameworks to the style of computation as it might be done by the brain.

The premise that PDP is using here is that traditional computer programs work very differently from brains, and that might be why computer programs had been (at that point) so bad at doing things that brains find easy (such as recognizing objects in pictures). The authors claimed that the PDP approach was "closer than other frameworks" to how the brain works, and therefore it might be better able to handle these kinds of tasks.

In fact, the approach laid out in PDP is very similar to the approach used in today's neural networks. The book defined parallel distributed processing as requiring the following:

- A set of *processing units*
- A *state of activation*
- An *output function* for each unit
- A *pattern of connectivity* among units

- A *propagation rule* for propagating patterns of activities through the network of connectivities
- An *activation rule* for combining the inputs impinging on a unit with the current state of that unit to produce an output for the unit
- A *learning rule* whereby patterns of connectivity are modified by experience
- An *environment* within which the system must operate

We will see in this book that modern neural networks handle each of these requirements.

In the 1980s, most models were built with a second layer of neurons, thus avoiding the problem that had been identified by Minsky and Papert (this was their "pattern of connectivity among units," to use the preceding framework). And indeed, neural networks were widely used during the '80s and '90s for real, practical projects. However, again a misunderstanding of the theoretical issues held back the field. In theory, adding just one extra layer of neurons was enough to allow any mathematical function to be approximated with these neural networks, but in practice such networks were often too big and too slow to be useful.

Although researchers showed 30 years ago that to get practical, good performance you need to use even more layers of neurons, it is only in the last decade that this principle has been more widely appreciated and applied. Neural networks are now finally living up to their potential, thanks to the use of more layers, coupled with the capacity to do so because of improvements in computer hardware, increases in data availability, and algorithmic tweaks that allow neural networks to be trained faster and more easily. We now have what Rosenblatt promised: "a machine capable of perceiving, recognizing, and identifying its surroundings without any human training or control."

This is what you will learn how to build in this book. But first, since we are going to be spending a lot of time together, let's get to know each other a bit...

Who We Are

We are Sylvain and Jeremy, your guides on this journey. We hope that you will find us well suited for this position.

Jeremy has been using and teaching machine learning for around 30 years. He started using neural networks 25 years ago. During this time, he has led many companies and projects that have machine learning at their core, including founding the first company to focus on deep learning and medicine, Enlitic, and taking on the role of president and chief scientist at the world's largest machine learning community, Kaggle. He is the cofounder, along with Dr. Rachel Thomas, of fast.ai, the organization that built the course this book is based on.

From time to time, you will hear directly from us in sidebars, like this one from Jeremy:

Jeremy Says

Hi, everybody; I'm Jeremy! You might be interested to know that I do not have any formal technical education. I completed a BA with a major in philosophy, and didn't have great grades. I was much more interested in doing real projects than theoretical studies, so I worked full time at a management consulting firm called McKinsey and Company throughout my university years. If you're somebody who would rather get their hands dirty building stuff than spend years learning abstract concepts, you will understand where I am coming from! Look out for sidebars from me to find information most suited to people with a less mathematical or formal technical background—that is, people like me...

Sylvain, on the other hand, knows a lot about formal technical education. He has written 10 math textbooks, covering the entire advanced French math curriculum!

Sylvain Says

Unlike Jeremy, I have not spent many years coding and applying machine learning algorithms. Rather, I recently came to the machine learning world by watching Jeremy's fast.ai course videos. So, if you are somebody who has not opened a terminal and written commands at the command line, you will understand where I am coming from! Look out for sidebars from me to find information most suited to people with a more mathematical or formal technical background, but less real-world coding experience—that is, people like me...

The fast.ai course has been studied by hundreds of thousands of students, from all walks of life, from all parts of the world. Sylvain stood out as the most impressive student of the course that Jeremy had ever seen, which led to him joining fast.ai and then becoming the coauthor, along with Jeremy, of the fastai software library.

All this means that between us, you have the best of both worlds: the people who know more about the software than anybody else, because they wrote it; an expert on math, and an expert on coding and machine learning; and also people who understand both what it feels like to be a relative outsider in math, and a relative outsider in coding and machine learning.

Anybody who has watched sports knows that if you have a two-person commentary team, you also need a third person to do "special comments." Our special commentator is Alexis Gallagher. Alexis has a very diverse background: he has been a researcher in mathematical biology, a screenplay writer, an improv performer, a McKinsey consultant (like Jeremy!), a Swift coder, and a CTO.

Alexis Says

I've decided it's time for me to learn about this AI stuff! After all, I've tried pretty much everything else....But I don't really have a background in building machine learning models. Still...how hard can it be? I'm going to be learning throughout this book, just like you are. Look out for my sidebars for learning tips that I found helpful on my journey, and hopefully you will find helpful too.

How to Learn Deep Learning

Harvard professor David Perkins, who wrote *Making Learning Whole* (Jossey-Bass), has much to say about teaching. The basic idea is to teach the *whole game*. That means that if you're teaching baseball, you first take people to a baseball game or get them to play it. You don't teach them how to wind twine to make a baseball from scratch, the physics of a parabola, or the coefficient of friction of a ball on a bat.

Paul Lockhart, a Columbia math PhD, former Brown professor, and K–12 math teacher, imagines in the influential essay "A Mathematician's Lament" (*https://oreil.ly/yNimZ*) a nightmare world where music and art are taught the way math is taught. Children are not allowed to listen to or play music until they have spent over a decade mastering music notation and theory, spending classes transposing sheet music into a different key. In art class, students study colors and applicators, but aren't allowed to actually paint until college. Sound absurd? This is how math is taught—we require students to spend years doing rote memorization and learning dry, disconnected *fundamentals* that we claim will pay off later, long after most of them quit the subject.

Unfortunately, this is where many teaching resources on deep learning begin—asking learners to follow along with the definition of the Hessian and theorems for the Taylor approximation of your loss functions, without ever giving examples of actual working code. We're not knocking calculus. We love calculus, and Sylvain has even taught it at the college level, but we don't think it's the best place to start when learning deep learning!

In deep learning, it really helps if you have the motivation to fix your model to get it to do better. That's when you start learning the relevant theory. But you need to have the model in the first place. We teach almost everything through real examples. As we build out those examples, we go deeper and deeper, and we'll show you how to make your projects better and better. This means that you'll be gradually learning all the theoretical foundations you need, in context, in such a way that you'll see why it matters and how it works.

So, here's our commitment to you. Throughout this book, we follow these principles:

Teaching the whole game
> We'll start off by showing you how to use a complete, working, usable, state-of-the-art deep learning network to solve real-world problems using simple, expressive tools. And then we'll gradually dig deeper and deeper into understanding how those tools are made, and how the tools that make those tools are made, and so on...

Always teaching through examples
> We'll ensure that there is a context and a purpose that you can understand intuitively, rather than starting with algebraic symbol manipulation.

Simplifying as much as possible
> We've spent years building tools and teaching methods that make previously complex topics simple.

Removing barriers
> Deep learning has, until now, been an exclusive game. We're breaking it open and ensuring that everyone can play.

The hardest part of deep learning is artisanal: how do you know if you've got enough data, whether it is in the right format, if your model is training properly, and, if it's not, what you should do about it? That is why we believe in learning by doing. As with basic data science skills, with deep learning you get better only through practical experience. Trying to spend too much time on the theory can be counterproductive. The key is to just code and try to solve problems: the theory can come later, when you have context and motivation.

There will be times when the journey feels hard. Times when you feel stuck. Don't give up! Rewind through the book to find the last bit where you definitely weren't stuck, and then read slowly through from there to find the first thing that isn't clear. Then try some code experiments yourself, and Google around for more tutorials on whatever the issue you're stuck with is—often you'll find a different angle on the material that might help it to click. Also, it's expected and normal to not understand everything (especially the code) on first reading. Trying to understand the material serially before proceeding can sometimes be hard. Sometimes things click into place after you get more context from parts down the road, from having a bigger picture. So if you do get stuck on a section, try moving on anyway and make a note to come back to it later.

Remember, you don't need any particular academic background to succeed at deep learning. Many important breakthroughs are made in research and industry by folks without a PhD, such as the paper "Unsupervised Representation Learning with Deep Convolutional Generative Adversarial Networks" (*https://oreil.ly/JV6rL*)—one of the most influential papers of the last decade, with over 5,000 citations—which was written by Alec Radford when he was an undergraduate. Even at Tesla, where they're trying to solve the extremely tough challenge of making a self-driving car, CEO Elon Musk says (*https://oreil.ly/nQCmO*):

> A PhD is definitely not required. All that matters is a deep understanding of AI & ability to implement NNs in a way that is actually useful (latter point is what's truly hard). Don't care if you even graduated high school.

What you will need to do to succeed, however, is to apply what you learn in this book to a personal project, and always persevere.

Your Projects and Your Mindset

Whether you're excited to identify if plants are diseased from pictures of their leaves, autogenerate knitting patterns, diagnose TB from X-rays, or determine when a raccoon is using your cat door, we will get you using deep learning on your own problems (via pretrained models from others) as quickly as possible, and then will progressively drill into more details. You'll learn how to use deep learning to solve your own problems at state-of-the-art accuracy within the first 30 minutes of the next chapter! (And feel free to skip straight there now if you're dying to get coding right away.) There is a pernicious myth out there that you need to have computing resources and datasets the size of those at Google to be able to do deep learning, but it's not true.

So, what sorts of tasks make for good test cases? You could train your model to distinguish between Picasso and Monet paintings or to pick out pictures of your daughter instead of pictures of your son. It helps to focus on your hobbies and passions—setting yourself four or five little projects rather than striving to solve a big, grand problem tends to work better when you're getting started. Since it is easy to get stuck, trying to be too ambitious too early can often backfire. Then, once you've got the basics mastered, aim to complete something you're really proud of!

Jeremy Says

Deep learning can be set to work on almost any problem. For instance, my first startup was a company called FastMail, which provided enhanced email services when it launched in 1999 (and still does to this day). In 2002, I set it up to use a primitive form of deep learning, single-layer neural networks, to help categorize emails and stop customers from receiving spam.

Common character traits in the people who do well at deep learning include playfulness and curiosity. The late physicist Richard Feynman is an example of someone we'd expect to be great at deep learning: his development of an understanding of the movement of subatomic particles came from his amusement at how plates wobble when they spin in the air.

Let's now focus on what you will learn, starting with the software.

The Software: PyTorch, fastai, and Jupyter (And Why It Doesn't Matter)

We've completed hundreds of machine learning projects using dozens of packages, and many programming languages. At fast.ai, we have written courses using most of the main deep learning and machine learning packages used today. After PyTorch came out in 2017, we spent over a thousand hours testing it before deciding that we would use it for future courses, software development, and research. Since that time, PyTorch has become the world's fastest-growing deep learning library and is already used for most research papers at top conferences. This is generally a leading indicator of usage in industry, because these are the papers that end up getting used in products and services commercially. We have found that PyTorch is the most flexible and expressive library for deep learning. It does not trade off speed for simplicity, but provides both.

PyTorch works best as a low-level foundation library, providing the basic operations for higher-level functionality. The fastai library is the most popular library for adding this higher-level functionality on top of PyTorch. It's also particularly well suited to the purposes of this book, because it is unique in providing a deeply layered software architecture (there's even a peer-reviewed academic paper (*https://oreil.ly/Uo3GR*) about this layered API). In this book, as we go deeper and deeper into the foundations of deep learning, we will also go deeper and deeper into the layers of fastai. This book covers version 2 of the fastai library, which is a from-scratch rewrite providing many unique features.

However, it doesn't really matter what software you learn, because it takes only a few days to learn to switch from one library to another. What really matters is learning the deep learning foundations and techniques properly. Our focus will be on using code that, as clearly as possible, expresses the concepts that you need to learn. Where we are teaching high-level concepts, we will use high-level fastai code. Where we are teaching low-level concepts, we will use low-level PyTorch or even pure Python code.

Though it may seem like new deep learning libraries are appearing at a rapid pace nowadays, you need to be prepared for a much faster rate of change in the coming months and years. As more people enter the field, they will bring more skills and ideas, and try more things. You should assume that whatever specific libraries and software you learn today will be obsolete in a year or two. Just think about the number of changes in libraries and technology stacks that occur all the time in the world of web programming—a much more mature and slow-growing area than deep learning. We strongly believe that the focus in learning needs to be on understanding the underlying techniques and how to apply them in practice, and how to quickly build expertise in new tools and techniques as they are released.

By the end of the book, you'll understand nearly all the code that's inside fastai (and much of PyTorch too), because in each chapter we'll be digging a level deeper to show you exactly what's going on as we build and train our models. This means that you'll have learned the most important best practices used in modern deep learning—not just how to use them, but how they really work and are implemented. If you want to use those approaches in another framework, you'll have the knowledge you need to do so if needed.

Since the most important thing for learning deep learning is writing code and experimenting, it's important that you have a great platform for experimenting with code. The most popular programming experimentation platform is called Jupyter (*https://jupyter.org*). This is what we will be using throughout this book. We will show you how you can use Jupyter to train and experiment with models and introspect every stage of the data preprocessing and model development pipeline. Jupyter is the most popular tool for doing data science in Python, for good reason. It is powerful, flexible, and easy to use. We think you will love it!

Let's see it in practice and train our first model.

Your First Model

As we said before, we will teach you how to do things before we explain why they work. Following this top-down approach, we will begin by actually training an image classifier to recognize dogs and cats with almost 100% accuracy. To train this model and run our experiments, you will need to do some initial setup. Don't worry; it's not as hard as it looks.

Sylvain Says

Do not skip the setup part even if it looks intimidating at first, especially if you have little or no experience using things like a terminal or the command line. Most of that is not necessary, and you will find that the easiest servers can be set up with just your usual web browser. It is crucial that you run your own experiments in parallel with this book in order to learn.

Getting a GPU Deep Learning Server

To do nearly everything in this book, you'll need access to a computer with an NVIDIA GPU (unfortunately, other brands of GPU are not fully supported by the main deep learning libraries). However, we don't recommend you buy one; in fact, even if you already have one, we don't suggest you use it just yet! Setting up a computer takes time and energy, and you want all your energy to focus on deep learning right now. Therefore, we instead suggest you rent access to a computer that already has everything you need preinstalled and ready to go. Costs can be as little as $0.25 per hour while you're using it, and some options are even free.

Jargon: Graphics Processing Unit (GPU)

Also known as a *graphics card*. A special kind of processor in your computer that can handle thousands of single tasks at the same time, especially designed for displaying 3D environments on a computer for playing games. These same basic tasks are very similar to what neural networks do, such that GPUs can run neural networks hundreds of times faster than regular CPUs. All modern computers contain a GPU, but few contain the right kind of GPU necessary for deep learning.

The best choice of GPU servers to use with this book will change over time, as companies come and go and prices change. We maintain a list of our recommended options on the book's website (*https://book.fast.ai*), so go there now and follow the instructions to get connected to a GPU deep learning server. Don't worry; it takes only about two minutes to get set up on most platforms, and many don't even require any payment or even a credit card to get started.

Alexis Says

My two cents: heed this advice! If you like computers, you will be tempted to set up your own box. Beware! It is feasible but surprisingly involved and distracting. There is a good reason this book is not titled *Everything You Ever Wanted to Know About Ubuntu System Administration, NVIDIA Driver Installation, apt-get, conda, pip, and Jupyter Notebook Configuration*. That would be a book of its own. Having designed and deployed our production machine learning infrastructure at work, I can testify it has its satisfactions, but it is as unrelated to modeling as maintaining an airplane is to flying one.

Each option shown on the website includes a tutorial; after completing the tutorial, you will end up with a screen looking like Figure 1-2.

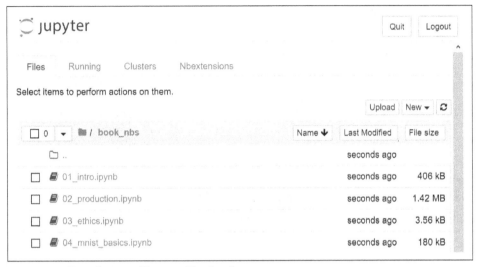

Figure 1-2. Initial view of Jupyter Notebook

You are now ready to run your first Jupyter notebook!

Jargon: Jupyter Notebook

A piece of software that allows you to include formatted text, code, images, videos, and much more, all within a single interactive document. Jupyter received the highest honor for software, the ACM Software System Award, thanks to its wide use and enormous impact in many academic fields and in industry. Jupyter Notebook is the software most widely used by data scientists for developing and interacting with deep learning models.

Running Your First Notebook

The notebooks are numbered by chapter in the same order as they are presented in this book. So, the very first notebook you will see listed is the notebook that you need to use now. You will be using this notebook to train a model that can recognize dog and cat photos. To do this, you'll be downloading a dataset of dog and cat photos, and using that to *train a model*.

A *dataset* is simply a bunch of data—it could be images, emails, financial indicators, sounds, or anything else. There are many datasets made freely available that are suitable for training models. Many of these datasets are created by academics to help advance research, many are made available for competitions (there are competitions where data scientists can compete to see who has the most accurate model!), and some are byproducts of other processes (such as financial filings).

Full and Stripped Notebooks

There are two versions of the notebooks. The root of the repo contains the exact notebooks used to create the book you're reading now, with all the prose and outputs. The *clean* folder has the same headings and code cells, but all outputs and prose have been removed. After reading a section of the book, we recommend working through the clean notebooks, with the book closed, and seeing if you can figure out what each cell will show before you execute it. Also try to recall what the code is demonstrating.

To open a notebook, just click it. The notebook will open, and it will look something like Figure 1-3 (note that there may be slight differences in details across different platforms; you can ignore those differences).

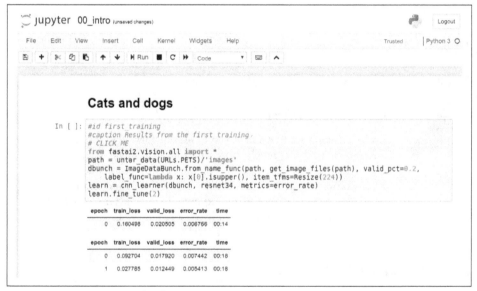

Figure 1-3. A Jupyter notebook

A notebook consists of *cells*. There are two main types of cell:

- Cells containing formatted text, images, and so forth. These use a format called *Markdown*, which you will learn about soon.

- Cells containing code that can be executed, and outputs will appear immediately underneath (which could be plain text, tables, images, animations, sounds, or even interactive applications).

Jupyter notebooks can be in one of two modes: edit mode or command mode. In edit mode, typing on your keyboard enters the letters into the cell in the usual way. However, in command mode, you will not see any flashing cursor, and each key on your keyboard will have a special function.

Before continuing, press the Escape key on your keyboard to switch to command mode (if you are already in command mode, this does nothing, so press it now just in case). To see a complete list of all the functions available, press H; press Escape to remove this help screen. Notice that in command mode, unlike in most programs, commands do not require you to hold down Control, Alt, or similar—you simply press the required letter key.

You can make a copy of a cell by pressing C (the cell needs to be selected first, indicated with an outline around it; if it is not already selected, click it once). Then press V to paste a copy of it.

Click the cell that begins with the line "# CLICK ME" to select it. The first character in that line indicates that what follows is a comment in Python, so it is ignored when executing the cell. The rest of the cell is, believe it or not, a complete system for creating and training a state-of-the-art model for recognizing cats versus dogs. So, let's train it now! To do so, just press Shift-Enter on your keyboard, or click the Play button on the toolbar. Then wait a few minutes while the following things happen:

1. A dataset called the Oxford-IIIT Pet Dataset (*https://oreil.ly/c_4Bv*) that contains 7,349 images of cats and dogs from 37 breeds will be downloaded from the fast.ai datasets collection to the GPU server you are using, and will then be extracted.

2. A *pretrained model* that has already been trained on 1.3 million images using a competition-winning model will be downloaded from the internet.

3. The pretrained model will be *fine-tuned* using the latest advances in transfer learning to create a model that is specially customized for recognizing dogs and cats.

The first two steps need to be run only once on your GPU server. If you run the cell again, it will use the dataset and model that have already been downloaded, rather than downloading them again. Let's take a look at the contents of the cell and the results (Table 1-2):

```
# CLICK ME
from fastai.vision.all import *
path = untar_data(URLs.PETS)/'images'

def is_cat(x): return x[0].isupper()
dls = ImageDataLoaders.from_name_func(
    path, get_image_files(path), valid_pct=0.2, seed=42,
    label_func=is_cat, item_tfms=Resize(224))
```

```
learn = cnn_learner(dls, resnet34, metrics=error_rate)
learn.fine_tune(1)
```

Table 1-2. Results from the first training

epoch	train_loss	valid_loss	error_rate	time
0	0.169390	0.021388	0.005413	00:14

epoch	train_loss	valid_loss	error_rate	time
0	0.058748	0.009240	0.002706	00:19

You will probably not see exactly the same results shown here. A lot of sources of small random variation are involved in training models. We generally see an error rate of well less than 0.02 in this example, however.

Training Time

Depending on your network speed, it might take a few minutes to download the pretrained model and dataset. Running `fine_tune` might take a minute or so. Often models in this book take a few minutes to train, as will your own models, so it's a good idea to come up with good techniques to make the most of this time. For instance, keep reading the next section while your model trains, or open up another notebook and use it for some coding experiments.

This Book Was Written in Jupyter Notebooks

We wrote this book using Jupyter notebooks, so for nearly every chart, table, and calculation in this book, we'll be showing you the exact code required to replicate it yourself. That's why very often in this book, you will see some code immediately followed by a table, a picture, or just some text. If you go on the book's website (*https://book.fast.ai*), you will find all the code, and you can try running and modifying every example yourself.

You just saw how a cell that outputs a table looks in the book. Here is an example of a cell that outputs text:

```
1+1
```

```
2
```

Jupyter will always print or show the result of the last line (if there is one). For instance, here is an example of a cell that outputs an image:

```
img = PILImage.create(image_cat())
img.to_thumb(192)
```

So, how do we know if this model is any good? In the last column of the table, you can see the *error rate*, which is the proportion of images that were incorrectly identified. The error rate serves as our metric—our measure of model quality, chosen to be intuitive and comprehensible. As you can see, the model is nearly perfect, even though the training time was only a few seconds (not including the one-time downloading of the dataset and the pretrained model). In fact, the accuracy you've achieved already is far better than anybody had ever achieved just 10 years ago!

Finally, let's check that this model actually works. Go and get a photo of a dog or a cat; if you don't have one handy, just search Google Images and download an image that you find there. Now execute the cell with `uploader` defined. It will output a button you can click, so you can select the image you want to classify:

```
uploader = widgets.FileUpload()
uploader
```

⬆ Upload (0)

Now you can pass the uploaded file to the model. Make sure that it is a clear photo of a single dog or a cat, and not a line drawing, cartoon, or similar. The notebook will tell you whether it thinks it is a dog or a cat, and how confident it is. Hopefully, you'll find that your model did a great job:

```
img = PILImage.create(uploader.data[0])
is_cat,_,probs = learn.predict(img)
print(f"Is this a cat?: {is_cat}.")
print(f"Probability it's a cat: {probs[1].item():.6f}")
```

```
Is this a cat?: True.
Probability it's a cat: 0.999986
```

Congratulations on your first classifier!

But what does this mean? What did you actually do? In order to explain this, let's zoom out again to take in the big picture.

What Is Machine Learning?

Your classifier is a deep learning model. As was already mentioned, deep learning models use neural networks, which originally date from the 1950s and have become powerful very recently thanks to recent advancements.

Another key piece of context is that deep learning is just a modern area in the more general discipline of *machine learning*. To understand the essence of what you did when you trained your own classification model, you don't need to understand deep learning. It is enough to see how your model and your training process are examples of the concepts that apply to machine learning in general.

So in this section, we will describe machine learning. We will explore the key concepts and see how they can be traced back to the original essay that introduced them.

Machine learning is, like regular programming, a way to get computers to complete a specific task. But how would we use regular programming to do what we just did in the preceding section: recognize dogs versus cats in photos? We would have to write down for the computer the exact steps necessary to complete the task.

Normally, it's easy enough for us to write down the steps to complete a task when we're writing a program. We just think about the steps we'd take if we had to do the task by hand, and then we translate them into code. For instance, we can write a function that sorts a list. In general, we'd write a function that looks something like Figure 1-4 (where *inputs* might be an unsorted list, and *results* a sorted list).

Figure 1-4. A traditional program

But for recognizing objects in a photo, that's a bit tricky; what *are* the steps we take when we recognize an object in a picture? We really don't know, since it all happens in our brain without us being consciously aware of it!

Right back at the dawn of computing, in 1949, an IBM researcher named Arthur Samuel started working on a different way to get computers to complete tasks, which he called *machine learning*. In his classic 1962 essay "Artificial Intelligence: A Frontier of Automation," he wrote:

> Programming a computer for such computations is, at best, a difficult task, not primarily because of any inherent complexity in the computer itself but, rather, because of the need to spell out every minute step of the process in the most exasperating detail. Computers, as any programmer will tell you, are giant morons, not giant brains.

His basic idea was this: instead of telling the computer the exact steps required to solve a problem, show it examples of the problem to solve, and let it figure out how to solve it itself. This turned out to be very effective: by 1961, his checkers-playing program had learned so much that it beat the Connecticut state champion! Here's how he described his idea (from the same essay as noted previously):

> Suppose we arrange for some automatic means of testing the effectiveness of any current weight assignment in terms of actual performance and provide a mechanism for altering the weight assignment so as to maximize the performance. We need not go into the details of such a procedure to see that it could be made entirely automatic and to see that a machine so programmed would "learn" from its experience.

There are a number of powerful concepts embedded in this short statement:

- The idea of a "weight assignment"
- The fact that every weight assignment has some "actual performance"
- The requirement that there be an "automatic means" of testing that performance
- The need for a "mechanism" (i.e., another automatic process) for improving the performance by changing the weight assignments

Let's take these concepts one by one, in order to understand how they fit together in practice. First, we need to understand what Samuel means by a *weight assignment*.

Weights are just variables, and a weight assignment is a particular choice of values for those variables. The program's inputs are values that it processes in order to produce its results—for instance, taking image pixels as inputs, and returning the classification "dog" as a result. The program's weight assignments are other values that define how the program will operate.

Because they will affect the program, they are in a sense another kind of input. We will update our basic picture in Figure 1-4 and replace it with Figure 1-5 in order to take this into account.

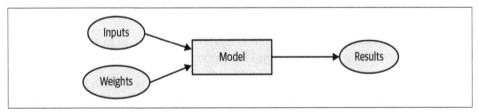

Figure 1-5. A program using weight assignment

We've changed the name of our box from *program* to *model*. This is to follow modern terminology and to reflect that the *model* is a special kind of program: it's one that can do *many different things*, depending on the *weights*. It can be implemented in many different ways. For instance, in Samuel's checkers program, different values of the weights would result in different checkers-playing strategies.

(By the way, what Samuel called "weights" are most generally referred to as model *parameters* these days, in case you have encountered that term. The term *weights* is reserved for a particular type of model parameter.)

Next, Samuel said we need an *automatic means of testing the effectiveness of any current weight assignment in terms of actual performance.* In the case of his checkers program, the "actual performance" of a model would be how well it plays. And you could automatically test the performance of two models by setting them to play against each other, and seeing which one usually wins.

Finally, he says we need *a mechanism for altering the weight assignment so as to maximize the performance.* For instance, we could look at the difference in weights between the winning model and the losing model, and adjust the weights a little further in the winning direction.

We can now see why he said that such a procedure *could be made entirely automatic and...a machine so programmed would "learn" from its experience.* Learning would become entirely automatic when the adjustment of the weights was also automatic—when instead of us improving a model by adjusting its weights manually, we relied on an automated mechanism that produced adjustments based on performance.

Figure 1-6 shows the full picture of Samuel's idea of training a machine learning model.

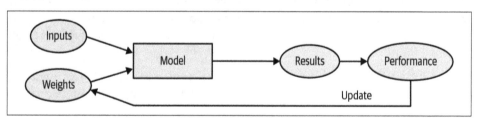

Figure 1-6. Training a machine learning model

Notice the distinction between the model's *results* (e.g., the moves in a checkers game) and its *performance* (e.g., whether it wins the game, or how quickly it wins).

Also note that once the model is trained—that is, once we've chosen our final, best, favorite weight assignment—then we can think of the weights as being *part of the model*, since we're not varying them anymore.

Therefore, actually *using* a model after it's trained looks like Figure 1-7.

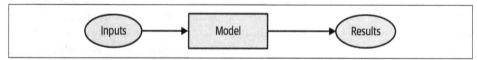

Figure 1-7. Using a trained model as a program

This looks identical to our original diagram in Figure 1-4, just with the word *program* replaced with *model*. This is an important insight: *a trained model can be treated just like a regular computer program.*

Jargon: Machine Learning

The training of programs developed by allowing a computer to learn from its experience, rather than through manually coding the individual steps.

What Is a Neural Network?

It's not too hard to imagine what the model might look like for a checkers program. There might be a range of checkers strategies encoded, and some kind of search mechanism, and then the weights could vary how strategies are selected, what parts of the board are focused on during a search, and so forth. But it's not at all obvious what the model might look like for an image recognition program, or for understanding text, or for many other interesting problems we might imagine.

What we would like is some kind of function that is so flexible that it could be used to solve any given problem, just by varying its weights. Amazingly enough, this function actually exists! It's the neural network, which we already discussed. That is, if you regard a neural network as a mathematical function, it turns out to be a function that is extremely flexible depending on its weights. A mathematical proof called the *universal approximation theorem* shows that this function can solve any problem to any level of accuracy, in theory. The fact that neural networks are so flexible means that, in practice, they are often a suitable kind of model, and you can focus your effort on the process of training them—that is, of finding good weight assignments.

But what about that process? One could imagine that you might need to find a new "mechanism" for automatically updating weights for every problem. This would be laborious. What we'd like here as well is a completely general way to update the weights of a neural network, to make it improve at any given task. Conveniently, this also exists!

This is called *stochastic gradient descent* (SGD). We'll see how neural networks and SGD work in detail in Chapter 4, as well as explaining the universal approximation theorem. For now, however, we will instead use Samuel's own words: *We need not go into the details of such a procedure to see that it could be made entirely automatic and to see that a machine so programmed would "learn" from its experience.*

Jeremy Says

Don't worry; neither SGD nor neural nets are mathematically complex. Both nearly entirely rely on addition and multiplication to do their work (but they do a *lot* of addition and multiplication!). The main reaction we hear from students when they see the details is: "Is that all it is?"

In other words, to recap, a neural network is a particular kind of machine learning model, which fits right in to Samuel's original conception. Neural networks are special because they are highly flexible, which means they can solve an unusually wide range of problems just by finding the right weights. This is powerful, because stochastic gradient descent provides us a way to find those weight values automatically.

Having zoomed out, let's now zoom back in and revisit our image classification problem using Samuel's framework.

Our inputs are the images. Our weights are the weights in the neural net. Our model is a neural net. Our results are the values that are calculated by the neural net, like "dog" or "cat."

What about the next piece, an *automatic means of testing the effectiveness of any current weight assignment in terms of actual performance*? Determining "actual performance" is easy enough: we can simply define our model's performance as its accuracy at predicting the correct answers.

Putting this all together, and assuming that SGD is our mechanism for updating the weight assignments, we can see how our image classifier is a machine learning model, much like Samuel envisioned.

A Bit of Deep Learning Jargon

Samuel was working in the 1960s, and since then terminology has changed. Here is the modern deep learning terminology for all the pieces we have discussed:

- The functional form of the *model* is called its *architecture* (but be careful—sometimes people use *model* as a synonym of *architecture*, so this can get confusing).
- The *weights* are called *parameters*.
- The *predictions* are calculated from the *independent variable*, which is the *data* not including the *labels*.
- The *results* of the model are called *predictions*.
- The measure of *performance* is called the *loss*.

- The loss depends not only on the predictions, but also on the correct *labels* (also known as *targets* or the *dependent variable*); e.g., "dog" or "cat."

After making these changes, our diagram in Figure 1-6 looks like Figure 1-8.

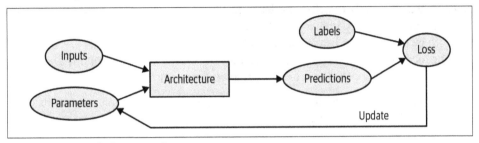

Figure 1-8. Detailed training loop

Limitations Inherent to Machine Learning

From this picture, we can now see some fundamental things about training a deep learning model:

- A model cannot be created without data.
- A model can learn to operate on only the patterns seen in the input data used to train it.
- This learning approach creates only *predictions*, not recommended *actions*.
- It's not enough to just have examples of input data; we need *labels* for that data too (e.g., pictures of dogs and cats aren't enough to train a model; we need a label for each one, saying which ones are dogs and which are cats).

Generally speaking, we've seen that most organizations that say they don't have enough data actually mean they don't have enough *labeled* data. If any organization is interested in doing something in practice with a model, then presumably they have some inputs they plan to run their model against. And presumably they've been doing that some other way for a while (e.g., manually, or with some heuristic program), so they have data from those processes! For instance, a radiology practice will almost certainly have an archive of medical scans (since they need to be able to check how their patients are progressing over time), but those scans may not have structured labels containing a list of diagnoses or interventions (since radiologists generally create free-text natural language reports, not structured data). We'll be discussing labeling approaches a lot in this book, because it's such an important issue in practice.

Since these kinds of machine learning models can only make *predictions* (i.e., attempt to replicate labels), this can result in a significant gap between organizational goals and model capabilities. For instance, in this book you'll learn how to create a *recommendation system* that can predict what products a user might purchase. This is often used in ecommerce, such as to customize products shown on a home page by showing the highest-ranked items. But such a model is generally created by looking at a user and their buying history (*inputs*) and what they went on to buy or look at (*labels*), which means that the model is likely to tell you about products the user already has, or already knows about, rather than new products that they are most likely to be interested in hearing about. That's very different from what, say, an expert at your local bookseller might do, where they ask questions to figure out your taste, and then tell you about authors or series that you've never heard of before.

Another critical insight comes from considering how a model interacts with its environment. This can create *feedback loops*, as described here:

1. A *predictive policing* model is created based on where arrests have been made in the past. In practice, this is not actually predicting crime, but rather predicting arrests, and is therefore partially simply reflecting biases in existing policing processes.

2. Law enforcement officers then might use that model to decide where to focus their policing activity, resulting in increased arrests in those areas.

3. Data on these additional arrests would then be fed back in to retrain future versions of the model.

This is a *positive feedback loop*: the more the model is used, the more biased the data becomes, making the model even more biased, and so forth.

Feedback loops can also create problems in commercial settings. For instance, a video recommendation system might be biased toward recommending content consumed by the biggest watchers of video (e.g., conspiracy theorists and extremists tend to watch more online video content than the average), resulting in those users increasing their video consumption, resulting in more of those kinds of videos being recommended. We'll consider this topic in more detail in Chapter 3.

Now that you have seen the base of the theory, let's go back to our code example and see in detail how the code corresponds to the process we just described.

How Our Image Recognizer Works

Let's see just how our image recognizer code maps to these ideas. We'll put each line into a separate cell, and look at what each one is doing (we won't explain every detail of every parameter yet, but will give a description of the important bits; full details will come later in the book). The first line imports all of the fastai.vision library:

```
from fastai.vision.all import *
```

This gives us all of the functions and classes we will need to create a wide variety of computer vision models.

Jeremy Says

A lot of Python coders recommend avoiding importing a whole library like this (using the import * syntax) because in large software projects it can cause problems. However, for interactive work such as in a Jupyter notebook, it works great. The fastai library is specially designed to support this kind of interactive use, and it will import only the necessary pieces into your environment.

The second line downloads a standard dataset from the fast.ai datasets collection (*https://course.fast.ai/datasets*) (if not previously downloaded) to your server, extracts it (if not previously extracted), and returns a Path object with the extracted location:

```
path = untar_data(URLs.PETS)/'images'
```

Sylvain Says

Throughout my time studying at fast.ai, and even still today, I've learned a lot about productive coding practices. The fastai library and fast.ai notebooks are full of great little tips that have helped make me a better programmer. For instance, notice that the fastai library doesn't just return a string containing the path to the dataset, but a Path object. This is a really useful class from the Python 3 standard library that makes accessing files and directories much easier. If you haven't come across it before, be sure to check out its documentation or a tutorial and try it out. Note that the book's website (*https://book.fast.ai*) contains links to recommended tutorials for each chapter. I'll keep letting you know about little coding tips I've found useful as we come across them.

In the third line, we define a function, is_cat, that labels cats based on a filename rule provided by the dataset's creators:

```
def is_cat(x): return x[0].isupper()
```

We use that function in the fourth line, which tells fastai what kind of dataset we have and how it is structured:

```
dls = ImageDataLoaders.from_name_func(
    path, get_image_files(path), valid_pct=0.2, seed=42,
    label_func=is_cat, item_tfms=Resize(224))
```

There are various classes for different kinds of deep learning datasets and problems—here we're using ImageDataLoaders. The first part of the class name will generally be the type of data you have, such as image or text.

The other important piece of information that we have to tell fastai is how to get the labels from the dataset. Computer vision datasets are normally structured in such a way that the label for an image is part of the filename or path—most commonly the parent folder name. fastai comes with a number of standardized labeling methods, and ways to write your own. Here we're telling fastai to use the is_cat function we just defined.

Finally, we define the Transforms that we need. A Transform contains code that is applied automatically during training; fastai includes many predefined Transforms, and adding new ones is as simple as creating a Python function. There are two kinds: item_tfms are applied to each item (in this case, each item is resized to a 224-pixel square), while batch_tfms are applied to a *batch* of items at a time using the GPU, so they're particularly fast (we'll see many examples of these throughout this book).

Why 224 pixels? This is the standard size for historical reasons (old pretrained models require this size exactly), but you can pass pretty much anything. If you increase the size, you'll often get a model with better results (since it will be able to focus on more details), but at the price of speed and memory consumption; the opposite is true if you decrease the size.

Jargon: Classification and Regression

Classification and *regression* have very specific meanings in machine learning. These are the two main types of model that we will be investigating in this book. A *classification model* is one that attempts to predict a class, or category. That is, it's predicting from a number of discrete possibilities, such as "dog" or "cat." A *regression model* is one that attempts to predict one or more numeric quantities, such as a temperature or a location. Sometimes people use the word *regression* to refer to a particular kind of model called a *linear regression model*; this is a bad practice, and we won't be using that terminology in this book!

The Pet dataset contains 7,390 pictures of dogs and cats, consisting of 37 breeds. Each image is labeled using its filename: for instance, the file *great_pyrenees_173.jpg* is the 173rd example of an image of a Great Pyrenees breed dog in the dataset. The filenames start with an uppercase letter if the image is a cat, and a lowercase letter otherwise. We have to tell fastai how to get labels from the filenames, which we do by calling from_name_func (which means that labels can be extracted using a function applied to the filename) and passing is_cat, which returns x[0].isupper(), which evaluates to True if the first letter is uppercase (i.e., it's a cat).

The most important parameter to mention here is valid_pct=0.2. This tells fastai to hold out 20% of the data and *not use it for training the model at all*. This 20% of the data is called the *validation set*; the remaining 80% is called the *training set*. The validation set is used to measure the accuracy of the model. By default, the 20% that is held out is selected randomly. The parameter `seed=42` sets the *random seed* to the same value every time we run this code, which means we get the same validation set every time we run it—this way, if we change our model and retrain it, we know that any differences are due to the changes to the model, not due to having a different random validation set.

fastai will *always* show you your model's accuracy using *only* the validation set, *never* the training set. This is absolutely critical, because if you train a large enough model for a long enough time, it will eventually memorize the label of every item in your dataset! The result will not be a useful model, because what we care about is how well our model works on *previously unseen images*. That is always our goal when creating a model: for it to be useful on data that the model sees only in the future, after it has been trained.

Even when your model has not fully memorized all your data, earlier on in training it may have memorized certain parts of it. As a result, the longer you train for, the better your accuracy will get on the training set; the validation set accuracy will also improve for a while, but eventually it will start getting worse as the model starts to memorize the training set rather than finding generalizable underlying patterns in the data. When this happens, we say that the model is *overfitting*.

Figure 1-9 shows what happens when you overfit, using a simplified example where we have just one parameter and some randomly generated data based on the function x**2. As you see, although the predictions in the overfit model are accurate for data near the observed data points, they are way off when outside of that range.

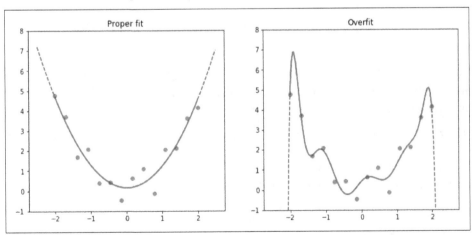

Figure 1-9. Example of overfitting

Overfitting is the single most important and challenging issue when training for all machine learning practitioners, and all algorithms. As you will see, it is easy to create a model that does a great job at making predictions on the exact data it has been trained on, but it is much harder to make accurate predictions on data the model has never seen before. And of course, this is the data that will matter in practice. For instance, if you create a handwritten digit classifier (as we will soon!) and use it to recognize numbers written on checks, then you are never going to see any of the numbers that the model was trained on—every check will have slightly different variations of writing to deal with.

You will learn many methods to avoid overfitting in this book. However, you should use those methods only after you have confirmed that overfitting is occurring (i.e., if you have observed the validation accuracy getting worse during training). We often see practitioners using overfitting avoidance techniques even when they have enough data that they didn't need to do so, ending up with a model that may be less accurate than what they could have achieved.

Validation Set

When you train a model, you must *always* have both a training set and a validation set, and you must measure the accuracy of your model only on the validation set. If you train for too long, with not enough data, you will see the accuracy of your model start to get worse; this is called *overfitting*. fastai defaults `valid_pct` to `0.2`, so even if you forget, fastai will create a validation set for you!

The fifth line of the code training our image recognizer tells fastai to create a *convolutional neural network* (CNN) and specifies what *architecture* to use (i.e., what kind of model to create), what data we want to train it on, and what *metric* to use:

```
learn = cnn_learner(dls, resnet34, metrics=error_rate)
```

Why a CNN? It's the current state-of-the-art approach to creating computer vision models. We'll be learning all about how CNNs work in this book. Their structure is inspired by how the human vision system works.

There are many architectures in fastai, which we will introduce in this book (as well as discussing how to create your own). Most of the time, however, picking an architecture isn't a very important part of the deep learning process. It's something that academics love to talk about, but in practice it is unlikely to be something you need to spend much time on. There are some standard architectures that work most of the time, and in this case we're using one called *ResNet* that we'll be talking a lot about in the book; it is both fast and accurate for many datasets and problems. The 34 in `resnet34` refers to the number of layers in this variant of the architecture (other options are 18, 50, 101, and 152). Models using architectures with more layers take longer to train and are more prone to overfitting (i.e., you can't train them for as many epochs before the accuracy on the validation set starts getting worse). On the other hand, when using more data, they can be quite a bit more accurate.

What is a metric? A *metric* is a function that measures the quality of the model's predictions using the validation set, and will be printed at the end of each epoch. In this case, we're using `error_rate`, which is a function provided by fastai that does just what it says: tells you what percentage of images in the validation set are being classified incorrectly. Another common metric for classification is `accuracy` (which is just `1.0 - error_rate`). fastai provides many more, which will be discussed throughout this book.

The concept of a metric may remind you of *loss*, but there is an important distinction. The entire purpose of loss is to define a "measure of performance" that the training system can use to update weights automatically. In other words, a good choice for loss is a choice that is easy for stochastic gradient descent to use. But a metric is defined for human consumption, so a good metric is one that is easy for you to understand, and that hews as closely as possible to what you want the model to do. At times, you might decide that the loss function is a suitable metric, but that is not necessarily the case.

`cnn_learner` also has a parameter `pretrained`, which defaults to `True` (so it's used in this case, even though we haven't specified it), which sets the weights in your model to values that have already been trained by experts to recognize a thousand different categories across 1.3 million photos (using the famous *ImageNet* (*http://www.image-net.org*) dataset). A model that has weights that have already been trained on another dataset is called a *pretrained model*. You should nearly always use a pretrained model, because it means that your model, before you've even shown it any of your data, is already very capable. And as you'll see, in a deep learning model, many of these capabilities are things you'll need, almost regardless of the details of your project. For instance, parts of pretrained models will handle edge, gradient, and color detection, which are needed for many tasks.

When using a pretrained model, `cnn_learner` will remove the last layer, since that is always specifically customized to the original training task (i.e., ImageNet dataset classification), and replace it with one or more new layers with randomized weights, of an appropriate size for the dataset you are working with. This last part of the model is known as the *head*.

Using pretrained models is the *most* important method we have to allow us to train more accurate models, more quickly, with less data and less time and money. You might think that would mean that using pretrained models would be the most studied area in academic deep learning…but you'd be very, very wrong! The importance of pretrained models is generally not recognized or discussed in most courses, books, or software library features, and is rarely considered in academic papers. As we write this at the start of 2020, things are just starting to change, but it's likely to take a while. So be careful: most people you speak to will probably greatly underestimate what you can do in deep learning with few resources, because they probably won't deeply understand how to use pretrained models.

Using a pretrained model for a task different from what it was originally trained for is known as *transfer learning*. Unfortunately, because transfer learning is so understudied, few domains have pretrained models available. For instance, few pretrained models are currently available in medicine, making transfer learning challenging to use in that domain. In addition, it is not yet well understood how to use transfer learning for tasks such as time series analysis.

Jargon: Transfer Learning

Using a pretrained model for a task different from what it was originally trained for.

The sixth line of our code tells fastai how to *fit* the model:

```
learn.fine_tune(1)
```

As we've discussed, the architecture only describes a *template* for a mathematical function; it doesn't actually do anything until we provide values for the millions of parameters it contains.

This is the key to deep learning—determining how to fit the parameters of a model to get it to solve your problem. To fit a model, we have to provide at least one piece of information: how many times to look at each image (known as number of *epochs*). The number of epochs you select will largely depend on how much time you have available, and how long you find it takes in practice to fit your model. If you select a number that is too small, you can always train for more epochs later.

But why is the method called `fine_tune`, and not `fit`? fastai *does* have a method called `fit`, which does indeed fit a model (i.e., look at images in the training set multiple times, each time updating the parameters to make the predictions closer and closer to the target labels). But in this case, we've started with a pretrained model, and we don't want to throw away all those capabilities that it already has. As you'll learn in this book, there are some important tricks to adapt a pretrained model for a new dataset—a process called *fine-tuning*.

Jargon: Fine-Tuning

A transfer learning technique that updates the parameters of a pretrained model by training for additional epochs using a different task from that used for pretraining.

When you use the `fine_tune` method, fastai will use these tricks for you. There are a few parameters you can set (which we'll discuss later), but in the default form shown here, it does two steps:

1. Use one epoch to fit just those parts of the model necessary to get the new random head to work correctly with your dataset.

2. Use the number of epochs requested when calling the method to fit the entire model, updating the weights of the later layers (especially the head) faster than the earlier layers (which, as we'll see, generally don't require many changes from the pretrained weights).

The *head* of a model is the part that is newly added to be specific to the new dataset. An *epoch* is one complete pass through the dataset. After calling `fit`, the results after each epoch are printed, showing the epoch number, the training and validation set losses (the "measure of performance" used for training the model), and any *metrics* you've requested (error rate, in this case).

So, with all this code, our model learned to recognize cats and dogs just from labeled examples. But how did it do it?

What Our Image Recognizer Learned

At this stage, we have an image recognizer that is working well, but we have no idea what it is doing! Although many people complain that deep learning results in impenetrable "black box" models (that is, something that gives predictions but that no one can understand), this really couldn't be further from the truth. There is a vast body of research showing how to deeply inspect deep learning models and get rich insights from them. Having said that, all kinds of machine learning models (including deep learning and traditional statistical models) can be challenging to fully understand, especially when considering how they will behave when coming across data that is very different from the data used to train them. We'll be discussing this issue throughout this book.

In 2013, PhD student Matt Zeiler and his supervisor, Rob Fergus, published "Visualizing and Understanding Convolutional Networks" (*https://oreil.ly/iP8cr*), which showed how to visualize the neural network weights learned in each layer of a model. They carefully analyzed the model that won the 2012 ImageNet competition, and used this analysis to greatly improve the model, such that they were able to go on to win the 2013 competition! Figure 1-10 is the picture that they published of the first layer's weights.

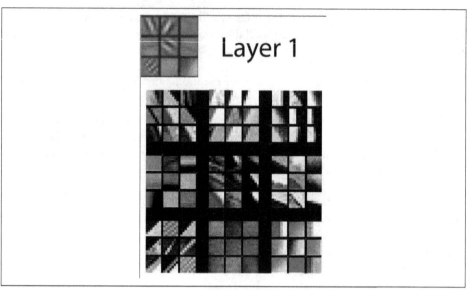

Figure 1-10. Activations of the first layer of a CNN (courtesy of Matthew D. Zeiler and Rob Fergus)

This picture requires some explanation. For each layer, the image part with the light gray background shows the reconstructed weights, and the larger section at the bottom shows the parts of the training images that most strongly matched each set of weights. For layer 1, what we can see is that the model has discovered weights that represent diagonal, horizontal, and vertical edges, as well as various gradients. (Note that for each layer, only a subset of the features is shown; in practice there are thousands across all of the layers.)

These are the basic building blocks that the model has learned for computer vision. They have been widely analyzed by neuroscientists and computer vision researchers, and it turns out that these learned building blocks are very similar to the basic visual machinery in the human eye, as well as the handcrafted computer vision features that were developed prior to the days of deep learning. The next layer is represented in Figure 1-11.

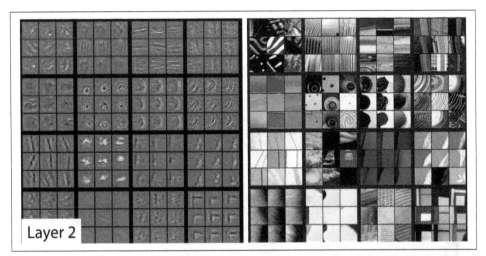

Figure 1-11. Activations of the second layer of a CNN (courtesy of Matthew D. Zeiler and Rob Fergus)

For layer 2, there are nine examples of weight reconstructions for each of the features found by the model. We can see that the model has learned to create feature detectors that look for corners, repeating lines, circles, and other simple patterns. These are built from the basic building blocks developed in the first layer. For each of these, the righthand side of the picture shows small patches from actual images that these features most closely match. For instance, the particular pattern in row 2, column 1 matches the gradients and textures associated with sunsets.

Figure 1-12 shows the image from the paper showing the results of reconstructing the features of layer 3.

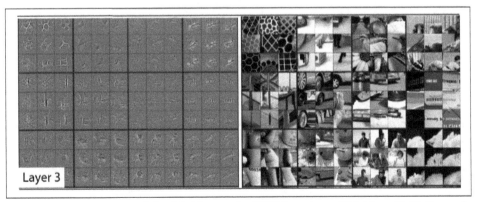

Figure 1-12. Activations of the third layer of a CNN (courtesy of Matthew D. Zeiler and Rob Fergus)

As you can see by looking at the righthand side of this picture, the features are now able to identify and match with higher-level semantic components, such as car wheels, text, and flower petals. Using these components, layers 4 and 5 can identify even higher-level concepts, as shown in Figure 1-13.

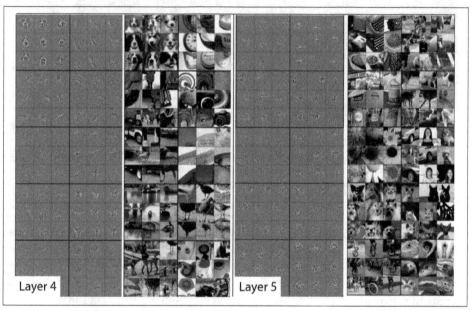

Figure 1-13. Activations of the fourth and fifth layers of a CNN (courtesy of Matthew D. Zeiler and Rob Fergus)

This article was studying an older model called *AlexNet* that contained only five layers. Networks developed since then can have hundreds of layers—so you can imagine how rich the features developed by these models can be!

When we fine-tuned our pretrained model earlier, we adapted what those last layers focus on (flowers, humans, animals) to specialize on the cats versus dogs problem. More generally, we could specialize such a pretrained model on many different tasks. Let's have a look at some examples.

Image Recognizers Can Tackle Non-Image Tasks

An image recognizer can, as its name suggests, only recognize images. But a lot of things can be represented as images, which means that an image recognizer can learn to complete many tasks.

For instance, a sound can be converted to a spectrogram, which is a chart that shows the amount of each frequency at each time in an audio file. Fast.ai student Ethan Sutin used this approach to easily beat the published accuracy of a state-of-the-art environmental sound detection model (*https://oreil.ly/747uv*) using a dataset of 8,732 urban sounds. fastai's `show_batch` clearly shows how each sound has a quite distinctive spectrogram, as you can see in Figure 1-14.

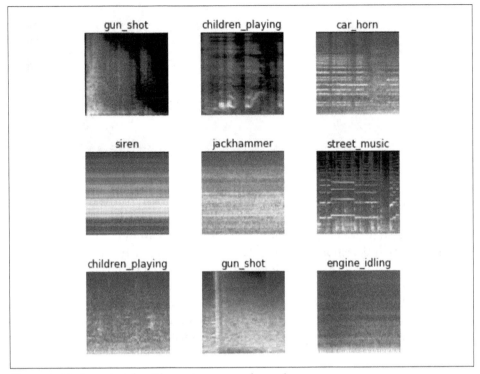

Figure 1-14. show_batch with spectrograms of sounds

A time series can easily be converted into an image by simply plotting the time series on a graph. However, it is often a good idea to try to represent your data in a way that makes it as easy as possible to pull out the most important components. In a time series, things like seasonality and anomalies are most likely to be of interest.

Various transformations are available for time series data. For instance, fast.ai student Ignacio Oguiza created images from a time series dataset for olive oil classification, using a technique called Gramian Angular Difference Field (GADF); you can see the result in Figure 1-15. He then fed those images to an image classification model just like the one you see in this chapter. His results, despite having only 30 training set images, were well over 90% accurate, and close to the state of the art.

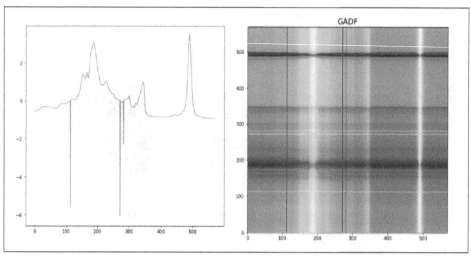

Figure 1-15. Converting a time series into an image

Another interesting fast.ai student project example comes from Gleb Esman. He was working on fraud detection at Splunk, using a dataset of users' mouse movements and mouse clicks. He turned these into pictures by drawing an image displaying the position, speed, and acceleration of the mouse pointer by using colored lines, and the clicks were displayed using small colored circles (*https://oreil.ly/6-I_X*), as shown in Figure 1-16. He fed this into an image recognition model just like the one we've used in this chapter, and it worked so well that it led to a patent for this approach to fraud analytics!

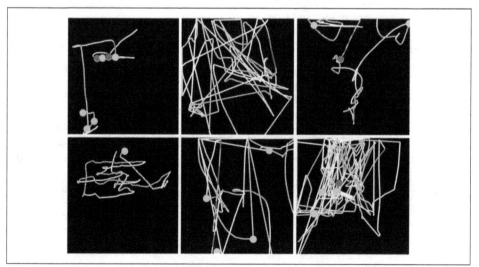

Figure 1-16. Converting computer mouse behavior to an image

Another example comes from the paper "Malware Classification with Deep Convolutional Neural Networks" (*https://oreil.ly/l_knA*) by Mahmoud Kalash et al., which explains that "the malware binary file is divided into 8-bit sequences which are then converted to equivalent decimal values. This decimal vector is reshaped and [a] grayscale image is generated that represent[s] the malware sample," in Figure 1-17.

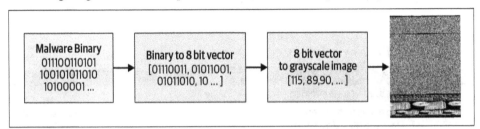

Figure 1-17. Malware classification process

The authors then show "pictures" generated through this process of malware in different categories, as shown in Figure 1-18.

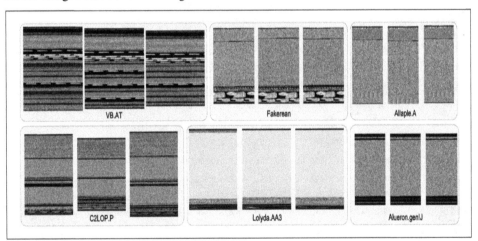

Figure 1-18. Malware examples

As you can see, the different types of malware look very distinctive to the human eye. The model the researchers trained based on this image representation was more accurate at malware classification than any previous approach shown in the academic literature. This suggests a good rule of thumb for converting a dataset into an image representation: if the human eye can recognize categories from the images, then a deep learning model should be able to do so too.

In general, you'll find that a small number of general approaches in deep learning can go a long way, if you're a bit creative in how you represent your data! You shouldn't think of approaches like the ones described here as "hacky workarounds," because they often (as here) beat previously state-of-the-art results. These really are the right ways to think about these problem domains.

Jargon Recap

We just covered a lot of information, so let's recap briefly. Table 1-3 provides a handy vocabulary list.

Table 1-3. Deep learning vocabulary

Term	Meaning
Label	The data that we're trying to predict, such as "dog" or "cat"
Architecture	The *template* of the model that we're trying to fit; i.e., the actual mathematical function that we're passing the input data and parameters to
Model	The combination of the architecture with a particular set of parameters
Parameters	The values in the model that change what task it can do and that are updated through model training
Fit	Update the parameters of the model such that the predictions of the model using the input data match the target labels
Train	A synonym for *fit*
Pretrained model	A model that has already been trained, generally using a large dataset, and will be fine-tuned
Fine-tune	Update a pretrained model for a different task
Epoch	One complete pass through the input data
Loss	A measure of how good the model is, chosen to drive training via SGD
Metric	A measurement of how good the model is using the validation set, chosen for human consumption
Validation set	A set of data held out from training, used only for measuring how good the model is
Training set	The data used for fitting the model; does not include any data from the validation set
Overfitting	Training a model in such a way that it *remembers* specific features of the input data, rather than generalizing well to data not seen during training
CNN	Convolutional neural network; a type of neural network that works particularly well for computer vision tasks

With this vocabulary in hand, we are now in a position to bring together all the key concepts introduced so far. Take a moment to review those definitions and read the following summary. If you can follow the explanation, you're well equipped to understand the discussions to come.

Machine learning is a discipline in which we define a program not by writing it entirely ourselves, but by learning from data. *Deep learning* is a specialty within machine learning that uses *neural networks* with multiple *layers*. *Image classification* is a representative example (also known as *image recognition*). We start with *labeled data* —a set of images for which we have assigned a *label* to each image, indicating what it represents. Our goal is to produce a program, called a *model*, that, given a new image, will make an accurate *prediction* regarding what that new image represents.

Every model starts with a choice of *architecture*, a general template for how that kind of model works internally. The process of *training* (or *fitting*) the model is the process of finding a set of *parameter values* (or *weights*) that specialize that general architecture into a model that works well for our particular kind of data. To define how well a model does on a single prediction, we need to define a *loss function*, which determines how we score a prediction as good or bad.

To make the training process go faster, we might start with a *pretrained model*—a model that has already been trained on someone else's data. We can then adapt it to our data by training it a bit more on our data, a process called *fine-tuning*.

When we train a model, a key concern is to ensure that our model *generalizes*: it learns general lessons from our data that also apply to new items it will encounter, so it can make good predictions on those items. The risk is that if we train our model badly, instead of learning general lessons, it effectively memorizes what it has already seen, and then it will make poor predictions about new images. Such a failure is called *overfitting*.

To avoid this, we always divide our data into two parts, the *training set* and the *validation set*. We train the model by showing it only the training set, and then we evaluate how well the model is doing by seeing how well it performs on items from the validation set. In this way, we check if the lessons the model learns from the training set are lessons that generalize to the validation set. In order for a person to assess how well the model is doing on the validation set overall, we define a *metric*. During the training process, when the model has seen every item in the training set, we call that an *epoch*.

All these concepts apply to machine learning in general. They apply to all sorts of schemes for defining a model by training it with data. What makes deep learning distinctive is a particular class of architectures: the architectures based on *neural networks*. In particular, tasks like image classification rely heavily on *convolutional neural networks*, which we will discuss shortly.

Deep Learning Is Not Just for Image Classification

Deep learning's effectiveness for classifying images has been widely discussed in recent years, even showing *superhuman* results on complex tasks like recognizing malignant tumors in CT scans. But it can do a lot more than this, as we will show here.

For instance, let's talk about something that is critically important for autonomous vehicles: localizing objects in a picture. If a self-driving car doesn't know where a pedestrian is, then it doesn't know how to avoid one! Creating a model that can recognize the content of every individual pixel in an image is called *segmentation*. Here is how we can train a segmentation model with fastai, using a subset of the *CamVid* dataset (*https://oreil.ly/rDy1i*) from the paper "Semantic Object Classes in Video: A High-Definition Ground Truth Database" (*https://oreil.ly/Mqclf*) by Gabriel J. Brostow et al.:

```
path = untar_data(URLs.CAMVID_TINY)
dls = SegmentationDataLoaders.from_label_func(
    path, bs=8, fnames = get_image_files(path/"images"),
    label_func = lambda o: path/'labels'/f'{o.stem}_P{o.suffix}',
    codes = np.loadtxt(path/'codes.txt', dtype=str)
)

learn = unet_learner(dls, resnet34)
learn.fine_tune(8)
```

epoch	train_loss	valid_loss	time
0	2.906601	2.347491	00:02

epoch	train_loss	valid_loss	time
0	1.988776	1.765969	00:02
1	1.703356	1.265247	00:02
2	1.591550	1.309860	00:02
3	1.459745	1.102660	00:02
4	1.324229	0.948472	00:02
5	1.205859	0.894631	00:02
6	1.102528	0.809563	00:02
7	1.020853	0.805135	00:02

We are not even going to walk through this code line by line, because it is nearly identical to our previous example! (We will be doing a deep dive into segmentation models in Chapter 15, along with all of the other models that we are briefly introducing in this chapter and many, many more.)

We can visualize how well it achieved its task by asking the model to color-code each pixel of an image. As you can see, it nearly perfectly classifies every pixel in every object. For instance, notice that all of the cars are overlaid with the same color, and all of the trees are overlaid with the same color (in each pair of images, the lefthand image is the ground truth label, and the right is the prediction from the model):

```
learn.show_results(max_n=6, figsize=(7,8))
```

One other area where deep learning has dramatically improved in the last couple of years is natural language processing (NLP). Computers can now generate text, translate automatically from one language to another, analyze comments, label words in sentences, and much more. Here is all of the code necessary to train a model that can classify the sentiment of a movie review better than anything that existed in the world just five years ago:

```
from fastai.text.all import *

dls = TextDataLoaders.from_folder(untar_data(URLs.IMDB), valid='test')
learn = text_classifier_learner(dls, AWD_LSTM, drop_mult=0.5, metrics=accuracy)
learn.fine_tune(4, 1e-2)
```

epoch	train_loss	valid_loss	accuracy	time
0	0.594912	0.407416	0.823640	01:35

epoch	train_loss	valid_loss	accuracy	time
0	0.268259	0.316242	0.876000	03:03
1	0.184861	0.246242	0.898080	03:10
2	0.136392	0.220086	0.918200	03:16
3	0.106423	0.191092	0.931360	03:15

This model is using the IMDb Large Movie Review dataset (*https://oreil.ly/tl-wp*) from "Learning Word Vectors for Sentiment Analysis" (*https://oreil.ly/L9vre*) by Andrew Maas et al. It works well with movie reviews of many thousands of words, but let's test it on a short one to see how it works:

```
learn.predict("I really liked that movie!")
```

```
('pos', tensor(1), tensor([0.0041, 0.9959]))
```

Here we can see the model has considered the review to be positive. The second part of the result is the index of "pos" in our data vocabulary, and the last part is the probabilities attributed to each class (99.6% for "pos" and 0.4% for "neg").

Now it's your turn! Write your own mini movie review, or copy one from the internet, and you can see what this model thinks about it.

The Order Matters

In a Jupyter notebook, the order you execute each cell is important. It's not like Excel, where everything gets updated as soon as you type something anywhere—it has an inner state that gets updated each time you execute a cell. For instance, when you run the first cell of the notebook (with the "CLICK ME" comment), you create an object called learn that contains a model and data for an image classification problem.

If we were to run the cell just shown in the text (the one that predicts whether a review is good) straight after, we would get an error as this learn object does not contain a text classification model. This cell needs to be run after the one containing this:

```
from fastai.text.all import *

dls = TextDataLoaders.from_folder(untar_data(URLs.IMDB), valid='test')
learn = text_classifier_learner(dls, AWD_LSTM, drop_mult=0.5,
                                metrics=accuracy)
learn.fine_tune(4, 1e-2)
```

The outputs themselves can be deceiving, because they include the results of the last time the cell was executed; if you change the code inside a cell without executing it, the old (misleading) results will remain.

Except when we mention it explicitly, the notebooks provided on the book's website (*https://book.fast.ai*) are meant to be run in order, from top to bottom. In general, when experimenting, you will find yourself executing cells in any order to go fast (which is a super neat feature of Jupyter Notebook), but once you have explored and arrived at the final version of your code, make sure you can run the cells of your notebooks in order (your future self won't necessarily remember the convoluted path you took otherwise!).

In command mode, typing 0 twice will restart the *kernel* (which is the engine powering your notebook). This will wipe your state clean and make it as if you had just

---

started in the notebook. Choose Run All Above from the Cell menu to run all cells above the point where you are. We have found this to be useful when developing the fastai library.

If you ever have any questions about a fastai method, you should use the function doc, passing it the method name:

```
doc(learn.predict)
```

Learner.predict	[source]
Learner.predict (**item** , **rm_type_tfms** = *None* , **with_input** = *False*)	
Return the prediction on item , fully decoded, loss function decoded and probabilities	
Show in docs	

A window pops up containing a brief one-line explanation. The "Show in docs" link takes you to the full documentation (*https://docs.fast.ai*), where you'll find all the details and lots of examples. Also, most of fastai's methods are just a handful of lines, so you can click the "source" link to see exactly what's going on behind the scenes.

Let's move on to something much less sexy, but perhaps significantly more widely commercially useful: building models from plain *tabular* data.

Jargon: Tabular

Data that is in the form of a table, such as from a spreadsheet, database, or a comma-separated values (CSV) file. A tabular model is a model that tries to predict one column of a table based on information in other columns of the table.

It turns out that looks very similar too. Here is the code necessary to train a model that will predict whether a person is a high-income earner, based on their socioeconomic background:

```
from fastai.tabular.all import *
path = untar_data(URLs.ADULT_SAMPLE)

dls = TabularDataLoaders.from_csv(path/'adult.csv', path=path, y_names="salary",
    cat_names = ['workclass', 'education', 'marital-status', 'occupation',
                 'relationship', 'race'],
    cont_names = ['age', 'fnlwgt', 'education-num'],
    procs = [Categorify, FillMissing, Normalize])

learn = tabular_learner(dls, metrics=accuracy)
```

As you see, we had to tell fastai which columns are *categorical* (contain values that are one of a discrete set of choices, such as `occupation`) versus *continuous* (contain a number that represents a quantity, such as `age`).

There is no pretrained model available for this task (in general, pretrained models are not widely available for any tabular modeling tasks, although some organizations have created them for internal use), so we don't use `fine_tune` in this case. Instead, we use `fit_one_cycle`, the most commonly used method for training fastai models *from scratch* (i.e., without transfer learning):

```
learn.fit_one_cycle(3)
```

epoch	train_loss	valid_loss	accuracy	time
0	0.359960	0.357917	0.831388	00:11
1	0.353458	0.349657	0.837991	00:10
2	0.338368	0.346997	0.843213	00:10

This model is using the *Adult* (*https://oreil.ly/Gc0AR*) dataset from the paper "Scaling Up the Accuracy of Naive-Bayes Classifiers: a Decision-Tree Hybrid" (*https://oreil.ly/qFOSc*) by Ron Kohavi, which contains some demographic data about individuals (like their education, marital status, race, sex and whether they have an annual income greater than $50k). The model is over 80% accurate and took around 30 seconds to train.

Let's look at one more. Recommendation systems are important, particularly in ecommerce. Companies like Amazon and Netflix try hard to recommend products or movies that users might like. Here's how to train a model that will predict movies people might like based on their previous viewing habits, using the MovieLens dataset (*https://oreil.ly/LCfwH*):

```
from fastai.collab import *
path = untar_data(URLs.ML_SAMPLE)
dls = CollabDataLoaders.from_csv(path/'ratings.csv')
learn = collab_learner(dls, y_range=(0.5,5.5))
learn.fine_tune(10)
```

epoch	train_loss	valid_loss	time
0	1.554056	1.428071	00:01

epoch	train_loss	valid_loss	time
0	1.393103	1.361342	00:01
1	1.297930	1.159169	00:00
2	1.052705	0.827934	00:01
3	0.810124	0.668735	00:01

epoch	train_loss	valid_loss	time
4	0.711552	0.627836	00:01
5	0.657402	0.611715	00:01
6	0.633079	0.605733	00:01
7	0.622399	0.602674	00:01
8	0.629075	0.601671	00:00
9	0.619955	0.601550	00:01

This model is predicting movie ratings on a scale of 0.5 to 5.0 to within around 0.6 average error. Since we're predicting a continuous number, rather than a category, we have to tell fastai what range our target has, using the y_range parameter.

Although we're not actually using a pretrained model (for the same reason that we didn't for the tabular model), this example shows that fastai lets us use fine_tune anyway in this case (you'll learn how and why this works in Chapter 5). Sometimes it's best to experiment with fine_tune versus fit_one_cycle to see which works best for your dataset.

We can use the same show_results call we saw earlier to view a few examples of user and movie IDs, actual ratings, and predictions:

```
learn.show_results()
```

	userId	movieId	rating	rating_pred
0	157	1200	4.0	3.558502
1	23	344	2.0	2.700709
2	19	1221	5.0	4.390801
3	430	592	3.5	3.944848
4	547	858	4.0	4.076881
5	292	39	4.5	3.753513
6	529	1265	4.0	3.349463
7	19	231	3.0	2.881087
8	475	4963	4.0	4.023387
9	130	260	4.5	3.979703

Datasets: Food for Models

You've already seen quite a few models in this section, each one trained using a different dataset to do a different task. In machine learning and deep learning, we can't do anything without data. So, the people who create datasets for us to train our models on are the (often underappreciated) heroes. Some of the most useful and important datasets are those that become important *academic baselines*— datasets that are widely studied by researchers and used to compare algorithmic changes. Some of these become household names (at least, among households that train models!), such as MNIST, CIFAR-10, and ImageNet.

The datasets used in this book have been selected because they provide great examples of the kinds of data that you are likely to encounter, and the academic literature has many examples of model results using these datasets to which you can compare your work.

Most datasets used in this book took the creators a lot of work to build. For instance, later in the book we'll be showing you how to create a model that can translate between French and English. The key input to this is a French/English parallel text corpus prepared in 2009 by Professor Chris Callison-Burch of the University of Pennsylvania. This dataset contains over 20 million sentence pairs in French and English. He built the dataset in a really clever way: by crawling millions of Canadian web pages (which are often multilingual) and then using a set of simple heuristics to transform URLs of French content to URLs pointing to the same content in English.

As you look at datasets throughout this book, think about where they might have come from and how they might have been curated. Then think about what kinds of interesting datasets you could create for your own projects. (We'll even take you step by step through the process of creating your own image dataset soon.)

fast.ai has spent a lot of time creating cut-down versions of popular datasets that are specially designed to support rapid prototyping and experimentation, and to be easier to learn with. In this book, we will often start by using one of the cut-down versions and later scale up to the full-size version (just as we're doing in this chapter!). This is how the world's top practitioners do their modeling in practice; they do most of their experimentation and prototyping with subsets of their data, and use the full dataset only when they have a good understanding of what they have to do.

Each of the models we trained showed a training and validation loss. A good validation set is one of the most important pieces of the training process. Let's see why and learn how to create one.

Validation Sets and Test Sets

As we've discussed, the goal of a model is to make predictions about data. But the model training process is fundamentally dumb. If we trained a model with all our data and then evaluated the model using that same data, we would not be able to tell how well our model can perform on data it hasn't seen. Without this very valuable piece of information to guide us in training our model, there is a very good chance it would become good at making predictions about that data but would perform poorly on new data.

To avoid this, our first step was to split our dataset into two sets: the *training set* (which our model sees in training) and the *validation set*, also known as the *development set* (which is used only for evaluation). This lets us test that the model learns lessons from the training data that generalize to new data, the validation data.

One way to understand this situation is that, in a sense, we don't want our model to get good results by "cheating." If it makes an accurate prediction for a data item, that should be because it has learned characteristics of that kind of item, and not because the model has been shaped by *actually having seen that particular item.*

Splitting off our validation data means our model never sees it in training and so is completely untainted by it, and is not cheating in any way. Right?

In fact, not necessarily. The situation is more subtle. This is because in realistic scenarios we rarely build a model just by training its parameters once. Instead, we are likely to explore many versions of a model through various modeling choices regarding network architecture, learning rates, data augmentation strategies, and other factors we will discuss in upcoming chapters. Many of these choices can be described as choices of *hyperparameters.* The word reflects that they are parameters about parameters, since they are the higher-level choices that govern the meaning of the weight parameters.

The problem is that even though the ordinary training process is looking at only predictions on the training data when it learns values for the weight parameters, the same is not true of us. We, as modelers, are evaluating the model by looking at predictions on the validation data when we decide to explore new hyperparameter values! So subsequent versions of the model are, indirectly, shaped by us having seen the validation data. Just as the automatic training process is in danger of overfitting the training data, we are in danger of overfitting the validation data through human trial and error and exploration.

The solution to this conundrum is to introduce another level of even more highly reserved data: the *test set.* Just as we hold back the validation data from the training process, we must hold back the test set data even from ourselves. It cannot be used to improve the model; it can be used only to evaluate the model at the very end of our efforts. In effect, we define a hierarchy of cuts of our data, based on how fully we want to hide it from training and modeling processes: training data is fully exposed, the validation data is less exposed, and test data is totally hidden. This hierarchy parallels the different kinds of modeling and evaluation processes themselves—the automatic training process with backpropagation, the more manual process of trying different hyperparameters between training sessions, and the assessment of our final result.

The test and validation sets should have enough data to ensure that you get a good estimate of your accuracy. If you're creating a cat detector, for instance, you generally want at least 30 cats in your validation set. That means that if you have a dataset with thousands of items, using the default 20% validation set size may be more than you need. On the other hand, if you have lots of data, using some of it for validation probably doesn't have any downsides.

Having two levels of "reserved data"—a validation set and a test set, with one level representing data that you are virtually hiding from yourself—may seem a bit extreme. But it is often necessary because models tend to gravitate toward the simplest way to do good predictions (memorization), and we as fallible humans tend to gravitate toward fooling ourselves about how well our models are performing. The discipline of the test set helps us keep ourselves intellectually honest. That doesn't mean we *always* need a separate test set—if you have very little data, you may need just a validation set—but generally it's best to use one if at all possible.

This same discipline can be critical if you intend to hire a third party to perform modeling work on your behalf. A third party might not understand your requirements accurately, or their incentives might even encourage them to misunderstand them. A good test set can greatly mitigate these risks and let you evaluate whether their work solves your actual problem.

To put it bluntly, if you're a senior decision maker in your organization (or you're advising senior decision makers), the most important takeaway is this: if you ensure that you really understand what test and validation sets are and why they're important, you'll avoid the single biggest source of failures we've seen when organizations decide to use AI. For instance, if you're considering bringing in an external vendor or service, make sure that you hold out some test data that the vendor *never gets to see*. Then *you* check their model on your test data, using a metric that *you* choose based on what actually matters to you in practice, and *you* decide what level of performance is adequate. (It's also a good idea for you to try out simple baseline yourself, so you know what a really simple model can achieve. Often it'll turn out that your simple model performs just as well as one produced by an external "expert"!)

Use Judgment in Defining Test Sets

To do a good job of defining a validation set (and possibly a test set), you will sometimes want to do more than just randomly grab a fraction of your original dataset. Remember: a key property of the validation and test sets is that they must be representative of the new data you will see in the future. This may sound like an impossible order! By definition, you haven't seen this data yet. But you usually still do know some things.

It's instructive to look at a few example cases. Many of these examples come from predictive modeling competitions on the *Kaggle* platform (*https://www.kaggle.com*), which is a good representation of problems and methods you might see in practice.

One case might be if you are looking at time series data. For a time series, choosing a random subset of the data will be both too easy (you can look at the data both before and after the dates you are trying to predict) and not representative of most business use cases (where you are using historical data to build a model for use in the future). If your data includes the date and you are building a model to use in the future, you will want to choose a continuous section with the latest dates as your validation set (for instance, the last two weeks or last month of available data).

Suppose you want to split the time series data in Figure 1-19 into training and validation sets.

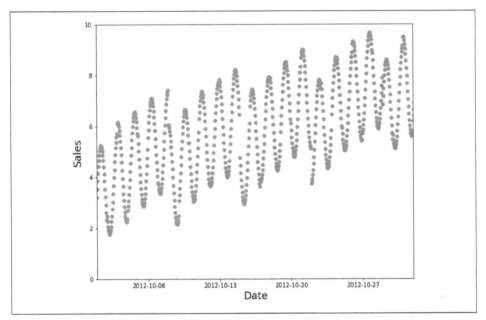

Figure 1-19. A time series

A random subset is a poor choice (too easy to fill in the gaps, and not indicative of what you'll need in production), as we can see in Figure 1-20.

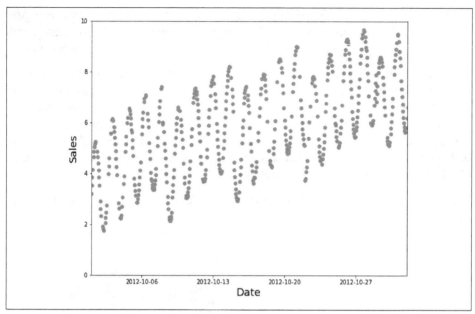

Figure 1-20. A poor training subset

Instead, use the earlier data as your training set (and the later data for the validation set), as shown in Figure 1-21.

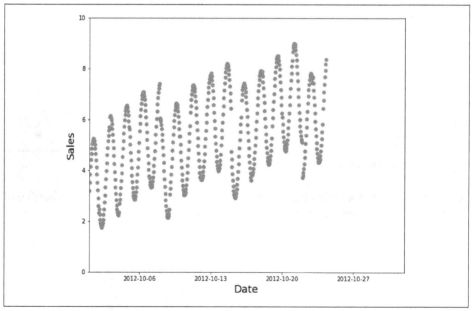

Figure 1-21. A good training subset

For example, Kaggle had a competition to predict the sales in a chain of Ecuadorian grocery stores (*https://oreil.ly/UQoXe*). Kaggle's training data ran from Jan 1, 2013 to Aug 15, 2017, and the test data spanned from Aug 16, 2017 to Aug 31, 2017. That way, the competition organizer ensured that entrants were making predictions for a time period that was *in the future*, from the perspective of their model. This is similar to the way quantitative hedge fund traders do *backtesting* to check whether their models are predictive of future periods, based on past data.

A second common case occurs when you can easily anticipate ways the data you will be making predictions for in production may be *qualitatively different* from the data you have to train your model with.

In the Kaggle distracted driver competition (*https://oreil.ly/zT_tC*), the independent variables are pictures of drivers at the wheel of a car, and the dependent variables are categories such as texting, eating, or safely looking ahead. Lots of pictures are of the same drivers in different positions, as we can see in Figure 1-22. If you were an insurance company building a model from this data, note that you would be most interested in how the model performs on drivers it hasn't seen before (since you would likely have training data for only a small group of people). In recognition of this, the test data for the competition consists of images of people that don't appear in the training set.

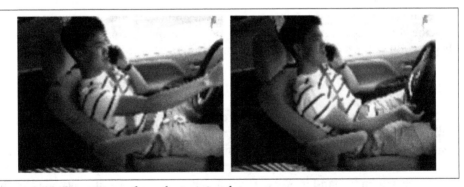

Figure 1-22. Two pictures from the training data

If you put one of the images in Figure 1-22 in your training set and one in the validation set, your model will have an easy time making a prediction for the one in the validation set, so it will seem to be performing better than it would on new people. Another perspective is that if you used all the people in training your model, your model might be overfitting to particularities of those specific people and not just learning the states (texting, eating, etc.).

A similar dynamic was at work in the Kaggle fisheries competition (*https://oreil.ly/iJwFf*) to identify the species of fish caught by fishing boats in order to reduce illegal fishing of endangered populations. The test set consisted of images from boats that didn't appear in the training data, so in this case you'd want your validation set to also include boats that are not in the training set.

Sometimes it may not be clear how your validation data will differ. For instance, for a problem using satellite imagery, you'd need to gather more information on whether the training set contained just certain geographic locations or came from geographically scattered data.

Now that you have gotten a taste of how to build a model, you can decide what you want to dig into next.

A *Choose Your Own Adventure* Moment

If you would like to learn more about how to use deep learning models in practice, including how to identify and fix errors, create a real working web application, and avoid your model causing unexpected harm to your organization or society more generally, then keep reading the next two chapters. If you would like to start learning the foundations of how deep learning works under the hood, skip to Chapter 4. (Did you ever read *Choose Your Own Adventure* books as a kid? Well, this is kind of like that…except with more deep learning than that book series contained.)

You will need to read all these chapters to progress further in the book, but the order in which you read them is totally up to you. They don't depend on each other. If you skip ahead to Chapter 4, we will remind you at the end to come back and read the chapters you skipped over before you go any further.

Questionnaire

After reading pages and pages of prose, it can be hard to know which key things you really need to focus on and remember. So, we've prepared a list of questions and suggested steps to complete at the end of each chapter. All the answers are in the text of the chapter, so if you're not sure about anything here, reread that part of the text and make sure you understand it. Answers to all these questions are also available on the book's website (*https://book.fast.ai*). You can also visit the forums (*https://forums.fast.ai*) if you get stuck to get help from other folks studying this material.

For more questions, including detailed answers and links to the video timeline, have a look at Radek Osmulski's aiquizzes (*http://aiquizzes.com/howto*).

1. Do you need these for deep learning?
   - Lots of math T/F
   - Lots of data T/F
   - Lots of expensive computers T/F

- A PhD T/F

2. Name five areas where deep learning is now the best tool in the world.

3. What was the name of the first device that was based on the principle of the artificial neuron?

4. Based on the book of the same name, what are the requirements for parallel distributed processing (PDP)?

5. What were the two theoretical misunderstandings that held back the field of neural networks?

6. What is a GPU?

7. Open a notebook and execute a cell containing: 1+1. What happens?

8. Follow through each cell of the stripped version of the notebook for this chapter. Before executing each cell, guess what will happen.

9. Complete the Jupyter Notebook online appendix (*https://oreil.ly/9uPZe*).

10. Why is it hard to use a traditional computer program to recognize images in a photo?

11. What did Samuel mean by "weight assignment"?

12. What term do we normally use in deep learning for what Samuel called "weights"?

13. Draw a picture that summarizes Samuel's view of a machine learning model.

14. Why is it hard to understand why a deep learning model makes a particular prediction?

15. What is the name of the theorem that shows that a neural network can solve any mathematical problem to any level of accuracy?

16. What do you need in order to train a model?

17. How could a feedback loop impact the rollout of a predictive policing model?

18. Do we always have to use 224×224-pixel images with the cat recognition model?

19. What is the difference between classification and regression?

20. What is a validation set? What is a test set? Why do we need them?

21. What will fastai do if you don't provide a validation set?

22. Can we always use a random sample for a validation set? Why or why not?

23. What is overfitting? Provide an example.

24. What is a metric? How does it differ from loss?

25. How can pretrained models help?

26. What is the "head" of a model?

27. What kinds of features do the early layers of a CNN find? How about the later layers?

28. Are image models useful only for photos?

29. What is an architecture?

30. What is segmentation?

31. What is y_range used for? When do we need it?

32. What are hyperparameters?

33. What's the best way to avoid failures when using AI in an organization?

Further Research

Each chapter also has a "Further Research" section that poses some questions that aren't fully answered in the text, or gives more advanced assignments. Answers to these questions aren't on the book's website; you'll need to do your own research!

1. Why is a GPU useful for deep learning? How is a CPU different, and why is it less effective for deep learning?

2. Try to think of three areas where feedback loops might impact the use of machine learning. See if you can find documented examples of that happening in practice.

CHAPTER 2

From Model to Production

The six lines of code we saw in Chapter 1 are just one small part of the process of using deep learning in practice. In this chapter, we're going to use a computer vision example to look at the end-to-end process of creating a deep learning application. More specifically, we're going to build a bear classifier! In the process, we'll discuss the capabilities and constraints of deep learning, explore how to create datasets, look at possible gotchas when using deep learning in practice, and more. Many of the key points will apply equally well to other deep learning problems, such as those in Chapter 1. If you work through a problem similar in key respects to our example problems, we expect you to get excellent results with little code, quickly.

Let's start with how you should frame your problem.

The Practice of Deep Learning

We've seen that deep learning can solve a lot of challenging problems quickly and with little code. As a beginner, there's a sweet spot of problems that are similar enough to our example problems that you can very quickly get extremely useful results. However, deep learning isn't magic! The same six lines of code won't work for every problem anyone can think of today.

Underestimating the constraints and overestimating the capabilities of deep learning may lead to frustratingly poor results, at least until you gain some experience and can solve the problems that arise. Conversely, overestimating the constraints and underestimating the capabilities of deep learning may mean you do not attempt a solvable problem because you talk yourself out of it.

We often talk to people who underestimate both the constraints and the capabilities of deep learning. Both of these can be problems: underestimating the capabilities means that you might not even try things that could be very beneficial, and underestimating the constraints might mean that you fail to consider and react to important issues.

The best thing to do is to keep an open mind. If you remain open to the possibility that deep learning might solve part of your problem with less data or complexity than you expect, you can design a process through which you can find the specific capabilities and constraints related to your particular problem. This doesn't mean making any risky bets—we will show you how you can gradually roll out models so that they don't create significant risks, and can even backtest them prior to putting them in production.

Starting Your Project

So where should you start your deep learning journey? The most important thing is to ensure that you have a project to work on—it is only through working on your own projects that you will get real experience building and using models. When selecting a project, the most important consideration is data availability.

Regardless of whether you are doing a project just for your own learning or for practical application in your organization, you want to be able to start quickly. We have seen many students, researchers, and industry practitioners waste months or years while they attempt to find their perfect dataset. The goal is not to find the "perfect" dataset or project, but just to get started and iterate from there. If you take this approach, you will be on your third iteration of learning and improving while the perfectionists are still in the planning stages!

We also suggest that you iterate from end to end in your project; don't spend months fine-tuning your model, or polishing the perfect GUI, or labeling the perfect dataset. …Instead, complete every step as well as you can in a reasonable amount of time, all the way to the end. For instance, if your final goal is an application that runs on a mobile phone, that should be what you have after each iteration. But perhaps in the early iterations you take shortcuts; for instance, by doing all of the processing on a remote server and using a simple responsive web application. By completing the project end to end, you will see where the trickiest bits are, and which bits make the biggest difference to the final result.

As you work through this book, we suggest that you complete lots of small experiments, by running and adjusting the notebooks we provide, at the same time that you gradually develop your own projects. That way, you will be getting experience with all of the tools and techniques that we're explaining as we discuss them.

Sylvain Says

To make the most of this book, take the time to experiment between each chapter, whether on your own project or by exploring the notebooks we provide. Then try rewriting those notebooks from scratch on a new dataset. It's only by practicing (and failing) a lot that you will develop intuition of how to train a model.

By using the end-to-end iteration approach, you will also get a better understanding of how much data you really need. For instance, you may find you can easily get only 200 labeled data items, and you can't really know until you try whether that's enough to get the performance you need for your application to work well in practice.

In an organizational context, you will be able to show your colleagues that your idea can work by showing them a real working prototype. We have repeatedly observed that this is the secret to getting good organizational buy-in for a project.

Since it is easiest to get started on a project for which you already have data available, that means it's probably easiest to get started on a project related to something you are already doing, because you already have data about things that you are doing. For instance, if you work in the music business, you may have access to many recordings. If you work as a radiologist, you probably have access to lots of medical images. If you are interested in wildlife preservation, you may have access to lots of images of wildlife.

Sometimes you have to get a bit creative. Maybe you can find a previous machine learning project, such as a Kaggle competition, that is related to your field of interest. Sometimes you have to compromise. Maybe you can't find the exact data you need for the precise project you have in mind; but you might be able to find something from a similar domain, or measured in a different way, tackling a slightly different problem. Working on these kinds of similar projects will still give you a good understanding of the overall process, and may help you identify other shortcuts, data sources, and so forth.

Especially when you are just starting out with deep learning, it's not a good idea to branch out into very different areas, to places that deep learning has not been applied to before. That's because if your model does not work at first, you will not know whether it is because you have made a mistake, or if the very problem you are trying to solve is simply not solvable with deep learning. And you won't know where to look to get help. Therefore, it is best at first to start by finding an example online of something that somebody has had good results with and that is at least somewhat similar to what you are trying to achieve, by converting your data into a format similar to what someone else has used before (such as creating an image from your data). Let's have a look at the state of deep learning, just so you know what kinds of things deep learning is good at right now.

The State of Deep Learning

Let's start by considering whether deep learning can be any good at the problem you are looking to work on. This section provides a summary of the state of deep learning at the start of 2020. However, things move very fast, and by the time you read this, some of these constraints may no longer exist. We will try to keep the book's website up-to-date; in addition, a Google search for "what can AI do now" is likely to provide current information.

Computer vision

There are many domains in which deep learning has not been used to analyze images yet, but those where it has been tried have nearly universally shown that computers can recognize items in an image at least as well as people can—even specially trained people, such as radiologists. This is known as *object recognition*. Deep learning is also good at recognizing where objects in an image are, and can highlight their locations and name each found object. This is known as *object detection* (in a variant of this that we saw in Chapter 1, every pixel is categorized based on the kind of object it is part of—this is called *segmentation*).

Deep learning algorithms are generally not good at recognizing images that are significantly different in structure or style from those used to train the model. For instance, if there were no black-and-white images in the training data, the model may do poorly on black-and-white images. Similarly, if the training data did not contain hand-drawn images, the model will probably do poorly on hand-drawn images. There is no general way to check which types of images are missing in your training set, but we will show in this chapter some ways to try to recognize when unexpected image types arise in the data when the model is being used in production (this is known as checking for *out-of-domain* data).

One major challenge for object detection systems is that image labeling can be slow and expensive. There is a lot of work at the moment going into tools to try to make this labeling faster and easier, and to require fewer handcrafted labels to train accurate object detection models. One approach that is particularly helpful is to synthetically generate variations of input images, such as by rotating them or changing their brightness and contrast; this is called *data augmentation* and also works well for text and other types of models. We will be discussing it in detail in this chapter.

Another point to consider is that although your problem might not look like a computer vision problem, it might be possible with a little imagination to turn it into one. For instance, if what you are trying to classify are sounds, you might try converting the sounds into images of their acoustic waveforms and then training a model on those images.

Text (natural language processing)

Computers are good at classifying both short and long documents based on categories such as spam or not spam, sentiment (e.g., is the review positive or negative), author, source website, and so forth. We are not aware of any rigorous work done in this area to compare computers to humans, but anecdotally it seems to us that deep learning performance is similar to human performance on these tasks.

Deep learning is also good at generating context-appropriate text, such as replies to social media posts, and imitating a particular author's style. It's good at making this content compelling to humans too—in fact, even more compelling than human-generated text. However, deep learning is not good at generating *correct* responses! We don't have a reliable way to, for instance, combine a knowledge base of medical information with a deep learning model for generating medically correct natural language responses. This is dangerous, because it is so easy to create content that appears to a layman to be compelling, but actually is entirely incorrect.

Another concern is that context-appropriate, highly compelling responses on social media could be used at massive scale—thousands of times greater than any troll farm previously seen—to spread disinformation, create unrest, and encourage conflict. As a rule of thumb, text generation models will always be technologically a bit ahead of models for recognizing automatically generated text. For instance, it is possible to use a model that can recognize artificially generated content to actually improve the generator that creates that content, until the classification model is no longer able to complete its task.

Despite these issues, deep learning has many applications in NLP: it can be used to translate text from one language to another, summarize long documents into something that can be digested more quickly, find all mentions of a concept of interest, and more. Unfortunately, the translation or summary could well include completely incorrect information! However, the performance is already good enough that many people are using these systems—for instance, Google's online translation system (and every other online service we are aware of) is based on deep learning.

Combining text and images

The ability of deep learning to combine text and images into a single model is, generally, far better than most people intuitively expect. For example, a deep learning model can be trained on input images with output captions written in English, and can learn to generate surprisingly appropriate captions automatically for new images! But again, we have the same warning that we discussed in the previous section: there is no guarantee that these captions will be correct.

Because of this serious issue, we generally recommend that deep learning be used not as an entirely automated process, but as part of a process in which the model and a human user interact closely. This can potentially make humans orders of magnitude more productive than they would be with entirely manual methods, and result in more accurate processes than using a human alone.

For instance, an automatic system can be used to identify potential stroke victims directly from CT scans, and send a high-priority alert to have those scans looked at quickly. There is only a three-hour window to treat strokes, so this fast feedback loop could save lives. At the same time, however, all scans could continue to be sent to radiologists in the usual way, so there would be no reduction in human input. Other deep learning models could automatically measure items seen on the scans and insert those measurements into reports, warning the radiologists about findings that they may have missed and telling them about other cases that might be relevant.

Tabular data

For analyzing time series and tabular data, deep learning has recently been making great strides. However, deep learning is generally used as part of an ensemble of multiple types of model. If you already have a system that is using random forests or gradient boosting machines (popular tabular modeling tools that you will learn about soon), then switching to or adding deep learning may not result in any dramatic improvement.

Deep learning does greatly increase the variety of columns that you can include—for example, columns containing natural language (book titles, reviews, etc.) and high-cardinality categorical columns (i.e., something that contains a large number of discrete choices, such as zip code or product ID). On the down side, deep learning models generally take longer to train than random forests or gradient boosting machines, although this is changing thanks to libraries such as RAPIDS (*https:// rapids.ai*), which provides GPU acceleration for the whole modeling pipeline. We cover the pros and cons of all these methods in detail in Chapter 9.

Recommendation systems

Recommendation systems are really just a special type of tabular data. In particular, they generally have a high-cardinality categorical variable representing users, and another one representing products (or something similar). A company like Amazon represents every purchase that has ever been made by its customers as a giant sparse matrix, with customers as the rows and products as the columns. Once they have the data in this format, data scientists apply some form of collaborative filtering to *fill in the matrix*. For example, if customer A buys products 1 and 10, and customer B buys products 1, 2, 4, and 10, the engine will recommend that A buy 2 and 4.

Because deep learning models are good at handling high-cardinality categorical variables, they are quite good at handling recommendation systems. They particularly come into their own, just like for tabular data, when combining these variables with other kinds of data, such as natural language or images. They can also do a good job of combining all of these types of information with additional metadata represented as tables, such as user information, previous transactions, and so forth.

However, nearly all machine learning approaches have the downside that they tell you only which products a particular user might like, rather than what recommendations would be helpful for a user. Many kinds of recommendations for products a user might like may not be at all helpful—for instance, if the user is already familiar with the products, or if they are simply different packagings of products they have already purchased (such as a boxed set of novels, when they already have each of the items in that set). Jeremy likes reading books by Terry Pratchett, and for a while Amazon was recommending nothing but Terry Pratchett books to him (see Figure 2-1), which really wasn't helpful because he was already aware of these books!

Figure 2-1. A not-so-useful recommendation

Other data types

Often you will find that domain-specific data types fit very nicely into existing categories. For instance, protein chains look a lot like natural language documents, in that they are long sequences of discrete tokens with complex relationships and meaning throughout the sequence. And indeed, it does turn out that using NLP deep learning methods is the current state-of-the-art approach for many types of protein analysis. As another example, sounds can be represented as spectrograms, which can be treated as images; standard deep learning approaches for images turn out to work really well on spectrograms.

The Drivetrain Approach

Many accurate models are of no use to anyone, and many inaccurate models are highly useful. To ensure that your modeling work is useful in practice, you need to consider how your work will be used. In 2012, Jeremy, along with Margit Zwemer and Mike Loukides, introduced a method called *the Drivetrain Approach* for thinking about this issue.

The Drivetrain Approach, illustrated in Figure 2-2, was described in detail in "Designing Great Data Products" (*https://oreil.ly/KJIIa*). The basic idea is to start with considering your objective, then think about what actions you can take to meet that objective and what data you have (or can acquire) that can help, and then build a model that you can use to determine the best actions to take to get the best results in terms of your objective.

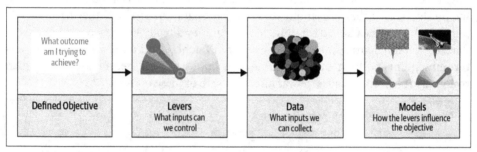

Figure 2-2. The Drivetrain Approach

Consider a model in an autonomous vehicle: you want to help a car drive safely from point A to point B without human intervention. Great predictive modeling is an important part of the solution, but it doesn't stand on its own; as products become more sophisticated, it disappears into the plumbing. Someone using a self-driving car is completely unaware of the hundreds (if not thousands) of models and the petabytes of data that make it work. But as data scientists build increasingly sophisticated products, they need a systematic design approach.

We use data not just to generate more data (in the form of predictions), but to produce *actionable outcomes*. That is the goal of the Drivetrain Approach. Start by defining a clear *objective*. For instance, Google, when creating its first search engine, considered "What is the user's main objective in typing in a search query?" This led to Google's objective, which was to "show the most relevant search result." The next step is to consider what *levers* you can pull (i.e., what actions you can take) to better achieve that objective. In Google's case, that was the ranking of the search results. The third step was to consider what new *data* they would need to produce such a ranking; they realized that the implicit information regarding which pages linked to which other pages could be used for this purpose.

Only after these first three steps do we begin thinking about building the predictive *models*. Our objective and available levers, what data we already have and what additional data we will need to collect, determine the models we can build. The models will take both the levers and any uncontrollable variables as their inputs; the outputs from the models can be combined to predict the final state for our objective.

Let's consider another example: recommendation systems. The *objective* of a recommendation engine is to drive additional sales by surprising and delighting the customer with recommendations of items they would not have purchased without the recommendation. The *lever* is the ranking of the recommendations. New *data* must be collected to generate recommendations that will *cause new sales*. This will require conducting many randomized experiments in order to collect data about a wide range of recommendations for a wide range of customers. This is a step that few organizations take; but without it, you don't have the information you need to optimize recommendations based on your true objective (more sales!).

Finally, you could build two *models* for purchase probabilities, conditional on seeing or not seeing a recommendation. The difference between these two probabilities is a utility function for a given recommendation to a customer. It will be low in cases where the algorithm recommends a familiar book that the customer has already rejected (both components are small) or a book that they would have bought even without the recommendation (both components are large and cancel each other out).

As you can see, in practice often the practical implementation of your models will require a lot more than just training a model! You'll often need to run experiments to collect more data, and consider how to incorporate your models into the overall system you're developing. Speaking of data, let's now focus on how to find data for your project.

Gathering Data

For many types of projects, you may be able to find all the data you need online. The project we'll be completing in this chapter is a *bear detector*. It will discriminate between three types of bear: grizzly, black, and teddy bears. There are many images on the internet of each type of bear that we can use. We just need a way to find them and download them.

We've provided a tool you can use for this purpose, so you can follow along with this chapter and create your own image recognition application for whatever kinds of objects you're interested in. In the fast.ai course, thousands of students have presented their work in the course forums, displaying everything from hummingbird varieties in Trinidad to bus types in Panama—one student even created an application that would help his fiancée recognize his 16 cousins during Christmas vacation!

At the time of writing, Bing Image Search is the best option we know of for finding and downloading images. It's free for up to 1,000 queries per month, and each query can download up to 150 images. However, something better might have come along between when we wrote this and when you're reading the book, so be sure to check out this book's website (*https://book.fast.ai*) for our current recommendation.

Keeping in Touch with the Latest Services

Services that can be used for creating datasets come and go all the time, and their features, interfaces, and pricing change regularly too. In this section, we'll show how to use the Bing Image Search API (*https://oreil.ly/P8VtT*) available as part of Azure Cognitive Services at the time this book was written.

To download images with Bing Image Search, sign up at Microsoft Azure (*https://oreil.ly/qCZku*) for a free account. You will be given a key, which you can copy and enter in a cell as follows (replacing *XXX* with your key and executing it):

```
key = os.environ.get('AZURE_SEARCH_KEY', 'XXX')
```

Or, if you're comfortable at the command line, you can set it in your terminal with

```
export AZURE_SEARCH_KEY=your_key_here
```

and then restart Jupyter Notebook, and use the above line without editing it.

Once you've set key, you can use search_images_bing. This function is provided by the small utils class included with the notebooks online (if you're not sure where a function is defined, you can just type it in your notebook to find out, as shown here):

```
search_images_bing
```

```
<function utils.search_images_bing(key, term, min_sz=128)>
```

Let's try this function out:

```
results = search_images_bing(key, 'grizzly bear')
ims = results.attrgot('content_url')
len(ims)
```

```
150
```

We've successfully downloaded the URLs of 150 grizzly bears (or, at least, images that Bing Image Search finds for that search term). Let's look at one:

```
dest = 'images/grizzly.jpg'
download_url(ims[0], dest)

im = Image.open(dest)
im.to_thumb(128,128)
```

This seems to have worked nicely, so let's use fastai's `download_images` to download all the URLs for each of our search terms. We'll put each in a separate folder:

```
bear_types = 'grizzly','black','teddy'
path = Path('bears')

if not path.exists():
    path.mkdir()
    for o in bear_types:
        dest = (path/o)
        dest.mkdir(exist_ok=True)
        results = search_images_bing(key, f'{o} bear')
        download_images(dest, urls=results.attrgot('contentUrl'))
```

Our folder has image files, as we'd expect:

```
fns = get_image_files(path)
fns
```

```
(#421) [Path('bears/black/00000095.jpg'),Path('bears/black/00000133.jpg'),Path('
 > bears/black/00000062.jpg'),Path('bears/black/00000023.jpg'),Path('bears/black
 > /00000029.jpg'),Path('bears/black/00000094.jpg'),Path('bears/black/00000124.j
 > pg'),Path('bears/black/00000056.jpeg'),Path('bears/black/00000046.jpg'),Path(
 > 'bears/black/00000045.jpg')...]
```

 Jeremy Says

I just love this about working in Jupyter notebooks! It's so easy to gradually build what I want, and check my work every step of the way. I make a *lot* of mistakes, so this is really helpful to me.

Often when we download files from the internet, a few are corrupt. Let's check:

```
failed = verify_images(fns)
failed
```

```
(#0) []
```

To remove all the failed images, you can use `unlink`. Like most fastai functions that return a collection, `verify_images` returns an object of type L, which includes the `map` method. This calls the passed function on each element of the collection:

```
failed.map(Path.unlink);
```

Getting Help in Jupyter Notebooks

Jupyter notebooks are great for experimenting and immediately seeing the results of each function, but there is also a lot of functionality to help you figure out how to use different functions, or even directly look at their source code. For instance, say you type this in a cell:

```
??verify_images
```

A window will pop up with this:

```
Signature: verify_images(fns)
Source:
def verify_images(fns):
    "Find images in `fns` that can't be opened"
    return L(fns[i] for i,o in
             enumerate(parallel(verify_image, fns)) if not o)
File:      ~/git/fastai/fastai/vision/utils.py
Type:      function
```

This tells us what argument the function accepts (fns), and then shows us the source code and the file it comes from. Looking at that source code, we can see it applies the function verify_image in parallel and keeps only the image files for which the result of that function is False, which is consistent with the doc string: it finds the images in fns that can't be opened.

Here are some other features that are very useful in Jupyter notebooks:

- At any point, if you don't remember the exact spelling of a function or argument name, you can press Tab to get autocompletion suggestions.

- When inside the parentheses of a function, pressing Shift and Tab simultaneously will display a window with the signature of the function and a short description. Pressing these keys twice will expand the documentation, and pressing them three times will open a full window with the same information at the bottom of your screen.

- In a cell, typing ?func_name and executing will open a window with the signature of the function and a short description.

- In a cell, typing ??func_name and executing will open a window with the signature of the function, a short description, and the source code.

- If you are using the fastai library, we added a doc function for you: executing doc(func_name) in a cell will open a window with the signature of the function, a short description, and links to the source code on GitHub and the full documentation of the function in the library docs (https://docs.fast.ai).

- Unrelated to the documentation but still very useful: to get help at any point if you get an error, type %debug in the next cell and execute to open the Python debugger (https://oreil.ly/RShnP), which will let you inspect the content of every variable.

One thing to be aware of in this process: as we discussed in Chapter 1, models can reflect only the data used to train them. And the world is full of biased data, which ends up reflected in, for example, Bing Image Search (which we used to create our dataset). For instance, let's say you were interested in creating an app that could help users figure out whether they had healthy skin, so you trained a model on the results of searches for (say) "healthy skin." Figure 2-3 shows you kind of the results you would get.

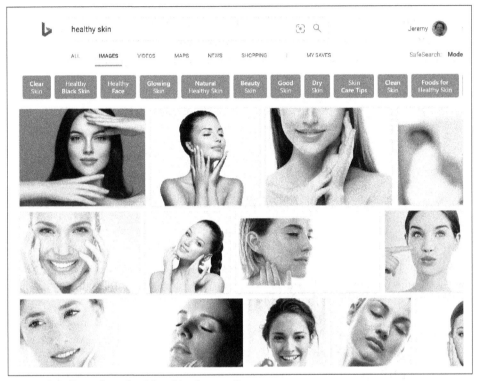

Figure 2-3. Data for a healthy skin detector?

With this as your training data, you would end up not with a healthy skin detector, but a *young white woman touching her face* detector! Be sure to think carefully about the types of data that you might expect to see in practice in your application, and check carefully to ensure that all these types are reflected in your model's source data. (Thanks to Deb Raji, who came up with the healthy skin example. See her paper "Actionable Auditing: Investigating the Impact of Publicly Naming Biased Performance Results of Commercial AI Products" (*https://oreil.ly/POS_C*) for more fascinating insights into model bias.)

Now that we have downloaded some data, we need to assemble it in a format suitable for model training. In fastai, that means creating an object called DataLoaders.

From Data to DataLoaders

DataLoaders is a thin class that just stores whatever DataLoader objects you pass to it and makes them available as train and valid. Although it's a simple class, it's important in fastai: it provides the data for your model. The key functionality in DataLoad ers is provided with just these four lines of code (it has some other minor functionality we'll skip over for now):

```
class DataLoaders(GetAttr):
    def __init__(self, *loaders): self.loaders = loaders
    def __getitem__(self, i): return self.loaders[i]
    train,valid = add_props(lambda i,self: self[i])
```

Jargon: DataLoaders

A fastai class that stores multiple DataLoader objects you pass to it —normally a train and a valid, although it's possible to have as many as you like. The first two are made available as properties.

Later in the book, you'll also learn about the Dataset and Datasets classes, which have the same relationship. To turn our downloaded data into a DataLoaders object, we need to tell fastai at least four things:

- What kinds of data we are working with
- How to get the list of items
- How to label these items
- How to create the validation set

So far we have seen a number of *factory methods* for particular combinations of these things, which are convenient when you have an application and data structure that happen to fit into those predefined methods. For when you don't, fastai has an extremely flexible system called the *data block API*. With this API, you can fully customize every stage of the creation of your DataLoaders. Here is what we need to create a DataLoaders for the dataset that we just downloaded:

```
bears = DataBlock(
    blocks=(ImageBlock, CategoryBlock),
    get_items=get_image_files,
    splitter=RandomSplitter(valid_pct=0.2, seed=42),
    get_y=parent_label,
    item_tfms=Resize(128))
```

Let's look at each of these arguments in turn. First we provide a tuple specifying the types we want for the independent and dependent variables:

```
blocks=(ImageBlock, CategoryBlock)
```

The *independent variable* is the thing we are using to make predictions from, and the *dependent variable* is our target. In this case, our independent variable is a set of images, and our dependent variables are the categories (type of bear) for each image. We will see many other types of block in the rest of this book.

For this `DataLoaders`, our underlying items will be file paths. We have to tell fastai how to get a list of those files. The `get_image_files` function takes a path, and returns a list of all of the images in that path (recursively, by default):

```
get_items=get_image_files
```

Often, datasets that you download will already have a validation set defined. Sometimes this is done by placing the images for the training and validation sets into different folders. Sometimes it is done by providing a CSV file in which each filename is listed along with which dataset it should be in. There are many ways that this can be done, and fastai provides a general approach that allows you to use one of its predefined classes for this or to write your own.

In this case, we want to split our training and validation sets randomly. However, we would like to have the same training/validation split each time we run this notebook, so we fix the random seed (computers don't really know how to create random numbers at all, but simply create lists of numbers that look random; if you provide the same starting point for that list each time—called the *seed*—then you will get the exact same list each time).

```
splitter=RandomSplitter(valid_pct=0.2, seed=42)
```

The independent variable is often referred to as x, and the dependent variable is often referred to as y. Here, we are telling fastai what function to call to create the labels in our dataset:

```
get_y=parent_label
```

`parent_label` is a function provided by fastai that simply gets the name of the folder a file is in. Because we put each of our bear images into folders based on the type of bear, this is going to give us the labels that we need.

Our images are all different sizes, and this is a problem for deep learning: we don't feed the model one image at a time but several of them (what we call a *mini-batch*). To group them in a big array (usually called a *tensor*) that is going to go through our model, they all need to be of the same size. So, we need to add a transform that will resize these images to the same size. *Item transforms* are pieces of code that run on each individual item, whether it be an image, category, or so forth. fastai includes many predefined transforms; we use the `Resize` transform here and specify a size of 128 pixels:

```
item_tfms=Resize(128)
```

This command has given us a `DataBlock` object. This is like a *template* for creating a `DataLoaders`. We still need to tell fastai the actual source of our data—in this case, the path where the images can be found:

```
dls = bears.dataloaders(path)
```

A `DataLoaders` includes validation and training `DataLoaders`. A `DataLoader` is a class that provides batches of a few items at a time to the GPU. We'll be learning a lot more about this class in the next chapter. When you loop through a `DataLoader`, fastai will give you 64 (by default) items at a time, all stacked up into a single tensor. We can take a look at a few of those items by calling the `show_batch` method on a `DataLoader`:

```
dls.valid.show_batch(max_n=4, nrows=1)
```

grizzly   grizzly   teddy   grizzly

By default, `Resize` *crops* the images to fit a square shape of the size requested, using the full width or height. This can result in losing some important details. Alternatively, you can ask fastai to pad the images with zeros (black), or squish/stretch them:

```
bears = bears.new(item_tfms=Resize(128, ResizeMethod.Squish))
dls = bears.dataloaders(path)
dls.valid.show_batch(max_n=4, nrows=1)
```

grizzly   grizzly   teddy   grizzly

```
bears = bears.new(item_tfms=Resize(128, ResizeMethod.Pad, pad_mode='zeros'))
dls = bears.dataloaders(path)
dls.valid.show_batch(max_n=4, nrows=1)
```

grizzly   grizzly   teddy   grizzly

All of these approaches seem somewhat wasteful or problematic. If we squish or stretch the images, they end up as unrealistic shapes, leading to a model that learns that things look different from how they actually are, which we would expect to result in lower accuracy. If we crop the images, we remove some of the features that allow us to perform recognition. For instance, if we were trying to recognize breeds of dog or cat, we might end up cropping out a key part of the body or the face necessary to distinguish between similar breeds. If we pad the images, we have a whole lot of empty space, which is just wasted computation for our model and results in a lower effective resolution for the part of the image we actually use.

Instead, what we normally do in practice is to randomly select part of the image and then crop to just that part. On each epoch (which is one complete pass through all of our images in the dataset), we randomly select a different part of each image. This means that our model can learn to focus on, and recognize, different features in our images. It also reflects how images work in the real world: different photos of the same thing may be framed in slightly different ways.

In fact, an entirely untrained neural network knows nothing whatsoever about how images behave. It doesn't even recognize that when an object is rotated by one degree, it still is a picture of the same thing! So training the neural network with examples of images in which the objects are in slightly different places and are slightly different sizes helps it to understand the basic concept of what an object is, and how it can be represented in an image.

Here is another example where we replace `Resize` with `RandomResizedCrop`, which is the transform that provides the behavior just described. The most important parameter to pass in is `min_scale`, which determines how much of the image to select at minimum each time:

```
bears = bears.new(item_tfms=RandomResizedCrop(128, min_scale=0.3))
dls = bears.dataloaders(path)
dls.train.show_batch(max_n=4, nrows=1, unique=True)
```

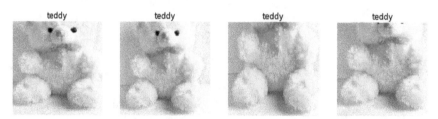

Here, we used unique=True to have the same image repeated with different versions
of this RandomResizedCrop transform.

RandomResizedCrop is a specific example of a more general technique, called data
augmentation.

Data Augmentation

Data augmentation refers to creating random variations of our input data, such that
they appear different but do not change the meaning of the data. Examples of common data augmentation techniques for images are rotation, flipping, perspective
warping, brightness changes, and contrast changes. For natural photo images such as
the ones we are using here, a standard set of augmentations that we have found work
pretty well are provided with the aug_transforms function.

Because our images are now all the same size, we can apply these augmentations to an
entire batch of them using the GPU, which will save a lot of time. To tell fastai we
want to use these transforms on a batch, we use the batch_tfms parameter (note that
we're not using RandomResizedCrop in this example, so you can see the differences
more clearly; we're also using double the amount of augmentation compared to the
default, for the same reason):

```
bears = bears.new(item_tfms=Resize(128), batch_tfms=aug_transforms(mult=2))
dls = bears.dataloaders(path)
dls.train.show_batch(max_n=8, nrows=2, unique=True)
```

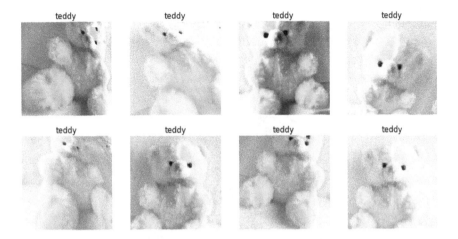

Now that we have assembled our data in a format fit for model training, let's train an image classifier using it.

Training Your Model, and Using It to Clean Your Data

Time to use the same lines of code as in Chapter 1 to train our bear classifier. We don't have a lot of data for our problem (150 pictures of each sort of bear at most), so to train our model, we'll use RandomResizedCrop, an image size of 224 pixels, which is fairly standard for image classification, and the default aug_transforms:

```
bears = bears.new(
    item_tfms=RandomResizedCrop(224, min_scale=0.5),
    batch_tfms=aug_transforms())
dls = bears.dataloaders(path)
```

We can now create our Learner and fine-tune it in the usual way:

```
learn = cnn_learner(dls, resnet18, metrics=error_rate)
learn.fine_tune(4)
```

epoch	train_loss	valid_loss	error_rate	time
0	1.235733	0.212541	0.087302	00:05

epoch	train_loss	valid_loss	error_rate	time
0	0.213371	0.112450	0.023810	00:05
1	0.173855	0.072306	0.023810	00:06
2	0.147096	0.039068	0.015873	00:06
3	0.123984	0.026801	0.015873	00:06

Now let's see whether the mistakes the model is making are mainly thinking that grizzlies are teddies (that would be bad for safety!), or that grizzlies are black bears, or something else. To visualize this, we can create a *confusion matrix*:

```
interp = ClassificationInterpretation.from_learner(learn)
interp.plot_confusion_matrix()
```

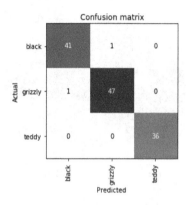

The rows represent all the black, grizzly, and teddy bears in our dataset, respectively. The columns represent the images that the model predicted as black, grizzly, and teddy bears, respectively. Therefore, the diagonal of the matrix shows the images that were classified correctly, and the off-diagonal cells represent those that were classified incorrectly. This is one of the many ways that fastai allows you to view the results of your model. It is (of course!) calculated using the validation set. With the color-coding, the goal is to have white everywhere except the diagonal, where we want dark blue. Our bear classifier isn't making many mistakes!

It's helpful to see where exactly our errors are occurring, to see whether they're due to a dataset problem (e.g., images that aren't bears at all, or are labeled incorrectly) or a model problem (perhaps it isn't handling images taken with unusual lighting, or from a different angle, etc.). To do this, we can sort our images by their loss.

The *loss* is a number that is higher if the model is incorrect (especially if it's also confident of its incorrect answer), or if it's correct but not confident of its correct answer. In the beginning of Part II, we'll learn in depth how loss is calculated and used in the training process. For now, `plot_top_losses` shows us the images with the highest loss in our dataset. As the title of the output says, each image is labeled with four things: prediction, actual (target label), loss, and probability. The *probability* here is the confidence level, from zero to one, that the model has assigned to its prediction:

```
interp.plot_top_losses(5, nrows=1)
```

grizzly/black / 1.37 / 0.74   black/grizzly / 0.94 / 0.61   black/black / 0.56 / 0.57   grizzly/grizzly / 0.14 / 0.87   grizzly/grizzly / 0.11 / 0.90

This output shows that the image with the highest loss is one that has been predicted as "grizzly" with high confidence. However, it's labeled (based on our Bing image search) as "black." We're not bear experts, but it sure looks to us like this label is incorrect! We should probably change its label to "grizzly."

The intuitive approach to doing data cleaning is to do it *before* you train a model. But as you've seen in this case, a model can help you find data issues more quickly and easily. So, we normally prefer to train a quick and simple model first, and then use it to help us with data cleaning.

fastai includes a handy GUI for data cleaning called `ImageClassifierCleaner` that allows you to choose a category and the training versus validation set and view the highest-loss images (in order), along with menus to allow images to be selected for removal or relabeling:

```
cleaner = ImageClassifierCleaner(learn)
cleaner
```

We can see that among our "black bears" is an image that contains two bears: one grizzly, one black. So, we should choose `<Delete>` in the menu under this image. `ImageClassifierCleaner` doesn't do the deleting or changing of labels for you; it just returns the indices of items to change. So, for instance, to delete (`unlink`) all images selected for deletion, we would run this:

```
for idx in cleaner.delete(): cleaner.fns[idx].unlink()
```

To move images for which we've selected a different category, we would run this:

```
for idx,cat in cleaner.change(): shutil.move(str(cleaner.fns[idx]), path/cat)
```

Sylvain Says

Cleaning the data and getting it ready for your model are two of the biggest challenges for data scientists; they say it takes 90% of their time. The fastai library aims to provide tools that make it as easy as possible.

We'll be seeing more examples of model-driven data cleaning throughout this book. Once we've cleaned up our data, we can retrain our model. Try it yourself, and see if your accuracy improves!

No Need for Big Data

After cleaning the dataset using these steps, we generally are seeing 100% accuracy on this task. We even see that result when we download a lot fewer images than the 150 per class we're using here. As you can see, the common complaint that *you need massive amounts of data to do deep learning* can be a very long way from the truth!

Now that we have trained our model, let's see how we can deploy it to be used in practice.

Turning Your Model into an Online Application

We are now going to look at what it takes to turn this model into a working online application. We will just go as far as creating a basic working prototype; we do not have the scope in this book to teach you all the details of web application development generally.

Using the Model for Inference

Once you've got a model you're happy with, you need to save it so you can then copy it over to a server where you'll use it in production. Remember that a model consists of two parts: the *architecture* and the trained *parameters*. The easiest way to save a model is to save both of these, because that way, when you load the model, you can be sure that you have the matching architecture and parameters. To save both parts, use the export method.

This method even saves the definition of how to create your `DataLoaders`. This is important, because otherwise you would have to redefine how to transform your data in order to use your model in production. fastai automatically uses your validation set `DataLoader` for inference by default, so your data augmentation will not be applied, which is generally what you want.

When you call `export`, fastai will save a file called *export.pkl*:

```
learn.export()
```

Let's check that the file exists, by using the `ls` method that fastai adds to Python's `Path` class:

```
path = Path()
path.ls(file_exts='.pkl')
```

```
(#1) [Path('export.pkl')]
```

You'll need this file wherever you deploy your app to. For now, let's try to create a simple app within our notebook.

When we use a model for getting predictions, instead of training, we call it *inference*. To create our inference learner from the exported file, we use `load_learner` (in this case, this isn't really necessary, since we already have a working `Learner` in our notebook; we're doing it here so you can see the whole process end to end):

```
learn_inf = load_learner(path/'export.pkl')
```

When we're doing inference, we're generally getting predictions for just one image at a time. To do this, pass a filename to `predict`:

```
learn_inf.predict('images/grizzly.jpg')
```

```
('grizzly', tensor(1), tensor([9.0767e-06, 9.9999e-01, 1.5748e-07]))
```

This has returned three things: the predicted category in the same format you originally provided (in this case, that's a string), the index of the predicted category, and the probabilities of each category. The last two are based on the order of categories in the *vocab* of the `DataLoaders`; that is, the stored list of all possible categories. At inference time, you can access the `DataLoaders` as an attribute of the `Learner`:

```
learn_inf.dls.vocab
```

```
(#3) ['black','grizzly','teddy']
```

We can see here that if we index into the vocab with the integer returned by `predict`, we get back "grizzly," as expected. Also, note that if we index into the list of probabilities, we see a nearly 1.00 probability that this is a grizzly.

We know how to make predictions from our saved model, so we have everything we need to start building our app. We can do it directly in a Jupyter notebook.

Creating a Notebook App from the Model

To use our model in an application, we can simply treat the `predict` method as a regular function. Therefore, creating an app from the model can be done using any of the myriad of frameworks and techniques available to application developers.

However, most data scientists are not familiar with the world of web application development. So let's try using something that you do, at this point, know: it turns out that we can create a complete working web application using nothing but Jupyter notebooks! The two things we need to make this happen are as follows:

- IPython widgets (ipywidgets)
- Voilà

IPython widgets are GUI components that bring together JavaScript and Python functionality in a web browser, and can be created and used within a Jupyter notebook. For instance, the image cleaner that we saw earlier in this chapter is entirely written with IPython widgets. However, we don't want to require users of our application to run Jupyter themselves.

That is why *Voilà* exists. It is a system for making applications consisting of IPython widgets available to end users, without them having to use Jupyter at all. Voilà is taking advantage of the fact that a notebook *already is* a kind of web application, just a rather complex one that depends on another web application: Jupyter itself. Essentially, it helps us automatically convert the complex web application we've already implicitly made (the notebook) into a simpler, easier-to-deploy web application, which functions like a normal web application rather than like a notebook.

But we still have the advantage of developing in a notebook, so with ipywidgets, we can build up our GUI step by step. We will use this approach to create a simple image classifier. First, we need a file upload widget:

```
btn_upload = widgets.FileUpload()
btn_upload
```

                        ⬆ Upload (0)

Now we can grab the image:

```
img = PILImage.create(btn_upload.data[-1])
```

We can use an `Output` widget to display it:

```
out_pl = widgets.Output()
out_pl.clear_output()
with out_pl: display(img.to_thumb(128,128))
out_pl
```

Then we can get our predictions:

```
pred,pred_idx,probs = learn_inf.predict(img)
```

And use a `Label` to display them:

```
lbl_pred = widgets.Label()
lbl_pred.value = f'Prediction: {pred}; Probability: {probs[pred_idx]:.04f}'
lbl_pred
```

Prediction: grizzly; Probability: 1.0000

We'll need a button to do the classification. It looks exactly like the Upload button:

```
btn_run = widgets.Button(description='Classify')
btn_run
```

We'll also need a *click event handler*; that is, a function that will be called when it's pressed. We can just copy over the previous lines of code:

```
def on_click_classify(change):
    img = PILImage.create(btn_upload.data[-1])
    out_pl.clear_output()
    with out_pl: display(img.to_thumb(128,128))
    pred,pred_idx,probs = learn_inf.predict(img)
    lbl_pred.value = f'Prediction: {pred}; Probability: {probs[pred_idx]:.04f}'

btn_run.on_click(on_click_classify)
```

You can test the button now by clicking it, and you should see the image and predictions update automatically!

We can now put them all in a vertical box (VBox) to complete our GUI:

```
VBox([widgets.Label('Select your bear!'),
      btn_upload, btn_run, out_pl, lbl_pred])
```

Select your bear!

⬆ Upload (0)

Classify

Prediction: grizzly; Probability: 1.0000

We have written all the code necessary for our app. The next step is to convert it into something we can deploy.

Turning Your Notebook into a Real App

Now that we have everything working in this Jupyter notebook, we can create our application. To do this, start a new notebook and add to it only the code needed to create and show the widgets that you need, and Markdown for any text that you want to appear. Have a look at the *bear_classifier* notebook in the book's repo to see the simple notebook application we created.

Next, install Voilà if you haven't already by copying these lines into a notebook cell and executing it:

```
!pip install voila
!jupyter serverextension enable --sys-prefix voila
```

Cells that begin with a ! do not contain Python code, but instead contain code that is passed to your shell (bash, Windows PowerShell, etc.). If you are comfortable using the command line, which we'll discuss more in this book, you can of course simply type these two lines (without the ! prefix) directly into your terminal. In this case, the first line installs the voila library and application, and the second connects it to your existing Jupyter notebook.

Voilà runs Jupyter notebooks just like the Jupyter notebook server you are using now does, but it also does something very important: it removes all of the cell inputs, and shows only output (including ipywidgets), along with your Markdown cells. So what's left is a web application! To view your notebook as a Voilà web application, replace the word "notebooks" in your browser's URL with "voila/render". You will see the same content as your notebook, but without any of the code cells.

Of course, you don't need to use Voilà or ipywidgets. Your model is just a function you can call (pred,pred_idx,probs = learn.predict(img)), so you can use it with any framework, hosted on any platform. And you can take something you've prototyped in ipywidgets and Voilà and later convert it into a regular web application. We're showing you this approach in the book because we think it's a great way for data scientists and other folks who aren't web development experts to create applications from their models.

We have our app; now let's deploy it!

Deploying Your App

As you now know, you need a GPU to train nearly any useful deep learning model. So, do you need a GPU to use that model in production? No! You almost certainly *do not need a GPU to serve your model in production*. There are a few reasons for this:

- As we've seen, GPUs are useful only when they do lots of identical work in parallel. If you're doing (say) image classification, you'll normally be classifying just one user's image at a time, and there isn't normally enough work to do in a single image to keep a GPU busy for long enough for it to be very efficient. So, a CPU will often be more cost-effective.

- An alternative could be to wait for a few users to submit their images, and then batch them up and process them all at once on a GPU. But then you're asking your users to wait, rather than getting answers straight away! And you need a high-volume site for this to be workable. If you do need this functionality, you can use a tool such as Microsoft's ONNX Runtime (*https://oreil.ly/nj-6f*) or AWS SageMaker (*https://oreil.ly/ajcaP*).

- The complexities of dealing with GPU inference are significant. In particular, the GPU's memory will need careful manual management, and you'll need a careful queueing system to ensure you process only one batch at a time.

- There's a lot more market competition in CPU than GPU servers, and as a result, there are much cheaper options available for CPU servers.

Because of the complexity of GPU serving, many systems have sprung up to try to automate this. However, managing and running these systems is also complex, and generally requires compiling your model into a different form that's specialized for that system. It's typically preferable to avoid dealing with this complexity until/unless your app gets popular enough that it makes clear financial sense for you to do so.

For at least the initial prototype of your application, and for any hobby projects that you want to show off, you can easily host them for free. The best place and the best way to do this will vary over time, so check the book's website for the most up-to-date recommendations. As we're writing this book in early 2020, the simplest (and free!) approach is to use Binder (*https://mybinder.org*). To publish your web app on Binder, you follow these steps:

1. Add your notebook to a GitHub repository (*http://github.com*).

2. Paste the URL of that repo into Binder's URL field, as shown in Figure 2-4.

3. Change the File drop-down to instead select URL.

4. In the "URL to open" field, enter `/voila/render/`*name*`.ipynb` (replacing *name* with the name of your notebook).

5. Click the clipboard button at the bottom right to copy the URL and paste it somewhere safe.

6. Click Launch.

Figure 2-4. Deploying to Binder

The first time you do this, Binder will take around 5 minutes to build your site. Behind the scenes, it is finding a virtual machine that can run your app, allocating storage, and collecting the files needed for Jupyter, for your notebook, and for presenting your notebook as a web application.

Finally, once it has started the app running, it will navigate your browser to your new web app. You can share the URL you copied to allow others to access your app as well.

For other (both free and paid) options for deploying your web app, be sure to take a look at the book's website (*https://book.fast.ai*).

You may well want to deploy your application onto mobile devices, or edge devices such as a Raspberry Pi. There are a lot of libraries and frameworks that allow you to integrate a model directly into a mobile application. However, these approaches tend to require a lot of extra steps and boilerplate, and do not always support all the PyTorch and fastai layers that your model might use. In addition, the work you do will depend on the kinds of mobile devices you are targeting for deployment—you might need to do some work to run on iOS devices, different work to run on newer Android devices, different work for older Android devices, etc. Instead, we recommend wherever possible that you deploy the model itself to a server, and have your mobile or edge application connect to it as a web service.

There are quite a few upsides to this approach. The initial installation is easier, because you have to deploy only a small GUI application, which connects to the server to do all the heavy lifting. More importantly perhaps, upgrades of that core logic can happen on your server, rather than needing to be distributed to all of your users. Your server will have a lot more memory and processing capacity than most edge devices, and it is far easier to scale those resources if your model becomes more demanding. The hardware that you will have on a server is also going to be more standard and more easily supported by fastai and PyTorch, so you don't have to compile your model into a different form.

There are downsides too, of course. Your application will require a network connection, and there will be some latency each time the model is called. (It takes a while for a neural network model to run anyway, so this additional network latency may not make a big difference to your users in practice. In fact, since you can use better hardware on the server, the overall latency may even be less than if it were running locally!) Also, if your application uses sensitive data, your users may be concerned about an approach that sends that data to a remote server, so sometimes privacy considerations will mean that you need to run the model on the edge device (it may be possible to avoid this by having an *on-premise* server, such as inside a company's firewall). Managing the complexity and scaling the server can create additional overhead too, whereas if your model runs on the edge devices, each user is bringing their own compute resources, which leads to easier scaling with an increasing number of users (also known as *horizontal scaling*).

Alexis Says

I've had a chance to see up close how the mobile ML landscape is changing in my work. We offer an iPhone app that depends on computer vision, and for years we ran our own computer vision models in the cloud. This was the only way to do it then since those models needed significant memory and compute resources and took minutes to process inputs. This approach required building not only the models (fun!), but also the infrastructure to ensure a certain number of "compute worker machines" were absolutely always running (scary), that more machines would automatically come online if traffic increased, that there was stable storage for large inputs and outputs, that the iOS app could know and tell the user how their job was doing, etc. Nowadays Apple provides APIs for converting models to run efficiently on devices, and most iOS devices have dedicated ML hardware, so that's the strategy we use for our newer models. It's still not easy, but in our case it's worth it for a faster user experience and to worry less about servers. What works for you will depend, realistically, on the user experience you're trying to create and what you personally find is easy to do. If you really know how to run servers, do it. If you really know how to build native mobile apps, do that. There are many roads up the hill.

Overall, we'd recommend using a simple CPU-based server approach where possible, for as long as you can get away with it. If you're lucky enough to have a very successful application, you'll be able to justify the investment in more complex deployment approaches at that time.

Congratulations—you have successfully built a deep learning model and deployed it! Now is a good time to take a pause and think about what could go wrong.

How to Avoid Disaster

In practice, a deep learning model will be just one piece of a much bigger system. As we discussed at the start of this chapter, building a data product requires thinking about the entire end-to-end process, from conception to use in production. In this book, we can't hope to cover all the complexity of managing deployed data products, such as managing multiple versions of models, A/B testing, canarying, refreshing the data (should we just grow and grow our datasets all the time, or should we regularly remove some of the old data?), handling data labeling, monitoring all this, detecting model rot, and so forth.

In this section, we will give an overview of some of the most important issues to consider; for a more detailed discussion of deployment issues, we refer you to the excellent *Building Machine Learning Powered Applications* by Emmanuel Ameisin (O'Reilly).

One of the biggest issues to consider is that understanding and testing the behavior of a deep learning model is much more difficult than with most other code you write. With normal software development, you can analyze the exact steps that the software is taking, and carefully study which of these steps match the desired behavior that you are trying to create. But with a neural network, the behavior emerges from the model's attempt to match the training data, rather than being exactly defined.

This can result in disaster! For instance, let's say we really were rolling out a bear detection system that will be attached to video cameras around campsites in national parks and will warn campers of incoming bears. If we used a model trained with the dataset we downloaded, there would be all kinds of problems in practice, such as these:

- Working with video data instead of images
- Handling nighttime images, which may not appear in this dataset
- Dealing with low-resolution camera images
- Ensuring results are returned fast enough to be useful in practice
- Recognizing bears in positions that are rarely seen in photos that people post online (for example from behind, partially covered by bushes, or a long way away from the camera)

A big part of the issue is that the kinds of photos that people are most likely to upload to the internet are the kinds of photos that do a good job of clearly and artistically displaying their subject matter—which isn't the kind of input this system is going to be getting. So, we may need to do a lot of our own data collection and labeling to create a useful system.

This is just one example of the more general problem of *out-of-domain* data. That is to say, there may be data that our model sees in production that is very different from what it saw during training. There isn't a complete technical solution to this problem; instead, we have to be careful about our approach to rolling out the technology.

There are other reasons we need to be careful too. One very common problem is *domain shift*, whereby the type of data that our model sees changes over time. For instance, an insurance company may use a deep learning model as part of its pricing and risk algorithm, but over time the types of customers the company attracts and the types of risks it represents may change so much that the original training data is no longer relevant.

Out-of-domain data and domain shift are examples of a larger problem: that you can never fully understand all the possible behaviors of a neural network, because they have far too many parameters. This is the natural downside of their best feature—their flexibility, which enables them to solve complex problems where we may not even be able to fully specify our preferred solution approaches. The good news, however, is that there are ways to mitigate these risks using a carefully thought-out process. The details of this will vary depending on the details of the problem you are solving, but we will attempt to lay out a high-level approach, summarized in Figure 2-5, which we hope will provide useful guidance.

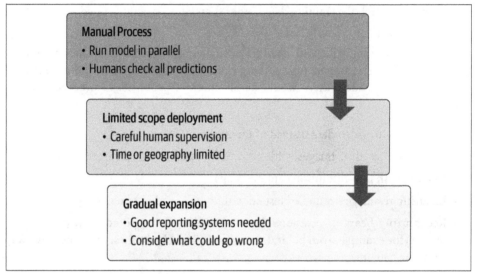

Figure 2-5. Deployment process

Where possible, the first step is to use an entirely manual process, with your deep learning model approach running in parallel but not being used directly to drive any actions. The humans involved in the manual process should look at the deep learning outputs and check whether they make sense. For instance, with our bear classifier, a park ranger could have a screen displaying video feeds from all the cameras, with any possible bear sightings simply highlighted in red. The park ranger would still be expected to be just as alert as before the model was deployed; the model is simply helping to check for problems at this point.

The second step is to try to limit the scope of the model, and have it carefully supervised by people. For instance, do a small geographically and time-constrained trial of the model-driven approach. Rather than rolling out our bear classifier in every national park throughout the country, we could pick a single observation post, for a one-week period, and have a park ranger check each alert before it goes out.

Then, gradually increase the scope of your rollout. As you do so, ensure that you have really good reporting systems in place, to make sure that you are aware of any significant changes to the actions being taken compared to your manual process. For instance, if the number of bear alerts doubles or halves after rollout of the new system in some location, you should be very concerned. Try to think about all the ways in which your system could go wrong, and then think about what measure or report or picture could reflect that problem, and ensure that your regular reporting includes that information.

Jeremy Says

I started a company 20 years ago called Optimal Decisions that used machine learning and optimization to help giant insurance companies set their pricing, impacting tens of billions of dollars of risks. We used the approaches described here to manage the potential downsides of something going wrong. Also, before we worked with our clients to put anything in production, we tried to simulate the impact by testing the end-to-end system on their previous year's data. It was always quite a nerve-wracking process putting these new algorithms into production, but every rollout was successful.

Unforeseen Consequences and Feedback Loops

One of the biggest challenges in rolling out a model is that your model may change the behavior of the system it is a part of. For instance, consider a "predictive policing" algorithm that predicts more crime in certain neighborhoods, causing more police officers to be sent to those neighborhoods, which can result in more crimes being recorded in those neighborhoods, and so on. In the Royal Statistical Society paper "To Predict and Serve?" (*https://oreil.ly/3YEWH*) Kristian Lum and William Isaac observe that "predictive policing is aptly named: it is predicting future policing, not future crime."

Part of the issue in this case is that in the presence of bias (which we'll discuss in depth in the next chapter), *feedback loops* can result in negative implications of that bias getting worse and worse. For instance, there are concerns that this is already happening in the US, where there is significant bias in arrest rates on racial grounds. According to the ACLU (*https://oreil.ly/A9ijk*), "despite roughly equal usage rates, Blacks are 3.73 times more likely than whites to be arrested for marijuana." The impact of this bias, along with the rollout of predictive policing algorithms in many parts of the United States, led Bärí Williams to write in the *New York Times* (*https://oreil.ly/xR0di*): "The same technology that's the source of so much excitement in my career is being used in law enforcement in ways that could mean that in the coming years, my son, who is 7 now, is more likely to be profiled or arrested—or worse—for no reason other than his race and where we live."

A helpful exercise prior to rolling out a significant machine learning system is to consider this question: "What would happen if it went really, really well?" In other words, what if the predictive power was extremely high, and its ability to influence behavior was extremely significant? In that case, who would be most impacted? What would the most extreme results potentially look like? How would you know what was really going on?

Such a thought exercise might help you to construct a more careful rollout plan, with ongoing monitoring systems and human oversight. Of course, human oversight isn't useful if it isn't listened to, so make sure that reliable and resilient communication channels exist so that the right people will be aware of issues and will have the power to fix them.

Get Writing!

One of the things our students have found most helpful to solidify their understanding of this material is to write it down. There is no better test of your understanding of a topic than attempting to teach it to somebody else. This is helpful even if you never show your writing to anybody—but it's even better if you share it! So we recommend that, if you haven't already, you start a blog. Now that you've completed this chapter and have learned how to train and deploy models, you're well placed to write your first blog post about your deep learning journey. What's surprised you? What opportunities do you see for deep learning in your field? What obstacles do you see?

Rachel Thomas, cofounder of fast.ai, wrote in the article "Why You (Yes, You) Should Blog" (*https://oreil.ly/X9-3L*):

> The top advice I would give my younger self would be to start blogging sooner. Here are some reasons to blog:
>
> - It's like a resume, only better. I know of a few people who have had blog posts lead to job offers!
>
> - Helps you learn. Organizing knowledge always helps me synthesize my own ideas. One of the tests of whether you understand something is whether you can explain it to someone else. A blog post is a great way to do that.
>
> - I've gotten invitations to conferences and invitations to speak from my blog posts. I was invited to the TensorFlow Dev Summit (which was awesome!) for writing a blog post about how I don't like TensorFlow.
>
> - Meet new people. I've met several people who have responded to blog posts I wrote.

- Saves time. Any time you answer a question multiple times through email, you should turn it into a blog post, which makes it easier for you to share the next time someone asks.

Perhaps her most important tip is this:

> You are best positioned to help people one step behind you. The material is still fresh in your mind. Many experts have forgotten what it was like to be a beginner (or an intermediate) and have forgotten why the topic is hard to understand when you first hear it. The context of your particular background, your particular style, and your knowledge level will give a different twist to what you're writing about.

We've provided full details on how to set up a blog in Appendix A. If you don't have a blog already, take a look at that now, because we've got a really great approach for you to start blogging for free, with no ads—and you can even use Jupyter Notebook!

Questionnaire

1. Where do text models currently have a major deficiency?
2. What are possible negative societal implications of text generation models?
3. In situations where a model might make mistakes, and those mistakes could be harmful, what is a good alternative to automating a process?
4. What kind of tabular data is deep learning particularly good at?
5. What's a key downside of directly using a deep learning model for recommendation systems?
6. What are the steps of the Drivetrain Approach?
7. How do the steps of the Drivetrain Approach map to a recommendation system?
8. Create an image recognition model using data you curate, and deploy it on the web.
9. What is `DataLoaders`?
10. What four things do we need to tell fastai to create `DataLoaders`?
11. What does the `splitter` parameter to `DataBlock` do?
12. How do we ensure a random split always gives the same validation set?
13. What letters are often used to signify the independent and dependent variables?
14. What's the difference between the crop, pad, and squish resize approaches? When might you choose one over the others?
15. What is data augmentation? Why is it needed?
16. Provide an example of where the bear classification model might work poorly in production, due to structural or style differences in the training data.

17. What is the difference between `item_tfms` and `batch_tfms`?

18. What is a confusion matrix?

19. What does `export` save?

20. What is it called when we use a model for making predictions, instead of training?

21. What are IPython widgets?

22. When would you use a CPU for deployment? When might a GPU be better?

23. What are the downsides of deploying your app to a server, instead of to a client (or edge) device such as a phone or PC?

24. What are three examples of problems that could occur when rolling out a bear warning system in practice?

25. What is out-of-domain data?

26. What is domain shift?

27. What are the three steps in the deployment process?

Further Research

1. Consider how the Drivetrain Approach maps to a project or problem you're interested in.

2. When might it be best to avoid certain types of data augmentation?

3. For a project you're interested in applying deep learning to, consider the thought experiment, "What would happen if it went really, really well?"

4. Start a blog and write your first blog post. For instance, write about what you think deep learning might be useful for in a domain you're interested in.

CHAPTER 3

Data Ethics

Acknowledgment: Dr. Rachel Thomas

This chapter was coauthored by Dr. Rachel Thomas, the cofounder of fast.ai and founding director of the Center for Applied Data Ethics at the University of San Francisco. It largely follows a subset of the syllabus she developed for the Introduction to Data Ethics course (*https://ethics.fast.ai*).

As we discussed in Chapters 1 and 2, sometimes machine learning models can go wrong. They can have bugs. They can be presented with data that they haven't seen before and behave in ways we don't expect. Or they could work exactly as designed, but be used for something that we would much prefer they were never, ever used for.

Because deep learning is such a powerful tool and can be used for so many things, it becomes particularly important that we consider the consequences of our choices. The philosophical study of *ethics* is the study of right and wrong, including how we can define those terms, recognize right and wrong actions, and understand the connection between actions and consequences. The field of *data ethics* has been around for a long time, and many academics are focused on this field. It is being used to help define policy in many jurisdictions; it is being used in companies big and small to consider how best to ensure good societal outcomes from product development; and it is being used by researchers who want to make sure that the work they are doing is used for good, and not for bad.

As a deep learning practitioner, therefore, you will likely at some point be put in a situation requiring you to consider data ethics. So what is data ethics? It's a subfield of ethics, so let's start there.

Jeremy Says

At university, philosophy of ethics was my main thing (it would have been the topic of my thesis, if I'd finished it, instead of dropping out to join the real world). Based on the years I spent studying ethics, I can tell you this: no one really agrees on what right and wrong are, whether they exist, how to spot them, which people are good and which bad, or pretty much anything else. So don't expect too much from the theory! We're going to focus on examples and thought starters here, not theory.

In answering the question "What Is Ethics?" (*https://oreil.ly/nyVh4*) the Markkula Center for Applied Ethics says that the term refers to the following:

- Well-founded standards of right and wrong that prescribe what humans should do
- The study and development of one's ethical standards

There is no list of right answers. There is no list of dos and don'ts. Ethics is complicated and context-dependent. It involves the perspectives of many stakeholders. Ethics is a muscle that you have to develop and practice. In this chapter, our goal is to provide some signposts to help you on that journey.

Spotting ethical issues is best to do as part of a collaborative team. This is the only way you can really incorporate different perspectives. Different people's backgrounds will help them to see things that may not be obvious to you. Working with a team is helpful for many "muscle-building" activities, including this one.

This chapter is certainly not the only part of the book where we talk about data ethics, but it's good to have a place where we focus on it for a while. To get oriented, it's perhaps easiest to look at a few examples. So, we picked out three that we think illustrate effectively some of the key topics.

Key Examples for Data Ethics

We are going to start with three specific examples that illustrate three common ethical issues in tech (we'll study these issues in more depth later in the chapter):

Recourse processes
  Arkansas's buggy healthcare algorithms left patients stranded.

Feedback loops
  YouTube's recommendation system helped unleash a conspiracy theory boom.

Bias

> When a traditionally African-American name is searched for on Google, it displays ads for criminal background checks.

In fact, for every concept that we introduce in this chapter, we are going to provide at least one specific example. For each one, think about what you could have done in this situation, and what kinds of obstructions there might have been to you getting that done. How would you deal with them? What would you look out for?

Bugs and Recourse: Buggy Algorithm Used for Healthcare Benefits

The Verge investigated software used in over half of the US states to determine how much healthcare people receive, and documented its findings in the article "What Happens When an Algorithm Cuts Your Healthcare" (*https://oreil.ly/25drC*). After implementation of the algorithm in Arkansas, hundreds of people (many with severe disabilities) had their healthcare drastically cut.

For instance, Tammy Dobbs, a woman with cerebral palsy who needs an aide to help her to get out of bed, to go to the bathroom, to get food, and more, had her hours of help suddenly reduced by 20 hours a week. She couldn't get any explanation for why her healthcare was cut. Eventually, a court case revealed that there were mistakes in the software implementation of the algorithm, negatively impacting people with diabetes or cerebral palsy. However, Dobbs and many other people reliant on these health-care benefits live in fear that their benefits could again be cut suddenly and inexplicably.

Feedback Loops: YouTube's Recommendation System

Feedback loops can occur when your model is controlling the next round of data you get. The data that is returned quickly becomes flawed by the software itself.

For instance, YouTube has 1.9 billion users, who watch over 1 billion hours of YouTube videos a day. Its recommendation algorithm (built by Google), which was designed to optimize watch time, is responsible for around 70% of the content that is watched. But there was a problem: it led to out-of-control feedback loops, leading the *New York Times* to run the headline "YouTube Unleashed a Conspiracy Theory Boom. Can It Be Contained?" (*https://oreil.ly/Lt3aU*) in February 2019. Ostensibly, recommendation systems are predicting what content people will like, but they also have a lot of power in determining what content people even see.

Bias: Professor Latanya Sweeney "Arrested"

Dr. Latanya Sweeney is a professor at Harvard and director of the university's data privacy lab. In the paper "Discrimination in Online Ad Delivery" (*https://oreil.ly/1qBxU*) (see Figure 3-1), she describes her discovery that Googling her name resulted in advertisements saying "Latanya Sweeney, Arrested?" even though she is the only known Latanya Sweeney and has never been arrested. However, when she Googled other names, such as "Kirsten Lindquist," she got more neutral ads, even though Kirsten Lindquist has been arrested three times.

Figure 3-1. Google search showing ads about Professor Latanya Sweeney's (nonexistent) arrest record

Being a computer scientist, she studied this systematically and looked at over 2,000 names. She found a clear pattern: historically Black names received advertisements suggesting that the person had a criminal record, whereas traditionally white names had more neutral advertisements.

This is an example of bias. It can make a big difference to people's lives—for instance, if a job applicant is Googled, it may appear that they have a criminal record when they do not.

Why Does This Matter?

One very natural reaction to considering these issues is: "So what? What's that got to do with me? I'm a data scientist, not a politician. I'm not one of the senior executives at my company who make the decisions about what we do. I'm just trying to build the most predictive model I can."

These are very reasonable questions. But we're going to try to convince you that the answer is that everybody who is training models absolutely needs to consider how their models will be used, and consider how to best ensure that they are used as positively as possible. There are things you can do. And if you don't do them, things can go pretty badly.

One particularly hideous example of what happens when technologists focus on technology at all costs is the story of IBM and Nazi Germany. In 2001, a Swiss judge ruled that it was not unreasonable "to deduce that IBM's technical assistance facilitated the tasks of the Nazis in the commission of their crimes against humanity, acts also involving accountancy and classification by IBM machines and utilized in the concentration camps themselves."

IBM, you see, supplied the Nazis with data tabulation products necessary to track the extermination of Jews and other groups on a massive scale. This was driven from the top of the company, with marketing to Hitler and his leadership team. Company President Thomas Watson personally approved the 1939 release of special IBM alphabetizing machines to help organize the deportation of Polish Jews. Pictured in Figure 3-2 is Adolf Hitler (far left) meeting with IBM CEO Tom Watson Sr. (second from left), shortly before Hitler awarded Watson a special "Service to the Reich" medal in 1937.

Figure 3-2. IBM CEO Tom Watson Sr. meeting with Adolf Hitler

But this was not an isolated incident—the organization's involvement was extensive. IBM and its subsidiaries provided regular training and maintenance onsite at the concentration camps: printing off cards, configuring machines, and repairing them as they broke frequently. IBM set up categorizations on its punch card system for the way that each person was killed, which group they were assigned to, and the logistical information necessary to track them through the vast Holocaust system (see Figure 3-3). IBM's code for Jews in the concentration camps was 8: some 6,000,000 were killed. Its code for Romanis was 12 (they were labeled by the Nazis as "asocials," with over 300,000 killed in the *Zigeunerlager*, or "Gypsy camp"). General executions were coded as 4, death in the gas chambers as 6.

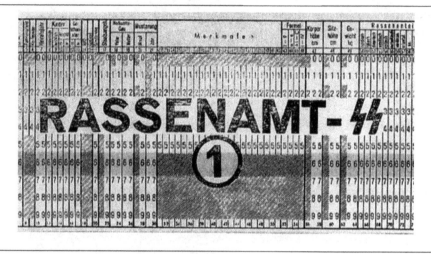

Figure 3-3. A punch card used by IBM in concentration camps

Of course, the project managers and engineers and technicians involved were just living their ordinary lives. Caring for their families, going to the church on Sunday, doing their jobs the best they could. Following orders. The marketers were just doing what they could to meet their business development goals. As Edwin Black, author of *IBM and the Holocaust* (Dialog Press) observed: "To the blind technocrat, the means were more important than the ends. The destruction of the Jewish people became even less important because the invigorating nature of IBM's technical achievement was only heightened by the fantastical profits to be made at a time when bread lines stretched across the world."

Step back for a moment and consider: How would you feel if you discovered that you had been part of a system that ended up hurting society? Would you be open to finding out? How can you help make sure this doesn't happen? We have described the most extreme situation here, but there are many negative societal consequences linked to AI and machine learning being observed today, some of which we'll describe in this chapter.

It's not just a moral burden, either. Sometimes technologists pay very directly for their actions. For instance, the first person who was jailed as a result of the Volkswagen scandal, in which the car company was revealed to have cheated on its diesel emissions tests, was not the manager who oversaw the project, or an executive at the helm of the company. It was one of the engineers, James Liang, who just did what he was told.

Of course, it's not all bad—if a project you are involved in turns out to make a huge positive impact on even one person, this is going to make you feel pretty great!

OK, so hopefully we have convinced you that you ought to care. But what should you do? As data scientists, we're naturally inclined to focus on making our models better by optimizing some metric or other. But optimizing that metric may not lead to better outcomes. And even if it *does* help create better outcomes, it almost certainly won't be the only thing that matters. Consider the pipeline of steps that occurs between the development of a model or an algorithm by a researcher or practitioner, and the point at which this work is used to make a decision. This entire pipeline needs to be considered *as a whole* if we're to have a hope of getting the kinds of outcomes we want.

Normally, there is a very long chain from one end to the other. This is especially true if you are a researcher who might not even know if your research will ever get used for anything, or if you're involved in data collection, which is even earlier in the pipeline. But no one is better placed to inform everyone involved in this chain about the capabilities, constraints, and details of your work than you are. Although there's no "silver bullet" that can ensure your work is used the right way, by getting involved in the process, and asking the right questions, you can at the very least ensure that the right issues are being considered.

Sometimes, the right response to being asked to do a piece of work is to just say "no." Often, however, the response we hear is, "If I don't do it, someone else will." But consider this: if you've been picked for the job, you're the best person they've found to do it—so if you don't do it, the best person isn't working on that project. If the first five people they ask all say no too, so much the better!

Integrating Machine Learning with Product Design

Presumably, the reason you're doing this work is that you hope it will be used for something. Otherwise, you're just wasting your time. So, let's start with the assumption that your work will end up somewhere. Now, as you are collecting your data and developing your model, you are making lots of decisions. What level of aggregation will you store your data at? What loss function should you use? What validation and training sets should you use? Should you focus on simplicity of implementation, speed of inference, or accuracy of the model? How will your model handle out-of-domain data items? Can it be fine-tuned, or must it be retrained from scratch over time?

These are not just algorithm questions. They are data product design questions. But the product managers, executives, judges, journalists, doctors—whoever ends up developing and using the system of which your model is a part—will not be well-placed to understand the decisions that you made, let alone change them.

For instance, two studies found that Amazon's facial recognition software produced inaccurate (*https://oreil.ly/bL5D9*) and racially biased (*https://oreil.ly/cDYqz*) results. Amazon claimed that the researchers should have changed the default parameters, without explaining how this would have changed the biased results. Furthermore, it turned out that Amazon was not instructing police departments (*https://oreil.ly/I5OAj*) that used its software to do this either. There was, presumably, a big distance between the researchers who developed these algorithms and the Amazon documentation staff who wrote the guidelines provided to the police.

A lack of tight integration led to serious problems for society at large, the police, and Amazon. It turned out that its system erroneously matched 28 members of Congress to criminal mugshots! (And the Congresspeople wrongly matched to criminal mugshots were disproportionately people of color, as seen in Figure 3-4.)

Figure 3-4. Congresspeople matched to criminal mugshots by Amazon software

Data scientists need to be part of a cross-disciplinary team. And researchers need to work closely with the kinds of people who will end up using their research. Better still, domain experts themselves could learn enough to be able to train and debug some models themselves—hopefully, a few of you are reading this book right now!

The modern workplace is a very specialized place. Everybody tends to have well-defined jobs to perform. Especially in large companies, it can be hard to know all the pieces of the puzzle. Sometimes companies even intentionally obscure the overall project goals being worked on, if they know that employees are not going to like the answers. This is sometimes done by compartmentalizing pieces as much as possible.

In other words, we're not saying that any of this is easy. It's hard. It's really hard. We all have to do our best. And we have often seen that the people who do get involved in the higher-level context of these projects, and attempt to develop cross-disciplinary capabilities and teams, become some of the most important and well rewarded members of their organizations. It's the kind of work that tends to be highly appreciated by senior executives, even if it is sometimes considered rather uncomfortable by middle management.

Topics in Data Ethics

Data ethics is a big field, and we can't cover everything. Instead, we're going to pick a few topics that we think are particularly relevant:

- The need for recourse and accountability
- Feedback loops
- Bias
- Disinformation

Let's look at each in turn.

Recourse and Accountability

In a complex system, it is easy for no one person to feel responsible for outcomes. While this is understandable, it does not lead to good results. In the earlier example of the Arkansas healthcare system in which a bug led to people with cerebral palsy losing access to needed care, the creator of the algorithm blamed government officials, and government officials blamed those who implemented the software. NYU professor Danah Boyd (*https://oreil.ly/KK5Hf*) described this phenomenon: "Bureaucracy has often been used to shift or evade responsibility....Today's algorithmic systems are extending bureaucracy."

An additional reason why recourse is so necessary is that data often contains errors. Mechanisms for audits and error correction are crucial. A database of suspected gang members maintained by California law enforcement officials was found to be full of errors, including 42 babies who had been added to the database when they were less than 1 year old (28 of whom were marked as "admitting to being gang members"). In this case, there was no process in place for correcting mistakes or removing people after they'd been added. Another example is the US credit report system: a large-scale study of credit reports by the Federal Trade Commission (FTC) in 2012 found that

26% of consumers had at least one mistake in their files, and 5% had errors that could be devastating.

Yet, the process of getting such errors corrected is incredibly slow and opaque. When public radio reporter Bobby Allyn (*https://oreil.ly/BUD6h*) discovered that he was erroneously listed as having a firearms conviction, it took him "more than a dozen phone calls, the handiwork of a county court clerk and six weeks to solve the problem. And that was only after I contacted the company's communications department as a journalist."

As machine learning practitioners, we do not always think of it as our responsibility to understand how our algorithms end up being implemented in practice. But we need to.

Feedback Loops

We explained in Chapter 1 how an algorithm can interact with its environment to create a feedback loop, making predictions that reinforce actions taken in the real world, which lead to predictions even more pronounced in the same direction. As an example, let's again consider YouTube's recommendation system. A couple of years ago, the Google team talked about how they had introduced reinforcement learning (closely related to deep learning, but your loss function represents a result potentially a long time after an action occurs) to improve YouTube's recommendation system. They described how they used an algorithm that made recommendations such that watch time would be optimized.

However, human beings tend to be drawn to controversial content. This meant that videos about things like conspiracy theories started to get recommended more and more by the recommendation system. Furthermore, it turns out that the kinds of people who are interested in conspiracy theories are also people who watch a lot of online videos! So, they started to get drawn more and more toward YouTube. The increasing number of conspiracy theorists watching videos on YouTube resulted in the algorithm recommending more and more conspiracy theory and other extremist content, which resulted in more extremists watching videos on YouTube, and more people watching YouTube developing extremist views, which led to the algorithm recommending more extremist content. The system was spiraling out of control.

And this phenomenon was not contained to this particular type of content. In June 2019, the *New York Times* published an article on YouTube's recommendation system titled "On YouTube's Digital Playground, an Open Gate for Pedophiles" (*https:// oreil.ly/81BEy*). The article started with this chilling story:

> Christiane C. didn't think anything of it when her 10-year-old daughter and a friend uploaded a video of themselves playing in a backyard pool…A few days later…the video had thousands of views. Before long, it had ticked up to 400,000…"I saw the video again and I got scared by the number of views," Christiane said. She had reason to be. YouTube's automated recommendation system…had begun showing the video to users who watched other videos of prepubescent, partially clothed children, a team of researchers has found.

> On its own, each video might be perfectly innocent, a home movie, say, made by a child. Any revealing frames are fleeting and appear accidental. But, grouped together, their shared features become unmistakable.

YouTube's recommendation algorithm had begun curating playlists for pedophiles, picking out innocent home videos that happened to contain prepubescent, partially clothed children.

No one at Google planned to create a system that turned family videos into porn for pedophiles. So what happened?

Part of the problem here is the centrality of metrics in driving a financially important system. When an algorithm has a metric to optimize, as you have seen, it will do everything it can to optimize that number. This tends to lead to all kinds of edge cases, and humans interacting with a system will search for, find, and exploit these edge cases and feedback loops for their advantage.

There are signs that this is exactly what has happened with YouTube's recommendation system in 2018. *The Guardian* ran an article called "How an Ex-YouTube Insider Investigated Its Secret Algorithm" (*https://oreil.ly/yjnPT*) about Guillaume Chaslot, an ex-YouTube engineer who created a website (*https://algotransparency.org*) that tracks these issues. Chaslot published the chart in Figure 3-5 following the release of Robert Mueller's "Report on the Investigation Into Russian Interference in the 2016 Presidential Election."

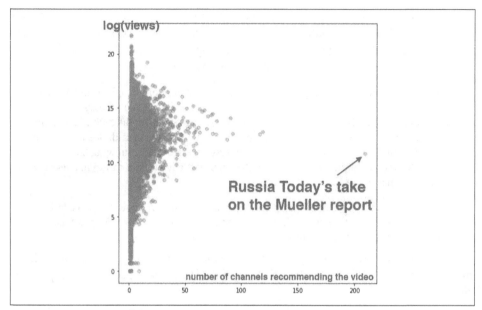

Figure 3-5. Coverage of the Mueller report

Russia Today's coverage of the Mueller report was an extreme outlier in terms of how many channels were recommending it. This suggests the possibility that Russia Today, a state-owned Russia media outlet, has been successful in gaming YouTube's recommendation algorithm. Unfortunately, the lack of transparency of systems like this makes it hard to uncover the kinds of problems that we're discussing.

One of our reviewers for this book, Aurélien Géron, led YouTube's video classification team from 2013 to 2016 (well before the events discussed here). He pointed out that it's not just feedback loops involving humans that are a problem. There can also be feedback loops without humans! He told us about an example from YouTube:

> One important signal to classify the main topic of a video is the channel it comes from. For example, a video uploaded to a cooking channel is very likely to be a cooking video. But how do we know what topic a channel is about? Well…in part by looking at the topics of the videos it contains! Do you see the loop? For example, many videos have a description which indicates what camera was used to shoot the video. As a result, some of these videos might get classified as videos about "photography." If a channel has such a misclassified video, it might be classified as a "photography" channel, making it even more likely for future videos on this channel to be wrongly classified as "photography." This could even lead to runaway virus-like classifications! One way to break this feedback loop is to classify videos with and without the channel signal. Then when classifying the channels, you can only use the classes obtained without the channel signal. This way, the feedback loop is broken.

There are positive examples of people and organizations attempting to combat these problems. Evan Estola, lead machine learning engineer at Meetup, discussed the example (*https://oreil.ly/QfHzT*) of men expressing more interest than women in tech meetups. Taking gender into account could therefore cause Meetup's algorithm to recommend fewer tech meetups to women, and as a result, fewer women would find out about and attend tech meetups, which could cause the algorithm to suggest even fewer tech meetups to women, and so on in a self-reinforcing feedback loop. So, Evan and his team made the ethical decision for their recommendation algorithm to not create such a feedback loop, by explicitly not using gender for that part of their model. It is encouraging to see a company not just unthinkingly optimize a metric, but consider its impact. According to Evan, "You need to decide which feature not to use in your algorithm… the most optimal algorithm is perhaps not the best one to launch into production."

While Meetup chose to avoid such an outcome, Facebook provides an example of allowing a runaway feedback loop to run wild. Like YouTube, it tends to radicalize users interested in one conspiracy theory by introducing them to more. As Renee DiResta, a researcher on proliferation of disinformation, writes (*https://oreil.ly/svgOt*):

> Once people join a single conspiracy-minded [Facebook] group, they are algorithmically routed to a plethora of others. Join an anti-vaccine group, and your suggestions will include anti-GMO, chemtrail watch, flat Earther (yes, really), and "curing cancer naturally" groups. Rather than pulling a user out of the rabbit hole, the recommendation engine pushes them further in.

It is extremely important to keep in mind that this kind of behavior can happen, and to either anticipate a feedback loop or take positive action to break it when you see the first signs of it in your own projects. Another thing to keep in mind is *bias*, which, as we discussed briefly in the previous chapter, can interact with feedback loops in very troublesome ways.

Bias

Discussions of bias online tend to get pretty confusing pretty fast. The word "bias" means so many different things. Statisticians often think when data ethicists are talking about bias that they're talking about the statistical definition of the term bias—but they're not. And they're certainly not talking about the biases that appear in the weights and biases that are the parameters of your model!

What they're talking about is the social science concept of bias. In "A Framework for Understanding Unintended Consequences of Machine Learning" (*https://oreil.ly/aF33V*) MIT's Harini Suresh and John Guttag describe six types of bias in machine learning, summarized in Figure 3-6.

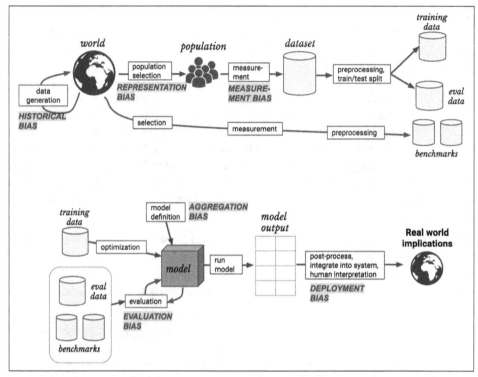

Figure 3-6. Bias in machine learning can come from multiple sources (courtesy of Harini Suresh and John V. Guttag)

We'll discuss four of these types of bias, those that we've found most helpful in our own work (see the paper for details on the others).

Historical bias

Historical bias comes from the fact that people are biased, processes are biased, and society is biased. Suresh and Guttag say: "Historical bias is a fundamental, structural issue with the first step of the data generation process and can exist even given perfect sampling and feature selection."

For instance, here are a few examples of historical *race bias* in the US, from the *New York Times* article "Racial Bias, Even When We Have Good Intentions" (*https://oreil.ly/cBQop*) by the University of Chicago's Sendhil Mullainathan:

- When doctors were shown identical files, they were much less likely to recommend cardiac catheterization (a helpful procedure) to Black patients.
- When bargaining for a used car, Black people were offered initial prices $700 higher and received far smaller concessions.

- Responding to apartment rental ads on Craigslist with a Black name elicited fewer responses than with a white name.
- An all-white jury was 16 percentage points more likely to convict a Black defendant than a white one, but when a jury had one Black member, it convicted both at the same rate.

The COMPAS algorithm, widely used for sentencing and bail decisions in the US, is an example of an important algorithm that, when tested by ProPublica (*https://oreil.ly/1XocO*), showed clear racial bias in practice (Figure 3-7).

Prediction Fails Differently for Black Defendants		
	WHITE	AFRICAN AMERICAN
Labeled Higher Risk, But Didn't Re-Offend	23.5%	44.9%
Labeled Lower Risk, Yet Did Re-Offend	47.7%	28.0%

Figure 3-7. Results of the COMPAS algorithm

Any dataset involving humans can have this kind of bias: medical data, sales data, housing data, political data, and so on. Because underlying bias is so pervasive, bias in datasets is very pervasive. Racial bias even turns up in computer vision, as shown in the example of autocategorized photos shared on Twitter by a Google Photos user shown in Figure 3-8.

Figure 3-8. One of these labels is very wrong…

Yes, that is showing what you think it is: Google Photos classified a Black user's photo with their friend as "gorillas"! This algorithmic misstep got a lot of attention in the media. "We're appalled and genuinely sorry that this happened," a company spokeswoman said. "There is still clearly a lot of work to do with automatic image labeling, and we're looking at how we can prevent these types of mistakes from happening in the future."

Unfortunately, fixing problems in machine learning systems when the input data has problems is hard. Google's first attempt didn't inspire confidence, as coverage by *The Guardian* suggested (Figure 3-9).

Figure 3-9. Google's first response to the problem

These kinds of problems are certainly not limited to Google. MIT researchers studied the most popular online computer vision APIs to see how accurate they were. But they didn't just calculate a single accuracy number—instead, they looked at the accuracy across four groups, as illustrated in Figure 3-10.

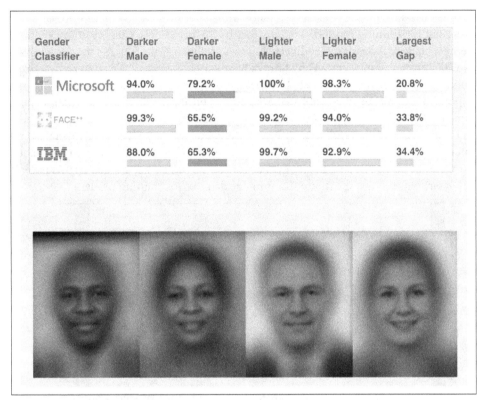

Gender Classifier	Darker Male	Darker Female	Lighter Male	Lighter Female	Largest Gap
Microsoft	94.0%	79.2%	100%	98.3%	20.8%
FACE⁺⁺	99.3%	65.5%	99.2%	94.0%	33.8%
IBM	88.0%	65.3%	99.7%	92.9%	34.4%

Figure 3-10. Error rate per gender and race for various facial recognition systems

IBM's system, for instance, had a 34.7% error rate for darker females, versus 0.3% for lighter males—over 100 times more errors! Some people incorrectly reacted to these experiments by claiming that the difference was simply because darker skin is harder for computers to recognize. However, what happened was that, after the negative publicity that this result created, all of the companies in question dramatically improved their models for darker skin, such that one year later, they were nearly as good as for lighter skin. So what this showed is that the developers failed to utilize datasets containing enough darker faces, or test their product with darker faces.

One of the MIT researchers, Joy Buolamwini, warned: "We have entered the age of automation overconfident yet underprepared. If we fail to make ethical and inclusive artificial intelligence, we risk losing gains made in civil rights and gender equity under the guise of machine neutrality."

Part of the issue appears to be a systematic imbalance in the makeup of popular data-sets used for training models. The abstract of the paper "No Classification Without Representation: Assessing Geodiversity Issues in Open Data Sets for the Developing World" (*https://oreil.ly/VqtOA*) by Shreya Shankar et al. states, "We analyze two large, publicly available image data sets to assess geo-diversity and find that these data sets appear to exhibit an observable amerocentric and eurocentric representation bias. Further, we analyze classifiers trained on these data sets to assess the impact of these training distributions and find strong differences in the relative performance on images from different locales." Figure 3-11 shows one of the charts from the paper, showing the geographic makeup of what were at the time (and still are, as this book is being written) the two most important image datasets for training models.

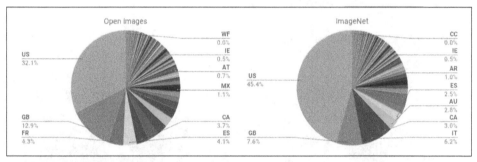

Figure 3-11. Image provenance in popular training sets

The vast majority of the images are from the US and other Western countries, leading to models trained on ImageNet performing worse on scenes from other countries and cultures. For instance, research found that such models are worse at identifying household items (such as soap, spices, sofas, or beds) from lower-income countries. Figure 3-12 shows an image from the paper "Does Object Recognition Work for Everyone?" (*https://oreil.ly/BkFjL*) by Terrance DeVries et al. of Facebook AI Research that illustrates this point.

Ground truth: Soap Nepal, 288 $/month

Azure: food, cheese, bread, cake, sandwich
Clarifai: food, wood, cooking, delicious, healthy
Google: food, dish, cuisine, comfort food, spam
Amazon: food, confectionary, sweets, burger
Watson: food, food product, turmeric, seasoning
Tencent: food, dish, matter, fast food, nutriment

Ground truth: Soap UK, 1890 $/month

Azure: toilet, design, art, sink
Clarifai: people, faucet, healthcare, lavatory, wash closet
Google: product, liquid, water, fluid, bathroom accessory
Amazon: sink, indoors, bottle, sink faucet
Watson: gas tank, storage tank, toiletry, dispenser, soap dispenser
Tencent: lotion, toiletry, soap dispenser, dispenser, after shave

Ground truth: Spices Phillipines, 262 $/month

Azure: bottle, beer, counter, drink, open
Clarifai: container, food, bottle, drink, stock
Google: product, yellow, drink, bottle, plastic bottle
Amazon: beverage, beer, alcohol, drink, bottle
Watson: food, larder food supply, pantry, condiment, food seasoning
Tencent: condiment, sauce, flavorer, catsup, hot sauce

Ground truth: Spices USA, 4559 $/month

Azure: bottle, wall, counter, food
Clarifai: container, food, can, medicine, stock
Google: seasoning, seasoned salt, ingredient, spice, spice rack
Amazon: shelf, tin, pantry, furniture, aluminium
Watson: tin, food, pantry, paint, can
Tencent: spice rack, chili sauce, condiment, canned food, rack

Figure 3-12. Object detection in action

In this example, we can see that the lower-income soap example is a very long way away from being accurate, with every commercial image recognition service predicting "food" as the most likely answer!

As we will discuss shortly, in addition, the vast majority of AI researchers and developers are young white men. Most projects that we have seen do most user testing using friends and families of the immediate product development group. Given this, the kinds of problems we just discussed should not be surprising.

Similar historical bias is found in the texts used as data for natural language processing models. This crops up in downstream machine learning tasks in many ways. For instance, it was widely reported (*https://oreil.ly/Vt_vT*) that until last year, Google Translate showed systematic bias in how it translated the Turkish gender-neutral pronoun "o" into English: when applied to jobs that are often associated with males, it used "he," and when applied to jobs that are often associated with females, it used "she" (Figure 3-13).

Figure 3-13. Gender bias in text datasets

We also see this kind of bias in online advertisements. For instance, a study (*https://oreil.ly/UGxuh*) in 2019 by Muhammad Ali et al. found that even when the person placing the ad does not intentionally discriminate, Facebook will show ads to very different audiences based on race and gender. Housing ads with the same text but picturing either a white or a Black family were shown to racially different audiences.

Measurement bias

In "Does Machine Learning Automate Moral Hazard and Error" (*https://oreil.ly/79Qtn*) in *American Economic Review*, Sendhil Mullainathan and Ziad Obermeyer look at a model that tries to answer this question: using historical electronic health record (EHR) data, what factors are most predictive of stroke? These are the top predictors from the model:

- Prior stroke
- Cardiovascular disease
- Accidental injury
- Benign breast lump
- Colonoscopy
- Sinusitis

However, only the top two have anything to do with a stroke! Based on what we've studied so far, you can probably guess why. We haven't really measured *stroke*, which occurs when a region of the brain is denied oxygen due to an interruption in the blood supply. What we've measured is who had symptoms, went to a doctor, got the appropriate tests, *and* received a diagnosis of stroke. Actually having a stroke is not the only thing correlated with this complete list—it's also correlated with being the kind of person who goes to the doctor (which is influenced by who has access to healthcare, can afford their co-pay, doesn't experience racial or gender-based medical discrimination, and more)! If you are likely to go to the doctor for an *accidental injury*, you are likely to also go the doctor when you are having a stroke.

This is an example of *measurement bias*. It occurs when our models make mistakes because we are measuring the wrong thing, or measuring it in the wrong way, or incorporating that measurement into the model inappropriately.

Aggregation bias

Aggregation bias occurs when models do not aggregate data in a way that incorporates all of the appropriate factors, or when a model does not include the necessary interaction terms, nonlinearities, or so forth. This can particularly occur in medical settings. For instance, the way diabetes is treated is often based on simple univariate statistics and studies involving small groups of heterogeneous people. Analysis of results is often done in a way that does not take into account different ethnicities or genders. However, it turns out that diabetes patients have different complications across ethnicities (*https://oreil.ly/gNS39*), and HbA1c levels (widely used to diagnose and monitor diabetes) differ in complex ways across ethnicities and genders (*https://oreil.ly/nR4fx*). This can result in people being misdiagnosed or incorrectly treated because medical decisions are based on a model that does not include these important variables and interactions.

Representation bias

The abstract of the paper "Bias in Bios: A Case Study of Semantic Representation Bias in a High-Stakes Setting" (*https://oreil.ly/0iowq*) by Maria De-Arteaga et al. notes that there is gender imbalance in occupations (e.g., females are more likely to be nurses, and males are more likely to be pastors), and says that "differences in true positive rates between genders are correlated with existing gender imbalances in occupations, which may compound these imbalances."

In other words, the researchers noticed that models predicting occupation did not only *reflect* the actual gender imbalance in the underlying population, but *amplified* it! This type of *representation bias* is quite common, particularly for simple models. When there is a clear, easy-to-see underlying relationship, a simple model will often assume that this relationship holds all the time. As Figure 3-14 from the paper shows, for occupations that had a higher percentage of females, the model tended to overestimate the prevalence of that occupation.

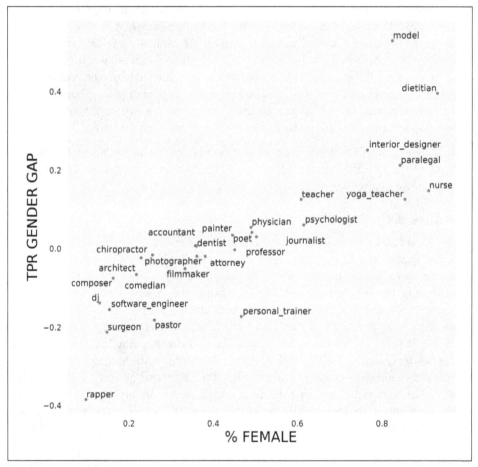

Figure 3-14. Model error in predicting occupation plotted against percentage of women in said occupation

For example, in the training dataset 14.6% of surgeons were women, yet in the model predictions only 11.6% of the true positives were women. The model is thus amplifying the bias existing in the training set.

Now that we've seen that those biases exist, what can we do to mitigate them?

Addressing different types of bias

Different types of bias require different approaches for mitigation. While gathering a more diverse dataset can address representation bias, this would not help with historical bias or measurement bias. All datasets contain bias. There is no such thing as a completely debiased dataset. Many researchers in the field have been converging on a set of proposals to enable better documentation of the decisions, context, and specifics about how and why a particular dataset was created, what scenarios it is appropriate to use in, and what the limitations are. This way, those using a particular dataset will not be caught off guard by its biases and limitations.

We often hear the question, "Humans are biased, so does algorithmic bias even matter?" This comes up so often, there must be some reasoning that makes sense to the people who ask it, but it doesn't seem very logically sound to us! Independently of whether this is logically sound, it's important to realize that algorithms (particularly machine learning algorithms!) and people are different. Consider these points about machine learning algorithms:

Machine learning can create feedback loops
  Small amounts of bias can rapidly increase exponentially because of feedback loops.

Machine learning can amplify bias
  Human bias can lead to larger amounts of machine learning bias.

Algorithms and humans are used differently
  Human decision makers and algorithmic decision makers are not used in a plug-and-play interchangeable way in practice. These examples are given in the list on the next page.

Technology is power
  And with that comes responsibility.

As the Arkansas healthcare example showed, machine learning is often implemented in practice not because it leads to better outcomes, but because it is cheaper and more efficient. Cathy O'Neill, in her book *Weapons of Math Destruction* (Crown), described a pattern in which the privileged are processed by people, whereas the poor are processed by algorithms. This is just one of a number of ways that algorithms are used differently than human decision makers. Others include the following:

- People are more likely to assume algorithms are objective or error-free (even if they're given the option of a human override).
- Algorithms are more likely to be implemented with no appeals process in place.
- Algorithms are often used at scale.
- Algorithmic systems are cheap.

Even in the absence of bias, algorithms (and deep learning especially, since it is such an effective and scalable algorithm) can lead to negative societal problems, such as when used for *disinformation*.

Disinformation

Disinformation has a history stretching back hundreds or even thousands of years. It is not necessarily about getting someone to believe something false, but rather often used to sow disharmony and uncertainty, and to get people to give up on seeking the truth. Receiving conflicting accounts can lead people to assume that they can never know whom or what to trust.

Some people think disinformation is primarily about false information or *fake news*, but in reality, disinformation can often contain seeds of truth, or half-truths taken out of context. Ladislav Bittman was an intelligence officer in the USSR who later defected to the US and wrote some books in the 1970s and 1980s on the role of disinformation in Soviet propaganda operations. In *The KGB and Soviet Disinformation* (Pergamon), he wrote "Most campaigns are a carefully designed mixture of facts, half-truths, exaggerations, and deliberate lies."

In the US, this has hit close to home in recent years, with the FBI detailing a massive disinformation campaign linked to Russia in the 2016 election. Understanding the disinformation that was used in this campaign is very educational. For instance, the FBI found that the Russian disinformation campaign often organized two separate fake "grass roots" protests, one for each side of an issue, and got them to protest at the same time! The Houston Chronicle (*https://oreil.ly/VyCkL*) reported on one of these odd events (Figure 3-15):

> A group that called itself the "Heart of Texas" had organized it on social media—a protest, they said, against the "Islamization" of Texas. On one side of Travis Street, I found about 10 protesters. On the other side, I found around 50 counterprotesters. But I couldn't find the rally organizers. No "Heart of Texas." I thought that was odd, and mentioned it in the article: What kind of group is a no-show at its own event? Now I know why. Apparently, the rally's organizers were in Saint Petersburg, Russia, at the time. "Heart of Texas" is one of the internet troll groups cited in Special Prosecutor Robert Mueller's recent indictment of Russians attempting to tamper with the US presidential election.

Figure 3-15. Event organized by the group Heart of Texas

Disinformation often involves coordinated campaigns of inauthentic behavior. For instance, fraudulent accounts may try to make it seem like many people hold a particular viewpoint. While most of us like to think of ourselves as independent-minded, in reality we evolved to be influenced by others in our in-group, and in opposition to those in our out-group. Online discussions can influence our viewpoints, or alter the range of what we consider acceptable viewpoints. Humans are social animals, and as social animals, we are extremely influenced by the people around us. Increasingly, radicalization occurs in online environments; so influence is coming from people in the virtual space of online forums and social networks.

Disinformation through autogenerated text is a particularly significant issue, due to the greatly increased capability provided by deep learning. We discuss this issue in depth when we delve into creating language models in Chapter 10.

One proposed approach is to develop some form of digital signature, to implement it in a seamless way, and to create norms that we should trust only content that has been verified. The head of the Allen Institute on AI, Oren Etzioni, wrote such a proposal in an article titled "How Will We Prevent AI-Based Forgery?" (*https://oreil.ly/8z7wm*): "AI is poised to make high-fidelity forgery inexpensive and automated, leading to potentially disastrous consequences for democracy, security, and society. The specter of AI forgery means that we need to act to make digital signatures de rigueur as a means of authentication of digital content."

While we can't hope to discuss all the ethical issues that deep learning, and algorithms more generally, bring up, hopefully this brief introduction has been a useful starting point you can build on. We'll now move on to the questions of how to identify ethical issues and what to do about them.

Identifying and Addressing Ethical Issues

Mistakes happen. Finding out about them, and dealing with them, needs to be part of the design of any system that includes machine learning (and many other systems too). The issues raised within data ethics are often complex and interdisciplinary, but it is crucial that we work to address them.

So what can we do? This is a big topic, but here are a few steps toward addressing ethical issues:

- Analyze a project you are working on.
- Implement processes at your company to find and address ethical risks.
- Support good policy.
- Increase diversity.

Let's walk through each step, starting with analyzing a project you are working on.

Analyze a Project You Are Working On

It's easy to miss important issues when considering ethical implications of your work. One thing that helps enormously is simply asking the right questions. Rachel Thomas recommends considering the following questions throughout the development of a data project:

- Should we even be doing this?
- What bias is in the data?
- Can the code and data be audited?
- What are the error rates for different subgroups?
- What is the accuracy of a simple rule-based alternative?
- What processes are in place to handle appeals or mistakes?
- How diverse is the team that built it?

These questions may be able to help you identify outstanding issues, and possible alternatives that are easier to understand and control. In addition to asking the right questions, it's also important to consider practices and processes to implement.

One thing to consider at this stage is what data you are collecting and storing. Data often ends up being used for different purposes the original intent. For instance, IBM began selling to Nazi Germany well before the Holocaust, including helping with Germany's 1933 census conducted by Adolf Hitler, which was effective at identifying far more Jewish people than had previously been recognized in Germany. Similarly, US census data was used to round up Japanese-Americans (who were US citizens) for internment during World War II. It is important to recognize how data and images collected can be weaponized later. Columbia professor Tim Wu wrote (*https://oreil.ly/6L0QM*) "You must assume that any personal data that Facebook or Android keeps are data that governments around the world will try to get or that thieves will try to steal."

Processes to Implement

The Markkula Center has released An Ethical Toolkit for Engineering/Design Practice (*https://oreil.ly/vDGGC*) that includes concrete practices to implement at your company, including regularly scheduled sweeps to proactively search for ethical risks (in a manner similar to cybersecurity penetration testing), expanding the ethical circle to include the perspectives of a variety of stakeholders, and considering the terrible people (how could bad actors abuse, steal, misinterpret, hack, destroy, or weaponize what you are building?).

Even if you don't have a diverse team, you can still try to proactively include the perspectives of a wider group, considering questions such as these (provided by the Markkula Center):

- Whose interests, desires, skills, experiences, and values have we simply assumed, rather than actually consulted?

- Who are all the stakeholders who will be directly affected by our product? How have their interests been protected? How do we know what their interests really are—have we asked?

- Who/which groups and individuals will be indirectly affected in significant ways?

- Who might use this product that we didn't expect to use it, or for purposes we didn't initially intend?

Ethical lenses

Another useful resource from the Markkula Center is its Conceptual Frameworks in Technology and Engineering Practice (*https://oreil.ly/bowax*). This considers how different foundational ethical lenses can help identify concrete issues, and lays out the following approaches and key questions:

The rights approach
> Which option best respects the rights of all who have a stake?

The justice approach
> Which option treats people equally or proportionately?

The utilitarian approach
> Which option will produce the most good and do the least harm?

The common good approach
> Which option best serves the community as a whole, not just some members?

The virtue approach
> Which option leads me to act as the sort of person I want to be?

Markkula's recommendations include a deeper dive into each of these perspectives, including looking at a project through the lens of its *consequences*:

- Who will be directly affected by this project? Who will be indirectly affected?
- Will the effects in aggregate likely create more good than harm, and what types of good and harm?
- Are we thinking about all relevant types of harm/benefit (psychological, political, environmental, moral, cognitive, emotional, institutional, cultural)?
- How might future generations be affected by this project?
- Do the risks of harm from this project fall disproportionately on the least powerful in society? Will the benefits go disproportionately to the well-off?
- Have we adequately considered "dual-use" and unintended downstream effects?

The alternative lens to this is the *deontological* perspective, which focuses on basic concepts of *right* and *wrong*:

- What rights of others and duties to others must we respect?
- How might the dignity and autonomy of each stakeholder be impacted by this project?
- What considerations of trust and of justice are relevant to this design/project?
- Does this project involve any conflicting moral duties to others, or conflicting stakeholder rights? How can we prioritize these?

One of the best ways to help come up with complete and thoughtful answers to questions like these is to ensure that the people asking the questions are *diverse*.

The Power of Diversity

Currently, less than 12% of AI researchers are women, according to a study from Element AI (*https://oreil.ly/sO09p*). The statistics are similarly dire when it comes to race and age. When everybody on a team has similar backgrounds, they are likely to have similar blind spots around ethical risks. The *Harvard Business Review* (HBR) has published a number of studies showing many benefits of diverse teams, including the following:

- "How Diversity Can Drive Innovation" (*https://oreil.ly/WRFSm*)
- "Teams Solve Problems Faster When They're More Cognitively Diverse" (*https://oreil.ly/vKy5b*)
- "Why Diverse Teams Are Smarter" (*https://oreil.ly/SFVBF*)
- "Defend Your Research: What Makes a Team Smarter? More Women" (*https://oreil.ly/A1A5n*)

Diversity can lead to problems being identified earlier, and a wider range of solutions being considered. For instance, Tracy Chou was an early engineer at Quora. She wrote of her experiences (*https://oreil.ly/n7WSn*), describing how she advocated internally for adding a feature that would allow trolls and other bad actors to be blocked. Chou recounts, "I was eager to work on the feature because I personally felt antagonized and abused on the site (gender isn't an unlikely reason as to why)…But if I hadn't had that personal perspective, it's possible that the Quora team wouldn't have prioritized building a block button so early in its existence." Harassment often drives people from marginalized groups off online platforms, so this functionality has been important for maintaining the health of Quora's community.

A crucial aspect to understand is that women leave the tech industry at over twice the rate that men do. According to the Harvard Business Review (*https://oreil.ly/ZIC7t*), 41% of women working in tech leave, compared to 17% of men. An analysis of over 200 books, whitepapers, and articles found that the reason they leave is that "they're treated unfairly; underpaid, less likely to be fast-tracked than their male colleagues, and unable to advance."

Studies have confirmed a number of the factors that make it harder for women to advance in the workplace. Women receive more vague feedback and personality criticism in performance evaluations, whereas men receive actionable advice tied to business outcomes (which is more useful). Women frequently experience being excluded from more creative and innovative roles, and not receiving high-visibility "stretch" assignments that are helpful in getting promoted. One study found that men's voices are perceived as more persuasive, fact-based, and logical than women's voices, even when reading identical scripts.

Receiving mentorship has been statistically shown to help men advance, but not women. The reason behind this is that when women receive mentorship, it's advice on how they should change and gain more self-knowledge. When men receive mentorship, it's public endorsement of their authority. Guess which is more useful in getting promoted?

As long as qualified women keep dropping out of tech, teaching more girls to code will not solve the diversity issues plaguing the field. Diversity initiatives often end up focusing primarily on white women, even though women of color face many additional barriers. In interviews (*https://oreil.ly/t5C6b*) with 60 women of color who work in STEM research, 100% had experienced discrimination.

The hiring process is particularly broken in tech. One study indicative of the disfunction comes from Triplebyte, a company that helps place software engineers in companies, conducting a standardized technical interview as part of this process. The company has a fascinating dataset: the results of how over 300 engineers did on their exam, coupled with the results of how those engineers did during the interview process for a variety of companies. The number one finding from Triplebyte's research (*https://oreil.ly/2Wtw4*) is that "the types of programmers that each company looks for often have little to do with what the company needs or does. Rather, they reflect company culture and the backgrounds of the founders."

This is a challenge for those trying to break into the world of deep learning, since most companies' deep learning groups today were founded by academics. These groups tend to look for people "like them"—that is, people who can solve complex math problems and understand dense jargon. They don't always know how to spot people who are actually good at solving real problems using deep learning.

This leaves a big opportunity for companies that are ready to look beyond status and pedigree, and focus on results!

Fairness, Accountability, and Transparency

The professional society for computer scientists, the ACM, runs a data ethics conference called the Conference on Fairness, Accountability, and Transparency (ACM FAccT), which used to go under the acronym FAT but now uses the less objectionable FAccT. Microsoft also has a group focused on Fairness, Accountability, Transparency, and Ethics in AI (FATE). In this section, we'll use the acronym FAccT to refer to the concepts of fairness, accountability, and transparency.

FAccT is a lens some people have used for considering ethical issues. One helpful resource for this is the free online book *Fairness and Machine Learning: Limitations and Opportunities* (*https://fairmlbook.org*) by Solon Barocas et al., which "gives a perspective on machine learning that treats fairness as a central concern rather than an afterthought." It also warns, however, that it "is intentionally narrow in scope...A narrow framing of machine learning ethics might be tempting to technologists and businesses as a way to focus on technical interventions while sidestepping deeper questions about power and accountability. We caution against this temptation." Rather than provide an overview of the FAccT approach to ethics (which is better done in books such as that one), our focus here will be on the limitations of this kind of narrow framing.

One great way to consider whether an ethical lens is complete is to try to come up with an example in which the lens and our own ethical intuitions give diverging results. Os Keyes et al. explored this in a graphic way in their paper "A Mulching Proposal: Analysing and Improving an Algorithmic System for Turning the Elderly into High-Nutrient Slurry" (*https://oreil.ly/_qug9*). The paper's abstract says:

> The ethical implications of algorithmic systems have been much discussed in both HCI and the broader community of those interested in technology design, development, and policy. In this paper, we explore the application of one prominent ethical framework—Fairness, Accountability, and Transparency—to a proposed algorithm that resolves various societal issues around food security and population aging. Using various standardised forms of algorithmic audit and evaluation, we drastically increase the algorithm's adherence to the FAT framework, resulting in a more ethical and beneficent system. We discuss how this might serve as a guide to other researchers or practitioners looking to ensure better ethical outcomes from algorithmic systems in their line of work.

In this paper, the rather controversial proposal ("Turning the Elderly into High-Nutrient Slurry") and the results ("drastically increase the algorithm's adherence to the FAT framework, resulting in a more ethical and beneficent system") are at odds… to say the least!

In philosophy, and especially philosophy of ethics, this is one of the most effective tools: first, come up with a process, definition, set of questions, etc., which is designed to resolve a problem. Then try to come up with an example in which that apparent solution results in a proposal that no one would consider acceptable. This can then lead to a further refinement of the solution.

So far, we've focused on things that you and your organization can do. But sometimes individual or organizational action is not enough. Sometimes governments also need to consider policy implications.

Role of Policy

We often talk to people who are eager for technical or design fixes to be a full solution to the kinds of problems that we've been discussing; for instance, a technical approach to debias data, or design guidelines for making technology less addictive. While such measures can be useful, they will not be sufficient to address the underlying problems that have led to our current state. For example, as long as it is profitable to create addictive technology, companies will continue to do so, regardless of whether this has the side effect of promoting conspiracy theories and polluting our information ecosystem. While individual designers may try to tweak product designs, we will not see substantial changes until the underlying profit incentives change.

The Effectiveness of Regulation

To look at what can cause companies to take concrete action, consider the following two examples of how Facebook has behaved. In 2018, a UN investigation found that Facebook had played a "determining role" in the ongoing genocide of the Rohingya, an ethnic minority in Mynamar described by UN Secretary-General Antonio Guterres as "one of, if not the, most discriminated people in the world." Local activists had been warning Facebook executives that their platform was being used to spread hate speech and incite violence since as early as 2013. In 2015, they were warned that Facebook could play the same role in Myanmar that the radio broadcasts played during the Rwandan genocide (where a million people were killed). Yet, by the end of 2015, Facebook employed only four contractors who spoke Burmese. As one person close to the matter said, "That's not 20/20 hindsight. The scale of this problem was significant and it was already apparent." Zuckerberg promised during the congressional hearings to hire "dozens" to address the genocide in Myanmar (in 2018, years after the genocide had begun, including the destruction by fire of at least 288 villages in northern Rakhine state after August 2017).

This stands in stark contrast to Facebook quickly hiring 1,200 people in Germany (*https://oreil.ly/q_8Dz*) to try to avoid expensive penalties (of up to 50 million euros) under a new German law against hate speech. Clearly, in this case, Facebook was more reactive to the threat of a financial penalty than to the systematic destruction of an ethnic minority.

In an article on privacy issues (*https://oreil.ly/K5YKf*), Maciej Ceglowski draws parallels with the environmental movement:

> This regulatory project has been so successful in the First World that we risk forgetting what life was like before it. Choking smog of the kind that today kills thousands in Jakarta and Delhi was once emblematic of London (*https://oreil.ly/pLzU7*). The Cuyahoga River in Ohio used to reliably catch fire (*https://oreil.ly/qrU5v*). In a particularly horrific example of unforeseen consequences, tetraethyl lead added to gasoline raised violent crime rates (*https://oreil.ly/4ngvr*) worldwide for fifty years. None of these harms could have been fixed by telling people to vote with their wallet, or carefully review the environmental policies of every company they gave their business to, or to stop using the technologies in question. It took coordinated, and sometimes highly technical, regulation across jurisdictional boundaries to fix them. In some cases, like the ban on commercial refrigerants (*https://oreil.ly/o839J*) that depleted the ozone layer, that regulation required a worldwide consensus. We're at the point where we need a similar shift in perspective in our privacy law.

Rights and Policy

Clean air and clean drinking water are public goods that are nearly impossible to protect through individual market decisions, but rather require coordinated regulatory action. Similarly, many of the harms resulting from unintended consequences of misuses of technology involve public goods, such as a polluted information environment or deteriorated ambient privacy. Too often privacy is framed as an individual right, yet there are societal impacts to widespread surveillance (which would still be the case even if it was possible for a few individuals to opt out).

Many of the issues we are seeing in tech are human rights issues, such as when a biased algorithm recommends that Black defendants have longer prison sentences, when particular job ads are shown only to young people, or when police use facial recognition to identify protesters. The appropriate venue to address human rights issues is typically through the law.

We need both regulatory and legal changes, *and* the ethical behavior of individuals. Individual behavior change can't address misaligned profit incentives, externalities (where corporations reap large profits while offloading their costs and harms to the broader society), or systemic failures. However, the law will never cover all edge cases, and it is important that individual software developers and data scientists are equipped to make ethical decisions in practice.

Cars: A Historical Precedent

The problems we are facing are complex, and there are no simple solutions. This can be discouraging, but we find hope in considering other large challenges that people have tackled throughout history. One example is the movement to increase car safety, covered as a case study in "Datasheets for Datasets" (*https://oreil.ly/nqG_r*) by Timnit Gebru et al. and in the design podcast 99% Invisible (*https://oreil.ly/2HGPd*). Early cars had no seatbelts, metal knobs on the dashboard that could lodge in people's skulls during a crash, regular plate glass windows that shattered in dangerous ways, and noncollapsible steering columns that impaled drivers. However, car companies were resistant to even discussing safety as something they could help address, and the widespread belief was that cars are just the way they are, and that it was the people using them who caused problems.

It took consumer safety activists and advocates decades of work to change the national conversation to consider that perhaps car companies had some responsibility that should be addressed through regulation. When the collapsible steering column was invented, it was not implemented for several years as there was no financial incentive to do so. Major car company General Motors hired private detectives to try to dig up dirt on consumer safety advocate Ralph Nader. The requirement of seatbelts, crash test dummies, and collapsible steering columns were major victories. It was only in 2011 that car companies were required to start using crash test dummies that would represent the average woman, and not just average men's bodies; prior to this, women were 40% more likely to be injured in a car crash of the same impact compared to a man. This is a vivid example of the ways that bias, policy, and technology have important consequences.

Conclusion

Coming from a background of working with binary logic, the lack of clear answers in ethics can be frustrating at first. Yet, the implications of how our work impacts the world, including unintended consequences and the work becoming weaponized by bad actors, are some of the most important questions we can (and should!) consider. Even though there aren't any easy answers, there are definite pitfalls to avoid and practices to follow to move toward more ethical behavior.

Many people (including us!) are looking for more satisfying, solid answers about how to address harmful impacts of technology. However, given the complex, far-reaching, and interdisciplinary nature of the problems we are facing, there are no simple solutions. Julia Angwin, former senior reporter at ProPublica who focuses on issues of algorithmic bias and surveillance (and one of the 2016 investigators of the COMPAS recidivism algorithm that helped spark the field of FAccT) said in a 2019 interview (*https://oreil.ly/o7FpP*):

> I strongly believe that in order to solve a problem, you have to diagnose it, and that we're still in the diagnosis phase of this. If you think about the turn of the century and industrialization, we had, I don't know, 30 years of child labor, unlimited work hours, terrible working conditions, and it took a lot of journalist muckraking and advocacy to diagnose the problem and have some understanding of what it was, and then the activism to get laws changed. I feel like we're in a second industrialization of data information… I see my role as trying to make as clear as possible what the downsides are, and diagnosing them really accurately so that they can be solvable. That's hard work, and lots more people need to be doing it.

It's reassuring that Angwin thinks we are largely still in the diagnosis phase: if your understanding of these problems feels incomplete, that is normal and natural. Nobody has a "cure" yet, although it is vital that we continue working to better understand and address the problems we are facing.

One of our reviewers for this book, Fred Monroe, used to work in hedge fund trading. He told us, after reading this chapter, that many of the issues discussed here (distribution of data being dramatically different from what a model was trained on, the impact of feedback loops on a model once deployed and at scale, and so forth) were also key issues for building profitable trading models. The kinds of things you need to do to consider societal consequences are going to have a lot of overlap with things you need to do to consider organizational, market, and customer consequences—so thinking carefully about ethics can also help you think carefully about how to make your data product successful more generally!

Questionnaire

1. Does ethics provide a list of "right answers"?
2. How can working with people of different backgrounds help when considering ethical questions?
3. What was the role of IBM in Nazi Germany? Why did the company participate as it did? Why did the workers participate?
4. What was the role of the first person jailed in the Volkswagen diesel scandal?
5. What was the problem with a database of suspected gang members maintained by California law enforcement officials?
6. Why did YouTube's recommendation algorithm recommend videos of partially clothed children to pedophiles, even though no employee at Google had programmed this feature?
7. What are the problems with the centrality of metrics?
8. Why did Meetup.com not include gender in its recommendation system for tech meetups?
9. What are the six types of bias in machine learning, according to Suresh and Guttag?
10. Give two examples of historical race bias in the US.
11. Where are most images in ImageNet from?
12. In the paper "Does Machine Learning Automate Moral Hazard and Error?" why is sinusitis found to be predictive of a stroke?
13. What is representation bias?
14. How are machines and people different, in terms of their use for making decisions?
15. Is disinformation the same as "fake news"?
16. Why is disinformation through autogenerated text a particularly significant issue?
17. What are the five ethical lenses described by the Markkula Center?
18. Where is policy an appropriate tool for addressing data ethics issues?

Further Research

1. Read the article "What Happens When an Algorithm Cuts Your Healthcare" (*https://oreil.ly/5Ziok*). How could problems like this be avoided in the future?

2. Research to find out more about YouTube's recommendation system and its societal impacts. Do you think recommendation systems must always have feedback loops with negative results? What approaches could Google take to avoid them? What about the government?

3. Read the paper "Discrimination in Online Ad Delivery" (*https://oreil.ly/jgKpM*). Do you think Google should be considered responsible for what happened to Dr. Sweeney? What would be an appropriate response?

4. How can a cross-disciplinary team help avoid negative consequences?

5. Read the paper "Does Machine Learning Automate Moral Hazard and Error?" (*https://oreil.ly/tLLOf*) What actions do you think should be taken to deal with the issues identified in this paper?

6. Read the article "How Will We Prevent AI-Based Forgery?" (*https://oreil.ly/6MQe4*) Do you think Etzioni's proposed approach could work? Why?

7. Complete the section "Analyze a Project You Are Working On" on page 118.

8. Consider whether your team could be more diverse. If so, what approaches might help?

Deep Learning in Practice: That's a Wrap!

Congratulations! You've made it to the end of the first section of the book. In this section, we've tried to show you what deep learning can do, and how you can use it to create real applications and products. At this point, you will get a lot more out of the book if you spend some time trying out what you've learned. Perhaps you have already been doing this as you go along—in which case, great! If not, that's no problem either—now is a great time to start experimenting yourself.

If you haven't been to the book's website (*https://book.fast.ai*) yet, head over there now. It's really important that you get yourself set up to run the notebooks. Becoming an effective deep learning practitioner is all about practice, so you need to be training models. So, please go get the notebooks running now if you haven't already! And have a look on the website for any important updates or notices; deep learning changes fast, and we can't change the words that are printed in this book, so the website is where you need to look to ensure you have the most up-to-date information.

Make sure that you have completed the following steps:

1. Connect to one of the GPU Jupyter servers recommended on the book's website.
2. Run the first notebook yourself.
3. Upload an image that you find in the first notebook; then try a few images of different kinds to see what happens.
4. Run the second notebook, collecting your own dataset based on image search queries that you come up with.
5. Think about how you can use deep learning to help you with your own projects, including what kinds of data you could use, what kinds of problems may come up, and how you might be able to mitigate these issues in practice.

In the next section of the book, you will learn about how and why deep learning works, instead of just seeing how you can use it in practice. Understanding the how and why is important for both practitioners and researchers, because in this fairly new field, nearly every project requires some level of customization and debugging. The better you understand the foundations of deep learning, the better your models will be. These foundations are less important for executives, product managers, and so forth (although still useful, so feel free to keep reading!), but they are critical for anybody who is training and deploying models themselves.

PART II

Understanding fastai's Applications

CHAPTER 4

Under the Hood: Training a Digit Classifier

Having seen what it looks like to train a variety of models in Chapter 2, let's now look under the hood and see exactly what is going on. We'll start by using computer vision to introduce fundamental tools and concepts for deep learning.

To be exact, we'll discuss the roles of arrays and tensors and of broadcasting, a powerful technique for using them expressively. We'll explain stochastic gradient descent (SGD), the mechanism for learning by updating weights automatically. We'll discuss the choice of a loss function for our basic classification task, and the role of minibatches. We'll also describe the math that a basic neural network is doing. Finally, we'll put all these pieces together.

In future chapters, we'll do deep dives into other applications as well, and see how these concepts and tools generalize. But this chapter is about laying foundation stones. To be frank, that also makes this one of the hardest chapters, because of how these concepts all depend on each other. Like an arch, all the stones need to be in place for the structure to stay up. Also like an arch, once that happens, it's a powerful structure that can support other things. But it requires some patience to assemble.

Let's begin. The first step is to consider how images are represented in a computer.

Pixels: The Foundations of Computer Vision

To understand what happens in a computer vision model, we first have to understand how computers handle images. We'll use one of the most famous datasets in computer vision, MNIST (*https://oreil.ly/g3RDg*), for our experiments. MNIST contains images of handwritten digits, collected by the National Institute of Standards and Technology and collated into a machine learning dataset by Yann Lecun and his colleagues. Lecun used MNIST in 1998 in LeNet-5 (*https://oreil.ly/LCNEx*), the first computer system to demonstrate practically useful recognition of handwritten digit sequences. This was one of the most important breakthroughs in the history of AI.

Tenacity and Deep Learning

The story of deep learning is one of tenacity and grit by a handful of dedicated researchers. After early hopes (and hype!), neural networks went out of favor in the 1990s and 2000s, and just a handful of researchers kept trying to make them work well. Three of them, Yann Lecun, Yoshua Bengio, and Geoffrey Hinton, were awarded the highest honor in computer science, the Turing Award (generally considered the "Nobel Prize of computer science"), in 2018 after triumphing despite the deep skepticism and disinterest of the wider machine learning and statistics community.

Hinton has told of how academic papers showing dramatically better results than anything previously published would be rejected by top journals and conferences, just because they used a neural network. Lecun's work on convolutional neural networks, which we will study in the next section, showed that these models could read hand-written text—something that had never been achieved before. However, his break-through was ignored by most researchers, even as it was used commercially to read 10% of the checks in the US!

In addition to these three Turing Award winners, many other researchers have battled to get us to where we are today. For instance, Jurgen Schmidhuber (who many believe should have shared in the Turing Award) pioneered many important ideas, including working with his student Sepp Hochreiter on the long short-term memory (LSTM) architecture (widely used for speech recognition and other text modeling tasks, and used in the IMDb example in Chapter 1). Perhaps most important of all, Paul Werbos in 1974 invented backpropagation for neural networks, the technique shown in this chapter and used universally for training neural networks (Werbos 1994 (*https:// oreil.ly/wWIWp*)). His development was almost entirely ignored for decades, but today it is considered the most important foundation of modern AI.

There is a lesson here for all of us! On your deep learning journey, you will face many obstacles, both technical and (even more difficult) posed by people around you who don't believe you'll be successful. There's one *guaranteed* way to fail, and that's to stop trying. We've seen that the only consistent trait among every fast.ai student who's gone on to be a world-class practitioner is that they are all very tenacious.

For this initial tutorial, we are just going to try to create a model that can classify any image as a 3 or a 7. So let's download a sample of MNIST that contains images of just these digits:

```
path = untar_data(URLs.MNIST_SAMPLE)
```

We can see what's in this directory by using `ls`, a method added by fastai. This method returns an object of a special fastai class called L, which has all the same functionality of Python's built-in `list`, plus a lot more. One of its handy features is that, when printed, it displays the count of items before listing the items themselves (if there are more than 10 items, it shows just the first few):

```
path.ls()
```

```
(#9) [Path('cleaned.csv'),Path('item_list.txt'),Path('trained_model.pkl'),Path('
 > models'),Path('valid'),Path('labels.csv'),Path('export.pkl'),Path('history.cs
 > v'),Path('train')]
```

The MNIST dataset follows a common layout for machine learning datasets: separate folders for the training set and the validation (and/or test) set. Let's see what's inside the training set:

```
(path/'train').ls()
```

```
(#2) [Path('train/7'),Path('train/3')]
```

There's a folder of 3s, and a folder of 7s. In machine learning parlance, we say that "3" and "7" are the *labels* (or targets) in this dataset. Let's take a look in one of these folders (using `sorted` to ensure we all get the same order of files):

```
threes = (path/'train'/'3').ls().sorted()
sevens = (path/'train'/'7').ls().sorted()
threes
```

```
(#6131) [Path('train/3/10.png'),Path('train/3/10000.png'),Path('train/3/10011.pn
 > g'),Path('train/3/10031.png'),Path('train/3/10034.png'),Path('train/3/10042.p
 > ng'),Path('train/3/10052.png'),Path('train/3/1007.png'),Path('train/3/10074.p
 > ng'),Path('train/3/10091.png')...]
```

As we might expect, it's full of image files. Let's take a look at one now. Here's an image of a handwritten number 3, taken from the famous MNIST dataset of handwritten numbers:

```
im3_path = threes[1]
im3 = Image.open(im3_path)
im3
```

Here we are using the `Image` class from the *Python Imaging Library* (PIL), which is the most widely used Python package for opening, manipulating, and viewing images. Jupyter knows about PIL images, so it displays the image for us automatically.

In a computer, everything is represented as a number. To view the numbers that make up this image, we have to convert it to a *NumPy array* or a *PyTorch tensor*. For instance, here's what a section of the image looks like converted to a NumPy array:

```
array(im3)[4:10,4:10]

array([[   0,    0,    0,    0,    0,    0],
       [   0,    0,    0,    0,    0,   29],
       [   0,    0,    0,   48,  166,  224],
       [   0,   93,  244,  249,  253,  187],
       [   0,  107,  253,  253,  230,   48],
       [   0,    3,   20,   20,   15,    0]], dtype=uint8)
```

The 4:10 indicates we requested the rows from index 4 (inclusive) to 10 (noninclusive), and the same for the columns. NumPy indexes from top to bottom and from left to right, so this section is located near the top-left corner of the image. Here's the same thing as a PyTorch tensor:

```
tensor(im3)[4:10,4:10]

tensor([[   0,    0,    0,    0,    0,    0],
        [   0,    0,    0,    0,    0,   29],
        [   0,    0,    0,   48,  166,  224],
        [   0,   93,  244,  249,  253,  187],
        [   0,  107,  253,  253,  230,   48],
        [   0,    3,   20,   20,   15,    0]], dtype=torch.uint8)
```

We can slice the array to pick just the part with the top of the digit in it, and then use a Pandas DataFrame to color-code the values using a gradient, which shows us clearly how the image is created from the pixel values:

```
im3_t = tensor(im3)
df = pd.DataFrame(im3_t[4:15,4:22])
df.style.set_properties(**{'font-size':'6pt'}).background_gradient('Greys')
```

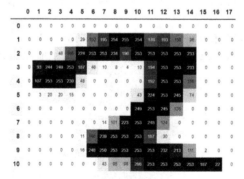

You can see that the background white pixels are stored as the number 0, black is the number 255, and shades of gray are between the two. The entire image contains 28 pixels across and 28 pixels down, for a total of 784 pixels. (This is much smaller than an image that you would get from a phone camera, which has millions of pixels, but is a convenient size for our initial learning and experiments. We will build up to bigger, full-color images soon.)

So, now you've seen what an image looks like to a computer, let's recall our goal: create a model that can recognize 3s and 7s. How might you go about getting a computer to do that?

Stop and Think!

Before you read on, take a moment to think about how a computer might be able to recognize these two digits. What kinds of features might it be able to look at? How might it be able to identify these features? How could it combine them? Learning works best when you try to solve problems yourself, rather than just reading somebody else's answers; so step away from this book for a few minutes, grab a piece of paper and pen, and jot some ideas down.

First Try: Pixel Similarity

So, here is a first idea: how about we find the average pixel value for every pixel of the 3s, then do the same for the 7s. This will give us two group averages, defining what we might call the "ideal" 3 and 7. Then, to classify an image as one digit or the other, we see which of these two ideal digits the image is most similar to. This certainly seems like it should be better than nothing, so it will make a good baseline.

Jargon: Baseline

A simple model that you are confident should perform reasonably well. It should be simple to implement and easy to test, so that you can then test each of your improved ideas and make sure they are always better than your baseline. Without starting with a sensible baseline, it is difficult to know whether your super-fancy models are any good. One good approach to creating a baseline is doing what we have done here: think of a simple, easy-to-implement model. Another good approach is to search around to find other people who have solved problems similar to yours, and download and run their code on your dataset. Ideally, try both of these!

Step 1 for our simple model is to get the average of pixel values for each of our two groups. In the process of doing this, we will learn a lot of neat Python numeric programming tricks!

Let's create a tensor containing all of our 3s stacked together. We already know how to create a tensor containing a single image. To create a tensor containing all the images in a directory, we will first use a Python list comprehension to create a plain list of the single image tensors.

We will use Jupyter to do some little checks of our work along the way—in this case, making sure that the number of returned items seems reasonable:

```
seven_tensors = [tensor(Image.open(o)) for o in sevens]
three_tensors = [tensor(Image.open(o)) for o in threes]
len(three_tensors),len(seven_tensors)
```

```
(6131, 6265)
```

List Comprehensions

List and dictionary comprehensions are a wonderful feature of Python. Many Python programmers use them every day, including the authors of this book—they are part of "idiomatic Python." But programmers coming from other languages may have never seen them before. A lot of great tutorials are just a web search away, so we won't spend a long time discussing them now. Here is a quick explanation and example to get you started. A list comprehension looks like this: `new_list = [f(o) for o in a_list if o>0]`. This will return every element of `a_list` that is greater than 0, after passing it to the function `f`. There are three parts here: the collection you are iterating over (`a_list`), an optional filter (`if o>0`), and something to do to each element (`f(o)`). It's not only shorter to write, but also way faster than the alternative ways of creating the same list with a loop.

We'll also check that one of the images looks OK. Since we now have tensors (which Jupyter by default will print as values), rather than PIL images (which Jupyter by default will display images), we need to use fastai's `show_image` function to display it:

```
show_image(three_tensors[1]);
```

3

For every pixel position, we want to compute the average over all the images of the intensity of that pixel. To do this, we first combine all the images in this list into a single three-dimensional tensor. The most common way to describe such a tensor is to call it a *rank-3 tensor*. We often need to stack up individual tensors in a collection into a single tensor. Unsurprisingly, PyTorch comes with a function called `stack` that we can use for this purpose.

Some operations in PyTorch, such as taking a mean, require us to *cast* our integer types to float types. Since we'll be needing this later, we'll also cast our stacked tensor to `float` now. Casting in PyTorch is as simple as writing the name of the type you wish to cast to, and treating it as a method.

Generally, when images are floats, the pixel values are expected to be between 0 and 1, so we will also divide by 255 here:

```
stacked_sevens = torch.stack(seven_tensors).float()/255
stacked_threes = torch.stack(three_tensors).float()/255
stacked_threes.shape
```

```
torch.Size([6131, 28, 28])
```

Perhaps the most important attribute of a tensor is its *shape*. This tells you the length of each axis. In this case, we can see that we have 6,131 images, each of size 28×28 pixels. There is nothing specifically about this tensor that says that the first axis is the number of images, the second is the height, and the third is the width—the semantics of a tensor are entirely up to us, and how we construct it. As far as PyTorch is concerned, it is just a bunch of numbers in memory.

The *length* of a tensor's shape is its rank:

```
len(stacked_threes.shape)
```

```
3
```

It is really important for you to commit to memory and practice these bits of tensor jargon: *rank* is the number of axes or dimensions in a tensor; *shape* is the size of each axis of a tensor.

 Alexis Says

Watch out because the term "dimension" is sometimes used in two ways. Consider that we live in "three-dimensional space," where a physical position can be described by a vector v, of length 3. But according to PyTorch, the attribute `v.ndim` (which sure looks like the "number of dimensions" of v) equals one, not three! Why? Because v is a vector, which is a tensor of rank one, meaning that it has only one *axis* (even if that axis has a length of three). In other words, sometimes dimension is used for the size of an axis ("space is three-dimensional"), while other times it is used for the rank, or the number of axes ("a matrix has two dimensions"). When confused, I find it helpful to translate all statements into terms of rank, axis, and length, which are unambiguous terms.

We can also get a tensor's rank directly with `ndim`:

```
stacked_threes.ndim
```

```
3
```

Finally, we can compute what the ideal 3 looks like. We calculate the mean of all the image tensors by taking the mean along dimension 0 of our stacked, rank-3 tensor. This is the dimension that indexes over all the images.

In other words, for every pixel position, this will compute the average of that pixel over all images. The result will be one value for every pixel position, or a single image. Here it is:

```
mean3 = stacked_threes.mean(0)
show_image(mean3);
```

3

According to this dataset, this is the ideal number 3! (You may not like it, but this is what peak number 3 performance looks like.) You can see how it's very dark where all the images agree it should be dark, but it becomes wispy and blurry where the images disagree.

Let's do the same thing for the 7s, but put all the steps together at once to save time:

```
mean7 = stacked_sevens.mean(0)
show_image(mean7);
```

7

Let's now pick an arbitrary 3 and measure its *distance* from our "ideal digits."

Stop and Think!

How would you calculate how similar a particular image is to each of our ideal digits? Remember to step away from this book and jot down some ideas before you move on! Research shows that recall and understanding improve dramatically when you are engaged with the learning process by solving problems, experimenting, and trying new ideas yourself.

Here's a sample 3:

```
a_3 = stacked_threes[1]
show_image(a_3);
```

3

How can we determine its distance from our ideal 3? We can't just add up the differences between the pixels of this image and the ideal digit. Some differences will be positive, while others will be negative, and these differences will cancel out, resulting in a situation where an image that is too dark in some places and too light in others might be shown as having zero total differences from the ideal. That would be misleading!

To avoid this, data scientists use two main ways to measure distance in this context:

- Take the mean of the *absolute value* of differences (absolute value is the function that replaces negative values with positive values). This is called the *mean absolute difference* or *L1 norm*.

- Take the mean of the *square* of differences (which makes everything positive) and then take the *square root* (which undoes the squaring). This is called the *root mean squared error* (RMSE) or *L2 norm*.

It's OK to Have Forgotten Your Math

In this book, we generally assume that you have completed high school math, and remember at least some of it—but everybody forgets some things! It all depends on what you happen to have had reason to practice in the meantime. Perhaps you have forgotten what a *square root* is, or exactly how they work. No problem! Anytime you come across a math concept that is not explained fully in this book, don't just keep moving on; instead, stop and look it up. Make sure you understand the basic idea, how it works, and why we might be using it. One of the best places to refresh your understanding is Khan Academy. For instance, Khan Academy has a great introduction to square roots (*https://oreil.ly/T7mxH*).

Let's try both of these now:

```
dist_3_abs = (a_3 - mean3).abs().mean()
dist_3_sqr = ((a_3 - mean3)**2).mean().sqrt()
dist_3_abs,dist_3_sqr

(tensor(0.1114), tensor(0.2021))

dist_7_abs = (a_3 - mean7).abs().mean()
dist_7_sqr = ((a_3 - mean7)**2).mean().sqrt()
dist_7_abs,dist_7_sqr

(tensor(0.1586), tensor(0.3021))
```

In both cases, the distance between our 3 and the "ideal" 3 is less than the distance to the ideal 7, so our simple model will give the right prediction in this case.

PyTorch already provides both of these as *loss functions*. You'll find these inside `torch.nn.functional`, which the PyTorch team recommends importing as `F` (and is available by default under that name in fastai):

```
F.l1_loss(a_3.float(),mean7), F.mse_loss(a_3,mean7).sqrt()

(tensor(0.1586), tensor(0.3021))
```

Here, `MSE` stands for *mean squared error*, and `l1` refers to the standard mathematical jargon for *mean absolute value* (in math it's called the *L1 norm*).

Sylvain Says

Intuitively, the difference between L1 norm and mean squared error (MSE) is that the latter will penalize bigger mistakes more heavily than the former (and be more lenient with small mistakes).

Jeremy Says

When I first came across this L1 thingie, I looked it up to see what on earth it meant. I found on Google that it is a *vector norm* using *absolute value*, so I looked up "vector norm" and started reading: *Given a vector space V over a field F of the real or complex numbers, a norm on V is a nonnegative-valued any function p: V → \[0,+∞) with the following properties: For all a ∈ F and all u, v ∈ V, p(u + v) ≤ p(u) + p(v)…* Then I stopped reading. "Ugh, I'll never understand math!" I thought, for the thousandth time. Since then, I've learned that every time these complex mathy bits of jargon come up in practice, it turns out I can replace them with a tiny bit of code! Like, the *L1 loss* is just equal to `(a-b).abs().mean()`, where a and b are tensors. I guess mathy folks just think differently than I do… I'll make sure in this book that every time some mathy jargon comes up, I'll give you the little bit of code it's equal to as well, and explain in common-sense terms what's going on.

We just completed various mathematical operations on PyTorch tensors. If you've done numeric programming in NumPy before, you may recognize these as being similar to NumPy arrays. Let's have a look at those two important data structures.

NumPy Arrays and PyTorch Tensors

NumPy (*https://numpy.org*) is the most widely used library for scientific and numeric programming in Python. It provides similar functionality and a similar API to that provided by PyTorch; however, it does not support using the GPU or calculating gradients, which are both critical for deep learning. Therefore, in this book, we will generally use PyTorch tensors instead of NumPy arrays, where possible.

(Note that fastai adds some features to NumPy and PyTorch to make them a bit more similar to each other. If any code in this book doesn't work on your computer, it's possible that you forgot to include a line like this at the start of your notebook: `from fastai.vision.all import *`.)

But what are arrays and tensors, and why should you care?

Python is slow compared to many languages. Anything fast in Python, NumPy, or PyTorch is likely to be a wrapper for a compiled object written (and optimized) in another language—specifically, C. In fact, *NumPy arrays and PyTorch tensors can finish computations many thousands of times faster than using pure Python.*

A NumPy array is a multidimensional table of data, with all items of the same type. Since that can be any type at all, they can even be arrays of arrays, with the innermost arrays potentially being different sizes—this is called a *jagged array*. By "multidimensional table," we mean, for instance, a list (dimension of one), a table or matrix (dimension of two), a table of tables or cube (dimension of three), and so forth. If the items are all of simple type such as integer or float, NumPy will store them as a compact C data structure in memory. This is where NumPy shines. NumPy has a wide variety of operators and methods that can run computations on these compact structures at the same speed as optimized C, because they are written in optimized C.

A PyTorch tensor is nearly the same thing as a NumPy array, but with an additional restriction that unlocks additional capabilities. It's the same in that it, too, is a multidimensional table of data, with all items of the same type. However, the restriction is that a tensor cannot use just any old type—it has to use a single basic numeric type for all components. As a result, a tensor is not as flexible as a genuine array of arrays. For example, a PyTorch tensor cannot be jagged. It is always a regularly shaped multidimensional rectangular structure.

The vast majority of methods and operators supported by NumPy on these structures are also supported by PyTorch, but PyTorch tensors have additional capabilities. One major capability is that these structures can live on the GPU, in which case their computation will be optimized for the GPU and can run much faster (given lots of values to work on). In addition, PyTorch can automatically calculate derivatives of these operations, including combinations of operations. As you'll see, it would be impossible to do deep learning in practice without this capability.

Sylvain Says

If you don't know what C is, don't worry: you won't need it at all. In a nutshell, it's a low-level (low-level means more similar to the language that computers use internally) language that is very fast compared to Python. To take advantage of its speed while programming in Python, try to avoid as much as possible writing loops, and replace them by commands that work directly on arrays or tensors.

Perhaps the most important new coding skill for a Python programmer to learn is how to effectively use the array/tensor APIs. We will be showing lots more tricks later in this book, but here's a summary of the key things you need to know for now.

To create an array or tensor, pass a list (or list of lists, or list of lists of lists, etc.) to array or tensor:

```
data = [[1,2,3],[4,5,6]]
arr = array (data)
tns = tensor(data)

arr   # numpy

array([[1, 2, 3],
       [4, 5, 6]])

tns   # pytorch

tensor([[1, 2, 3],
        [4, 5, 6]])
```

All the operations that follow are shown on tensors, but the syntax and results for NumPy arrays are identical.

You can select a row (note that, like lists in Python, tensors are 0-indexed, so 1 refers to the second row/column):

```
tns[1]

tensor([4, 5, 6])
```

Or a column, by using : to indicate *all of the first axis* (we sometimes refer to the dimensions of tensors/arrays as *axes*):

```
tns[:,1]

tensor([2, 5])
```

You can combine these with Python slice syntax ([*start*:*end*], with *end* being excluded) to select part of a row or column:

```
tns[1,1:3]
```

```
tensor([5, 6])
```

And you can use the standard operators, such as +, -, *, and /:

```
tns+1
```

```
tensor([[2, 3, 4],
        [5, 6, 7]])
```

Tensors have a type:

```
tns.type()
```

```
'torch.LongTensor'
```

And will automatically change that type as needed; for example, from int to float:

```
tns*1.5
```

```
tensor([[1.5000, 3.0000, 4.5000],
        [6.0000, 7.5000, 9.0000]])
```

So, is our baseline model any good? To quantify this, we must define a metric.

Computing Metrics Using Broadcasting

Recall that a *metric* is a number that is calculated based on the predictions of our model and the correct labels in our dataset, in order to tell us how good our model is. For instance, we could use either of the functions we saw in the previous section, mean squared error or mean absolute error, and take the average of them over the whole dataset. However, neither of these are numbers that are very understandable to most people; in practice, we normally use *accuracy* as the metric for classification models.

As we've discussed, we want to calculate our metric over a *validation set*. This is so that we don't inadvertently overfit—that is, train a model to work well only on our training data. This is not really a risk with the pixel similarity model we're using here as a first try, since it has no trained components, but we'll use a validation set anyway to follow normal practices and to be ready for our second try later.

To get a validation set, we need to remove some of the data from training entirely, so it is not seen by the model at all. As it turns out, the creators of the MNIST dataset have already done this for us. Do you remember how there was a whole separate directory called *valid*? That's what this directory is for!

So to start, let's create tensors for our 3s and 7s from that directory. These are the tensors we will use to calculate a metric measuring the quality of our first-try model, which measures distance from an ideal image:

```
valid_3_tens = torch.stack([tensor(Image.open(o))
                            for o in (path/'valid'/'3').ls()])
valid_3_tens = valid_3_tens.float()/255
valid_7_tens = torch.stack([tensor(Image.open(o))
                            for o in (path/'valid'/'7').ls()])
valid_7_tens = valid_7_tens.float()/255
valid_3_tens.shape,valid_7_tens.shape
```

```
(torch.Size([1010, 28, 28]), torch.Size([1028, 28, 28]))
```

It's good to get in the habit of checking shapes as you go. Here we see two tensors, one representing the 3s validation set of 1,010 images of size 28×28, and one representing the 7s validation set of 1,028 images of size 28×28.

We ultimately want to write a function, is_3, that will decide whether an arbitrary image is a 3 or a 7. It will do this by deciding which of our two "ideal digits" that arbitrary image is closer to. For that we need to define a notion of *distance*—that is, a function that calculates the distance between two images.

We can write a simple function that calculates the mean absolute error using an expression very similar to the one we wrote in the last section:

```
def mnist_distance(a,b): return (a-b).abs().mean((-1,-2))
mnist_distance(a_3, mean3)
```

```
tensor(0.1114)
```

This is the same value we previously calculated for the distance between these two images, the ideal 3 mean3 and the arbitrary sample 3 a_3, which are both single-image tensors with a shape of [28,28].

But to calculate a metric for overall accuracy, we will need to calculate the distance to the ideal 3 for *every* image in the validation set. How do we do that calculation? We could write a loop over all of the single-image tensors that are stacked within our validation set tensor, valid_3_tens, which has a shape of [1010,28,28] representing 1,010 images. But there is a better way.

Something interesting happens when we take this exact same distance function, designed for comparing two single images, but pass in as an argument valid_3_tens, the tensor that represents the 3s validation set:

```
valid_3_dist = mnist_distance(valid_3_tens, mean3)
valid_3_dist, valid_3_dist.shape
```

```
(tensor([0.1050, 0.1526, 0.1186,  ..., 0.1122, 0.1170, 0.1086]),
 torch.Size([1010]))
```

Instead of complaining about shapes not matching, it returned the distance for every single image as a vector (i.e., a rank-1 tensor) of length 1,010 (the number of 3s in our validation set). How did that happen?

Take another look at our function `mnist_distance`, and you'll see we have there the subtraction (`a-b`). The magic trick is that PyTorch, when it tries to perform a simple subtraction operation between two tensors of different ranks, will use *broadcasting*: it will automatically expand the tensor with the smaller rank to have the same size as the one with the larger rank. Broadcasting is an important capability that makes tensor code much easier to write.

After broadcasting so the two argument tensors have the same rank, PyTorch applies its usual logic for two tensors of the same rank: it performs the operation on each corresponding element of the two tensors, and returns the tensor result. For instance:

```
tensor([1,2,3]) + tensor(1)

tensor([2, 3, 4])
```

So in this case, PyTorch treats `mean3`, a rank-2 tensor representing a single image, as if it were 1,010 copies of the same image, and then subtracts each of those copies from each 3 in our validation set. What shape would you expect this tensor to have? Try to figure it out yourself before you look at the answer here:

```
(valid_3_tens-mean3).shape

torch.Size([1010, 28, 28])
```

We are calculating the difference between our ideal 3 and each of the 1,010 3s in the validation set, for each of 28×28 images, resulting in the shape [`1010,28,28`].

There are a couple of important points about how broadcasting is implemented, which make it valuable not just for expressivity but also for performance:

- PyTorch doesn't *actually* copy `mean3` 1,010 times. It *pretends* it were a tensor of that shape, but doesn't allocate any additional memory.
- It does the whole calculation in C (or, if you're using a GPU, in CUDA, the equivalent of C on the GPU), tens of thousands of times faster than pure Python (up to millions of times faster on a GPU!).

This is true of all broadcasting and elementwise operations and functions done in PyTorch. *It's the most important technique for you to know to create efficient PyTorch code.*

Next in `mnist_distance` we see `abs`. You might be able to guess now what this does when applied to a tensor. It applies the method to each individual element in the tensor, and returns a tensor of the results (that is, it applies the method *elementwise*). So in this case, we'll get back 1,010 matrices of absolute values.

Finally, our function calls mean((-1,-2)). The tuple (-1,-2) represents a range of axes. In Python, -1 refers to the last element, and -2 refers to the second-to-last. So in this case, this tells PyTorch that we want to take the mean ranging over the values indexed by the last two axes of the tensor. The last two axes are the horizontal and vertical dimensions of an image. After taking the mean over the last two axes, we are left with just the first tensor axis, which indexes over our images, which is why our final size was (1010). In other words, for every image, we averaged the intensity of all the pixels in that image.

We'll be learning lots more about broadcasting throughout this book, especially in Chapter 17, and will be practicing it regularly too.

We can use mnist_distance to figure out whether an image is a 3 by using the following logic: if the distance between the digit in question and the ideal 3 is less than the distance to the ideal 7, then it's a 3. This function will automatically do broadcasting and be applied elementwise, just like all PyTorch functions and operators:

```
def is_3(x): return mnist_distance(x,mean3) < mnist_distance(x,mean7)
```

Let's test it on our example case:

```
is_3(a_3), is_3(a_3).float()
```

```
(tensor(True), tensor(1.))
```

Note that when we convert the Boolean response to a float, we get 1.0 for True and 0.0 for False.

Thanks to broadcasting, we can also test it on the full validation set of 3s:

```
is_3(valid_3_tens)
```

```
tensor([True, True, True,  ..., True, True, True])
```

Now we can calculate the accuracy for each of the 3s and 7s, by taking the average of that function for all 3s and its inverse for all 7s:

```
accuracy_3s =      is_3(valid_3_tens).float() .mean()
accuracy_7s = (1 - is_3(valid_7_tens).float()).mean()

accuracy_3s,accuracy_7s,(accuracy_3s+accuracy_7s)/2
```

```
(tensor(0.9168), tensor(0.9854), tensor(0.9511))
```

This looks like a pretty good start! We're getting over 90% accuracy on both 3s and 7s, and we've seen how to define a metric conveniently using broadcasting. But let's be honest: 3s and 7s are very different-looking digits. And we're classifying only 2 out of the 10 possible digits so far. So we're going to need to do better!

To do better, perhaps it is time to try a system that does some real learning—one that can automatically modify itself to improve its performance. In other words, it's time to talk about the training process and SGD.

Stochastic Gradient Descent

Do you remember the way that Arthur Samuel described machine learning, which we quoted in Chapter 1?

> Suppose we arrange for some automatic means of testing the effectiveness of any current weight assignment in terms of actual performance and provide a mechanism for altering the weight assignment so as to maximize the performance. We need not go into the details of such a procedure to see that it could be made entirely automatic and to see that a machine so programmed would "learn" from its experience.

As we discussed, this is the key to allowing us to have a model that can get better and better—that can learn. But our pixel similarity approach does not really do this. We do not have any kind of weight assignment, or any way of improving based on testing the effectiveness of a weight assignment. In other words, we can't really improve our pixel similarity approach by modifying a set of parameters. To take advantage of the power of deep learning, we will first have to represent our task in the way that Samuel described it.

Instead of trying to find the similarity between an image and an "ideal image," we could instead look at each individual pixel and come up with a set of weights for each, such that the highest weights are associated with those pixels most likely to be black for a particular category. For instance, pixels toward the bottom right are not very likely to be activated for a 7, so they should have a low weight for a 7, but they are likely to be activated for an 3, so they should have a high weight for an 3. This can be represented as a function and set of weight values for each possible category—for instance, the probability of being the number 3:

```
def pr_three(x, w): return (x*w).sum()
```

Here we are assuming that x is the image, represented as a vector—in other words, with all of the rows stacked up end to end into a single long line. And we are assuming that the weights are a vector w. If we have this function, we just need some way to update the weights to make them a little bit better. With such an approach, we can repeat that step a number of times, making the weights better and better, until they are as good as we can make them.

We want to find the specific values for the vector w that cause the result of our function to be high for those images that are 3s, and low for those images that are not. Searching for the best vector w is a way to search for the best function for recognizing 3s. (Because we are not yet using a deep neural network, we are limited by what our function can do—we are going to fix that constraint later in this chapter.)

To be more specific, here are the steps required to turn this function into a machine learning classifier:

1. *Initialize* the weights.
2. For each image, use these weights to *predict* whether it appears to be a 3 or a 7.
3. Based on these predictions, calculate how good the model is (its *loss*).
4. Calculate the *gradient*, which measures for each weight how changing that weight would change the loss.
5. *Step* (that is, change) all the weights based on that calculation.
6. Go back to step 2 and *repeat* the process.
7. Iterate until you decide to *stop* the training process (for instance, because the model is good enough or you don't want to wait any longer).

These seven steps, illustrated in Figure 4-1, are the key to the training of all deep learning models. That deep learning turns out to rely entirely on these steps is extremely surprising and counterintuitive. It's amazing that this process can solve such complex problems. But, as you'll see, it really does!

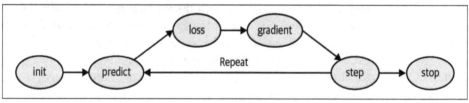

Figure 4-1. The gradient descent process

There are many ways to do each of these seven steps, and we will be learning about them throughout the rest of this book. These are the details that make a big difference for deep learning practitioners, but it turns out that the general approach to each one follows some basic principles. Here are a few guidelines:

Initialize

We initialize the parameters to random values. This may sound surprising. There are certainly other choices we could make, such as initializing them to the percentage of times that pixel is activated for that category—but since we already know that we have a routine to improve these weights, it turns out that just starting with random weights works perfectly well.

Loss

This is what Samuel referred to when he spoke of *testing the effectiveness of any current weight assignment in terms of actual performance*. We need a function that will return a number that is small if the performance of the model is good (the standard approach is to treat a small loss as good and a large loss as bad, although this is just a convention).

Step

A simple way to figure out whether a weight should be increased a bit or decreased a bit would be just to try it: increase the weight by a small amount, and see if the loss goes up or down. Once you find the correct direction, you could then change that amount by a bit more, or a bit less, until you find an amount that works well. However, this is slow! As we will see, the magic of calculus allows us to directly figure out in which direction, and by roughly how much, to change each weight, without having to try all these small changes. The way to do this is by calculating *gradients*. This is just a performance optimization; we would get exactly the same results by using the slower manual process as well.

Stop

Once we've decided how many epochs to train the model for (a few suggestions for this were given in the earlier list), we apply that decision. For our digit classifier, we would keep training until the accuracy of the model started getting worse, or we ran out of time.

Before applying these steps to our image classification problem, let's illustrate what they look like in a simpler case. First we will define a very simple function, the quadratic—let's pretend that this is our loss function, and x is a weight parameter of the function:

```
def f(x): return x**2
```

Here is a graph of that function:

```
plot_function(f, 'x', 'x**2')
```

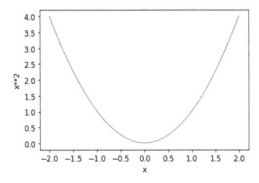

The sequence of steps we described earlier starts by picking a random value for a parameter, and calculating the value of the loss:

```
plot_function(f, 'x', 'x**2')
plt.scatter(-1.5, f(-1.5), color='red');
```

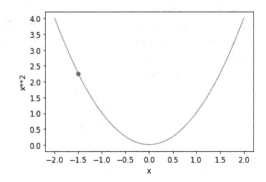

Now we look to see what would happen if we increased or decreased our parameter by a little bit—the *adjustment*. This is simply the slope at a particular point:

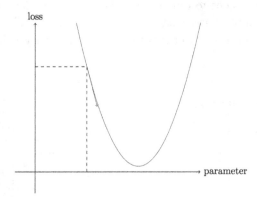

We can change our weight by a little in the direction of the slope, calculate our loss and adjustment again, and repeat this a few times. Eventually, we will get to the lowest point on our curve:

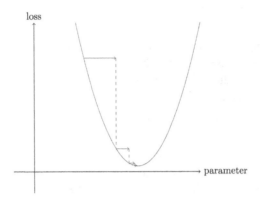

This basic idea goes all the way back to Isaac Newton, who pointed out that we can optimize arbitrary functions in this way. Regardless of how complicated our functions become, this basic approach of gradient descent will not significantly change. The only minor changes we will see later in this book are some handy ways we can make it faster, by finding better steps.

Calculating Gradients

The one magic step is the bit where we calculate the gradients. As we mentioned, we use calculus as a performance optimization; it allows us to more quickly calculate whether our loss will go up or down when we adjust our parameters up or down. In other words, the gradients will tell us how much we have to change each weight to make our model better.

You may remember from your high school calculus class that the *derivative* of a function tells you how much a change in its parameters will change its result. If not, don't worry; lots of us forget calculus once high school is behind us! But you will need some intuitive understanding of what a derivative is before you continue, so if this is all very fuzzy in your head, head over to Khan Academy and complete the lessons on basic derivatives (*https://oreil.ly/nyd0R*). You won't have to know how to calculate them yourself; you just have to know what a derivative is.

The key point about a derivative is this: for any function, such as the quadratic function we saw in the previous section, we can calculate its derivative. The derivative is another function. It calculates the change, rather than the value. For instance, the derivative of the quadratic function at the value 3 tells us how rapidly the function changes at the value 3. More specifically, you may recall that gradient is defined as *rise/run*; that is, the change in the value of the function, divided by the change in the value of the parameter. When we know how our function will change, we know what we need to do to make it smaller. This is the key to machine learning: having a way to change the parameters of a function to make it smaller. Calculus provides us with a computational shortcut, the derivative, which lets us directly calculate the gradients of our functions.

One important thing to be aware of is that our function has lots of weights that we need to adjust, so when we calculate the derivative, we won't get back one number, but lots of them—a gradient for every weight. But there is nothing mathematically tricky here; you can calculate the derivative with respect to one weight and treat all the other ones as constant, and then repeat that for each other weight. This is how all of the gradients are calculated, for every weight.

We mentioned just now that you won't have to calculate any gradients yourself. How can that be? Amazingly enough, PyTorch is able to automatically compute the derivative of nearly any function! What's more, it does it very fast. Most of the time, it will be at least as fast as any derivative function that you can create by hand. Let's see an example.

First, let's pick a tensor value at which we want gradients:

```
xt = tensor(3.).requires_grad_()
```

Notice the special method `requires_grad_`? That's the magical incantation we use to tell PyTorch that we want to calculate gradients with respect to that variable at that value. It is essentially tagging the variable, so PyTorch will remember to keep track of how to compute gradients of the other direct calculations on it that you will ask for.

 Alexis Says

This API might throw you off if you're coming from math or physics. In those contexts, the "gradient" of a function is just another function (i.e., its derivative), so you might expect gradient-related APIs to give you a new function. But in deep learning, "gradient" usually means the *value* of a function's derivative at a particular argument value. The PyTorch API also puts the focus on the argument, not the function you're actually computing the gradients of. It may feel backward at first, but it's just a different perspective.

Now we calculate our function with that value. Notice how PyTorch prints not just the value calculated, but also a note that it has a gradient function it'll be using to calculate our gradients when needed:

```
yt = f(xt)
yt

tensor(9., grad_fn=<PowBackward0>)
```

Finally, we tell PyTorch to calculate the gradients for us:

```
yt.backward()
```

The "backward" here refers to *backpropagation*, which is the name given to the process of calculating the derivative of each layer. We'll see how this is done exactly in Chapter 17, when we calculate the gradients of a deep neural net from scratch. This is called the *backward pass* of the network, as opposed to the *forward pass*, which is where the activations are calculated. Life would probably be easier if backward was just called calculate_grad, but deep learning folks really do like to add jargon everywhere they can!

We can now view the gradients by checking the grad attribute of our tensor:

```
xt.grad
```

```
tensor(6.)
```

If you remember your high school calculus rules, the derivative of x**2 is 2*x, and we have x=3, so the gradients should be 2*3=6, which is what PyTorch calculated for us!

Now we'll repeat the preceding steps, but with a vector argument for our function:

```
xt = tensor([3.,4.,10.]).requires_grad_()
xt
```

```
tensor([ 3.,   4.,  10.], requires_grad=True)
```

And we'll add sum to our function so it can take a vector (i.e., a rank-1 tensor) and return a scalar (i.e., a rank-0 tensor):

```
def f(x): return (x**2).sum()
```

```
yt = f(xt)
yt
```

```
tensor(125., grad_fn=<SumBackward0>)
```

Our gradients are 2*xt, as we'd expect!

```
yt.backward()
xt.grad
```

```
tensor([ 6.,   8.,  20.])
```

The gradients tell us only the slope of our function; they don't tell us exactly how far to adjust the parameters. But they do give us some idea of how far: if the slope is very large, that may suggest that we have more adjustments to do, whereas if the slope is very small, that may suggest that we are close to the optimal value.

Stepping with a Learning Rate

Deciding how to change our parameters based on the values of the gradients is an important part of the deep learning process. Nearly all approaches start with the basic idea of multiplying the gradient by some small number, called the *learning rate* (LR). The learning rate is often a number between 0.001 and 0.1, although it could be anything. Often people select a learning rate just by trying a few, and finding which results in the best model after training (we'll show you a better approach later in this book, called the *learning rate finder*). Once you've picked a learning rate, you can adjust your parameters using this simple function:

```
w -= w.grad * lr
```

This is known as *stepping* your parameters, using an *optimization step*.

If you pick a learning rate that's too low, it can mean having to do a lot of steps. Figure 4-2 illustrates that.

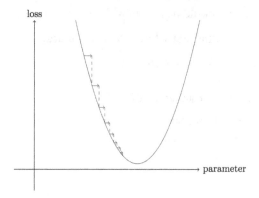

Figure 4-2. Gradient descent with low LR

But picking a learning rate that's too high is even worse—it can result in the loss getting *worse*, as we see in Figure 4-3!

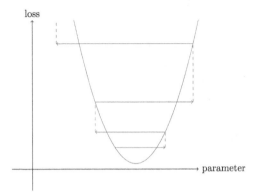

Figure 4-3. Gradient descent with high LR

If the learning rate is too high, it may also "bounce" around, rather than diverging; Figure 4-4 shows how this results in taking many steps to train successfully.

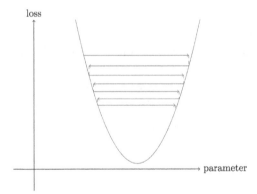

Figure 4-4. Gradient descent with bouncy LR

Now let's apply all of this in an end-to-end example.

An End-to-End SGD Example

We've seen how to use gradients to minimize our loss. Now it's time to look at an SGD example and see how finding a minimum can be used to train a model to fit data better.

Let's start with a simple, synthetic example model. Imagine you were measuring the speed of a roller coaster as it went over the top of a hump. It would start fast, and then get slower as it went up the hill; it would be slowest at the top, and it would then speed up again as it went downhill. You want to build a model of how the speed changes over time. If you were measuring the speed manually every second for 20 seconds, it might look something like this:

```
time = torch.arange(0,20).float(); time
```

```
tensor([ 0.,   1.,   2.,   3.,   4.,   5.,   6.,   7.,   8.,   9.,  10.,  11.,  12.,  13.,
    > 14.,  15.,  16.,  17.,  18.,  19.])
```

```
speed = torch.randn(20)*3 + 0.75*(time-9.5)**2 + 1
plt.scatter(time,speed);
```

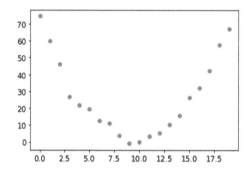

We've added a bit of random noise, since measuring things manually isn't precise. This means it's not that easy to answer the question: what was the roller coaster's speed? Using SGD, we can try to find a function that matches our observations. We can't consider every possible function, so let's use a guess that it will be quadratic; i.e., a function of the form a*(time**2)+(b*time)+c.

We want to distinguish clearly between the function's input (the time when we are measuring the coaster's speed) and its parameters (the values that define *which* quadratic we're trying). So let's collect the parameters in one argument and thus separate the input, t, and the parameters, params, in the function's signature:

```
def f(t, params):
    a,b,c = params
    return a*(t**2) + (b*t) + c
```

In other words, we've restricted the problem of finding the best imaginable function that fits the data to finding the best *quadratic* function. This greatly simplifies the problem, since every quadratic function is fully defined by the three parameters a, b, and c. Thus, to find the best quadratic function, we need to find only the best values for a, b, and c.

If we can solve this problem for the three parameters of a quadratic function, we'll be able to apply the same approach for other, more complex functions with more parameters—such as a neural net. Let's find the parameters for f first, and then we'll come back and do the same thing for the MNIST dataset with a neural net.

We need to define first what we mean by "best." We define this precisely by choosing a *loss function*, which will return a value based on a prediction and a target, where lower values of the function correspond to "better" predictions. For continuous data, it's common to use *mean squared error*:

```
def mse(preds, targets): return ((preds-targets)**2).mean().sqrt()
```

Now, let's work through our seven-step process.

Step 1: Initialize the parameters

First, we initialize the parameters to random values and tell PyTorch that we want to track their gradients using `requires_grad_`:

```
params = torch.randn(3).requires_grad_()
```

Step 2: Calculate the predictions

Next, we calculate the predictions:

```
preds = f(time, params)
```

Let's create a little function to see how close our predictions are to our targets, and take a look:

```
def show_preds(preds, ax=None):
    if ax is None: ax=plt.subplots()[1]
    ax.scatter(time, speed)
    ax.scatter(time, to_np(preds), color='red')
    ax.set_ylim(-300,100)

show_preds(preds)
```

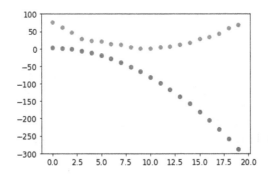

This doesn't look very close—our random parameters suggest that the roller coaster will end up going backward, since we have negative speeds!

Step 3: Calculate the loss

We calculate the loss as follows:

```
loss = mse(preds, speed)
loss
```

```
tensor(25823.8086, grad_fn=<MeanBackward0>)
```

Our goal is now to improve this. To do that, we'll need to know the gradients.

Step 4: Calculate the gradients

The next step is to calculate the gradients, or an approximation of how the parameters need to change:

```
loss.backward()
params.grad
```

```
tensor([-53195.8594,   -3419.7146,   -253.8908])
```

```
params.grad * 1e-5
```

```
tensor([-0.5320, -0.0342, -0.0025])
```

We can use these gradients to improve our parameters. We'll need to pick a learning rate (we'll discuss how to do that in practice in the next chapter; for now, we'll just use 1e-5 or 0.00001):

```
params
```

```
tensor([-0.7658, -0.7506,  1.3525], requires_grad=True)
```

Step 5: Step the weights

Now we need to update the parameters based on the gradients we just calculated:

```
lr = 1e-5
params.data -= lr * params.grad.data
params.grad = None
```

Alexis Says

Understanding this bit depends on remembering recent history. To calculate the gradients, we call backward on the loss. But this loss was itself calculated by mse, which in turn took preds as an input, which was calculated using f taking as an input params, which was the object on which we originally called required_grads_—which is the original call that now allows us to call backward on loss. This chain of function calls represents the mathematical composition of functions, which enables PyTorch to use calculus's chain rule under the hood to calculate these gradients.

Let's see if the loss has improved:

```
preds = f(time,params)
mse(preds, speed)
```

```
tensor(5435.5366, grad_fn=<MeanBackward0>)
```

And take a look at the plot:

```
show_preds(preds)
```

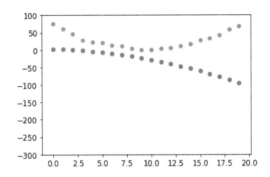

We need to repeat this a few times, so we'll create a function to apply one step:

```
def apply_step(params, prn=True):
    preds = f(time, params)
    loss = mse(preds, speed)
    loss.backward()
    params.data -= lr * params.grad.data
    params.grad = None
    if prn: print(loss.item())
    return preds
```

Step 6: Repeat the process

Now we iterate. By looping and performing many improvements, we hope to reach a good result:

```
for i in range(10): apply_step(params)
```

```
5435.53662109375
1577.4495849609375
847.3780517578125
709.22265625
683.0757446289062
678.12451171875
677.1839599609375
677.0025024414062
676.96435546875
676.9537353515625
```

The loss is going down, just as we hoped! But looking only at these loss numbers disguises the fact that each iteration represents an entirely different quadratic function being tried, on the way to finding the best possible quadratic function. We can see this process visually if, instead of printing out the loss function, we plot the function at every step. Then we can see how the shape is approaching the best possible quadratic function for our data:

```
_,axs = plt.subplots(1,4,figsize=(12,3))
for ax in axs: show_preds(apply_step(params, False), ax)
plt.tight_layout()
```

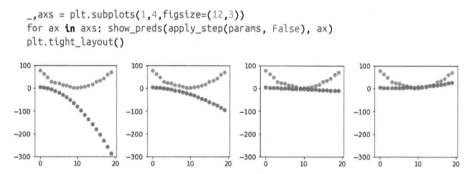

Step 7: Stop

We just decided to stop after 10 epochs arbitrarily. In practice, we would watch the training and validation losses and our metrics to decide when to stop, as we've discussed.

Summarizing Gradient Descent

Now that you've seen what happens in each step, let's take another look at our graphical representation of the gradient descent process (Figure 4-5) and do a quick recap.

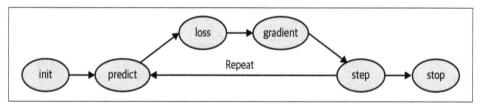

Figure 4-5. The gradient descent process

At the beginning, the weights of our model can be random (training *from scratch*) or come from a pretrained model (*transfer learning*). In the first case, the output we will get from our inputs won't have anything to do with what we want, and even in the second case, it's likely the pretrained model won't be very good at the specific task we are targeting. So the model will need to *learn* better weights.

We begin by comparing the outputs the model gives us with our targets (we have labeled data, so we know what result the model should give) using a *loss function*, which returns a number that we want to make as low as possible by improving our weights. To do this, we take a few data items (such as images) from the training set and feed them to our model. We compare the corresponding targets using our loss function, and the score we get tells us how wrong our predictions were. We then change the weights a little bit to make it slightly better.

To find how to change the weights to make the loss a bit better, we use calculus to calculate the *gradients*. (Actually, we let PyTorch do it for us!) Let's consider an analogy. Imagine you are lost in the mountains with your car parked at the lowest point. To find your way back to it, you might wander in a random direction, but that probably wouldn't help much. Since you know your vehicle is at the lowest point, you would be better off going downhill. By always taking a step in the direction of the steepest downward slope, you should eventually arrive at your destination. We use the magnitude of the gradient (i.e., the steepness of the slope) to tell us how big a step to take; specifically, we multiply the gradient by a number we choose called the *learning rate* to decide on the step size. We then *iterate* until we have reached the lowest point, which will be our parking lot; then we can *stop*.

All of what we just saw can be transposed directly to the MNIST dataset, except for the loss function. Let's now see how we can define a good training objective.

The MNIST Loss Function

We already have our xs—that is, our independent variables, the images themselves. We'll concatenate them all into a single tensor, and also change them from a list of matrices (a rank-3 tensor) to a list of vectors (a rank-2 tensor). We can do this using view, which is a PyTorch method that changes the shape of a tensor without changing its contents. -1 is a special parameter to view that means "make this axis as big as necessary to fit all the data":

```
train_x = torch.cat([stacked_threes, stacked_sevens]).view(-1, 28*28)
```

We need a label for each image. We'll use 1 for 3s and 0 for 7s:

```
train_y = tensor([1]*len(threes) + [0]*len(sevens)).unsqueeze(1)
train_x.shape,train_y.shape
```

```
(torch.Size([12396, 784]), torch.Size([12396, 1]))
```

A `Dataset` in PyTorch is required to return a tuple of (x,y) when indexed. Python provides a `zip` function that, when combined with `list`, provides a simple way to get this functionality:

```
dset = list(zip(train_x,train_y))
x,y = dset[0]
x.shape,y

(torch.Size([784]), tensor([1]))

valid_x = torch.cat([valid_3_tens, valid_7_tens]).view(-1, 28*28)
valid_y = tensor([1]*len(valid_3_tens) + [0]*len(valid_7_tens)).unsqueeze(1)
valid_dset = list(zip(valid_x,valid_y))
```

Now we need an (initially random) weight for every pixel (this is the *initialize* step in our seven-step process):

```
def init_params(size, std=1.0): return (torch.randn(size)*std).requires_grad_()

weights = init_params((28*28,1))
```

The function `weights*pixels` won't be flexible enough—it is always equal to 0 when the pixels are equal to 0 (i.e., its *intercept* is 0). You might remember from high school math that the formula for a line is y=w*x+b; we still need the b. We'll initialize it to a random number too:

```
bias = init_params(1)
```

In neural networks, the w in the equation y=w*x+b is called the *weights*, and the b is called the *bias*. Together, the weights and bias make up the *parameters*.

Jargon: Parameters

The *weights* and *biases* of a model. The weights are the w in the equation w*x+b, and the biases are the b in that equation.

We can now calculate a prediction for one image:

```
(train_x[0]*weights.T).sum() + bias

tensor([20.2336], grad_fn=<AddBackward0>)
```

While we could use a Python `for` loop to calculate the prediction for each image, that would be very slow. Because Python loops don't run on the GPU, and because Python is a slow language for loops in general, we need to represent as much of the computation in a model as possible using higher-level functions.

In this case, there's an extremely convenient mathematical operation that calculates w*x for every row of a matrix—it's called *matrix multiplication*. Figure 4-6 shows what matrix multiplication looks like.

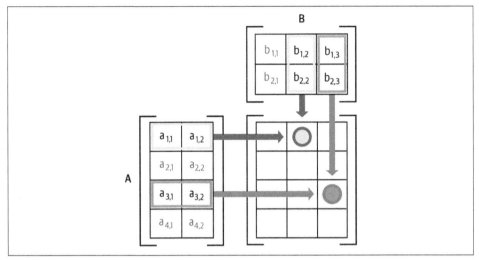

Figure 4-6. Matrix multiplication

This image shows two matrices, A and B, being multiplied together. Each item of the result, which we'll call AB, contains each item of its corresponding row of A multiplied by each item of its corresponding column of B, added together. For instance, row 1, column 2 (the yellow dot with a red border) is calculated as $a_{1,1} * b_{1,2} + a_{1,2} * b_{2,2}$. If you need a refresher on matrix multiplication, we suggest you take a look at the "Intro to Matrix Multiplication" (*https://oreil.ly/w0XKS*) on Khan Academy, since this is the most important mathematical operation in deep learning.

In Python, matrix multiplication is represented with the @ operator. Let's try it:

```
def linear1(xb): return xb@weights + bias
preds = linear1(train_x)
preds

tensor([[20.2336],
        [17.0644],
        [15.2384],
        ...,
        [18.3804],
        [23.8567],
        [28.6816]], grad_fn=<AddBackward0>)
```

The first element is the same as we calculated before, as we'd expect. This equation, batch @ weights + bias, is one of the two fundamental equations of any neural network (the other one is the *activation function*, which we'll see in a moment).

Let's check our accuracy. To decide if an output represents a 3 or a 7, we can just check whether it's greater than 0, so our accuracy for each item can be calculated (using broadcasting, so no loops!) as follows:

```
corrects = (preds>0.0).float() == train_y
corrects
```

```
tensor([[ True],
        [ True],
        [ True],
        ...,
        [False],
        [False],
        [False]])
```

```
corrects.float().mean().item()
```

```
0.4912068545818329
```

Now let's see what the change in accuracy is for a small change in one of the weights:

```
weights[0] *= 1.0001
```

```
preds = linear1(train_x)
((preds>0.0).float() == train_y).float().mean().item()
```

```
0.4912068545818329
```

As we've seen, we need gradients in order to improve our model using SGD, and in order to calculate gradients we need a *loss function* that represents how good our model is. That is because the gradients are a measure of how that loss function changes with small tweaks to the weights.

So, we need to choose a loss function. The obvious approach would be to use accuracy, which is our metric, as our loss function as well. In this case, we would calculate our prediction for each image, collect these values to calculate an overall accuracy, and then calculate the gradients of each weight with respect to that overall accuracy.

Unfortunately, we have a significant technical problem here. The gradient of a function is its *slope*, or its steepness, which can be defined as *rise over run*—that is, how much the value of the function goes up or down, divided by how much we changed the input. We can write this mathematically as:

```
(y_new - y_old) / (x_new - x_old)
```

This gives a good approximation of the gradient when x_new is very similar to x_old, meaning that their difference is very small. But accuracy changes at all only when a prediction changes from a 3 to a 7, or vice versa. The problem is that a small change in weights from x_old to x_new isn't likely to cause any prediction to change, so (y_new - y_old) will almost always be 0. In other words, the gradient is 0 almost everywhere.

A very small change in the value of a weight will often not change the accuracy at all. This means it is not useful to use accuracy as a loss function—if we do, most of the time our gradients will be 0, and the model will not be able to learn from that number.

Sylvain Says

In mathematical terms, accuracy is a function that is constant almost everywhere (except at the threshold, 0.5), so its derivative is nil almost everywhere (and infinity at the threshold). This then gives gradients that are 0 or infinite, which are useless for updating the model.

Instead, we need a loss function that, when our weights result in slightly better predictions, gives us a slightly better loss. So what does a "slightly better prediction" look like, exactly? Well, in this case, it means that if the correct answer is a 3, the score is a little higher, or if the correct answer is a 7, the score is a little lower.

Let's write such a function now. What form does it take?

The loss function receives not the images themselves, but the predictions from the model. So let's make one argument, prds, of values between 0 and 1, where each value is the prediction that an image is a 3. It is a vector (i.e., a rank-1 tensor) indexed over the images.

The purpose of the loss function is to measure the difference between predicted values and the true values—that is, the targets (aka labels). Let's therefore make another argument, trgts, with values of 0 or 1 that tells whether an image actually is a 3 or not. It is also a vector (i.e., another rank-1 tensor) indexed over the images.

For instance, suppose we had three images that we knew were a 3, a 7, and a 3. And suppose our model predicted with high confidence (0.9) that the first was a 3, with slight confidence (0.4) that the second was a 7, and with fair confidence (0.2), but incorrectly, that the last was a 7. This would mean our loss function would receive these values as its inputs:

```
trgts  = tensor([1,0,1])
prds   = tensor([0.9, 0.4, 0.2])
```

Here's a first try at a loss function that measures the distance between predictions and targets:

```
def mnist_loss(predictions, targets):
    return torch.where(targets==1, 1-predictions, predictions).mean()
```

We're using a new function, torch.where(a,b,c). This is the same as running the list comprehension [b[i] if a[i] else c[i] for i in range(len(a))], except it works on tensors, at C/CUDA speed. In plain English, this function will measure how distant each prediction is from 1 if it should be 1, and how distant it is from 0 if it should be 0, and then it will take the mean of all those distances.

Read the Docs

It's important to learn about PyTorch functions like this, because looping over tensors in Python performs at Python speed, not C/CUDA speed! Try running `help(torch.where)` now to read the docs for this function, or, better still, look it up on the PyTorch documentation site.

Let's try it on our `prds` and `trgts`:

```
torch.where(trgts==1, 1-prds, prds)
```

```
tensor([0.1000, 0.4000, 0.8000])
```

You can see that this function returns a lower number when predictions are more accurate, when accurate predictions are more confident (higher absolute values), and when inaccurate predictions are less confident. In PyTorch, we always assume that a lower value of a loss function is better. Since we need a scalar for the final loss, `mnist_loss` takes the mean of the previous tensor:

```
mnist_loss(prds,trgts)
```

```
tensor(0.4333)
```

For instance, if we change our prediction for the one "false" target from `0.2` to `0.8`, the loss will go down, indicating that this is a better prediction:

```
mnist_loss(tensor([0.9, 0.4, 0.8]),trgts)
```

```
tensor(0.2333)
```

One problem with `mnist_loss` as currently defined is that it assumes that predictions are always between 0 and 1. We need to ensure, then, that this is actually the case! As it happens, there is a function that does exactly that—let's take a look.

Sigmoid

The `sigmoid` function always outputs a number between 0 and 1. It's defined as follows:

```
def sigmoid(x): return 1/(1+torch.exp(-x))
```

PyTorch defines an accelerated version for us, so we don't really need our own. This is an important function in deep learning, since we often want to ensure that values are between 0 and 1. This is what it looks like:

```
plot_function(torch.sigmoid, title='Sigmoid', min=-4, max=4)
```

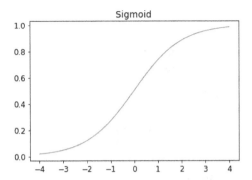

As you can see, it takes any input value, positive or negative, and smooshes it into an output value between 0 and 1. It's also a smooth curve that only goes up, which makes it easier for SGD to find meaningful gradients.

Let's update `mnist_loss` to first apply `sigmoid` to the inputs:

```
def mnist_loss(predictions, targets):
    predictions = predictions.sigmoid()
    return torch.where(targets==1, 1-predictions, predictions).mean()
```

Now we can be confident our loss function will work, even if the predictions are not between 0 and 1. All that is required is that a higher prediction corresponds to higher confidence.

Having defined a loss function, now is a good moment to recapitulate why we did this. After all, we already had a metric, which was overall accuracy. So why did we define a loss?

The key difference is that the metric is to drive human understanding and the loss is to drive automated learning. To drive automated learning, the loss must be a function that has a meaningful derivative. It can't have big flat sections and large jumps, but instead must be reasonably smooth. This is why we designed a loss function that would respond to small changes in confidence level. This requirement means that sometimes it does not really reflect exactly what we are trying to achieve, but is rather a compromise between our real goal and a function that can be optimized using its gradient. The loss function is calculated for each item in our dataset, and then at the end of an epoch, the loss values are all averaged and the overall mean is reported for the epoch.

Metrics, on the other hand, are the numbers that we care about. These are the values that are printed at the end of each epoch that tell us how our model is doing. It is important that we learn to focus on these metrics, rather than the loss, when judging the performance of a model.

SGD and Mini-Batches

Now that we have a loss function suitable for driving SGD, we can consider some of the details involved in the next phase of the learning process, which is to change or update the weights based on the gradients. This is called an *optimization step*.

To take an optimization step, we need to calculate the loss over one or more data items. How many should we use? We could calculate it for the whole dataset and take the average, or we could calculate it for a single data item. But neither of these is ideal. Calculating it for the whole dataset would take a long time. Calculating it for a single item would not use much information, so it would result in an imprecise and unstable gradient. You'd be going to the trouble of updating the weights, but taking into account only how that would improve the model's performance on that single item.

So instead we compromise: we calculate the average loss for a few data items at a time. This is called a *mini-batch*. The number of data items in the mini-batch is called the *batch size*. A larger batch size means that you will get a more accurate and stable estimate of your dataset's gradients from the loss function, but it will take longer, and you will process fewer mini-batches per epoch. Choosing a good batch size is one of the decisions you need to make as a deep learning practitioner to train your model quickly and accurately. We will talk about how to make this choice throughout this book.

Another good reason for using mini-batches rather than calculating the gradient on individual data items is that, in practice, we nearly always do our training on an accelerator such as a GPU. These accelerators perform well only if they have lots of work to do at a time, so it's helpful if we can give them lots of data items to work on. Using mini-batches is one of the best ways to do this. However, if you give them too much data to work on at once, they run out of memory—making GPUs happy is also tricky!

As you saw in our discussion of data augmentation in Chapter 2, we get better generalization if we can vary things during training. One simple and effective thing we can vary is what data items we put in each mini-batch. Rather than simply enumerating our dataset in order for every epoch, instead what we normally do is randomly shuffle it on every epoch, before we create mini-batches. PyTorch and fastai provide a class that will do the shuffling and mini-batch collation for you, called `DataLoader`.

A `DataLoader` can take any Python collection and turn it into an iterator over many batches, like so:

```
coll = range(15)
dl = DataLoader(coll, batch_size=5, shuffle=True)
list(dl)

[tensor([ 3, 12,  8, 10,  2]),
 tensor([ 9,  4,  7, 14,  5]),
 tensor([ 1, 13,  0,  6, 11])]
```

For training a model, we don't just want any Python collection, but a collection containing independent and dependent variables (the inputs and targets of the model). A collection that contains tuples of independent and dependent variables is known in PyTorch as a Dataset. Here's an example of an extremely simple Dataset:

```
ds = L(enumerate(string.ascii_lowercase))
ds

(#26) [(0, 'a'),(1, 'b'),(2, 'c'),(3, 'd'),(4, 'e'),(5, 'f'),(6, 'g'),(7,
 > 'h'),(8, 'i'),(9, 'j')...]
```

When we pass a Dataset to a DataLoader we will get back many batches that are themselves tuples of tensors representing batches of independent and dependent variables:

```
dl = DataLoader(ds, batch_size=6, shuffle=True)
list(dl)

[(tensor([17, 18, 10, 22,  8, 14]), ('r', 's', 'k', 'w', 'i', 'o')),
 (tensor([20, 15,  9, 13, 21, 12]), ('u', 'p', 'j', 'n', 'v', 'm')),
 (tensor([ 7, 25,  6,  5, 11, 23]), ('h', 'z', 'g', 'f', 'l', 'x')),
 (tensor([ 1,  3,  0, 24, 19, 16]), ('b', 'd', 'a', 'y', 't', 'q')),
 (tensor([2, 4]), ('c', 'e'))]
```

We are now ready to write our first training loop for a model using SGD!

Putting It All Together

It's time to implement the process we saw in Figure 4-1. In code, our process will be implemented something like this for each epoch:

```
for x,y in dl:
    pred = model(x)
    loss = loss_func(pred, y)
    loss.backward()
    parameters -= parameters.grad * lr
```

First, let's reinitialize our parameters:

```
weights = init_params((28*28,1))
bias = init_params(1)
```

A DataLoader can be created from a Dataset:

```
dl = DataLoader(dset, batch_size=256)
xb,yb = first(dl)
xb.shape,yb.shape

(torch.Size([256, 784]), torch.Size([256, 1]))
```

We'll do the same for the validation set:

```
valid_dl = DataLoader(valid_dset, batch_size=256)
```

Let's create a mini-batch of size 4 for testing:

```
batch = train_x[:4]
batch.shape
```

```
torch.Size([4, 784])
```

```
preds = linear1(batch)
preds
```

```
tensor([[-11.1002],
        [  5.9263],
        [  9.9627],
        [ -8.1484]], grad_fn=<AddBackward0>)
```

```
loss = mnist_loss(preds, train_y[:4])
loss
```

```
tensor(0.5006, grad_fn=<MeanBackward0>)
```

Now we can calculate the gradients:

```
loss.backward()
weights.grad.shape,weights.grad.mean(),bias.grad
```

```
(torch.Size([784, 1]), tensor(-0.0001), tensor([-0.0008]))
```

Let's put that all in a function:

```
def calc_grad(xb, yb, model):
    preds = model(xb)
    loss = mnist_loss(preds, yb)
    loss.backward()
```

And test it:

```
calc_grad(batch, train_y[:4], linear1)
weights.grad.mean(),bias.grad
```

```
(tensor(-0.0002), tensor([-0.0015]))
```

But look what happens if we call it twice:

```
calc_grad(batch, train_y[:4], linear1)
weights.grad.mean(),bias.grad
```

```
(tensor(-0.0003), tensor([-0.0023]))
```

The gradients have changed! The reason for this is that loss.backward *adds* the gradients of loss to any gradients that are currently stored. So, we have to set the current gradients to 0 first:

```
weights.grad.zero_()
bias.grad.zero_();
```

In-Place Operations

Methods in PyTorch whose names end in an underscore modify their objects *in place*. For instance, `bias.zero_` sets all elements of the tensor `bias` to 0.

Our only remaining step is to update the weights and biases based on the gradient and learning rate. When we do so, we have to tell PyTorch not to take the gradient of this step too—otherwise, things will get confusing when we try to compute the derivative at the next batch! If we assign to the `data` attribute of a tensor, PyTorch will not take the gradient of that step. Here's our basic training loop for an epoch:

```
def train_epoch(model, lr, params):
    for xb,yb in dl:
        calc_grad(xb, yb, model)
        for p in params:
            p.data -= p.grad*lr
            p.grad.zero_()
```

We also want to check how we're doing, by looking at the accuracy of the validation set. To decide if an output represents a 3 or a 7, we can just check whether it's greater than 0.5. So our accuracy for each item can be calculated (using broadcasting, so no loops!) as follows:

```
(preds>0.5).float() == train_y[:4]
```

```
tensor([[False],
        [ True],
        [ True],
        [False]])
```

That gives us this function to calculate our validation accuracy:

```
def batch_accuracy(xb, yb):
    preds = xb.sigmoid()
    correct = (preds>0.5) == yb
    return correct.float().mean()
```

We can check it works:

```
batch_accuracy(linear1(batch), train_y[:4])
```

```
tensor(0.5000)
```

And then put the batches together:

```
def validate_epoch(model):
    accs = [batch_accuracy(model(xb), yb) for xb,yb in valid_dl]
    return round(torch.stack(accs).mean().item(), 4)

validate_epoch(linear1)
```

```
0.5219
```

That's our starting point. Let's train for one epoch and see if the accuracy improves:

```
lr = 1.
params = weights,bias
train_epoch(linear1, lr, params)
validate_epoch(linear1)
```

```
0.6883
```

Then do a few more:

```
for i in range(20):
    train_epoch(linear1, lr, params)
    print(validate_epoch(linear1), end=' ')
```

```
0.8314 0.9017 0.9227 0.9349 0.9438 0.9501 0.9535 0.9564 0.9594 0.9618 0.9613
 > 0.9638 0.9643 0.9652 0.9662 0.9677 0.9687 0.9691 0.9691 0.9696
```

Looking good! We're already about at the same accuracy as our "pixel similarity" approach, and we've created a general-purpose foundation we can build on. Our next step will be to create an object that will handle the SGD step for us. In PyTorch, it's called an *optimizer*.

Creating an Optimizer

Because this is such a general foundation, PyTorch provides some useful classes to make it easier to implement. The first thing we can do is replace our `linear1` function with PyTorch's `nn.Linear` module. A *module* is an object of a class that inherits from the PyTorch `nn.Module` class. Objects of this class behave identically to standard Python functions, in that you can call them using parentheses, and they will return the activations of a model.

`nn.Linear` does the same thing as our `init_params` and `linear` together. It contains both the *weights* and *biases* in a single class. Here's how we replicate our model from the previous section:

```
linear_model = nn.Linear(28*28,1)
```

Every PyTorch module knows what parameters it has that can be trained; they are available through the `parameters` method:

```
w,b = linear_model.parameters()
w.shape,b.shape
```

```
(torch.Size([1, 784]), torch.Size([1]))
```

We can use this information to create an optimizer:

```
class BasicOptim:
    def __init__(self,params,lr): self.params,self.lr = list(params),lr

    def step(self, *args, **kwargs):
        for p in self.params: p.data -= p.grad.data * self.lr
```

```
def zero_grad(self, *args, **kwargs):
    for p in self.params: p.grad = None
```

We can create our optimizer by passing in the model's parameters:

```
opt = BasicOptim(linear_model.parameters(), lr)
```

Our training loop can now be simplified:

```
def train_epoch(model):
    for xb,yb in dl:
        calc_grad(xb, yb, model)
        opt.step()
        opt.zero_grad()
```

Our validation function doesn't need to change at all:

```
validate_epoch(linear_model)
```

```
0.4157
```

Let's put our little training loop in a function, to make things simpler:

```
def train_model(model, epochs):
    for i in range(epochs):
        train_epoch(model)
        print(validate_epoch(model), end=' ')
```

The results are the same as in the previous section:

```
train_model(linear_model, 20)
```

```
0.4932 0.8618 0.8203 0.9102 0.9331 0.9468 0.9555 0.9629 0.9658 0.9673 0.9687
 > 0.9707 0.9726 0.9751 0.9761 0.9761 0.9775 0.978 0.9785 0.9785
```

fastai provides the SGD class that, by default, does the same thing as our `BasicOptim`:

```
linear_model = nn.Linear(28*28,1)
opt = SGD(linear_model.parameters(), lr)
train_model(linear_model, 20)
```

```
0.4932 0.852 0.8335 0.9116 0.9326 0.9473 0.9555 0.9624 0.9648 0.9668 0.9692
 > 0.9712 0.9731 0.9746 0.9761 0.9765 0.9775 0.978 0.9785 0.9785
```

fastai also provides `Learner.fit`, which we can use instead of `train_model`. To create a `Learner`, we first need to create a `DataLoaders`, by passing in our training and validation `DataLoaders`:

```
dls = DataLoaders(dl, valid_dl)
```

To create a `Learner` without using an application (such as `cnn_learner`), we need to pass in all the elements that we've created in this chapter: the `DataLoaders`, the model, the optimization function (which will be passed the parameters), the loss function, and optionally any metrics to print:

```
learn = Learner(dls, nn.Linear(28*28,1), opt_func=SGD,
                loss_func=mnist_loss, metrics=batch_accuracy)
```

Now we can call `fit`:

```
learn.fit(10, lr=lr)
```

epoch	train_loss	valid_loss	batch_accuracy	time
0	0.636857	0.503549	0.495584	00:00
1	0.545725	0.170281	0.866045	00:00
2	0.199223	0.184893	0.831207	00:00
3	0.086580	0.107836	0.911187	00:00
4	0.045185	0.078481	0.932777	00:00
5	0.029108	0.062792	0.946516	00:00
6	0.022560	0.053017	0.955348	00:00
7	0.019687	0.046500	0.962218	00:00
8	0.018252	0.041929	0.965162	00:00
9	0.017402	0.038573	0.967615	00:00

As you can see, there's nothing magic about the PyTorch and fastai classes. They are just convenient prepackaged pieces that make your life a bit easier! (They also provide a lot of extra functionality we'll be using in future chapters.)

With these classes, we can now replace our linear model with a neural network.

Adding a Nonlinearity

So far, we have a general procedure for optimizing the parameters of a function, and we have tried it out on a boring function: a simple linear classifier. A linear classifier is constrained in terms of what it can do. To make it a bit more complex (and able to handle more tasks), we need to add something nonlinear (i.e., different from ax+b) between two linear classifiers—this is what gives us a neural network.

Here is the entire definition of a basic neural network:

```
def simple_net(xb):
    res = xb@w1 + b1
    res = res.max(tensor(0.0))
    res = res@w2 + b2
    return res
```

That's it! All we have in `simple_net` is two linear classifiers with a `max` function between them.

Here, w1 and w2 are weight tensors, and b1 and b2 are bias tensors; that is, parameters that are initially randomly initialized, just as we did in the previous section:

```
w1 = init_params((28*28,30))
b1 = init_params(30)
w2 = init_params((30,1))
b2 = init_params(1)
```

The key point is that w1 has 30 output activations (which means that w2 must have 30 input activations, so they match). That means that the first layer can construct 30 different features, each representing a different mix of pixels. You can change that 30 to anything you like, to make the model more or less complex.

That little function res.max(tensor(0.0)) is called a *rectified linear unit*, also known as *ReLU*. We think we can all agree that *rectified linear unit* sounds pretty fancy and complicated...But actually, there's nothing more to it than res.max(tensor(0.0))—in other words, replace every negative number with a zero. This tiny function is also available in PyTorch as F.relu:

```
plot_function(F.relu)
```

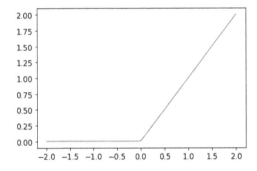

Jeremy Says

There is an enormous amount of jargon in deep learning, including terms like *rectified linear unit*. The vast majority of this jargon is no more complicated than can be implemented in a short line of code, as we saw in this example. The reality is that for academics to get their papers published, they need to make them sound as impressive and sophisticated as possible. One way that they do that is to introduce jargon. Unfortunately, this results in the field becoming far more intimidating and difficult to get into than it should be. You do have to learn the jargon, because otherwise papers and tutorials are not going to mean much to you. But that doesn't mean you have to find the jargon intimidating. Just remember, when you come across a word or phrase that you haven't seen before, it will almost certainly turn out to be referring to a very simple concept.

The basic idea is that by using more linear layers, we can have our model do more computation, and therefore model more complex functions. But there's no point in just putting one linear layer directly after another one, because when we multiply things together and then add them up multiple times, that could be replaced by multiplying different things together and adding them up just once! That is to say, a series of any number of linear layers in a row can be replaced with a single linear layer with a different set of parameters.

But if we put a nonlinear function between them, such as max, this is no longer true. Now each linear layer is somewhat decoupled from the other ones and can do its own useful work. The max function is particularly interesting, because it operates as a simple if statement.

Sylvain Says

Mathematically, we say the composition of two linear functions is another linear function. So, we can stack as many linear classifiers as we want on top of each other, and without nonlinear functions between them, it will just be the same as one linear classifier.

Amazingly enough, it can be mathematically proven that this little function can solve any computable problem to an arbitrarily high level of accuracy, if you can find the right parameters for w1 and w2 and if you make these matrices big enough. For any arbitrarily wiggly function, we can approximate it as a bunch of lines joined together; to make it closer to the wiggly function, we just have to use shorter lines. This is known as the *universal approximation theorem*. The three lines of code that we have here are known as *layers*. The first and third are known as *linear layers*, and the second line of code is known variously as a *nonlinearity*, or *activation function*.

Just as in the previous section, we can replace this code with something a bit simpler by taking advantage of PyTorch:

```
simple_net = nn.Sequential(
    nn.Linear(28*28,30),
    nn.ReLU(),
    nn.Linear(30,1)
)
```

nn.Sequential creates a module that will call each of the listed layers or functions in turn.

nn.ReLU is a PyTorch module that does exactly the same thing as the F.relu function. Most functions that can appear in a model also have identical forms that are modules. Generally, it's just a case of replacing F with nn and changing the capitalization. When using nn.Sequential, PyTorch requires us to use the module version. Since modules are classes, we have to instantiate them, which is why you see nn.ReLU in this example.

Because nn.Sequential is a module, we can get its parameters, which will return a list of all the parameters of all the modules it contains. Let's try it out! As this is a deeper model, we'll use a lower learning rate and a few more epochs:

```
learn = Learner(dls, simple_net, opt_func=SGD,
                loss_func=mnist_loss, metrics=batch_accuracy)

learn.fit(40, 0.1)
```

We're not showing the 40 lines of output here to save room; the training process is recorded in learn.recorder, with the table of output stored in the values attribute, so we can plot the accuracy over training:

```
plt.plot(L(learn.recorder.values).itemgot(2));
```

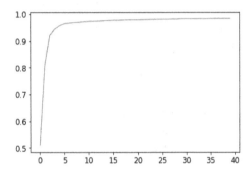

And we can view the final accuracy:

```
learn.recorder.values[-1][2]
```

```
0.982826292514801
```

At this point, we have something that is rather magical:

- A function that can solve any problem to any level of accuracy (the neural network) given the correct set of parameters
- A way to find the best set of parameters for any function (stochastic gradient descent)

This is why deep learning can do such fantastic things. Believing that this combination of simple techniques can really solve any problem is one of the biggest steps that we find many students have to take. It seems too good to be true—surely things should be more difficult and complicated than this? Our recommendation: try it out! We just tried it on the MNIST dataset, and you've seen the results. And since we are doing everything from scratch ourselves (except for calculating the gradients), you know that there is no special magic hiding behind the scenes.

Going Deeper

There is no need to stop at just two linear layers. We can add as many as we want, as long as we add a nonlinearity between each pair of linear layers. As you will learn, however, the deeper the model gets, the harder it is to optimize the parameters in practice. Later in this book, you will learn about some simple but brilliantly effective techniques for training deeper models.

We already know that a single nonlinearity with two linear layers is enough to approximate any function. So why would we use deeper models? The reason is performance. With a deeper model (one with more layers), we do not need to use as many parameters; it turns out that we can use smaller matrices, with more layers, and get better results than we would get with larger matrices and few layers.

That means that we can train the model more quickly, and it will take up less memory. In the 1990s, researchers were so focused on the universal approximation theorem that few were experimenting with more than one nonlinearity. This theoretical but not practical foundation held back the field for years. Some researchers, however, did experiment with deep models, and eventually were able to show that these models could perform much better in practice. Eventually, theoretical results were developed that showed why this happens. Today, it is extremely unusual to find anybody using a neural network with just one nonlinearity.

Here is what happens when we train an 18-layer model using the same approach we saw in Chapter 1:

```
dls = ImageDataLoaders.from_folder(path)
learn = cnn_learner(dls, resnet18, pretrained=False,
                    loss_func=F.cross_entropy, metrics=accuracy)
learn.fit_one_cycle(1, 0.1)
```

epoch	train_loss	valid_loss	accuracy	time
0	0.082089	0.009578	0.997056	00:11

Nearly 100% accuracy! That's a big difference compared to our simple neural net. But as you'll learn in the remainder of this book, there are just a few little tricks you need to use to get such great results from scratch yourself. You already know the key foundational pieces. (Of course, even when you know all the tricks, you'll nearly always want to work with the prebuilt classes provided by PyTorch and fastai, because they save you from having to think about all the little details yourself.)

Jargon Recap

Congratulations: you now know how to create and train a deep neural network from scratch! We've gone through quite a few steps to get to this point, but you might be surprised at how simple it really is.

Now that we are at this point, it is a good opportunity to define, and review, some jargon and key concepts.

A neural network contains a lot of numbers, but they are only of two types: numbers that are calculated, and the parameters that these numbers are calculated from. This gives us the two most important pieces of jargon to learn:

Activations
> Numbers that are calculated (both by linear and nonlinear layers)

Parameters
> Numbers that are randomly initialized, and optimized (that is, the numbers that define the model)

We will often talk in this book about activations and parameters. Remember that they have specific meanings. They are numbers. They are not abstract concepts, but they are actual specific numbers that are in your model. Part of becoming a good deep learning practitioner is getting used to the idea of looking at your activations and parameters, and plotting them and testing whether they are behaving correctly.

Our activations and parameters are all contained in *tensors*. These are simply regularly shaped arrays—for example, a matrix. Matrices have rows and columns; we call these the *axes* or *dimensions*. The number of dimensions of a tensor is its *rank*. There are some special tensors:

- Rank-0: scalar
- Rank-1: vector
- Rank-2: matrix

A neural network contains a number of layers. Each layer is either *linear* or *nonlinear*. We generally alternate between these two kinds of layers in a neural network. Sometimes people refer to both a linear layer and its subsequent nonlinearity together as a single layer. Yes, this is confusing. Sometimes a nonlinearity is referred to as an *activation function*.

Table 4-1 summarizes the key concepts related to SGD.

Table 4-1. Deep learning vocabulary

Term	Meaning
ReLU	Function that returns 0 for negative numbers and doesn't change positive numbers.
Mini-batch	A small group of inputs and labels gathered together in two arrays. A gradient descent step is updated on this batch (rather than a whole epoch).
Forward pass	Applying the model to some input and computing the predictions.
Loss	A value that represents how well (or badly) our model is doing.
Gradient	The derivative of the loss with respect to some parameter of the model.
Backward pass	Computing the gradients of the loss with respect to all model parameters.
Gradient descent	Taking a step in the direction opposite to the gradients to make the model parameters a little bit better.
Learning rate	The size of the step we take when applying SGD to update the parameters of the model.

Choose Your Own Adventure Reminder

Did you choose to skip over Chapters 2 and 3, in your excitement to peek under the hood? Well, here's your reminder to head back to Chapter 2 now, because you'll be needing to know that stuff soon!

Questionnaire

1. How is a grayscale image represented on a computer? How about a color image?
2. How are the files and folders in the MNIST_SAMPLE dataset structured? Why?
3. Explain how the "pixel similarity" approach to classifying digits works.
4. What is a list comprehension? Create one now that selects odd numbers from a list and doubles them.
5. What is a rank-3 tensor?
6. What is the difference between tensor rank and shape? How do you get the rank from the shape?
7. What are RMSE and L1 norm?
8. How can you apply a calculation on thousands of numbers at once, many thousands of times faster than a Python loop?
9. Create a 3×3 tensor or array containing the numbers from 1 to 9. Double it. Select the bottom-right four numbers.
10. What is broadcasting?
11. Are metrics generally calculated using the training set or the validation set? Why?

12. What is SGD?

13. Why does SGD use mini-batches?

14. What are the seven steps in SGD for machine learning?

15. How do we initialize the weights in a model?

16. What is loss?

17. Why can't we always use a high learning rate?

18. What is a gradient?

19. Do you need to know how to calculate gradients yourself?

20. Why can't we use accuracy as a loss function?

21. Draw the sigmoid function. What is special about its shape?

22. What is the difference between a loss function and a metric?

23. What is the function to calculate new weights using a learning rate?

24. What does the `DataLoader` class do?

25. Write pseudocode showing the basic steps taken in each epoch for SGD.

26. Create a function that, if passed two arguments `[1,2,3,4]` and `'abcd'`, returns `[(1, 'a'), (2, 'b'), (3, 'c'), (4, 'd')]`. What is special about that output data structure?

27. What does `view` do in PyTorch?

28. What are the bias parameters in a neural network? Why do we need them?

29. What does the `@` operator do in Python?

30. What does the `backward` method do?

31. Why do we have to zero the gradients?

32. What information do we have to pass to `Learner`?

33. Show Python or pseudocode for the basic steps of a training loop.

34. What is ReLU? Draw a plot of it for values from `-2` to `+2`.

35. What is an activation function?

36. What's the difference between `F.relu` and `nn.ReLU`?

37. The universal approximation theorem shows that any function can be approximated as closely as needed using just one nonlinearity. So why do we normally use more?

Further Research

1. Create your own implementation of Learner from scratch, based on the training loop shown in this chapter.

2. Complete all the steps in this chapter using the full MNIST datasets (for all digits, not just 3s and 7s). This is a significant project and will take you quite a bit of time to complete! You'll need to do some of your own research to figure out how to overcome obstacles you'll meet on the way.

CHAPTER 5

Image Classification

Now that you understand what deep learning is, what it's for, and how to create and deploy a model, it's time for us to go deeper! In an ideal world, deep learning practitioners wouldn't have to know every detail of how things work under the hood. But as yet, we don't live in an ideal world. The truth is, to make your model really work, and work reliably, there are a lot of details you have to get right, and a lot of details that you have to check. This process requires being able to look inside your neural network as it trains and as it makes predictions, find possible problems, and know how to fix them.

So, from here on in the book, we are going to do a deep dive into the mechanics of deep learning. What is the architecture of a computer vision model, an NLP model, a tabular model, and so on? How do you create an architecture that matches the needs of your particular domain? How do you get the best possible results from the training process? How do you make things faster? What do you have to change as your datasets change?

We will start by repeating the same basic applications that we looked at in the first chapter, but we are going to do two things:

- Make them better.
- Apply them to a wider variety of types of data.

To do these two things, we will have to learn all of the pieces of the deep learning puzzle. This includes different types of layers, regularization methods, optimizers, how to put layers together into architectures, labeling techniques, and much more. We are not just going to dump all of these things on you, though; we will introduce them progressively as needed, to solve actual problems related to the projects we are working on.

From Dogs and Cats to Pet Breeds

In our very first model, we learned how to classify dogs versus cats. Just a few years ago, this was considered a very challenging task—but today, it's far too easy! We will not be able to show you the nuances of training models with this problem, because we get a nearly perfect result without worrying about any of the details. But it turns out that the same dataset also allows us to work on a much more challenging problem: figuring out what breed of pet is shown in each image.

In Chapter 1, we presented the applications as already-solved problems. But this is not how things work in real life. We start with a dataset that we know nothing about. We then have to figure out how it is put together, how to extract the data we need from it, and what that data looks like. For the rest of this book, we will be showing you how to solve these problems in practice, including all of the intermediate steps necessary to understand the data that we are working with and test your modeling as you go.

We already downloaded the Pets dataset, and we can get a path to this dataset using the same code as in Chapter 1:

```
from fastai.vision.all import *
path = untar_data(URLs.PETS)
```

Now if we are going to understand how to extract the breed of each pet from each image, we're going to need to understand how this data is laid out. Such details of data layout are a vital piece of the deep learning puzzle. Data is usually provided in one of these two ways:

- Individual files representing items of data, such as text documents or images, possibly organized into folders or with filenames representing information about those items

- A table of data (e.g., in CSV format) in which each row is an item and may include filenames providing connections between the data in the table and data in other formats, such as text documents and images

There are exceptions to these rules—particularly in domains such as genomics, where there can be binary database formats or even network streams—but overall the vast majority of the datasets you'll work with will use some combination of these two formats.

To see what is in our dataset, we can use the `ls` method:

```
path.ls()
```

```
(#3) [Path('annotations'),Path('images'),Path('models')]
```

We can see that this dataset provides us with *images* and *annotations* directories. The website (*https://oreil.ly/xveoN*) for the dataset tells us that the *annotations* directory contains information about where the pets are rather than what they are. In this chapter, we will be doing classification, not localization, which is to say that we care about what the pets are, not where they are. Therefore, we will ignore the *annotations* directory for now. So, let's have a look inside the *images* directory:

```
(path/"images").ls()
```

```
(#7394) [Path('images/great_pyrenees_173.jpg'),Path('images/wheaten_terrier_46.j
 > pg'),Path('images/Ragdoll_262.jpg'),Path('images/german_shorthaired_3.jpg'),P
 > ath('images/american_bulldog_196.jpg'),Path('images/boxer_188.jpg'),Path('ima
 > ges/staffordshire_bull_terrier_173.jpg'),Path('images/basset_hound_71.jpg'),P
 > ath('images/staffordshire_bull_terrier_37.jpg'),Path('images/yorkshire_terrie
 > r_18.jpg')...]
```

Most functions and methods in fastai that return a collection use a class called L. This class can be thought of as an enhanced version of the ordinary Python list type, with added conveniences for common operations. For instance, when we display an object of this class in a notebook, it appears in the format shown here. The first thing that is shown is the number of items in the collection, prefixed with a #. You'll also see in the preceding output that the list is suffixed with an ellipsis. This means that only the first few items are displayed—which is a good thing, because we would not want more than 7,000 filenames on our screen!

By examining these filenames, we can see how they appear to be structured. Each filename contains the pet breed, then an underscore (_), a number, and finally the file extension. We need to create a piece of code that extracts the breed from a single Path. Jupyter notebooks make this easy, because we can gradually build up something that works, and then use it for the entire dataset. We do have to be careful to not make too many assumptions at this point. For instance, if you look carefully, you may notice that some of the pet breeds contain multiple words, so we cannot simply break at the first _ character that we find. To allow us to test our code, let's pick out one of these filenames:

```
fname = (path/"images").ls()[0]
```

The most powerful and flexible way to extract information from strings like this is to use a *regular expression*, also known as a *regex*. A regular expression is a special string, written in the regular expression language, which specifies a general rule for deciding whether another string passes a test (i.e., "matches" the regular expression), and also possibly for plucking a particular part or parts out of that other string. In this case, we need a regular expression that extracts the pet breed from the filename.

We do not have the space to give you a complete regular expression tutorial here, but many excellent ones are online and we know that many of you will already be familiar with this wonderful tool. If you're not, that is totally fine—this is a great opportunity for you to rectify that! We find that regular expressions are one of the most useful tools in our programming toolkit, and many of our students tell us that this is one of the things they are most excited to learn about. So head over to Google and search for "regular expressions tutorial" now, and then come back here after you've had a good look around. The book's website (*https://book.fast.ai*) also provides a list of our favorites.

Alexis Says

Not only are regular expressions dead handy, but they also have interesting roots. They are "regular" because they were originally examples of a "regular" language, the lowest rung within the Chomsky hierarchy. This is a grammar classification developed by linguist Noam Chomsky, who also wrote *Syntactic Structures*, the pioneering work searching for the formal grammar underlying human language. This is one of the charms of computing: the hammer you reach for every day may have, in fact, come from a spaceship.

When you are writing a regular expression, the best way to start is to try it against one example at first. Let's use the `findall` method to try a regular expression against the filename of the `fname` object:

```
re.findall(r'(.+)_\d+.jpg$', fname.name)
```

```
['great_pyrenees']
```

This regular expression plucks out all the characters leading up to the last underscore character, as long as the subsequent characters are numerical digits and then the JPEG file extension.

Now that we confirmed the regular expression works for the example, let's use it to label the whole dataset. fastai comes with many classes to help with labeling. For labeling with regular expressions, we can use the `RegexLabeller` class. In this example, we use the data block API that we saw in Chapter 2 (in fact, we nearly always use the data block API—it's so much more flexible than the simple factory methods we saw in Chapter 1):

```
pets = DataBlock(blocks = (ImageBlock, CategoryBlock),
                 get_items=get_image_files,
                 splitter=RandomSplitter(seed=42),
                 get_y=using_attr(RegexLabeller(r'(.+)_\d+.jpg$'), 'name'),
                 item_tfms=Resize(460),
                 batch_tfms=aug_transforms(size=224, min_scale=0.75))
dls = pets.dataloaders(path/"images")
```

One important piece of this `DataBlock` call that we haven't seen before is in these two lines:

```
item_tfms=Resize(460),
batch_tfms=aug_transforms(size=224, min_scale=0.75)
```

These lines implement a fastai data augmentation strategy that we call *presizing*. Presizing is a particular way to do image augmentation that is designed to minimize data destruction while maintaining good performance.

Presizing

We need our images to have the same dimensions, so that they can collate into tensors to be passed to the GPU. We also want to minimize the number of distinct augmentation computations we perform. The performance requirement suggests that we should, where possible, compose our augmentation transforms into fewer transforms (to reduce the number of computations and the number of lossy operations) and transform the images into uniform sizes (for more efficient processing on the GPU).

The challenge is that, if performed after resizing down to the augmented size, various common data augmentation transforms might introduce spurious empty zones, degrade data, or both. For instance, rotating an image by 45 degrees fills corner regions of the new bounds with emptiness, which will not teach the model anything. Many rotation and zooming operations will require interpolating to create pixels. These interpolated pixels are derived from the original image data but are still of lower quality.

To work around these challenges, presizing adopts two strategies that are shown in Figure 5-1:

1. Resize images to relatively "large" dimensions—that is, dimensions significantly larger than the target training dimensions.

2. Compose all of the common augmentation operations (including a resize to the final target size) into one, and perform the combined operation on the GPU only once at the end of processing, rather than performing the operations individually and interpolating multiple times.

The first step, the resize, creates images large enough that they have spare margin to allow further augmentation transforms on their inner regions without creating empty zones. This transformation works by resizing to a square, using a large crop size. On the training set, the crop area is chosen randomly, and the size of the crop is selected to cover the entire width or height of the image, whichever is smaller. In the second step, the GPU is used for all data augmentation, and all of the potentially destructive operations are done together, with a single interpolation at the end.

Figure 5-1. Presizing on the training set

This picture shows the two steps:

1. *Crop full width or height*: This is in `item_tfms`, so it's applied to each individual image before it is copied to the GPU. It's used to ensure all images are the same size. On the training set, the crop area is chosen randomly. On the validation set, the center square of the image is always chosen.

2. *Random crop and augment*: This is in `batch_tfms`, so it's applied to a batch all at once on the GPU, which means it's fast. On the validation set, only the resize to the final size needed for the model is done here. On the training set, the random crop and any other augmentations are done first.

To implement this process in fastai, you use `Resize` as an item transform with a large size, and `RandomResizedCrop` as a batch transform with a smaller size. `RandomResizedCrop` will be added for you if you include the `min_scale` parameter in your `aug_transforms` function, as was done in the `DataBlock` call in the previous section. Alternatively, you can use `pad` or `squish` instead of `crop` (the default) for the initial `Resize`.

Figure 5-2 shows the difference between an image that has been zoomed, interpolated, rotated, and then interpolated again (which is the approach used by all other deep learning libraries), shown here on the right, and an image that has been zoomed and rotated as one operation and then interpolated once (the fastai approach), shown here on the left.

Figure 5-2. A comparison of fastai's data augmentation strategy (left) and the traditional approach (right)

You can see that the image on the right is less well defined and has reflection padding artifacts in the bottom-left corner; also, the grass at the top left has disappeared entirely. We find that, in practice, using presizing significantly improves the accuracy of models and often results in speedups too.

The fastai library also provides simple ways to check how your data looks right before training your model, which is an extremely important step. We'll look at those next.

Checking and Debugging a DataBlock

We can never just assume that our code is working perfectly. Writing a `DataBlock` is like writing a blueprint. You will get an error message if you have a syntax error somewhere in your code, but you have no guarantee that your template is going to work on your data source as you intend. So, before training a model, you should always check your data.

You can do this using the `show_batch` method:

```
dls.show_batch(nrows=1, ncols=3)
```

beagle   yorkshire_terrier   leonberger

Take a look at each image, and check that each one seems to have the correct label for that breed of pet. Often, data scientists work with data with which they are not as familiar as domain experts may be: for instance, I actually don't know what a lot of these pet breeds are. Since I am not an expert on pet breeds, I would use Google images at this point to search for a few of these breeds, and make sure the images look similar to what I see in this output.

If you made a mistake while building your `DataBlock`, you likely won't see it before this step. To debug this, we encourage you to use the `summary` method. It will attempt to create a batch from the source you give it, with a lot of details. Also, if it fails, you will see exactly at which point the error happens, and the library will try to give you some help. For instance, one common mistake is to forget to use a `Resize` transform, so you end up with pictures of different sizes and are not able to batch them. Here is what the summary would look like in that case (note that the exact text may have changed since the time of writing, but it will give you an idea):

```
pets1 = DataBlock(blocks = (ImageBlock, CategoryBlock),
                  get_items=get_image_files,
                  splitter=RandomSplitter(seed=42),
                  get_y=using_attr(RegexLabeller(r'(.+)_\d+.jpg$'), 'name'))
pets1.summary(path/"images")
```

```
Setting-up type transforms pipelines
Collecting items from /home/sgugger/.fastai/data/oxford-iiit-pet/images
Found 7390 items
2 datasets of sizes 5912,1478
Setting up Pipeline: PILBase.create
Setting up Pipeline: partial -> Categorize

Building one sample
  Pipeline: PILBase.create
    starting from
      /home/sgugger/.fastai/data/oxford-iiit-pet/images/american_bulldog_83.jpg
    applying PILBase.create gives
      PILImage mode=RGB size=375x500
```

```
Pipeline: partial -> Categorize
  starting from
    /home/sgugger/.fastai/data/oxford-iiit-pet/images/american_bulldog_83.jpg
  applying partial gives
    american_bulldog
  applying Categorize gives
    TensorCategory(12)

Final sample: (PILImage mode=RGB size=375x500, TensorCategory(12))

Setting up after_item: Pipeline: ToTensor
Setting up before_batch: Pipeline:
Setting up after_batch: Pipeline: IntToFloatTensor

Building one batch
Applying item_tfms to the first sample:
  Pipeline: ToTensor
    starting from
      (PILImage mode=RGB size=375x500, TensorCategory(12))
    applying ToTensor gives
      (TensorImage of size 3x500x375, TensorCategory(12))

Adding the next 3 samples

No before_batch transform to apply

Collating items in a batch
Error! It's not possible to collate your items in a batch
Could not collate the 0-th members of your tuples because got the following
shapes:
torch.Size([3, 500, 375]),torch.Size([3, 375, 500]),torch.Size([3, 333, 500]),
torch.Size([3, 375, 500])
```

You can see exactly how we gathered the data and split it, how we went from a file-name to a *sample* (the tuple (image, category)), then what item transforms were applied and how it failed to collate those samples in a batch (because of the different shapes).

Once you think your data looks right, we generally recommend the next step should be using it to train a simple model. We often see people put off the training of an actual model for far too long. As a result, they don't find out what their baseline results look like. Perhaps your problem doesn't require lots of fancy domain-specific engineering. Or perhaps the data doesn't seem to train the model at all. These are things that you want to know as soon as possible.

For this initial test, we'll use the same simple model that we used in Chapter 1:

```
learn = cnn_learner(dls, resnet34, metrics=error_rate)
learn.fine_tune(2)
```

epoch	train_loss	valid_loss	error_rate	time
0	1.491732	0.337355	0.108254	00:18

epoch	train_loss	valid_loss	error_rate	time
0	0.503154	0.293404	0.096076	00:23
1	0.314759	0.225316	0.066306	00:23

As we've briefly discussed before, the table shown when we fit a model shows us the results after each epoch of training. Remember, an epoch is one complete pass through all of the images in the data. The columns shown are the average loss over the items of the training set, the loss on the validation set, and any metrics that we requested—in this case, the error rate.

Remember that *loss* is whatever function we've decided to use to optimize the parameters of our model. But we haven't actually told fastai what loss function we want to use. So what is it doing? fastai will generally try to select an appropriate loss function based on the kind of data and model you are using. In this case, we have image data and a categorical outcome, so fastai will default to using *cross-entropy loss*.

Cross-Entropy Loss

Cross-entropy loss is a loss function that is similar to the one we used in the previous chapter, but (as we'll see) has two benefits:

- It works even when our dependent variable has more than two categories.
- It results in faster and more reliable training.

To understand how cross-entropy loss works for dependent variables with more than two categories, we first have to understand what the actual data and activations that are seen by the loss function look like.

Viewing Activations and Labels

Let's take a look at the activations of our model. To get a batch of real data from our DataLoaders, we can use the one_batch method:

```
x,y = dls.one_batch()
```

As you see, this returns the dependent and independent variables, as a mini-batch. Let's see what is contained in our dependent variable:

```
y
```

```
TensorCategory([11,  0,  0,  5, 20,  4, 22, 31, 23, 10, 20,  2,  3, 27, 18, 23,
> 33,  5, 24,  7,  6, 12,  9, 11, 35, 14, 10, 15,  3,  3, 21,  5, 19, 14, 12,
> 15, 27,  1, 17, 10,  7,  6, 15, 23, 36,  1, 35,  6,
         4, 29, 24, 32,  2, 14, 26, 25, 21,  0, 29, 31, 18,  7,  7, 17],
> device='cuda:5')
```

Our batch size is 64, so we have 64 rows in this tensor. Each row is a single integer between 0 and 36, representing our 37 possible pet breeds. We can view the predictions (the activations of the final layer of our neural network) by using Learner.get_preds. This function takes either a dataset index (0 for train and 1 for valid) or an iterator of batches. Thus, we can pass it a simple list with our batch to get our predictions. It returns predictions and targets by default, but since we already have the targets, we can effectively ignore them by assigning to the special variable _:

```
preds,_ = learn.get_preds(dl=[(x,y)])
preds[0]
```

```
tensor([7.9069e-04, 6.2350e-05, 3.7607e-05, 2.9260e-06, 1.3032e-05, 2.5760e-05,
> 6.2341e-08, 3.6400e-07, 4.1311e-06, 1.3310e-04, 2.3090e-03, 9.9281e-01,
> 4.6494e-05, 6.4266e-07, 1.9780e-06, 5.7005e-07,
         3.3448e-06, 3.5691e-03, 3.4385e-06, 1.1578e-05, 1.5916e-06, 8.5567e-08,
> 5.0773e-08, 2.2978e-06, 1.4150e-06, 3.5459e-07, 1.4599e-04, 5.6198e-08,
> 3.4108e-07, 2.0813e-06, 8.0568e-07, 4.3381e-07,
         1.0069e-05, 9.1020e-07, 4.8714e-06, 1.2734e-06, 2.4735e-06])
```

The actual predictions are 37 probabilities between 0 and 1, which add up to 1 in total:

```
len(preds[0]),preds[0].sum()
```

```
(37, tensor(1.0000))
```

To transform the activations of our model into predictions like this, we used something called the *softmax* activation function.

Softmax

In our classification model, we use the softmax activation function in the final layer to ensure that the activations are all between 0 and 1, and that they sum to 1.

Softmax is similar to the sigmoid function, which we saw earlier. As a reminder, sigmoid looks like this:

```
plot_function(torch.sigmoid, min=-4,max=4)
```

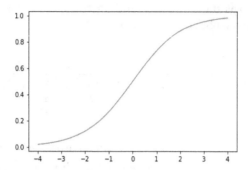

We can apply this function to a single column of activations from a neural network and get back a column of numbers between 0 and 1, so it's a very useful activation function for our final layer.

Now think about what happens if we want to have more categories in our target (such as our 37 pet breeds). That means we'll need more activations than just a single column: we need an activation *per category*. We can create, for instance, a neural net that predicts 3s and 7s that returns two activations, one for each class—this will be a good first step toward creating the more general approach. Let's just use some random numbers with a standard deviation of 2 (so we multiply randn by 2) for this example, assuming we have six images and two possible categories (where the first column represents 3s and the second is 7s):

```
acts = torch.randn((6,2))*2
acts
```

```
tensor([[ 0.6734,  0.2576],
        [ 0.4689,  0.4607],
        [-2.2457, -0.3727],
        [ 4.4164, -1.2760],
        [ 0.9233,  0.5347],
        [ 1.0698,  1.6187]])
```

We can't just take the sigmoid of this directly, since we don't get rows that add to 1 (we want the probability of being a 3 plus the probability of being a 7 to add up to 1):

```
acts.sigmoid()
```

```
tensor([[0.6623, 0.5641],
        [0.6151, 0.6132],
        [0.0957, 0.4079],
        [0.9881, 0.2182],
        [0.7157, 0.6306],
        [0.7446, 0.8346]])
```

In Chapter 4, our neural net created a single activation per image, which we passed through the sigmoid function. That single activation represented the model's confidence that the input was a 3. Binary problems are a special case of classification problem, because the target can be treated as a single Boolean value, as we did in `mnist_loss`. But binary problems can also be thought of in the context of the more general group of classifiers with any number of categories: in this case, we happen to have two categories. As we saw in the bear classifier, our neural net will return one activation per category.

So in the binary case, what do those activations really indicate? A single pair of activations simply indicates the *relative* confidence of the input being a 3 versus being a 7. The overall values, whether they are both high or both low, don't matter—all that matters is which is higher, and by how much.

We would expect that since this is just another way of representing the same problem, we would be able to use `sigmoid` directly on the two-activation version of our neural net. And indeed we can! We can just take the *difference* between the neural net activations, because that reflects how much more sure we are of the input being a 3 than a 7, and then take the sigmoid of that:

```
(acts[:,0]-acts[:,1]).sigmoid()
```

```
tensor([0.6025, 0.5021, 0.1332, 0.9966, 0.5959, 0.3661])
```

The second column (the probability of it being a 7) will then just be that value subtracted from 1. Now, we need a way to do all this that also works for more than two columns. It turns out that this function, called `softmax`, is exactly that:

```
def softmax(x): return exp(x) / exp(x).sum(dim=1, keepdim=True)
```

Jargon: Exponential Function (exp)

Defined as `e**x`, where `e` is a special number approximately equal to 2.718. It is the inverse of the natural logarithm function. Note that `exp` is always positive and increases *very* rapidly!

Let's check that `softmax` returns the same values as `sigmoid` for the first column, and those values subtracted from 1 for the second column:

```
sm_acts = torch.softmax(acts, dim=1)
sm_acts
```

```
tensor([[0.6025, 0.3975],
        [0.5021, 0.4979],
        [0.1332, 0.8668],
        [0.9966, 0.0034],
        [0.5959, 0.4041],
        [0.3661, 0.6339]])
```

`softmax` is the multi-category equivalent of `sigmoid`—we have to use it anytime we have more than two categories and the probabilities of the categories must add to 1, and we often use it even when there are just two categories, just to make things a bit more consistent. We could create other functions that have the properties that all activations are between 0 and 1, and sum to 1; however, no other function has the same relationship to the sigmoid function, which we've seen is smooth and symmetric. Also, we'll see shortly that the softmax function works well hand in hand with the loss function we will look at in the next section.

If we have three output activations, such as in our bear classifier, calculating softmax for a single bear image would then look something like Figure 5-3.

	output	exp	softmax
teddy	0.02	1.02	0.22
grizzly	-2.49	0.08	0.02
brown	1.25	3.49	0.76
		4.60	1.00

Figure 5-3. Example of softmax on the bear classifier

What does this function do in practice? Taking the exponential ensures all our numbers are positive, and then dividing by the sum ensures we are going to have a bunch of numbers that add up to 1. The exponential also has a nice property: if one of the numbers in our activations x is slightly bigger than the others, the exponential will amplify this (since it grows, well…exponentially), which means that in the softmax, that number will be closer to 1.

Intuitively, the softmax function *really* wants to pick one class among the others, so it's ideal for training a classifier when we know each picture has a definite label. (Note that it may be less ideal during inference, as you might want your model to sometimes tell you it doesn't recognize any of the classes that it has seen during training, and not pick a class because it has a slightly bigger activation score. In this case, it might be better to train a model using multiple binary output columns, each using a sigmoid activation.)

Softmax is the first part of the cross-entropy loss—the second part is log likelihood.

Log Likelihood

When we calculated the loss for our MNIST example in the preceding chapter, we used this:

```
def mnist_loss(inputs, targets):
    inputs = inputs.sigmoid()
    return torch.where(targets==1, 1-inputs, inputs).mean()
```

Just as we moved from sigmoid to softmax, we need to extend the loss function to work with more than just binary classification—it needs to be able to classify any number of categories (in this case, we have 37 categories). Our activations, after softmax, are between 0 and 1, and sum to 1 for each row in the batch of predictions. Our targets are integers between 0 and 36.

In the binary case, we used `torch.where` to select between `inputs` and `1-inputs`. When we treat a binary classification as a general classification problem with two categories, it becomes even easier, because (as we saw in the previous section) we now have two columns containing the equivalent of `inputs` and `1-inputs`. So, all we need to do is select from the appropriate column. Let's try to implement this in PyTorch. For our synthetic 3s and 7s example, let's say these are our labels:

```
targ = tensor([0,1,0,1,1,0])
```

And these are the softmax activations:

```
sm_acts
```

```
tensor([[0.6025, 0.3975],
        [0.5021, 0.4979],
        [0.1332, 0.8668],
        [0.9966, 0.0034],
        [0.5959, 0.4041],
        [0.3661, 0.6339]])
```

Then for each item of `targ`, we can use that to select the appropriate column of `sm_acts` using tensor indexing, like so:

```
idx = range(6)
sm_acts[idx, targ]
```

```
tensor([0.6025, 0.4979, 0.1332, 0.0034, 0.4041, 0.3661])
```

To see exactly what's happening here, let's put all the columns together in a table. Here, the first two columns are our activations, then we have the targets, the row index, and finally the result shown in the preceding code:

3	7	targ	idx	loss
0.602469	0.397531	0	0	0.602469
0.502065	0.497935	1	1	0.497935
0.133188	0.866811	0	2	0.133188
0.99664	0.00336017	1	3	0.00336017
0.595949	0.404051	1	4	0.404051
0.366118	0.633882	0	5	0.366118

Looking at this table, you can see that the final column can be calculated by taking the `targ` and `idx` columns as indices into the two-column matrix containing the 3 and 7 columns. That's what `sm_acts[idx, targ]` is doing.

The really interesting thing here is that this works just as well with more than two columns. To see this, consider what would happen if we added an activation column for every digit (0 through 9), and then targ contained a number from 0 to 9. As long as the activation columns sum to 1 (as they will, if we use softmax), we'll have a loss function that shows how well we're predicting each digit.

We're picking the loss only from the column containing the correct label. We don't need to consider the other columns, because by the definition of softmax, they add up to 1 minus the activation corresponding to the correct label. Therefore, making the activation for the correct label as high as possible must mean we're also decreasing the activations of the remaining columns.

PyTorch provides a function that does exactly the same thing as sm_acts[range(n), targ] (except it takes the negative, because when applying the log afterward, we will have negative numbers), called nll_loss (*NLL* stands for *negative log likelihood*):

```
-sm_acts[idx, targ]
tensor([-0.6025, -0.4979, -0.1332, -0.0034, -0.4041, -0.3661])
F.nll_loss(sm_acts, targ, reduction='none')
tensor([-0.6025, -0.4979, -0.1332, -0.0034, -0.4041, -0.3661])
```

Despite its name, this PyTorch function does not take the log. We'll see why in the next section, but first, let's see why taking the logarithm can be useful.

Taking the log

The function we saw in the previous section works quite well as a loss function, but we can make it a bit better. The problem is that we are using probabilities, and probabilities cannot be smaller than 0 or greater than 1. That means our model will not care whether it predicts 0.99 or 0.999. Indeed, those numbers are very close together —but in another sense, 0.999 is 10 times more confident than 0.99. So, we want to transform our numbers between 0 and 1 to instead be between negative infinity and 0. There is a mathematical function that does exactly this: the *logarithm* (available as torch.log). It is not defined for numbers less than 0 and looks like this:

```
plot_function(torch.log, min=0,max=4)
```

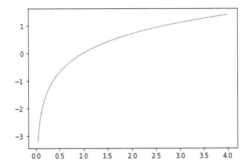

Does "logarithm" ring a bell? The logarithm function has this identity:

```
y = b**a
a = log(y,b)
```

In this case, we're assuming that log(y,b) returns *log y base b*. However, PyTorch doesn't define log this way: log in Python uses the special number e (2.718...) as the base.

Perhaps a logarithm is something that you have not thought about for the last 20 years or so. But it's a mathematical idea that is going to be really critical for many things in deep learning, so now would be a great time to refresh your memory. The key thing to know about logarithms is this relationship:

```
log(a*b) = log(a)+log(b)
```

When we see it in that format, it looks a bit boring; but think about what this really means. It means that logarithms increase linearly when the underlying signal increases exponentially or multiplicatively. This is used, for instance, in the Richter scale of earthquake severity and the dB scale of noise levels. It's also often used on financial charts, where we want to show compound growth rates more clearly. Computer scientists love using logarithms, because it means that multiplication, which can create really, really large and really, really small numbers, can be replaced by addition, which is much less likely to result in scales that are difficult for our computers to handle.

Sylvain Says

It's not just computer scientists who love logs! Until computers came along, engineers and scientists used a special ruler called a *slide rule* that did multiplication by adding logarithms. Logarithms are widely used in physics, for multiplying very big or very small numbers, and many other fields.

Taking the mean of the positive or negative log of our probabilities (depending on whether it's the correct or incorrect class) gives us the *negative log likelihood* loss. In PyTorch, `nll_loss` assumes that you already took the log of the softmax, so it doesn't do the logarithm for you.

Confusing Name, Beware

The "nll" in `nll_loss` stands for "negative log likelihood," but it doesn't actually take the log at all! It assumes you have *already* taken the log. PyTorch has a function called `log_softmax` that combines `log` and `softmax` in a fast and accurate way. `nll_loss` is designed to be used after `log_softmax`.

When we first take the softmax, and then the log likelihood of that, that combination is called *cross-entropy loss*. In PyTorch, this is available as `nn.CrossEntropyLoss` (which, in practice, does `log_softmax` and then `nll_loss`):

```
loss_func = nn.CrossEntropyLoss()
```

As you see, this is a class. Instantiating it gives you an object that behaves like a function:

```
loss_func(acts, targ)
```

```
tensor(1.8045)
```

All PyTorch loss functions are provided in two forms, the class form just shown as well as a plain functional form, available in the `F` namespace:

```
F.cross_entropy(acts, targ)
```

```
tensor(1.8045)
```

Either one works fine and can be used in any situation. We've noticed that most people tend to use the class version, and that's more often used in PyTorch's official docs and examples, so we'll tend to use that too.

By default, PyTorch loss functions take the mean of the loss of all items. You can use `reduction='none'` to disable that:

```
nn.CrossEntropyLoss(reduction='none')(acts, targ)
```

```
tensor([0.5067, 0.6973, 2.0160, 5.6958, 0.9062, 1.0048])
```

Sylvain Says

An interesting feature about cross-entropy loss appears when we consider its gradient. The gradient of `cross_entropy(a,b)` is `softmax(a)-b`. Since `softmax(a)` is the final activation of the model, that means that the gradient is proportional to the difference between the prediction and the target. This is the same as mean squared error in regression (assuming there's no final activation function such as that added by `y_range`), since the gradient of `(a-b)**2` is `2*(a-b)`. Because the gradient is linear, we won't see sudden jumps or exponential increases in gradients, which should lead to smoother training of models.

We have now seen all the pieces hidden behind our loss function. But while this puts a number on how well (or badly) our model is doing, it does nothing to help us know if it's any good. Let's now see some ways to interpret our model's predictions.

Model Interpretation

It's very hard to interpret loss functions directly, because they are designed to be things computers can differentiate and optimize, not things that people can understand. That's why we have metrics. These are not used in the optimization process, but just to help us poor humans understand what's going on. In this case, our accuracy is looking pretty good already! So where are we making mistakes?

We saw in Chapter 1 that we can use a confusion matrix to see where our model is doing well and where it's doing badly:

```
interp = ClassificationInterpretation.from_learner(learn)
interp.plot_confusion_matrix(figsize=(12,12), dpi=60)
```

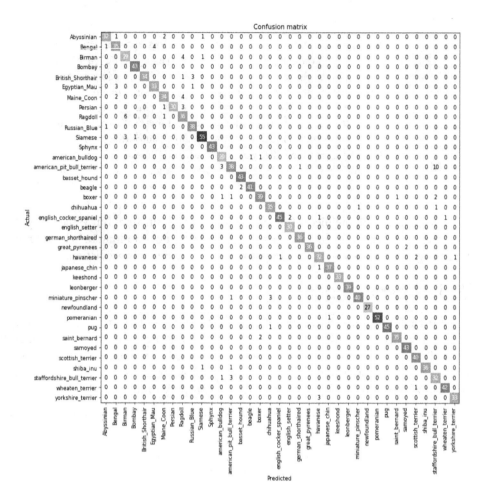

Confusion matrix

Oh, dear—in this case, a confusion matrix is very hard to read. We have 37 pet breeds, which means we have 37×37 entries in this giant matrix! Instead, we can use the `most_confused` method, which just shows us the cells of the confusion matrix with the most incorrect predictions (here, with at least 5 or more):

```
interp.most_confused(min_val=5)
```

```
[('american_pit_bull_terrier', 'staffordshire_bull_terrier', 10),
 ('Ragdoll', 'Birman', 6)]
```

Since we are not pet breed experts, it is hard for us to know whether these category errors reflect actual difficulties in recognizing breeds. So again, we turn to Google. A little bit of Googling tells us that the most common category errors shown here are breed differences that even expert breeders sometimes disagree about. So this gives us some comfort that we are on the right track.

We seem to have a good baseline. What can we do now to make it even better?

Improving Our Model

We will now look at a range of techniques to improve the training of our model and make it better. While doing so, we will explain a little bit more about transfer learning and how to fine-tune our pretrained model as best as possible, without breaking the pretrained weights.

The first thing we need to set when training a model is the learning rate. We saw in the previous chapter that it needs to be just right to train as efficiently as possible, so how do we pick a good one? fastai provides a tool for this.

The Learning Rate Finder

One of the most important things we can do when training a model is to make sure that we have the right learning rate. If our learning rate is too low, it can take many, many epochs to train our model. Not only does this waste time, but it also means that we may have problems with overfitting, because every time we do a complete pass through the data, we give our model a chance to memorize it.

So let's just make our learning rate really high, right? Sure, let's try that and see what happens:

```
learn = cnn_learner(dls, resnet34, metrics=error_rate)
learn.fine_tune(1, base_lr=0.1)
```

epoch	train_loss	valid_loss	error_rate	time
0	8.946717	47.954632	0.893775	00:20

epoch	train_loss	valid_loss	error_rate	time
0	7.231843	4.119265	0.954668	00:24

That doesn't look good. Here's what happened. The optimizer stepped in the correct direction, but it stepped so far that it totally overshot the minimum loss. Repeating that multiple times makes it get further and further away, not closer and closer!

What do we do to find the perfect learning rate—not too high and not too low? In 2015, researcher Leslie Smith came up with a brilliant idea, called the *learning rate finder*. His idea was to start with a very, very small learning rate, something so small that we would never expect it to be too big to handle. We use that for one mini-batch, find what the losses are afterward, and then increase the learning rate by a certain percentage (e.g., doubling it each time). Then we do another mini-batch, track the loss, and double the learning rate again. We keep doing this until the loss gets worse, instead of better. This is the point where we know we have gone too far. We then select a learning rate a bit lower than this point. Our advice is to pick either of these:

- One order of magnitude less than where the minimum loss was achieved (i.e., the minimum divided by 10)

- The last point where the loss was clearly decreasing

The learning rate finder computes those points on the curve to help you. Both these rules usually give around the same value. In the first chapter, we didn't specify a learning rate, using the default value from the fastai library (which is 1e-3):

```
learn = cnn_learner(dls, resnet34, metrics=error_rate)
lr_min,lr_steep = learn.lr_find()
```

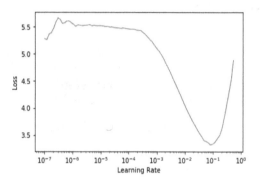

```
print(f"Minimum/10: {lr_min:.2e}, steepest point: {lr_steep:.2e}")
```

```
Minimum/10: 8.32e-03, steepest point: 6.31e-03
```

We can see on this plot that in the range 1e-6 to 1e-3, nothing really happens and the model doesn't train. Then the loss starts to decrease until it reaches a minimum, and then increases again. We don't want a learning rate greater than 1e-1, as it will cause training to diverge (you can try for yourself), but 1e-1 is already too high: at this stage, we've left the period where the loss was decreasing steadily.

In this learning rate plot, it appears that a learning rate around 3e-3 would be appropriate, so let's choose that:

```
learn = cnn_learner(dls, resnet34, metrics=error_rate)
learn.fine_tune(2, base_lr=3e-3)
```

epoch	train_loss	valid_loss	error_rate	time
0	1.071820	0.427476	0.133965	00:19

epoch	train_loss	valid_loss	error_rate	time
0	0.738273	0.541828	0.150880	00:24
1	0.401544	0.266623	0.081867	00:24

Logarithmic Scale

The learning rate finder plot has a logarithmic scale, which is why the middle point between 1e-3 and 1e-2 is between 3e-3 and 4e-3. This is because we care mostly about the order of magnitude of the learning rate.

It's interesting that the learning rate finder was discovered only in 2015, while neural networks have been under development since the 1950s. Throughout that time, finding a good learning rate has been, perhaps, the most important and challenging issue for practitioners. The solution does not require any advanced math, giant computing resources, huge datasets, or anything else that would make it inaccessible to any curious researcher. Furthermore, Smith was not part of some exclusive Silicon Valley lab, but was working as a naval researcher. All of this is to say: breakthrough work in deep learning absolutely does not require access to vast resources, elite teams, or advanced mathematical ideas. Lots of work remains to be done that requires just a bit of common sense, creativity, and tenacity.

Now that we have a good learning rate to train our model, let's look at how we can fine-tune the weights of a pretrained model.

Unfreezing and Transfer Learning

We discussed briefly in Chapter 1 how transfer learning works. We saw that the basic idea is that a pretrained model, trained potentially on millions of data points (such as ImageNet), is fine-tuned for another task. But what does this really mean?

We now know that a convolutional neural network consists of many linear layers with a nonlinear activation function between each pair, followed by one or more final linear layers with an activation function such as softmax at the very end. The final linear layer uses a matrix with enough columns such that the output size is the same as the number of classes in our model (assuming that we are doing classification).

This final linear layer is unlikely to be of any use for us when we are fine-tuning in a transfer learning setting, because it is specifically designed to classify the categories in the original pretraining dataset. So when we do transfer learning, we remove it, throw it away, and replace it with a new linear layer with the correct number of outputs for our desired task (in this case, there would be 37 activations).

This newly added linear layer will have entirely random weights. Therefore, our model prior to fine-tuning has entirely random outputs. But that does not mean that it is an entirely random model! All of the layers prior to the last one have been care-fully trained to be good at image classification tasks in general. As we saw in the images from the Zeiler and Fergus paper (*https://oreil.ly/aTRwE*) in Chapter 1 (see Figures 1-10 through 1-13), the first few layers encode general concepts, such as find-ing gradients and edges, and later layers encode concepts that are still useful for us, such as finding eyeballs and fur.

We want to train a model in such a way that we allow it to remember all of these gen-erally useful ideas from the pretrained model, use them to solve our particular task (classify pet breeds), and adjust them only as required for the specifics of our particu-lar task.

Our challenge when fine-tuning is to replace the random weights in our added linear layers with weights that correctly achieve our desired task (classifying pet breeds) without breaking the carefully pretrained weights and the other layers. A simple trick can allow this to happen: tell the optimizer to update the weights in only those ran-domly added final layers. Don't change the weights in the rest of the neural network at all. This is called *freezing* those pretrained layers.

When we create a model from a pretrained network, fastai automatically freezes all of the pretrained layers for us. When we call the `fine_tune` method, fastai does two things:

- Trains the randomly added layers for one epoch, with all other layers frozen
- Unfreezes all the layers, and trains them for the number of epochs requested

Although this is a reasonable default approach, it is likely that for your particular dataset, you may get better results by doing things slightly differently. The `fine_tune` method has parameters you can use to change its behavior, but it might be easiest for you to just call the underlying methods directly if you want to get custom behavior. Remember that you can see the source code for the method by using the following syntax:

```
learn.fine_tune??
```

So let's try doing this manually ourselves. First of all, we will train the randomly added layers for three epochs, using `fit_one_cycle`. As mentioned in Chapter 1, `fit_one_cycle` is the suggested way to train models without using `fine_tune`. We'll see why later in the book; in short, what `fit_one_cycle` does is to start training at a low learning rate, gradually increase it for the first section of training, and then grad-ually decrease it again for the last section of training:

```
learn = cnn_learner(dls, resnet34, metrics=error_rate)
learn.fit_one_cycle(3, 3e-3)
```

epoch	train_loss	valid_loss	error_rate	time
0	1.188042	0.355024	0.102842	00:20
1	0.534234	0.302453	0.094723	00:20
2	0.325031	0.222268	0.074425	00:20

Then we'll unfreeze the model:

```
learn.unfreeze()
```

and run `lr_find` again, because having more layers to train, and weights that have already been trained for three epochs, means our previously found learning rate isn't appropriate anymore:

```
learn.lr_find()
```

```
(1.0964782268274575e-05, 1.5848931980144698e-06)
```

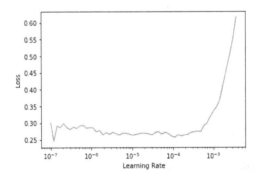

Note that the graph is a little different from when we had random weights: we don't have that sharp descent that indicates the model is training. That's because our model has been trained already. Here we have a somewhat flat area before a sharp increase, and we should take a point well before that sharp increase—for instance, 1e-5. The point with the maximum gradient isn't what we look for here and should be ignored.

Let's train at a suitable learning rate:

```
learn.fit_one_cycle(6, lr_max=1e-5)
```

epoch	train_loss	valid_loss	error_rate	time
0	0.263579	0.217419	0.069012	00:24
1	0.253060	0.210346	0.062923	00:24
2	0.224340	0.207357	0.060217	00:24
3	0.200195	0.207244	0.061570	00:24
4	0.194269	0.200149	0.059540	00:25
5	0.173164	0.202301	0.059540	00:25

This has improved our model a bit, but there's more we can do. The deepest layers of our pretrained model might not need as high a learning rate as the last ones, so we should probably use different learning rates for those—this is known as using *discriminative* learning rates.

Discriminative Learning Rates

Even after we unfreeze, we still care a lot about the quality of those pretrained weights. We would not expect that the best learning rate for those pretrained parameters would be as high as for the randomly added parameters, even after we have tuned those randomly added parameters for a few epochs. Remember, the pretrained weights have been trained for hundreds of epochs, on millions of images.

In addition, do you remember the images we saw in Chapter 1, showing what each layer learns? The first layer learns very simple foundations, like edge and gradient detectors; these are likely to be just as useful for nearly any task. The later layers learn much more complex concepts, like "eye" and "sunset," which might not be useful in your task at all (maybe you're classifying car models, for instance). So it makes sense to let the later layers fine-tune more quickly than earlier layers.

Therefore, fastai's default approach is to use discriminative learning rates. This technique was originally developed in the ULMFiT approach to NLP transfer learning that we will introduce in Chapter 10. Like many good ideas in deep learning, it is extremely simple: use a lower learning rate for the early layers of the neural network, and a higher learning rate for the later layers (and especially the randomly added layers). The idea is based on insights developed by Jason Yosinski et al. (*https://oreil.ly/j3640*), who showed in 2014 that with transfer learning, different layers of a neural network should train at different speeds, as seen in Figure 5-4.

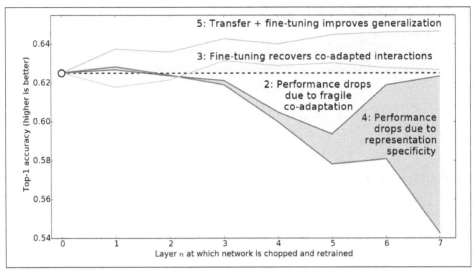

Figure 5-4. Impact of different layers and training methods on transfer learning (courtesy of Jason Yosinski et al.)

fastai lets you pass a Python `slice` object anywhere that a learning rate is expected. The first value passed will be the learning rate in the earliest layer of the neural network, and the second value will be the learning rate in the final layer. The layers in between will have learning rates that are multiplicatively equidistant throughout that range. Let's use this approach to replicate the previous training, but this time we'll set only the *lowest* layer of our net to a learning rate of 1e-6; the other layers will scale up to 1e-4. Let's train for a while and see what happens:

```
learn = cnn_learner(dls, resnet34, metrics=error_rate)
learn.fit_one_cycle(3, 3e-3)
learn.unfreeze()
learn.fit_one_cycle(12, lr_max=slice(1e-6,1e-4))
```

epoch	train_loss	valid_loss	error_rate	time
0	1.145300	0.345568	0.119756	00:20
1	0.533986	0.251944	0.077131	00:20
2	0.317696	0.208371	0.069012	00:20

epoch	train_loss	valid_loss	error_rate	time
0	0.257977	0.205400	0.067659	00:25
1	0.246763	0.205107	0.066306	00:25
2	0.240595	0.193848	0.062246	00:25
3	0.209988	0.198061	0.062923	00:25
4	0.194756	0.193130	0.064276	00:25

epoch	train_loss	valid_loss	error_rate	time
5	0.169985	0.187885	0.056157	00:25
6	0.153205	0.186145	0.058863	00:25
7	0.141480	0.185316	0.053451	00:25
8	0.128564	0.180999	0.051421	00:25
9	0.126941	0.186288	0.054127	00:25
10	0.130064	0.181764	0.054127	00:25
11	0.124281	0.181855	0.054127	00:25

Now the fine-tuning is working great!

fastai can show us a graph of the training and validation loss:

```
learn.recorder.plot_loss()
```

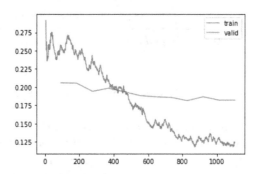

As you can see, the training loss keeps getting better and better. But notice that even-tually the validation loss improvement slows and sometimes even gets worse! This is the point at which the model is starting to overfit. In particular, the model is becom-ing overconfident of its predictions. But this does *not* mean that it is getting less accu-rate, necessarily. Take a look at the table of training results per epoch, and you will often see that the accuracy continues improving, even as the validation loss gets worse. In the end, what matters is your accuracy, or more generally your chosen met-rics, not the loss. The loss is just the function we've given the computer to help us to optimize.

Another decision you have to make when training the model is how long to train for. We'll consider that next.

Selecting the Number of Epochs

Often you will find that you are limited by time, rather than generalization and accu-racy, when choosing how many epochs to train for. So your first approach to training should be to simply pick a number of epochs that will train in the amount of time that you are happy to wait for. Then look at the training and validation loss plots, as shown previously, and in particular your metrics. If you see that they are still getting better even in your final epochs, you know that you have not trained for too long.

On the other hand, you may well see that the metrics you have chosen are really getting worse at the end of training. Remember, it's not just that we're looking for the validation loss to get worse, but the actual metrics. Your validation loss will first get worse during training because the model gets overconfident, and only later will get worse because it is incorrectly memorizing the data. We care in practice about only the latter issue. Remember, our loss function is something that we use to allow our optimizer to have something it can differentiate and optimize; it's not the thing we care about in practice.

Before the days of 1cycle training, it was common to save the model at the end of each epoch, and then select whichever model had the best accuracy out of all of the models saved in each epoch. This is known as *early stopping*. However, this is unlikely to give you the best answer, because those epochs in the middle occur before the learning rate has had a chance to reach the small values, where it can really find the best result. Therefore, if you find that you have overfit, what you should do is retrain your model from scratch, and this time select a total number of epochs based on where your previous best results were found.

If you have the time to train for more epochs, you may want to instead use that time to train more parameters—that is, use a deeper architecture.

Deeper Architectures

In general, a model with more parameters can model your data more accurately. (There are lots and lots of caveats to this generalization, and it depends on the specifics of the architectures you are using, but it is a reasonable rule of thumb for now.) For most of the architectures that we will be seeing in this book, you can create larger versions of them by simply adding more layers. However, since we want to use pretrained models, we need to make sure that we choose a number of layers that have already been pretrained for us.

This is why, in practice, architectures tend to come in a small number of variants. For instance, the ResNet architecture that we are using in this chapter comes in variants with 18, 34, 50, 101, and 152 layers, pretrained on ImageNet. A larger (more layers and parameters; sometimes described as the *capacity* of a model) version of a ResNet will always be able to give us a better training loss, but it can suffer more from overfitting, because it has more parameters to overfit with.

In general, a bigger model has the ability to better capture the real underlying relationships in your data, as well as to capture and memorize the specific details of your individual images.

However, using a deeper model is going to require more GPU RAM, so you may need to lower the size of your batches to avoid an *out-of-memory error*. This happens when you try to fit too much inside your GPU and looks like this:

```
Cuda runtime error: out of memory
```

You may have to restart your notebook when this happens. The way to solve it is to use a smaller batch size, which means passing smaller groups of images at any given time through your model. You can pass the batch size you want to the call by creating your `DataLoaders` with `bs=`.

The other downside of deeper architectures is that they take quite a bit longer to train. One technique that can speed things up a lot is *mixed-precision training*. This refers to using less-precise numbers (*half-precision floating point*, also called *fp16*) where possible during training. As we are writing these words in early 2020, nearly all current NVIDIA GPUs support a special feature called *tensor cores* that can dramatically speed up neural network training, by 2–3×. They also require a lot less GPU memory. To enable this feature in fastai, just add `to_fp16()` after your `Learner` creation (you also need to import the module).

You can't really know the best architecture for your particular problem ahead of time —you need to try training some. So let's try a ResNet-50 now with mixed precision:

```
from fastai.callback.fp16 import *
learn = cnn_learner(dls, resnet50, metrics=error_rate).to_fp16()
learn.fine_tune(6, freeze_epochs=3)
```

epoch	train_loss	valid_loss	error_rate	time
0	1.427505	0.310554	0.098782	00:21
1	0.606785	0.302325	0.094723	00:22
2	0.409267	0.294803	0.091340	00:21

epoch	train_loss	valid_loss	error_rate	time
0	0.261121	0.274507	0.083897	00:26
1	0.296653	0.318649	0.084574	00:26
2	0.242356	0.253677	0.069012	00:26
3	0.150684	0.251438	0.065629	00:26
4	0.094997	0.239772	0.064276	00:26
5	0.061144	0.228082	0.054804	00:26

You'll see here we've gone back to using `fine_tune`, since it's so handy! We can pass `freeze_epochs` to tell fastai how many epochs to train for while frozen. It will automatically change learning rates appropriately for most datasets.

In this case, we're not seeing a clear win from the deeper model. This is useful to remember—bigger models aren't necessarily better models for your particular case! Make sure you try small models before you start scaling up.

Conclusion

In this chapter, you learned some important practical tips, both for getting your image data ready for modeling (presizing, data block summary) and for fitting the model (learning rate finder, unfreezing, discriminative learning rates, setting the number of epochs, and using deeper architectures). Using these tools will help you to build more accurate image models, more quickly.

We also discussed cross-entropy loss. This part of the book is worth spending plenty of time on. You aren't likely to need to implement cross-entropy loss from scratch yourself in practice, but it's important you understand the inputs to and output from that function, because it (or a variant of it, as we'll see in the next chapter) is used in nearly every classification model. So when you want to debug a model, or put a model in production, or improve the accuracy of a model, you're going to need to be able to look at its activations and loss, and understand what's going on, and why. You can't do that properly if you don't understand your loss function.

If cross-entropy loss hasn't "clicked" for you just yet, don't worry—you'll get there! First, go back to the preceding chapter and make sure you really understand `mnist_loss`. Then work gradually through the cells of the notebook for this chapter, where we step through each piece of cross-entropy loss. Make sure you understand what each calculation is doing and why. Try creating some small tensors yourself and pass them into the functions, to see what they return.

Remember: the choices made in the implementation of cross-entropy loss are not the only possible choices that could have been made. Just as when we looked at regression we could choose between mean squared error and mean absolute difference (L1), we could change the details here too. If you have other ideas for possible functions that you think might work, feel free to give them a try in this chapter's notebook! (Fair warning, though: you'll probably find that the model will be slower to train and less accurate. That's because the gradient of cross-entropy loss is proportional to the difference between the activation and the target, so SGD always gets a nicely scaled step for the weights.)

Questionnaire

1. Why do we first resize to a large size on the CPU, and then to a smaller size on the GPU?

2. If you are not familiar with regular expressions, find a regular expression tutorial and some problem sets, and complete them. Have a look on the book's website for suggestions.

3. What are the two ways in which data is most commonly provided for most deep learning datasets?

4. Look up the documentation for L and try using a few of the new methods that it adds.

5. Look up the documentation for the Python `pathlib` module and try using a few methods of the `Path` class.

6. Give two examples of ways that image transformations can degrade the quality of the data.

7. What method does fastai provide to view the data in a `DataLoaders`?

8. What method does fastai provide to help you debug a `DataBlock`?

9. Should you hold off on training a model until you have thoroughly cleaned your data?

10. What are the two pieces that are combined into cross-entropy loss in PyTorch?

11. What are the two properties of activations that softmax ensures? Why is this important?

12. When might you want your activations to not have these two properties?

13. Calculate the `exp` and `softmax` columns of Figure 5-3 yourself (i.e., in a spreadsheet, with a calculator, or in a notebook).

14. Why can't we use `torch.where` to create a loss function for datasets where our label can have more than two categories?

15. What is the value of log(–2)? Why?

16. What are two good rules of thumb for picking a learning rate from the learning rate finder?

17. What two steps does the `fine_tune` method do?

18. In Jupyter Notebook, how do you get the source code for a method or function?

19. What are discriminative learning rates?

20. How is a Python `slice` object interpreted when passed as a learning rate to fastai?

21. Why is early stopping a poor choice when using 1cycle training?

22. What is the difference between `resnet50` and `resnet101`?

23. What does `to_fp16` do?

Further Research

1. Find the paper by Leslie Smith that introduced the learning rate finder, and read it.

2. See if you can improve the accuracy of the classifier in this chapter. What's the best accuracy you can achieve? Look on the forums and the book's website to see what other students have achieved with this dataset and how they did it.

CHAPTER 6

Other Computer Vision Problems

In the previous chapter, you learned some important practical techniques for training models in practice. Considerations like selecting learning rates and the number of epochs are very important to getting good results.

In this chapter, we are going to look at two other types of computer vision problems: multi-label classification and regression. The first one occurs when you want to predict more than one label per image (or sometimes none at all), and the second occurs when your labels are one or several numbers—a quantity instead of a category.

In the process, we will study more deeply the output activations, targets, and loss functions in deep learning models.

Multi-Label Classification

Multi-label classification refers to the problem of identifying the categories of objects in images that may not contain exactly one type of object. There may be more than one kind of object, or there may be no objects at all in the classes you are looking for.

For instance, this would have been a great approach for our bear classifier. One problem with the bear classifier that we rolled out in Chapter 2 was that if a user uploaded something that wasn't any kind of bear, the model would still say it was either a grizzly, black, or teddy bear—it had no ability to predict "not a bear at all." In fact, after we have completed this chapter, it would be a great exercise for you to go back to your image classifier application and try to retrain it using the multi-label technique, and then test it by passing in an image that is not of any of your recognized classes.

In practice, we have not seen many examples of people training multi-label classifiers for this purpose—but we often see both users and developers complaining about this problem. It appears that this simple solution is not at all widely understood or appreciated! Because in practice it is probably more common to have some images with zero matches or more than one match, we should probably expect in practice that multi-label classifiers are more widely applicable than single-label classifiers.

First let's see what a multi-label dataset looks like; then we'll explain how to get it ready for our model. You'll see that the architecture of the model does not change from the preceding chapter; only the loss function does. Let's start with the data.

The Data

For our example, we are going to use the PASCAL dataset, which can have more than one kind of classified object per image.

We begin by downloading and extracting the dataset as per usual:

```
from fastai.vision.all import *
path = untar_data(URLs.PASCAL_2007)
```

This dataset is different from the ones we have seen before, in that it is not structured by filename or folder but instead comes with a CSV file telling us what labels to use for each image. We can inspect the CSV file by reading it into a Pandas DataFrame:

```
df = pd.read_csv(path/'train.csv')
df.head()
```

	fname	labels	is_valid
0	000005.jpg	chair	True
1	000007.jpg	car	True
2	000009.jpg	horse person	True
3	000012.jpg	car	False
4	000016.jpg	bicycle	True

As you can see, the list of categories in each image is shown as a space-delimited string.

Pandas and DataFrames

No, it's not actually a panda! *Pandas* is a Python library that is used to manipulate and analyze tabular and time series data. The main class is DataFrame, which represents a table of rows and columns.

You can get a DataFrame from a CSV file, a database table, Python dictionaries, and many other sources. In Jupyter, a DataFrame is output as a formatted table, as shown here.

You can access rows and columns of a DataFrame with the `iloc` property, as if it were a matrix:

```
df.iloc[:,0]
```

```
0        000005.jpg
1        000007.jpg
2        000009.jpg
3        000012.jpg
4        000016.jpg
            ...
5006     009954.jpg
5007     009955.jpg
5008     009958.jpg
5009     009959.jpg
5010     009961.jpg
Name: fname, Length: 5011, dtype: object
```

```
df.iloc[0,:]
# Trailing :s are always optional (in numpy, pytorch, pandas, etc.),
#    so this is equivalent:
df.iloc[0]
```

```
fname           000005.jpg
labels               chair
is_valid              True
Name: 0, dtype: object
```

You can also grab a column by name by indexing into a DataFrame directly:

```
df['fname']
```

```
0        000005.jpg
1        000007.jpg
2        000009.jpg
3        000012.jpg
4        000016.jpg
            ...
5006     009954.jpg
5007     009955.jpg
5008     009958.jpg
5009     009959.jpg
5010     009961.jpg
Name: fname, Length: 5011, dtype: object
```

You can create new columns and do calculations using columns:

```
df1 = pd.DataFrame()
df1['a'] = [1,2,3,4]
df1
```

	a
0	1
1	2
2	3
3	4

```
df1['b'] = [10, 20, 30, 40]
df1['a'] + df1['b']

0    11
1    22
2    33
3    44
dtype: int64
```

Pandas is a fast and flexible library, and an important part of every data scientist's Python toolbox. Unfortunately, its API can be rather confusing and surprising, so it takes a while to get familiar with it. If you haven't used Pandas before, we suggest going through a tutorial; we are particularly fond of *Python for Data Analysis* (O'Reilly) by Wes McKinney, the creator of Pandas. It also covers other important libraries like `matplotlib` and `NumPy`. We will try to briefly describe Pandas functionality we use as we come across it, but will not go into the level of detail of McKinney's book.

Now that we have seen what the data looks like, let's make it ready for model training.

Constructing a DataBlock

How do we convert from a `DataFrame` object to a `DataLoaders` object? We generally suggest using the data block API for creating a `DataLoaders` object, where possible, since it provides a good mix of flexibility and simplicity. Here we will show you the steps that we take to use the data block API to construct a `DataLoaders` object in practice, using this dataset as an example.

As we have seen, PyTorch and fastai have two main classes for representing and accessing a training set or validation set:

Dataset
:   A collection that returns a tuple of your independent and dependent variable for a single item

DataLoader
:   An iterator that provides a stream of mini-batches, where each mini-batch is a tuple of a batch of independent variables and a batch of dependent variables

On top of these, fastai provides two classes for bringing your training and validation sets together:

Datasets
> An iterator that contains a training Dataset and a validation Dataset

DataLoaders
> An object that contains a training DataLoader and a validation DataLoader

Since a DataLoader builds on top of a Dataset and adds additional functionality to it (collating multiple items into a mini-batch), it's often easiest to start by creating and testing Datasets, and then look at DataLoaders after that's working.

When we create a DataBlock, we build up gradually, step by step, and use the notebook to check our data along the way. This is a great way to make sure that you maintain momentum as you are coding, and that you keep an eye out for any problems. It's easy to debug, because you know that if a problem arises, it is in the line of code you just typed!

Let's start with the simplest case, which is a data block created with no parameters:

```
dblock = DataBlock()
```

We can create a Datasets object from this. The only thing needed is a source—in this case, our DataFrame:

```
dsets = dblock.datasets(df)
```

This contains a train and a valid dataset, which we can index into:

```
dsets.train[0]
```

```
(fname       008663.jpg
 labels      car person
 is_valid    False
 Name: 4346, dtype: object,
 fname       008663.jpg
 labels      car person
 is_valid    False
 Name: 4346, dtype: object)
```

As you can see, this simply returns a row of the DataFrame, twice. This is because by default, the data block assumes we have two things: input and target. We are going to need to grab the appropriate fields from the DataFrame, which we can do by passing get_x and get_y functions:

```
dblock = DataBlock(get_x = lambda r: r['fname'], get_y = lambda r: r['labels'])
dsets = dblock.datasets(df)
dsets.train[0]

('005620.jpg', 'aeroplane')
```

As you can see, rather than defining a function in the usual way, we are using Python's `lambda` keyword. This is just a shortcut for defining and then referring to a function. The following more verbose approach is identical:

```
def get_x(r): return r['fname']
def get_y(r): return r['labels']
dblock = DataBlock(get_x = get_x, get_y = get_y)
dsets = dblock.datasets(df)
dsets.train[0]
```

```
('002549.jpg', 'tvmonitor')
```

Lambda functions are great for quickly iterating, but they are not compatible with serialization, so we advise you to use the more verbose approach if you want to export your `Learner` after training (lambdas are fine if you are just experimenting).

We can see that the independent variable will need to be converted into a complete path so that we can open it as an image, and the dependent variable will need to be split on the space character (which is the default for Python's `split` function) so that it becomes a list:

```
def get_x(r): return path/'train'/r['fname']
def get_y(r): return r['labels'].split(' ')
dblock = DataBlock(get_x = get_x, get_y = get_y)
dsets = dblock.datasets(df)
dsets.train[0]
```

```
(Path('/home/sgugger/.fastai/data/pascal_2007/train/008663.jpg'),
 ['car', 'person'])
```

To actually open the image and do the conversion to tensors, we will need to use a set of transforms; block types will provide us with those. We can use the same block types that we have used previously, with one exception: the `ImageBlock` will work fine again, because we have a path that points to a valid image, but the `CategoryBlock` is not going to work. The problem is that block returns a single integer, but we need to be able to have multiple labels for each item. To solve this, we use a `MultiCategory Block`. This type of block expects to receive a list of strings, as we have in this case, so let's test it out:

```
dblock = DataBlock(blocks=(ImageBlock, MultiCategoryBlock),
                   get_x = get_x, get_y = get_y)
dsets = dblock.datasets(df)
dsets.train[0]
```

```
(PILImage mode=RGB size=500x375,
 TensorMultiCategory([0., 0., 0., 0., 0., 0., 0., 0., 0., 0., 0., 1., 0., 0.,
 > 0., 0., 0., 0., 0., 0.]))
```

As you can see, our list of categories is not encoded in the same way that it was for the regular `CategoryBlock`. In that case, we had a single integer representing which category was present, based on its location in our vocab. In this case, however, we instead have a list of 0s, with a 1 in any position where that category is present. For example, if there is a 1 in the second and fourth positions, that means vocab items two and four are present in this image. This is known as *one-hot encoding*. The reason we can't easily just use a list of category indices is that each list would be a different length, and PyTorch requires tensors, where everything has to be the same length.

 Jargon: One-Hot Encoding

Using a vector of 0s, with a 1 in each location that is represented in the data, to encode a list of integers.

Let's check what the categories represent for this example (we are using the convenient `torch.where` function, which tells us all of the indices where our condition is true or false):

```
idxs = torch.where(dsets.train[0][1]==1.)[0]
dsets.train.vocab[idxs]
```

```
(#1) ['dog']
```

With NumPy arrays, PyTorch tensors, and fastai's L class, we can index directly using a list or vector, which makes a lot of code (such as this example) much clearer and more concise.

We have ignored the column `is_valid` up until now, which means that `DataBlock` has been using a random split by default. To explicitly choose the elements of our validation set, we need to write a function and pass it to `splitter` (or use one of fastai's predefined functions or classes). It will take the items (here our whole DataFrame) and must return two (or more) lists of integers:

```
def splitter(df):
    train = df.index[~df['is_valid']].tolist()
    valid = df.index[df['is_valid']].tolist()
    return train,valid

dblock = DataBlock(blocks=(ImageBlock, MultiCategoryBlock),
                   splitter=splitter,
                   get_x=get_x,
                   get_y=get_y)

dsets = dblock.datasets(df)
dsets.train[0]

(PILImage mode=RGB size=500x333,
 TensorMultiCategory([0., 0., 0., 0., 0., 0., 1., 0., 0., 0., 0., 0., 0., 0.,
 > 0., 0., 0., 0., 0., 0.]))
```

As we have discussed, a `DataLoader` collates the items from a `Dataset` into a mini-batch. This is a tuple of tensors, where each tensor simply stacks the items from that location in the `Dataset` item.

Now that we have confirmed that the individual items look OK, there's one more step, we need to ensure we can create our `DataLoaders`, which is to ensure that every item is of the same size. To do this, we can use `RandomResizedCrop`:

```
dblock = DataBlock(blocks=(ImageBlock, MultiCategoryBlock),
                   splitter=splitter,
                   get_x=get_x,
                   get_y=get_y,
                   item_tfms = RandomResizedCrop(128, min_scale=0.35))
dls = dblock.dataloaders(df)
```

And now we can display a sample of our data:

```
dls.show_batch(nrows=1, ncols=3)
```

car

bicycle;car;person

cat

Remember that if anything goes wrong when you create your `DataLoaders` from your `DataBlock`, or if you want to view exactly what happens with your `DataBlock`, you can use the `summary` method we presented in the previous chapter.

Our data is now ready for training a model. As we will see, nothing is going to change when we create our `Learner`, but behind the scenes the fastai library will pick a new loss function for us: binary cross entropy.

Binary Cross Entropy

Now we'll create our `Learner`. We saw in Chapter 4 that a `Learner` object contains four main things: the model, a `DataLoaders` object, an `Optimizer`, and the loss function to use. We already have our `DataLoaders`, we can leverage fastai's `resnet` models (which we'll learn how to create from scratch later), and we know how to create an SGD optimizer. So let's focus on ensuring we have a suitable loss function. To do this, let's use `cnn_learner` to create a `Learner`, so we can look at its activations:

```
learn = cnn_learner(dls, resnet18)
```

We also saw that the model in a `Learner` is generally an object of a class inheriting from `nn.Module`, and that we can call it using parentheses and it will return the activations of a model. You should pass it your independent variable, as a mini-batch. We can try it out by grabbing a mini-batch from our `DataLoader` and then passing it to the model:

```
x,y = dls.train.one_batch()
activs = learn.model(x)
activs.shape
```

```
torch.Size([64, 20])
```

Think about why `activs` has this shape—we have a batch size of 64, and we need to calculate the probability of each of 20 categories. Here's what one of those activations looks like:

```
activs[0]
```

```
tensor([ 2.0258, -1.3543,  1.4640,  1.7754, -1.2820, -5.8053,  3.6130,  0.7193,
>  -4.3683, -2.5001, -2.8373, -1.8037,  2.0122,  0.6189,  1.9729,  0.8999,
>  -2.6769, -0.3829,  1.2212,  1.6073],
        device='cuda:0', grad_fn=<SelectBackward>)
```

Getting Model Activations

Knowing how to manually get a mini-batch and pass it into a model, and look at the activations and loss, is really important for debugging your model. It is also very helpful for learning, so that you can see exactly what is going on.

They aren't yet scaled to between 0 and 1, but we learned how to do that in Chapter 4, using the `sigmoid` function. We also saw how to calculate a loss based on this—this is our loss function from Chapter 4, with the addition of `log` as discussed in the preceding chapter:

```
def binary_cross_entropy(inputs, targets):
    inputs = inputs.sigmoid()
    return -torch.where(targets==1, 1-inputs, inputs).log().mean()
```

Note that because we have a one-hot-encoded dependent variable, we can't directly use `nll_loss` or `softmax` (and therefore we can't use `cross_entropy`):

- `softmax`, as we saw, requires that all predictions sum to 1, and tends to push one activation to be much larger than the others (because of the use of `exp`); however, we may well have multiple objects that we're confident appear in an image, so restricting the maximum sum of activations to 1 is not a good idea. By the same reasoning, we may want the sum to be *less* than 1, if we don't think *any* of the categories appear in an image.

- `nll_loss`, as we saw, returns the value of just one activation: the single activation corresponding with the single label for an item. This doesn't make sense when we have multiple labels.

On the other hand, the `binary_cross_entropy` function, which is just `mnist_loss` along with `log`, provides just what we need, thanks to the magic of PyTorch's elementwise operations. Each activation will be compared to each target for each column, so we don't have to do anything to make this function work for multiple columns.

Jeremy Says

One of the things I really like about working with libraries like PyTorch, with broadcasting and elementwise operations, is that quite frequently I find I can write code that works equally well for a single item or a batch of items, without changes. `binary_cross_entropy` is a great example of this. By using these operations, we don't have to write loops ourselves, and can rely on PyTorch to do the looping we need as appropriate for the rank of the tensors we're working with.

PyTorch already provides this function for us. In fact, it provides a number of versions, with rather confusing names!

`F.binary_cross_entropy` and its module equivalent `nn.BCELoss` calculate cross entropy on a one-hot-encoded target, but do not include the initial `sigmoid`. Normally, for one-hot-encoded targets you'll want `F.binary_cross_entropy_with_log its` (or `nn.BCEWithLogitsLoss`), which do both sigmoid and binary cross entropy in a single function, as in the preceding example.

The equivalent for single-label datasets (like MNIST or the Pet dataset), where the target is encoded as a single integer, is `F.nll_loss` or `nn.NLLLoss` for the version without the initial softmax, and `F.cross_entropy` or `nn.CrossEntropyLoss` for the version with the initial softmax.

Since we have a one-hot-encoded target, we will use `BCEWithLogitsLoss`:

```
loss_func = nn.BCEWithLogitsLoss()
loss = loss_func(activs, y)
loss
```

```
tensor(1.0082, device='cuda:5', grad_fn=<BinaryCrossEntropyWithLogitsBackward>)
```

We don't need to tell fastai to use this loss function (although we can if we want) since it will be automatically chosen for us. fastai knows that the `DataLoaders` has multiple category labels, so it will use `nn.BCEWithLogitsLoss` by default.

One change compared to the preceding chapter is the metric we use: because this is a multilabel problem, we can't use the accuracy function. Why is that? Well, accuracy was comparing our outputs to our targets like so:

```
def accuracy(inp, targ, axis=-1):
    "Compute accuracy with `targ` when `pred` is bs * n_classes"
    pred = inp.argmax(dim=axis)
    return (pred == targ).float().mean()
```

The class predicted was the one with the highest activation (this is what argmax does). Here it doesn't work because we could have more than one prediction on a single image. After applying the sigmoid to our activations (to make them between 0 and 1), we need to decide which ones are 0s and which ones are 1s by picking a *threshold*. Each value above the threshold will be considered as a 1, and each value lower than the threshold will be considered a 0:

```
def accuracy_multi(inp, targ, thresh=0.5, sigmoid=True):
    "Compute accuracy when `inp` and `targ` are the same size."
    if sigmoid: inp = inp.sigmoid()
    return ((inp>thresh)==targ.bool()).float().mean()
```

If we pass accuracy_multi directly as a metric, it will use the default value for threshold, which is 0.5. We might want to adjust that default and create a new version of accuracy_multi that has a different default. To help with this, there is a function in Python called partial. It allows us to *bind* a function with some arguments or keyword arguments, making a new version of that function that, whenever it is called, always includes those arguments. For instance, here is a simple function taking two arguments:

```
def say_hello(name, say_what="Hello"): return f"{say_what} {name}."
say_hello('Jeremy'),say_hello('Jeremy', 'Ahoy!')
```

```
('Hello Jeremy.', 'Ahoy! Jeremy.')
```

We can switch to a French version of that function by using partial:

```
f = partial(say_hello, say_what="Bonjour")
f("Jeremy"),f("Sylvain")
```

```
('Bonjour Jeremy.', 'Bonjour Sylvain.')
```

We can now train our model. Let's try setting the accuracy threshold to 0.2 for our metric:

```
learn = cnn_learner(dls, resnet50, metrics=partial(accuracy_multi, thresh=0.2))
learn.fine_tune(3, base_lr=3e-3, freeze_epochs=4)
```

epoch	train_loss	valid_loss	accuracy_multi	time
0	0.903610	0.659728	0.263068	00:07
1	0.724266	0.346332	0.525458	00:07
2	0.415597	0.125662	0.937590	00:07
3	0.254987	0.116880	0.945418	00:07

epoch	train_loss	valid_loss	accuracy_multi	time
0	0.123872	0.132634	0.940179	00:08
1	0.112387	0.113758	0.949343	00:08
2	0.092151	0.104368	0.951195	00:08

Picking a threshold is important. If you pick a threshold that's too low, you'll often be failing to select correctly labeled objects. We can see this by changing our metric and then calling `validate`, which returns the validation loss and metrics:

```
learn.metrics = partial(accuracy_multi, thresh=0.1)
learn.validate()
```

```
(#2) [0.10436797887086868,0.93057781457901]
```

If you pick a threshold that's too high, you'll be selecting only the objects about which the model is very confident:

```
learn.metrics = partial(accuracy_multi, thresh=0.99)
learn.validate()
```

```
(#2) [0.10436797887086868,0.9416930675506592]
```

We can find the best threshold by trying a few levels and seeing what works best. This is much faster if we grab the predictions just once:

```
preds,targs = learn.get_preds()
```

Then we can call the metric directly. Note that by default `get_preds` applies the output activation function (sigmoid, in this case) for us, so we'll need to tell `accuracy_multi` to not apply it:

```
accuracy_multi(preds, targs, thresh=0.9, sigmoid=False)
```

```
TensorMultiCategory(0.9554)
```

We can now use this approach to find the best threshold level:

```
xs = torch.linspace(0.05,0.95,29)
accs = [accuracy_multi(preds, targs, thresh=i, sigmoid=False) for i in xs]
plt.plot(xs,accs);
```

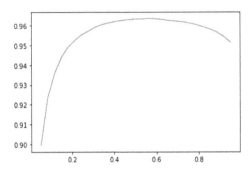

In this case, we're using the validation set to pick a hyperparameter (the threshold), which is the purpose of the validation set. Sometimes students have expressed their concern that we might be *overfitting* to the validation set, since we're trying lots of values to see which is the best. However, as you see in the plot, changing the threshold in this case results in a smooth curve, so we're clearly not picking an inappropriate outlier. This is a good example of where you have to be careful of the difference between theory (don't try lots of hyperparameter values or you might overfit the validation set) versus practice (if the relationship is smooth, it's fine to do this).

This concludes the part of this chapter dedicated to multi-label classification. Next, we'll take a look at a regression problem.

Regression

It's easy to think of deep learning models as being classified into domains, like *computer vision*, *NLP*, and so forth. And indeed, that's how fastai classifies its applications —largely because that's how most people are used to thinking of things.

But really, that's hiding a more interesting and deeper perspective. A model is defined by its independent and dependent variables, along with its loss function. That means that there's really a far wider array of models than just the simple domain-based split. Perhaps we have an independent variable that's an image, and a dependent that's text (e.g., generating a caption from an image); or perhaps we have an independent variable that's text and a dependent that's an image (e.g., generating an image from a caption—which is actually possible for deep learning to do!); or perhaps we've got images, texts, and tabular data as independent variables, and we're trying to predict product purchases…the possibilities really are endless.

To be able to move beyond fixed applications to crafting your own novel solutions to novel problems, it helps to really understand the data block API (and maybe also the mid-tier API, which we'll see later in the book). As an example, let's consider the problem of *image regression*. This refers to learning from a dataset in which the independent variable is an image, and the dependent variable is one or more floats. Often we see people treat image regression as a whole separate application—but as you'll see here, we can treat it as just another CNN on top of the data block API.

We're going to jump straight to a somewhat tricky variant of image regression, because we know you're ready for it! We're going to do a key point model. A *key point* refers to a specific location represented in an image—in this case, we'll use images of people and we'll be looking for the center of the person's face in each image. That means we'll actually be predicting *two* values for each image: the row and column of the face center.

Assembling the Data

We will use the Biwi Kinect Head Pose dataset (*https://oreil.ly/-4cO-*) for this section. We'll begin by downloading the dataset as usual:

```
path = untar_data(URLs.BIWI_HEAD_POSE)
```

Let's see what we've got!

```
path.ls()
```

```
(#50) [Path('13.obj'),Path('07.obj'),Path('06.obj'),Path('13'),Path('10'),Path('
 > 02'),Path('11'),Path('01'),Path('20.obj'),Path('17')...]
```

There are 24 directories numbered from 01 to 24 (they correspond to the different people photographed), and a corresponding *.obj* file for each (we won't need them here). Let's take a look inside one of these directories:

```
(path/'01').ls()
```

```
(#1000) [Path('01/frame_00281_pose.txt'),Path('01/frame_00078_pose.txt'),Path('0
 > 1/frame_00349_rgb.jpg'),Path('01/frame_00304_pose.txt'),Path('01/frame_00207_
 > pose.txt'),Path('01/frame_00116_rgb.jpg'),Path('01/frame_00084_rgb.jpg'),Path
 > ('01/frame_00070_rgb.jpg'),Path('01/frame_00125_pose.txt'),Path('01/frame_003
 > 24_rgb.jpg')...]
```

Inside the subdirectories, we have different frames. Each of them comes with an image (*_rgb.jpg*) and a pose file (*_pose.txt*). We can easily get all the image files recursively with `get_image_files`, and then write a function that converts an image filename to its associated pose file:

```
img_files = get_image_files(path)
def img2pose(x): return Path(f'{str(x)[:-7]}pose.txt')
img2pose(img_files[0])
```

```
Path('13/frame_00349_pose.txt')
```

Let's take a look at our first image:

```
im = PILImage.create(img_files[0])
im.shape
```

```
(480, 640)
```

```
im.to_thumb(160)
```

The Biwi dataset website (*https://oreil.ly/wHL28*) used to explain the format of the pose text file associated with each image, which shows the location of the center of the head. The details of this aren't important for our purposes, so we'll just show the function we use to extract the head center point:

```
cal = np.genfromtxt(path/'01'/'rgb.cal', skip_footer=6)
def get_ctr(f):
    ctr = np.genfromtxt(img2pose(f), skip_header=3)
    c1 = ctr[0] * cal[0][0]/ctr[2] + cal[0][2]
    c2 = ctr[1] * cal[1][1]/ctr[2] + cal[1][2]
    return tensor([c1,c2])
```

This function returns the coordinates as a tensor of two items:

```
get_ctr(img_files[0])
```

```
tensor([384.6370, 259.4787])
```

We can pass this function to DataBlock as get_y, since it is responsible for labeling each item. We'll resize the images to half their input size, to speed up training a bit.

One important point to note is that we should not just use a random splitter. The same people appear in multiple images in this dataset, but we want to ensure that our model can generalize to people that it hasn't seen yet. Each folder in the dataset contains the images for one person. Therefore, we can create a splitter function that returns True for just one person, resulting in a validation set containing just that person's images.

The only other difference from the previous data block examples is that the second block is a PointBlock. This is necessary so that fastai knows that the labels represent coordinates; that way, it knows that when doing data augmentation, it should do the same augmentation to these coordinates as it does to the images:

```
biwi = DataBlock(
    blocks=(ImageBlock, PointBlock),
    get_items=get_image_files,
    get_y=get_ctr,
    splitter=FuncSplitter(lambda o: o.parent.name=='13'),
    batch_tfms=[*aug_transforms(size=(240,320)),
                Normalize.from_stats(*imagenet_stats)]
)
```

Points and Data Augmentation

We're not aware of other libraries (except for fastai) that automatically and correctly apply data augmentation to coordinates. So, if you're working with another library, you may need to disable data augmentation for these kinds of problems.

Before doing any modeling, we should look at our data to confirm it seems OK:

```
dls = biwi.dataloaders(path)
dls.show_batch(max_n=9, figsize=(8,6))
```

That's looking good! As well as looking at the batch visually, it's a good idea to also look at the underlying tensors (especially as a student; it will help clarify your understanding of what your model is really seeing):

```
xb,yb = dls.one_batch()
xb.shape,yb.shape

(torch.Size([64, 3, 240, 320]), torch.Size([64, 1, 2]))
```

Make sure that you understand *why* these are the shapes for our mini-batches.

Here's an example of one row from the dependent variable:

```
yb[0]
```

```
tensor([[0.0111, 0.1810]], device='cuda:5')
```

As you can see, we haven't had to use a separate *image regression* application; all we've had to do is label the data and tell fastai what kinds of data the independent and dependent variables represent.

It's the same for creating our Learner. We will use the same function as before, with one new parameter, and we will be ready to train our model.

Training a Model

As usual, we can use cnn_learner to create our Learner. Remember way back in Chapter 1 how we used y_range to tell fastai the range of our targets? We'll do the same here (coordinates in fastai and PyTorch are always rescaled between –1 and +1):

```
learn = cnn_learner(dls, resnet18, y_range=(-1,1))
```

y_range is implemented in fastai using sigmoid_range, which is defined as follows:

```
def sigmoid_range(x, lo, hi): return torch.sigmoid(x) * (hi-lo) + lo
```

This is set as the final layer of the model, if y_range is defined. Take a moment to think about what this function does, and why it forces the model to output activations in the range (lo,hi).

Here's what it looks like:

```
plot_function(partial(sigmoid_range,lo=-1,hi=1), min=-4, max=4)
```

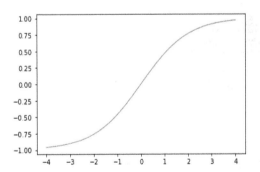

We didn't specify a loss function, which means we're getting whatever fastai chooses as the default. Let's see what it picked for us:

```
dls.loss_func
```

```
FlattenedLoss of MSELoss()
```

This makes sense, since when coordinates are used as the dependent variable, most of the time we're likely to be trying to predict something as close as possible; that's basically what MSELoss (mean squared error loss) does. If you want to use a different loss function, you can pass it to cnn_learner by using the loss_func parameter.

Note also that we didn't specify any metrics. That's because the MSE is already a useful metric for this task (although it's probably more interpretable after we take the square root).

We can pick a good learning rate with the learning rate finder:

```
learn.lr_find()
```

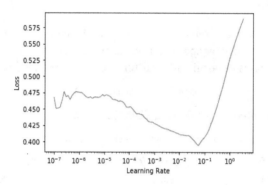

We'll try an LR of 1e-2:

```
lr = 1e-2
learn.fine_tune(3, lr)
```

epoch	train_loss	valid_loss	time
0	0.045840	0.012957	00:36
1	0.006369	0.001853	00:36
2	0.003000	0.000496	00:37
3	0.001963	0.000360	00:37
4	0.001584	0.000116	00:36

Generally, when we run this, we get a loss of around 0.0001, which corresponds to this average coordinate prediction error:

```
math.sqrt(0.0001)
```

```
0.01
```

This sounds very accurate! But it's important to take a look at our results with Learner.show_results. The left side has the actual (*ground truth*) coordinates and the right side has our model's predictions:

```
learn.show_results(ds_idx=1, max_n=3, figsize=(6,8))
```

It's quite amazing that with just a few minutes of computation, we've created such an accurate key points model, and without any special domain-specific application. This is the power of building on flexible APIs and using transfer learning! It's particularly striking that we've been able to use transfer learning so effectively, even between totally different tasks; our pretrained model was trained to do image classification, and we fine-tuned for image regression.

Conclusion

In problems that are at first glance completely different (single-label classification, multi-label classification, and regression), we end up using the same model with just different numbers of outputs. The loss function is the one thing that changes, which is why it's important to double-check that you are using the right loss function for your problem.

fastai will automatically try to pick the right one from the data you built, but if you are using pure PyTorch to build your DataLoaders, make sure you think hard about your choice of loss function, and remember that you most probably want the following:

- nn.CrossEntropyLoss for single-label classification
- nn.BCEWithLogitsLoss for multi-label classification
- nn.MSELoss for regression

Questionnaire

1. How could multi-label classification improve the usability of the bear classifier?
2. How do we encode the dependent variable in a multi-label classification problem?
3. How do you access the rows and columns of a DataFrame as if it were a matrix?
4. How do you get a column by name from a DataFrame?
5. What is the difference between a `Dataset` and `DataLoader`?
6. What does a `Datasets` object normally contain?
7. What does a `DataLoaders` object normally contain?
8. What does `lambda` do in Python?
9. What are the methods to customize how the independent and dependent variables are created with the data block API?
10. Why is softmax not an appropriate output activation function when using a one-hot-encoded target?
11. Why is `nll_loss` not an appropriate loss function when using a one-hot-encoded target?
12. What is the difference between `nn.BCELoss` and `nn.BCEWithLogitsLoss`?
13. Why can't we use regular accuracy in a multi-label problem?
14. When is it OK to tune a hyperparameter on the validation set?
15. How is `y_range` implemented in fastai? (See if you can implement it yourself and test it without peeking!)
16. What is a regression problem? What loss function should you use for such a problem?
17. What do you need to do to make sure the fastai library applies the same data augmentation to your input images and your target point coordinates?

Further Research

1. Read a tutorial about Pandas DataFrames and experiment with a few methods that look interesting to you. See the book's website for recommended tutorials.
2. Retrain the bear classifier using multi-label classification. See if you can make it work effectively with images that don't contain any bears, including showing that information in the web application. Try an image with two kinds of bears. Check whether the accuracy on the single-label dataset is impacted using multi-label classification.

CHAPTER 7

Training a State-of-the-Art Model

This chapter introduces more advanced techniques for training an image classification model and getting state-of-the-art results. You can skip it if you want to learn more about other applications of deep learning and come back to it later—knowledge of this material will not be assumed in later chapters.

We will look at what normalization is, a powerful data augmentation technique called Mixup, the progressive resizing approach, and test time augmentation. To show all of this, we are going to train a model from scratch (not using transfer learning) by using a subset of ImageNet called Imagenette (*https://oreil.ly/1uj3x*). It contains a subset of 10 very different categories from the original ImageNet dataset, making for quicker training when we want to experiment.

This is going to be much harder to do well than with our previous datasets because we're using full-size, full-color images, which are photos of objects of different sizes, in different orientations, in different lighting, and so forth. So, in this chapter we're going to introduce important techniques for getting the most out of your dataset, especially when you're training from scratch, or using transfer learning to train a model on a very different kind of dataset than the pretrained model used.

Imagenette

When fast.ai first started, people used three main datasets for building and testing computer vision models:

ImageNet
   1.3 million images of various sizes, around 500 pixels across, in 1,000 categories, which took a few days to train

MNIST

50,000 28×28-pixel grayscale handwritten digits

CIFAR10

60,000 32×32-pixel color images in 10 classes

The problem was that the smaller datasets didn't generalize effectively to the large ImageNet dataset. The approaches that worked well on ImageNet generally had to be developed and trained on ImageNet. This led to many people believing that only researchers with access to giant computing resources could effectively contribute to developing image classification algorithms.

We thought that seemed very unlikely to be true. We had never seen a study that showed that ImageNet happens to be exactly the right size, and that other datasets could not be developed that would provide useful insights. So we wanted to create a new dataset that researchers could test their algorithms on quickly and cheaply, but that would also provide insights likely to work on the full ImageNet dataset.

About three hours later, we had created Imagenette. We selected 10 classes from the full ImageNet that looked very different from one another. As we had hoped, we were able to quickly and cheaply create a classifier capable of recognizing these classes. We then tried out a few algorithmic tweaks to see how they impacted Imagenette. We found some that worked pretty well, and tested them on ImageNet as well—and we were pleased to find that our tweaks worked well on ImageNet too!

There is an important message here: the dataset you are given is not necessarily the dataset you want. It's particularly unlikely to be the dataset that you want to do your development and prototyping in. You should aim to have an iteration speed of no more than a couple of minutes—that is, when you come up with a new idea you want to try out, you should be able to train a model and see how it goes within a couple of minutes. If it's taking longer to do an experiment, think about how you could cut down your dataset, or simplify your model, to improve your experimentation speed. The more experiments you can do, the better!

Let's get started with this dataset:

```
from fastai.vision.all import *
path = untar_data(URLs.IMAGENETTE)
```

First we'll get our dataset into a `DataLoaders` object, using the *presizing* trick introduced in Chapter 5:

```
dblock = DataBlock(blocks=(ImageBlock(), CategoryBlock()),
                   get_items=get_image_files,
                   get_y=parent_label,
                   item_tfms=Resize(460),
                   batch_tfms=aug_transforms(size=224, min_scale=0.75))
dls = dblock.dataloaders(path, bs=64)
```

Then we'll do a training run that will serve as a baseline:

```
model = xresnet50(n_out=dls.c)
learn = Learner(dls, model, loss_func=CrossEntropyLossFlat(), metrics=accuracy)
learn.fit_one_cycle(5, 3e-3)
```

epoch	train_loss	valid_loss	accuracy	time
0	1.583403	2.064317	0.401792	01:03
1	1.208877	1.260106	0.601568	01:02
2	0.925265	1.036154	0.664302	01:03
3	0.730190	0.700906	0.777819	01:03
4	0.585707	0.541810	0.825243	01:03

That's a good baseline, since we are not using a pretrained model, but we can do better. When working with models that are being trained from scratch, or fine-tuned to a very different dataset from the one used for the pretraining, some additional techniques are really important. In the rest of the chapter, we'll consider some key approaches you'll want to be familiar with. The first one is *normalizing* your data.

Normalization

When training a model, it helps if your input data is *normalized*—that is, has a mean of 0 and a standard deviation of 1. But most images and computer vision libraries use values between 0 and 255 for pixels, or between 0 and 1; in either case, your data is not going to have a mean of 0 and a standard deviation of 1.

Let's grab a batch of our data and look at those values, by averaging over all axes except for the channel axis, which is axis 1:

```
x,y = dls.one_batch()
x.mean(dim=[0,2,3]),x.std(dim=[0,2,3])

(TensorImage([0.4842, 0.4711, 0.4511], device='cuda:5'),
 TensorImage([0.2873, 0.2893, 0.3110], device='cuda:5'))
```

As we expected, the mean and standard deviation are not very close to the desired values. Fortunately, normalizing the data is easy to do in fastai by adding the Normalize transform. This acts on a whole mini-batch at once, so you can add it to the batch_tfms section of your data block. You need to pass to this transform the mean and standard deviation that you want to use; fastai comes with the standard ImageNet mean and standard deviation already defined. (If you do not pass any statistics to the Normalize transform, fastai will automatically calculate them from a single batch of your data.)

Let's add this transform (using imagenet_stats, as Imagenette is a subset of Image-Net) and take a look at one batch now:

```
def get_dls(bs, size):
    dblock = DataBlock(blocks=(ImageBlock, CategoryBlock),
                       get_items=get_image_files,
                       get_y=parent_label,
                       item_tfms=Resize(460),
                       batch_tfms=[*aug_transforms(size=size, min_scale=0.75),
                                   Normalize.from_stats(*imagenet_stats)])
    return dblock.dataloaders(path, bs=bs)

dls = get_dls(64, 224)

x,y = dls.one_batch()
x.mean(dim=[0,2,3]),x.std(dim=[0,2,3])

(TensorImage([-0.0787,  0.0525,  0.2136], device='cuda:5'),
 TensorImage([1.2330, 1.2112, 1.3031], device='cuda:5'))
```

Let's check what effect this had on training our model:

```
model = xresnet50()
learn = Learner(dls, model, loss_func=CrossEntropyLossFlat(), metrics=accuracy)
learn.fit_one_cycle(5, 3e-3)
```

epoch	train_loss	valid_loss	accuracy	time
0	1.632865	2.250024	0.391337	01:02
1	1.294041	1.579932	0.517177	01:02
2	0.960535	1.069164	0.657207	01:04
3	0.730220	0.767433	0.771845	01:05
4	0.577889	0.550673	0.824496	01:06

Although it helped only a little here, normalization becomes especially important when using pretrained models. The pretrained model knows how to work with only data of the type that it has seen before. If the average pixel value was 0 in the data it was trained with, but your data has 0 as the minimum possible value of a pixel, then the model is going to be seeing something very different from what is intended!

This means that when you distribute a model, you need to also distribute the statistics used for normalization, since anyone using it for inference or transfer learning will need to use the same statistics. By the same token, if you're using a model that someone else has trained, make sure you find out what normalization statistics they used, and match them.

We didn't have to handle normalization in previous chapters because when using a pretrained model through cnn_learner, the fastai library automatically adds the proper Normalize transform; the model has been pretrained with certain statistics in Normalize (usually coming from the ImageNet dataset), so the library can fill those in for you. Note that this applies to only pretrained models, which is why we need to add this information manually here, when training from scratch.

All our training up until now has been done at size 224. We could have begun training at a smaller size before going to that. This is called *progressive resizing*.

Progressive Resizing

When fast.ai and its team of students won the DAWNBench competition (*https://oreil.ly/16tar*) in 2018, one of the most important innovations was something very simple: start training using small images, and end training using large images. Spending most of the epochs training with small images helps training complete much faster. Completing training using large images makes the final accuracy much higher. We call this approach *progressive resizing*.

Jargon: Progressive Resizing

Gradually using larger and larger images as you train.

As we have seen, the kinds of features that are learned by convolutional neural networks are not in any way specific to the size of the image—early layers find things like edges and gradients, and later layers may find things like noses and sunsets. So, when we change image size in the middle of training, it doesn't mean that we have to find totally different parameters for our model.

But clearly there are some differences between small images and big ones, so we shouldn't expect our model to continue working exactly as well, with no changes at all. Does this remind you of something? When we developed this idea, it reminded us of transfer learning! We are trying to get our model to learn to do something a little bit different from what it has learned to do before. Therefore, we should be able to use the fine_tune method after we resize our images.

Progressive resizing has an additional benefit: it is another form of data augmentation. Therefore, you should expect to see better generalization of your models that are trained with progressive resizing.

To implement progressive resizing, it is most convenient if you first create a get_dls function that takes an image size and a batch size, as we did in the previous section, and returns your DataLoaders.

Now you can create your DataLoaders with a small size and use and fit_one_cycle in the usual way, training for fewer epochs than you might otherwise do:

```
dls = get_dls(128, 128)
learn = Learner(dls, xresnet50(n_out=dls.c), loss_func=CrossEntropyLossFlat(),
                metrics=accuracy)
learn.fit_one_cycle(4, 3e-3)
```

epoch	train_loss	valid_loss	accuracy	time
0	1.902943	2.447006	0.401419	00:30
1	1.315203	1.572992	0.525765	00:30
2	1.001199	0.767886	0.759149	00:30
3	0.765864	0.665562	0.797984	00:30

Then you can replace the `DataLoaders` inside the `Learner`, and fine-tune:

```
learn.dls = get_dls(64, 224)
learn.fine_tune(5, 1e-3)
```

epoch	train_loss	valid_loss	accuracy	time
0	0.985213	1.654063	0.565721	01:06

epoch	train_loss	valid_loss	accuracy	time
0	0.706869	0.689622	0.784541	01:07
1	0.739217	0.928541	0.712472	01:07
2	0.629462	0.788906	0.764003	01:07
3	0.491912	0.502622	0.836445	01:06
4	0.414880	0.431332	0.863331	01:06

As you can see, we're getting much better performance, and the initial training on small images was much faster on each epoch.

You can repeat the process of increasing size and training more epochs as many times as you like, for as big an image as you wish—but of course, you will not get any benefit by using an image size larger than the size of your images on disk.

Note that for transfer learning, progressive resizing may actually hurt performance. This is most likely to happen if your pretrained model was quite similar to your transfer learning task and the dataset and was trained on similar-sized images, so the weights don't need to be changed much. In that case, training on smaller images may damage the pretrained weights.

On the other hand, if the transfer learning task is going to use images that are of different sizes, shapes, or styles than those used in the pretraining task, progressive resizing will probably help. As always, the answer to "Will it help?" is "Try it!"

Another thing we could try is applying data augmentation to the validation set. Up until now, we have applied it only on the training set; the validation set always gets the same images. But maybe we could try to make predictions for a few augmented versions of the validation set and average them. We'll consider this approach next.

Test Time Augmentation

We have been using random cropping as a way to get some useful data augmentation, which leads to better generalization, and results in a need for less training data. When we use random cropping, fastai will automatically use center-cropping for the validation set—that is, it will select the largest square area it can in the center of the image, without going past the image's edges.

This can often be problematic. For instance, in a multi-label dataset, sometimes there are small objects toward the edges of an image; these could be entirely cropped out by center cropping. Even for problems such as our pet breed classification example, it's possible that a critical feature necessary for identifying the correct breed, such as the color of the nose, could be cropped out.

One solution to this problem is to avoid random cropping entirely. Instead, we could simply squish or stretch the rectangular images to fit into a square space. But then we miss out on a very useful data augmentation, and we also make the image recognition more difficult for our model, because it has to learn how to recognize squished and squeezed images, rather than just correctly proportioned images.

Another solution is to not center crop for validation, but instead to select a number of areas to crop from the original rectangular image, pass each of them through our model, and take the maximum or average of the predictions. In fact, we could do this not just for different crops, but for different values across all of our test time augmentation parameters. This is known as *test time augmentation* (TTA).

Jargon: Test Time Augmentation (TTA)

During inference or validation, creating multiple versions of each image using data augmentation, and then taking the average or maximum of the predictions for each augmented version of the image.

Depending on the dataset, test time augmentation can result in dramatic improvements in accuracy. It does not change the time required to train at all, but will increase the amount of time required for validation or inference by the number of test-time-augmented images requested. By default, fastai will use the unaugmented center crop image plus four randomly augmented images.

You can pass any `DataLoader` to fastai's `tta` method; by default, it will use your validation set:

```
preds,targs = learn.tta()
accuracy(preds, targs).item()
```

```
0.8737863898277283
```

As we can see, using TTA gives us good a boost in performance, with no additional training required. However, it does make inference slower—if you're averaging five images for TTA, inference will be five times slower.

We've seen a few examples of how data augmentation helps train better models. Let's now focus on a new data augmentation technique called *Mixup*.

Mixup

Mixup, introduced in the 2017 paper "*mixup*: Beyond Empirical Risk Minimization" (*https://oreil.ly/UvIkN*) by Hongyi Zhang et al., is a powerful data augmentation technique that can provide dramatically higher accuracy, especially when you don't have much data and don't have a pretrained model that was trained on data similar to your dataset. The paper explains: "While data augmentation consistently leads to improved generalization, the procedure is dataset-dependent, and thus requires the use of expert knowledge." For instance, it's common to flip images as part of data augmentation, but should you flip only horizontally or also vertically? The answer is that it depends on your dataset. In addition, if flipping (for instance) doesn't provide enough data augmentation for you, you can't "flip more." It's helpful to have data augmentation techniques that "dial up" or "dial down" the amount of change, to see what works best for you.

Mixup works as follows, for each image:

1. Select another image from your dataset at random.
2. Pick a weight at random.
3. Take a weighted average (using the weight from step 2) of the selected image with your image; this will be your independent variable.
4. Take a weighted average (with the same weight) of this image's labels with your image's labels; this will be your dependent variable.

In pseudocode, we're doing this (where t is the weight for our weighted average):

```
image2,target2 = dataset[randint(0,len(dataset)]
t = random_float(0.5,1.0)
new_image = t * image1 + (1-t) * image2
new_target = t * target1 + (1-t) * target2
```

For this to work, our targets need to be one-hot encoded. The paper describes this using the equations in Figure 7-1 (where λ is the same as t in our pseudocode).

Contribution Motivated by these issues, we introduce a simple and data-agnostic data augmentation routine, termed *mixup* (Section 2). In a nutshell, *mixup* constructs virtual training examples

$$\tilde{x} = \lambda x_i + (1 - \lambda)x_j, \qquad \text{where } x_i, x_j \text{ are raw input vectors}$$
$$\tilde{y} = \lambda y_i + (1 - \lambda)y_j, \qquad \text{where } y_i, y_j \text{ are one-hot label encodings}$$

Figure 7-1. An excerpt from the Mixup paper

Papers and Math

We're going to be looking at more and more research papers from here on in the book. Now that you have the basic jargon, you might be surprised to discover how much of them you can understand, with a little practice! One issue you'll notice is that Greek letters, such as λ, appear in most papers. It's a good idea to learn the names of all the Greek letters, since otherwise it's hard to read the papers to yourself and remember them (or to read code based on them, since code often uses the names of the Greek letters spelled out, such as `lambda`).

The bigger issue with papers is that they use math, instead of code, to explain what's going on. If you don't have much of a math background, this will likely be intimidating and confusing at first. But remember: what is being shown in the math is something that will be implemented in code. It's just another way of talking about the same thing! After reading a few papers, you'll pick up more and more of the notation. If you don't know what a symbol is, try looking it up in Wikipedia's list of mathematical symbols (*https://oreil.ly/m5ad5*) or drawing it in Detexify (*https://oreil.ly/92u4d*), which (using machine learning!) will find the name of your hand-drawn symbol. Then you can search online for that name to find out what it's for.

Figure 7-2 shows what it looks like when we take a *linear combination* of images, as done in Mixup.

Figure 7-2. Mixing a church and a gas station

The third image is built by adding 0.3 times the first one and 0.7 times the second. In this example, should the model predict "church" or "gas station"? The right answer is 30% church and 70% gas station, since that's what we'll get if we take the linear combination of the one-hot-encoded targets. For instance, suppose we have 10 classes, and "church" is represented by the index 2 and "gas station" by the index 7. The one-hot-encoded representations are as follows:

```
[0, 0, 1, 0, 0, 0, 0, 0, 0, 0] and [0, 0, 0, 0, 0, 0, 0, 1, 0, 0]
```

So here is our final target:

```
[0, 0, 0.3, 0, 0, 0, 0, 0.7, 0, 0]
```

This all done for us inside fastai by adding a *callback* to our `Learner`. `Callbacks` are what is used inside fastai to inject custom behavior in the training loop (like a learning rate schedule, or training in mixed precision). You'll be learning all about callbacks, including how to make your own, in Chapter 16. For now, all you need to know is that you use the `cbs` parameter to `Learner` to pass callbacks.

Here is how we train a model with Mixup:

```
model = xresnet50(n_out=dls.c)
learn = Learner(dls, model, loss_func=CrossEntropyLossFlat(),
                metrics=accuracy, cbs=MixUp())
learn.fit_one_cycle(5, 3e-3)
```

What happens when we train a model with data that's "mixed up" in this way? Clearly, it's going to be harder to train, because it's harder to see what's in each image. And the model has to predict two labels per image, rather than just one, as well as figuring out how much each one is weighted. Overfitting seems less likely to be a problem, however, because we're not showing the same image in each epoch, but are instead showing a random combination of two images.

Mixup requires far more epochs to train to get better accuracy, compared to other augmentation approaches we've seen. You can try training Imagenette with and without Mixup by using the *examples/train_imagenette.py* script in the fastai repo (*https://oreil.ly/lrGXE*). At the time of writing, the leaderboard in the Imagenette repo (*https://oreil.ly/3Gt56*) is showing that Mixup is used for all leading results for trainings of >80 epochs, and for fewer epochs Mixup is not being used. This is in line with our experience of using Mixup too.

One of the reasons that Mixup is so exciting is that it can be applied to types of data other than photos. In fact, some people have even shown good results by using Mixup on activations *inside* their models, not just on inputs—this allows Mixup to be used for NLP and other data types too.

There's another subtle issue that Mixup deals with for us, which is that it's not actually possible with the models we've seen before for our loss to ever be perfect. The problem is that our labels are 1s and 0s, but the outputs of softmax and sigmoid can never equal 1 or 0. This means training our model pushes our activations ever closer to those values, such that the more epochs we do, the more extreme our activations become.

With Mixup, we no longer have that problem, because our labels will be exactly 1 or 0 only if we happen to "mix" with another image of the same class. The rest of the time, our labels will be a linear combination, such as the 0.7 and 0.3 we got in the church and gas station example earlier.

One issue with this, however, is that Mixup is "accidentally" making the labels bigger than 0 or smaller than 1. That is to say, we're not *explicitly* telling our model that we want to change the labels in this way. So, if we want to make the labels closer to or further away from 0 and 1, we have to change the amount of Mixup—which also changes the amount of data augmentation, which might not be what we want. There is, however, a way to handle this more directly, which is to use *label smoothing*.

Label Smoothing

In the theoretical expression of loss, in classification problems, our targets are one-hot encoded (in practice, we tend to avoid doing this to save memory, but what we compute is the same loss as if we had used one-hot encoding). That means the model is trained to return 0 for all categories but one, for which it is trained to return 1. Even 0.999 is not "good enough"; the model will get gradients and learn to predict activations with even higher confidence. This encourages overfitting and gives you at inference time a model that is not going to give meaningful probabilities: it will always say 1 for the predicted category even if it's not too sure, just because it was trained this way.

This can become very harmful if your data is not perfectly labeled. In the bear classifier we studied in Chapter 2, we saw that some of the images were mislabeled, or contained two different kinds of bears. In general, your data will never be perfect. Even if the labels were manually produced by humans, they could make mistakes, or have differences of opinions on images that are harder to label.

Instead, we could replace all our 1s with a number a bit less than 1, and our 0s with a number a bit more than 0, and then train. This is called *label smoothing*. By encouraging your model to be less confident, label smoothing will make your training more robust, even if there is mislabeled data. The result will be a model that generalizes better at inference.

This is how label smoothing works in practice: we start with one-hot-encoded labels, then replace all 0s with $\frac{\epsilon}{N}$ (that's the Greek letter *epsilon*, which is what was used in the paper that introduced label smoothing (*https://oreil.ly/L3ypf*) and is used in the fastai code), where N is the number of classes and ϵ is a parameter (usually 0.1, which would mean we are 10% unsure of our labels). Since we want the labels to add up to

1, we also replace the 1s with $1 - \epsilon + \frac{\epsilon}{N}$. This way, we don't encourage the model to predict something overconfidently. In our Imagenette example that has 10 classes, the targets become something like this (here for a target that corresponds to the index 3):

```
[0.01, 0.01, 0.01, 0.91, 0.01, 0.01, 0.01, 0.01, 0.01, 0.01]
```

In practice, we don't want to one-hot encode the labels, and fortunately we won't need to (the one-hot encoding is just good to explain label smoothing and visualize it).

Label Smoothing, the Paper

Here is how the reasoning behind label smoothing was explained in the paper by Christian Szegedy et al.:

> This maximum is not achievable for finite z_k but is approached if $z_y \gg z_k$ for all $k \neq y$—that is, if the logit corresponding to the ground-truth label is much [greater] than all other logits. This, however, can cause two problems. First, it may result in over-fitting: if the model learns to assign full probability to the ground-truth label for each training example, it is not guaranteed to generalize. Second, it encourages the differences between the largest logit and all others to become large, and this, combined with the bounded gradient $\frac{\partial \ell}{\partial z_k}$, reduces the ability of the model to adapt. Intuitively, this happens because the model becomes too confident about its predictions.

Let's practice our paper-reading skills to try to interpret this. "This maximum" is referring to the previous part of the paragraph, which talked about the fact that 1 is the value of the label for the positive class. So, it's not possible for any value (except infinity) to result in 1 after sigmoid or softmax. In a paper, you won't normally see "any value" written; instead, it will get a symbol, which in this case is z_k. This shorthand is helpful in a paper, because it can be referred to again later, and the reader will know which value is being discussed.

Then it says: "if $z_y \gg z_k$ for all $k \neq y$." In this case, the paper immediately follows the math with an English description, which is handy because you can just read that. In the math, the y is referring to the target (y is defined earlier in the paper; sometimes it's hard to find where symbols are defined, but nearly all papers will define all their symbols somewhere), and z_y is the activation corresponding to the target. So to get close to 1, this activation needs to be much higher than all the others for that prediction.

Next, consider the statement "if the model learns to assign full probability to the ground-truth label for each training example, it is not guaranteed to generalize." This is saying that making z_y really big means we'll need large weights and large activations throughout our model. Large weights lead to "bumpy" functions, where a small change in input results in a big change to predictions. This is really bad for generalization, because it means just one pixel changing a bit could change our prediction entirely!

Finally, we have "it encourages the differences between the largest logit and all others to become large, and this, combined with the bounded gradient $\frac{\partial \ell}{\partial z_k}$, reduces the ability of the model to adapt." The gradient of cross entropy, remember, is basically out put - target. Both output and target are between 0 and 1, so the difference is between -1 and 1, which is why the paper says the gradient is "bounded" (it can't be infinite). Therefore, our SGD steps are bounded too. "Reduces the ability of the model to adapt" means that it is hard for it to be updated in a transfer learning setting. This follows because the difference in loss due to incorrect predictions is unbounded, but we can take only a limited step each time.

To use this in practice, we just have to change the loss function in our call to Learner:

```
model = xresnet50(n_out=dls.c)
learn = Learner(dls, model, loss_func=LabelSmoothingCrossEntropy(),
                metrics=accuracy)
learn.fit_one_cycle(5, 3e-3)
```

As with Mixup, you won't generally see significant improvements from label smoothing until you train more epochs. Try it yourself and see: how many epochs do you have to train before label smoothing shows an improvement?

Conclusion

You have now seen everything you need to train a state-of-the-art model in computer vision, whether from scratch or using transfer learning. Now all you have to do is experiment on your own problems! See if training longer with Mixup and/or label smoothing avoids overfitting and gives you better results. Try progressive resizing and test time augmentation.

Most importantly, remember that if your dataset is big, there is no point prototyping on the whole thing. Find a small subset that is representative of the whole, as we did with Imagenette, and experiment on it.

In the next three chapters, we will look at the other applications directly supported by fastai: collaborative filtering, tabular modeling, and working with text. We will go back to computer vision in the next section of the book, with a deep dive into convolutional neural networks in Chapter 13.

Questionnaire

1. What is the difference between ImageNet and Imagenette? When is it better to experiment on one versus the other?

2. What is normalization?

3. Why didn't we have to care about normalization when using a pretrained model?

4. What is progressive resizing?

5. Implement progressive resizing in your own project. Did it help?

6. What is test time augmentation? How do you use it in fastai?

7. Is using TTA at inference slower or faster than regular inference? Why?

8. What is Mixup? How do you use it in fastai?

9. Why does Mixup prevent the model from being too confident?

10. Why does training with Mixup for five epochs end up worse than training without Mixup?

11. What is the idea behind label smoothing?

12. What problems in your data can label smoothing help with?

13. When using label smoothing with five categories, what is the target associated with the index 1?

14. What is the first step to take when you want to prototype quick experiments on a new dataset?

Further Research

1. Use the fastai documentation to build a function that crops an image to a square in each of the four corners; then implement a TTA method that averages the predictions on a center crop and those four crops. Did it help? Is it better than the TTA method of fastai?

2. Find the Mixup paper on arXiv and read it. Pick one or two more recent articles introducing variants of Mixup and read them; then try to implement them on your problem.

3. Find the script training Imagenette using Mixup and use it as an example to build a script for a long training on your own project. Execute it and see if it helps.

4. Read the sidebar "Label Smoothing, the Paper" on page 250; then look at the relevant section of the original paper and see if you can follow it. Don't be afraid to ask for help!

CHAPTER 8

Collaborative Filtering Deep Dive

One common problem to solve is having a number of users and a number of products, and you want to recommend which products are most likely to be useful for which users. Many variations exist: for example, recommending movies (such as on Netflix), figuring out what to highlight for a user on a home page, deciding what stories to show in a social media feed, and so forth. A general solution to this problem, called *collaborative filtering*, works like this: look at which products the current user has used or liked, find other users who have used or liked similar products, and then recommend other products that those users have used or liked.

For example, on Netflix, you may have watched lots of movies that are science fiction, full of action, and were made in the 1970s. Netflix may not know these particular properties of the films you have watched, but it will be able to see that other people who have watched the same movies that you watched also tended to watch other movies that are science fiction, full of action, and were made in the 1970s. In other words, to use this approach, we don't necessarily need to know anything about the movies except who likes to watch them.

There is a more general class of problems that this approach can solve, not necessarily involving users and products. Indeed, for collaborative filtering, we more commonly refer to *items*, rather than *products*. Items could be links that people click, diagnoses that are selected for patients, and so forth.

The key foundational idea is that of *latent factors*. In the Netflix example, we started with the assumption that you like old, action-packed sci-fi movies. But you never told Netflix that you like these kinds of movies. And Netflix never needed to add columns to its movies table saying which movies are of these types. Still, there must be some underlying concept of sci-fi, action, and movie age, and these concepts must be relevant for at least some people's movie-watching decisions.

For this chapter, we are going to work on this movie recommendation problem. We'll start by getting some data suitable for a collaborative filtering model.

A First Look at the Data

We do not have access to Netflix's entire dataset of movie watching history, but there is a great dataset that we can use, called MovieLens (*https://oreil.ly/gP3Q5*). This dataset contains tens of millions of movie rankings (a combination of a movie ID, a user ID, and a numeric rating), although we will just use a subset of 100,000 of them for our example. If you're interested, it would be a great learning project to try to replicate this approach on the full 25-million recommendation dataset, which you can get from their website.

The dataset is available through the usual fastai function:

```
from fastai.collab import *
from fastai.tabular.all import *
path = untar_data(URLs.ML_100k)
```

According to the *README*, the main table is in the file *u.data*. It is tab-separated and the columns are, respectively, user, movie, rating, and timestamp. Since those names are not encoded, we need to indicate them when reading the file with Pandas. Here is a way to open this table and take a look:

```
ratings = pd.read_csv(path/'u.data', delimiter='\t', header=None,
                      names=['user','movie','rating','timestamp'])
ratings.head()
```

	user	movie	rating	timestamp
0	196	242	3	881250949
1	186	302	3	891717742
2	22	377	1	878887116
3	244	51	2	880606923
4	166	346	1	886397596

Although this has all the information we need, it is not a particularly helpful way for humans to look at this data. Figure 8-1 shows the same data cross-tabulated into a human-friendly table.

userId \ movieId	27	49	57	72	79	89	92	99	143	179	180	197	402	417	505
14	3.0	5.0	1.0	3.0	4.0	4.0	5.0	2.0	5.0	5.0	4.0	5.0	5.0	2.0	5.0
29	5.0	5.0	5.0	4.0	5.0	4.0	4.0	5.0	4.0	4.0	5.0	5.0	3.0	4.0	5.0
72	4.0	5.0	5.0	4.0	5.0	3.0	4.5	5.0	4.5	5.0	5.0	5.0	4.5	5.0	4.0
211	5.0	4.0	4.0	3.0	5.0	3.0	4.0	4.5	4.0		3.0	3.0	5.0	3.0	
212	2.5		2.0	5.0		4.0	2.5		5.0	5.0	3.0	3.0	4.0	3.0	2.0
293	3.0		4.0	4.0	4.0	3.0		3.0	4.0	4.0	4.5	4.0	4.5	4.0	
310	3.0	3.0	5.0	4.5	5.0	4.5	2.0	4.5	4.0	3.0	4.5	4.5	4.0	3.0	4.0
379	5.0	5.0	5.0	4.0		4.0	5.0	4.0	4.0	4.0		3.0	5.0	4.0	4.0
451	4.0	5.0	4.0	5.0	4.0	4.0	5.0	5.0	4.0	4.0	4.0	4.0	2.0	3.5	5.0
467	3.0	3.5	3.0	2.5			3.0	3.5	3.5	3.0	3.5	3.0	3.0	4.0	4.0
508	5.0	5.0	4.0	3.0	5.0	2.0	4.0	4.0	5.0	5.0	5.0	3.0	4.5	3.0	4.5
546		5.0	2.0	3.0	5.0		5.0	5.0		2.5	2.0	3.5	3.5	3.5	5.0
563	1.0	5.0	3.0	5.0	4.0	5.0	5.0		2.0	5.0	5.0	3.0	3.0	4.0	5.0
579	4.5	4.5	3.5	3.0	4.0	4.5	4.0	4.0	4.0	4.0	3.5	3.0	4.5	4.0	4.5
623		5.0	3.0	3.0		3.0	5.0		5.0	5.0	5.0	5.0	2.0	5.0	4.0

Figure 8-1. Crosstab of movies and users

We have selected just a few of the most popular movies, and users who watch the most movies, for this crosstab example. The empty cells in this table are the things that we would like our model to learn to fill in. Those are the places where a user has not reviewed the movie yet, presumably because they have not watched it. For each user, we would like to figure out which of those movies they might be most likely to enjoy.

If we knew for each user to what degree they liked each important category that a movie might fall into, such as genre, age, preferred directors and actors, and so forth, and we knew the same information about each movie, then a simple way to fill in this table would be to multiply this information together for each movie and use a combination. For instance, assuming these factors range between –1 and +1, with positive numbers indicating stronger matches and negative numbers weaker ones, and the categories are science-fiction, action, and old movies, then we could represent the movie *The Rise of Skywalker* as follows:

```
rise_skywalker = np.array([0.98,0.9,-0.9])
```

Here, for instance, we are scoring *very science-fiction* as 0.98, *very action* as 0.9, and *very not old* as –0.9. We could represent a user who likes modern sci-fi action movies as follows:

```
user1 = np.array([0.9,0.8,-0.6])
```

We can now calculate the match between this combination:

```
(user1*rise_skywalker).sum()
```

```
2.1420000000000003
```

When we multiply two vectors together and add up the results, this is known as the *dot product*. It is used a lot in machine learning and forms the basis of matrix multiplication. We will be looking a lot more at matrix multiplication and dot products in Chapter 17.

Jargon: Dot Product

The mathematical operation of multiplying the elements of two vectors together, and then summing up the result.

On the other hand, we might represent the movie *Casablanca* as follows:

```
casablanca = np.array([-0.99,-0.3,0.8])
```

The match between this combination is shown here:

```
(user1*casablanca).sum()
```

```
-1.611
```

Since we don't know what the latent factors are, and we don't know how to score them for each user and movie, we should learn them.

Learning the Latent Factors

There is surprisingly little difference between specifying the structure of a model, as we did in the preceding section, and learning one, since we can just use our general gradient descent approach.

Step 1 of this approach is to randomly initialize some parameters. These parameters will be a set of latent factors for each user and movie. We will have to decide how many to use. We will discuss how to select this shortly, but for illustrative purposes, let's use 5 for now. Because each user will have a set of these factors, and each movie will have a set of these factors, we can show these randomly initialized values right next to the users and movies in our crosstab, and we can then fill in the dot products for each of these combinations in the middle. For example, Figure 8-2 shows what it looks like in Microsoft Excel, with the top-left cell formula displayed as an example.

Step 2 of this approach is to calculate our predictions. As we've discussed, we can do this by simply taking the dot product of each movie with each user. If, for instance, the first latent user factor represents how much the user likes action movies and the first latent movie factor represents whether the movie has a lot of action or not, the product of those will be particularly high if either the user likes action movies and the movie has a lot of action in it, or the user doesn't like action movies and the movie doesn't have any action in it. On the other hand, if we have a mismatch (a user loves action movies but the movie isn't an action film, or the user doesn't like action movies and it is one), the product will be very low.

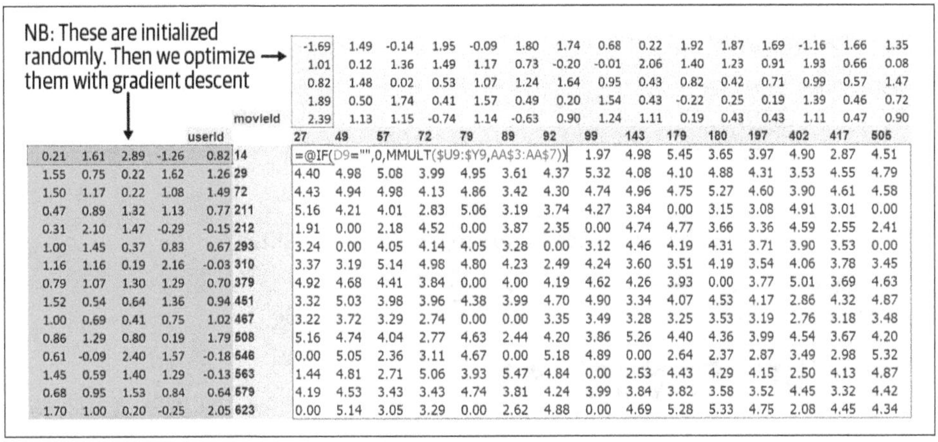

NB: These are initialized randomly. Then we optimize them with gradient descent →

-1.69	1.49	-0.14	1.95	-0.09	1.80	1.74	0.68	0.22	1.92	1.87	1.69	-1.16	1.66	1.35
1.01	0.12	1.36	1.49	1.17	0.73	-0.20	-0.01	2.06	1.40	1.23	0.91	1.93	0.66	0.08
0.82	1.48	0.02	0.53	1.07	1.24	1.64	0.95	0.43	0.82	0.42	0.71	0.99	0.57	1.47
1.89	0.50	1.74	0.41	1.57	0.49	0.20	1.54	0.43	-0.22	0.25	0.19	1.39	0.46	0.72
2.39	1.13	1.15	-0.74	1.14	-0.63	0.90	1.24	1.11	0.19	0.43	0.43	1.11	0.47	0.90

userId → / movieId

					movieId	27	49	57	72	79	89	92	99	143	179	180	197	402	417	505
0.21	1.61	2.89	-1.26	0.82	14	=@IF(D9="",0,MMULT($U9:$Y9,AA$3:AA$7))							1.97	4.98	5.45	3.65	3.97	4.90	2.87	4.51
1.55	0.75	0.22	1.62	1.26	29	4.40	4.98	5.08	3.99	4.95	3.61	4.37	5.32	4.08	4.10	4.88	4.31	3.53	4.55	4.79
1.50	1.17	0.22	1.08	1.49	72	4.43	4.94	4.98	4.13	4.86	3.42	4.30	4.74	4.96	4.75	5.27	4.60	3.90	4.61	4.58
0.47	0.89	1.32	1.13	0.77	211	5.16	4.21	4.01	2.83	5.06	3.19	3.74	4.27	3.84	0.00	3.15	3.08	4.91	3.01	0.00
0.31	2.10	1.47	-0.29	-0.15	212	1.91	0.00	2.18	4.52	0.00	3.87	2.35	0.00	4.74	4.77	3.66	3.36	4.59	2.55	2.41
1.00	1.45	0.37	0.83	0.67	293	3.24	0.00	4.05	4.14	4.05	3.28	0.00	3.12	4.46	4.19	4.31	3.71	3.90	3.53	0.00
1.16	1.16	0.19	2.16	-0.03	310	3.37	3.19	5.14	4.98	4.80	4.23	2.49	4.24	3.60	3.51	4.19	3.54	4.06	3.78	3.45
0.79	1.07	1.30	1.29	0.70	379	4.92	4.68	4.41	3.84	0.00	4.00	4.19	4.62	4.26	3.93	0.00	3.77	5.01	3.69	4.63
1.52	0.54	0.64	1.36	0.94	451	3.32	5.03	3.98	3.96	4.38	3.99	4.70	4.90	3.34	4.07	4.53	4.17	2.86	4.32	4.87
1.00	0.69	0.41	0.75	1.02	467	3.22	3.72	3.29	2.74	0.00	0.00	3.35	3.49	3.28	3.25	3.53	3.19	2.76	3.18	3.48
0.86	1.29	0.80	0.19	1.79	508	5.16	4.74	4.04	2.77	4.63	2.44	4.20	3.86	5.26	4.40	4.36	3.99	4.54	3.67	4.20
0.61	-0.09	2.40	1.57	-0.18	546	0.00	5.05	2.36	3.11	4.67	0.00	5.18	4.89	0.00	2.64	2.37	2.87	3.49	2.98	5.32
1.45	0.59	1.40	1.29	-0.13	563	1.44	4.81	2.71	5.06	3.93	5.47	4.84	0.00	2.53	4.43	4.29	4.15	2.50	4.13	4.87
0.68	0.95	1.53	0.84	0.64	579	4.19	4.53	3.43	3.43	4.74	3.81	4.24	3.99	3.84	3.82	3.58	3.52	4.45	3.32	4.42
1.70	1.00	0.20	-0.25	2.05	623	0.00	5.14	3.05	3.29	0.00	2.62	4.88	0.00	4.69	5.28	5.33	4.75	2.08	4.45	4.34

Figure 8-2. Latent factors with crosstab

Step 3 is to calculate our loss. We can use any loss function that we wish; let's pick mean squared error for now, since that is one reasonable way to represent the accuracy of a prediction.

That's all we need. With this in place, we can optimize our parameters (the latent factors) using stochastic gradient descent, such as to minimize the loss. At each step, the stochastic gradient descent optimizer will calculate the match between each movie and each user using the dot product, and will compare it to the actual rating that each user gave to each movie. It will then calculate the derivative of this value and step the weights by multiplying this by the learning rate. After doing this lots of times, the loss will get better and better, and the recommendations will also get better and better.

To use the usual `Learner.fit` function, we will need to get our data into a `DataLoaders`, so let's focus on that now.

Creating the DataLoaders

When showing the data, we would rather see movie titles than their IDs. The table `u.item` contains the correspondence of IDs to titles:

```
movies = pd.read_csv(path/'u.item',  delimiter='|', encoding='latin-1',
                    usecols=(0,1), names=('movie','title'), header=None)
movies.head()
```

	movie	title
0	1	Toy Story (1995)
1	2	GoldenEye (1995)
2	3	Four Rooms (1995)
3	4	Get Shorty (1995)
4	5	Copycat (1995)

We can merge this with our `ratings` table to get the user ratings by title:

```
ratings = ratings.merge(movies)
ratings.head()
```

	user	movie	rating	timestamp	title
0	196	242	3	881250949	Kolya (1996)
1	63	242	3	875747190	Kolya (1996)
2	226	242	5	883888671	Kolya (1996)
3	154	242	3	879138235	Kolya (1996)
4	306	242	5	876503793	Kolya (1996)

We can then build a `DataLoaders` object from this table. By default, it takes the first column for the user, the second column for the item (here our movies), and the third column for the ratings. We need to change the value of `item_name` in our case to use the titles instead of the IDs:

```
dls = CollabDataLoaders.from_df(ratings, item_name='title', bs=64)
dls.show_batch()
```

	user	title	rating
0	207	Four Weddings and a Funeral (1994)	3
1	565	Remains of the Day, The (1993)	5
2	506	Kids (1995)	1
3	845	Chasing Amy (1997)	3
4	798	Being Human (1993)	2
5	500	Down by Law (1986)	4
6	409	Much Ado About Nothing (1993)	3
7	721	Braveheart (1995)	5
8	316	Psycho (1960)	2
9	883	Judgment Night (1993)	5

To represent collaborative filtering in PyTorch, we can't just use the crosstab representation directly, especially if we want it to fit into our deep learning framework. We can represent our movie and user latent factor tables as simple matrices:

```
n_users  = len(dls.classes['user'])
n_movies = len(dls.classes['title'])
n_factors = 5

user_factors = torch.randn(n_users, n_factors)
movie_factors = torch.randn(n_movies, n_factors)
```

To calculate the result for a particular movie and user combination, we have to look up the index of the movie in our movie latent factor matrix, and the index of the user in our user latent factor matrix; then we can do our dot product between the two latent factor vectors. But *look up in an index* is not an operation our deep learning models know how to do. They know how to do matrix products and activation functions.

Fortunately, it turns out that we can represent *look up in an index* as a matrix product. The trick is to replace our indices with one-hot-encoded vectors. Here is an example of what happens if we multiply a vector by a one-hot-encoded vector representing the index 3:

```
one_hot_3 = one_hot(3, n_users).float()
user_factors.t() @ one_hot_3

tensor([-0.4586, -0.9915, -0.4052, -0.3621, -0.5908])
```

It gives us the same vector as the one at index 3 in the matrix:

```
user_factors[3]

tensor([-0.4586, -0.9915, -0.4052, -0.3621, -0.5908])
```

If we do that for a few indices at once, we will have a matrix of one-hot-encoded vectors, and that operation will be a matrix multiplication! This would be a perfectly acceptable way to build models using this kind of architecture, except that it would use a lot more memory and time than necessary. We know that there is no real underlying reason to store the one-hot-encoded vector, or to search through it to find the occurrence of the number 1—we should just be able to index into an array directly with an integer. Therefore, most deep learning libraries, including PyTorch, include a special layer that does just this; it indexes into a vector using an integer, but has its derivative calculated in such a way that it is identical to what it would have been if it had done a matrix multiplication with a one-hot-encoded vector. This is called an *embedding*.

Jargon: Embedding

Multiplying by a one-hot-encoded matrix, using the computational shortcut that it can be implemented by simply indexing directly. This is quite a fancy word for a very simple concept. The thing that you multiply the one-hot-encoded matrix by (or, using the computational shortcut, index into directly) is called the *embedding matrix*.

In computer vision, we have a very easy way to get all the information of a pixel through its RGB values: each pixel in a colored image is represented by three numbers. Those three numbers give us the redness, the greenness, and the blueness, which is enough to get our model to work afterward.

For the problem at hand, we don't have the same easy way to characterize a user or a movie. There are probably relations with genres: if a given user likes romance, they are likely to give higher scores to romance movies. Other factors might be whether the movie is more action-oriented versus heavy on dialogue, or the presence of a specific actor whom a user might particularly like.

How do we determine numbers to characterize those? The answer is, we don't. We will let our model *learn* them. By analyzing the existing relations between users and movies, our model can figure out itself the features that seem important or not.

This is what embeddings are. We will attribute to each of our users and each of our movies a random vector of a certain length (here, n_factors=5), and we will make those learnable parameters. That means that at each step, when we compute the loss by comparing our predictions to our targets, we will compute the gradients of the loss with respect to those embedding vectors and update them with the rules of SGD (or another optimizer).

At the beginning, those numbers don't mean anything since we have chosen them randomly, but by the end of training, they will. By learning on existing data about the relations between users and movies, without having any other information, we will see that they still get some important features, and can isolate blockbusters from independent films, action movies from romance, and so on.

We are now in a position to create our whole model from scratch.

Collaborative Filtering from Scratch

Before we can write a model in PyTorch, we first need to learn the basics of object-oriented programming and Python. If you haven't done any object-oriented programming before, we will give you a quick introduction here, but we would recommend looking up a tutorial and getting some practice before moving on.

The key idea in object-oriented programming is the *class*. We have been using classes throughout this book, such as `DataLoader`, `String`, and `Learner`. Python also makes it easy for us to create new classes. Here is an example of a simple class:

```
class Example:
    def __init__(self, a): self.a = a
    def say(self,x): return f'Hello {self.a}, {x}.'
```

The most important piece of this is the special method called `__init__` (pronounced *dunder init*). In Python, any method surrounded in double underscores like this is considered special. It indicates that some extra behavior is associated with this method name. In the case of `__init__`, this is the method Python will call when your new object is created. So, this is where you can set up any state that needs to be initialized upon object creation. Any parameters included when the user constructs an instance of your class will be passed to the `__init__` method as parameters. Note that the first parameter to any method defined inside a class is `self`, so you can use this to set and get any attributes that you will need:

```
ex = Example('Sylvain')
ex.say('nice to meet you')

'Hello Sylvain, nice to meet you.'
```

Also note that creating a new PyTorch module requires inheriting from `Module`. *Inheritance* is an important object-oriented concept that we will not discuss in detail here—in short, it means that we can add additional behavior to an existing class. PyTorch already provides a `Module` class, which provides some basic foundations that we want to build on. So, we add the name of this *superclass* after the name of the class that we are defining, as shown in the following examples.

The final thing that you need to know to create a new PyTorch module is that when your module is called, PyTorch will call a method in your class called `forward`, and will pass along to that any parameters that are included in the call. Here is the class defining our dot product model:

```
class DotProduct(Module):
    def __init__(self, n_users, n_movies, n_factors):
        self.user_factors = Embedding(n_users, n_factors)
        self.movie_factors = Embedding(n_movies, n_factors)

    def forward(self, x):
        users = self.user_factors(x[:,0])
        movies = self.movie_factors(x[:,1])
        return (users * movies).sum(dim=1)
```

If you haven't seen object-oriented programming before, don't worry; you won't need to use it much in this book. We are just mentioning this approach here because most online tutorials and documentation will use the object-oriented syntax.

Note that the input of the model is a tensor of shape `batch_size` x 2, where the first column (`x[:, 0]`) contains the user IDs, and the second column (`x[:, 1]`) contains the movie IDs. As explained before, we use the *embedding* layers to represent our matrices of user and movie latent factors:

```
x,y = dls.one_batch()
x.shape
```

```
torch.Size([64, 2])
```

Now that we have defined our architecture and created our parameter matrices, we need to create a `Learner` to optimize our model. In the past, we have used special functions, such as `cnn_learner`, which set up everything for us for a particular application. Since we are doing things from scratch here, we will use the plain `Learner` class:

```
model = DotProduct(n_users, n_movies, 50)
learn = Learner(dls, model, loss_func=MSELossFlat())
```

We are now ready to fit our model:

```
learn.fit_one_cycle(5, 5e-3)
```

epoch	train_loss	valid_loss	time
0	1.326261	1.295701	00:12
1	1.091352	1.091475	00:11
2	0.961574	0.977690	00:11
3	0.829995	0.893122	00:11
4	0.781661	0.876511	00:12

The first thing we can do to make this model a little bit better is to force those predictions to be between 0 and 5. For this, we just need to use `sigmoid_range`, as in Chapter 6. One thing we discovered empirically is that it's better to have the range go a little bit over 5, so we use (0, 5.5):

```
class DotProduct(Module):
    def __init__(self, n_users, n_movies, n_factors, y_range=(0,5.5)):
        self.user_factors = Embedding(n_users, n_factors)
        self.movie_factors = Embedding(n_movies, n_factors)
        self.y_range = y_range

    def forward(self, x):
        users = self.user_factors(x[:,0])
        movies = self.movie_factors(x[:,1])
        return sigmoid_range((users * movies).sum(dim=1), *self.y_range)

model = DotProduct(n_users, n_movies, 50)
learn = Learner(dls, model, loss_func=MSELossFlat())
learn.fit_one_cycle(5, 5e-3)
```

epoch	train_loss	valid_loss	time
0	0.976380	1.001455	00:12
1	0.875964	0.919960	00:12
2	0.685377	0.870664	00:12
3	0.483701	0.874071	00:12
4	0.385249	0.878055	00:12

This is a reasonable start, but we can do better. One obvious missing piece is that some users are just more positive or negative in their recommendations than others, and some movies are just plain better or worse than others. But in our dot product representation, we do not have any way to encode either of these things. If all you can say about a movie is, for instance, that it is very sci-fi, very action-oriented, and very not old, then you don't really have any way to say whether most people like it.

That's because at this point we have only weights; we do not have biases. If we have a single number for each user that we can add to our scores, and ditto for each movie, that will handle this missing piece very nicely. So first of all, let's adjust our model architecture:

```
class DotProductBias(Module):
    def __init__(self, n_users, n_movies, n_factors, y_range=(0,5.5)):
        self.user_factors = Embedding(n_users, n_factors)
        self.user_bias = Embedding(n_users, 1)
        self.movie_factors = Embedding(n_movies, n_factors)
        self.movie_bias = Embedding(n_movies, 1)
        self.y_range = y_range

    def forward(self, x):
        users = self.user_factors(x[:,0])
        movies = self.movie_factors(x[:,1])
        res = (users * movies).sum(dim=1, keepdim=True)
        res += self.user_bias(x[:,0]) + self.movie_bias(x[:,1])
        return sigmoid_range(res, *self.y_range)
```

Let's try training this and see how it goes:

```
model = DotProductBias(n_users, n_movies, 50)
learn = Learner(dls, model, loss_func=MSELossFlat())
learn.fit_one_cycle(5, 5e-3)
```

epoch	train_loss	valid_loss	time
0	0.929161	0.936303	00:13
1	0.820444	0.861306	00:13
2	0.621612	0.865306	00:14
3	0.404648	0.886448	00:13
4	0.292948	0.892580	00:13

Instead of being better, it ends up being worse (at least at the end of training). Why is that? If we look at both trainings carefully, we can see the validation loss stopped improving in the middle and started to get worse. As we've seen, this is a clear indication of overfitting. In this case, there is no way to use data augmentation, so we will have to use another regularization technique. One approach that can be helpful is *weight decay*.

Weight Decay

Weight decay, or *L2 regularization*, consists of adding to your loss function the sum of all the weights squared. Why do that? Because when we compute the gradients, it will add a contribution to them that will encourage the weights to be as small as possible.

Why would it prevent overfitting? The idea is that the larger the coefficients are, the sharper canyons we will have in the loss function. If we take the basic example of a parabola, y = a * (x**2), the larger a is, the more *narrow* the parabola is:

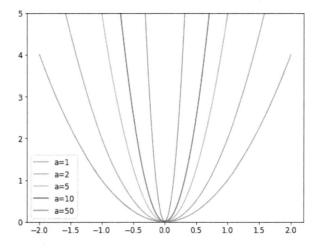

So, letting our model learn high parameters might cause it to fit all the data points in the training set with an overcomplex function that has very sharp changes, which will lead to overfitting.

Limiting our weights from growing too much is going to hinder the training of the model, but it will yield a state where it generalizes better. Going back to the theory briefly, weight decay (or just wd) is a parameter that controls that sum of squares we add to our loss (assuming parameters is a tensor of all parameters):

```
loss_with_wd = loss + wd * (parameters**2).sum()
```

In practice, though, it would be very inefficient (and maybe numerically unstable) to compute that big sum and add it to the loss. If you remember a little bit of high school math, you might recall that the derivative of p**2 with respect to p is 2*p, so adding that big sum to our loss is exactly the same as doing this:

```
parameters.grad += wd * 2 * parameters
```

In practice, since wd is a parameter that we choose, we can make it twice as big, so we don't even need the *2 in this equation. To use weight decay in fastai, pass wd in your call to fit or fit_one_cycle (it can be passed on both):

```
model = DotProductBias(n_users, n_movies, 50)
learn = Learner(dls, model, loss_func=MSELossFlat())
learn.fit_one_cycle(5, 5e-3, wd=0.1)
```

epoch	train_loss	valid_loss	time
0	0.972090	0.962366	00:13
1	0.875591	0.885106	00:13
2	0.723798	0.839880	00:13
3	0.586002	0.823225	00:13
4	0.490980	0.823060	00:13

Much better!

Creating Our Own Embedding Module

So far, we've used Embedding without thinking about how it really works. Let's re-create DotProductBias *without* using this class. We'll need a randomly initialized weight matrix for each of the embeddings. We have to be careful, however. Recall from Chapter 4 that optimizers require that they can get all the parameters of a module from the module's parameters method. However, this does not happen fully automatically. If we just add a tensor as an attribute to a Module, it will not be included in parameters:

```
class T(Module):
    def __init__(self): self.a = torch.ones(3)

L(T().parameters())

(#0) []
```

To tell `Module` that we want to treat a tensor as a parameter, we have to wrap it in the `nn.Parameter` class. This class doesn't add any functionality (other than automatically calling `requires_grad_` for us). It's used only as a "marker" to show what to include in `parameters`:

```
class T(Module):
    def __init__(self): self.a = nn.Parameter(torch.ones(3))

L(T().parameters())

(#1) [Parameter containing:
tensor([1., 1., 1.], requires_grad=True)]
```

All PyTorch modules use `nn.Parameter` for any trainable parameters, which is why we haven't needed to explicitly use this wrapper until now:

```
class T(Module):
    def __init__(self): self.a = nn.Linear(1, 3, bias=False)

t = T()
L(t.parameters())

(#1) [Parameter containing:
tensor([[-0.9595],
        [-0.8490],
        [ 0.8159]], requires_grad=True)]

type(t.a.weight)

torch.nn.parameter.Parameter
```

We can create a tensor as a parameter, with random initialization, like so:

```
def create_params(size):
    return nn.Parameter(torch.zeros(*size).normal_(0, 0.01))
```

Let's use this to create `DotProductBias` again, but without `Embedding`:

```
class DotProductBias(Module):
    def __init__(self, n_users, n_movies, n_factors, y_range=(0,5.5)):
        self.user_factors = create_params([n_users, n_factors])
        self.user_bias = create_params([n_users])
        self.movie_factors = create_params([n_movies, n_factors])
        self.movie_bias = create_params([n_movies])
        self.y_range = y_range

    def forward(self, x):
        users = self.user_factors[x[:,0]]
        movies = self.movie_factors[x[:,1]]
        res = (users*movies).sum(dim=1)
        res += self.user_bias[x[:,0]] + self.movie_bias[x[:,1]]
        return sigmoid_range(res, *self.y_range)
```

Then let's train it again to check we get around the same results we saw in the previous section:

```
model = DotProductBias(n_users, n_movies, 50)
learn = Learner(dls, model, loss_func=MSELossFlat())
learn.fit_one_cycle(5, 5e-3, wd=0.1)
```

epoch	train_loss	valid_loss	time
0	0.962146	0.936952	00:14
1	0.858084	0.884951	00:14
2	0.740883	0.838549	00:14
3	0.592497	0.823599	00:14
4	0.473570	0.824263	00:14

Now, let's take a look at what our model has learned.

Interpreting Embeddings and Biases

Our model is already useful, in that it can provide us with movie recommendations for our users—but it is also interesting to see what parameters it has discovered. The easiest to interpret are the biases. Here are the movies with the lowest values in the bias vector:

```
movie_bias = learn.model.movie_bias.squeeze()
idxs = movie_bias.argsort()[:5]
[dls.classes['title'][i] for i in idxs]
```

```
['Children of the Corn: The Gathering (1996)',
 'Lawnmower Man 2: Beyond Cyberspace (1996)',
 'Beautician and the Beast, The (1997)',
 'Crow: City of Angels, The (1996)',
 'Home Alone 3 (1997)']
```

Think about what this means. What it's saying is that for each of these movies, even when a user is very well matched to its latent factors (which, as we will see in a moment, tend to represent things like level of action, age of movie, and so forth), they still generally don't like it. We could have simply sorted the movies directly by their average rating, but looking at the learned bias tells us something much more interesting. It tells us not just whether a movie is of a kind that people tend not to enjoy watching, but that people tend to not like watching it even if it is of a kind that they would otherwise enjoy! By the same token, here are the movies with the highest bias:

```
idxs = movie_bias.argsort(descending=True)[:5]
[dls.classes['title'][i] for i in idxs]
```

```
['L.A. Confidential (1997)',
 'Titanic (1997)',
 'Silence of the Lambs, The (1991)',
 'Shawshank Redemption, The (1994)',
 'Star Wars (1977)']
```

So, for instance, even if you don't normally enjoy detective movies, you might enjoy *LA Confidential*!

It is not quite so easy to directly interpret the embedding matrices. There are just too many factors for a human to look at. But there is a technique that can pull out the most important underlying *directions* in such a matrix, called *principal component analysis* (PCA). We will not be going into this in detail in this book, because it is not particularly important for you to understand to be a deep learning practitioner, but if you are interested, we suggest you check out the fast.ai course Computational Linear Algebra for Coders (*https://oreil.ly/NLj2R*). Figure 8-3 shows what our movies look like based on two of the strongest PCA components.

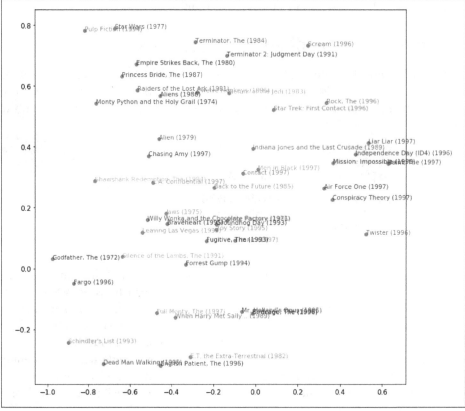

Figure 8-3. Representation of movies based on two strongest PCA components

We can see here that the model seems to have discovered a concept of *classic* versus *pop culture* movies, or perhaps it is *critically acclaimed* that is represented here.

Jeremy Says

No matter how many models I train, I never stop getting moved and surprised by how these randomly initialized bunches of numbers, trained with such simple mechanics, manage to discover things about my data all by themselves. It almost seems like cheating that I can create code that does useful things without ever actually telling it how to do those things!

We defined our model from scratch to teach you what is inside, but you can directly use the fastai library to build it. We'll look at how to do that next.

Using fastai.collab

We can create and train a collaborative filtering model using the exact structure shown earlier by using fastai's `collab_learner`:

```
learn = collab_learner(dls, n_factors=50, y_range=(0, 5.5))

learn.fit_one_cycle(5, 5e-3, wd=0.1)
```

epoch	train_loss	valid_loss	time
0	0.931751	0.953806	00:13
1	0.851826	0.878119	00:13
2	0.715254	0.834711	00:13
3	0.583173	0.821470	00:13
4	0.496625	0.821688	00:13

The names of the layers can be seen by printing the model:

```
learn.model

EmbeddingDotBias(
  (u_weight): Embedding(944, 50)
  (i_weight): Embedding(1635, 50)
  (u_bias): Embedding(944, 1)
  (i_bias): Embedding(1635, 1)
)
```

We can use these to replicate any of the analyses we did in the previous section—for instance:

```
movie_bias = learn.model.i_bias.weight.squeeze()
idxs = movie_bias.argsort(descending=True)[:5]
[dls.classes['title'][i] for i in idxs]

['Titanic (1997)',
 "Schindler's List (1993)",
 'Shawshank Redemption, The (1994)',
```

```
'L.A. Confidential (1997)',
'Silence of the Lambs, The (1991)']
```

Another interesting thing we can do with these learned embeddings is to look at *distance*.

Embedding Distance

On a two-dimensional map, we can calculate the distance between two coordinates by using the formula of Pythagoras: $\sqrt{x^2 + y^2}$ (assuming that x and y are the distances between the coordinates on each axis). For a 50-dimensional embedding, we can do exactly the same thing, except that we add up the squares of all 50 of the coordinate distances.

If there were two movies that were nearly identical, their embedding vectors would also have to be nearly identical, because the users who would like them would be nearly exactly the same. There is a more general idea here: movie similarity can be defined by the similarity of users who like those movies. And that directly means that the distance between two movies' embedding vectors can define that similarity. We can use this to find the most similar movie to *Silence of the Lambs*:

```
movie_factors = learn.model.i_weight.weight
idx = dls.classes['title'].o2i['Silence of the Lambs, The (1991)']
distances = nn.CosineSimilarity(dim=1)(movie_factors, movie_factors[idx][None])
idx = distances.argsort(descending=True)[1]
dls.classes['title'][idx]
```

```
'Dial M for Murder (1954)'
```

Now that we have successfully trained a model, let's see how to deal with the situation of having no data for a user. How can we make recommendations to new users?

Bootstrapping a Collaborative Filtering Model

The biggest challenge with using collaborative filtering models in practice is the *bootstrapping problem*. The most extreme version of this problem is having no users, and therefore no history to learn from. What products do you recommend to your very first user?

But even if you are a well-established company with a long history of user transactions, you still have the question: what do you do when a new user signs up? And indeed, what do you do when you add a new product to your portfolio? There is no magic solution to this problem, and really the solutions that we suggest are just variations of *use your common sense*. You could assign new users the mean of all of the embedding vectors of your other users, but this has the problem that that particular combination of latent factors may be not at all common (for instance, the average for the science-fiction factor may be high, and the average for the action factor may be low, but it is not that common to find people who like science-fiction without action). It would probably be better to pick a particular user to represent *average taste*.

Better still is to use a tabular model based on user metadata to construct your initial embedding vector. When a user signs up, think about what questions you could ask to help you understand their tastes. Then you can create a model in which the dependent variable is a user's embedding vector, and the independent variables are the results of the questions that you ask them, along with their signup metadata. We will see in the next section how to create these kinds of tabular models. (You may have noticed that when you sign up for services such as Pandora and Netflix, they tend to ask you a few questions about what genres of movie or music you like; this is how they come up with your initial collaborative filtering recommendations.)

One thing to be careful of is that a small number of extremely enthusiastic users may end up effectively setting the recommendations for your whole user base. This is a very common problem, for instance, in movie recommendation systems. People who watch anime tend to watch a whole lot of it, and don't watch very much else, and spend a lot of time putting their ratings on websites. As a result, anime tends to be heavily overrepresented in a lot of *best ever movies* lists. In this particular case, it can be fairly obvious that you have a problem of representation bias, but if the bias is occurring in the latent factors, it may not be obvious at all.

Such a problem can change the entire makeup of your user base, and the behavior of your system. This is particularly true because of positive feedback loops. If a small number of your users tend to set the direction of your recommendation system, they are naturally going to end up attracting more people like them to your system. And that will, of course, amplify the original representation bias. This type of bias is a natural tendency to be amplified exponentially. You may have seen examples of company executives expressing surprise at how their online platforms rapidly deteriorated in such a way that they expressed values at odds with the values of the founders. In the presence of these kinds of feedback loops, it is easy to see how such a divergence can happen both quickly and in a way that is hidden until it is too late.

In a self-reinforcing system like this, we should probably expect these kinds of feedback loops to be the norm, not the exception. Therefore, you should assume that you will see them, plan for that, and identify up front how you will deal with these issues. Try to think about all of the ways in which feedback loops may be represented in your system, and how you might be able to identify them in your data. In the end, this is coming back to our original advice about how to avoid disaster when rolling out any kind of machine learning system. It's all about ensuring that there are humans in the loop; that there is careful monitoring, and a gradual and thoughtful rollout.

Our dot product model works quite well, and it is the basis of many successful real-world recommendation systems. This approach to collaborative filtering is known as *probabilistic matrix factorization* (PMF). Another approach, which generally works similarly well given the same data, is deep learning.

Deep Learning for Collaborative Filtering

To turn our architecture into a deep learning model, the first step is to take the results of the embedding lookup and concatenate those activations together. This gives us a matrix that we can then pass through linear layers and nonlinearities in the usual way.

Since we'll be concatenating the embeddings, rather than taking their dot product, the two embedding matrices can have different sizes (different numbers of latent factors). fastai has a function `get_emb_sz` that returns recommended sizes for embedding matrices for your data, based on a heuristic that fast.ai has found tends to work well in practice:

```
embs = get_emb_sz(dls)
embs
```

```
[(944, 74), (1635, 101)]
```

Let's implement this class:

```
class CollabNN(Module):
    def __init__(self, user_sz, item_sz, y_range=(0,5.5), n_act=100):
        self.user_factors = Embedding(*user_sz)
        self.item_factors = Embedding(*item_sz)
        self.layers = nn.Sequential(
            nn.Linear(user_sz[1]+item_sz[1], n_act),
            nn.ReLU(),
            nn.Linear(n_act, 1))
        self.y_range = y_range

    def forward(self, x):
        embs = self.user_factors(x[:,0]),self.item_factors(x[:,1])
        x = self.layers(torch.cat(embs, dim=1))
        return sigmoid_range(x, *self.y_range)
```

And use it to create a model:

```
model = CollabNN(*embs)
```

CollabNN creates our Embedding layers in the same way as previous classes in this chapter, except that we now use the embs sizes. self.layers is identical to the mini-neural net we created in Chapter 4 for MNIST. Then, in forward, we apply the embeddings, concatenate the results, and pass this through the mini-neural net. Finally, we apply sigmoid_range as we have in previous models.

Let's see if it trains:

```
learn = Learner(dls, model, loss_func=MSELossFlat())
learn.fit_one_cycle(5, 5e-3, wd=0.01)
```

epoch	train_loss	valid_loss	time
0	0.940104	0.959786	00:15
1	0.893943	0.905222	00:14
2	0.865591	0.875238	00:14
3	0.800177	0.867468	00:14
4	0.760255	0.867455	00:14

fastai provides this model in `fastai.collab` if you pass `use_nn=True` in your call to `collab_learner` (including calling `get_emb_sz` for you), and it lets you easily create more layers. For instance, here we're creating two hidden layers, of size 100 and 50, respectively:

```
learn = collab_learner(dls, use_nn=True, y_range=(0, 5.5), layers=[100,50])
learn.fit_one_cycle(5, 5e-3, wd=0.1)
```

epoch	train_loss	valid_loss	time
0	1.002747	0.972392	00:16
1	0.926903	0.922348	00:16
2	0.877160	0.893401	00:16
3	0.838334	0.865040	00:16
4	0.781666	0.864936	00:16

`learn.model` is an object of type `EmbeddingNN`. Let's take a look at fastai's code for this class:

```
@delegates(TabularModel)
class EmbeddingNN(TabularModel):
    def __init__(self, emb_szs, layers, **kwargs):
        super().__init__(emb_szs, layers=layers, n_cont=0, out_sz=1, **kwargs)
```

Wow, that's not a lot of code! This class *inherits* from `TabularModel`, which is where it gets all its functionality from. In `__init__`, it calls the same method in `TabularModel`, passing `n_cont=0` and `out_sz=1`; other than that, it passes along only whatever arguments it received.

kwargs and Delegates

`EmbeddingNN` includes `**kwargs` as a parameter to `__init__`. In Python, `**kwargs` in a parameter list means "put any additional keyword arguments into a dict called kwargs." And `**kwargs` in an argument list means "insert all key/value pairs in the kwargs dict as named arguments here." This approach is used in many popular libraries, such as `matplotlib`, in which the main `plot` function simply has the signature plot(*args, **kwargs). The plot documentation (*https://oreil.ly/P9A8T*) says "The kwargs are Line2D properties" and then lists those properties.

We're using **kwargs in EmbeddingNN to avoid having to write all the arguments to TabularModel a second time, and keep them in sync. However, this makes our API quite difficult to work with, because now Jupyter Notebook doesn't know what parameters are available. Consequently, things like tab completion of parameter names and pop-up lists of signatures won't work.

fastai resolves this by providing a special @delegates decorator, which automatically changes the signature of the class or function (EmbeddingNN in this case) to insert all of its keyword arguments into the signature.

Although the results of EmbeddingNN are a bit worse than the dot product approach (which shows the power of carefully constructing an architecture for a domain), it does allow us to do something very important: we can now directly incorporate other user and movie information, date and time information, or any other information that may be relevant to the recommendation. That's exactly what TabularModel does. In fact, we've now seen that EmbeddingNN is just a TabularModel, with n_cont=0 and out_sz=1. So, we'd better spend some time learning about TabularModel, and how to use it to get great results! We'll do that in the next chapter.

Conclusion

For our first non–computer vision application, we looked at recommendation systems and saw how gradient descent can learn intrinsic factors or biases about items from a history of ratings. Those can then give us information about the data.

We also built our first model in PyTorch. We will do a lot more of this in the next section of the book, but first, let's finish our dive into the other general applications of deep learning, continuing with tabular data.

Questionnaire

1. What problem does collaborative filtering solve?
2. How does it solve it?
3. Why might a collaborative filtering predictive model fail to be a very useful recommendation system?
4. What does a crosstab representation of collaborative filtering data look like?
5. Write the code to create a crosstab representation of the MovieLens data (you might need to do some web searching!).

6. What is a latent factor? Why is it "latent"?

7. What is a dot product? Calculate a dot product manually using pure Python with lists.

8. What does `pandas.DataFrame.merge` do?

9. What is an embedding matrix?

10. What is the relationship between an embedding and a matrix of one-hot-encoded vectors?

11. Why do we need `Embedding` if we could use one-hot-encoded vectors for the same thing?

12. What does an embedding contain before we start training (assuming we're not using a pretrained model)?

13. Create a class (without peeking, if possible!) and use it.

14. What does `x[:,0]` return?

15. Rewrite the `DotProduct` class (without peeking, if possible!) and train a model with it.

16. What is a good loss function to use for MovieLens? Why?

17. What would happen if we used cross-entropy loss with MovieLens? How would we need to change the model?

18. What is the use of bias in a dot product model?

19. What is another name for weight decay?

20. Write the equation for weight decay (without peeking!).

21. Write the equation for the gradient of weight decay. Why does it help reduce weights?

22. Why does reducing weights lead to better generalization?

23. What does `argsort` do in PyTorch?

24. Does sorting the movie biases give the same result as averaging overall movie ratings by movie? Why/why not?

25. How do you print the names and details of the layers in a model?

26. What is the "bootstrapping problem" in collaborative filtering?

27. How could you deal with the bootstrapping problem for new users? For new movies?

28. How can feedback loops impact collaborative filtering systems?

29. When using a neural network in collaborative filtering, why can we have different numbers of factors for movies and users?

30. Why is there an `nn.Sequential` in the `CollabNN` model?

31. What kind of model should we use if we want to add metadata about users and items, or information such as date and time, to a collaborative filtering model?

Further Research

1. Take a look at all the differences between the `Embedding` version of `DotProduct Bias` and the `create_params` version, and try to understand why each of those changes is required. If you're not sure, try reverting each change to see what happens. (NB: even the type of brackets used in `forward` has changed!)

2. Find three other areas where collaborative filtering is being used, and identify the pros and cons of this approach in those areas.

3. Complete this notebook using the full MovieLens dataset, and compare your results to online benchmarks. See if you can improve your accuracy. Look on the book's website and the fast.ai forums for ideas. Note that there are more columns in the full dataset—see if you can use those too (the next chapter might give you ideas).

4. Create a model for MovieLens that works with cross-entropy loss, and compare it to the model in this chapter.

CHAPTER 9

Tabular Modeling Deep Dive

Tabular modeling takes data in the form of a table (like a spreadsheet or CSV). The objective is to predict the value in one column based on the values in the other columns. In this chapter, we will look at not only deep learning, but also more general machine learning techniques like random forests, as they can give better results depending on your problem.

We will look at how we should preprocess and clean the data as well as how to interpret the result of our models after training, but first we will see how we can feed columns that contain categories into a model that expects numbers by using embeddings.

Categorical Embeddings

In tabular data, some columns may contain numerical data, like "age," while others contain string values, like "sex." The numerical data can be directly fed to the model (with some optional preprocessing), but the other columns need to be converted to numbers. Since the values in those correspond to different categories, we often call this type of variables *categorical variables*. The first type are called *continuous variables*.

Jargon: Continuous and Categorical Variables

Continuous variables are numerical data, such as "age," that can be directly fed to the model, since you can add and multiply them directly. Categorical variables contain a number of discrete levels, such as "movie ID," for which addition and multiplication don't have meaning (even if they're stored as numbers).

At the end of 2015, the Rossmann sales competition (*https://oreil.ly/U85_1*) ran on Kaggle. Competitors were given a wide range of information about various stores in Germany, and were tasked with trying to predict sales on a number of days. The goal was to help the company manage stock properly and be able to satisfy demand without holding unnecessary inventory. The official training set provided a lot of information about the stores. It was also permitted for competitors to use additional data, as long as that data was made public and available to all participants.

One of the gold medalists used deep learning, in one of the earliest known examples of a state-of-the-art deep learning tabular model. Their method involved far less feature engineering, based on domain knowledge, than those of the other gold medalists. The paper "Entity Embeddings of Categorical Variables" (*https://oreil.ly/VmgoU*) describes their approach. In an online-only chapter on the book's website (*https://book.fast.ai*), we show how to replicate it from scratch and attain the same accuracy shown in the paper. In the abstract of the paper, the authors (Cheng Guo and Felix Bekhahn) say:

> Entity embedding not only reduces memory usage and speeds up neural networks compared with one-hot encoding, but more importantly by mapping similar values close to each other in the embedding space it reveals the intrinsic properties of the categorical variables...[It] is especially useful for datasets with lots of high cardinality features, where other methods tend to overfit...As entity embedding defines a distance measure for categorical variables, it can be used for visualizing categorical data and for data clustering.

We have already noticed all of these points when we built our collaborative filtering model. We can clearly see that these insights go far beyond just collaborative filtering, however.

The paper also points out that (as we discussed in the preceding chapter) an embedding layer is exactly equivalent to placing an ordinary linear layer after every one-hot-encoded input layer. The authors used the diagram in Figure 9-1 to show this equivalence. Note that "dense layer" is a term with the same meaning as "linear layer," and the one-hot encoding layers represent inputs.

The insight is important because we already know how to train linear layers, so this shows that from the point of view of the architecture and our training algorithm, the embedding layer is just another layer. We also saw this in practice in the preceding chapter, when we built a collaborative filtering neural network that looks exactly like this diagram.

Just as we analyzed the embedding weights for movie reviews, the authors of the entity embeddings paper analyzed the embedding weights for their sales prediction model. What they found was quite amazing, and illustrates their second key insight: the embedding transforms the categorical variables into inputs that are both continuous and meaningful.

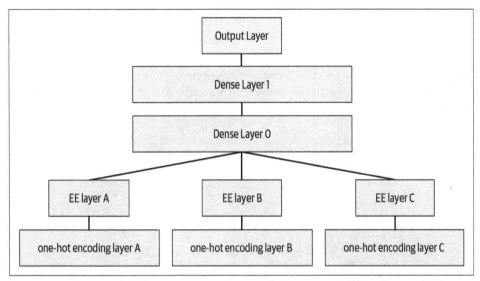

Figure 9-1. Entity embeddings in a neural network (courtesy of Cheng Guo and Felix Berkhahn)

The images in Figure 9-2 illustrate these ideas. They are based on the approaches used in the paper, along with some analysis we have added.

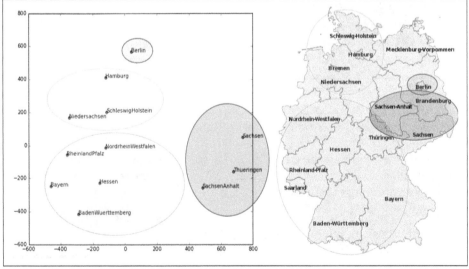

Figure 9-2. State embeddings and map (courtesy of Cheng Guo and Felix Berkhahn)

On the left is a plot of the embedding matrix for the possible values of the State category. For a categorical variable, we call the possible values of the variable its "levels" (or "categories" or "classes"), so here one level is "Berlin," another is "Hamburg," etc. On the right is a map of Germany. The actual physical locations of the German states were not part of the provided data, yet the model itself learned where they must be, based only on the behavior of store sales!

Do you remember how we talked about *distance* between embeddings? The authors of the paper plotted the distance between store embeddings against the actual geographic distance between the stores (see Figure 9-3). They found that they matched very closely!

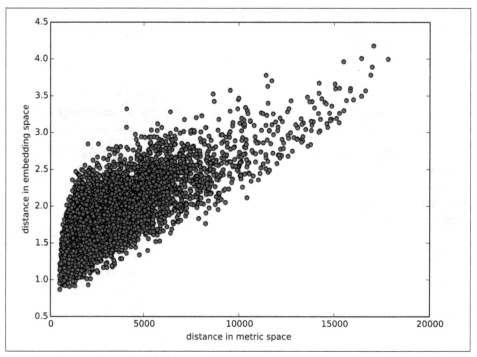

Figure 9-3. Store distances (courtesy of Cheng Guo and Felix Berkhahn)

We've even tried plotting the embeddings for days of the week and months of the year, and found that days and months that are near each other on the calendar ended up close as embeddings too, as shown in Figure 9-4.

What stands out in these two examples is that we provide the model fundamentally categorical data about discrete entities (e.g., German states or days of the week), and then the model learns an embedding for these entities that defines a continuous notion of distance between them. Because the embedding distance was learned based on real patterns in the data, that distance tends to match up with our intuitions.

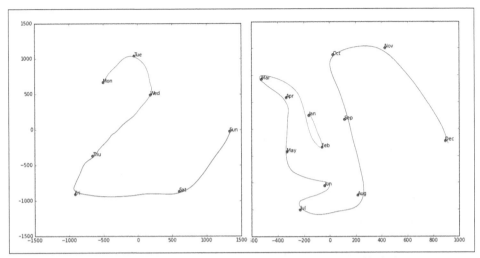

Figure 9-4. Date embeddings (courtesy of Cheng Guo and Felix Berkhahn)

In addition, it is valuable in its own right that embeddings are continuous, because models are better at understanding continuous variables. This is unsurprising considering models are built of many continuous parameter weights and continuous activation values, which are updated via gradient descent (a learning algorithm for finding the minimums of continuous functions).

Another benefit is that we can combine our continuous embedding values with truly continuous input data in a straightforward manner: we just concatenate the variables and feed the concatenation into our first dense layer. In other words, the raw categorical data is transformed by an embedding layer before it interacts with the raw continuous input data. This is how fastai and Guo and Berkhahn handle tabular models containing continuous and categorical variables.

An example using this concatenation approach is how Google does its recommendations on Google Play, as explained in the paper "Wide & Deep Learning for Recommender Systems" (*https://oreil.ly/wsnvQ*). Figure 9-5 illustrates this.

Interestingly, the Google team combined both approaches we saw in the previous chapter: the dot product (which they call *cross product*) and neural network approaches.

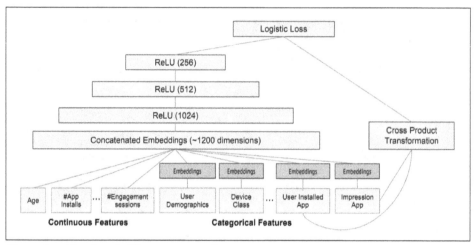

Figure 9-5. The Google Play recommendation system

Let's pause for a moment. So far, the solution to all of our modeling problems has been to *train a deep learning model*. And indeed, that is a pretty good rule of thumb for complex unstructured data like images, sounds, natural language text, and so forth. Deep learning also works very well for collaborative filtering. But it is not always the best starting point for analyzing tabular data.

Beyond Deep Learning

Most machine learning courses will throw dozens of algorithms at you, with a brief technical description of the math behind them and maybe a toy example. You're left confused by the enormous range of techniques shown and have little practical understanding of how to apply them.

The good news is that modern machine learning can be distilled down to a couple of key techniques that are widely applicable. Recent studies have shown that the vast majority of datasets can be best modeled with just two methods:

- Ensembles of decision trees (i.e., random forests and gradient boosting machines), mainly for structured data (such as you might find in a database table at most companies)
- Multilayered neural networks learned with SGD (i.e., shallow and/or deep learning), mainly for unstructured data (such as audio, images, and natural language)

Although deep learning is nearly always clearly superior for unstructured data, these two approaches tend to give quite similar results for many kinds of structured data. But ensembles of decision trees tend to train faster, are often easier to interpret, do not require special GPU hardware for inference at scale, and often require less hyperparameter tuning. They have also been popular for quite a lot longer than deep learning, so there is a more mature ecosystem of tooling and documentation around them.

Most importantly, the critical step of interpreting a model of tabular data is significantly easier for decision tree ensembles. There are tools and methods for answering the pertinent questions, like these: Which columns in the dataset were the most important for your predictions? How are they related to the dependent variable? How do they interact with each other? And which particular features were most important for some particular observation?

Therefore, ensembles of decision trees are our first approach for analyzing a new tabular dataset.

The exception to this guideline is when the dataset meets one of these conditions:

- There are some high-cardinality categorical variables that are very important ("cardinality" refers to the number of discrete levels representing categories, so a high-cardinality categorical variable is something like a zip code, which can take on thousands of possible levels).
- There are some columns that contain data that would be best understood with a neural network, such as plain text data.

In practice, when we deal with datasets that meet these exceptional conditions, we always try both decision tree ensembles and deep learning to see which works best. Deep learning will likely be a useful approach in our example of collaborative filtering, as we have at least two high-cardinality categorical variables: the users and the movies. But in practice, things tend to be less cut-and-dried, and there will often be a mixture of high- and low-cardinality categorical variables and continuous variables.

Either way, it's clear that we are going to need to add decision tree ensembles to our modeling toolbox!

Up to now, we've used PyTorch and fastai for pretty much all of our heavy lifting. But these libraries are mainly designed for algorithms that do lots of matrix multiplication and derivatives (that is, stuff like deep learning!). Decision trees don't depend on these operations at all, so PyTorch isn't much use.

Instead, we will be largely relying on a library called *scikit-learn* (also known as *sklearn*). Scikit-learn is a popular library for creating machine learning models, using approaches that are not covered by deep learning. In addition, we'll need to do some tabular data processing and querying, so we'll want to use the Pandas library. Finally, we'll also need NumPy, since that's the main numeric programming library that both sklearn and Pandas rely on.

We don't have time to do a deep dive into all these libraries in this book, so we'll just be touching on some of the main parts of each. For a far more in-depth discussion, we strongly suggest Wes McKinney's *Python for Data Analysis* (O'Reilly). McKinney is the creator of Pandas, so you can be sure that the information is accurate!

First, let's gather the data we will use.

The Dataset

The dataset we use in this chapter is from the Blue Book for Bulldozers Kaggle competition, which has the following description: "The goal of the contest is to predict the sale price of a particular piece of heavy equipment at auction based on its usage, equipment type, and configuration. The data is sourced from auction result postings and includes information on usage and equipment configurations."

This is a very common type of dataset and prediction problem, similar to what you may see in your project or workplace. The dataset is available for download on Kaggle, a website that hosts data science competitions.

Kaggle Competitions

Kaggle is an awesome resource for aspiring data scientists or anyone looking to improve their machine learning skills. There is nothing like getting hands-on practice and receiving real-time feedback to help you improve your skills.

Kaggle provides the following:

- Interesting datasets
- Feedback on how you're doing
- A leaderboard to see what's good, what's possible, and what's state-of-the-art
- Blog posts by winning contestants sharing useful tips and techniques

Until now, all our datasets have been available to download through fastai's integrated dataset system. However, the dataset we will be using in this chapter is available only from Kaggle. Therefore, you will need to register on the site, then go to the page for the competition (*https://oreil.ly/B9wfd*). On that page click Rules, and then I Understand and Accept. (Although the competition has finished, and you will not be entering it, you still have to agree to the rules to be allowed to download the data.)

The easiest way to download Kaggle datasets is to use the Kaggle API. You can install this by using `pip` and running this in a notebook cell:

```
!pip install kaggle
```

You need an API key to use the Kaggle API; to get one, click your profile picture on the Kaggle website and choose My Account; then click Create New API Token. This will save a file called *kaggle.json* to your PC. You need to copy this key on your GPU server. To do so, open the file you downloaded, copy the contents, and paste them inside the single quotes in the following cell in the notebook associated with this chapter (e.g., `creds = '{"username":"xxx","key":"xxx"}'`):

```
creds = ''
```

Then execute this cell (this needs to be run only once):

```
cred_path = Path('~/.kaggle/kaggle.json').expanduser()
if not cred_path.exists():
    cred_path.parent.mkdir(exist_ok=True)
    cred_path.write(creds)
    cred_path.chmod(0o600)
```

Now you can download datasets from Kaggle! Pick a path to download the dataset to:

```
path = URLs.path('bluebook')
path
```

```
Path('/home/sgugger/.fastai/archive/bluebook')
```

And use the Kaggle API to download the dataset to that path and extract it:

```
if not path.exists():
    path.mkdir()
    api.competition_download_cli('bluebook-for-bulldozers', path=path)
    file_extract(path/'bluebook-for-bulldozers.zip')

path.ls(file_type='text')
```

```
(#7) [Path('Valid.csv'),Path('Machine_Appendix.csv'),Path('ValidSolution.csv'),P
 > ath('TrainAndValid.csv'),Path('random_forest_benchmark_test.csv'),Path('Test.
 > csv'),Path('median_benchmark.csv')]
```

Now that we have downloaded our dataset, let's take a look at it!

Look at the Data

Kaggle provides information about some of the fields of our dataset. The Data page (*https://oreil.ly/oSrBi*) explains that the key fields in *train.csv* are as follows:

SalesID
    The unique identifier of the sale.

MachineID
    The unique identifier of a machine. A machine can be sold multiple times.

saleprice
    What the machine sold for at auction (provided only in *train.csv*).

```
saledate
```
   The date of the sale.

In any sort of data science work, it's important to *look at your data directly* to make sure you understand the format, how it's stored, what types of values it holds, etc. Even if you've read a description of the data, the actual data may not be what you expect. We'll start by reading the training set into a Pandas DataFrame. Generally, it's a good idea to also specify `low_memory=False` unless Pandas actually runs out of memory and returns an error. The `low_memory` parameter, which is `True` by default, tells Pandas to look at only a few rows of data at a time to figure out what type of data is in each column. This means that Pandas can end up using different data types for different rows, which generally leads to data processing errors or model training problems later.

Let's load our data and have a look at the columns:

```
df = pd.read_csv(path/'TrainAndValid.csv', low_memory=False)

df.columns

Index(['SalesID', 'SalePrice', 'MachineID', 'ModelID', 'datasource',
       'auctioneerID', 'YearMade', 'MachineHoursCurrentMeter', 'UsageBand',
       'saledate', 'fiModelDesc', 'fiBaseModel', 'fiSecondaryDesc',
       'fiModelSeries', 'fiModelDescriptor', 'ProductSize',
       'fiProductClassDesc', 'state', 'ProductGroup', 'ProductGroupDesc',
       'Drive_System', 'Enclosure', 'Forks', 'Pad_Type', 'Ride_Control',
       'Stick', 'Transmission', 'Turbocharged', 'Blade_Extension',
       'Blade_Width', 'Enclosure_Type', 'Engine_Horsepower', 'Hydraulics',
       'Pushblock', 'Ripper', 'Scarifier', 'Tip_Control', 'Tire_Size',
       'Coupler', 'Coupler_System', 'Grouser_Tracks', 'Hydraulics_Flow',
       'Track_Type', 'Undercarriage_Pad_Width', 'Stick_Length', 'Thumb',
       'Pattern_Changer', 'Grouser_Type', 'Backhoe_Mounting', 'Blade_Type',
       'Travel_Controls', 'Differential_Type', 'Steering_Controls'],
      dtype='object')
```

That's a lot of columns for us to look at! Try looking through the dataset to get a sense of what kind of information is in each one. We'll shortly see how to "zero in" on the most interesting bits.

At this point, a good next step is to handle *ordinal columns*. This refers to columns containing strings or similar, but where those strings have a natural ordering. For instance, here are the levels of `ProductSize`:

```
df['ProductSize'].unique()

array([nan, 'Medium', 'Small', 'Large / Medium', 'Mini', 'Large', 'Compact'],
 > dtype=object)
```

We can tell Pandas about a suitable ordering of these levels like so:

```
sizes = 'Large','Large / Medium','Medium','Small','Mini','Compact'
df['ProductSize'] = df['ProductSize'].astype('category')
df['ProductSize'].cat.set_categories(sizes, ordered=True, inplace=True)
```

The most important data column is the dependent variable—the one we want to predict. Recall that a model's metric is a function that reflects how good the predictions are. It's important to note what metric is being used for a project. Generally, selecting the metric is an important part of the project setup. In many cases, choosing a good metric will require more than just selecting a variable that already exists. It is more like a design process. You should think carefully about which metric, or set of metric, actually measures the notion of model quality that matters to you. If no variable represents that metric, you should see if you can build the metric from the variables that are available.

However, in this case, Kaggle tells us what metric to use: the root mean squared log error (RMLSE) between the actual and predicted auction prices. We need do only a small amount of processing to use this: we take the log of the prices, so that the m_rmse of that value will give us what we ultimately need:

```
dep_var = 'SalePrice'
df[dep_var] = np.log(df[dep_var])
```

We are now ready to explore our first machine learning algorithm for tabular data: decision trees.

Decision Trees

Decision tree ensembles, as the name suggests, rely on decision trees. So let's start there! A decision tree asks a series of binary (yes or no) questions about the data. After each question, the data at that part of the tree is split between a Yes and a No branch, as shown in Figure 9-6. After one or more questions, either a prediction can be made on the basis of all previous answers or another question is required.

This sequence of questions is now a procedure for taking any data item, whether an item from the training set or a new one, and assigning that item to a group. Namely, after asking and answering the questions, we can say the item belongs to the same group as all the other training data items that yielded the same set of answers to the questions. But what good is this? The goal of our model is to predict values for items, not to assign them into groups from the training dataset. The value is that we can now assign a prediction value for each of these groups—for regression, we take the target mean of the items in the group.

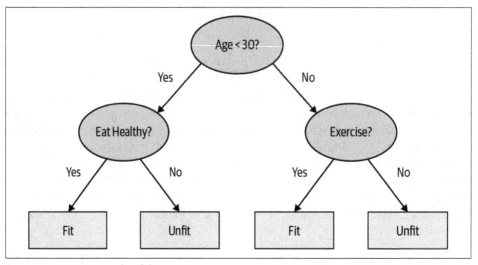

Figure 9-6. An example of decision tree

Let's consider how we find the right questions to ask. Of course, we wouldn't want to have to create all these questions ourselves—that's what computers are for! The basic steps to train a decision tree can be written down very easily:

1. Loop through each column of the dataset in turn.

2. For each column, loop through each possible level of that column in turn.

3. Try splitting the data into two groups, based on whether they are greater than or less than that value (or if it is a categorical variable, based on whether they are equal to or not equal to that level of that categorical variable).

4. Find the average sale price for each of those two groups, and see how close that is to the actual sale price of each of the items of equipment in that group. Treat this as a very simple "model" in which our predictions are simply the average sale price of the item's group.

5. After looping through all of the columns and all the possible levels for each, pick the split point that gave the best predictions using that simple model.

6. We now have two groups for our data, based on this selected split. Treat each group as a separate dataset, and find the best split for each by going back to step 1 for each group.

7. Continue this process recursively, until you have reached some stopping criterion for each group—for instance, stop splitting a group further when it has only 20 items in it.

Although this is an easy enough algorithm to implement yourself (and it is a good exercise to do so), we can save some time by using the implementation built into sklearn.

First, however, we need to do a little data preparation.

Alexis Says

Here's a productive question to ponder. If you consider that the procedure for defining a decision tree essentially chooses one *sequence of splitting questions about variables*, you might ask yourself, how do we know this procedure chooses the *correct sequence*? The rule is to choose the splitting question that produces the best split (i.e., that most accurately separates the items into two distinct categories), and then to apply the same rule to the groups that split produces, and so on. This is known in computer science as a "greedy" approach. Can you imagine a scenario in which asking a "less powerful" splitting question would enable a better split down the road (or should I say down the trunk!) and lead to a better result overall?

Handling Dates

The first piece of data preparation we need to do is to enrich our representation of dates. The fundamental basis of the decision tree that we just described is *bisection*—dividing a group into two. We look at the ordinal variables and divide the dataset based on whether the variable's value is greater (or lower) than a threshold, and we look at the categorical variables and divide the dataset based on whether the variable's level is a particular level. So this algorithm has a way of dividing the dataset based on both ordinal and categorical data.

But how does this apply to a common data type, the date? You might want to treat a date as an ordinal value, because it is meaningful to say that one date is greater than another. However, dates are a bit different from most ordinal values in that some dates are qualitatively different from others in a way that that is often relevant to the systems we are modeling.

To help our algorithm handle dates intelligently, we'd like our model to know more than whether a date is more recent or less recent than another. We might want our model to make decisions based on that date's day of the week, on whether a day is a holiday, on what month it is in, and so forth. To do this, we replace every date column with a set of date metadata columns, such as holiday, day of week, and month. These columns provide categorical data that we suspect will be useful.

fastai comes with a function that will do this for us—we just have to pass a column name that contains dates:

```
df = add_datepart(df, 'saledate')
```

Let's do the same for the test set while we're there:

```
df_test = pd.read_csv(path/'Test.csv', low_memory=False)
df_test = add_datepart(df_test, 'saledate')
```

We can see that there are now lots of new columns in our DataFrame:

```
' '.join(o for o in df.columns if o.startswith('sale'))
```

```
'saleYear saleMonth saleWeek saleDay saleDayofweek saleDayofyear
> saleIs_month_end saleIs_month_start saleIs_quarter_end saleIs_quarter_start
> saleIs_year_end saleIs_year_start saleElapsed'
```

This is a good first step, but we will need to do a bit more cleaning. For this, we will use fastai objects called `TabularPandas` and `TabularProc`.

Using TabularPandas and TabularProc

A second piece of preparatory processing is to be sure we can handle strings and missing data. Out of the box, sklearn cannot do either. Instead we will use fastai's class `TabularPandas`, which wraps a Pandas DataFrame and provides a few conveniences. To populate a `TabularPandas`, we will use two `TabularProcs`, `Categorify` and `FillMissing`. A `TabularProc` is like a regular `Transform`, except for the following:

- It returns the exact same object that's passed to it, after modifying the object in place.
- It runs the transform once, when data is first passed in, rather than lazily as the data is accessed.

`Categorify` is a `TabularProc` that replaces a column with a numeric categorical column. `FillMissing` is a `TabularProc` that replaces missing values with the median of the column, and creates a new Boolean column that is set to `True` for any row where the value was missing. These two transforms are needed for nearly every tabular dataset you will use, so this is a good starting point for your data processing:

```
procs = [Categorify, FillMissing]
```

`TabularPandas` will also handle splitting the dataset into training and validation sets for us. However, we need to be very careful about our validation set. We want to design it so that it is like the *test set* Kaggle will use to judge the contest.

Recall the distinction between a validation set and a test set, as discussed in Chapter 1. A *validation set* is data we hold back from training in order to ensure that the training process does not overfit on the training data. A *test set* is data that is held back even more deeply, from us ourselves, in order to ensure that *we* don't overfit on the validation data as we explore various model architectures and hyperparameters.

We don't get to see the test set. But we do want to define our validation data so that it has the same sort of relationship to the training data as the test set will have.

In some cases, just randomly choosing a subset of your data points will do that. This is not one of those cases, because it is a time series.

If you look at the date range represented in the test set, you will discover that it covers a six-month period from May 2012, which is later in time than any date in the training set. This is a good design, because the competition sponsor will want to ensure that a model is able to predict the future. But it means that if we are going to have a useful validation set, we also want the validation set to be later in time than the training set. The Kaggle training data ends in April 2012, so we will define a narrower training dataset that consists only of the Kaggle training data from before November 2011, and we'll define a validation set consisting of data from after November 2011.

To do this we use `np.where`, a useful function that returns (as the first element of a tuple) the indices of all `True` values:

```
cond = (df.saleYear<2011) | (df.saleMonth<10)
train_idx = np.where( cond)[0]
valid_idx = np.where(~cond)[0]

splits = (list(train_idx),list(valid_idx))
```

`TabularPandas` needs to be told which columns are continuous and which are categorical. We can handle that automatically using the helper function `cont_cat_split`:

```
cont,cat = cont_cat_split(df, 1, dep_var=dep_var)

to = TabularPandas(df, procs, cat, cont, y_names=dep_var, splits=splits)
```

A `TabularPandas` behaves a lot like a fastai `Datasets` object, including providing `train` and `valid` attributes:

```
len(to.train),len(to.valid)
```

```
(404710, 7988)
```

We can see that the data is still displayed as strings for categories (we show only a few columns here because the full table is too big to fit on a page):

```
to.show(3)
```

	state	ProductGroup	Drive_System	Enclosure	SalePrice
0	Alabama	WL	#na#	EROPS w AC	11.097410
1	North Carolina	WL	#na#	EROPS w AC	10.950807
2	New York	SSL	#na#	OROPS	9.210340

However, the underlying items are all numeric:

```
to.items.head(3)
```

	state	ProductGroup	Drive_System	Enclosure
0	1	6	0	3
1	33	6	0	3
2	32	3	0	6

The conversion of categorical columns to numbers is done by simply replacing each unique level with a number. The numbers associated with the levels are chosen consecutively as they are seen in a column, so there's no particular meaning to the numbers in categorical columns after conversion. The exception is if you first convert a column to a Pandas ordered category (as we did for ProductSize earlier), in which case the ordering you chose is used. We can see the mapping by looking at the classes attribute:

```
to.classes['ProductSize']
```

```
(#7) ['#na#','Large','Large / Medium','Medium','Small','Mini','Compact']
```

Since it takes a minute or so to process the data to get to this point, we should save it —that way, in the future, we can continue our work from here without rerunning the previous steps. fastai provides a **save** method that uses Python's *pickle* system to save nearly any Python object:

```
(path/'to.pkl').save(to)
```

To read this back later, you would type this:

```
to = (path/'to.pkl').load()
```

Now that all this preprocessing is done, we are ready to create a decision tree.

Creating the Decision Tree

To begin, we define our independent and dependent variables:

```
xs,y = to.train.xs,to.train.y
valid_xs,valid_y = to.valid.xs,to.valid.y
```

Now that our data is all numeric, and there are no missing values, we can create a decision tree:

```
m = DecisionTreeRegressor(max_leaf_nodes=4)
m.fit(xs, y);
```

To keep it simple, we've told sklearn to create just four *leaf nodes*. To see what it's learned, we can display the tree:

```
draw_tree(m, xs, size=7, leaves_parallel=True, precision=2)
```

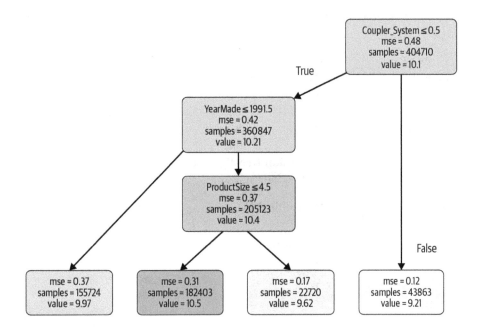

Understanding this picture is one of the best ways to understand decision trees, so we will start at the top and explain each part step by step.

The top node represents the *initial model* before any splits have been done, when all the data is in one group. This is the simplest possible model. It is the result of asking zero questions and will always predict the value to be the average value of the whole dataset. In this case, we can see it predicts a value of 10.1 for the logarithm of the sales price. It gives a mean squared error of 0.48. The square root of this is 0.69. (Remember that unless you see m_rmse, or a *root mean squared error*, the value you are looking at is before taking the square root, so it is just the average of the square of the differences.) We can also see that there are 404,710 auction records in this group—that is the total size of our training set. The final piece of information shown here is the decision criterion for the best split that was found, which is to split based on the coupler_system column.

Moving down and to the left, this node shows us that there were 360,847 auction records for equipment where coupler_system was less than 0.5. The average value of our dependent variable in this group is 10.21. Moving down and to the right from the initial model takes us to the records where coupler_system was greater than 0.5.

The bottom row contains our *leaf nodes*: the nodes with no answers coming out of them, because there are no more questions to be answered. At the far right of this row is the node containing records where coupler_system was greater than 0.5. The average value is 9.21, so we can see the decision tree algorithm did find a single binary decision that separated high-value from low-value auction results. Asking only about `coupler_system` predicts an average value of 9.21 versus 10.1.

Returning back to the top node after the first decision point, we can see that a second binary decision split has been made, based on asking whether `YearMade` is less than or equal to 1991.5. For the group where this is true (remember, this is now following two binary decisions, based on `coupler_system` and `YearMade`), the average value is 9.97, and there are 155,724 auction records in this group. For the group of auctions where this decision is false, the average value is 10.4, and there are 205,123 records. So again, we can see that the decision tree algorithm has successfully split our more expensive auction records into two more groups that differ in value significantly.

We can show the same information using Terence Parr's powerful dtreeviz library (*https://oreil.ly/e9KrM*):

```
samp_idx = np.random.permutation(len(y))[:500]
dtreeviz(m, xs.iloc[samp_idx], y.iloc[samp_idx], xs.columns, dep_var,
        fontname='DejaVu Sans', scale=1.6, label_fontsize=10,
        orientation='LR')
```

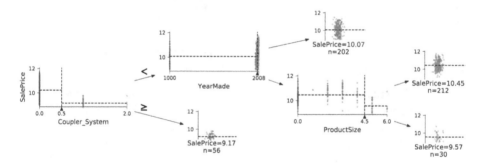

This shows a chart of the distribution of the data for each split point. We can clearly see that there's a problem with our `YearMade` data: there are bulldozers made in the year 1000, apparently! Presumably, this is just a missing value code (a value that doesn't otherwise appear in the data and that is used as a placeholder in cases where a value is missing). For modeling purposes, 1000 is fine, but as you can see, this outlier makes visualizing the values we are interested in more difficult. So, let's replace it with 1950:

```
xs.loc[xs['YearMade']<1900, 'YearMade'] = 1950
valid_xs.loc[valid_xs['YearMade']<1900, 'YearMade'] = 1950
```

That change makes the split much clearer in the tree visualization, even although it doesn't change the result of the model in any significant way. This is a great example of how resilient decision trees are to data issues!

```
m = DecisionTreeRegressor(max_leaf_nodes=4).fit(xs, y)
dtreeviz(m, xs.iloc[samp_idx], y.iloc[samp_idx], xs.columns, dep_var,
        fontname='DejaVu Sans', scale=1.6, label_fontsize=10,
        orientation='LR')
```

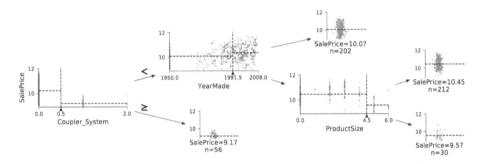

Let's now have the decision tree algorithm build a bigger tree. Here, we are not passing in any stopping criteria such as max_leaf_nodes:

```
m = DecisionTreeRegressor()
m.fit(xs, y);
```

We'll create a little function to check the root mean squared error of our model (m_rmse), since that's how the competition was judged:

```
def r_mse(pred,y): return round(math.sqrt(((pred-y)**2).mean()), 6)
def m_rmse(m, xs, y): return r_mse(m.predict(xs), y)

m_rmse(m, xs, y)
```

```
0.0
```

So, our model is perfect, right? Not so fast…remember, we really need to check the validation set, to ensure we're not overfitting:

```
m_rmse(m, valid_xs, valid_y)
```

```
0.337727
```

Oops—it looks like we might be overfitting pretty badly. Here's why:

```
m.get_n_leaves(), len(xs)
```

```
(340909, 404710)
```

We have nearly as many leaf nodes as data points! That seems a little over-enthusiastic. Indeed, sklearn's default settings allow it to continue splitting nodes until there is only one item in each leaf node. Let's change the stopping rule to tell sklearn to ensure every leaf node contains at least 25 auction records:

```
m = DecisionTreeRegressor(min_samples_leaf=25)
m.fit(to.train.xs, to.train.y)
m_rmse(m, xs, y), m_rmse(m, valid_xs, valid_y)
```

```
(0.248562, 0.32368)
```

That looks much better. Let's check the number of leaves again:

```
m.get_n_leaves()
```

```
12397
```

Much more reasonable!

Alexis Says

Here's my intuition for an overfitting decision tree with more leaf nodes than data items. Consider the game Twenty Questions. In that game, the chooser secretly imagines an object (like, "our television set"), and the guesser gets to pose 20 yes or no questions to try to guess what the object is (like "Is it bigger than a breadbox?"). The guesser is not trying to predict a numerical value, but just to identify a particular object out of the set of all imaginable objects. When your decision tree has more leaves than there are possible objects in your domain, it is essentially a well-trained guesser. It has learned the sequence of questions needed to identify a particular data item in the training set, and it is "predicting" only by describing that item's value. This is a way of memorizing the training set—i.e., of overfitting.

Building a decision tree is a good way to create a model of our data. It is very flexible, since it can clearly handle nonlinear relationships and interactions between variables. But we can see there is a fundamental compromise between how well it generalizes (which we can achieve by creating small trees) and how accurate it is on the training set (which we can achieve by using large trees).

So how do we get the best of both worlds? We'll show you right after we handle an important missing detail: how to handle categorical variables.

Categorical Variables

In the previous chapter, when working with deep learning networks, we dealt with categorical variables by one-hot encoding them and feeding them to an embedding layer. The embedding layer helped the model to discover the meaning of the different levels of these variables (the levels of a categorical variable do not have an intrinsic meaning, unless we manually specify an ordering using Pandas). In a decision tree, we don't have embedding layers—so how can these untreated categorical variables do anything useful in a decision tree? For instance, how could something like a product code be used?

The short answer is: it just works! Think about a situation in which one product code is far more expensive at auction than any other one. In that case, any binary split will result in that one product code being in some group, and that group will be more expensive than the other group. Therefore, our simple decision tree building algorithm will choose that split. Later, during training, the algorithm will be able to further split the subgroup that contains the expensive product code, and over time, the tree will home in on that one expensive product.

It is also possible to use one-hot encoding to replace a single categorical variable with multiple one-hot-encoded columns, where each column represents a possible level of the variable. Pandas has a `get_dummies` method that does just that.

However, there is not really any evidence that such an approach improves the end result. So, we generally avoid it where possible, because it does end up making your dataset harder to work with. In 2019, this issue was explored in the paper "Splitting on Categorical Predictors in Random Forests" (*https://oreil.ly/ojzKJ*) by Marvin Wright and Inke König:

> The standard approach for nominal predictors is to consider all $2^{k-1} - 1$ 2-partitions of the k predictor categories. However, this exponential relationship produces a large number of potential splits to be evaluated, increasing computational complexity and restricting the possible number of categories in most implementations. For binary classification and regression, it was shown that ordering the predictor categories in each split leads to exactly the same splits as the standard approach. This reduces computational complexity because only $k - 1$ splits have to be considered for a nominal predictor with k categories.

Now that you understand how decision trees work, it's time for that best-of-both-worlds solution: random forests.

Random Forests

In 1994, Berkeley professor Leo Breiman, one year after his retirement, published a small technical report called "Bagging Predictors" (*https://oreil.ly/6gMuG*), which turned out to be one of the most influential ideas in modern machine learning. The report began:

> Bagging predictors is a method for generating multiple versions of a predictor and using these to get an aggregated predictor. The aggregation averages over the versions...The multiple versions are formed by making bootstrap replicates of the learning set and using these as new learning sets. Tests...show that bagging can give substantial gains in accuracy. The vital element is the instability of the prediction method. If perturbing the learning set can cause significant changes in the predictor constructed, then bagging can improve accuracy.

Here is the procedure that Breiman is proposing:

1. Randomly choose a subset of the rows of your data (i.e., "bootstrap replicates of your learning set").
2. Train a model using this subset.
3. Save that model, and then return to step 1 a few times.
4. This will give you multiple trained models. To make a prediction, predict using all of the models, and then take the average of each of those model's predictions.

This procedure is known as *bagging*. It is based on a deep and important insight: although each of the models trained on a subset of data will make more errors than a model trained on the full dataset, those errors will not be correlated with each other. Different models will make different errors. The average of those errors, therefore, is zero! So if we take the average of all of the models' predictions, we should end up with a prediction that gets closer and closer to the correct answer, the more models we have. This is an extraordinary result—it means that we can improve the accuracy of nearly any kind of machine learning algorithm by training it multiple times, each time on a different random subset of the data, and averaging its predictions.

In 2001, Breiman went on to demonstrate that this approach to building models, when applied to decision tree building algorithms, was particularly powerful. He went even further than just randomly choosing rows for each model's training, but also randomly selected from a subset of columns when choosing each split in each decision tree. He called this method the *random forest*. Today it is, perhaps, the most widely used and practically important machine learning method.

In essence, a random forest is a model that averages the predictions of a large number of decision trees, which are generated by randomly varying various parameters that specify what data is used to train the tree and other tree parameters. Bagging is a particular approach to *ensembling*, or combining the results of multiple models together. To see how it works in practice, let's get started on creating our own random forest!

Creating a Random Forest

We can create a random forest just like we created a decision tree, except now we are also specifying parameters that indicate how many trees should be in the forest, how we should subset the data items (the rows), and how we should subset the fields (the columns).

In the following function definition, n_estimators defines the number of trees we want, max_samples defines how many rows to sample for training each tree, and max_features defines how many columns to sample at each split point (where 0.5 means "take half the total number of columns"). We can also specify when to stop splitting the tree nodes, effectively limiting the depth of the tree, by including the same min_samples_leaf parameter we used in the preceding section. Finally, we pass n_jobs=-1 to tell sklearn to use all our CPUs to build the trees in parallel. By creating a little function for this, we can more quickly try variations in the rest of this chapter:

```
def rf(xs, y, n_estimators=40, max_samples=200_000,
       max_features=0.5, min_samples_leaf=5, **kwargs):
    return RandomForestRegressor(n_jobs=-1, n_estimators=n_estimators,
        max_samples=max_samples, max_features=max_features,
        min_samples_leaf=min_samples_leaf, oob_score=True).fit(xs, y)

m = rf(xs, y);
```

Our validation RMSE is now much improved over our last result produced by the DecisionTreeRegressor, which made just one tree using all the available data:

```
m_rmse(m, xs, y), m_rmse(m, valid_xs, valid_y)

(0.170896, 0.233502)
```

One of the most important properties of random forests is that they aren't very sensitive to the hyperparameter choices, such as max_features. You can set n_estimators to as high a number as you have time to train—the more trees you have, the more accurate the model will be. max_samples can often be left at its default, unless you have over 200,000 data points, in which case setting it to 200,000 will make it train faster with little impact on accuracy. max_features=0.5 and min_samples_leaf=4 both tend to work well, although sklearn's defaults work well too.

The sklearn docs show an example (*https://oreil.ly/E0Och*) of the effects of different `max_features` choices, with increasing numbers of trees. In the plot, the blue plot line uses the fewest features, and the green line uses the most (it uses all the features). As you can see in Figure 9-7, the models with the lowest error result from using a subset of features but with a larger number of trees.

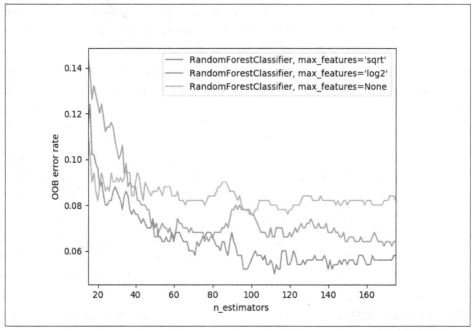

Figure 9-7. Error based on max features and number of trees (source: https://oreil.ly/ E0Och)

To see the impact of `n_estimators`, let's get the predictions from each individual tree in our forest (these are in the `estimators_` attribute):

```
preds = np.stack([t.predict(valid_xs) for t in m.estimators_])
```

As you can see, `preds.mean(0)` gives the same results as our random forest:

```
r_mse(preds.mean(0), valid_y)
```

```
0.233502
```

Let's see what happens to the RMSE as we add more and more trees. As you can see, the improvement levels off quite a bit after around 30 trees:

```
plt.plot([r_mse(preds[:i+1].mean(0), valid_y) for i in range(40)]);
```

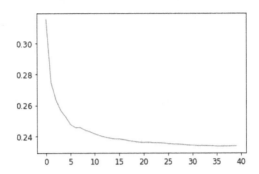

The performance on our validation set is worse than on our training set. But is that because we're overfitting, or because the validation set covers a different time period, or a bit of both? With the existing information we've seen, we can't tell. However, random forests have a very clever trick called *out-of-bag* (OOB) error that can help us with this (and more!).

Out-of-Bag Error

Recall that in a random forest, each tree is trained on a different subset of the training data. The OOB error is a way of measuring prediction error in the training dataset by including in the calculation of a row's error trees only where that row was *not* included in training. This allows us to see whether the model is overfitting, without needing a separate validation set.

Alexis Says

My intuition for this is that, since every tree was trained with a different randomly selected subset of rows, out-of-bag error is a little like imagining that every tree therefore also has its own validation set. That validation set is simply the rows that were not selected for that tree's training.

This is particularly beneficial in cases where we have only a small amount of training data, as it allows us to see whether our model generalizes without removing items to create a validation set. The OOB predictions are available in the `oob_prediction_` attribute. Note that we compare them to the training labels, since this is being calculated on trees using the training set:

```
r_mse(m.oob_prediction_, y)
```

```
0.210686
```

We can see that our OOB error is much lower than our validation set error. This means that something else is causing that error, in *addition* to normal generalization error. We'll discuss the reasons for this later in this chapter.

This is one way to interpret our model's predictions—let's focus on more of those now.

Model Interpretation

For tabular data, model interpretation is particularly important. For a given model, we are most likely to be interested in are the following:

- How confident are we in our predictions using a particular row of data?
- For predicting with a particular row of data, what were the most important factors, and how did they influence that prediction?
- Which columns are the strongest predictors, which can we ignore?
- Which columns are effectively redundant with each other, for purposes of prediction?
- How do predictions vary as we vary these columns?

As we will see, random forests are particularly well suited to answering these questions. Let's start with the first one!

Tree Variance for Prediction Confidence

We saw how the model averages the individual tree's predictions to get an overall prediction—that is, an estimate of the value. But how can we know the confidence of the estimate? One simple way is to use the standard deviation of predictions across the trees, instead of just the mean. This tells us the *relative* confidence of predictions. In general, we would want to be more cautious of using the results for rows where trees give very different results (higher standard deviations), compared to cases where they are more consistent (lower standard deviations).

In "Creating a Random Forest" on page 299, we saw how to get predictions over the validation set, using a Python list comprehension to do this for each tree in the forest:

```
preds = np.stack([t.predict(valid_xs) for t in m.estimators_])
preds.shape
```

```
(40, 7988)
```

Now we have a prediction for every tree and every auction in the validation set (40 trees and 7,988 auctions).

Using this, we can get the standard deviation of the predictions over all the trees, for each auction:

```
preds_std = preds.std(0)
```

Here are the standard deviations for the predictions for the first five auctions—that is, the first five rows of the validation set:

```
preds_std[:5]
```

```
array([0.21529149, 0.10351274, 0.08901878, 0.28374773, 0.11977206])
```

As you can see, the confidence in the predictions varies widely. For some auctions, there is a low standard deviation because the trees agree. For others, it's higher, as the trees don't agree. This is information that would be useful in a production setting; for instance, if you were using this model to decide which items to bid on at auction, a low-confidence prediction might cause you to look more carefully at an item before you made a bid.

Feature Importance

It's not normally enough just to know that a model can make accurate predictions—we also want to know *how* it's making predictions. The *feature importances* give us this insight. We can get these directly from sklearn's random forest by looking in the `feature_importances_` attribute. Here's a simple function we can use to pop them into a DataFrame and sort them:

```
def rf_feat_importance(m, df):
    return pd.DataFrame({'cols':df.columns, 'imp':m.feature_importances_}
                       ).sort_values('imp', ascending=False)
```

The feature importances for our model show that the first few most important columns have much higher importance scores than the rest, with (not surprisingly) `Year Made` and `ProductSize` being at the top of the list:

```
fi = rf_feat_importance(m, xs)
fi[:10]
```

	cols	imp
69	YearMade	0.182890
6	ProductSize	0.127268
30	Coupler_System	0.117698
7	fiProductClassDesc	0.069939
66	ModelID	0.057263
77	saleElapsed	0.050113
32	Hydraulics_Flow	0.047091
3	fiSecondaryDesc	0.041225
31	Grouser_Tracks	0.031988
1	fiModelDesc	0.031838

A plot of the feature importances shows the relative importances more clearly:

```
def plot_fi(fi):
    return fi.plot('cols', 'imp', 'barh', figsize=(12,7), legend=False)

plot_fi(fi[:30]);
```

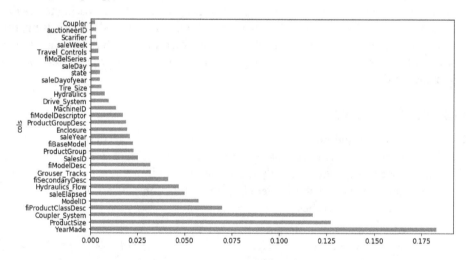

The way these importances are calculated is quite simple yet elegant. The feature importance algorithm loops through each tree, and then recursively explores each branch. At each branch, it looks to see what feature was used for that split, and how much the model improves as a result of that split. The improvement (weighted by the number of rows in that group) is added to the importance score for that feature. This is summed across all branches of all trees, and finally the scores are normalized such that they add to 1.

Removing Low-Importance Variables

It seems likely that we could use a subset of the columns by removing the variables of low importance and still get good results. Let's try keeping just those with a feature importance greater than 0.005:

```
to_keep = fi[fi.imp>0.005].cols
len(to_keep)
```

```
21
```

We can retrain our model using just this subset of the columns:

```
xs_imp = xs[to_keep]
valid_xs_imp = valid_xs[to_keep]

m = rf(xs_imp, y)
```

And here's the result:

```
m_rmse(m, xs_imp, y), m_rmse(m, valid_xs_imp, valid_y)
```

```
(0.181208, 0.232323)
```

Our accuracy is about the same, but we have far fewer columns to study:

```
len(xs.columns), len(xs_imp.columns)
```

```
(78, 21)
```

We've found that generally the first step to improving a model is simplifying it—78 columns was too many for us to study them all in depth! Furthermore, in practice, often a simpler, more interpretable model is easier to roll out and maintain.

This also makes our feature importance plot easier to interpret. Let's look at it again:

```
plot_fi(rf_feat_importance(m, xs_imp));
```

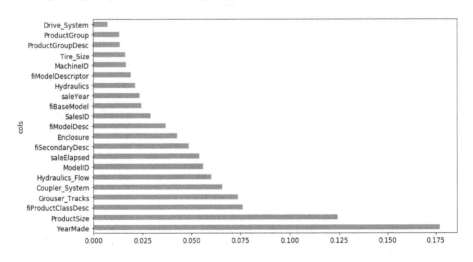

One thing that makes this harder to interpret is that there seem to be some variables with very similar meanings: for example, `ProductGroup` and `ProductGroupDesc`. Let's try to remove any redundant features.

Removing Redundant Features

Let's start with this:

```
cluster_columns(xs_imp)
```

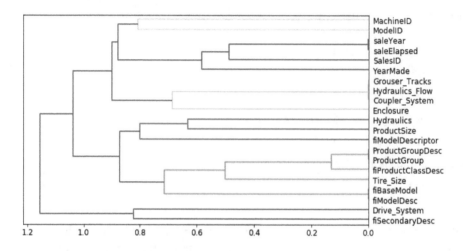

In this chart, the pairs of columns that are most similar are the ones that were merged together early, far from the "root" of the tree at the left. Unsurprisingly, the fields `Pro ductGroup` and `ProductGroupDesc` were merged quite early, as were `saleYear` and `saleElapsed`, and `fiModelDesc` and `fiBaseModel`. These might be so closely correlated they are practically synonyms for each other.

Determining Similarity

The most similar pairs are found by calculating the *rank correlation*, which means that all the values are replaced with their *rank* (first, second, third, etc. within the column), and then the *correlation* is calculated. (Feel free to skip over this minor detail though, since it's not going to come up again in the book!)

Let's try removing some of these closely related features to see if the model can be simplified without impacting the accuracy. First, we create a function that quickly trains a random forest and returns the OOB score, by using a lower `max_samples` and higher `min_samples_leaf`. The OOB score is a number returned by sklearn that ranges between 1.0 for a perfect model and 0.0 for a random model. (In statistics it's called R^2, although the details aren't important for this explanation.) We don't need it to be very accurate—we're just going to use it to compare different models, based on removing some of the possibly redundant columns:

```
def get_oob(df):
    m = RandomForestRegressor(n_estimators=40, min_samples_leaf=15,
        max_samples=50000, max_features=0.5, n_jobs=-1, oob_score=True)
    m.fit(df, y)
    return m.oob_score_
```

Here's our baseline:

```
get_oob(xs_imp)
```

```
0.8771039618198545
```

Now we try removing each of our potentially redundant variables, one at a time:

```
{c:get_oob(xs_imp.drop(c, axis=1)) for c in (
    'saleYear', 'saleElapsed', 'ProductGroupDesc','ProductGroup',
    'fiModelDesc', 'fiBaseModel',
    'Hydraulics_Flow','Grouser_Tracks', 'Coupler_System')}
```

```
{'saleYear': 0.8759666979317242,
 'saleElapsed': 0.8728423449081594,
 'ProductGroupDesc': 0.877877012281002,
 'ProductGroup': 0.8772503407182847,
 'fiModelDesc': 0.8756415073829513,
 'fiBaseModel': 0.8765165299438019,
 'Hydraulics_Flow': 0.8778545895742573,
 'Grouser_Tracks': 0.8773718142788077,
 'Coupler_System': 0.8778016988955392}
```

Now let's try dropping multiple variables. We'll drop one from each of the tightly aligned pairs we noticed earlier. Let's see what that does:

```
to_drop = ['saleYear', 'ProductGroupDesc', 'fiBaseModel', 'Grouser_Tracks']
get_oob(xs_imp.drop(to_drop, axis=1))
```

```
0.8739605718147015
```

Looking good! This is really not much worse than the model with all the fields. Let's create DataFrames without these columns, and save them:

```
xs_final = xs_imp.drop(to_drop, axis=1)
valid_xs_final = valid_xs_imp.drop(to_drop, axis=1)

(path/'xs_final.pkl').save(xs_final)
(path/'valid_xs_final.pkl').save(valid_xs_final)
```

We can load them back later:

```
xs_final = (path/'xs_final.pkl').load()
valid_xs_final = (path/'valid_xs_final.pkl').load()
```

Now we can check our RMSE again, to confirm that the accuracy hasn't substantially changed:

```
m = rf(xs_final, y)
m_rmse(m, xs_final, y), m_rmse(m, valid_xs_final, valid_y)
```

```
(0.183263, 0.233846)
```

By focusing on the most important variables and removing some redundant ones, we've greatly simplified our model. Now, let's see how those variables affect our predictions using partial dependence plots.

Partial Dependence

As we've seen, the two most important predictors are `ProductSize` and `YearMade`. We'd like to understand the relationship between these predictors and sale price. It's a good idea to first check the count of values per category (provided by the Pandas `value_counts` method), to see how common each category is:

```
p = valid_xs_final['ProductSize'].value_counts(sort=False).plot.barh()
c = to.classes['ProductSize']
plt.yticks(range(len(c)), c);
```

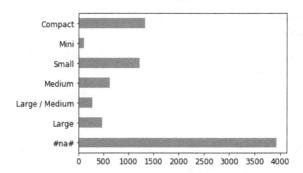

The largest group is #na#, which is the label fastai applies to missing values.

Let's do the same thing for YearMade. Since this is a numeric feature, we'll need to draw a histogram, which groups the year values into a few discrete bins:

```
ax = valid_xs_final['YearMade'].hist()
```

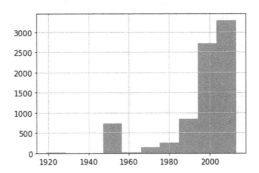

Other than the special value 1950, which we used for coding missing year values, most of the data is from after 1990.

Now we're ready to look at *partial dependence plots*. Partial dependence plots try to answer the question: if a row varied on nothing other than the feature in question, how would it impact the dependent variable?

For instance, how does YearMade impact sale price, all other things being equal? To answer this question, we can't just take the average sale price for each YearMade. The problem with that approach is that many other things vary from year to year as well, such as which products are sold, how many products have air-conditioning, inflation, and so forth. So, merely averaging over all the auctions that have the same YearMade would also capture the effect of how every other field also changed along with Year Made and how that overall change affected price.

Instead, what we do is replace every single value in the YearMade column with 1950, and then calculate the predicted sale price for every auction, and take the average over all auctions. Then we do the same for 1951, 1952, and so forth until our final year of 2011. This isolates the effect of only YearMade (even if it does so by averaging over some imagined records where we assign a YearMade value that might never actually exist alongside some other values).

Alexis Says

If you are philosophically minded, it is somewhat dizzying to contemplate the different kinds of hypotheticality that we are juggling to make this calculation. First, there's the fact that *every* prediction is hypothetical, because we are not noting empirical data. Second, there's the point that we're *not* merely interested in asking how sale price would change if we changed `YearMade` and everything else along with it. Rather, we're very specifically asking how sale price would change in a hypothetical world where only `YearMade` changed. Phew! It is impressive that we can ask such questions. I recommend Judea Pearl and Dana Mackenzie's recent book on causality, *The Book of Why* (Basic Books), if you're interested in more deeply exploring formalisms for analyzing these subtleties.

With these averages, we can then plot each year on the x-axis, and each prediction on the y-axis. This, finally, is a partial dependence plot. Let's take a look:

```
from sklearn.inspection import plot_partial_dependence

fig,ax = plt.subplots(figsize=(12, 4))
plot_partial_dependence(m, valid_xs_final, ['YearMade','ProductSize'],
                        grid_resolution=20, ax=ax);
```

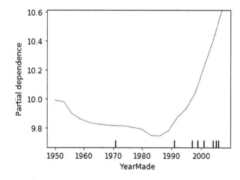 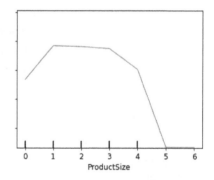

Looking first of all at the `YearMade` plot, and specifically at the section covering the years after 1990 (since, as we noted, this is where we have the most data), we can see a nearly linear relationship between year and price. Remember that our dependent variable is after taking the logarithm, so this means that in practice there is an exponential increase in price. This is what we would expect: depreciation is generally recognized as being a multiplicative factor over time, so for a given sale date, varying the year made ought to show an exponential relationship with sale price.

The `ProductSize` partial plot is a bit concerning. It shows that the final group, which we saw is for missing values, has the lowest price. To use this insight in practice, we would want to find out *why* it's missing so often and what that *means*. Missing values can sometimes be useful predictors—it entirely depends on what causes them to be missing. Sometimes, however, they can indicate *data leakage*.

Data Leakage

In the paper "Leakage in Data Mining: Formulation, Detection, and Avoidance" (*https://oreil.ly/XwvYf*), Shachar Kaufman et al. describe leakage as follows:

> The introduction of information about the target of a data mining problem, which should not be legitimately available to mine from. A trivial example of leakage would be a model that uses the target itself as an input, thus concluding for example that "it rains on rainy days." In practice, the introduction of this illegitimate information is unintentional, and facilitated by the data collection, aggregation, and preparation process.

They give as an example:

> A real-life business intelligence project at IBM where potential customers for certain products were identified, among other things, based on keywords found on their websites. This turned out to be leakage since the website content used for training had been sampled at the point in time where the potential customer has already become a customer, and where the website contained traces of the IBM products purchased, such as the word "Websphere" (e.g., in a press release about the purchase or a specific product feature the client uses).

Data leakage is subtle and can take many forms. In particular, missing values often represent data leakage.

For instance, Jeremy competed in a Kaggle competition designed to predict which researchers would end up receiving research grants. The information was provided by a university and included thousands of examples of research projects, along with information about the researchers involved and data on whether or not each grant was eventually accepted. The university hoped to be able to use the models developed in this competition to rank which grant applications were most likely to succeed, so it could prioritize its processing.

Jeremy used a random forest to model the data, and then used feature importance to find out which features were most predictive. He noticed three surprising things:

- The model was able to correctly predict who would receive grants over 95% of the time.
- Apparently meaningless identifier columns were the most important predictors.
- The day of week and day of year columns were also highly predictive; for instance, the vast majority of grant applications dated on a Sunday were accepted, and many accepted grant applications were dated on January 1.

For the identifier columns, a partial dependence plot showed that when the information was missing, the application was almost always rejected. It turned out that in practice, the university filled out much of this information only *after* a grant application was accepted. Often, for applications that were not accepted, it was just left blank. Therefore, this information was not something that was available at the time that the application was received, and it would not be available for a predictive model —it was data leakage.

In the same way, the final processing of successful applications was often done automatically as a batch at the end of the week, or the end of the year. It was this final processing date that ended up in the data, so again, this information, while predictive, was not actually available at the time that the application was received.

This example showcases the most practical and simple approaches to identifying data leakage, which are to build a model and then do the following:

- Check whether the accuracy of the model is *too good to be true*.
- Look for important predictors that don't make sense in practice.
- Look for partial dependence plot results that don't make sense in practice.

Thinking back to our bear detector, this mirrors the advice that we provided in Chapter 2—it is often a good idea to build a model first and then do your data cleaning, rather than vice versa. The model can help you identify potentially problematic data issues.

It can also help you identify which factors influence specific predictions, with tree interpreters.

Tree Interpreter

At the start of this section, we said that we wanted to be able to answer five questions:

- How confident are we in our predictions using a particular row of data?
- For predicting with a particular row of data, what were the most important factors, and how did they influence that prediction?
- Which columns are the strongest predictors?
- Which columns are effectively redundant with each other, for purposes of prediction?
- How do predictions vary as we vary these columns?

We've handled four of these already; only the second question remains. To answer this question, we need to use the *treeinterpreter* library. We'll also use the *waterfall-charts* library to draw the chart of the results. You can install these by running these commands in a notebook cell:

```
!pip install treeinterpreter
!pip install waterfallcharts
```

We have already seen how to compute feature importances across the entire random forest. The basic idea was to look at the contribution of each variable to improving the model, at each branch of every tree, and then add up all of these contributions per variable.

We can do exactly the same thing, but for just a single row of data. For instance, let's say we are looking at a particular item at auction. Our model might predict that this item will be very expensive, and we want to know why. So, we take that one row of data and put it through the first decision tree, looking to see what split is used at each point throughout the tree. For each split, we find the increase or decrease in the addition, compared to the parent node of the tree. We do this for every tree, and add up the total change in importance by split variable.

For instance, let's pick the first few rows of our validation set:

```
row = valid_xs_final.iloc[:5]
```

We can then pass these to `treeinterpreter`:

```
prediction,bias,contributions = treeinterpreter.predict(m, row.values)
```

`prediction` is simply the prediction that the random forest makes. `bias` is the prediction based on taking the mean of the dependent variable (i.e., the *model* that is the root of every tree). `contributions` is the most interesting bit—it tells us the total change in prediction due to each of the independent variables. Therefore, the sum of `contributions` plus `bias` must equal the `prediction`, for each row. Let's look at just the first row:

```
prediction[0], bias[0], contributions[0].sum()
```

```
(array([9.98234598]), 10.104309759725059, -0.12196378442186026)
```

The clearest way to display the contributions is with a *waterfall plot*. This shows how the positive and negative contributions from all the independent variables sum up to create the final prediction, which is the righthand column labeled "net" here:

```
waterfall(valid_xs_final.columns, contributions[0], threshold=0.08,
          rotation_value=45,formatting='{:,.3f}');
```

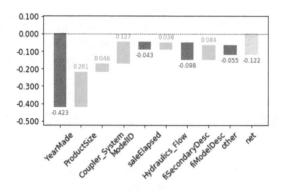

This kind of information is most useful in production, rather than during model development. You can use it to provide useful information to users of your data product about the underlying reasoning behind the predictions.

Now that we covered some classic machine learning techniques to solve this problem, let's see how deep learning can help!

Extrapolation and Neural Networks

A problem with random forests, like all machine learning or deep learning algorithms, is that they don't always generalize well to new data. We'll see in which situations neural networks generalize better, but first, let's look at the extrapolation problem that random forests have and how they can help identify out-of-domain data.

The Extrapolation Problem

Let's consider the simple task of making predictions from 40 data points showing a slightly noisy linear relationship:

```
x_lin = torch.linspace(0,20, steps=40)
y_lin = x_lin + torch.randn_like(x_lin)
plt.scatter(x_lin, y_lin);
```

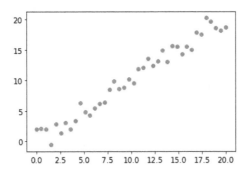

Although we have only a single independent variable, sklearn expects a matrix of independent variables, not a single vector. So we have to turn our vector into a matrix with one column. In other words, we have to change the *shape* from [40] to [40,1]. One way to do that is with the unsqueeze method, which adds a new unit axis to a tensor at the requested dimension:

```
xs_lin = x_lin.unsqueeze(1)
x_lin.shape,xs_lin.shape
```

```
(torch.Size([40]), torch.Size([40, 1]))
```

A more flexible approach is to slice an array or tensor with the special value None, which introduces an additional unit axis at that location:

```
x_lin[:,None].shape
```

```
torch.Size([40, 1])
```

We can now create a random forest for this data. We'll use only the first 30 rows to train the model:

```
m_lin = RandomForestRegressor().fit(xs_lin[:30],y_lin[:30])
```

Then we'll test the model on the full dataset. The blue dots are the training data, and the red dots are the predictions:

```
plt.scatter(x_lin, y_lin, 20)
plt.scatter(x_lin, m_lin.predict(xs_lin), color='red', alpha=0.5);
```

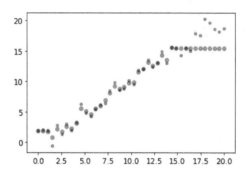

We have a big problem! Our predictions outside the domain that our training data covered are all too low. Why do you suppose this is?

Remember, a random forest just averages the predictions of a number of trees. And a tree simply predicts the average value of the rows in a leaf. Therefore, a tree and a random forest can never predict values outside the range of the training data. This is particularly problematic for data indicating a trend over time, such as inflation, and you wish to make predictions for a future time. Your predictions will be systematically too low.

But the problem extends beyond time variables. Random forests are not able to extrapolate outside the types of data they have seen, in a more general sense. That's why we need to make sure our validation set does not contain out-of-domain data.

Finding Out-of-Domain Data

Sometimes it is hard to know whether your test set is distributed in the same way as your training data, or, if it is different, which columns reflect that difference. There's an easy way to figure this out, which is to use a random forest!

But in this case, we don't use the random forest to predict our actual dependent variable. Instead, we try to predict whether a row is in the validation set or the training set. To see this in action, let's combine our training and validation sets, create a dependent variable that represents which dataset each row comes from, build a random forest using that data, and get its feature importance:

```
df_dom = pd.concat([xs_final, valid_xs_final])
is_valid = np.array([0]*len(xs_final) + [1]*len(valid_xs_final))

m = rf(df_dom, is_valid)
rf_feat_importance(m, df_dom)[:6]
```

	cols	imp
5	saleElapsed	0.859446
9	SalesID	0.119325
13	MachineID	0.014259
0	YearMade	0.001793
8	fiModelDesc	0.001740
11	Enclosure	0.000657

This shows that three columns differ significantly between the training and validation sets: saleElapsed, SalesID, and MachineID. It's fairly obvious why this is the case for saleElapsed: it's the number of days between the start of the dataset and each row, so it directly encodes the date. The difference in SalesID suggests that identifiers for auction sales might increment over time. MachineID suggests something similar might be happening for individual items sold in those auctions.

Let's get a baseline of the original random forest model's RMSE, and then determine the effect of removing each of these columns in turn:

```
m = rf(xs_final, y)
print('orig', m_rmse(m, valid_xs_final, valid_y))

for c in ('SalesID','saleElapsed','MachineID'):
    m = rf(xs_final.drop(c,axis=1), y)
    print(c, m_rmse(m, valid_xs_final.drop(c,axis=1), valid_y))

orig 0.232795
SalesID 0.23109
saleElapsed 0.236221
MachineID 0.233492
```

It looks like we should be able to remove SalesID and MachineID without losing any accuracy. Let's check:

```
time_vars = ['SalesID','MachineID']
xs_final_time = xs_final.drop(time_vars, axis=1)
valid_xs_time = valid_xs_final.drop(time_vars, axis=1)

m = rf(xs_final_time, y)
m_rmse(m, valid_xs_time, valid_y)

0.231307
```

Removing these variables has slightly improved the model's accuracy; but more importantly, it should make it more resilient over time, and easier to maintain and understand. We recommend that for all datasets, you try building a model in which your dependent variable is is_valid, as we did here. It can often uncover subtle *domain shift* issues that you may otherwise miss.

One thing that might help in our case is to simply avoid using old data. Often, old data shows relationships that just aren't valid anymore. Let's try just using the most recent few years of the data:

```
xs['saleYear'].hist();
```

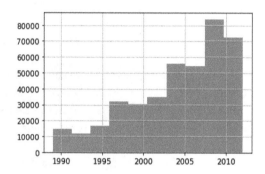

Here's the result of training on this subset:

```
filt = xs['saleYear']>2004
xs_filt = xs_final_time[filt]
y_filt = y[filt]

m = rf(xs_filt, y_filt)
m_rmse(m, xs_filt, y_filt), m_rmse(m, valid_xs_time, valid_y)
```

```
(0.17768, 0.230631)
```

It's a tiny bit better, which shows that you shouldn't always use your entire dataset; sometimes a subset can be better.

Let's see if using a neural network helps.

Using a Neural Network

We can use the same approach to build a neural network model. Let's first replicate the steps we took to set up the TabularPandas object:

```
df_nn = pd.read_csv(path/'TrainAndValid.csv', low_memory=False)
df_nn['ProductSize'] = df_nn['ProductSize'].astype('category')
df_nn['ProductSize'].cat.set_categories(sizes, ordered=True, inplace=True)
df_nn[dep_var] = np.log(df_nn[dep_var])
df_nn = add_datepart(df_nn, 'saledate')
```

We can leverage the work we did to trim unwanted columns in the random forest by using the same set of columns for our neural network:

```
df_nn_final = df_nn[list(xs_final_time.columns) + [dep_var]]
```

Categorical columns are handled very differently in neural networks, compared to decision tree approaches. As we saw in Chapter 8, in a neutral net, a great way to handle categorical variables is by using embeddings. To create embeddings, fastai needs to determine which columns should be treated as categorical variables. It does this by comparing the number of distinct levels in the variable to the value of the max_card parameter. If it's lower, fastai will treat the variable as categorical. Embedding sizes larger than 10,000 should generally be used only after you've tested whether there are better ways to group the variable, so we'll use 9,000 as our max_card value:

```
cont_nn,cat_nn = cont_cat_split(df_nn_final, max_card=9000, dep_var=dep_var)
```

In this case, however, there's one variable that we absolutely do not want to treat as categorical: saleElapsed. A categorical variable cannot, by definition, extrapolate outside the range of values that it has seen, but we want to be able to predict auction sale prices in the future. Let's verify that cont_cat_split did the correct thing:

```
cont_nn.append('saleElapsed')
cat_nn.remove('saleElapsed')
```

Let's take a look at the cardinality of each of the categorical variables that we have chosen so far:

```
df_nn_final[cat_nn].nunique()
```

```
YearMade             73
ProductSize           6
Coupler_System        2
fiProductClassDesc    74
ModelID            5281
Hydraulics_Flow       3
fiSecondaryDesc     177
fiModelDesc        5059
ProductGroup          6
Enclosure             6
fiModelDescriptor   140
Drive_System          4
Hydraulics           12
Tire_Size            17
dtype: int64
```

The fact that there are two variables pertaining to the "model" of the equipment, both with similar very high cardinalities, suggests that they may contain similar, redundant information. Note that we would not necessarily catch this when analyzing redundant features, since that relies on similar variables being sorted in the same order (that is, they need to have similarly named levels). Having a column with 5,000 levels means needing 5,000 columns in our embedding matrix, which would be nice to avoid if possible. Let's see what the impact of removing one of these model columns has on the random forest:

```
xs_filt2 = xs_filt.drop('fiModelDescriptor', axis=1)
valid_xs_time2 = valid_xs_time.drop('fiModelDescriptor', axis=1)
m2 = rf(xs_filt2, y_filt)
m_rmse(m2, xs_filt2, y_filt), m_rmse(m2, valid_xs_time2, valid_y)
```

```
(0.176706, 0.230642)
```

There's minimal impact, so we will remove it as a predictor for our neural network:

```
cat_nn.remove('fiModelDescriptor')
```

We can create our `TabularPandas` object in the same way as when we created our random forest, with one very important addition: normalization. A random forest does not need any normalization—the tree building procedure cares only about the order of values in a variable, not at all about how they are scaled. But as we have seen, a neural network definitely does care about this. Therefore, we add the `Normalize` processor when we build our `TabularPandas` object:

```
procs_nn = [Categorify, FillMissing, Normalize]
to_nn = TabularPandas(df_nn_final, procs_nn, cat_nn, cont_nn,
                      splits=splits, y_names=dep_var)
```

Tabular models and data don't generally require much GPU RAM, so we can use larger batch sizes:

```
dls = to_nn.dataloaders(1024)
```

As we've discussed, it's a good idea to set `y_range` for regression models, so let's find the min and max of our dependent variable:

```
y = to_nn.train.y
y.min(),y.max()
```

```
(8.465899897028686, 11.863582336583399)
```

We can now create the `Learner` to create this tabular model. As usual, we use the application-specific learner function, to take advantage of its application-customized defaults. We set the loss function to MSE, since that's what this competition uses.

By default, for tabular data fastai creates a neural network with two hidden layers, with 200 and 100 activations, respectively. This works quite well for small datasets, but here we've got quite a large dataset, so we increase the layer sizes to 500 and 250:

```
from fastai.tabular.all import *
```

```
learn = tabular_learner(dls, y_range=(8,12), layers=[500,250],
                        n_out=1, loss_func=F.mse_loss)
```

```
learn.lr_find()
```

```
(0.005754399299621582, 0.0002754228771664202)
```

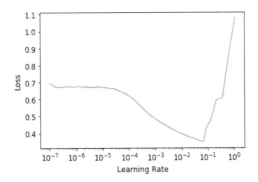

There's no need to use `fine_tune`, so we'll train with `fit_one_cycle` for a few epochs and see how it looks:

```
learn.fit_one_cycle(5, 1e-2)
```

epoch	train_loss	valid_loss	time
0	0.069705	0.062389	00:11
1	0.056253	0.058489	00:11
2	0.048385	0.052256	00:11
3	0.043400	0.050743	00:11
4	0.040358	0.050986	00:11

We can use our `r_mse` function to compare the result to the random forest result we got earlier:

```
preds,targs = learn.get_preds()
r_mse(preds,targs)
```

```
0.2258
```

It's quite a bit better than the random forest (although it took longer to train, and it's fussier about hyperparameter tuning).

Before we move on, let's save our model in case we want to come back to it again later:

```
learn.save('nn')
```

fastai's Tabular Classes

In fastai, a tabular model is simply a model that takes columns of continuous or categorical data, and predicts a category (a classification model) or a continuous value (a regression model). Categorical independent variables are passed through an embedding and concatenated, as we saw in the neural net we used for collaborative filtering, and then continuous variables are concatenated as well.

The model created in `tabular_learner` is an object of class `TabularModel`. Take a look at the source for `tabular_learner` now (remember, that's `tabular_learner??` in Jupyter). You'll see that like `collab_learner`, it first calls `get_emb_sz` to calculate appropriate embedding sizes (you can override these by using the `emb_szs` parameter, which is a dictionary containing any column names you want to set sizes for manually), and it sets a few other defaults. Other than that, it creates the `TabularModel` and passes that to `TabularLearner` (note that `TabularLearner` is identical to `Learner`, except for a customized `predict` method).

That means that really all the work is happening in `TabularModel`, so take a look at the source for that now. With the exception of the `BatchNorm1d` and `Dropout` layers (which we'll be learning about shortly), you now have the knowledge required to understand this whole class. Take a look at the discussion of `EmbeddingNN` at the end of the preceding chapter. Recall that it passed `n_cont=0` to `TabularModel`. We now can see why that was: because there are zero continuous variables (in fastai, the `n_` prefix means "number of," and `cont` is an abbreviation for "continuous").

Another thing that can help with generalization is to use several models and average their predictions—a technique, as mentioned earlier, known as *ensembling*.

Ensembling

Think back to the original reasoning behind why random forests work so well: each tree has errors, but those errors are not correlated with each other, so the average of those errors should tend toward zero once there are enough trees. Similar reasoning could be used to consider averaging the predictions of models trained using different algorithms.

In our case, we have two very different models, trained using very different algorithms: a random forest and a neural network. It would be reasonable to expect that the kinds of errors that each one makes would be quite different. Therefore, we might expect that the average of their predictions would be better than either one's individual predictions.

As we saw earlier, a random forest is itself an ensemble. But we can then include a random forest in *another* ensemble—an ensemble of the random forest and the neural network! While ensembling won't make the difference between a successful and an unsuccessful modeling process, it can certainly add a nice little boost to any models that you have built.

One minor issue we have to be aware of is that our PyTorch model and our sklearn model create data of different types: PyTorch gives us a rank-2 tensor (a column matrix), whereas NumPy gives us a rank-1 array (a vector). `squeeze` removes any unit axes from a tensor, and `to_np` converts it into a NumPy array:

```
rf_preds = m.predict(valid_xs_time)
ens_preds = (to_np(preds.squeeze()) + rf_preds) /2
```

This gives us a better result than either model achieved on its own:

```
r_mse(ens_preds,valid_y)
```

```
0.22291
```

In fact, this result is better than any score shown on the Kaggle leaderboard. It's not directly comparable, however, because the Kaggle leaderboard uses a separate dataset that we do not have access to. Kaggle does not allow us to submit to this old competition to find out how we would have done, but our results certainly look encouraging!

Boosting

So far, our approach to ensembling has been to use *bagging*, which involves combining many models (each trained on a different data subset) by averaging them. As we saw, when this is applied to decision trees, this is called a *random forest*.

In another important approach to ensembling, called *boosting*, where we add models instead of averaging them. Here is how boosting works:

1. Train a small model that underfits your dataset.
2. Calculate the predictions in the training set for this model.
3. Subtract the predictions from the targets; these are called the *residuals* and represent the error for each point in the training set.
4. Go back to step 1, but instead of using the original targets, use the residuals as the targets for the training.
5. Continue doing this until you reach a stopping criterion, such as a maximum number of trees, or you observe your validation set error getting worse.

Using this approach, each new tree will be attempting to fit the error of all of the previous trees combined. Because we are continually creating new residuals by subtracting the predictions of each new tree from the residuals from the previous tree, the residuals will get smaller and smaller.

To make predictions with an ensemble of boosted trees, we calculate the predictions from each tree and then add them all together. There are many models following this basic approach, and many names for the same models. *Gradient boosting machines* (GBMs) and *gradient boosted decision trees* (GBDTs) are the terms you're most likely to come across, or you may see the names of specific libraries implementing these; at the time of writing, *XGBoost* is the most popular.

Note that, unlike with random forests, with this approach, there is nothing to stop us from overfitting. Using more trees in a random forest does not lead to overfitting, because each tree is independent of the others. But in a boosted ensemble, the more trees you have, the better the training error becomes, and eventually you will see overfitting on the validation set.

We are not going to go into detail on how to train a gradient boosted tree ensemble here, because the field is moving rapidly, and any guidance we give will almost certainly be outdated by the time you read this. As we write this, sklearn has just added a `HistGradientBoostingRegressor` class that provides excellent performance. There are many hyperparameters to tweak for this class, and for all gradient boosted tree methods we have seen. Unlike random forests, gradient boosted trees are extremely sensitive to the choices of these hyperparameters; in practice, most people use a loop that tries a range of hyperparameters to find the ones that work best.

One more technique that has gotten great results is to use embeddings learned by a neural net in a machine learning model.

Combining Embeddings with Other Methods

The abstract of the entity embedding paper we mentioned at the start of this chapter states: "The embeddings obtained from the trained neural network boost the performance of all tested machine learning methods considerably when used as the input features instead." It includes the very interesting table shown in Figure 9-8.

method	MAPE	MAPE (with EE)
KNN	0.290	0.116
random forest	0.158	0.108
gradient boosted trees	0.152	0.115
neural network	0.101	0.093

Figure 9-8. Effects of using neural network embeddings as input to other machine learning methods (courtesy of Cheng Guo and Felix Berkhahn)

This is showing the mean average percent error (MAPE) compared among four modeling techniques, three of which we have already seen, along with k-nearest neighbors (KNN), which is a very simple baseline method. The first numeric column contains the results of using the methods on the data provided in the competition; the second column shows what happens if you first train a neural network with categorical embeddings, and then use those categorical embeddings instead of the raw categorical columns in the model. As you see, in every case, the models are dramatically improved by using the embeddings instead of the raw categories.

This is a really important result, because it shows that you can get much of the performance improvement of a neural network without having to use a neural network at inference time. You could just use an embedding, which is literally just an array lookup, along with a small decision tree ensemble.

These embeddings need not even be necessarily learned separately for each model or task in an organization. Instead, once a set of embeddings are learned for a column for a particular task, they could be stored in a central place and reused across multiple models. In fact, we know from private communication with other practitioners at large companies that this is already happening in many places.

Conclusion

We have discussed two approaches to tabular modeling: decision tree ensembles and neural networks. We've also mentioned two decision tree ensembles: random forests and gradient boosting machines. Each is effective but also requires compromises:

- *Random forests* are the easiest to train, because they are extremely resilient to hyperparameter choices and require little preprocessing. They are fast to train, and should not overfit if you have enough trees. But they can be a little less accurate, especially if extrapolation is required, such as predicting future time periods.

- *Gradient boosting machines* in theory are just as fast to train as random forests, but in practice you will have to try lots of hyperparameters. They can overfit, but they are often a little more accurate than random forests.

- *Neural networks* take the longest time to train and require extra preprocessing, such as normalization; this normalization needs to be used at inference time as well. They can provide great results and extrapolate well, but only if you are careful with your hyperparameters and take care to avoid overfitting.

We suggest starting your analysis with a random forest. This will give you a strong baseline, and you can be confident that it's a reasonable starting point. You can then use that model for feature selection and partial dependence analysis, to get a better understanding of your data.

From that foundation, you can try neural nets and GBMs, and if they give you significantly better results on your validation set in a reasonable amount of time, you can use them. If decision tree ensembles are working well for you, try adding the embeddings for the categorical variables to the data, and see if that helps your decision trees learn better.

Questionnaire

1. What is a continuous variable?
2. What is a categorical variable?
3. Provide two of the words that are used for the possible values of a categorical variable.
4. What is a dense layer?
5. How do entity embeddings reduce memory usage and speed up neural networks?
6. What kinds of datasets are entity embeddings especially useful for?
7. What are the two main families of machine learning algorithms?
8. Why do some categorical columns need a special ordering in their classes? How do you do this in Pandas?
9. Summarize what a decision tree algorithm does.
10. Why is a date different from a regular categorical or continuous variable, and how can you preprocess it to allow it to be used in a model?
11. Should you pick a random validation set in the bulldozer competition? If no, what kind of validation set should you pick?
12. What is pickle and what is it useful for?
13. How are `mse`, `samples`, and `values` calculated in the decision tree drawn in this chapter?
14. How do we deal with outliers before building a decision tree?
15. How do we handle categorical variables in a decision tree?
16. What is bagging?
17. What is the difference between `max_samples` and `max_features` when creating a random forest?
18. If you increase `n_estimators` to a very high value, can that lead to overfitting? Why or why not?
19. In the section "Creating a Random Forest", after Figure 9-7, why did `preds.mean(0)` give the same result as our random forest?
20. What is out-of-bag error?

21. List the reasons that a model's validation set error might be worse than the OOB error. How could you test your hypotheses?

22. Explain why random forests are well suited to answering each of the following questions:
    - How confident are we in our predictions using a particular row of data?
    - For predicting with a particular row of data, what were the most important factors, and how did they influence that prediction?
    - Which columns are the strongest predictors?
    - How do predictions vary as we vary these columns?

23. What's the purpose of removing unimportant variables?

24. What's a good type of plot for showing tree interpreter results?

25. What is the extrapolation problem?

26. How can you tell if your test or validation set is distributed in a different way than your training set?

27. Why do we ensure that `saleElapsed` is a continuous variable, even though it has fewer than 9,000 distinct values?

28. What is boosting?

29. How could we use embeddings with a random forest? Would we expect this to help?

30. Why might we not always use a neural net for tabular modeling?

Further Research

1. Pick a competition on Kaggle with tabular data (current or past) and try to adapt the techniques seen in this chapter to get the best possible results. Compare your results to the private leaderboard.

2. Implement the decision tree algorithm in this chapter from scratch yourself, and try it on the dataset you used in the first exercise.

3. Use the embeddings from the neural net in this chapter in a random forest, and see if you can improve on the random forest results we saw.

4. Explain what each line of the source of `TabularModel` does (with the exception of the `BatchNorm1d` and `Dropout` layers).

CHAPTER 10

NLP Deep Dive: RNNs

In Chapter 1, we saw that deep learning can be used to get great results with natural language datasets. Our example relied on using a pretrained language model and fine-tuning it to classify reviews. That example highlighted a difference between transfer learning in NLP and computer vision: in general, in NLP the pretrained model is trained on a different task.

What we call a *language model* is a model that has been trained to guess the next word in a text (having read the ones before). This kind of task is called *self-supervised learning*: we do not need to give labels to our model, just feed it lots and lots of texts. It has a process to automatically get labels from the data, and this task isn't trivial: to properly guess the next word in a sentence, the model will have to develop an understanding of the English (or other) language. Self-supervised learning can also be used in other domains; for instance, see "Self-Supervised Learning and Computer Vision" (*https://oreil.ly/ECjff*) for an introduction to vision applications. Self-supervised learning is not usually used for the model that is trained directly, but instead is used for pretraining a model used for transfer learning.

Jargon: Self-Supervised Learning

Training a model using labels that are embedded in the independent variable, rather than requiring external labels. For instance, training a model to predict the next word in a text.

The language model we used in Chapter 1 to classify IMDb reviews was pretrained on Wikipedia. We got great results by directly fine-tuning this language model to a movie review classifier, but with one extra step, we can do even better. The Wikipedia English is slightly different from the IMDb English, so instead of jumping directly to the classifier, we could fine-tune our pretrained language model to the IMDb corpus and then use *that* as the base for our classifier.

Even if our language model knows the basics of the language we are using in the task (e.g., our pretrained model is in English), it helps to get used to the style of the corpus we are targeting. It may be more informal language, or more technical, with new words to learn or different ways of composing sentences. In the case of the IMDb dataset, there will be lots of names of movie directors and actors, and often a less formal style of language than that seen in Wikipedia.

We already saw that with fastai, we can download a pretrained English language model and use it to get state-of-the-art results for NLP classification. (We expect pretrained models in many more languages to be available soon; they might well be available by the time you are reading this book, in fact.) So, why are we learning how to train a language model in detail?

One reason, of course, is that it is helpful to understand the foundations of the models that you are using. But there is another very practical reason, which is that you get even better results if you fine-tune the (sequence-based) language model prior to fine-tuning the classification model. For instance, for the IMDb sentiment analysis task, the dataset includes 50,000 additional movie reviews that do not have any positive or negative labels attached. Since there are 25,000 labeled reviews in the training set and 25,000 in the validation set, that makes 100,000 movie reviews altogether. We can use all of these reviews to fine-tune the pretrained language model, which was trained only on Wikipedia articles; this will result in a language model that is particularly good at predicting the next word of a movie review.

This is known as the Universal Language Model Fine-tuning (ULMFiT) approach. The paper introducing it (*https://oreil.ly/rET-C*) showed that this extra stage of fine-tuning the language model, prior to transfer learning to a classification task, resulted in significantly better predictions. Using this approach, we have three stages for transfer learning in NLP, as summarized in Figure 10-1.

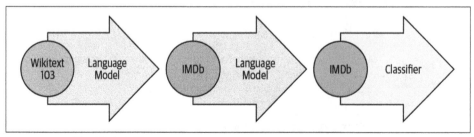

Figure 10-1. The ULMFiT process

We'll now explore how to apply a neural network to this language modeling problem, using the concepts introduced in the preceding two chapters. But before reading further, pause and think about how *you* would approach this.

Text Preprocessing

It's not at all obvious how we're going to use what we've learned so far to build a language model. Sentences can be different lengths, and documents can be long. So how can we predict the next word of a sentence using a neural network? Let's find out!

We've already seen how categorical variables can be used as independent variables for a neural network. Here's the approach we took for a single categorical variable:

1. Make a list of all possible levels of that categorical variable (we'll call this list the *vocab*).
2. Replace each level with its index in the vocab.
3. Create an embedding matrix for this containing a row for each level (i.e., for each item of the vocab).
4. Use this embedding matrix as the first layer of a neural network. (A dedicated embedding matrix can take as inputs the raw vocab indexes created in step 2; this is equivalent to, but faster and more efficient than, a matrix that takes as input one-hot-encoded vectors representing the indexes.)

We can do nearly the same thing with text! What is new is the idea of a sequence. First we concatenate all of the documents in our dataset into one big long string and split it into words (or *tokens*), giving us a very long list of words. Our independent variable will be the sequence of words starting with the first word in our very long list and ending with the second to last, and our dependent variable will be the sequence of words starting with the second word and ending with the last word.

Our vocab will consist of a mix of common words that are already in the vocabulary of our pretrained model and new words specific to our corpus (cinematographic terms or actor's names, for instance). Our embedding matrix will be built accordingly: for words that are in the vocabulary of our pretrained model, we will take the corresponding row in the embedding matrix of the pretrained model; but for new words, we won't have anything, so we will just initialize the corresponding row with a random vector.

Each of the steps necessary to create a language model has jargon associated with it from the world of natural language processing, and fastai and PyTorch classes available to help. The steps are as follows:

Tokenization
> Convert the text into a list of words (or characters, or substrings, depending on the granularity of your model).

Numericalization
> List all of the unique words that appear (the vocab), and convert each word into a number by looking up its index in the vocab.

Language model data loader creation
> fastai provides an `LMDataLoader` class that automatically handles creating a dependent variable that is offset from the independent variable by one token. It also handles some important details, such as how to shuffle the training data in such a way that the dependent and independent variables maintain their structure as required.

Language model creation
> We need a special kind of model that does something we haven't seen before: handles input lists that could be arbitrarily big or small. There are a number of ways to do this; in this chapter, we will be using a *recurrent neural network* (RNN). We will get to the details of RNNs in Chapter 12, but for now, you can think of it as just another deep neural network.

Let's take a look at how each step works in detail.

Tokenization

When we said "convert the text into a list of words," we left out a lot of details. For instance, what do we do with punctuation? How do we deal with a word like "don't"? Is it one word or two? What about long medical or chemical words? Should they be split into their separate pieces of meaning? How about hyphenated words? What about languages like German and Polish, which can create really long words from many, many pieces? What about languages like Japanese and Chinese that don't use bases at all, and don't really have a well-defined idea of *word*?

Because there is no one correct answer to these questions, there is no one approach to tokenization. There are three main approaches:

Word-based
> Split a sentence on spaces, as well as applying language-specific rules to try to separate parts of meaning even when there are no spaces (such as turning "don't" into "do n't"). Generally, punctuation marks are also split into separate tokens.

Subword based
> Split words into smaller parts, based on the most commonly occurring substrings. For instance, "occasion" might be tokenized as "o c ca sion".

Character-based

Split a sentence into its individual characters.

We'll look at word and subword tokenization here, and we'll leave character-based tokenization for you to implement in the questionnaire at the end of this chapter.

Jargon: Token

One element of a list created by the tokenization process. It could be a word, part of a word (a *subword*), or a single character.

Word Tokenization with fastai

Rather than providing its own tokenizers, fastai provides a consistent interface to a range of tokenizers in external libraries. Tokenization is an active field of research, and new and improved tokenizers are coming out all the time, so the defaults that fastai uses change too. However, the API and options shouldn't change too much, since fastai tries to maintain a consistent API even as the underlying technology changes.

Let's try it out with the IMDb dataset that we used in Chapter 1:

```
from fastai.text.all import *
path = untar_data(URLs.IMDB)
```

We'll need to grab the text files in order to try out a tokenizer. Just as `get_image_files` (which we've used many times already), gets all the image files in a path, `get_text_files` gets all the text files in a path. We can also optionally pass `folders` to restrict the search to a particular list of subfolders:

```
files = get_text_files(path, folders = ['train', 'test', 'unsup'])
```

Here's a review that we'll tokenize (we'll print just the start of it here to save space):

```
txt = files[0].open().read(); txt[:75]
```

```
'This movie, which I just discovered at the video store, has apparently sit '
```

As we write this book, the default English word tokenizer for fastai uses a library called *spaCy*. It has a sophisticated rules engine with special rules for URLs, individual special English words, and much more. Rather than directly using `SpacyTokenizer`, however, we'll use `WordTokenizer`, since that will always point to fastai's current default word tokenizer (which may not necessarily be spaCy, depending when you're reading this).

Let's try it out. We'll use fastai's `coll_repr(collection,n)` function to display the results. This displays the first *n* items of *collection*, along with the full size—it's what L uses by default. Note that fastai's tokenizers take a collection of documents to tokenize, so we have to wrap txt in a list:

```
spacy = WordTokenizer()
toks = first(spacy([txt]))
print(coll_repr(toks, 30))
```

```
(#201) ['This','movie',',','which','I','just','discovered','at','the','video','s
 > tore',',','has','apparently','sit','around','for','a','couple','of','years','
 > without','a','distributor','.','It','"'s"','easy','to','see'...]
```

As you see, spaCy has mainly just separated out the words and punctuation. But it does something else here too: it has split "it's" into "it" and "'s". That makes intuitive sense; these are separate words, really. Tokenization is a surprisingly subtle task, when you think about all the little details that have to be handled. Fortunately, spaCy handles these pretty well for us—for instance, here we see that "." is separated when it terminates a sentence, but not in an acronym or number:

```
first(spacy(['The U.S. dollar $1 is $1.00.']))
```

```
(#9) ['The','U.S.','dollar','$','1','is','$','1.00','.']
```

fastai then adds some additional functionality to the tokenization process with the Tokenizer class:

```
tkn = Tokenizer(spacy)
print(coll_repr(tkn(txt), 31))
```

```
(#228) ['xxbos','xxmaj','this','movie',',','which','i','just','discovered','at',
 > 'the','video','store',',','has','apparently','sit','around','for','a','couple
 > ',','of','years','without','a','distributor','.','xxmaj','it','"'s"','easy'...]
```

Notice that there are now some tokens that start with the characters "xx", which is not a common word prefix in English. These are *special tokens*.

For example, the first item in the list, xxbos, is a special token that indicates the start of a new text ("BOS" is a standard NLP acronym that means "beginning of stream"). By recognizing this start token, the model will be able to learn it needs to "forget" what was said previously and focus on upcoming words.

These special tokens don't come from spaCy directly. They are there because fastai adds them by default, by applying a number of rules when processing text. These rules are designed to make it easier for a model to recognize the important parts of a sentence. In a sense, we are translating the original English language sequence into a simplified tokenized language—a language that is designed to be easy for a model to learn.

For instance, the rules will replace a sequence of four exclamation points with a special *repeated character* token, followed by the number four, and then a single exclamation point. In this way, the model's embedding matrix can encode information about general concepts such as repeated punctuation rather than requiring a separate token for every number of repetitions of every punctuation mark. Similarly, a capitalized word will be replaced with a special capitalization token, followed by the lowercase version of the word. This way, the embedding matrix needs only the lowercase versions of the words, saving compute and memory resources, but can still learn the concept of capitalization.

Here are some of the main special tokens you'll see:

xxbos
> Indicates the beginning of a text (here, a review)

xxmaj
> Indicates the next word begins with a capital (since we lowercased everything)

xxunk
> Indicates this word is unknown

To see the rules that were used, you can check the default rules:

```
defaults.text_proc_rules
[<function fastai.text.core.fix_html(x)>,
 <function fastai.text.core.replace_rep(t)>,
 <function fastai.text.core.replace_wrep(t)>,
 <function fastai.text.core.spec_add_spaces(t)>,
 <function fastai.text.core.rm_useless_spaces(t)>,
 <function fastai.text.core.replace_all_caps(t)>,
 <function fastai.text.core.replace_maj(t)>,
 <function fastai.text.core.lowercase(t, add_bos=True, add_eos=False)>]
```

As always, you can look at the source code for each of them in a notebook by typing the following:

```
??replace_rep
```

Here is a brief summary of what each does:

fix_html
> Replaces special HTML characters with a readable version (IMDb reviews have quite a few of these)

replace_rep
> Replaces any character repeated three times or more with a special token for repetition (xxrep), the number of times it's repeated, then the character

replace_wrep
> Replaces any word repeated three times or more with a special token for word repetition (xxwrep), the number of times it's repeated, then the word

spec_add_spaces
> Adds spaces around / and #

`rm_useless_spaces`
> Removes all repetitions of the space character

`replace_all_caps`
> Lowercases a word written in all caps and adds a special token for all caps (xxup) in front of it

`replace_maj`
> Lowercases a capitalized word and adds a special token for capitalized (xxmaj) in front of it

`lowercase`
> Lowercases all text and adds a special token at the beginning (xxbos) and/or the end (xxeos)

Let's take a look at a few of them in action:

```
coll_repr(tkn('&copy;   Fast.ai www.fast.ai/INDEX'), 31)
```

```
"(#11) ['xxbos','©','xxmaj','fast.ai','xxrep','3','w','.fast.ai','/','xxup','ind
> ex'...]"
```

Now let's take a look at how subword tokenization would work.

Subword Tokenization

In addition to the *word tokenization* approach seen in the preceding section, another popular tokenization method is *subword tokenization*. Word tokenization relies on an assumption that spaces provide a useful separation of components of meaning in a sentence. However, this assumption is not always appropriate. For instance, consider this sentence: 我的名字是郝杰瑞 ("My name is Jeremy Howard" in Chinese). That's not going to work very well with a word tokenizer, because there are no spaces in it! Languages like Chinese and Japanese don't use spaces, and in fact they don't even have a well-defined concept of a "word." Other languages, like Turkish and Hungarian, can add many subwords together without spaces, creating very long words that include a lot of separate pieces of information.

To handle these cases, it's generally best to use subword tokenization. This proceeds in two steps:

1. Analyze a corpus of documents to find the most commonly occurring groups of letters. These become the vocab.

2. Tokenize the corpus using this vocab of *subword units*.

Let's look at an example. For our corpus, we'll use the first 2,000 movie reviews:

```
txts = L(o.open().read() for o in files[:2000])
```

We instantiate our tokenizer, passing in the size of the vocab we want to create, and then we need to "train" it. That is, we need to have it read our documents and find the common sequences of characters to create the vocab. This is done with setup. As we'll see shortly, setup is a special fastai method that is called automatically in our usual data processing pipelines. Since we're doing everything manually at the moment, however, we have to call it ourselves. Here's a function that does these steps for a given vocab size and shows an example output:

```
def subword(sz):
    sp = SubwordTokenizer(vocab_sz=sz)
    sp.setup(txts)
    return ' '.join(first(sp([txt]))[:40])
```

Let's try it out:

```
subword(1000)
```

```
'_This _movie , _which _I _just _dis c over ed _at _the _video _st or e , _has
> _a p par ent ly _s it _around _for _a _couple _of _years _without _a _dis t
> ri but or . _It'
```

When using fastai's subword tokenizer, the special character _ represents a space character in the original text.

If we use a smaller vocab, each token will represent fewer characters, and it will take more tokens to represent a sentence:

```
subword(200)
```

```
'_ T h i s _movie , _w h i ch _I _ j us t _ d i s c o ver ed _a t _the _ v id e
> o _ st or e , _h a s'
```

On the other hand, if we use a larger vocab, most common English words will end up in the vocab themselves, and we will not need as many to represent a sentence:

```
subword(10000)
```

```
"_This _movie , _which _I _just _discover ed _at _the _video _store , _has
> _apparently _sit _around _for _a _couple _of _years _without _a _distributor
> . _It ' s _easy _to _see _why . _The _story _of _two _friends _living"
```

Picking a subword vocab size represents a compromise: a larger vocab means fewer tokens per sentence, which means faster training, less memory, and less state for the model to remember; but on the downside, it means larger embedding matrices, which require more data to learn.

Overall, subword tokenization provides a way to easily scale between character tokenization (i.e., using a small subword vocab) and word tokenization (i.e., using a large subword vocab), and handles every human language without needing language-specific algorithms to be developed. It can even handle other "languages" such as genomic sequences or MIDI music notation! For this reason, in the last year its popularity has soared, and it seems likely to become the most common tokenization approach (it may well already be, by the time you read this!).

Once our texts have been split into tokens, we need to convert them to numbers. We'll look at that next.

Numericalization with fastai

Numericalization is the process of mapping tokens to integers. The steps are basically identical to those necessary to create a `Category` variable, such as the dependent variable of digits in MNIST:

1. Make a list of all possible levels of that categorical variable (the vocab).
2. Replace each level with its index in the vocab.

Let's take a look at this in action on the word-tokenized text we saw earlier:

```
toks = tkn(txt)
print(coll_repr(tkn(txt), 31))
```

```
(#228) ['xxbos','xxmaj','this','movie',',',',','which','i','just','discovered','at',
 > 'the','video','store',',',',','has','apparently','sit','around','for','a','couple
 > ',','of','years','without','a','distributor','.','xxmaj','it','"'s",'easy'...]
```

Just as with `SubwordTokenizer`, we need to call `setup` on `Numericalize`; this is how we create the vocab. That means we'll need our tokenized corpus first. Since tokenization takes a while, it's done in parallel by fastai; but for this manual walk-through, we'll use a small subset:

```
toks200 = txts[:200].map(tkn)
toks200[0]
```

```
(#228)
 > ['xxbos','xxmaj','this','movie',',',',','which','i','just','discovered','at'...]
```

We can pass this to `setup` to create our vocab:

```
num = Numericalize()
num.setup(toks200)
coll_repr(num.vocab,20)
```

```
"(#2000) ['xxunk','xxpad','xxbos','xxeos','xxfld','xxrep','xxwrep','xxup','xxmaj
 > ',','the','.',',','a','and','of','to','is','in','i','it'...]"
```

Our special rules tokens appear first, and then every word appears once, in frequency order. The defaults to `Numericalize` are `min_freq=3` and `max_vocab=60000`. `max_vocab=60000` results in fastai replacing all words other than the most common 60,000 with a special *unknown word* token, `xxunk`. This is useful to avoid having an overly large embedding matrix, since that can slow down training and use up too much memory, and can also mean that there isn't enough data to train useful representations for rare words. However, this last issue is better handled by setting `min_freq`; the default `min_freq=3` means that any word appearing fewer than three times is replaced with xxunk.

fastai can also numericalize your dataset using a vocab that you provide, by passing a list of words as the `vocab` parameter.

Once we've created our `Numericalize` object, we can use it as if it were a function:

```
nums = num(toks)[:20]; nums
```

```
tensor([  2,   8,  21,  28,  11,  90,  18,  59,   0,  45,   9, 351, 499,  11,
> 72, 533, 584, 146,  29,  12])
```

This time, our tokens have been converted to a tensor of integers that our model can receive. We can check that they map back to the original text:

```
' '.join(num.vocab[o] for o in nums)
```

```
'xxbos xxmaj this movie , which i just xxunk at the video store , has apparently
> sit around for a'
```

Now that we have numbers, we need to put them in batches for our model.

Putting Our Texts into Batches for a Language Model

When dealing with images, we needed to resize them all to the same height and width before grouping them together in a mini-batch so they could stack together efficiently in a single tensor. Here it's going to be a little different, because one cannot simply resize text to a desired length. Also, we want our language model to read text in order, so that it can efficiently predict what the next word is. This means each new batch should begin precisely where the previous one left off.

Suppose we have the following text:

> In this chapter, we will go back over the example of classifying movie reviews we studied in chapter 1 and dig deeper under the surface. First we will look at the processing steps necessary to convert text into numbers and how to customize it. By doing this, we'll have another example of the PreProcessor used in the data block API.
>
> Then we will study how we build a language model and train it for a while.

The tokenization process will add special tokens and deal with punctuation to return this text:

> xxbos xxmaj in this chapter , we will go back over the example of classifying movie reviews we studied in chapter 1 and dig deeper under the surface . xxmaj first we will look at the processing steps necessary to convert text into numbers and how to customize it . xxmaj by doing this , we 'll have another example of the preprocessor used in the data block xxup api . \n xxmaj then we will study how we build a language model and train it for a while .

We now have 90 tokens, separated by spaces. Let's say we want a batch size of 6. We need to break this text into 6 contiguous parts of length 15:

xxbos	xxmaj	in	this	chapter	,	we	will	go	back	over	the	example	of	classifying
movie	reviews	we	studied	in	chapter	1	and	dig	deeper	under	the	surface	.	xxmaj
first	we	will	look	at	the	processing	steps	necessary	to	convert	text	into	numbers	and
how	to	customize	it	.	xxmaj	by	doing	this	,	we	'll	have	another	example
of	the	preprocessor	used	in	the	data	block	xxup	api	.	\n	xxmaj	then	we
will	study	how	we	build	a	language	model	and	train	it	for	a	while	.

In a perfect world, we could then give this one batch to our model. But that approach doesn't scale, because outside this toy example, it's unlikely that a single batch containing all the tokens would fit in our GPU memory (here we have 90 tokens, but all the IMDb reviews together give several million).

So, we need to divide this array more finely into subarrays of a fixed sequence length. It is important to maintain order within and across these subarrays, because we will use a model that maintains a state so that it remembers what it read previously when predicting what comes next.

Going back to our previous example with 6 batches of length 15, if we chose a sequence length of 5, that would mean we first feed the following array:

xxbos	xxmaj	in	this	chapter
movie	reviews	we	studied	in
first	we	will	look	at
how	to	customize	it	.
of	the	preprocessor	used	in
will	study	how	we	build

Then, this one:

,	we	will	go	back
chapter	1	and	dig	deeper
the	processing	steps	necessary	to
xxmaj	by	doing	this	,
the	data	block	xxup	api
a	language	model	and	train

And finally:

over	the	example	of	classifying
under	the	surface	.	xxmaj
convert	text	into	numbers	and
we	'll	have	another	example
.	\n	xxmaj	then	we
it	for	a	while	.

Going back to our movie reviews dataset, the first step is to transform the individual texts into a stream by concatenating them together. As with images, it's best to randomize the order of the inputs, so at the beginning of each epoch we will shuffle the entries to make a new stream (we shuffle the order of the documents, not the order of the words inside them, or the texts would not make sense anymore!).

We then cut this stream into a certain number of chunks of contiguous text (which is our *batch size*). For instance, if the stream has 50,000 tokens and we set a batch size of 10, this will give us 10 mini-streams of 5,000 tokens. What is important is that we preserve the order of the tokens (so from 1 to 5,000 for the first mini-stream, then from 5,001 to 10,000...), because we want the model to read continuous rows of text (as in the preceding example). An xxbos token is added at the start of each text during preprocessing, so that the model knows when it reads the stream when a new entry is beginning.

So to recap, at every epoch we shuffle our collection of documents and concatenate them into a stream of tokens. We then cut that stream into a batch of fixed-size consecutive mini-streams. Our model will then read the mini-streams in order, and thanks to an inner state, it will produce the same activation, whatever sequence length we picked.

This is all done behind the scenes by the fastai library when we create an LMDataLoader. We do this by first applying our Numericalize object to the tokenized texts

```
nums200 = toks200.map(num)
```

and then passing that to LMDataLoader:

```
dl = LMDataLoader(nums200)
```

Let's confirm that this gives the expected results, by grabbing the first batch

```
x,y = first(dl)
x.shape,y.shape
```

```
(torch.Size([64, 72]), torch.Size([64, 72]))
```

and then looking at the first row of the independent variable, which should be the start of the first text:

```
' '.join(num.vocab[o] for o in x[0][:20])
```

```
'xxbos xxmaj this movie , which i just xxunk at the video store , has apparently
> sit around for a'
```

The dependent variable is the same thing offset by one token:

```
' '.join(num.vocab[o] for o in y[0][:20])
```

```
'xxmaj this movie , which i just xxunk at the video store , has apparently sit
> around for a couple'
```

This concludes all the preprocessing steps we need to apply to our data. We are now ready to train our text classifier.

Training a Text Classifier

As we saw at the beginning of this chapter, there are two steps to training a state-of-the-art text classifier using transfer learning: first we need to fine-tune our language model pretrained on Wikipedia to the corpus of IMDb reviews, and then we can use that model to train a classifier.

As usual, let's start with assembling our data.

Language Model Using DataBlock

fastai handles tokenization and numericalization automatically when `TextBlock` is passed to `DataBlock`. All of the arguments that can be passed to `Tokenizer` and `Numericalize` can also be passed to `TextBlock`. In the next chapter, we'll discuss the easiest ways to run each of these steps separately, to ease debugging, but you can always just debug by running them manually on a subset of your data as shown in the previous sections. And don't forget about `DataBlock`'s handy `summary` method, which is very useful for debugging data issues.

Here's how we use `TextBlock` to create a language model, using fastai's defaults:

```
get_imdb = partial(get_text_files, folders=['train', 'test', 'unsup'])

dls_lm = DataBlock(
    blocks=TextBlock.from_folder(path, is_lm=True),
    get_items=get_imdb, splitter=RandomSplitter(0.1)
).dataloaders(path, path=path, bs=128, seq_len=80)
```

One thing that's different from previous types we've used in `DataBlock` is that we're not just using the class directly (i.e., `TextBlock(...)`, but instead are calling a *class method*. A class method is a Python method that, as the name suggests, belongs to a *class* rather than an *object*. (Be sure to search online for more information about class methods if you're not familiar with them, since they're commonly used in many Python libraries and applications; we've used them a few times previously in the book, but haven't called attention to them.) The reason that `TextBlock` is special is that setting up the numericalizer's vocab can take a long time (we have to read and tokenize every document to get the vocab).

To be as efficient as possible, fastai performs a few optimizations:

- It saves the tokenized documents in a temporary folder, so it doesn't have to tokenize them more than once.
- It runs multiple tokenization processes in parallel, to take advantage of your computer's CPUs.

We need to tell `TextBlock` how to access the texts, so that it can do this initial preprocessing—that's what `from_folder` does.

`show_batch` then works in the usual way:

```
dls_lm.show_batch(max_n=2)
```

	text	text_
0	xxbos xxmaj it 's awesome ! xxmaj in xxmaj story xxmaj mode , your going from punk to pro . xxmaj you have to complete goals that involve skating , driving , and walking . xxmaj you create your own skater and give it a name , and you can make it look stupid or realistic . xxmaj you are with your friend xxmaj eric throughout the game until he betrays you and gets you kicked off of the skateboard	xxmaj it 's awesome ! xxmaj in xxmaj story xxmaj mode , your going from punk to pro . xxmaj you have to complete goals that involve skating , driving , and walking . xxmaj you create your own skater and give it a name , and you can make it look stupid or realistic . xxmaj you are with your friend xxmaj eric throughout the game until he betrays you and gets you kicked off the skateboard xxunk
1	what xxmaj i 've read , xxmaj death xxmaj bed is based on an actual dream , xxmaj george xxmaj barry , the director , successfully transferred dream to film , only a genius could accomplish such a task . \n\n xxmaj old mansions make for good quality horror , as do portraits , not sure what to make of the killer bed with its killer yellow liquid , quite a bizarre dream , indeed . xxmaj also , this	xxmaj i 've read , xxmaj death xxmaj bed is based on an actual dream , xxmaj george xxmaj barry , the director , successfully transferred dream to film , only a genius could accomplish such a task . \n\n xxmaj old mansions make for good quality horror , as do portraits , not sure what to make of the killer bed with its killer yellow liquid , quite a bizarre dream , indeed . xxmaj also , this is

Now that our data is ready, we can fine-tune the pretrained language model.

Fine-Tuning the Language Model

To convert the integer word indices into activations that we can use for our neural network, we will use embeddings, just as we did for collaborative filtering and tabular modeling. Then we'll feed those embeddings into a *recurrent neural network* (RNN), using an architecture called *AWD-LSTM* (we will show you how to write such a model from scratch in Chapter 12). As we discussed earlier, the embeddings in the pretrained model are merged with random embeddings added for words that weren't in the pretraining vocabulary. This is handled automatically inside `language_model_learner`:

```
learn = language_model_learner(
    dls_lm, AWD_LSTM, drop_mult=0.3,
    metrics=[accuracy, Perplexity()]).to_fp16()
```

The loss function used by default is cross-entropy loss, since we essentially have a classification problem (the different categories being the words in our vocab). The *perplexity* metric used here is often used in NLP for language models: it is the exponential of the loss (i.e., `torch.exp(cross_entropy)`). We also include the accuracy metric to see how many times our model is right when trying to predict the next word, since cross entropy (as we've seen) is both hard to interpret and tells us more about the model's confidence than its accuracy.

Let's go back to the process diagram from the beginning of this chapter. The first arrow has been completed for us and made available as a pretrained model in fastai, and we've just built the `DataLoaders` and `Learner` for the second stage. Now we're ready to fine-tune our language model!

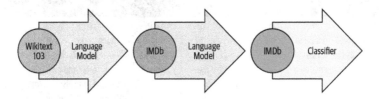

It takes quite a while to train each epoch, so we'll be saving the intermediate model results during the training process. Since `fine_tune` doesn't do that for us, we'll use `fit_one_cycle`. Just like `cnn_learner`, `language_model_learner` automatically calls `freeze` when using a pretrained model (which is the default), so this will train only the embeddings (the only part of the model that contains randomly initialized weights—i.e., embeddings for words that are in our IMDb vocab, but aren't in the pretrained model vocab):

```
learn.fit_one_cycle(1, 2e-2)
```

epoch	train_loss	valid_loss	accuracy	perplexity	time
0	4.120048	3.912788	0.299565	50.038246	11:39

This model takes a while to train, so it's a good opportunity to talk about saving intermediary results.

Saving and Loading Models

You can easily save the state of your model like so:

```
learn.save('1epoch')
```

This will create a file in *learn.path/models/* named *1epoch.pth*. If you want to load your model in another machine after creating your Learner the same way, or resume training later, you can load the content of this file as follows:

```
learn = learn.load('1epoch')
```

Once the initial training has completed, we can continue fine-tuning the model after unfreezing:

```
learn.unfreeze()
learn.fit_one_cycle(10, 2e-3)
```

epoch	train_loss	valid_loss	accuracy	perplexity	time
0	3.893486	3.772820	0.317104	43.502548	12:37
1	3.820479	3.717197	0.323790	41.148880	12:30
2	3.735622	3.659760	0.330321	38.851997	12:09
3	3.677086	3.624794	0.333960	37.516987	12:12
4	3.636646	3.601300	0.337017	36.645859	12:05
5	3.553636	3.584241	0.339355	36.026001	12:04
6	3.507634	3.571892	0.341353	35.583862	12:08
7	3.444101	3.565988	0.342194	35.374371	12:08
8	3.398597	3.566283	0.342647	35.384815	12:11
9	3.375563	3.568166	0.342528	35.451500	12:05

Once this is done, we save all of our model except the final layer that converts activations to probabilities of picking each token in our vocabulary. The model not including the final layer is called the *encoder*. We can save it with **save_encoder**:

```
learn.save_encoder('finetuned')
```

Jargon: Encoder

The model not including the task-specific final layer(s). This term means much the same thing as "body" when applied to vision CNNs, but "encoder" tends to be more used for NLP and generative models.

This completes the second stage of the text classification process: fine-tuning the language model. We can now use it to fine-tune a classifier using the IMDb sentiment labels. Before we move on to fine-tuning the classifier, however, let's quickly try something different: using our model to generate random reviews.

Text Generation

Because our model is trained to guess the next word of the sentence, we can use it to write new reviews:

```
TEXT = "I liked this movie because"
N_WORDS = 40
N_SENTENCES = 2
preds = [learn.predict(TEXT, N_WORDS, temperature=0.75)
         for _ in range(N_SENTENCES)]

print("\n".join(preds))
```

```
i liked this movie because of its story and characters . The story line was very
 > strong , very good for a sci - fi film . The main character , Alucard , was
 > very well developed and brought the whole story
i liked this movie because i like the idea of the premise of the movie , the (
 > very ) convenient virus ( which , when you have to kill a few people , the "
 > evil " machine has to be used to protect
```

As you can see, we add some randomness (we pick a random word based on the probabilities returned by the model) so we don't get exactly the same review twice. Our model doesn't have any programmed knowledge of the structure of a sentence or grammar rules, yet it has clearly learned a lot about English sentences: we can see it capitalizes properly (*I* is transformed to *i* because our rules require two characters or more to consider a word as capitalized, so it's normal to see it lowercased) and is using consistent tense. The general review makes sense at first glance, and it's only if you read carefully that you can notice something is a bit off. Not bad for a model trained in a couple of hours!

But our end goal wasn't to train a model to generate reviews, but to classify them…so let's use this model to do just that.

Creating the Classifier DataLoaders

We're now moving from language model fine-tuning to classifier fine-tuning. To re-cap, a language model predicts the next word of a document, so it doesn't need any external labels. A classifier, however, predicts an external label—in the case of IMDb, it's the sentiment of a document.

This means that the structure of our `DataBlock` for NLP classification will look very familiar. It's nearly the same as we've seen for the many image classification datasets we've worked with:

```
dls_clas = DataBlock(
    blocks=(TextBlock.from_folder(path, vocab=dls_lm.vocab),CategoryBlock),
    get_y = parent_label,
```

```
      get_items=partial(get_text_files, folders=['train', 'test']),
      splitter=GrandparentSplitter(valid_name='test')
).dataloaders(path, path=path, bs=128, seq_len=72)
```

Just as with image classification, `show_batch` shows the dependent variable (sentiment, in this case) with each independent variable (movie review text):

```
dls_clas.show_batch(max_n=3)
```

	text	category
0	xxbos i rate this movie with 3 skulls , only coz the girls knew how to scream , this could 've been a better movie , if actors were better , the twins were xxup ok , i believed they were evil , but the eldest and youngest brother , they sucked really bad , it seemed like they were reading the scripts instead of acting them .... spoiler : if they 're vampire 's why do they freeze the blood ? vampires ca n't drink frozen blood , the sister in the movie says let 's drink her while she is alive ... .but then when they 're moving to another house , they take on a cooler they 're frozen blood . end of spoiler \n\n it was a huge waste of time , and that made me mad coz i read all the reviews of how	neg
1	xxbos i have read all of the xxmaj love xxmaj come xxmaj softly books . xxmaj knowing full well that movies can not use all aspects of the book , but generally they at least have the main point of the book . i was highly disappointed in this movie . xxmaj the only thing that they have in this movie that is in the book is that xxmaj missy 's father comes to xxunk in the book both parents come) . xxmaj that is all . xxmaj the story line was so twisted and far fetch and yes , sad , from the book , that i just could n't enjoy it . xxmaj even if i did n't read the book it was too sad . i do know that xxmaj pioneer life was rough , but the whole movie was a downer . xxmaj the rating	neg
2	xxbos xxmaj this , for lack of a better term , movie is lousy . xxmaj where do i start ... ... \n\n xxmaj cinemaphotography - xxmaj this was , perhaps , the worst xxmaj i 've seen this year . xxmaj it looked like the camera was being tossed from camera man to camera man . xxmaj maybe they only had one camera . xxmaj it gives you the sensation of being a volleyball . \n\n xxmaj there are a bunch of scenes , haphazardly , thrown in with no continuity at all . xxmaj when they did the ' split screen ' , it was absurd . xxmaj everything was squished flat , it looked ridiculous . \n\n xxmaj the color tones were way off . xxmaj these people need to learn how to balance a camera . xxmaj this ' movie ' is poorly made , and	neg

Looking at the `DataBlock` definition, every piece is familiar from previous data blocks we've built, with two important exceptions:

- `TextBlock.from_folder` no longer has the `is_lm=True` parameter.
- We pass the `vocab` we created for the language model fine-tuning.

The reason that we pass the `vocab` of the language model is to make sure we use the same correspondence of token to index. Otherwise, the embeddings we learned in our fine-tuned language model won't make any sense to this model, and the fine-tuning step won't be of any use.

By passing `is_lm=False` (or not passing `is_lm` at all, since it defaults to `False`), we tell `TextBlock` that we have regular labeled data, rather than using the next tokens as labels. There is one challenge we have to deal with, however, which has to do with collating multiple documents into a mini-batch. Let's see with an example, by trying to create a mini-batch containing the first 10 documents. First we'll numericalize them:

```
nums_samp = toks200[:10].map(num)
```

Let's now look at how many tokens each of these 10 movie reviews has:

```
nums_samp.map(len)
```

```
(#10) [228,238,121,290,196,194,533,124,581,155]
```

Remember, PyTorch `DataLoaders` need to collate all the items in a batch into a single tensor, and a single tensor has a fixed shape (i.e., it has a particular length on every axis, and all items must be consistent). This should sound familiar: we had the same issue with images. In that case, we used cropping, padding, and/or squishing to make all the inputs the same size. Cropping might not be a good idea for documents, because it seems likely we'd remove some key information (having said that, the same issue is true for images, and we use cropping there; data augmentation hasn't been well explored for NLP yet, so perhaps there are actually opportunities to use cropping in NLP too!). You can't really "squish" a document. So that leaves padding!

We will expand the shortest texts to make them all the same size. To do this, we use a special padding token that will be ignored by our model. Additionally, to avoid memory issues and improve performance, we will batch together texts that are roughly the same lengths (with some shuffling for the training set). We do this by (approximately, for the training set) sorting the documents by length prior to each epoch. The result is that the documents collated into a single batch will tend of be of similar lengths. We won't pad every batch to the same size, but will instead use the size of the largest document in each batch as the target size.

Dynamically Resize Images

It is possible to do something similar with images, which is especially useful for irregularly sized rectangular images, but at the time of writing no library provides good support for this yet, and there aren't any papers covering it. It's something we're planning to add to fastai soon, however, so keep an eye on the book's website; we'll add information about this as soon as we have it working well.

The sorting and padding are automatically done by the data block API for us when using a `TextBlock` with `is_lm=False`. (We don't have this same issue for language model data, since we concatenate all the documents together first and then split them into equally sized sections.)

We can now create a model to classify our texts:

```
learn = text_classifier_learner(dls_clas, AWD_LSTM, drop_mult=0.5,
                                metrics=accuracy).to_fp16()
```

The final step prior to training the classifier is to load the encoder from our fine-tuned language model. We use `load_encoder` instead of `load` because we have only pretrained weights available for the encoder; `load` by default raises an exception if an incomplete model is loaded:

```
learn = learn.load_encoder('finetuned')
```

Fine-Tuning the Classifier

The last step is to train with discriminative learning rates and *gradual unfreezing*. In computer vision, we often unfreeze the model all at once, but for NLP classifiers, we find that unfreezing a few layers at a time makes a real difference:

```
learn.fit_one_cycle(1, 2e-2)
```

epoch	train_loss	valid_loss	accuracy	time
0	0.347427	0.184480	0.929320	00:33

In just one epoch, we get the same result as our training in Chapter 1—not too bad! We can pass -2 to `freeze_to` to freeze all except the last two parameter groups:

```
learn.freeze_to(-2)
learn.fit_one_cycle(1, slice(1e-2/(2.6**4),1e-2))
```

epoch	train_loss	valid_loss	accuracy	time
0	0.247763	0.171683	0.934640	00:37

Then we can unfreeze a bit more and continue training:

```
learn.freeze_to(-3)
learn.fit_one_cycle(1, slice(5e-3/(2.6**4),5e-3))
```

epoch	train_loss	valid_loss	accuracy	time
0	0.193377	0.156696	0.941200	00:45

And finally, the whole model!

```
learn.unfreeze()
learn.fit_one_cycle(2, slice(1e-3/(2.6**4),1e-3))
```

epoch	train_loss	valid_loss	accuracy	time
0	0.172888	0.153770	0.943120	01:01
1	0.161492	0.155567	0.942640	00:57

We reached 94.3% accuracy, which was state-of-the-art performance just three years ago. By training another model on all the texts read backward and averaging the predictions of those two models, we can even get to 95.1% accuracy, which was the state of the art introduced by the ULMFiT paper. It was beaten only a few months ago, by fine-tuning a much bigger model and using expensive data augmentation techniques (translating sentences in another language and back, using another model for translation).

Using a pretrained model let us build a fine-tuned language model that is pretty powerful, to either generate fake reviews or help classify them. This is exciting stuff, but it's good to remember that this technology can also be used for malign purposes.

Disinformation and Language Models

Even simple algorithms based on rules, before the days of widely available deep learning language models, could be used to create fraudulent accounts and try to influence policymakers. Jeff Kao, now a computational journalist at ProPublica, analyzed the comments that were sent to the US Federal Communications Commission (FCC) regarding a 2017 proposal to repeal net neutrality. In his article "More than a Million Pro-Repeal Net Neutrality Comments Were Likely Faked" (*https://oreil.ly/ptq8B*), he reports how he discovered a large cluster of comments opposing net neutrality that seemed to have been generated by some sort of Mad Libs–style mail merge. In Figure 10-2, the fake comments have been helpfully color-coded by Kao to highlight their formulaic nature.

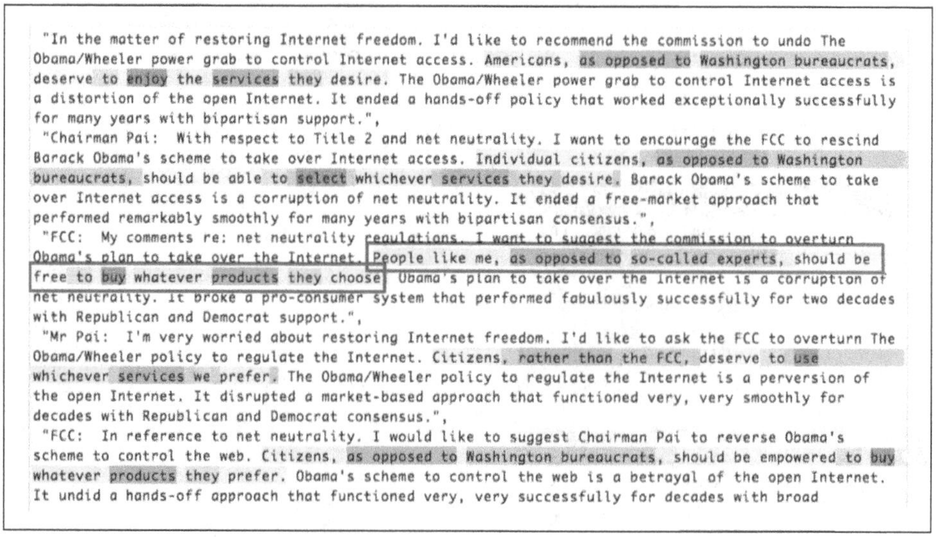

```
    "In the matter of restoring Internet freedom. I'd like to recommend the commission to undo The
Obama/Wheeler power grab to control Internet access. Americans, as opposed to Washington bureaucrats,
deserve to enjoy the services they desire. The Obama/Wheeler power grab to control Internet access is
a distortion of the open Internet. It ended a hands-off policy that worked exceptionally successfully
for many years with bipartisan support.",
    "Chairman Pai: With respect to Title 2 and net neutrality. I want to encourage the FCC to rescind
Barack Obama's scheme to take over Internet access. Individual citizens, as opposed to Washington
bureaucrats, should be able to select whichever services they desire. Barack Obama's scheme to take
over Internet access is a corruption of net neutrality. It ended a free-market approach that
performed remarkably smoothly for many years with bipartisan consensus.",
    "FCC: My comments re: net neutrality regulations. I want to suggest the commission to overturn
Obama's plan to take over the Internet. People like me, as opposed to so-called experts, should be
free to buy whatever products they choose. Obama's plan to take over the Internet is a corruption of
net neutrality. It broke a pro-consumer system that performed fabulously successfully for two decades
with Republican and Democrat support.",
    "Mr Pai: I'm very worried about restoring Internet freedom. I'd like to ask the FCC to overturn The
Obama/Wheeler policy to regulate the Internet. Citizens, rather than the FCC, deserve to use
whichever services we prefer. The Obama/Wheeler policy to regulate the Internet is a perversion of
the open Internet. It disrupted a market-based approach that functioned very, very smoothly for
decades with Republican and Democrat consensus.",
    "FCC: In reference to net neutrality. I would like to suggest Chairman Pai to reverse Obama's
scheme to control the web. Citizens, as opposed to Washington bureaucrats, should be empowered to buy
whatever products they prefer. Obama's scheme to control the web is a betrayal of the open Internet.
It undid a hands-off approach that functioned very, very successfully for decades with broad
```

Figure 10-2. Comments received by the FCC during the net neutrality debate

Kao estimated that "less than 800,000 of the 22M+ comments…could be considered truly unique" and that "more than 99% of the truly unique comments were in favor of keeping net neutrality."

Given advances in language modeling that have occurred since 2017, such fraudulent campaigns could be nearly impossible to catch now. You now have all the necessary tools at your disposal to create a compelling language model—something that can generate context-appropriate, believable text. It won't necessarily be perfectly accurate or correct, but it will be plausible. Think about what this technology would mean when put together with the kinds of disinformation campaigns we have learned about in recent years. Take a look at the Reddit dialogue shown in Figure 10-3, where a language model based on OpenAI's GPT-2 algorithm is having a conversation with itself about whether the US government should cut defense spending.

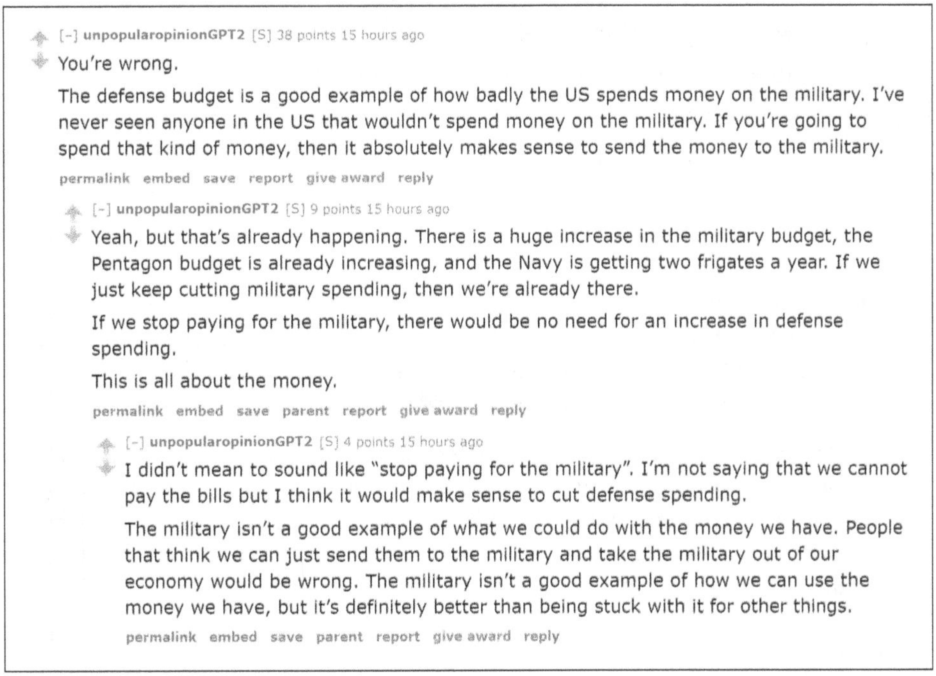

[-] unpopularopinionGPT2 [S] 38 points 15 hours ago
You're wrong.

The defense budget is a good example of how badly the US spends money on the military. I've never seen anyone in the US that wouldn't spend money on the military. If you're going to spend that kind of money, then it absolutely makes sense to send the money to the military.

permalink embed save report give award reply

[-] unpopularopinionGPT2 [S] 9 points 15 hours ago
Yeah, but that's already happening. There is a huge increase in the military budget, the Pentagon budget is already increasing, and the Navy is getting two frigates a year. If we just keep cutting military spending, then we're already there.

If we stop paying for the military, there would be no need for an increase in defense spending.

This is all about the money.

permalink embed save parent report give award reply

[-] unpopularopinionGPT2 [S] 4 points 15 hours ago
I didn't mean to sound like "stop paying for the military". I'm not saying that we cannot pay the bills but I think it would make sense to cut defense spending.

The military isn't a good example of what we could do with the money we have. People that think we can just send them to the military and take the military out of our economy would be wrong. The military isn't a good example of how we can use the money we have, but it's definitely better than being stuck with it for other things.

permalink embed save parent report give award reply

Figure 10-3. An algorithm talking to itself on Reddit

In this case, it was explained that an algorithm was being used to generate the dialogue. But imagine what would happen if a bad actor decided to release such an algorithm across social networks—they could do it slowly and carefully, allowing the algorithm to gradually develop followers and trust over time. It would not take many resources to have literally millions of accounts doing this. In such a situation, we could easily imagine getting to a point where the vast majority of discourse online was from bots, and nobody would have any idea that it was happening.

We are already starting to see examples of machine learning being used to generate identities. For example, Figure 10-4 shows a LinkedIn profile for Katie Jones.

Figure 10-4. Katie Jones's LinkedIn profile

Katie Jones was connected on LinkedIn to several members of mainstream Washington think tanks. But she didn't exist. That image you see was autogenerated by a generative adversarial network, and somebody named Katie Jones has not, in fact, graduated from the Center for Strategic and International Studies.

Many people assume or hope that algorithms will come to our defense here—that we will develop classification algorithms that can automatically recognize autogenerated content. The problem, however, is that this will always be an arms race, in which better classification (or discriminator) algorithms can be used to create better generation algorithms.

Conclusion

In this chapter, we explored the last application covered out of the box by the fastai library: text. We saw two types of models: language models that can generate texts, and a classifier that determines whether a review is positive or negative. To build a state-of-the art classifier, we used a pretrained language model, fine-tuned it to the corpus of our task, then used its body (the encoder) with a new head to do the classification.

Before we end this part of the book, we'll take a look at how the fastai library can help you assemble your data for your specific problems.

Questionnaire

1. What is self-supervised learning?

2. What is a language model?

3. Why is a language model considered self-supervised?

4. What are self-supervised models usually used for?

5. Why do we fine-tune language models?

6. What are the three steps to create a state-of-the-art text classifier?

7. How do the 50,000 unlabeled movie reviews help create a better text classifier for the IMDb dataset?

8. What are the three steps to prepare your data for a language model?

9. What is tokenization? Why do we need it?

10. Name three approaches to tokenization.

11. What is xxbos?

12. List four rules that fastai applies to text during tokenization.

13. Why are repeated characters replaced with a token showing the number of repetitions and the character that's repeated?

14. What is numericalization?

15. Why might there be words that are replaced with the "unknown word" token?

16. With a batch size of 64, the first row of the tensor representing the first batch contains the first 64 tokens for the dataset. What does the second row of that tensor contain? What does the first row of the second batch contain? (Careful—students often get this one wrong! Be sure to check your answer on the book's website.)

17. Why do we need padding for text classification? Why don't we need it for language modeling?

18. What does an embedding matrix for NLP contain? What is its shape?

19. What is perplexity?

20. Why do we have to pass the vocabulary of the language model to the classifier data block?

21. What is gradual unfreezing?

22. Why is text generation always likely to be ahead of automatic identification of machine-generated texts?

Further Research

1. See what you can learn about language models and disinformation. What are the best language models today? Take a look at some of their outputs. Do you find them convincing? How could a bad actor best use such a model to create conflict and uncertainty?

2. Given the limitation that models are unlikely to be able to consistently recognize machine-generated texts, what other approaches may be needed to handle large-scale disinformation campaigns that leverage deep learning?

CHAPTER 11

Data Munging with fastai's Mid-Level API

We have seen what `Tokenizer` and `Numericalize` do to a collection of texts, and how they're used inside the data block API, which handles those transforms for us directly using the `TextBlock`. But what if we want to apply only one of those transforms, either to see intermediate results or because we have already tokenized texts? More generally, what can we do when the data block API is not flexible enough to accommodate our particular use case? For this, we need to use fastai's *mid-level API* for processing data. The data block API is built on top of that layer, so it will allow you to do everything the data block API does, and much much more.

Going Deeper into fastai's Layered API

The fastai library is built on a *layered API*. In the very top layer are *applications* that allow us to train a model in five lines of code, as we saw in Chapter 1. In the case of creating `DataLoaders` for a text classifier, for instance, we used this line:

```
from fastai.text.all import *

dls = TextDataLoaders.from_folder(untar_data(URLs.IMDB), valid='test')
```

The factory method `TextDataLoaders.from_folder` is very convenient when your data is arranged the exact same way as the IMDb dataset, but in practice, that often won't be the case. The data block API offers more flexibility. As we saw in the preceding chapter, we can get the same result with the following:

```
path = untar_data(URLs.IMDB)
dls = DataBlock(
    blocks=(TextBlock.from_folder(path),CategoryBlock),
    get_y = parent_label,
    get_items=partial(get_text_files, folders=['train', 'test']),
    splitter=GrandparentSplitter(valid_name='test')
).dataloaders(path)
```

But it's sometimes not flexible enough. For debugging purposes, for instance, we might need to apply just parts of the transforms that come with this data block. Or we might want to create a `DataLoaders` for an application that isn't directly supported by fastai. In this section, we'll dig into the pieces that are used inside fastai to implement the data block API. Understanding these will enable you to leverage the power and flexibility of this mid-tier API.

Mid-Level API

The mid-level API does not contain only functionality for creating `DataLoaders`. It also has the *callback* system, which allows us to customize the training loop any way we like, and the *general optimizer*. Both will be covered in Chapter 16.

Transforms

When we studied tokenization and numericalization in the preceding chapter, we started by grabbing a bunch of texts:

```
files = get_text_files(path, folders = ['train', 'test'])
txts = L(o.open().read() for o in files[:2000])
```

We then showed how to tokenize them with a `Tokenizer`

```
tok = Tokenizer.from_folder(path)
tok.setup(txts)
toks = txts.map(tok)
toks[0]
```

```
(#374) ['xxbos','xxmaj','well',',',',','"','cube','"','(','1997',')'...]
```

and how to numericalize, including automatically creating the vocab for our corpus:

```
num = Numericalize()
num.setup(toks)
nums = toks.map(num)
nums[0][:10]
```

```
tensor([   2,    8,   76,   10,   23, 3112,   23,   34, 3113,   33])
```

The classes also have a `decode` method. For instance, `Numericalize.decode` gives us back the string tokens:

```
nums_dec = num.decode(nums[0][:10]); nums_dec
```

```
(#10) ['xxbos','xxmaj','well',',',',','"','cube','"','(','1997',')']
```

`Tokenizer.decode` turns this back into a single string (it may not, however, be exactly the same as the original string; this depends on whether the tokenizer is *reversible*, which the default word tokenizer is not at the time we're writing this book):

```
tok.decode(nums_dec)
```

```
'xxbos xxmaj well , " cube " ( 1997 )'
```

decode is used by fastai's show_batch and show_results, as well as some other inference methods, to convert predictions and mini-batches into a human-understandable representation.

For each of tok or num in the preceding examples, we created an object called the setup method (which trains the tokenizer if needed for tok and creates the vocab for num), applied it to our raw texts (by calling the object as a function), and then finally decoded the result back to an understandable representation. These steps are needed for most data preprocessing tasks, so fastai provides a class that encapsulates them. This is the Transform class. Both Tokenize and Numericalize are Transforms.

In general, a Transform is an object that behaves like a function and has an optional setup method that will initialize an inner state (like the vocab inside num) and an optional decode method that will reverse the function (this reversal may not be perfect, as we saw with tok).

A good example of decode is found in the Normalize transform that we saw in Chapter 7: to be able to plot the images, its decode method undoes the normalization (i.e., it multiplies by the standard deviation and adds back the mean). On the other hand, data augmentation transforms do not have a decode method, since we want to show the effects on images to make sure the data augmentation is working as we want.

A special behavior of Transforms is that they always get applied over tuples. In general, our data is always a tuple (input,target) (sometimes with more than one input or more than one target). When applying a transform on an item like this, such as Resize, we don't want to resize the tuple as a whole; instead, we want to resize the input (if applicable) and the target (if applicable) separately. It's the same for batch transforms that do data augmentation: when the input is an image and the target is a segmentation mask, the transform needs to be applied (the same way) to the input and the target.

We can see this behavior if we pass a tuple of texts to tok:

```
tok((txts[0], txts[1]))
```

```
((#374) ['xxbos','xxmaj','well',',',',','"','cube','"','(','1997',')'...],
 (#207)
> ['xxbos','xxmaj','conrad','xxmaj','hall','went','out','with','a','bang'...])
```

Writing Your Own Transform

If you want to write a custom transform to apply to your data, the easiest way is to write a function. As you can see in this example, a Transform will be applied only to a matching type, if a type is provided (otherwise, it will always be applied). In the following code, the :int in the function signature means that f gets applied only to ints. That's why tfm(2.0) returns 2.0, but tfm(2) returns 3 here:

```
def f(x:int): return x+1
tfm = Transform(f)
tfm(2),tfm(2.0)
```

```
(3, 2.0)
```

Here, f is converted to a Transform with no setup and no decode method.

Python has a special syntax for passing a function (like f) to another function (or something that behaves like a function, known as a *callable* in Python), called a *decorator*. A decorator is used by prepending a callable with @ and placing it before a function definition (there are lots of good online tutorials about Python decorators, so take a look at one if this is a new concept for you). The following is identical to the previous code:

```
@Transform
def f(x:int): return x+1
f(2),f(2.0)
```

```
(3, 2.0)
```

If you need either setup or decode, you will need to subclass Transform to implement the actual encoding behavior in encodes, then (optionally) the setup behavior in setups and the decoding behavior in decodes:

```
class NormalizeMean(Transform):
    def setups(self, items): self.mean = sum(items)/len(items)
    def encodes(self, x): return x-self.mean
    def decodes(self, x): return x+self.mean
```

Here, NormalizeMean will initialize a certain state during the setup (the mean of all elements passed); then the transformation is to subtract that mean. For decoding purposes, we implement the reverse of that transformation by adding the mean. Here is an example of NormalizeMean in action:

```
tfm = NormalizeMean()
tfm.setup([1,2,3,4,5])
start = 2
y = tfm(start)
z = tfm.decode(y)
tfm.mean,y,z
```

```
(3.0, -1.0, 2.0)
```

Note that the method called and the method implemented are different, for each of these methods:

Class	To call	To implement
nn.Module (PyTorch)	() (i.e., call as function)	forward
Transform	()	encodes
Transform	decode()	decodes
Transform	setup()	setups

So, for instance, you would never call `setups` directly, but instead would call `setup`. The reason is that `setup` does some work before and after calling `setups` for you. To learn more about `Transforms` and how you can use them to implement different behavior depending on the type of input, be sure to check the tutorials in the fastai docs.

Pipeline

To compose several transforms together, fastai provides the `Pipeline` class. We define a `Pipeline` by passing it a list of `Transforms`; it will then compose the transforms inside it. When you call a `Pipeline` on an object, it will automatically call the transforms inside, in order:

```
tfms = Pipeline([tok, num])
t = tfms(txts[0]); t[:20]

tensor([   2,    8,   76,   10,   23, 3112,   23,   34, 3113,   33,   10,    8,
> 4477,   22,   88,   32,   10,   27,   42,   14])
```

And you can call `decode` on the result of your encoding, to get back something you can display and analyze:

```
tfms.decode(t)[:100]

'xxbos xxmaj well , " cube " ( 1997 ) , xxmaj vincenzo \'s first movie , was one
> of the most interesti'
```

The only part that doesn't work the same way as in `Transform` is the setup. To properly set up a `Pipeline` of `Transforms` on some data, you need to use a `TfmdLists`.

TfmdLists and Datasets: Transformed Collections

Your data is usually a set of raw items (like filenames, or rows in a DataFrame) to which you want to apply a succession of transformations. We just saw that a succession of transformations is represented by a `Pipeline` in fastai. The class that groups this `Pipeline` with your raw items is called `TfmdLists`.

TfmdLists

Here is the short way of doing the transformation we saw in the previous section:

```
tls = TfmdLists(files, [Tokenizer.from_folder(path), Numericalize])
```

At initialization, the `TfmdLists` will automatically call the `setup` method of each `Transform` in order, providing each not with the raw items but the items transformed by all the previous `Transforms`, in order. We can get the result of our `Pipeline` on any raw element just by indexing into the `TfmdLists`:

```
t = tls[0]; t[:20]
```

```
tensor([    2,    8,   91,   11,   22, 5793,   22,   37, 4910,   34,
>    11,    8, 13042,   23,  107,   30,   11,   25,   44,   14])
```

And the `TfmdLists` knows how to decode for show purposes:

```
tls.decode(t)[:100]
```

```
'xxbos xxmaj well , " cube " ( 1997 ) , xxmaj vincenzo \'s first movie , was one
> of the most interesti'
```

In fact, it even has a `show` method:

```
tls.show(t)
```

```
xxbos xxmaj well , " cube " ( 1997 ) , xxmaj vincenzo 's first movie , was one
> of the most interesting and tricky ideas that xxmaj i 've ever seen when
> talking about movies . xxmaj they had just one scenery , a bunch of actors
> and a plot . xxmaj so , what made it so special were all the effective
> direction , great dialogs and a bizarre condition that characters had to deal
> like rats in a labyrinth . xxmaj his second movie , " cypher " ( 2002 ) , was
> all about its story , but it was n't so good as " cube " but here are the
> characters being tested like rats again .

" nothing " is something very interesting and gets xxmaj vincenzo coming back
> to his ' cube days ' , locking the characters once again in a very different
> space with no time once more playing with the characters like playing with
> rats in an experience room . xxmaj but instead of a thriller sci - fi ( even
> some of the promotional teasers and trailers erroneous seemed like that ) , "
> nothing " is a loose and light comedy that for sure can be called a modern
> satire about our society and also about the intolerant world we 're living .
> xxmaj once again xxmaj xxunk amaze us with a great idea into a so small kind
> of thing . 2 actors and a blinding white scenario , that 's all you got most
> part of time and you do n't need more than that . xxmaj while " cube " is a
> claustrophobic experience and " cypher " confusing , " nothing " is
> completely the opposite but at the same time also desperate .

xxmaj this movie proves once again that a smart idea means much more than just
> a millionaire budget . xxmaj of course that the movie fails sometimes , but
> its prime idea means a lot and offsets any flaws . xxmaj there 's nothing
> more to be said about this movie because everything is a brilliant surprise
> and a totally different experience that i had in movies since " cube " .
```

The TfmdLists is named with an "s" because it can handle a training and a validation set with a splits argument. You just need to pass the indices of the elements that are in the training set and the indices of the elements that are in the validation set:

```
cut = int(len(files)*0.8)
splits = [list(range(cut)), list(range(cut,len(files)))]
tls = TfmdLists(files, [Tokenizer.from_folder(path), Numericalize],
                splits=splits)
```

You can then access them through the train and valid attributes:

```
tls.valid[0][:20]
```

```
tensor([    2,    8,   20,   30,   87,  510, 1570,   12,  408,  379,
      > 4196,   10,    8,   20,   30,   16,   13, 12216,  202,  509])
```

If you have manually written a Transform that performs all of your preprocessing at once, turning raw items into a tuple with inputs and targets, then TfmdLists is the class you need. You can directly convert it to a DataLoaders object with the dataload ers method. This is what we will do in our Siamese example later in this chapter.

In general, though, you will have two (or more) parallel pipelines of transforms: one for processing your raw items into inputs and one to process your raw items into targets. For instance, here, the pipeline we defined processes only the raw text into inputs. If we want to do text classification, we also have to process the labels into targets.

For this, we need to do two things. First we take the label name from the parent folder. There is a function, parent_label, for this:

```
lbls = files.map(parent_label)
lbls
```

```
(#50000) ['pos','pos','pos','pos','pos','pos','pos','pos','pos','pos'...]
```

Then we need a Transform that will grab the unique items and build a vocab with them during setup, then transform the string labels into integers when called. fastai provides this for us; it's called Categorize:

```
cat = Categorize()
cat.setup(lbls)
cat.vocab, cat(lbls[0])
```

```
((#2) ['neg','pos'], TensorCategory(1))
```

To do the whole setup automatically on our list of files, we can create a TfmdLists as before:

```
tls_y = TfmdLists(files, [parent_label, Categorize()])
tls_y[0]
```

```
TensorCategory(1)
```

But then we end up with two separate objects for our inputs and targets, which is not what we want. This is where `Datasets` comes to the rescue.

Datasets

`Datasets` will apply two (or more) pipelines in parallel to the same raw object and build a tuple with the result. Like `TfmdLists`, it will automatically do the setup for us, and when we index into a `Datasets`, it will return us a tuple with the results of each pipeline:

```
x_tfms = [Tokenizer.from_folder(path), Numericalize]
y_tfms = [parent_label, Categorize()]
dsets = Datasets(files, [x_tfms, y_tfms])
x,y = dsets[0]
x[:20],y
```

Like a `TfmdLists`, we can pass along `splits` to a `Datasets` to split our data between training and validation sets:

```
x_tfms = [Tokenizer.from_folder(path), Numericalize]
y_tfms = [parent_label, Categorize()]
dsets = Datasets(files, [x_tfms, y_tfms], splits=splits)
x,y = dsets.valid[0]
x[:20],y
```

```
(tensor([    2,     8,    20,    30,    87,   510,  1570,    12,   408,   379,
>  4196,    10,     8,    20,    30,    16,    13, 12216,   202,   509]),
 TensorCategory(0))
```

It can also decode any processed tuple or show it directly:

```
t = dsets.valid[0]
dsets.decode(t)
```

```
('xxbos xxmaj this movie had horrible lighting and terrible camera movements .
> xxmaj this movie is a jumpy horror flick with no meaning at all . xxmaj the
> slashes are totally fake looking . xxmaj it looks like some 17 year - old
> idiot wrote this movie and a 10 year old kid shot it . xxmaj with the worst
> acting you can ever find . xxmaj people are tired of knives . xxmaj at least
> move on to guns or fire . xxmaj it has almost exact lines from " when a xxmaj
> stranger xxmaj calls " . xxmaj with gruesome killings , only crazy people
> would enjoy this movie . xxmaj it is obvious the writer does n\'t have kids
> or even care for them . i mean at show some mercy . xxmaj just to sum it up ,
> this movie is a " b " movie and it sucked . xxmaj just for your own sake , do
> n\'t even think about wasting your time watching this crappy movie .',
 'neg')
```

The last step is to convert our `Datasets` object to a `DataLoaders`, which can be done with the `dataloaders` method. Here we need to pass along a special argument to take care of the padding problem (as we saw in the preceding chapter). This needs to happen just before we batch the elements, so we pass it to `before_batch`:

```
dls = dsets.dataloaders(bs=64, before_batch=pad_input)
```

`dataloaders` directly calls `DataLoader` on each subset of our `Datasets`. fastai's `DataLoader` expands the PyTorch class of the same name and is responsible for collating the items from our datasets into batches. It has a lot of points of customization, but the most important ones that you should know are as follows:

`after_item`
: Applied on each item after grabbing it inside the dataset. This is the equivalent of `item_tfms` in `DataBlock`.

`before_batch`
: Applied on the list of items before they are collated. This is the ideal place to pad items to the same size.

`after_batch`
: Applied on the batch as a whole after its construction. This is the equivalent of `batch_tfms` in `DataBlock`.

As a conclusion, here is the full code necessary to prepare the data for text classification:

```
tfms = [[Tokenizer.from_folder(path), Numericalize], [parent_label, Categorize]]
files = get_text_files(path, folders = ['train', 'test'])
splits = GrandparentSplitter(valid_name='test')(files)
dsets = Datasets(files, tfms, splits=splits)
dls = dsets.dataloaders(dl_type=SortedDL, before_batch=pad_input)
```

The two differences from the previous code are the use of `GrandparentSplitter` to split our training and validation data, and the `dl_type` argument. This is to tell `dataloaders` to use the `SortedDL` class of `DataLoader`, and not the usual one. `SortedDL` constructs batches by putting samples of roughly the same lengths into batches.

This does the exact same thing as our previous `DataBlock`:

```
path = untar_data(URLs.IMDB)
dls = DataBlock(
    blocks=(TextBlock.from_folder(path),CategoryBlock),
    get_y = parent_label,
    get_items=partial(get_text_files, folders=['train', 'test']),
    splitter=GrandparentSplitter(valid_name='test')
).dataloaders(path)
```

But now you know how to customize every single piece of it!

Let's practice what we just learned about using this mid-level API for data preprocessing on a computer vision example now.

Applying the Mid-Level Data API: SiamesePair

A *Siamese model* takes two images and has to determine whether they are of the same class. For this example, we will use the Pet dataset again and prepare the data for a model that will have to predict whether two images of pets are of the same breed. We will explain here how to prepare the data for such a model, and then we will train that model in Chapter 15.

First things first—let's get the images in our dataset:

```
from fastai.vision.all import *
path = untar_data(URLs.PETS)
files = get_image_files(path/"images")
```

If we didn't care about showing our objects at all, we could directly create one transform to completely preprocess that list of files. We will want to look at those images, though, so we need to create a custom type. When you call the show method on a TfmdLists or a Datasets object, it will decode items until it reaches a type that contains a show method and use it to show the object. That show method gets passed a ctx, which could be a matplotlib axis for images or a row of a DataFrame for texts.

Here we create a SiameseImage object that subclasses fastuple and is intended to contain three things: two images, and a Boolean that's True if the images are of the same breed. We also implement the special show method, such that it concatenates the two images with a black line in the middle. Don't worry too much about the part that is in the if test (which is to show the SiameseImage when the images are Python images, not tensors); the important part is in the last three lines:

```
class SiameseImage(fastuple):
    def show(self, ctx=None, **kwargs):
        img1,img2,same_breed = self
        if not isinstance(img1, Tensor):
            if img2.size != img1.size: img2 = img2.resize(img1.size)
            t1,t2 = tensor(img1),tensor(img2)
            t1,t2 = t1.permute(2,0,1),t2.permute(2,0,1)
        else: t1,t2 = img1,img2
        line = t1.new_zeros(t1.shape[0], t1.shape[1], 10)
        return show_image(torch.cat([t1,line,t2], dim=2),
                          title=same_breed, ctx=ctx)
```

Let's create a first `SiameseImage` and check that our `show` method works:

```
img = PILImage.create(files[0])
s = SiameseImage(img, img, True)
s.show();
```

True

We can also try with a second image that's not from the same class:

```
img1 = PILImage.create(files[1])
s1 = SiameseImage(img, img1, False)
s1.show();
```

False

The important thing with transforms that we saw before is that they dispatch over tuples or their subclasses. That's precisely why we chose to subclass `fastuple` in this instance—this way, we can apply any transform that works on images to our `Siamese Image`, and it will be applied on each image in the tuple:

```
s2 = Resize(224)(s1)
s2.show();
```

False

Here the `Resize` transform is applied to each of the two images, but not the Boolean flag. Even if we have a custom type, we can thus benefit from all the data augmentation transforms inside the library.

We are now ready to build the `Transform` that we will use to get our data ready for a Siamese model. First, we will need a function to determine the classes of all our images:

```
def label_func(fname):
    return re.match(r'^(.*)_\d+.jpg$', fname.name).groups()[0]
```

For each image, our transform will, with a probability of 0.5, draw an image from the same class and return a `SiameseImage` with a true label, or draw an image from another class and return a `SiameseImage` with a false label. This is all done in the private `_draw` function. There is one difference between the training and validation sets, which is why the transform needs to be initialized with the splits: on the training set, we will make that random pick each time we read an image, whereas on the validation set, we make this random pick once and for all at initialization. This way, we get more varied samples during training, but always the same validation set:

```
class SiameseTransform(Transform):
    def __init__(self, files, label_func, splits):
        self.labels = files.map(label_func).unique()
        self.lbl2files = {l: L(f for f in files if label_func(f) == l)
                          for l in self.labels}
        self.label_func = label_func
        self.valid = {f: self._draw(f) for f in files[splits[1]]}

    def encodes(self, f):
        f2,t = self.valid.get(f, self._draw(f))
        img1,img2 = PILImage.create(f),PILImage.create(f2)
        return SiameseImage(img1, img2, t)

    def _draw(self, f):
        same = random.random() < 0.5
        cls = self.label_func(f)
        if not same:
            cls = random.choice(L(l for l in self.labels if l != cls))
        return random.choice(self.lbl2files[cls]),same
```

We can then create our main transform:

```
splits = RandomSplitter()(files)
tfm = SiameseTransform(files, label_func, splits)
tfm(files[0]).show();
```

True

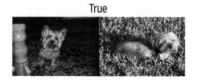

In the mid-level API for data collection, we have two objects that can help us apply transforms on a set of items: TfmdLists and Datasets. If you remember what we have just seen, one applies a Pipeline of transforms and the other applies several Pipelines of transforms in parallel, to build tuples. Here, our main transform already builds the tuples, so we use TfmdLists:

```
tls = TfmdLists(files, tfm, splits=splits)
show_at(tls.valid, 0);
```

True

And we can finally get our data in DataLoaders by calling the dataloaders method. One thing to be careful of here is that this method does not take item_tfms and batch_tfms like a DataBlock. The fastai DataLoader has several hooks that are named after events; here what we apply on the items after they are grabbed is called after_item, and what we apply on the batch once it's built is called after_batch:

```
dls = tls.dataloaders(after_item=[Resize(224), ToTensor],
    after_batch=[IntToFloatTensor, Normalize.from_stats(*imagenet_stats)])
```

Note that we need to pass more transforms than usual—that's because the data block API usually adds them automatically:

- ToTensor is the one that converts images to tensors (again, it's applied on every part of the tuple).

- IntToFloatTensor converts the tensor of images containing integers from 0 to 255 to a tensor of floats, and divides by 255 to make the values between 0 and 1.

We can now train a model using this DataLoaders. It will need a bit more customization than the usual model provided by cnn_learner since it has to take two images instead of one, but we will see how to create such a model and train it in Chapter 15.

Conclusion

fastai provides a layered API. It takes one line of code to grab the data when it's in one of the usual settings, making it easy for beginners to focus on training a model without spending too much time assembling the data. Then, the high-level data block API gives you more flexibility by allowing you to mix and match building blocks. Underneath it, the mid-level API gives you greater flexibility to apply transformations on your items. In your real-world problems, this is probably what you will need to use, and we hope it makes the step of data-munging as easy as possible.

Questionnaire

1. Why do we say that fastai has a "layered" API? What does it mean?

2. Why does a Transform have a decode method? What does it do?

3. Why does a Transform have a setup method? What does it do?

4. How does a Transform work when called on a tuple?

5. Which methods do you need to implement when writing your own Transform?

6. Write a Normalize transform that fully normalizes items (subtract the mean and divide by the standard deviation of the dataset), and that can decode that behavior. Try not to peek!

7. Write a Transform that does the numericalization of tokenized texts (it should set its vocab automatically from the dataset seen and have a decode method). Look at the source code of fastai if you need help.

8. What is a Pipeline?

9. What is a TfmdLists?

10. What is a Datasets? How is it different from a TfmdLists?

11. Why are TfmdLists and Datasets named with an "s"?

12. How can you build a DataLoaders from a TfmdLists or a Datasets?

13. How do you pass item_tfms and batch_tfms when building a DataLoaders from a TfmdLists or a Datasets?

14. What do you need to do when you want to have your custom items work with methods like show_batch or show_results?

15. Why can we easily apply fastai data augmentation transforms to the SiamesePair we built?

Further Research

1. Use the mid-level API to prepare the data in `DataLoaders` on your own datasets. Try this with the Pet dataset and the Adult dataset from Chapter 1.

2. Look at the Siamese tutorial in the fastai documentation (*https://docs.fast.ai*) to learn how to customize the behavior of `show_batch` and `show_results` for new types of items. Implement it in your own project.

Understanding fastai's Applications: Wrap Up

Congratulations—you've completed all of the chapters in this book that cover the key practical parts of training models and using deep learning! You know how to use all of fastai's built-in applications, and how to customize them using the data block API and loss functions. You even know how to create a neural network from scratch and train it! (And hopefully you now know some of the questions to ask to make sure your creations help improve society too.)

The knowledge you already have is enough to create full working prototypes of many types of neural network application. More importantly, it will help you understand the capabilities and limitations of deep learning models, and how to design a system that's well adapted to them.

In the rest of this book, we will be pulling apart those applications, piece by piece, to understand the foundations they are built on. This is important knowledge for a deep learning practitioner, because it allows you to inspect and debug models that you build and to create new applications that are customized for your particular projects.

PART III

Foundations of Deep Learning

CHAPTER 12

A Language Model from Scratch

We're now ready to go deep...deep into deep learning! You already learned how to train a basic neural network, but how do you go from there to creating state-of-the-art models? In this part of the book, we're going to uncover all of the mysteries, starting with language models.

You saw in Chapter 10 how to fine-tune a pretrained language model to build a text classifier. In this chapter, we will explain exactly what is inside that model and what an RNN is. First, let's gather some data that will allow us to quickly prototype our various models.

The Data

Whenever we start working on a new problem, we always first try to think of the simplest dataset we can that will allow us to try out methods quickly and easily, and interpret the results. When we started working on language modeling a few years ago, we didn't find any datasets that would allow for quick prototyping, so we made one. We call it *Human Numbers*, and it simply contains the first 10,000 numbers written out in English.

Jeremy Says

One of the most common practical mistakes I see even among highly experienced practitioners is failing to use appropriate datasets at appropriate times during the analysis process. In particular, most people tend to start with datasets that are too big and too complicated.

We can download, extract, and take a look at our dataset in the usual way:

```
from fastai.text.all import *
path = untar_data(URLs.HUMAN_NUMBERS)

path.ls()

(#2) [Path('train.txt'),Path('valid.txt')]
```

Let's open those two files and see what's inside. At first, we'll join all of the texts together and ignore the train/valid split given by the dataset (we'll come back to that later):

```
lines = L()
with open(path/'train.txt') as f: lines += L(*f.readlines())
with open(path/'valid.txt') as f: lines += L(*f.readlines())
lines

(#9998) ['one \n','two \n','three \n','four \n','five \n','six \n','seven
 > \n','eight \n','nine \n','ten \n'...]
```

We take all those lines and concatenate them in one big stream. To mark when we go from one number to the next, we use a . as a separator:

```
text = ' . '.join([l.strip() for l in lines])
text[:100]

'one . two . three . four . five . six . seven . eight . nine . ten . eleven .
 > twelve . thirteen . fo'
```

We can tokenize this dataset by splitting on spaces:

```
tokens = text.split(' ')
tokens[:10]

['one', '.', 'two', '.', 'three', '.', 'four', '.', 'five', '.']
```

To numericalize, we have to create a list of all the unique tokens (our *vocab*):

```
vocab = L(*tokens).unique()
vocab

(#30) ['one','.','two','three','four','five','six','seven','eight','nine'...]
```

Then we can convert our tokens into numbers by looking up the index of each in the vocab:

```
word2idx = {w:i for i,w in enumerate(vocab)}
nums = L(word2idx[i] for i in tokens)
nums

(#63095) [0,1,2,1,3,1,4,1,5,1...]
```

Now that we have a small dataset on which language modeling should be an easy task, we can build our first model.

Our First Language Model from Scratch

One simple way to turn this into a neural network would be to specify that we are going to predict each word based on the previous three words. We could create a list of every sequence of three words as our independent variables, and the next word after each sequence as the dependent variable.

We can do that with plain Python. Let's do it first with tokens just to confirm what it looks like:

```
L((tokens[i:i+3], tokens[i+3]) for i in range(0,len(tokens)-4,3))

(#21031) [((['one', '.', 'two'], '.'),(['.', 'three', '.'], 'four'),(['four',
 > '.', 'five'], '.'),(['.', 'six', '.'], 'seven'),(['seven', '.', 'eight'],
 > '.'),(['.', 'nine', '.'], 'ten'),(['ten', '.', 'eleven'], '.'),(['.',
 > 'twelve', '.'], 'thirteen'),(['thirteen', '.', 'fourteen'], '.'),(['.',
 > 'fifteen', '.'], 'sixteen')...]
```

Now we will do it with tensors of the numericalized values, which is what the model will actually use:

```
seqs = L((tensor(nums[i:i+3]), nums[i+3]) for i in range(0,len(nums)-4,3))
seqs

(#21031) [(tensor([0, 1, 2]), 1),(tensor([1, 3, 1]), 4),(tensor([4, 1, 5]),
 > 1),(tensor([1, 6, 1]), 7),(tensor([7, 1, 8]), 1),(tensor([1, 9, 1]),
 > 10),(tensor([10,  1, 11]), 1),(tensor([ 1, 12,  1]), 13),(tensor([13,  1,
 > 14]), 1),(tensor([ 1, 15,  1]), 16)...]
```

We can batch those easily using the `DataLoader` class. For now, we will split the sequences randomly:

```
bs = 64
cut = int(len(seqs) * 0.8)
dls = DataLoaders.from_dsets(seqs[:cut], seqs[cut:], bs=64, shuffle=False)
```

We can now create a neural network architecture that takes three words as input, and returns a prediction of the probability of each possible next word in the vocab. We will use three standard linear layers, but with two tweaks.

The first tweak is that the first linear layer will use only the first word's embedding as activations, the second layer will use the second word's embedding plus the first layer's output activations, and the third layer will use the third word's embedding plus the second layer's output activations. The key effect is that every word is interpreted in the information context of any words preceding it.

The second tweak is that each of these three layers will use the same weight matrix. The way that one word impacts the activations from previous words should not change depending on the position of a word. In other words, activation values will change as data moves through the layers, but the layer weights themselves will not change from layer to layer. So, a layer does not learn one sequence position; it must learn to handle all positions.

Since layer weights do not change, you might think of the sequential layers as "the same layer" repeated. In fact, PyTorch makes this concrete; we can create just one layer and use it multiple times.

Our Language Model in PyTorch

We can now create the language model module that we described earlier:

```
class LMModel1(Module):
    def __init__(self, vocab_sz, n_hidden):
        self.i_h = nn.Embedding(vocab_sz, n_hidden)
        self.h_h = nn.Linear(n_hidden, n_hidden)
        self.h_o = nn.Linear(n_hidden,vocab_sz)

    def forward(self, x):
        h = F.relu(self.h_h(self.i_h(x[:,0])))
        h = h + self.i_h(x[:,1])
        h = F.relu(self.h_h(h))
        h = h + self.i_h(x[:,2])
        h = F.relu(self.h_h(h))
        return self.h_o(h)
```

As you see, we have created three layers:

- The embedding layer (i_h, for *input* to *hidden*)
- The linear layer to create the activations for the next word (h_h, for *hidden* to *hidden*)
- A final linear layer to predict the fourth word (h_o, for *hidden* to *output*)

This might be easier to represent in pictorial form, so let's define a simple pictorial representation of basic neural networks. Figure 12-1 shows how we're going to represent a neural net with one hidden layer.

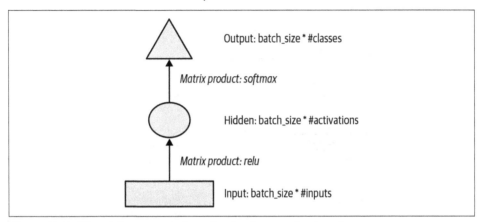

Figure 12-1. Pictorial representation of a simple neural network

Each shape represents activations: rectangle for input, circle for hidden (inner) layer activations, and triangle for output activations. We will use those shapes (summarized in Figure 12-2) in all the diagrams in this chapter.

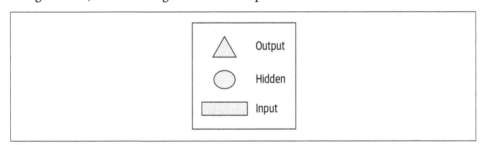

Figure 12-2. Shapes used in our pictorial representations

An arrow represents the actual layer computation—i.e., the linear layer followed by the activation function. Using this notation, Figure 12-3 shows what our simple language model looks like.

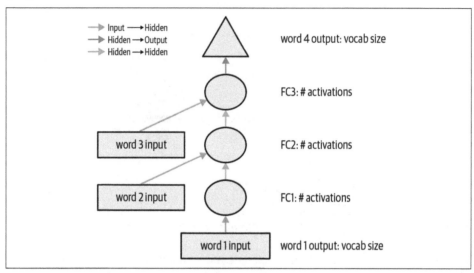

Figure 12-3. Representation of our basic language model

To simplify things, we've removed the details of the layer computation from each arrow. We've also color-coded the arrows, such that all arrows with the same color have the same weight matrix. For instance, all the input layers use the same embedding matrix, so they all have the same color (green).

Let's try training this model and see how it goes:

```
learn = Learner(dls, LMModel1(len(vocab), 64), loss_func=F.cross_entropy,
                metrics=accuracy)
learn.fit_one_cycle(4, 1e-3)
```

epoch	train_loss	valid_loss	accuracy	time
0	1.824297	1.970941	0.467554	00:02
1	1.386973	1.823242	0.467554	00:02
2	1.417556	1.654497	0.494414	00:02
3	1.376440	1.650849	0.494414	00:02

To see if this is any good, let's check what a very simple model would give us. In this case, we could always predict the most common token, so let's find out which token is most often the target in our validation set:

```
n,counts = 0,torch.zeros(len(vocab))
for x,y in dls.valid:
    n += y.shape[0]
    for i in range_of(vocab): counts[i] += (y==i).long().sum()
idx = torch.argmax(counts)
idx, vocab[idx.item()], counts[idx].item()/n
```

```
(tensor(29), 'thousand', 0.15165200855716662)
```

The most common token has the index 29, which corresponds to the token thousand. Always predicting this token would give us an accuracy of roughly 15%, so we are faring way better!

Alexis Says

My first guess was that the separator would be the most common token, since there is one for every number. But looking at tokens reminded me that large numbers are written with many words, so on the way to 10,000 you write "thousand" a lot: five thousand, five thousand and one, five thousand and two, etc. Oops! Looking at your data is great for noticing subtle features as well as embarrassingly obvious ones.

This is a nice first baseline. Let's see how we can refactor it with a loop.

Our First Recurrent Neural Network

Looking at the code for our module, we could simplify it by replacing the duplicated code that calls the layers with a for loop. In addition to making our code simpler, this will have the benefit that we will be able to apply our module equally well to token sequences of different lengths—we won't be restricted to token lists of length three:

```
class LMModel2(Module):
    def __init__(self, vocab_sz, n_hidden):
        self.i_h = nn.Embedding(vocab_sz, n_hidden)
        self.h_h = nn.Linear(n_hidden, n_hidden)
        self.h_o = nn.Linear(n_hidden,vocab_sz)

    def forward(self, x):
        h = 0
        for i in range(3):
            h = h + self.i_h(x[:,i])
            h = F.relu(self.h_h(h))
        return self.h_o(h)
```

Let's check that we get the same results using this refactoring:

```
learn = Learner(dls, LMModel2(len(vocab), 64), loss_func=F.cross_entropy,
                metrics=accuracy)
learn.fit_one_cycle(4, 1e-3)
```

epoch	train_loss	valid_loss	accuracy	time
0	1.816274	1.964143	0.460185	00:02
1	1.423805	1.739964	0.473259	00:02
2	1.430327	1.685172	0.485382	00:02
3	1.388390	1.657033	0.470406	00:02

We can also refactor our pictorial representation in exactly the same way, as shown in Figure 12-4 (we're also removing the details of activation sizes here, and using the same arrow colors as in Figure 12-3).

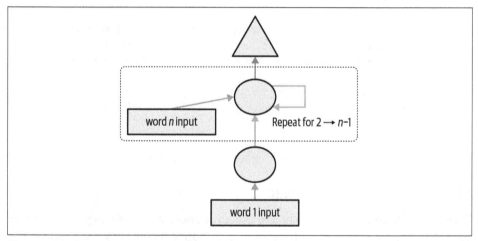

Figure 12-4. Basic recurrent neural network

You will see that a set of activations is being updated each time through the loop, stored in the variable h—this is called the *hidden state*.

Jargon: Hidden State

The activations that are updated at each step of a recurrent neural network.

A neural network that is defined using a loop like this is called a *recurrent neural network* (RNN). It is important to realize that an RNN is not a complicated new architecture, but simply a refactoring of a multilayer neural network using a for loop.

Alexis Says

My true opinion: if they were called "looping neural networks," or LNNs, they would seem 50% less daunting!

Now that we know what an RNN is, let's try to make it a little bit better.

Improving the RNN

Looking at the code for our RNN, one thing that seems problematic is that we are initializing our hidden state to zero for every new input sequence. Why is that a problem? We made our sample sequences short so they would fit easily into batches. But if we order those samples correctly, the sample sequences will be read in order by the model, exposing the model to long stretches of the original sequence.

Another thing we can look at is having more signal: why predict only the fourth word when we could use the intermediate predictions to also predict the second and third words? Let's see how we can implement those changes, starting with adding some state.

Maintaining the State of an RNN

Because we initialize the model's hidden state to zero for each new sample, we are throwing away all the information we have about the sentences we have seen so far, which means that our model doesn't actually know where we are up to in the overall counting sequence. This is easily fixed; we can simply move the initialization of the hidden state to `__init__`.

But this fix will create its own subtle, but important, problem. It effectively makes our neural network as deep as the entire number of tokens in our document. For instance, if there were 10,000 tokens in our dataset, we would be creating a 10,000-layer neural network.

To see why this is the case, consider the original pictorial representation of our recurrent neural network in Figure 12-3, before refactoring it with a for loop. You can see each layer corresponds with one token input. When we talk about the representation of a recurrent neural network before refactoring with the for loop, we call this the *unrolled representation*. It is often helpful to consider the unrolled representation when trying to understand an RNN.

The problem with a 10,000-layer neural network is that if and when you get to the 10,000th word of the dataset, you will still need to calculate the derivatives all the way back to the first layer. This is going to be slow indeed, and memory-intensive. It is unlikely that you'll be able to store even one mini-batch on your GPU.

The solution to this problem is to tell PyTorch that we do not want to backpropagate the derivatives through the entire implicit neural network. Instead, we will keep just the last three layers of gradients. To remove all of the gradient history in PyTorch, we use the detach method.

Here is the new version of our RNN. It is now stateful, because it remembers its activations between different calls to forward, which represent its use for different samples in the batch:

```
class LMModel3(Module):
    def __init__(self, vocab_sz, n_hidden):
        self.i_h = nn.Embedding(vocab_sz, n_hidden)
        self.h_h = nn.Linear(n_hidden, n_hidden)
        self.h_o = nn.Linear(n_hidden,vocab_sz)
        self.h = 0

    def forward(self, x):
        for i in range(3):
            self.h = self.h + self.i_h(x[:,i])
            self.h = F.relu(self.h_h(self.h))
        out = self.h_o(self.h)
        self.h = self.h.detach()
        return out

    def reset(self): self.h = 0
```

This model will have the same activations whatever sequence length we pick, because the hidden state will remember the last activation from the previous batch. The only thing that will be different is the gradients computed at each step: they will be calculated on only sequence length tokens in the past, instead of the whole stream. This approach is called *backpropagation through time* (BPTT).

 Jargon: Backpropagation Through Time

Treating a neural net with effectively one layer per time step (usually refactored using a loop) as one big model, and calculating gradients on it in the usual way. To avoid running out of memory and time, we usually use *truncated* BPTT, which "detaches" the history of computation steps in the hidden state every few time steps.

To use LMModel3, we need to make sure the samples are going to be seen in a certain order. As we saw in Chapter 10, if the first line of the first batch is our dset[0], the second batch should have dset[1] as the first line, so that the model sees the text flowing.

LMDataLoader was doing this for us in Chapter 10. This time we're going to do it ourselves.

To do this, we are going to rearrange our dataset. First we divide the samples into `m = len(dset) // bs` groups (this is the equivalent of splitting the whole concatenated dataset into, for example, 64 equally sized pieces, since we're using `bs=64` here). `m` is the length of each of these pieces. For instance, if we're using our whole dataset (although we'll actually split it into train versus valid in a moment), we have this:

```
m = len(seqs)//bs
m,bs,len(seqs)
```

```
(328, 64, 21031)
```

The first batch will be composed of the samples

```
(0, m, 2*m, ..., (bs-1)*m)
```

the second batch of the samples

```
(1, m+1, 2*m+1, ..., (bs-1)*m+1)
```

and so forth. This way, at each epoch, the model will see a chunk of contiguous text of size `3*m` (since each text is of size 3) on each line of the batch.

The following function does that reindexing:

```
def group_chunks(ds, bs):
    m = len(ds) // bs
    new_ds = L()
    for i in range(m): new_ds += L(ds[i + m*j] for j in range(bs))
    return new_ds
```

Then we just pass `drop_last=True` when building our `DataLoaders` to drop the last batch that does not have a shape of `bs`. We also pass `shuffle=False` to make sure the texts are read in order:

```
cut = int(len(seqs) * 0.8)
dls = DataLoaders.from_dsets(
    group_chunks(seqs[:cut], bs),
    group_chunks(seqs[cut:], bs),
    bs=bs, drop_last=True, shuffle=False)
```

The last thing we add is a little tweak of the training loop via a `Callback`. We will talk more about callbacks in Chapter 16; this one will call the `reset` method of our model at the beginning of each epoch and before each validation phase. Since we implemented that method to set the hidden state of the model to zero, this will make sure we start with a clean state before reading those continuous chunks of text. We can also start training a bit longer:

```
learn = Learner(dls, LMModel3(len(vocab), 64), loss_func=F.cross_entropy,
                metrics=accuracy, cbs=ModelResetter)
learn.fit_one_cycle(10, 3e-3)
```

epoch	train_loss	valid_loss	accuracy	time
0	1.677074	1.827367	0.467548	00:02
1	1.282722	1.870913	0.388942	00:02
2	1.090705	1.651793	0.462500	00:02
3	1.005092	1.613794	0.516587	00:02
4	0.965975	1.560775	0.551202	00:02
5	0.916182	1.595857	0.560577	00:02
6	0.897657	1.539733	0.574279	00:02
7	0.836274	1.585141	0.583173	00:02
8	0.805877	1.629808	0.586779	00:02
9	0.795096	1.651267	0.588942	00:02

This is already better! The next step is to use more targets and compare them to the intermediate predictions.

Creating More Signal

Another problem with our current approach is that we predict only one output word for each three input words. As a result, the amount of signal that we are feeding back to update weights with is not as large as it could be. It would be better if we predicted the next word after every single word, rather than every three words, as shown in Figure 12-5.

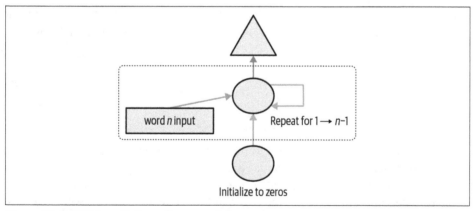

Figure 12-5. RNN predicting after every token

This is easy enough to add. We need to first change our data so that the dependent variable has each of the three next words after each of our three input words. Instead of 3, we use an attribute, `sl` (for sequence length), and make it a bit bigger:

```
sl = 16
seqs = L((tensor(nums[i:i+sl]), tensor(nums[i+1:i+sl+1]))
        for i in range(0,len(nums)-sl-1,sl))
cut = int(len(seqs) * 0.8)
dls = DataLoaders.from_dsets(group_chunks(seqs[:cut], bs),
                             group_chunks(seqs[cut:], bs),
                             bs=bs, drop_last=True, shuffle=False)
```

Looking at the first element of `seqs`, we can see that it contains two lists of the same size. The second list is the same as the first, but offset by one element:

```
[L(vocab[o] for o in s) for s in seqs[0]]
```

```
[(#16) ['one','.','two','.','three','.','four','.','five','.'...],
 (#16) ['.','two','.','three','.','four','.','five','.','six'...]]
```

Now we need to modify our model so that it outputs a prediction after every word, rather than just at the end of a three-word sequence:

```
class LMModel4(Module):
    def __init__(self, vocab_sz, n_hidden):
        self.i_h = nn.Embedding(vocab_sz, n_hidden)
        self.h_h = nn.Linear(n_hidden, n_hidden)
        self.h_o = nn.Linear(n_hidden,vocab_sz)
        self.h = 0

    def forward(self, x):
        outs = []
        for i in range(sl):
            self.h = self.h + self.i_h(x[:,i])
            self.h = F.relu(self.h_h(self.h))
            outs.append(self.h_o(self.h))
        self.h = self.h.detach()
        return torch.stack(outs, dim=1)

    def reset(self): self.h = 0
```

This model will return outputs of shape `bs x sl x vocab_sz` (since we stacked on `dim=1`). Our targets are of shape `bs x sl`, so we need to flatten those before using them in `F.cross_entropy`:

```
def loss_func(inp, targ):
    return F.cross_entropy(inp.view(-1, len(vocab)), targ.view(-1))
```

We can now use this loss function to train the model:

```
learn = Learner(dls, LMModel4(len(vocab), 64), loss_func=loss_func,
                metrics=accuracy, cbs=ModelResetter)
learn.fit_one_cycle(15, 3e-3)
```

epoch	train_loss	valid_loss	accuracy	time
0	3.103298	2.874341	0.212565	00:01
1	2.231964	1.971280	0.462158	00:01
2	1.711358	1.813547	0.461182	00:01
3	1.448516	1.828176	0.483236	00:01
4	1.288630	1.659564	0.520671	00:01
5	1.161470	1.714023	0.554932	00:01
6	1.055568	1.660916	0.575033	00:01
7	0.960765	1.719624	0.591064	00:01
8	0.870153	1.839560	0.614665	00:01
9	0.808545	1.770278	0.624349	00:01
10	0.758084	1.842931	0.610758	00:01
11	0.719320	1.799527	0.646566	00:01
12	0.683439	1.917928	0.649821	00:01
13	0.660283	1.874712	0.628581	00:01
14	0.646154	1.877519	0.640055	00:01

We need to train for longer, since the task has changed a bit and is more complicated now. But we end up with a good result…at least, sometimes. If you run it a few times, you'll see that you can get quite different results on different runs. That's because effectively we have a very deep network here, which can result in very large or very small gradients. We'll see in the next part of this chapter how to deal with this.

Now, the obvious way to get a better model is to go deeper: we have only one linear layer between the hidden state and the output activations in our basic RNN, so maybe we'll get better results with more.

Multilayer RNNs

In a multilayer RNN, we pass the activations from our recurrent neural network into a second recurrent neural network, as in Figure 12-6.

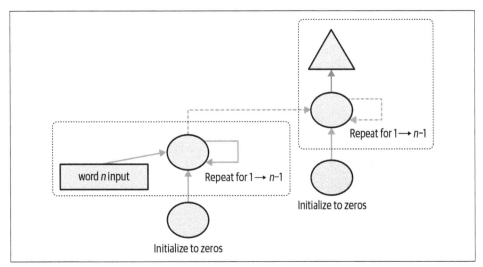

Figure 12-6. 2-layer RNN

The unrolled representation is shown in Figure 12-7 (similar to Figure 12-3).

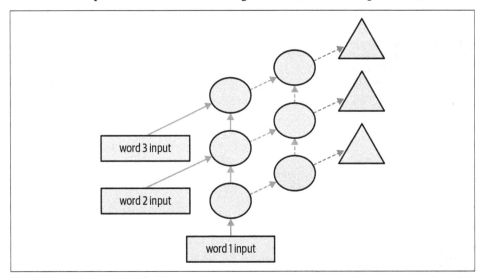

Figure 12-7. 2-layer unrolled RNN

Let's see how to implement this in practice.

The Model

We can save some time by using PyTorch's RNN class, which implements exactly what we created earlier, but also gives us the option to stack multiple RNNs, as we have discussed:

```
class LMModel5(Module):
    def __init__(self, vocab_sz, n_hidden, n_layers):
        self.i_h = nn.Embedding(vocab_sz, n_hidden)
        self.rnn = nn.RNN(n_hidden, n_hidden, n_layers, batch_first=True)
        self.h_o = nn.Linear(n_hidden, vocab_sz)
        self.h = torch.zeros(n_layers, bs, n_hidden)

    def forward(self, x):
        res,h = self.rnn(self.i_h(x), self.h)
        self.h = h.detach()
        return self.h_o(res)

    def reset(self): self.h.zero_()

learn = Learner(dls, LMModel5(len(vocab), 64, 2),
                loss_func=CrossEntropyLossFlat(),
                metrics=accuracy, cbs=ModelResetter)
learn.fit_one_cycle(15, 3e-3)
```

epoch	train_loss	valid_loss	accuracy	time
0	3.055853	2.591640	0.437907	00:01
1	2.162359	1.787310	0.471598	00:01
2	1.710663	1.941807	0.321777	00:01
3	1.520783	1.999726	0.312012	00:01
4	1.330846	2.012902	0.413249	00:01
5	1.163297	1.896192	0.450684	00:01
6	1.033813	2.005209	0.434814	00:01
7	0.919090	2.047083	0.456706	00:01
8	0.822939	2.068031	0.468831	00:01
9	0.750180	2.136064	0.475098	00:01
10	0.695120	2.139140	0.485433	00:01
11	0.655752	2.155081	0.493652	00:01
12	0.629650	2.162583	0.498535	00:01
13	0.613583	2.171649	0.491048	00:01
14	0.604309	2.180355	0.487874	00:01

Now that's disappointing…our previous single-layer RNN performed better. Why? The reason is that we have a deeper model, leading to exploding or vanishing activations.

Exploding or Disappearing Activations

In practice, creating accurate models from this kind of RNN is difficult. We will get better results if we call detach less often, and have more layers—this gives our RNN a longer time horizon to learn from and richer features to create. But it also means we have a deeper model to train. The key challenge in the development of deep learning has been figuring out how to train these kinds of models.

This is challenging because of what happens when you multiply by a matrix many times. Think about what happens when you multiply by a number many times. For example, if you multiply by 2, starting at 1, you get the sequence 1, 2, 4, 8,...and after 32 steps, you are already at 4,294,967,296. A similar issue happens if you multiply by 0.5: you get 0.5, 0.25, 0.125...and after 32 steps, it's 0.00000000023. As you can see, multiplying by a number even slightly higher or lower than 1 results in an explosion or disappearance of our starting number, after just a few repeated multiplications.

Because matrix multiplication is just multiplying numbers and adding them up, exactly the same thing happens with repeated matrix multiplications. And that's all a deep neural network is—each extra layer is another matrix multiplication. This means that it is very easy for a deep neural network to end up with extremely large or extremely small numbers.

This is a problem, because the way computers store numbers (known as *floating point*) means that they become less and less accurate the further away the numbers get from zero. The diagram in Figure 12-8, from the excellent article "What You Never Wanted to Know about Floating Point but Will Be Forced to Find Out" (*https://oreil.ly/c_kG9*), shows how the precision of floating-point numbers varies over the number line.

Figure 12-8. Precision of floating-point numbers

This inaccuracy means that often the gradients calculated for updating the weights end up as zero or infinity for deep networks. This is commonly referred to as the *vanishing gradients* or *exploding gradients* problem. It means that in SGD, the weights are either not updated at all or jump to infinity. Either way, they won't improve with training.

Researchers have developed ways to tackle this problem, which we will be discussing later in the book. One option is to change the definition of a layer in a way that makes it less likely to have exploding activations. We'll look at the details of how this is done in Chapter 13, when we discuss batch normalization, and Chapter 14, when we discuss ResNets, although these details don't generally matter in practice (unless you are a researcher who is creating new approaches to solving this problem). Another strategy for dealing with this is by being careful about initialization, which is a topic we'll investigate in Chapter 17.

For RNNs, two types of layers are frequently used to avoid exploding activations: *gated recurrent units* (GRUs) and *long short-term memory* (LSTM) layers. Both of these are available in PyTorch and are drop-in replacements for the RNN layer. We will cover only LSTMs in this book; plenty of good tutorials online explain GRUs, which are a minor variant on the LSTM design.

LSTM

LSTM is an architecture that was introduced back in 1997 by Jürgen Schmidhuber and Sepp Hochreiter. In this architecture, there are not one, but two, hidden states. In our base RNN, the hidden state is the output of the RNN at the previous time step. That hidden state is then responsible for two things:

- Having the right information for the output layer to predict the correct next token
- Retaining memory of everything that happened in the sentence

Consider, for example, the sentences "Henry has a dog and he likes his dog very much" and "Sophie has a dog and she likes her dog very much." It's very clear that the RNN needs to remember the name at the beginning of the sentence to be able to predict *he/she* or *his/her*.

In practice, RNNs are really bad at retaining memory of what happened much earlier in the sentence, which is the motivation to have another hidden state (called *cell state*) in the LSTM. The cell state will be responsible for keeping *long short-term memory*, while the hidden state will focus on the next token to predict. Let's take a closer look at how this is achieved and build an LSTM from scratch.

Building an LSTM from Scratch

In order to build an LSTM, we first have to understand its architecture. Figure 12-9 shows its inner structure.

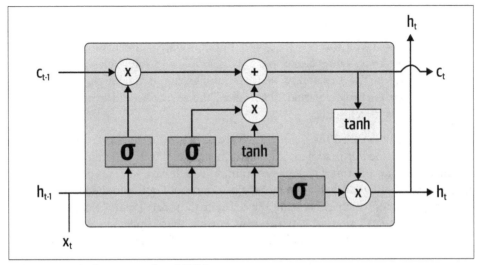

Figure 12-9. Architecture of an LSTM

In this picture, our input x_t enters on the left with the previous hidden state (h_{t-1}) and cell state (c_{t-1}). The four orange boxes represent four layers (our neural nets), with the activation being either sigmoid (σ) or tanh. tanh is just a sigmoid function rescaled to the range -1 to 1. Its mathematical expression can be written like this:

$$\tanh(x) = \frac{e^x - e^{-x}}{e^x + e^{-x}} = 2\sigma(2x) - 1$$

where σ is the sigmoid function. The green circles in the figure are elementwise operations. What goes out on the right is the new hidden state (h_t) and new cell state (c_t), ready for our next input. The new hidden state is also used as output, which is why the arrow splits to go up.

Let's go over the four neural nets (called *gates*) one by one and explain the diagram—but before this, notice how very little the cell state (at the top) is changed. It doesn't even go directly through a neural net! This is exactly why it will carry on a longer-term state.

First, the arrows for input and old hidden state are joined together. In the RNN we wrote earlier in this chapter, we were adding them together. In the LSTM, we stack them in one big tensor. This means the dimension of our embeddings (which is the dimension of x_t) can be different from the dimension of our hidden state. If we call those n_in and n_hid, the arrow at the bottom is of size n_in + n_hid; thus all the neural nets (orange boxes) are linear layers with n_in + n_hid inputs and n_hid outputs.

The first gate (looking from left to right) is called the *forget gate*. Since it's a linear layer followed by a sigmoid, its output will consist of scalars between 0 and 1. We multiply this result by the cell state to determine which information to keep and which to throw away: values closer to 0 are discarded, and values closer to 1 are kept. This gives the LSTM the ability to forget things about its long-term state. For instance, when crossing a period or an xxbos token, we would expect it to (have learned to) reset its cell state.

The second gate is called the *input gate*. It works with the third gate (which doesn't really have a name but is sometimes called the *cell gate*) to update the cell state. For instance, we may see a new gender pronoun, in which case we'll need to replace the information about gender that the forget gate removed. Similar to the forget gate, the input gate decides which elements of the cell state to update (values close to 1) or not (values close to 0). The third gate determines what those updated values are, in the range of –1 to 1 (thanks to the tanh function). The result is added to the cell state.

The last gate is the *output gate*. It determines which information from the cell state to use to generate the output. The cell state goes through a tanh before being combined with the sigmoid output from the output gate, and the result is the new hidden state. In terms of code, we can write the same steps like this:

```
class LSTMCell(Module):
    def __init__(self, ni, nh):
        self.forget_gate = nn.Linear(ni + nh, nh)
        self.input_gate  = nn.Linear(ni + nh, nh)
        self.cell_gate   = nn.Linear(ni + nh, nh)
        self.output_gate = nn.Linear(ni + nh, nh)

    def forward(self, input, state):
        h,c = state
        h = torch.cat([h, input], dim=1)
        forget = torch.sigmoid(self.forget_gate(h))
        c = c * forget
        inp = torch.sigmoid(self.input_gate(h))
        cell = torch.tanh(self.cell_gate(h))
        c = c + inp * cell
        out = torch.sigmoid(self.output_gate(h))
        h = out * torch.tanh(c)
        return h, (h,c)
```

In practice, we can then refactor the code. Also, in terms of performance, it's better to do one big matrix multiplication than four smaller ones (that's because we launch the special fast kernel on the GPU only once, and it gives the GPU more work to do in parallel). The stacking takes a bit of time (since we have to move one of the tensors around on the GPU to have it all in a contiguous array), so we use two separate layers for the input and the hidden state. The optimized and refactored code then looks like this:

```
class LSTMCell(Module):
    def __init__(self, ni, nh):
        self.ih = nn.Linear(ni,4*nh)
        self.hh = nn.Linear(nh,4*nh)

    def forward(self, input, state):
        h,c = state
        # One big multiplication for all the gates is better than 4 smaller ones
        gates = (self.ih(input) + self.hh(h)).chunk(4, 1)
        ingate,forgetgate,outgate = map(torch.sigmoid, gates[:3])
        cellgate = gates[3].tanh()

        c = (forgetgate*c) + (ingate*cellgate)
        h = outgate * c.tanh()
        return h, (h,c)
```

Here we use the PyTorch chunk method to split our tensor into four pieces. It works like this:

```
t = torch.arange(0,10); t
```

```
tensor([0, 1, 2, 3, 4, 5, 6, 7, 8, 9])
```

```
t.chunk(2)
```

```
(tensor([0, 1, 2, 3, 4]), tensor([5, 6, 7, 8, 9]))
```

Let's now use this architecture to train a language model!

Training a Language Model Using LSTMs

Here is the same network as LMModel5, using a two-layer LSTM. We can train it at a higher learning rate, for a shorter time, and get better accuracy:

```
class LMModel6(Module):
    def __init__(self, vocab_sz, n_hidden, n_layers):
        self.i_h = nn.Embedding(vocab_sz, n_hidden)
        self.rnn = nn.LSTM(n_hidden, n_hidden, n_layers, batch_first=True)
        self.h_o = nn.Linear(n_hidden, vocab_sz)
        self.h = [torch.zeros(n_layers, bs, n_hidden) for _ in range(2)]

    def forward(self, x):
        res,h = self.rnn(self.i_h(x), self.h)
        self.h = [h_.detach() for h_ in h]
        return self.h_o(res)

    def reset(self):
        for h in self.h: h.zero_()

learn = Learner(dls, LMModel6(len(vocab), 64, 2),
                loss_func=CrossEntropyLossFlat(),
                metrics=accuracy, cbs=ModelResetter)
learn.fit_one_cycle(15, 1e-2)
```

epoch	train_loss	valid_loss	accuracy	time
0	3.000821	2.663942	0.438314	00:02
1	2.139642	2.184780	0.240479	00:02
2	1.607275	1.812682	0.439779	00:02
3	1.347711	1.830982	0.497477	00:02
4	1.123113	1.937766	0.594401	00:02
5	0.852042	2.012127	0.631592	00:02
6	0.565494	1.312742	0.725749	00:02
7	0.347445	1.297934	0.711263	00:02
8	0.208191	1.441269	0.731201	00:02
9	0.126335	1.569952	0.737305	00:02
10	0.079761	1.427187	0.754150	00:02
11	0.052990	1.494990	0.745117	00:02
12	0.039008	1.393731	0.757894	00:02
13	0.031502	1.373210	0.758464	00:02
14	0.028068	1.368083	0.758464	00:02

Now that's better than a multilayer RNN! We can still see there is a bit of overfitting, however, which is a sign that a bit of regularization might help.

Regularizing an LSTM

Recurrent neural networks, in general, are hard to train, because of the problem of vanishing activations and gradients we saw before. Using LSTM (or GRU) cells makes training easier than with vanilla RNNs, but they are still very prone to overfitting. Data augmentation, while a possibility, is less often used for text data than for images because in most cases it requires another model to generate random augmentations (e.g., by translating the text into another language and then back into the original language). Overall, data augmentation for text data is currently not a well-explored space.

However, we can use other regularization techniques instead to reduce overfitting, which were thoroughly studied for use with LSTMs in the paper "Regularizing and Optimizing LSTM Language Models" (*https://oreil.ly/Rf-OG*) by Stephen Merity et al. This paper showed how effective use of dropout, activation regularization, and temporal activation regularization could allow an LSTM to beat state-of-the-art results that previously required much more complicated models. The authors called an LSTM using these techniques an *AWD-LSTM*. We'll look at each of these techniques in turn.

Dropout

Dropout is a regularization technique that was introduced by Geoffrey Hinton et al. in "Improving Neural Networks by Preventing Co-Adaptation of Feature Detectors" (*https://oreil.ly/-_xie*). The basic idea is to randomly change some activations to zero at training time. This makes sure all neurons actively work toward the output, as seen in Figure 12-10 (from "Dropout: A Simple Way to Prevent Neural Networks from Overfitting" (*https://oreil.ly/pYNxF*) by Nitish Srivastava et al.).

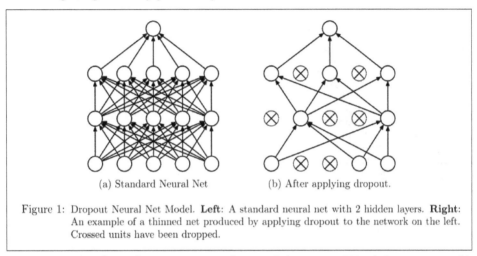

(a) Standard Neural Net   (b) After applying dropout.

Figure 1: Dropout Neural Net Model. **Left**: A standard neural net with 2 hidden layers. **Right**: An example of a thinned net produced by applying dropout to the network on the left. Crossed units have been dropped.

Figure 12-10. Applying dropout in a neural network (courtesy of Nitish Srivastava et al.)

Hinton used a nice metaphor when he explained, in an interview, the inspiration for dropout:

> I went to my bank. The tellers kept changing, and I asked one of them why. He said he didn't know but they got moved around a lot. I figured it must be because it would require cooperation between employees to successfully defraud the bank. This made me realize that randomly removing a different subset of neurons on each example would prevent conspiracies and thus reduce overfitting.

In the same interview, he also explained that neuroscience provided additional inspiration:

> We don't really know why neurons spike. One theory is that they want to be noisy so as to regularize, because we have many more parameters than we have data points. The idea of dropout is that if you have noisy activations, you can afford to use a much bigger model.

This explains the idea behind why dropout helps to generalize: first it helps the neurons to cooperate better together; then it makes the activations more noisy, thus making the model more robust.

We can see, however, that if we were to just zero those activations without doing anything else, our model would have problems training: if we go from the sum of five activations (that are all positive numbers since we apply a ReLU) to just two, this won't have the same scale. Therefore, if we apply dropout with a probability p, we rescale all activations by dividing them by 1-p (on average p will be zeroed, so it leaves 1-p), as shown in Figure 12-11.

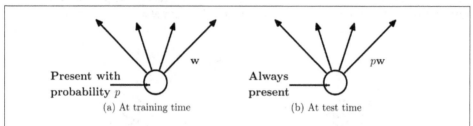

(a) At training time   (b) At test time

Figure 2: **Left**: A unit at training time that is present with probability p and is connected to units in the next layer with weights **w**. **Right**: At test time, the unit is always present and the weights are multiplied by p. The output at test time is same as the expected output at training time.

Figure 12-11. Why we scale the activations when applying dropout (courtesy of Nitish Srivastava et al.)

This is a full implementation of the dropout layer in PyTorch (although PyTorch's native layer is actually written in C, not Python):

```
class Dropout(Module):
    def __init__(self, p): self.p = p
    def forward(self, x):
        if not self.training: return x
        mask = x.new(*x.shape).bernoulli_(1-p)
        return x * mask.div_(1-p)
```

The bernoulli_ method is creating a tensor of random zeros (with probability p) and ones (with probability 1-p), which is then multiplied with our input before dividing by 1-p. Note the use of the training attribute, which is available in any PyTorch nn.Module, and tells us if we are doing training or inference.

Do Your Own Experiments

In previous chapters of the book, we'd be adding a code example for `bernoulli_` here, so you can see exactly how it works. But now that you know enough to do this yourself, we're going to be doing fewer and fewer examples for you, and instead expecting you to do your own experiments to see how things work. In this case, you'll see in the end-of-chapter questionnaire that we're asking you to experiment with `bernoulli_`—but don't wait for us to ask you to experiment to develop your understanding of the code we're studying; go ahead and do it anyway!

Using dropout before passing the output of our LSTM to the final layer will help reduce overfitting. Dropout is also used in many other models, including the default CNN head used in `fastai.vision`, and is available in `fastai.tabular` by passing the `ps` parameter (where each "p" is passed to each added `Dropout` layer), as we'll see in Chapter 15.

Dropout has different behavior in training and validation mode, which we specified using the `training` attribute in `Dropout`. Calling the `train` method on a `Module` sets `training` to `True` (both for the module you call the method on and for every module it recursively contains), and `eval` sets it to `False`. This is done automatically when calling the methods of `Learner`, but if you are not using that class, remember to switch from one to the other as needed.

Activation Regularization and Temporal Activation Regularization

Activation regularization (AR) and *temporal activation regularization* (TAR) are two regularization methods very similar to weight decay, discussed in Chapter 8. When applying weight decay, we add a small penalty to the loss that aims at making the weights as small as possible. For activation regularization, it's the final activations produced by the LSTM that we will try to make as small as possible, instead of the weights.

To regularize the final activations, we have to store those somewhere, then add the means of the squares of them to the loss (along with a multiplier `alpha`, which is just like `wd` for weight decay):

```
loss += alpha * activations.pow(2).mean()
```

Temporal activation regularization is linked to the fact we are predicting tokens in a sentence. That means it's likely that the outputs of our LSTMs should somewhat make sense when we read them in order. TAR is there to encourage that behavior by adding a penalty to the loss to make the difference between two consecutive activations as small as possible: our activations tensor has a shape `bs x sl x n_hid`, and we read consecutive activations on the sequence length axis (the dimension in the middle). With this, TAR can be expressed as follows:

```
loss += beta * (activations[:,1:] - activations[:,:-1]).pow(2).mean()
```

`alpha` and `beta` are then two hyperparameters to tune. To make this work, we need our model with dropout to return three things: the proper output, the activations of the LSTM pre-dropout, and the activations of the LSTM post-dropout. AR is often applied on the dropped-out activations (to not penalize the activations we turned into zeros afterward), while TAR is applied on the non-dropped-out activations (because those zeros create big differences between two consecutive time steps). A callback called `RNNRegularizer` will then apply this regularization for us.

Training a Weight-Tied Regularized LSTM

We can combine dropout (applied before we go into our output layer) with AR and TAR to train our previous LSTM. We just need to return three things instead of one: the normal output of our LSTM, the dropped-out activations, and the activations from our LSTMs. The last two will be picked up by the callback `RNNRegularization` for the contributions it has to make to the loss.

Another useful trick we can add from the AWD-LSTM paper (*https://oreil.ly/ETQ5X*) is *weight tying*. In a language model, the input embeddings represent a mapping from English words to activations, and the output hidden layer represents a mapping from activations to English words. We might expect, intuitively, that these mappings could be the same. We can represent this in PyTorch by assigning the same weight matrix to each of these layers:

```
self.h_o.weight = self.i_h.weight
```

In `LMModel7`, we include these final tweaks:

```
class LMModel7(Module):
    def __init__(self, vocab_sz, n_hidden, n_layers, p):
        self.i_h = nn.Embedding(vocab_sz, n_hidden)
        self.rnn = nn.LSTM(n_hidden, n_hidden, n_layers, batch_first=True)
        self.drop = nn.Dropout(p)
        self.h_o = nn.Linear(n_hidden, vocab_sz)
        self.h_o.weight = self.i_h.weight
        self.h = [torch.zeros(n_layers, bs, n_hidden) for _ in range(2)]

    def forward(self, x):
        raw,h = self.rnn(self.i_h(x), self.h)
        out = self.drop(raw)
        self.h = [h_.detach() for h_ in h]
        return self.h_o(out),raw,out

    def reset(self):
        for h in self.h: h.zero_()
```

We can create a regularized `Learner` using the `RNNRegularizer` callback:

```
learn = Learner(dls, LMModel7(len(vocab), 64, 2, 0.5),
                loss_func=CrossEntropyLossFlat(), metrics=accuracy,
                cbs=[ModelResetter, RNNRegularizer(alpha=2, beta=1)])
```

A `TextLearner` automatically adds those two callbacks for us (with those values for `alpha` and `beta` as defaults), so we can simplify the preceding line:

```
learn = TextLearner(dls, LMModel7(len(vocab), 64, 2, 0.4),
                    loss_func=CrossEntropyLossFlat(), metrics=accuracy)
```

We can then train the model, and add additional regularization by increasing the weight decay to `0.1`:

```
learn.fit_one_cycle(15, 1e-2, wd=0.1)
```

epoch	train_loss	valid_loss	accuracy	time
0	2.693885	2.013484	0.466634	00:02
1	1.685549	1.187310	0.629313	00:02
2	0.973307	0.791398	0.745605	00:02
3	0.555823	0.640412	0.794108	00:02
4	0.351802	0.557247	0.836100	00:02
5	0.244986	0.594977	0.807292	00:02
6	0.192231	0.511690	0.846761	00:02
7	0.162456	0.520370	0.858073	00:02
8	0.142664	0.525918	0.842285	00:02
9	0.128493	0.495029	0.858073	00:02
10	0.117589	0.464236	0.867188	00:02
11	0.109808	0.466550	0.869303	00:02
12	0.104216	0.455151	0.871826	00:02
13	0.100271	0.452659	0.873617	00:02
14	0.098121	0.458372	0.869385	00:02

Now this is far better than our previous model!

Conclusion

You have now seen everything that is inside the AWD-LSTM architecture we used in text classification in Chapter 10. It uses dropout in a lot more places:

- Embedding dropout (inside the embedding layer, drops some random lines of embeddings)
- Input dropout (applied after the embedding layer)

- Weight dropout (applied to the weights of the LSTM at each training step)
- Hidden dropout (applied to the hidden state between two layers)

This makes it even more regularized. Since fine-tuning those five dropout values (including the dropout before the output layer) is complicated, we have determined good defaults and allow the magnitude of dropout to be tuned overall with the drop_mult parameter you saw in that chapter (which is multiplied by each dropout).

Another architecture that is very powerful, especially in "sequence-to-sequence" problems (problems in which the dependent variable is itself a variable-length sequence, such as language translation), is the Transformers architecture. You can find it in a bonus chapter on the book's website (*https://book.fast.ai*).

Questionnaire

1. If the dataset for your project is so big and complicated that working with it takes a significant amount of time, what should you do?

2. Why do we concatenate the documents in our dataset before creating a language model?

3. To use a standard fully connected network to predict the fourth word given the previous three words, what two tweaks do we need to make to our model?

4. How can we share a weight matrix across multiple layers in PyTorch?

5. Write a module that predicts the third word given the previous two words of a sentence, without peeking.

6. What is a recurrent neural network?

7. What is hidden state?

8. What is the equivalent of hidden state in LMModel1?

9. To maintain the state in an RNN, why is it important to pass the text to the model in order?

10. What is an "unrolled" representation of an RNN?

11. Why can maintaining the hidden state in an RNN lead to memory and performance problems? How do we fix this problem?

12. What is BPTT?

13. Write code to print out the first few batches of the validation set, including converting the token IDs back into English strings, as we showed for batches of IMDb data in Chapter 10.

14. What does the ModelResetter callback do? Why do we need it?

15. What are the downsides of predicting just one output word for each three input words?

16. Why do we need a custom loss function for `LMModel4`?

17. Why is the training of `LMModel4` unstable?

18. In the unrolled representation, we can see that a recurrent neural network has many layers. So why do we need to stack RNNs to get better results?

19. Draw a representation of a stacked (multilayer) RNN.

20. Why should we get better results in an RNN if we call `detach` less often? Why might this not happen in practice with a simple RNN?

21. Why can a deep network result in very large or very small activations? Why does this matter?

22. In a computer's floating-point representation of numbers, which numbers are the most precise?

23. Why do vanishing gradients prevent training?

24. Why does it help to have two hidden states in the LSTM architecture? What is the purpose of each one?

25. What are these two states called in an LSTM?

26. What is tanh, and how is it related to sigmoid?

27. What is the purpose of this code in `LSTMCell`:

```
h = torch.cat([h, input], dim=1)
```

28. What does chunk do in PyTorch?

29. Study the refactored version of `LSTMCell` carefully to ensure you understand how and why it does the same thing as the nonrefactored version.

30. Why can we use a higher learning rate for `LMModel6`?

31. What are the three regularization techniques used in an AWD-LSTM model?

32. What is dropout?

33. Why do we scale the activations with dropout? Is this applied during training, inference, or both?

34. What is the purpose of this line from `Dropout`:

```
if not self.training: return x
```

35. Experiment with `bernoulli_` to understand how it works.

36. How do you set your model in training mode in PyTorch? In evaluation mode?

37. Write the equation for activation regularization (in math or code, as you prefer). How is it different from weight decay?

38. Write the equation for temporal activation regularization (in math or code, as you prefer). Why wouldn't we use this for computer vision problems?

39. What is weight tying in a language model?

Further Research

1. In `LMModel2`, why can forward start with h=0? Why don't we need to say `h=torch.zeros(...)`?

2. Write the code for an LSTM from scratch (you may refer to Figure 12-9).

3. Search the internet for the GRU architecture and implement it from scratch, and try training a model. See if you can get results similar to those we saw in this chapter. Compare your results to the results of PyTorch's built-in `GRU` module.

4. Take a look at the source code for AWD-LSTM in fastai, and try to map each of the lines of code to the concepts shown in this chapter.

CHAPTER 13

Convolutional Neural Networks

In Chapter 4, we learned how to create a neural network recognizing images. We were able to achieve a bit over 98% accuracy at distinguishing 3s from 7s—but we also saw that fastai's built-in classes were able to get close to 100%. Let's start trying to close the gap.

In this chapter, we will begin by digging into what convolutions are and building a CNN from scratch. We will then study a range of techniques to improve training stability and learn all the tweaks the library usually applies for us to get great results.

The Magic of Convolutions

One of the most powerful tools that machine learning practitioners have at their disposal is *feature engineering*. A *feature* is a transformation of the data that is designed to make it easier to model. For instance, the `add_datepart` function that we used for our tabular dataset preprocessing in Chapter 9 added date features to the Bulldozers dataset. What kinds of features might we be able to create from images?

Jargon: Feature Engineering

Creating new transformations of the input data in order to make it easier to model.

In the context of an image, a feature is a visually distinctive attribute. For example, the number 7 is characterized by a horizontal edge near the top of the digit, and a top-right to bottom-left diagonal edge underneath that. On the other hand, the number 3 is characterized by a diagonal edge in one direction at the top left and bottom right of the digit, the opposite diagonal at the bottom left and top right, horizontal edges at the middle, top, and bottom, and so forth. So what if we could extract information about where the edges occur in each image, and then use that information as our features, instead of raw pixels?

It turns out that finding the edges in an image is a very common task in computer vision and is surprisingly straightforward. To do it, we use something called a *convolution*. A convolution requires nothing more than multiplication and addition—two operations that are responsible for the vast majority of work that we will see in every single deep learning model in this book!

A convolution applies a *kernel* across an image. A kernel is a little matrix, such as the 3×3 matrix in the top right of Figure 13-1.

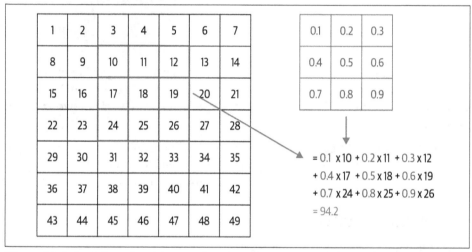

Figure 13-1. Applying a kernel to one location

The 7×7 grid to the left is the *image* we're going to apply the kernel to. The convolution operation multiplies each element of the kernel by each element of a 3×3 block of the image. The results of these multiplications are then added together. The diagram in Figure 13-1 shows an example of applying a kernel to a single location in the image, the 3×3 block around cell 18.

Let's do this with code. First, we create a little 3×3 matrix like so:

```
top_edge = tensor([[-1,-1,-1],
                   [ 0,  0,  0],
                   [ 1,  1,  1]]).float()
```

We're going to call this our kernel (because that's what fancy computer vision researchers call these). And we'll need an image, of course:

```
path = untar_data(URLs.MNIST_SAMPLE)

im3 = Image.open(path/'train'/'3'/'12.png')
show_image(im3);
```

3

Now we're going to take the top 3×3-pixel square of our image, and multiply each of those values by each item in our kernel. Then we'll add them up, like so:

```
im3_t = tensor(im3)
im3_t[0:3,0:3] * top_edge

tensor([[-0., -0., -0.],
        [0., 0., 0.],
        [0., 0., 0.]])

(im3_t[0:3,0:3] * top_edge).sum()

tensor(0.)
```

Not very interesting so far—all the pixels in the top-left corner are white. But let's pick a couple of more interesting spots:

```
df = pd.DataFrame(im3_t[:10,:20])
df.style.set_properties(**{'font-size':'6pt'}).background_gradient('Greys')
```

	0	1	2	3	4	5	6	7	8	9	10	11	12	13	14	15	16	17	18	19
0	0	0	0	0	0	0	0	0	0	0	0	0	0	0	0	0	0	0	0	0
1	0	0	0	0	0	0	0	0	0	0	0	0	0	0	0	0	0	0	0	0
2	0	0	0	0	0	0	0	0	0	0	0	0	0	0	0	0	0	0	0	0
3	0	0	0	0	0	0	0	0	0	0	0	0	0	0	0	0	0	0	0	0
4	0	0	0	0	0	0	0	0	0	0	0	0	0	0	0	0	0	0	0	0
5	0	0	0	12	99	91	142	155	246	182	155	155	155	155	131	52	0	0	0	0
6	0	0	0	138	254	254	254	254	254	254	254	254	254	254	254	252	210	122	33	0
7	0	0	0	220	254	254	254	235	189	189	189	189	150	189	205	254	254	254	75	0
8	0	0	0	35	74	35	35	25	0	0	0	0	0	0	13	224	254	254	153	0
9	0	0	0	0	0	0	0	0	0	0	0	0	0	0	90	254	254	247	53	0

There's a top edge at cell 5,8. Let's repeat our calculation there:

```
(im3_t[4:7,6:9] * top_edge).sum()
```

```
tensor(762.)
```

There's a right edge at cell 8,18. What does that give us?

```
(im3_t[7:10,17:20] * top_edge).sum()
```

```
tensor(-29.)
```

As you can see, this little calculation is returning a high number where the 3×3-pixel square represents a top edge (i.e., where there are low values at the top of the square and high values immediately underneath). That's because the -1 values in our kernel have little impact in that case, but the 1 values have a lot.

Let's look a tiny bit at the math. The filter will take any window of size 3×3 in our images, and if we name the pixel values like this

$a1$ $a2$ $a3$
$a4$ $a5$ $a6$
$a7$ $a8$ $a9$

it will return $a1 + a2 + a3 - a7 - a8 - a9$. If we are in a part of the image where $a1$, $a2$, and $a3$ add up to the same as $a7$, $a8$, and $a9$, then the terms will cancel each other out and we will get 0. However, if $a1$ is greater than $a7$, $a2$ is greater than $a8$, and $a3$ is greater than $a9$, we will get a bigger number as a result. So this filter detects horizontal edges—more precisely, edges where we go from bright parts of the image at the top to darker parts at the bottom.

Changing our filter to have the row of 1s at the top and the -1s at the bottom would detect horizontal edges that go from dark to light. Putting the 1s and -1s in columns versus rows would give us filters that detect vertical edges. Each set of weights will produce a different kind of outcome.

Let's create a function to do this for one location, and check that it matches our result from before:

```
def apply_kernel(row, col, kernel):
    return (im3_t[row-1:row+2,col-1:col+2] * kernel).sum()
```

```
apply_kernel(5,7,top_edge)
```

```
tensor(762.)
```

But note that we can't apply it to the corner (e.g., location 0,0), since there isn't a complete 3×3 square there.

Mapping a Convolutional Kernel

We can map `apply_kernel()` across the coordinate grid. That is, we'll be taking our 3×3 kernel and applying it to each 3×3 section of our image. For instance, Figure 13-2 shows the positions a 3×3 kernel can be applied to in the first row of a 5×5 image.

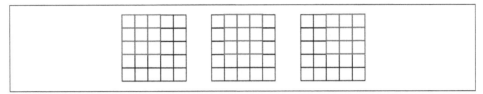

Figure 13-2. Applying a kernel across a grid

To get a grid of coordinates, we can use a *nested list comprehension*, like so:

```
[[(i,j) for j in range(1,5)] for i in range(1,5)]

[[(1, 1), (1, 2), (1, 3), (1, 4)],
 [(2, 1), (2, 2), (2, 3), (2, 4)],
 [(3, 1), (3, 2), (3, 3), (3, 4)],
 [(4, 1), (4, 2), (4, 3), (4, 4)]]
```

Nested List Comprehensions

Nested list comprehensions are used a lot in Python, so if you haven't seen them before, take a few minutes to make sure you understand what's happening here, and experiment with writing your own nested list comprehensions.

Here's the result of applying our kernel over a coordinate grid:

```
rng = range(1,27)
top_edge3 = tensor([[apply_kernel(i,j,top_edge) for j in rng] for i in rng])

show_image(top_edge3);
```

Looking good! Our top edges are black, and bottom edges are white (since they are the *opposite* of top edges). Now that our image contains negative numbers too, `mat plotlib` has automatically changed our colors so that white is the smallest number in the image, black the highest, and zeros appear as gray.

We can try the same thing for left edges:

```
left_edge = tensor([[-1,1,0],
                    [-1,1,0],
                    [-1,1,0]]).float()

left_edge3 = tensor([[apply_kernel(i,j,left_edge) for j in rng] for i in rng])

show_image(left_edge3);
```

As we mentioned before, a convolution is the operation of applying such a kernel over a grid. Vincent Dumoulin and Francesco Visin's paper "A Guide to Convolution Arithmetic for Deep Learning" (*https://oreil.ly/les1R*) has many great diagrams showing how image kernels can be applied. Figure 13-3 is an example from the paper showing (at the bottom) a light blue 4×4 image with a dark blue 3×3 kernel being applied, creating a 2×2 green output activation map at the top.

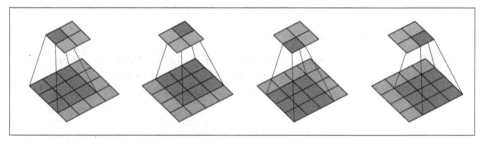

Figure 13-3. Result of applying a 3×3 kernel to a 4×4 image (courtesy of Vincent Dumoulin and Francesco Visin)

Look at the shape of the result. If the original image has a height of h and a width of w, how many 3×3 windows can we find? As you can see from the example, there are h-2 by w-2 windows, so the image we get as a result has a height of h-2 and a width of w-2.

We won't implement this convolution function from scratch, but use PyTorch's implementation instead (it is way faster than anything we could do in Python).

Convolutions in PyTorch

Convolution is such an important and widely used operation that PyTorch has it built in. It's called F.conv2d (recall that F is a fastai import from torch.nn.functional, as recommended by PyTorch). PyTorch docs tell us that it includes these parameters:

```
input
```
   input tensor of shape (minibatch, in_channels, iH, iW)

```
weight
```
   filters of shape (out_channels, in_channels, kH, kW)

Here iH,iW is the height and width of the image (i.e., 28,28), and kH,kW is the height and width of our kernel (3,3). But apparently PyTorch is expecting rank-4 tensors for both these arguments, whereas currently we have only rank-2 tensors (i.e., matrices, or arrays with two axes).

The reason for these extra axes is that PyTorch has a few tricks up its sleeve. The first trick is that PyTorch can apply a convolution to multiple images at the same time. That means we can call it on every item in a batch at once!

The second trick is that PyTorch can apply multiple kernels at the same time. So let's create the diagonal-edge kernels too, and then stack all four of our edge kernels into a single tensor:

```
diag1_edge = tensor([[ 0,-1, 1],
                     [-1, 1, 0],
                     [ 1, 0, 0]]).float()
diag2_edge = tensor([[ 1,-1, 0],
                     [ 0, 1,-1],
                     [ 0, 0, 1]]).float()

edge_kernels = torch.stack([left_edge, top_edge, diag1_edge, diag2_edge])
edge_kernels.shape
```
```
torch.Size([4, 3, 3])
```

To test this, we'll need a DataLoader and a sample mini-batch. Let's use the data block API:

```
mnist = DataBlock((ImageBlock(cls=PILImageBW), CategoryBlock),
                  get_items=get_image_files,
                  splitter=GrandparentSplitter(),
                  get_y=parent_label)

dls = mnist.dataloaders(path)
xb,yb = first(dls.valid)
xb.shape
```
```
torch.Size([64, 1, 28, 28])
```

By default, fastai puts data on the GPU when using data blocks. Let's move it to the CPU for our examples:

```
xb,yb = to_cpu(xb),to_cpu(yb)
```

One batch contains 64 images, each of 1 channel, with 28×28 pixels. F.conv2d can handle multichannel (color) images too. A *channel* is a single basic color in an image —for regular full-color images, there are three channels, red, green, and blue. PyTorch represents an image as a rank-3 tensor, with these dimensions:

```
[channels, rows, columns]
```

We'll see how to handle more than one channel later in this chapter. Kernels passed to F.conv2d need to be rank-4 tensors:

```
[features_out, channels_in, rows, columns]
```

edge_kernels is currently missing one of these: we need to tell PyTorch that the number of input channels in the kernel is one, which we can do by inserting an axis of size one (this is known as a *unit axis*) in the first location, where the PyTorch docs show in_channels is expected. To insert a unit axis into a tensor, we use the unsqueeze method:

```
edge_kernels.shape,edge_kernels.unsqueeze(1).shape
```

```
(torch.Size([4, 3, 3]), torch.Size([4, 1, 3, 3]))
```

This is now the correct shape for edge_kernels. Let's pass this all to conv2d:

```
edge_kernels = edge_kernels.unsqueeze(1)

batch_features = F.conv2d(xb, edge_kernels)
batch_features.shape
```

```
torch.Size([64, 4, 26, 26])
```

The output shape shows we have 64 images in the mini-batch, 4 kernels, and 26×26 edge maps (we started with 28×28 images, but lost one pixel from each side as discussed earlier). We can see we get the same results as when we did this manually:

```
show_image(batch_features[0,0]);
```

The most important trick that PyTorch has up its sleeve is that it can use the GPU to do all this work in parallel—applying multiple kernels to multiple images, across multiple channels. Doing lots of work in parallel is critical to getting GPUs to work efficiently; if we did each of these operations one at a time, we'd often run hundreds of times slower (and if we used our manual convolution loop from the previous section, we'd be millions of times slower!). Therefore, to become a strong deep learning practitioner, one skill to practice is giving your GPU plenty of work to do at a time.

It would be nice to not lose those two pixels on each axis. The way we do that is to add *padding*, which is simply additional pixels added around the outside of our image. Most commonly, pixels of zeros are added.

Strides and Padding

With appropriate padding, we can ensure that the output activation map is the same size as the original image, which can make things a lot simpler when we construct our architectures. Figure 13-4 shows how adding padding allows us to apply the kernel in the image corners.

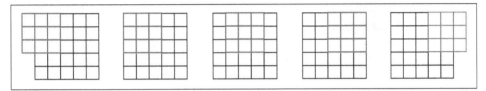

Figure 13-4. A convolution with padding

With a 5×5 input, 4×4 kernel, and 2 pixels of padding, we end up with a 6×6 activation map, as we can see in Figure 13-5.

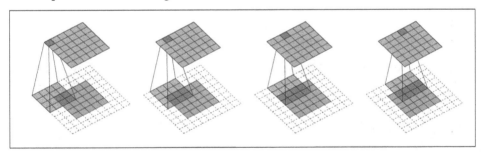

Figure 13-5. A 4×4 kernel with 5×5 input and 2 pixels of padding (courtesy of Vincent Dumoulin and Francesco Visin)

If we add a kernel of size `ks` by `ks` (with `ks` an odd number), the necessary padding on each side to keep the same shape is `ks//2`. An even number for `ks` would require a different amount of padding on the top/bottom and left/right, but in practice we almost never use an even filter size.

So far, when we have applied the kernel to the grid, we have moved it one pixel over at a time. But we can jump further; for instance, we could move over two pixels after each kernel application, as in Figure 13-6. This is known as a *stride-2* convolution. The most common kernel size in practice is 3×3, and the most common padding is 1. As you'll see, stride-2 convolutions are useful for decreasing the size of our outputs, and stride-1 convolutions are useful for adding layers without changing the output size.

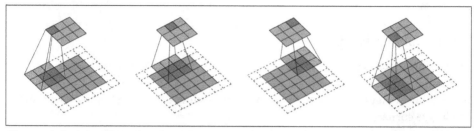

Figure 13-6. A 3×3 kernel with 5×5 input, stride-2 convolution, and 1 pixel of padding (courtesy of Vincent Dumoulin and Francesco Visin)

In an image of size h by w, using a padding of 1 and a stride of 2 will give us a result of size (h+1)//2 by (w+1)//2. The general formula for each dimension is

```
(n + 2*pad - ks) // stride + 1
```

where pad is the padding, ks is the size of our kernel, and stride is the stride.

Let's now take a look at how the pixel values of the result of our convolutions are computed.

Understanding the Convolution Equations

To explain the math behind convolutions, fast.ai student Matt Kleinsmith came up with the very clever idea of showing CNNs from different viewpoints (*https://oreil.ly/wZuBs*). In fact, it's so clever, and so helpful, we're going to show it here too!

Here's our 3×3-pixel image, with each pixel labeled with a letter:

A	B	C
D	E	F
G	H	J

And here's our kernel, with each weight labeled with a Greek letter:

Since the filter fits in the image four times, we have four results:

Figure 13-7 shows how we applied the kernel to each section of the image to yield each result.

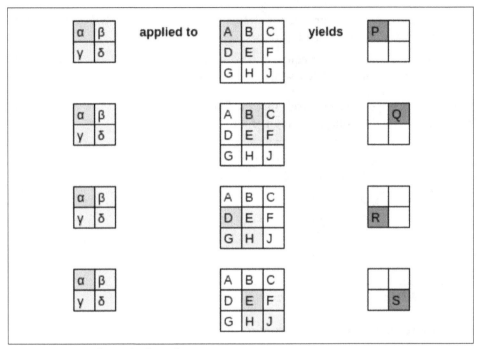

Figure 13-7. Applying the kernel

The equation view is in Figure 13-8.

$$\alpha * A + \beta * B + \gamma * D + \delta * E + b = P$$

$$\alpha * B + \beta * C + \gamma * E + \delta * F + b = Q$$

$$\alpha * D + \beta * E + \gamma * G + \delta * H + b = R$$

$$\alpha * E + \beta * F + \gamma * H + \delta * J + b = S$$

Figure 13-8. The equation

Notice that the bias term, *b*, is the same for each section of the image. You can consider the bias as part of the filter, just as the weights (α, β, γ, δ) are part of the filter.

Here's an interesting insight—a convolution can be represented as a special kind of matrix multiplication, as illustrated in Figure 13-9. The weight matrix is just like the ones from traditional neural networks. However, this weight matrix has two special properties:

1. The zeros shown in gray are untrainable. This means that they'll stay zero throughout the optimization process.

2. Some of the weights are equal, and while they are trainable (i.e., changeable), they must remain equal. These are called *shared weights*.

The zeros correspond to the pixels that the filter can't touch. Each row of the weight matrix corresponds to one application of the filter.

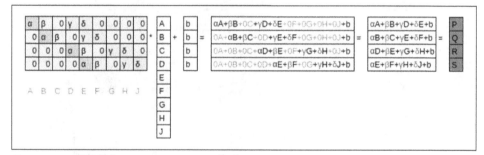

Figure 13-9. Convolution as matrix multiplication

Now that we understand what convolutions are, let's use them to build a neural net.

Our First Convolutional Neural Network

There is no reason to believe that some particular edge filters are the most useful kernels for image recognition. Furthermore, we've seen that in later layers, convolutional kernels become complex transformations of features from lower levels, but we don't have a good idea of how to manually construct these.

Instead, it would be best to learn the values of the kernels. We already know how to do this—SGD! In effect, the model will learn the features that are useful for classification. When we use convolutions instead of (or in addition to) regular linear layers, we create a *convolutional neural network* (CNN).

Creating the CNN

Let's go back to the basic neural network we had in Chapter 4. It was defined like this:

```
simple_net = nn.Sequential(
    nn.Linear(28*28,30),
    nn.ReLU(),
    nn.Linear(30,1)
)
```

We can view a model's definition:

```
simple_net
```

```
Sequential(
  (0): Linear(in_features=784, out_features=30, bias=True)
  (1): ReLU()
  (2): Linear(in_features=30, out_features=1, bias=True)
)
```

We now want to create a similar architecture to this linear model, but using convolutional layers instead of linear. nn.Conv2d is the module equivalent of F.conv2d. It's more convenient than F.conv2d when creating an architecture, because it creates the weight matrix for us automatically when we instantiate it.

Here's a possible architecture:

```
broken_cnn = sequential(
    nn.Conv2d(1,30, kernel_size=3, padding=1),
    nn.ReLU(),
    nn.Conv2d(30,1, kernel_size=3, padding=1)
)
```

One thing to note here is that we didn't need to specify 28*28 as the input size. That's because a linear layer needs a weight in the weight matrix for every pixel, so it needs to know how many pixels there are, but a convolution is applied over each pixel automatically. The weights depend only on the number of input and output channels and the kernel size, as we saw in the previous section.

Think about what the output shape is going to be; then let's try it and see:

```
broken_cnn(xb).shape
```

```
torch.Size([64, 1, 28, 28])
```

This is not something we can use to do classification, since we need a single output activation per image, not a 28×28 map of activations. One way to deal with this is to use enough stride-2 convolutions such that the final layer is size 1. After one stride-2 convolution, the size will be 14×14; after two, it will be 7×7; then 4×4, 2×2, and finally size 1.

Let's try that now. First, we'll define a function with the basic parameters we'll use in each convolution:

```
def conv(ni, nf, ks=3, act=True):
    res = nn.Conv2d(ni, nf, stride=2, kernel_size=ks, padding=ks//2)
    if act: res = nn.Sequential(res, nn.ReLU())
    return res
```

Refactoring

Refactoring parts of your neural networks like this makes it much less likely you'll get errors due to inconsistencies in your architectures, and makes it more obvious to the reader which parts of your layers are actually changing.

When we use a stride-2 convolution, we often increase the number of features at the same time. This is because we're decreasing the number of activations in the activation map by a factor of 4; we don't want to decrease the capacity of a layer by too much at a time.

Jargon: Channels and Features

These two terms are largely used interchangeably and refer to the size of the second axis of a weight matrix, which is the number of activations per grid cell after a convolution. *Features* is never used to refer to the input data, but *channels* can refer to either the input data (generally, channels are colors) or activations inside the network.

Here is how we can build a simple CNN:

```
simple_cnn = sequential(
    conv(1 ,4),             #14x14
    conv(4 ,8),             #7x7
    conv(8 ,16),            #4x4
    conv(16,32),            #2x2
    conv(32,2, act=False),  #1x1
    Flatten(),
)
```

Jeremy Says

I like to add comments like the ones here after each convolution to show how large the activation map will be after each layer. These comments assume that the input size is 28×28.

Now the network outputs two activations, which map to the two possible levels in our labels:

```
simple_cnn(xb).shape
```

```
torch.Size([64, 2])
```

We can now create our `Learner`:

```
learn = Learner(dls, simple_cnn, loss_func=F.cross_entropy, metrics=accuracy)
```

To see exactly what's going on in the model, we can use `summary`:

```
learn.summary()
```

```
Sequential (Input shape: ['64 x 1 x 28 x 28'])
```

Layer (type)	Output Shape	Param #	Trainable
Conv2d	64 x 4 x 14 x 14	40	True
ReLU	64 x 4 x 14 x 14	0	False
Conv2d	64 x 8 x 7 x 7	296	True
ReLU	64 x 8 x 7 x 7	0	False
Conv2d	64 x 16 x 4 x 4	1,168	True
ReLU	64 x 16 x 4 x 4	0	False
Conv2d	64 x 32 x 2 x 2	4,640	True
ReLU	64 x 32 x 2 x 2	0	False
Conv2d	64 x 2 x 1 x 1	578	True
Flatten	64 x 2	0	False

```
Total params: 6,722
Total trainable params: 6,722
Total non-trainable params: 0

Optimizer used: <function Adam at 0x7fbc9c258cb0>
Loss function: <function cross_entropy at 0x7fbca9ba0170>

Callbacks:
  - TrainEvalCallback
  - Recorder
  - ProgressCallback
```

Note that the output of the final `Conv2d` layer is 64x2x1x1. We need to remove those extra 1x1 axes; that's what `Flatten` does. It's basically the same as PyTorch's `squeeze` method, but as a module.

Let's see if this trains! Since this is a deeper network than we've built from scratch before, we'll use a lower learning rate and more epochs:

```
learn.fit_one_cycle(2, 0.01)
```

epoch	train_loss	valid_loss	accuracy	time
0	0.072684	0.045110	0.990186	00:05
1	0.022580	0.030775	0.990186	00:05

Success! It's getting closer to the `resnet18` result we had, although it's not quite there yet, and it's taking more epochs, and we're needing to use a lower learning rate. We still have a few more tricks to learn, but we're getting closer and closer to being able to create a modern CNN from scratch.

Understanding Convolution Arithmetic

We can see from the summary that we have an input of size 64x1x28x28. The axes are `batch,channel,height,width`. This is often represented as NCHW (where N refers to batch size). TensorFlow, on the other hand, uses NHWC axis order. Here is the first layer:

```
m = learn.model[0]
m

Sequential(
  (0): Conv2d(1, 4, kernel_size=(3, 3), stride=(2, 2), padding=(1, 1))
  (1): ReLU()
)
```

So we have 1 input channel, 4 output channels, and a 3×3 kernel. Let's check the weights of the first convolution:

```
m[0].weight.shape

torch.Size([4, 1, 3, 3])
```

The summary shows we have 40 parameters, and 4*1*3*3 is 36. What are the other four parameters? Let's see what the bias contains:

```
m[0].bias.shape

torch.Size([4])
```

We can now use this information to clarify our statement in the previous section: "When we use a stride-2 convolution, we often increase the number of features because we're decreasing the number of activations in the activation map by a factor of 4; we don't want to decrease the capacity of a layer by too much at a time."

There is one bias for each channel. (Sometimes channels are called *features* or *filters* when they are not input channels.) The output shape is 64x4x14x14, and this will therefore become the input shape to the next layer. The next layer, according to summary, has 296 parameters. Let's ignore the batch axis to keep things simple. So, for each of 14*14=196 locations, we are multiplying 296-8=288 weights (ignoring the bias for simplicity), so that's 196*288=56_448 multiplications at this layer. The next layer will have 7*7*(1168-16)=56_448 multiplications.

What happened here is that our stride-2 convolution halved the *grid size* from 14x14 to 7x7, and we doubled the *number of filters* from 8 to 16, resulting in no overall change in the amount of computation. If we left the number of channels the same in each stride-2 layer, the amount of computation being done in the net would get less and less as it gets deeper. But we know that the deeper layers have to compute semantically rich features (such as eyes or fur), so we wouldn't expect that doing *less* computation would make sense.

Another way to think of this is based on receptive fields.

Receptive Fields

The *receptive field* is the area of an image that is involved in the calculation of a layer. On the book's website (*https://book.fast.ai*), you'll find an Excel spreadsheet called *conv-example.xlsx* that shows the calculation of two stride-2 convolutional layers using an MNIST digit. Each layer has a single kernel. Figure 13-10 shows what we see if we click one of the cells in the *conv2* section, which shows the output of the second convolutional layer, and click *trace precedents*.

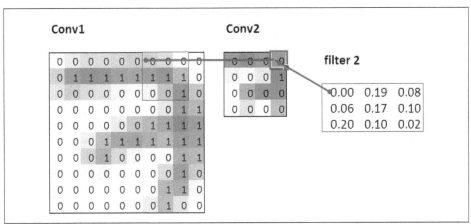

Figure 13-10. Immediate precedents of Conv2 layer

Here, the cell with the green border is the cell we clicked, and the blue highlighted cells are its *precedents*—the cells used to calculate its value. These cells are the corresponding 3×3 area of cells from the input layer (on the left), and the cells from the filter (on the right). Let's now click *trace precedents* again, to see what cells are used to calculate these inputs. Figure 13-11 shows what happens.

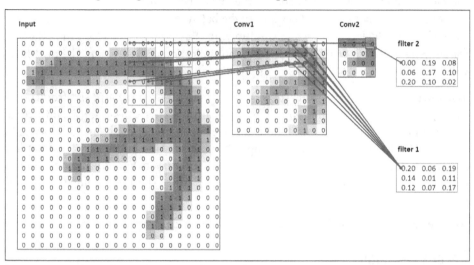

Figure 13-11. Secondary precedents of Conv2 layer

In this example, we have just two convolutional layers, each of stride 2, so this is now tracing right back to the input image. We can see that a 7×7 area of cells in the input layer is used to calculate the single green cell in the Conv2 layer. This 7×7 area is the *receptive field* in the input of the green activation in Conv2. We can also see that a second filter kernel is needed now, since we have two layers.

As you see from this example, the deeper we are in the network (specifically, the more stride-2 convs we have before a layer), the larger the receptive field for an activation in that layer is. A large receptive field means that a large amount of the input image is used to calculate each activation in that layer. We now know that in the deeper layers of the network, we have semantically rich features, corresponding to larger receptive fields. Therefore, we'd expect that we'd need more weights for each of our features to handle this increasing complexity. This is another way of saying the same thing we mentioned in the previous section: when we introduce a stride-2 conv in our network, we should also increase the number of channels.

When writing this particular chapter, we had a lot of questions we needed answers for, to be able to explain CNNs to you as best we could. Believe it or not, we found most of the answers on Twitter. We're going to take a quick break to talk to you about that now, before we move on to color images.

A Note About Twitter

We are not, to say the least, big users of social networks in general. But our goal in writing this book is to help you become the best deep learning practitioner you can, and we would be remiss not to mention how important Twitter has been in our own deep learning journeys.

You see, there's another part of Twitter, far away from Donald Trump and the Kardashians, where deep learning researchers and practitioners talk shop every day. As we were writing this section, Jeremy wanted to double-check that what we were saying about stride-2 convolutions was accurate, so he asked on Twitter:

Jeremy Howard
@jeremyphoward

I forget: why did we move from stride 1 convs with maxpool to stride 2 convs? And why don't we use stride 1 convs with avgpool (or do some modern nets do that)? Is it just an empirical thing, or is there some deeper reason? Has someone done the ablation studies?

11:21 AM · Feb 23, 2020 · Twitter Web App

A few minutes later, this answer popped up:

Christian Szegedy
@ChrSzegedy

Replying to @jeremyphoward

This depends on a lot of factors: the overall network architecture, the accelerator (CPU vs GPU vs TPU) etc. Some Inception models used concatenation of (conv + max/avg/l2 pooling). The quality differences were marginal. Some pooling methods are more residual friendly.

11:39 AM · Feb 23, 2020 · Twitter Web App

Christian Szegedy is the first author of Inception (*https://oreil.ly/hGE_Y*), the 2014 ImageNet winner, and source of many key insights used in modern neural networks. Two hours later, this appeared:

Yann LeCun
@ylecun

Replying to @jeremyphoward

My original early 1989 NeurComp paper on ConvNet used stride 2, no pooling, simply because the computation was fast.
The 2nd paper (NIPS 1989) used stride +average pooling/tanh.
It worked better on zipcode digits. But it could have been due to many reasons.

1:35 PM · Feb 23, 2020 · Twitter for Android

Do you recognize that name? You saw it in Chapter 2, when we were talking about the Turing Award winners who established the foundations of deep learning today!

Jeremy also asked on Twitter for help checking that our description of label smoothing in Chapter 7 was accurate, and got a response again directly from Christian Szegedy (label smoothing was originally introduced in the Inception paper):

Christian Szegedy
@ChrSzegedy

Replying to @jeremyphoward

It was mostly written by Sergey, so he might be the best person to ask. IMO, yours is a fair motivation of label-smoothing. It interprets the passage correctly.

5:24 PM · Feb 21, 2020 · Twitter Web App

Many of the top people in deep learning today are Twitter regulars, and are very open about interacting with the wider community. One good way to get started is to look at a list of Jeremy's recent Twitter likes (*https://oreil.ly/sqOl7*), or Sylvain's (*https://oreil.ly/VWYHY*). That way, you can see a list of Twitter users whom we think have interesting and useful things to say.

Twitter is the main way we both stay up to date with interesting papers, software releases, and other deep learning news. For making connections with the deep learning community, we recommend getting involved both in the fast.ai forums (*https://forums.fast.ai*) and on Twitter.

That said, let's get back to the meat of this chapter. Up until now, we have shown you examples of pictures in only black and white, with one value per pixel. In practice, most colored images have three values per pixel to define their color. We'll look at working with color images next.

Color Images

A color picture is a rank-3 tensor:

```
im = image2tensor(Image.open(image_bear()))
im.shape
```

```
torch.Size([3, 1000, 846])
```

```
show_image(im);
```

The first axis contains the channels red, green, and blue (here highlighted with the corresponding color maps):

```
_,axs = subplots(1,3)
for bear,ax,color in zip(im,axs,('Reds','Greens','Blues')):
    show_image(255-bear, ax=ax, cmap=color)
```

We saw what the convolution operation was for one filter on one channel of the image (our examples were done on a square). A convolutional layer will take an image with a certain number of channels (three for the first layer for regular RGB color images) and output an image with a different number of channels. As with our hidden size that represented the numbers of neurons in a linear layer, we can decide to have as many filters as we want, and each will be able to specialize (some to detect horizontal edges, others to detect vertical edges, and so forth) to give something like the examples we studied in Chapter 2.

In one sliding window, we have a certain number of channels and we need as many filters (we don't use the same kernel for all the channels). So our kernel doesn't have a size of 3×3, but ch_in (for channels in) is 3×3. On each channel, we multiply the elements of our window by the elements of the corresponding filter, and then sum the results (as we saw before) and sum over all the filters. In the example given in Figure 13-12, the result of our conv layer on that window is red + green + blue.

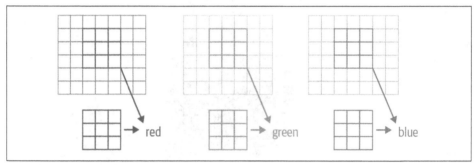

Figure 13-12. Convolution over an RGB image

So, in order to apply a convolution to a color picture, we require a kernel tensor with a size that matches the first axis. At each location, the corresponding parts of the kernel and the image patch are multiplied together.

These are then all added together to produce a single number for each grid location for each output feature, as shown in Figure 13-13.

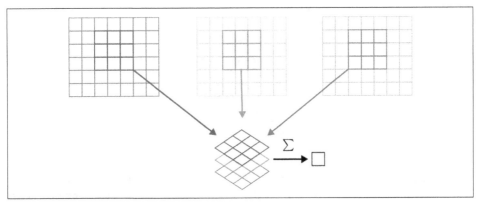

Figure 13-13. Adding the RGB filters

Then we have `ch_out` filters like this, so in the end, the result of our convolutional layer will be a batch of images with `ch_out` channels and a height and width given by the formula outlined earlier. This give us `ch_out` tensors of size `ch_in x ks x ks` that we represent in one big tensor of four dimensions. In PyTorch, the order of the dimensions for those weights is `ch_out x ch_in x ks x ks`.

Additionally, we may want to have a bias for each filter. In the preceding example, the final result for our convolutional layer would be $y_R + y_G + y_B + b$ in that case. As in a linear layer, there are as many biases as we have kernels, so the bias is a vector of size `ch_out`.

No special mechanisms are required when setting up a CNN for training with color images. Just make sure your first layer has three inputs.

There are lots of ways of processing color images. For instance, you can change them to black and white, change from RGB to HSV (hue, saturation, and value) color space, and so forth. In general, it turns out experimentally that changing the encoding of colors won't make any difference to your model results, as long as you don't lose information in the transformation. So, transforming to black and white is a bad idea, since it removes the color information entirely (and this can be critical; for instance, a pet breed may have a distinctive color); but converting to HSV generally won't make any difference.

Now you know what those pictures in Chapter 1 of "what a neural net learns" from the Zeiler and Fergus paper (*https://oreil.ly/Y6dzZ*) mean! As a reminder, this is their picture of some of the layer 1 weights:

This is taking the three slices of the convolutional kernel, for each output feature, and displaying them as images. We can see that even though the creators of the neural net never explicitly created kernels to find edges, for instance, the neural net automatically discovered these features using SGD.

Now let's see how we can train these CNNs, and show you all the techniques fastai uses under the hood for efficient training.

Improving Training Stability

Since we are so good at recognizing 3s from 7s, let's move on to something harder—recognizing all 10 digits. That means we'll need to use MNIST instead of MNIST_SAMPLE:

```
path = untar_data(URLs.MNIST)

path.ls()

(#2) [Path('testing'),Path('training')]
```

The data is in two folders named *training* and *testing*, so we have to tell GrandparentSplitter about that (it defaults to train and valid). We do that in the get_dls function, which we define to make it easy to change our batch size later:

```
def get_dls(bs=64):
    return DataBlock(
        blocks=(ImageBlock(cls=PILImageBW), CategoryBlock),
        get_items=get_image_files,
        splitter=GrandparentSplitter('training','testing'),
        get_y=parent_label,
        batch_tfms=Normalize()
    ).dataloaders(path, bs=bs)

dls = get_dls()
```

Remember, it's always a good idea to look at your data before you use it:

```
dls.show_batch(max_n=9, figsize=(4,4))
```

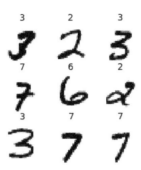

Now that we have our data ready, we can train a simple model on it.

A Simple Baseline

Earlier in this chapter, we built a model based on a conv function like this:

```
def conv(ni, nf, ks=3, act=True):
    res = nn.Conv2d(ni, nf, stride=2, kernel_size=ks, padding=ks//2)
    if act: res = nn.Sequential(res, nn.ReLU())
    return res
```

Let's start with a basic CNN as a baseline. We'll use the same one as earlier, but with one tweak: we'll use more activations. Since we have more numbers to differentiate, we'll likely need to learn more filters.

As we discussed, we generally want to double the number of filters each time we have a stride-2 layer. One way to increase the number of filters throughout our network is to double the number of activations in the first layer—then every layer after that will end up twice as big as in the previous version as well.

But this creates a subtle problem. Consider the kernel that is being applied to each pixel. By default, we use a 3×3-pixel kernel. Therefore, there are a total of 3 × 3 = 9 pixels that the kernel is being applied to at each location. Previously, our first layer had four output filters. So four values were being computed from nine pixels at each location. Think about what happens if we double this output to eight filters. Then when we apply our kernel, we will be using nine pixels to calculate eight numbers. That means it isn't really learning much at all: the output size is almost the same as the input size. Neural networks will create useful features only if they're forced to do so—that is, if the number of outputs from an operation is significantly smaller than the number of inputs.

To fix this, we can use a larger kernel in the first layer. If we use a kernel of 5×5 pixels, 25 pixels are being used at each kernel application. Creating eight filters from this will mean the neural net will have to find some useful features:

```
def simple_cnn():
    return sequential(
        conv(1 ,8, ks=5),        #14x14
        conv(8 ,16),             #7x7
        conv(16,32),             #4x4
        conv(32,64),             #2x2
        conv(64,10, act=False),  #1x1
        Flatten(),
    )
```

As you'll see in a moment, we can look inside our models while they're training in order to try to find ways to make them train better. To do this, we use the Activation Stats callback, which records the mean, standard deviation, and histogram of activations of every trainable layer (as we've seen, callbacks are used to add behavior to the training loop; we'll explore how they work in Chapter 16):

```
from fastai.callback.hook import *
```

We want to train quickly, so that means training at a high learning rate. Let's see how we go at 0.06:

```
def fit(epochs=1):
    learn = Learner(dls, simple_cnn(), loss_func=F.cross_entropy,
                    metrics=accuracy, cbs=ActivationStats(with_hist=True))
    learn.fit(epochs, 0.06)
    return learn

learn = fit()
```

epoch	train_loss	valid_loss	accuracy	time
0	2.307071	2.305865	0.113500	00:16

This didn't train at all well! Let's find out why.

One handy feature of the callbacks passed to Learner is that they are made available automatically, with the same name as the callback class, except in snake_case. So, our ActivationStats callback can be accessed through activation_stats. I'm sure you remember learn.recorder...can you guess how that is implemented? That's right, it's a callback called Recorder!

ActivationStats includes some handy utilities for plotting the activations during training. plot_layer_stats(idx) plots the mean and standard deviation of the activations of layer number idx, along with the percentage of activations near zero. Here's the first layer's plot:

```
learn.activation_stats.plot_layer_stats(0)
```

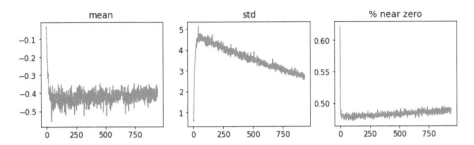

Generally our model should have a consistent, or at least smooth, mean and standard deviation of layer activations during training. Activations near zero are particularly problematic, because it means we have computation in the model that's doing nothing at all (since multiplying by zero gives zero). When you have some zeros in one layer, they will therefore generally carry over to the next layer...which will then create more zeros. Here's the penultimate layer of our network:

```
learn.activation_stats.plot_layer_stats(-2)
```

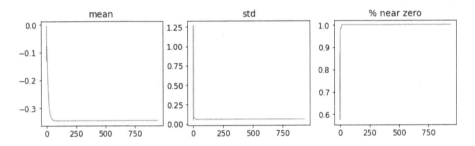

As expected, the problems get worse toward the end of the network, as the instability and zero activations compound over layers. Let's look at what we can do to make training more stable.

Increase Batch Size

One way to make training more stable is to increase the batch size. Larger batches have gradients that are more accurate, since they're calculated from more data. On the downside, though, a larger batch size means fewer batches per epoch, which means fewer opportunities for your model to update weights. Let's see if a batch size of 512 helps:

```
dls = get_dls(512)
learn = fit()
```

epoch	train_loss	valid_loss	accuracy	time
0	2.309385	2.302744	0.113500	00:08

Let's see what the penultimate layer looks like:

```
learn.activation_stats.plot_layer_stats(-2)
```

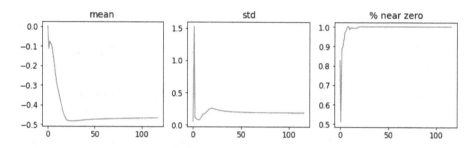

Again, we've got most of our activations near zero. Let's see what else we can do to improve training stability.

1cycle Training

Our initial weights are not well suited to the task we're trying to solve. Therefore, it is dangerous to begin training with a high learning rate: we may very well make the training diverge instantly, as we've seen. We probably don't want to end training with a high learning rate either, so that we don't skip over a minimum. But we want to train at a high learning rate for the rest of the training period, because we'll be able to train more quickly that way. Therefore, we should change the learning rate during training, from low, to high, and then back to low again.

Leslie Smith (yes, the same guy who invented the learning rate finder!) developed this idea in his article "Super-Convergence: Very Fast Training of Neural Networks Using Large Learning Rates" (*https://oreil.ly/EB8NU*). He designed a schedule for learning rate separated into two phases: one where the learning rate grows from the minimum value to the maximum value (*warmup*), and one where it decreases back to the minimum value (*annealing*). Smith called this combination of approaches *1cycle training*.

1cycle training allows us to use a much higher maximum learning rate than other types of training, which gives two benefits:

- By training with higher learning rates, we train faster—a phenomenon Smith calls *super-convergence*.

- By training with higher learning rates, we overfit less because we skip over the sharp local minima to end up in a smoother (and therefore more generalizable) part of the loss.

The second point is an interesting and subtle one; it is based on the observation that a model that generalizes well is one whose loss would not change very much if you changed the input by a small amount. If a model trains at a large learning rate for quite a while, and can find a good loss when doing so, it must have found an area that also generalizes well, because it is jumping around a lot from batch to batch (that is basically the definition of a high learning rate). The problem is that, as we have discussed, just jumping to a high learning rate is more likely to result in diverging losses, rather than seeing your losses improve. So we don't jump straight to a high learning rate. Instead, we start at a low learning rate, where our losses do not diverge, and we allow the optimizer to gradually find smoother and smoother areas of our parameters by gradually going to higher and higher learning rates.

Then, once we have found a nice smooth area for our parameters, we want to find the very best part of that area, which means we have to bring our learning rates down again. This is why 1cycle training has a gradual learning rate warmup, and a gradual learning rate cooldown. Many researchers have found that in practice this approach leads to more accurate models and trains more quickly. That is why it is the approach that is used by default for `fine_tune` in fastai.

In Chapter 16, we'll learn all about *momentum* in SGD. Briefly, momentum is a technique whereby the optimizer takes a step not only in the direction of the gradients, but also that continues in the direction of previous steps. Leslie Smith introduced the idea of *cyclical momentum* in "A Disciplined Approach to Neural Network Hyper-Parameters: Part 1" (*https://oreil.ly/oL7GT*). It suggests that the momentum varies in the opposite direction of the learning rate: when we are at high learning rates, we use less momentum, and we use more again in the annealing phase.

We can use 1cycle training in fastai by calling `fit_one_cycle`:

```
def fit(epochs=1, lr=0.06):
    learn = Learner(dls, simple_cnn(), loss_func=F.cross_entropy,
                    metrics=accuracy, cbs=ActivationStats(with_hist=True))
    learn.fit_one_cycle(epochs, lr)
    return learn

learn = fit()
```

epoch	train_loss	valid_loss	accuracy	time
0	0.210838	0.084827	0.974300	00:08

We're finally making some progress! It's giving us a reasonable accuracy now.

We can view the learning rate and momentum throughout training by calling plot_sched on learn.recorder. learn.recorder (as the name suggests) records everything that happens during training, including losses, metrics, and hyperparameters such as learning rate and momentum:

```
learn.recorder.plot_sched()
```

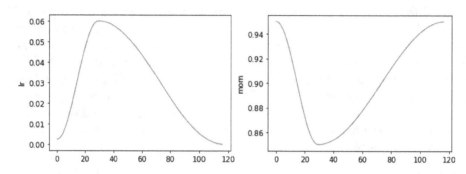

Smith's original 1cycle paper used a linear warmup and linear annealing. As you can see, we adapted the approach in fastai by combining it with another popular approach: cosine annealing. fit_one_cycle provides the following parameters you can adjust:

lr_max
: The highest learning rate that will be used (this can also be a list of learning rates for each layer group, or a Python slice object containing the first and last layer group learning rates)

div
: How much to divide lr_max by to get the starting learning rate

div_final
: How much to divide lr_max by to get the ending learning rate

pct_start
: What percentage of the batches to use for the warmup

moms
: A tuple (*mom1*,*mom2*,*mom3*), where *mom1* is the initial momentum, *mom2* is the minimum momentum, and *mom3* is the final momentum

Let's take a look at our layer stats again:

```
learn.activation_stats.plot_layer_stats(-2)
```

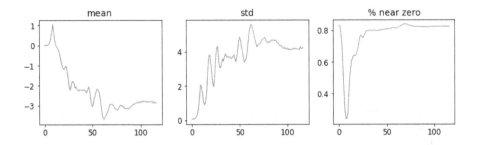

The percentage of near-zero weights is getting much better, although it's still quite high. We can see even more about what's going on in our training by using color_dim, passing it a layer index:

```
learn.activation_stats.color_dim(-2)
```

color_dim was developed by fast.ai in conjunction with a student, Stefano Giomo. Giomo, who refers to the idea as the *colorful dimension*, provides an in-depth explanation (*https://oreil.ly/bPXGw*) of the history and details behind the method. The basic idea is to create a histogram of the activations of a layer, which we would hope would follow a smooth pattern such as the normal distribution (Figure 13-14).

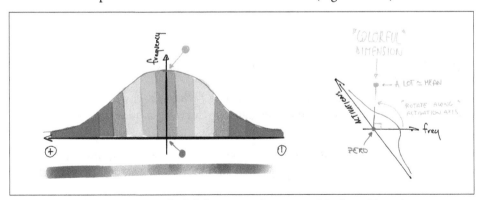

Figure 13-14. Histogram in colorful dimension (courtesy of Stefano Giomo)

To create color_dim, we take the histogram shown on the left here and convert it into just the colored representation shown at the bottom. Then we flip it on its side, as shown on the right. We found that the distribution is clearer if we take the log of the histogram values. Then, Giomo describes:

> The final plot for each layer is made by stacking the histogram of the activations from each batch along the horizontal axis. So each vertical slice in the visualisation represents the histogram of activations for a single batch. The color intensity corresponds to the height of the histogram; in other words, the number of activations in each histogram bin.

Figure 13-15 shows how this all fits together.

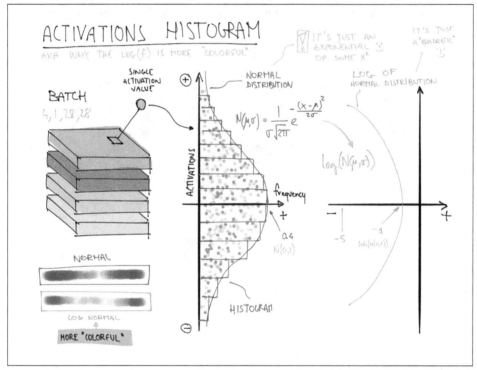

Figure 13-15. Summary of the colorful dimension (courtesy of Stefano Giomo)

This illustrates why log(*f*) is more colorful than *f* when *f* follows a normal distribution, because taking a log changes the Gaussian curve in a quadratic, which isn't as narrow.

So with that in mind, let's take another look at the result for the penultimate layer:

```
learn.activation_stats.color_dim(-2)
```

This shows a classic picture of "bad training." We start with nearly all activations at zero—that's what we see at the far left, with all the dark blue. The bright yellow at the bottom represents the near-zero activations. Then, over the first few batches, we see the number of nonzero activations exponentially increasing. But it goes too far and collapses! We see the dark blue return, and the bottom becomes bright yellow again. It almost looks like training restarts from scratch. Then we see the activations increase again and collapse again. After repeating this a few times, eventually we see a spread of activations throughout the range.

It's much better if training can be smooth from the start. The cycles of exponential increase and then collapse tend to result in a lot of near-zero activations, resulting in slow training and poor final results. One way to solve this problem is to use batch normalization.

Batch Normalization

To fix the slow training and poor final results we ended up with in the previous section, we need to fix the initial large percentage of near-zero activations, and then try to maintain a good distribution of activations throughout training.

Sergey Ioffe and Christian Szegedy presented a solution to this problem in the 2015 paper "Batch Normalization: Accelerating Deep Network Training by Reducing Internal Covariate Shift" (*https://oreil.ly/MTZJL*). In the abstract, they describe just the problem that we've seen:

> Training Deep Neural Networks is complicated by the fact that the distribution of each layer's inputs changes during training, as the parameters of the previous layers change. This slows down the training by requiring lower learning rates and careful parameter initialization…We refer to this phenomenon as internal covariate shift, and address the problem by normalizing layer inputs.

Their solution, they say is as follows:

> Making normalization a part of the model architecture and performing the normalization for each training mini-batch. Batch Normalization allows us to use much higher learning rates and be less careful about initialization.

The paper caused great excitement as soon as it was released, because it included the chart in Figure 13-16, which clearly demonstrated that batch normalization could train a model that was even more accurate than the current state of the art (the *Inception* architecture) and around 5× faster.

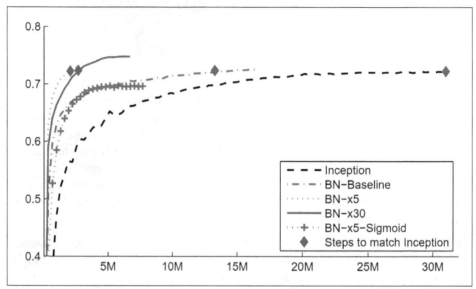

Figure 13-16. Impact of batch normalization (courtesy of Sergey Ioffe and Christian Szegedy)

Batch normalization (often called *batchnorm*) works by taking an average of the mean and standard deviations of the activations of a layer and using those to normalize the activations. However, this can cause problems because the network might want some activations to be really high in order to make accurate predictions. So they also added two learnable parameters (meaning they will be updated in the SGD step), usually called gamma and beta. After normalizing the activations to get some new activation vector y, a batchnorm layer returns gamma*y + beta.

That's why our activations can have any mean or variance, independent from the mean and standard deviation of the results of the previous layer. Those statistics are learned separately, making training easier on our model. The behavior is different during training and validation: during training we use the mean and standard deviation of the batch to normalize the data, while during validation we instead use a running mean of the statistics calculated during training.

Let's add a batchnorm layer to conv:

```
def conv(ni, nf, ks=3, act=True):
    layers = [nn.Conv2d(ni, nf, stride=2, kernel_size=ks, padding=ks//2)]
    layers.append(nn.BatchNorm2d(nf))
    if act: layers.append(nn.ReLU())
    return nn.Sequential(*layers)
```

and fit our model:

```
learn = fit()
```

epoch	train_loss	valid_loss	accuracy	time
0	0.130036	0.055021	0.986400	00:10

That's a great result! Let's take a look at color_dim:

```
learn.activation_stats.color_dim(-4)
```

This is just what we hope to see: a smooth development of activations, with no "crashes." Batchnorm has really delivered on its promise here! In fact, batchnorm has been so successful that we see it (or something very similar) in nearly all modern neural networks.

An interesting observation about models containing batch normalization layers is that they tend to generalize better than models that don't contain them. Although we haven't as yet seen a rigorous analysis of what's going on here, most researchers believe that the reason is that batch normalization adds some extra randomness to the training process. Each mini-batch will have a somewhat different mean and standard deviation than other mini-batches. Therefore, the activations will be normalized by different values each time. In order for the model to make accurate predictions, it will have to learn to become robust to these variations. In general, adding additional randomization to the training process often helps.

Since things are going so well, let's train for a few more epochs and see how it goes. In fact, let's *increase* the learning rate, since the abstract of the batchnorm paper claimed we should be able to "train at much higher learning rates":

```
learn = fit(5, lr=0.1)
```

epoch	train_loss	valid_loss	accuracy	time
0	0.191731	0.121738	0.960900	00:11
1	0.083739	0.055808	0.981800	00:10
2	0.053161	0.044485	0.987100	00:10
3	0.034433	0.030233	0.990200	00:10
4	0.017646	0.025407	0.991200	00:10

```
learn = fit(5, lr=0.1)
```

epoch	train_loss	valid_loss	accuracy	time
0	0.183244	0.084025	0.975800	00:13
1	0.080774	0.067060	0.978800	00:12
2	0.050215	0.062595	0.981300	00:12
3	0.030020	0.030315	0.990700	00:12
4	0.015131	0.025148	0.992100	00:12

At this point, I think it's fair to say we know how to recognize digits! It's time to move on to something harder…

Conclusion

We've seen that convolutions are just a type of matrix multiplication, with two constraints on the weight matrix: some elements are always zero, and some elements are tied (forced to always have the same value). In Chapter 1, we saw the eight requirements from the 1986 book *Parallel Distributed Processing*; one of them was "A pattern of connectivity among units." That's exactly what these constraints do: they enforce a certain pattern of connectivity.

These constraints allow us to use far fewer parameters in our model, without sacrificing the ability to represent complex visual features. That means we can train deeper models faster, with less overfitting. Although the universal approximation theorem shows that it should be *possible* to represent anything in a fully connected network in one hidden layer, we've seen now that in *practice* we can train much better models by being thoughtful about network architecture.

Convolutions are by far the most common pattern of connectivity we see in neural nets (along with regular linear layers, which we refer to as *fully connected*), but it's likely that many more will be discovered.

We've also seen how to interpret the activations of layers in the network to see whether training is going well or not, and how batchnorm helps regularize the training and makes it smoother. In the next chapter, we will use both of those layers to build the most popular architecture in computer vision: a residual network.

Questionnaire

1. What is a feature?
2. Write out the convolutional kernel matrix for a top edge detector.
3. Write out the mathematical operation applied by a 3×3 kernel to a single pixel in an image.
4. What is the value of a convolutional kernel applied to a 3×3 matrix of zeros?
5. What is padding?
6. What is stride?
7. Create a nested list comprehension to complete any task that you choose.
8. What are the shapes of the `input` and `weight` parameters to PyTorch's 2D convolution?
9. What is a channel?
10. What is the relationship between a convolution and a matrix multiplication?
11. What is a convolutional neural network?
12. What is the benefit of refactoring parts of your neural network definition?
13. What is `Flatten`? Where does it need to be included in the MNIST CNN? Why?
14. What does NCHW mean?
15. Why does the third layer of the MNIST CNN have `7*7*(1168-16)` multiplications?
16. What is a receptive field?
17. What is the size of the receptive field of an activation after two stride-2 convolutions? Why?
18. Run *conv-example.xlsx* yourself and experiment with *trace precedents*.
19. Have a look at Jeremy or Sylvain's list of recent Twitter "likes," and see if you find any interesting resources or ideas there.
20. How is a color image represented as a tensor?
21. How does a convolution work with a color input?
22. What method can we use to see that data in `DataLoaders`?
23. Why do we double the number of filters after each stride-2 conv?
24. Why do we use a larger kernel in the first conv with MNIST (with `simple_cnn`)?

25. What information does `ActivationStats` save for each layer?

26. How can we access a learner's callback after training?

27. What are the three statistics plotted by `plot_layer_stats`? What does the x-axis represent?

28. Why are activations near zero problematic?

29. What are the upsides and downsides of training with a larger batch size?

30. Why should we avoid using a high learning rate at the start of training?

31. What is 1cycle training?

32. What are the benefits of training with a high learning rate?

33. Why do we want to use a low learning rate at the end of training?

34. What is cyclical momentum?

35. What callback tracks hyperparameter values during training (along with other information)?

36. What does one column of pixels in the `color_dim` plot represent?

37. What does "bad training" look like in `color_dim`? Why?

38. What trainable parameters does a batch normalization layer contain?

39. What statistics are used to normalize in batch normalization during training? How about during validation?

40. Why do models with batch normalization layers generalize better?

Further Research

1. What features other than edge detectors have been used in computer vision (especially before deep learning became popular)?

2. Other normalization layers are available in PyTorch. Try them out and see what works best. Learn about why other normalization layers have been developed and how they differ from batch normalization.

3. Try moving the activation function after the batch normalization layer in conv. Does it make a difference? See what you can find out about what order is recommended and why.

CHAPTER 14

ResNets

In this chapter, we will build on top of the CNNs introduced in the previous chapter and explain to you the ResNet (residual network) architecture. It was introduced in 2015 by Kaiming He et al. in the article "Deep Residual Learning for Image Recognition" (*https://oreil.ly/b68K8*) and is by far the most used model architecture nowadays. More recent developments in image models almost always use the same trick of residual connections, and most of the time, they are just a tweak of the original ResNet.

We will first show you the basic ResNet as it was first designed and then explain the modern tweaks that make it more performant. But first, we will need a problem a little bit more difficult than the MNIST dataset, since we are already close to 100% accuracy with a regular CNN on it.

Going Back to Imagenette

It's going to be tough to judge any improvements we make to our models when we are already at an accuracy that is as high as we saw on MNIST in the previous chapter, so we will tackle a tougher image classification problem by going back to Imagenette. We'll stick with small images to keep things reasonably fast.

Let's grab the data—we'll use the already-resized 160 px version to make things faster still, and will random crop to 128 px:

```
def get_data(url, presize, resize):
    path = untar_data(url)
    return DataBlock(
        blocks=(ImageBlock, CategoryBlock), get_items=get_image_files,
        splitter=GrandparentSplitter(valid_name='val'),
        get_y=parent_label, item_tfms=Resize(presize),
        batch_tfms=[*aug_transforms(min_scale=0.5, size=resize),
                    Normalize.from_stats(*imagenet_stats)],
    ).dataloaders(path, bs=128)

dls = get_data(URLs.IMAGENETTE_160, 160, 128)

dls.show_batch(max_n=4)
```

When we looked at MNIST, we were dealing with 28×28-pixel images. For Image-nette, we are going to be training with 128×128-pixel images. Later, we would like to be able to use larger images as well—at least as big as 224×224-pixels, the ImageNet standard. Do you recall how we managed to get a single vector of activations for each image out of the MNIST convolutional neural network?

The approach we used was to ensure that there were enough stride-2 convolutions such that the final layer would have a grid size of 1. Then we just flattened out the unit axes that we ended up with, to get a vector for each image (so, a matrix of activations for a mini-batch). We could do the same thing for Imagenette, but that would cause two problems:

- We'd need lots of stride-2 layers to make our grid 1×1 at the end—perhaps more than we would otherwise choose.

- The model would not work on images of any size other than the size we originally trained on.

One approach to dealing with the first issue would be to flatten the final convolutional layer in a way that handles a grid size other than 1×1. We could simply flatten a matrix into a vector as we have done before, by laying out each row after the previous row. In fact, this is the approach that convolutional neural networks up until 2013 nearly always took. The most famous example is the 2013 ImageNet winner VGG, still sometimes used today. But there was another problem with this architecture: it not only did not work with images other than those of the same size used in the training set, but also required a lot of memory, because flattening out the convolutional layer resulted in many activations being fed into the final layers. Therefore, the weight matrices of the final layers were enormous.

This problem was solved through the creation of *fully convolutional networks*. The trick in fully convolutional networks is to take the average of activations across a convolutional grid. In other words, we can simply use this function:

```
def avg_pool(x): return x.mean((2,3))
```

As you see, it is taking the mean over the x- and y-axes. This function will always convert a grid of activations into a single activation per image. PyTorch provides a slightly more versatile module called nn.AdaptiveAvgPool2d, which averages a grid of activations into whatever sized destination you require (although we nearly always use a size of 1).

A fully convolutional network, therefore, has a number of convolutional layers, some of which will be stride 2, at the end of which is an adaptive average pooling layer, a flatten layer to remove the unit axes, and finally a linear layer. Here is our first fully convolutional network:

```
def block(ni, nf): return ConvLayer(ni, nf, stride=2)
def get_model():
    return nn.Sequential(
        block(3, 16),
        block(16, 32),
        block(32, 64),
        block(64, 128),
        block(128, 256),
        nn.AdaptiveAvgPool2d(1),
        Flatten(),
        nn.Linear(256, dls.c))
```

We're going to be replacing the implementation of block in the network with other variants in a moment, which is why we're not calling it conv anymore. We're also saving some time by taking advantage of fastai's ConvLayer, which already provides the functionality of conv from the preceding chapter (plus a lot more!).

Stop and Think

Consider this question: would this approach make sense for an optical character recognition (OCR) problem such as MNIST? The vast majority of practitioners tackling OCR and similar problems tend to use fully convolutional networks, because that's what nearly everybody learns nowadays. But it really doesn't make any sense! You can't decide, for instance, whether a number is a 3 or an 8 by slicing it into small pieces, jumbling them up, and deciding whether on average each piece looks like a 3 or an 8. But that's what adaptive average pooling effectively does! Fully convolutional networks are really a good choice only for objects that don't have a single correct orientation or size (e.g., like most natural photos).

Once we are done with our convolutional layers, we will get activations of size bs x ch x h x w (batch size, a certain number of channels, height, and width). We want to convert this to a tensor of size bs x ch, so we take the average over the last two dimensions and flatten the trailing 1×1 dimension as we did in our previous model.

This is different from regular pooling in the sense that those layers will generally take the average (for average pooling) or the maximum (for max pooling) of a window of a given size. For instance, max pooling layers of size 2, which were very popular in older CNNs, reduce the size of our image by half on each dimension by taking the maximum of each 2×2 window (with a stride of 2).

As before, we can define a `Learner` with our custom model and then train it on the data we grabbed earlier:

```
def get_learner(m):
    return Learner(dls, m, loss_func=nn.CrossEntropyLoss(), metrics=accuracy
                  ).to_fp16()

learn = get_learner(get_model())

learn.lr_find()

(0.47863011360168456, 3.981071710586548)
```

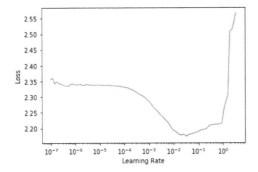

3e-3 is often a good learning rate for CNNs, and that appears to be the case here too, so let's try that:

```
learn.fit_one_cycle(5, 3e-3)
```

epoch	train_loss	valid_loss	accuracy	time
0	1.901582	2.155090	0.325350	00:07
1	1.559855	1.586795	0.507771	00:07
2	1.296350	1.295499	0.571720	00:07
3	1.144139	1.139257	0.639236	00:07
4	1.049770	1.092619	0.659108	00:07

That's a pretty good start, considering we have to pick the correct one of 10 categories, and we're training from scratch for just 5 epochs! We can do way better than this using a deeper model, but just stacking new layers won't really improve our results (you can try and see for yourself!). To work around this problem, ResNets introduce the idea of *skip connections*. We'll explore those and other aspects of ResNets in the next section.

Building a Modern CNN: ResNet

We now have all the pieces we need to build the models we have been using in our computer vision tasks since the beginning of this book: ResNets. We'll introduce the main idea behind them and show how it improves accuracy on Imagenette compared to our previous model, before building a version with all the recent tweaks.

Skip Connections

In 2015, the authors of the ResNet paper noticed something that they found curious. Even after using batchnorm, they saw that a network using more layers was doing less well than a network using fewer layers—and there were no other differences between the models. Most interestingly, the difference was observed not only in the validation set, but also in the training set; so it wasn't just a generalization issue, but a training issue. As the paper explains:

> Unexpectedly, such degradation is not caused by overfitting, and adding more layers to a suitably deep model leads to higher training error, as [previously reported] and thoroughly verified by our experiments.

This phenomenon was illustrated by the graph in Figure 14-1, with training error on the left and test error on the right.

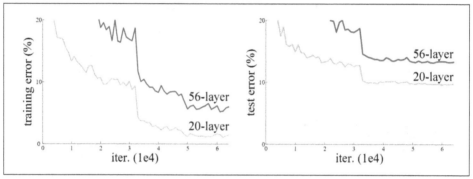

Figure 14-1. Training of networks of different depth (courtesy of Kaiming He et al.)

As the authors mention here, they are not the first people to have noticed this curious fact. But they were the first to make a very important leap:

> Let us consider a shallower architecture and its deeper counterpart that adds more layers onto it. There exists a solution by construction to the deeper model: the added layers are identity mapping, and the other layers are copied from the learned shallower model.

As this is an academic paper, this process is described in a rather inaccessible way, but the concept is actually very simple: start with a 20-layer neural network that is trained well, and add another 36 layers that do nothing at all (for instance, they could be linear layers with a single weight equal to 1, and bias equal to 0). The result will be a 56-layer network that does exactly the same thing as the 20-layer network, proving that there are always deep networks that should be *at least as good* as any shallow network. But for some reason, SGD does not seem able to find them.

Jargon: Identity Mapping

Returning the input without changing it at all. This process is performed by an *identity function*.

Actually, there is another way to create those extra 36 layers, which is much more interesting. What if we replaced every occurrence of conv(x) with x + conv(x), where conv is the function from the previous chapter that adds a second convolution, then a batchnorm layer, then a ReLU. Furthermore, recall that batchnorm does gamma*y + beta. What if we initialized gamma to zero for every one of those final batchnorm layers? Since beta is already initialized to zero, our conv(x) for those extra 36 layers will always be equal to zero, which means x+conv(x) will always be equal to x.

What has that gained us? The key thing is that those 36 extra layers, as they stand, are an *identity mapping*, but they have *parameters*, which means they are *trainable*. So, we can start with our best 20-layer model, add these 36 extra layers that initially do nothing at all, and then *fine-tune the whole 56-layer model*. Those extra 36 layers can then learn the parameters that make them most useful!

The ResNet paper proposed a variant of this, which is to instead "skip over" every second convolution, so effectively we get x+conv2(conv1(x)). This is shown by the diagram in Figure 14-2 (from the paper).

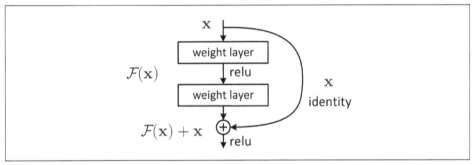

Figure 14-2. A simple ResNet block (courtesy of Kaiming He et al.)

That arrow on the right is just the x part of x+conv2(conv1(x)) and is known as the *identity branch*, or *skip connection*. The path on the left is the conv2(conv1(x)) part. You can think of the identity path as providing a direct route from the input to the output.

In a ResNet, we don't proceed by first training a smaller number of layers, and then adding new layers on the end and fine-tuning. Instead, we use ResNet blocks like the one in Figure 14-2 throughout the CNN, initialized from scratch in the usual way and trained with SGD in the usual way. We rely on the skip connections to make the network easier to train with SGD.

There's another (largely equivalent) way to think of these ResNet blocks. This is how the paper describes it:

Instead of hoping each few stacked layers directly fit a desired underlying mapping, we explicitly let these layers fit a residual mapping. Formally, denoting the desired underlying mapping as $H(x)$, we let the stacked nonlinear layers fit another mapping of $F(x) := H(x)-x$. The original mapping is recast into $F(x)+x$. We hypothesize that it is easier to optimize the residual mapping than to optimize the original, unreferenced mapping. To the extreme, if an identity mapping were optimal, it would be easier to push the residual to zero than to fit an identity mapping by a stack of nonlinear layers.

Again, this is rather inaccessible prose—so let's try to restate it in plain English! If the outcome of a given layer is x and we're using a ResNet block that returns y = x + block(x), we're not asking the block to predict y; we are asking it to predict the difference between y and x. So the job of those blocks isn't to predict certain features, but to minimize the error between x and the desired y. A ResNet is, therefore, good at learning about slight differences between doing nothing and passing through a block of two convolutional layers (with trainable weights). This is how these models got their name: they're predicting residuals (reminder: "residual" is prediction minus target).

One key concept that both of these two ways of thinking about ResNets share is the idea of ease of learning. This is an important theme. Recall the universal approximation theorem, which states that a sufficiently large network can learn anything. This is still true, but there turns out to be a very important difference between what a network *can learn* in principle, and what it is *easy for it to learn* with realistic data and training regimes. Many of the advances in neural networks over the last decade have been like the ResNet block: the result of realizing how to make something that was always possible actually feasible.

 True Identity Path

The original paper didn't actually do the trick of using zero for the initial value of gamma in the last batchnorm layer of each block; that came a couple of years later. So, the original version of ResNet didn't quite begin training with a true identity path through the ResNet blocks, but nonetheless having the ability to "navigate through" the skip connections did make it train better. Adding the batchnorm gamma init trick made the models train at even higher learning rates.

Here's the definition of a simple ResNet block (fastai initializes the gamma weights of the last batchnorm layer to zero because of norm_type=NormType.BatchZero):

```
class ResBlock(Module):
    def __init__(self, ni, nf):
        self.convs = nn.Sequential(
            ConvLayer(ni,nf),
            ConvLayer(nf,nf, norm_type=NormType.BatchZero))
```

```
def forward(self, x): return x + self.convs(x)
```

This has two problems, however: it can't handle a stride other than 1, and it requires that ni==nf. Stop for a moment to think carefully about why this is.

The issue is that with a stride of, say, 2 on one of the convolutions, the grid size of the output activations will be half the size on each axis of the input. So then we can't add that back to x in forward because x and the output activations have different dimensions. The same basic issue occurs if ni!=nf: the shapes of the input and output connections won't allow us to add them together.

To fix this, we need a way to change the shape of x to match the result of self.convs. Halving the grid size can be done using an average pooling layer with a stride of 2: that is, a layer that takes 2×2 patches from the input and replaces them with their average.

Changing the number of channels can be done by using a convolution. We want this skip connection to be as close to an identity map as possible, however, which means making this convolution as simple as possible. The simplest possible convolution is one with a kernel size of 1. That means that the kernel is size ni × nf × 1 × 1, so it's only doing a dot product over the channels of each input pixel—it's not combining across pixels at all. This kind of *1x1 convolution* is widely used in modern CNNs, so take a moment to think about how it works.

 Jargon: 1x1 Convolution

A convolution with a kernel size of 1.

Here's a ResBlock using these tricks to handle changing shape in the skip connection:

```
def _conv_block(ni,nf,stride):
    return nn.Sequential(
        ConvLayer(ni, nf, stride=stride),
        ConvLayer(nf, nf, act_cls=None, norm_type=NormType.BatchZero))

class ResBlock(Module):
    def __init__(self, ni, nf, stride=1):
        self.convs = _conv_block(ni,nf,stride)
        self.idconv = noop if ni==nf else ConvLayer(ni, nf, 1, act_cls=None)
        self.pool = noop if stride==1 else nn.AvgPool2d(2, ceil_mode=True)

    def forward(self, x):
        return F.relu(self.convs(x) + self.idconv(self.pool(x)))
```

Note that we're using the noop function here, which simply returns its input unchanged (*noop* is a computer science term that stands for "no operation"). In this case, `idconv` does nothing at all if `ni==nf`, and `pool` does nothing if `stride==1`, which is what we wanted in our skip connection.

Also, you'll see that we've removed the ReLU (`act_cls=None`) from the final convolution in `convs` and from `idconv`, and moved it to *after* we add the skip connection. The thinking behind this is that the whole ResNet block is like a layer, and you want your activation to be after your layer.

Let's replace our `block` with `ResBlock` and try it out:

```
def block(ni,nf): return ResBlock(ni, nf, stride=2)
learn = get_learner(get_model())

learn.fit_one_cycle(5, 3e-3)
```

epoch	train_loss	valid_loss	accuracy	time
0	1.973174	1.845491	0.373248	00:08
1	1.678627	1.778713	0.439236	00:08
2	1.386163	1.596503	0.507261	00:08
3	1.177839	1.102993	0.644841	00:09
4	1.052435	1.038013	0.667771	00:09

It's not much better. But the whole point of this was to allow us to train *deeper* models, and we're not really taking advantage of that yet. To create a model that's, say, twice as deep, all we need to do is replace our `block` with two `ResBlocks` in a row:

```
def block(ni, nf):
    return nn.Sequential(ResBlock(ni, nf, stride=2), ResBlock(nf, nf))

learn = get_learner(get_model())
learn.fit_one_cycle(5, 3e-3)
```

epoch	train_loss	valid_loss	accuracy	time
0	1.964076	1.864578	0.355159	00:12
1	1.636880	1.596789	0.502675	00:12
2	1.335378	1.304472	0.588535	00:12
3	1.089160	1.065063	0.663185	00:12
4	0.942904	0.963589	0.692739	00:12

Now we're making good progress!

The authors of the ResNet paper went on to win the 2015 ImageNet challenge. At the time, this was by far the most important annual event in computer vision. We have already seen another ImageNet winner: the 2013 winners, Zeiler and Fergus. It is interesting to note that in both cases, the starting points for the breakthroughs were experimental observations: observations about what layers actually learn, in the case of Zeiler and Fergus, and observations about which kinds of networks can be trained, in the case of the ResNet authors. This ability to design and analyze thoughtful experiments, or even just to see an unexpected result, say, "Hmmm, that's interesting," and then, most importantly, set about figuring out what on earth is going on, with great tenacity, is at the heart of many scientific discoveries. Deep learning is not like pure mathematics. It is a heavily experimental field, so it's important to be a strong practitioner, not just a theoretician.

Since the ResNet was introduced, it's been widely studied and applied to many domains. One of the most interesting papers, published in 2018, is "Visualizing the Loss Landscape of Neural Nets" (*https://oreil.ly/C9cFi*) by Hao Li et al. It shows that using skip connections helps smooth the loss function, which makes training easier as it avoids falling into a very sharp area. Figure 14-3 shows a stunning picture from the paper, illustrating the difference between the bumpy terrain that SGD has to navigate to optimize a regular CNN (left) versus the smooth surface of a ResNet (right).

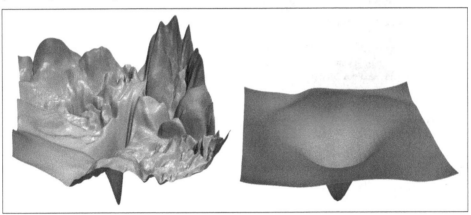

Figure 14-3. Impact of ResNet on loss landscape (courtesy of Hao Li et al.)

Our first model is already good, but further research has discovered more tricks we can apply to make it better. We'll look at those next.

A State-of-the-Art ResNet

In "Bag of Tricks for Image Classification with Convolutional Neural Networks" (*https://oreil.ly/n-qhd*), Tong He et al. study variations of the ResNet architecture that come at almost no additional cost in terms of number of parameters or computation. By using a tweaked ResNet-50 architecture and Mixup, they achieved 94.6% top-5 accuracy on ImageNet, in comparison to 92.2% with a regular ResNet-50 without Mixup. This result is better than that achieved by regular ResNet models that are twice as deep (and twice as slow, and much more likely to overfit).

Jargon: Top-5 Accuracy

A metric testing how often the label we want is in the top 5 predictions of our model. It was used in the ImageNet competition because many of the images contained multiple objects, or contained objects that could be easily confused or may even have been mislabeled with a similar label. In these situations, looking at top-1 accuracy may be inappropriate. However, recently CNNs have been getting so good that top-5 accuracy is nearly 100%, so some researchers are using top-1 accuracy for ImageNet too now.

We'll use this tweaked version as we scale up to the full ResNet, because it's substantially better. It differs a little bit from our previous implementation, in that instead of just starting with ResNet blocks, it begins with a few convolutional layers followed by a max pooling layer. This is what the first layers, called the *stem* of the network, look like:

```
def _resnet_stem(*sizes):
    return [
        ConvLayer(sizes[i], sizes[i+1], 3, stride = 2 if i==0 else 1)
            for i in range(len(sizes)-1)
    ] + [nn.MaxPool2d(kernel_size=3, stride=2, padding=1)]

_resnet_stem(3,32,32,64)

[ConvLayer(
    (0): Conv2d(3, 32, kernel_size=(3, 3), stride=(2, 2), padding=(1, 1))
    (1): BatchNorm2d(32, eps=1e-05, momentum=0.1)
    (2): ReLU()
 ), ConvLayer(
    (0): Conv2d(32, 32, kernel_size=(3, 3), stride=(1, 1), padding=(1, 1))
    (1): BatchNorm2d(32, eps=1e-05, momentum=0.1)
    (2): ReLU()
 ), ConvLayer(
    (0): Conv2d(32, 64, kernel_size=(3, 3), stride=(1, 1), padding=(1, 1))
    (1): BatchNorm2d(64, eps=1e-05, momentum=0.1)
    (2): ReLU()
 ), MaxPool2d(kernel_size=3, stride=2, padding=1, ceil_mode=False)]
```

Jargon: Stem

The first few layers of a CNN. Generally, the stem has a different structure than the main body of the CNN.

The reason that we have a stem of plain convolutional layers, instead of ResNet blocks, is based on an important insight about all deep convolutional neural networks: the vast majority of the computation occurs in the early layers. Therefore, we should keep the early layers as fast and simple as possible.

To see why so much computation occurs in the early layers, consider the very first convolution on a 128-pixel input image. If it is a stride-1 convolution, it will apply the kernel to every one of the 128×128 pixels. That's a lot of work! In the later layers, however, the grid size could be as small as 4×4 or even 2×2, so there are far fewer kernel applications to do.

On the other hand, the first-layer convolution has only 3 input features and 32 output features. Since it is a 3×3 kernel, this is 3×32×3×3 = 864 parameters in the weights. But the last convolution will have 256 input features and 512 output features, resulting in 1,179,648 weights! So the first layers contain the vast majority of the computation, but the last layers contain the vast majority of the parameters.

A ResNet block takes more computation than a plain convolutional block, since (in the stride-2 case) a ResNet block has three convolutions and a pooling layer. That's why we want to have plain convolutions to start off our ResNet.

We're now ready to show the implementation of a modern ResNet, with the "bag of tricks." It uses the four groups of ResNet blocks, with 64, 128, 256, then 512 filters. Each group starts with a stride-2 block, except for the first one, since it's just after a MaxPooling layer:

```python
class ResNet(nn.Sequential):
    def __init__(self, n_out, layers, expansion=1):
        stem = _resnet_stem(3,32,32,64)
        self.block_szs = [64, 64, 128, 256, 512]
        for i in range(1,5): self.block_szs[i] *= expansion
        blocks = [self._make_layer(*o) for o in enumerate(layers)]
        super().__init__(*stem, *blocks,
                         nn.AdaptiveAvgPool2d(1), Flatten(),
                         nn.Linear(self.block_szs[-1], n_out))

    def _make_layer(self, idx, n_layers):
        stride = 1 if idx==0 else 2
        ch_in,ch_out = self.block_szs[idx:idx+2]
        return nn.Sequential(*[
            ResBlock(ch_in if i==0 else ch_out, ch_out, stride if i==0 else 1)
            for i in range(n_layers)
        ])
```

The _make_layer function is just there to create a series of n_layers blocks. The first one is going from ch_in to ch_out with the indicated stride, and all the others are blocks of stride 1 with ch_out to ch_out tensors. Once the blocks are defined, our model is purely sequential, which is why we define it as a subclass of nn.Sequential. (Ignore the expansion parameter for now; we'll discuss it in the next section. For now, it'll be 1, so it doesn't do anything.)

The various versions of the models (ResNet-18, -34, -50, etc.) just change the number of blocks in each of those groups. This is the definition of a ResNet-18:

```
rn = ResNet(dls.c, [2,2,2,2])
```

Let's train it for a little bit and see how it fares compared to the previous model:

```
learn = get_learner(rn)
learn.fit_one_cycle(5, 3e-3)
```

epoch	train_loss	valid_loss	accuracy	time
0	1.673882	1.828394	0.413758	00:13
1	1.331675	1.572685	0.518217	00:13
2	1.087224	1.086102	0.650701	00:13
3	0.900428	0.968219	0.684331	00:12
4	0.760280	0.782558	0.757197	00:12

Even though we have more channels (and our model is therefore even more accurate), our training is just as fast as before thanks to our optimized stem.

To make our model deeper without taking too much compute or memory, we can use another kind of layer introduced by the ResNet paper for ResNets with a depth of 50 or more: the bottleneck layer.

Bottleneck Layers

Instead of stacking two convolutions with a kernel size of 3, bottleneck layers use three convolutions: two 1×1 (at the beginning and the end) and one 3×3, as shown on the right in Figure 14-4.

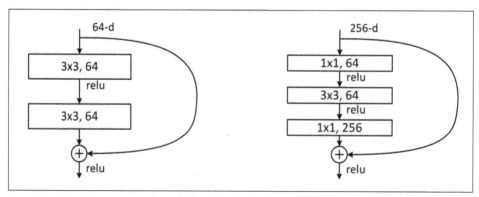

Figure 14-4. Comparison of regular and bottleneck ResNet blocks (courtesy of Kaiming He et al.)

Why is that useful? 1×1 convolutions are much faster, so even if this seems to be a more complex design, this block executes faster than the first ResNet block we saw. This then lets us use more filters: as we see in the illustration, the number of filters in and out is four times higher (256 instead of 64). The 1×1 convs diminish then restore the number of channels (hence the name *bottleneck*). The overall impact is that we can use more filters in the same amount of time.

Let's try replacing our `ResBlock` with this bottleneck design:

```
def _conv_block(ni,nf,stride):
    return nn.Sequential(
        ConvLayer(ni, nf//4, 1),
        ConvLayer(nf//4, nf//4, stride=stride),
        ConvLayer(nf//4, nf, 1, act_cls=None, norm_type=NormType.BatchZero))
```

We'll use this to create a ResNet-50 with group sizes of (3,4,6,3). We now need to pass 4 into the `expansion` parameter of `ResNet`, since we need to start with four times fewer channels and we'll end with four times more channels.

Deeper networks like this don't generally show improvements when training for only 5 epochs, so we'll bump it up to 20 epochs this time to make the most of our bigger model. And to really get great results, let's use bigger images too:

```
dls = get_data(URLs.IMAGENETTE_320, presize=320, resize=224)
```

We don't have to do anything to account for the larger 224-pixel images; thanks to our fully convolutional network, it just works. This is also why we were able to do *progressive resizing* earlier in the book—the models we used were fully convolutional, so we were even able to fine-tune models trained with different sizes. We can now train our model and see the effects:

```
rn = ResNet(dls.c, [3,4,6,3], 4)

learn = get_learner(rn)
learn.fit_one_cycle(20, 3e-3)
```

epoch	train_loss	valid_loss	accuracy	time
0	1.613448	1.473355	0.514140	00:31
1	1.359604	2.050794	0.397452	00:31
2	1.253112	4.511735	0.387006	00:31
3	1.133450	2.575221	0.396178	00:31
4	1.054752	1.264525	0.613758	00:32
5	0.927930	2.670484	0.422675	00:32
6	0.838268	1.724588	0.528662	00:32
7	0.748289	1.180668	0.666497	00:31
8	0.688637	1.245039	0.650446	00:32
9	0.645530	1.053691	0.674904	00:31

epoch	train_loss	valid_loss	accuracy	time
10	0.593401	1.180786	0.676433	00:32
11	0.536634	0.879937	0.713885	00:32
12	0.479208	0.798356	0.741656	00:32
13	0.440071	0.600644	0.806879	00:32
14	0.402952	0.450296	0.858599	00:32
15	0.359117	0.486126	0.846369	00:32
16	0.313642	0.442215	0.861911	00:32
17	0.294050	0.485967	0.853503	00:32
18	0.270583	0.408566	0.875924	00:32
19	0.266003	0.411752	0.872611	00:33

We're getting a great result now! Try adding Mixup, and then training this for a hundred epochs while you go get lunch. You'll have yourself a very accurate image classifier, trained from scratch.

The bottleneck design we've shown here is typically used in only ResNet-50, -101, and -152 models. ResNet-18 and -34 models usually use the non-bottleneck design seen in the previous section. However, we've noticed that the bottleneck layer generally works better even for the shallower networks. This just goes to show that the little details in papers tend to stick around for years, even if they're not quite the best design! Questioning assumptions and "stuff everyone knows" is always a good idea, because this is still a new field, and lots of details aren't always done well.

Conclusion

You have now seen how the models we have been using for computer vision since the first chapter are built, using skip connections to allow deeper models to be trained. Even though there has been a lot of research into better architectures, they all use one version or another of this trick to make a direct path from the input to the end of the network. When using transfer learning, the ResNet is the pretrained model. In the next chapter, we will look at the final details of how the models we used were built from it.

Questionnaire

1. How did we get to a single vector of activations in the CNNs used for MNIST in previous chapters? Why isn't that suitable for Imagenette?

2. What do we do for Imagenette instead?

3. What is adaptive pooling?

4. What is average pooling?

5. Why do we need `Flatten` after an adaptive average pooling layer?

6. What is a skip connection?

7. Why do skip connections allow us to train deeper models?

8. What does Figure 14-1 show? How did that lead to the idea of skip connections?

9. What is identity mapping?

10. What is the basic equation for a ResNet block (ignoring batchnorm and ReLU layers)?

11. What do ResNets have to do with residuals?

12. How do we deal with the skip connection when there is a stride-2 convolution? How about when the number of filters changes?

13. How can we express a 1×1 convolution in terms of a vector dot product?

14. Create a 1×1 convolution with `F.conv2d` or `nn.Conv2d` and apply it to an image. What happens to the shape of the image?

15. What does the `noop` function return?

16. Explain what is shown in Figure 14-3.

17. When is top-5 accuracy a better metric than top-1 accuracy?

18. What is the "stem" of a CNN?

19. Why do we use plain convolutions in the CNN stem instead of ResNet blocks?

20. How does a bottleneck block differ from a plain ResNet block?

21. Why is a bottleneck block faster?

22. How do fully convolutional nets (and nets with adaptive pooling in general) allow for progressive resizing?

Further Research

1. Try creating a fully convolutional net with adaptive average pooling for MNIST (note that you'll need fewer stride-2 layers). How does it compare to a network without such a pooling layer?

2. In Chapter 17, we introduce *Einstein summation notation*. Skip ahead to see how this works, and then write an implementation of the 1×1 convolution operation using `torch.einsum`. Compare it to the same operation using `torch.conv2d`.

3. Write a top-5 accuracy function using plain PyTorch or plain Python.

4. Train a model on Imagenette for more epochs, with and without label smoothing. Take a look at the Imagenette leaderboards and see how close you can get to the best results shown. Read the linked pages describing the leading approaches.

CHAPTER 15

Application Architectures Deep Dive

We are now in the exciting position that we can fully understand the architectures that we have been using for our state-of-the-art models for computer vision, natural language processing, and tabular analysis. In this chapter, we're going to fill in all the missing details on how fastai's application models work and show you how to build them.

We will also go back to the custom data preprocessing pipeline we saw in Chapter 11 for Siamese networks and show you how to use the components in the fastai library to build custom pretrained models for new tasks.

We'll start with computer vision.

Computer Vision

For computer vision applications, we use the functions `cnn_learner` and `unet_learner` to build our models, depending on the task. In this section, we'll explore how to build the `Learner` objects we used in Parts I and II of this book.

cnn_learner

Let's take a look at what happens when we use the `cnn_learner` function. We begin by passing this function an architecture to use for the *body* of the network. Most of the time, we use a ResNet, which you already know how to create, so we don't need to delve into that any further. Pretrained weights are downloaded as required and loaded into the ResNet.

Then, for transfer learning, the network needs to be *cut*. This refers to slicing off the final layer, which is responsible only for ImageNet-specific categorization. In fact, we do not slice off only this layer, but everything from the adaptive average pooling layer onward. The reason for this will become clear in just a moment. Since different architectures might use different types of pooling layers, or even completely different kinds of *heads*, we don't just search for the adaptive pooling layer to decide where to cut the pretrained model. Instead, we have a dictionary of information that is used for each model to determine where its body ends and its head starts. We call this `model_meta` —here it is for `resnet50`:

```
model_meta[resnet50]
```

```
{'cut': -2,
 'split': <function fastai.vision.learner._resnet_split(m)>,
 'stats': ([0.485, 0.456, 0.406], [0.229, 0.224, 0.225])}
```

Jargon: Body and Head

The head of a neural net is the part that is specialized for a particular task. For a CNN, it's generally the part after the adaptive average pooling layer. The body is everything else, and includes the stem (which we learned about in Chapter 14).

If we take all of the layers prior to the cut point of -2, we get the part of the model that fastai will keep for transfer learning. Now, we put on our new head. This is created using the function `create_head`:

```
create_head(20,2)
```

```
Sequential(
  (0): AdaptiveConcatPool2d(
    (ap): AdaptiveAvgPool2d(output_size=1)
    (mp): AdaptiveMaxPool2d(output_size=1)
  )
  (1): Flatten()
  (2): BatchNorm1d(20, eps=1e-05, momentum=0.1, affine=True)
  (3): Dropout(p=0.25, inplace=False)
  (4): Linear(in_features=20, out_features=512, bias=False)
  (5): ReLU(inplace=True)
  (6): BatchNorm1d(512, eps=1e-05, momentum=0.1, affine=True)
  (7): Dropout(p=0.5, inplace=False)
  (8): Linear(in_features=512, out_features=2, bias=False)
)
```

With this function, you can choose how many additional linear layers are added to the end, how much dropout to use after each one, and what kind of pooling to use. By default, fastai will apply both average pooling and max pooling, and will concatenate the two together (this is the `AdaptiveConcatPool2d` layer). This is not a particularly common approach, but it was developed independently at fastai and other research labs in recent years and tends to provide a small improvement over using just average pooling.

fastai is a bit different from most libraries in that by default it adds two linear layers, rather than one, in the CNN head. The reason is that transfer learning can still be useful even, as we have seen, when transferring the pretrained model to very different domains. However, just using a single linear layer is unlikely to be enough in these cases; we have found that using two linear layers can allow transfer learning to be used more quickly and easily, in more situations.

One Last Batchnorm

One parameter to `create_head` that is worth looking at is `bn_final`. Setting this to `True` will cause a batchnorm layer to be added as your final layer. This can be useful in helping your model scale appropriately for your output activations. We haven't seen this approach published anywhere as yet, but we have found that it works well in practice wherever we have used it.

Let's now take a look at what `unet_learner` did in the segmentation problem we showed in Chapter 1.

unet_learner

One of the most interesting architectures in deep learning is the one that we used for segmentation in Chapter 1. Segmentation is a challenging task, because the output required is really an image, or a pixel grid, containing the predicted label for every pixel. Other tasks share a similar basic design, such as increasing the resolution of an image (*super-resolution*), adding color to a black-and-white image (*colorization*), or converting a photo into a synthetic painting (*style transfer*)—these tasks are covered by an online chapter of this book (*https://book.fast.ai*), so be sure to check it out after you've read this chapter. In each case, we are starting with an image and converting it to another image of the same dimensions or aspect ratio, but with the pixels altered in some way. We refer to these as *generative vision models*.

The way we do this is to start with the exact same approach to developing a CNN head as we saw in the previous section. We start with a ResNet, for instance, and cut off the adaptive pooling layer and everything after that. Then we replace those layers with our custom head, which does the generative task.

There was a lot of handwaving in that last sentence! How on earth do we create a CNN head that generates an image? If we start with, say, a 224-pixel input image, then at the end of the ResNet body we will have a 7×7 grid of convolutional activations. How can we convert that into a 224-pixel segmentation mask?

Naturally, we do this with a neural network! So we need some kind of layer that can increase the grid size in a CNN. One simple approach is to replace every pixel in the 7×7 grid with four pixels in a 2×2 square. Each of those four pixels will have the same value—this is known as *nearest neighbor interpolation*. PyTorch provides a layer that does this for us, so one option is to create a head that contains stride-1 convolutional layers (along with batchnorm and ReLU layers as usual) interspersed with 2×2 nearest neighbor interpolation layers. In fact, you can try this now! See if you can create a custom head designed like this, and try it on the CamVid segmentation task. You should find that you get some reasonable results, although they won't be as good as our Chapter 1 results.

Another approach is to replace the nearest neighbor and convolution combination with a *transposed convolution*, otherwise known as a *stride half convolution*. This is identical to a regular convolution, but first zero padding is inserted between all the pixels in the input. This is easiest to see with a picture—Figure 15-1 shows a diagram from the excellent convolutional arithmetic paper (*https://oreil.ly/hu06c*) we discussed in Chapter 13, showing a 3×3 transposed convolution applied to a 3×3 image.

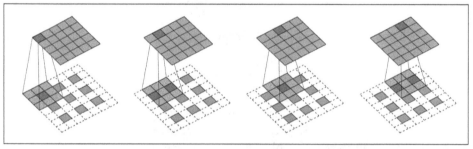

Figure 15-1. A transposed convolution (courtesy of Vincent Dumoulin and Francesco Visin)

As you see, the result is to increase the size of the input. You can try this out now by using fastai's ConvLayer class; pass the parameter transpose=True to create a transposed convolution, instead of a regular one, in your custom head.

Neither of these approaches, however, works really well. The problem is that our 7×7 grid simply doesn't have enough information to create a 224×224-pixel output. It's asking an awful lot of the activations of each of those grid cells to have enough information to fully regenerate every pixel in the output.

The solution is to use *skip connections*, as in a ResNet, but skipping from the activations in the body of the ResNet all the way over to the activations of the transposed convolution on the opposite side of the architecture. This approach, illustrated in Figure 15-2, was developed by Olaf Ronneberger et al. in the 2015 paper "U-Net: Convolutional Networks for Biomedical Image Segmentation" (*https://oreil.ly/6ely4*). Although the paper focused on medical applications, the U-Net has revolutionized all kinds of generative vision models.

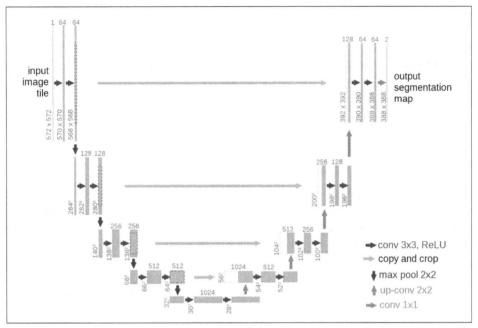

Figure 15-2. The U-Net architecture (courtesy of Olaf Ronneberger, Philipp Fischer, and Thomas Brox)

This picture shows the CNN body on the left (in this case, it's a regular CNN, not a ResNet, and they're using 2×2 max pooling instead of stride-2 convolutions, since this paper was written before ResNets came along) and the transposed convolutional ("up-conv") layers on the right. The extra skip connections are shown as gray arrows crossing from left to right (these are sometimes called *cross connections*). You can see why it's called a *U-Net*!

With this architecture, the input to the transposed convolutions is not just the lower-resolution grid in the preceding layer, but also the higher-resolution grid in the ResNet head. This allows the U-Net to use all of the information of the original image, as it is needed. One challenge with U-Nets is that the exact architecture depends on the image size. fastai has a unique `DynamicUnet` class that autogenerates an architecture of the right size based on the data provided.

Let's focus now on an example in which we leverage the fastai library to write a custom model.

A Siamese Network

Let's go back to the input pipeline we set up in Chapter 11 for a Siamese network. As you may remember, it consisted of a pair of images with the label being `True` or `False`, depending on whether they were in the same class.

Using what we just saw, let's build a custom model for this task and train it. How? We will use a pretrained architecture and pass our two images through it. Then we can concatenate the results and send them to a custom head that will return two predictions. In terms of modules, this looks like this:

```
class SiameseModel(Module):
    def __init__(self, encoder, head):
        self.encoder,self.head = encoder,head

    def forward(self, x1, x2):
        ftrs = torch.cat([self.encoder(x1), self.encoder(x2)], dim=1)
        return self.head(ftrs)
```

To create our encoder, we just need to take a pretrained model and cut it, as we explained before. The function `create_body` does that for us; we just have to pass it the place where we want to cut. As we saw earlier, per the dictionary of metadata for pretrained models, the cut value for a ResNet is `-2`:

```
encoder = create_body(resnet34, cut=-2)
```

Then we can create our head. A look at the encoder tells us the last layer has 512 features, so this head will need to receive `512*2`. Why 2? First we have to multiply by 2 because we have two images. Then we need a second multiplication by 2 because of our concat-pool trick. So we create the head as follows:

```
head = create_head(512*2, 2, ps=0.5)
```

With our encoder and head, we can now build our model:

```
model = SiameseModel(encoder, head)
```

Before using `Learner`, we have two more things to define. First, we must define the loss function we want to use. It's regular cross entropy, but since our targets are Booleans, we need to convert them to integers or PyTorch will throw an error:

```
def loss_func(out, targ):
    return nn.CrossEntropyLoss()(out, targ.long())
```

More importantly, to take full advantage of transfer learning, we have to define a custom *splitter*. A splitter is a function that tells the fastai library how to split the model into parameter groups. These are used behind the scenes to train only the head of a model when we do transfer learning.

Here we want two parameter groups: one for the encoder and one for the head. We can thus define the following splitter (`params` is just a function that returns all parameters of a given module):

```
def siamese_splitter(model):
    return [params(model.encoder), params(model.head)]
```

Then we can define our `Learner` by passing the data, model, loss function, splitter, and any metric we want. Since we are not using a convenience function from fastai for transfer learning (like `cnn_learner`), we have to call `learn.freeze` manually. This will make sure only the last parameter group (in this case, the head) is trained:

```
learn = Learner(dls, model, loss_func=loss_func,
                splitter=siamese_splitter, metrics=accuracy)
learn.freeze()
```

Then we can directly train our model with the usual method:

```
learn.fit_one_cycle(4, 3e-3)
```

epoch	train_loss	valid_loss	accuracy	time
0	0.367015	0.281242	0.885656	00:26
1	0.307688	0.214721	0.915426	00:26
2	0.275221	0.170615	0.936401	00:26
3	0.223771	0.159633	0.943843	00:26

Now we unfreeze and fine-tune the whole model a bit more with discriminative learning rates (that is, a lower learning rate for the body and a higher one for the head):

```
learn.unfreeze()
learn.fit_one_cycle(4, slice(1e-6,1e-4))
```

epoch	train_loss	valid_loss	accuracy	time
0	0.212744	0.159033	0.944520	00:35
1	0.201893	0.159615	0.942490	00:35
2	0.204606	0.152338	0.945196	00:36
3	0.213203	0.148346	0.947903	00:36

94.8% is very good when we remember that a classifier trained the same way (with no data augmentation) had an error rate of 7%.

Now that we've seen how to create complete state-of-the-art computer vision models, let's move on to NLP.

Natural Language Processing

Converting an AWD-LSTM language model into a transfer learning classifier, as we did in Chapter 10, follows a very similar process to what we did with `cnn_learner` in the first section of this chapter. We do not need a "meta" dictionary in this case, because we do not have such a variety of architectures to support in the body. All we need to do is select the stacked RNN for the encoder in the language model, which is a single PyTorch module. This encoder will provide an activation for every word of the input, because a language model needs to output a prediction for every next word.

To create a classifier from this, we use an approach described in the ULMFiT paper (*https://oreil.ly/3hdSj*) as "BPTT for Text Classification (BPT3C)":

> We divide the document into fixed-length batches of size *b*. At the beginning of each batch, the model is initialized with the final state of the previous batch; we keep track of the hidden states for mean and max-pooling; gradients are back-propagated to the batches whose hidden states contributed to the final prediction. In practice, we use variable length backpropagation sequences.

In other words, the classifier contains a `for` loop, which loops over each batch of a sequence. The state is maintained across batches, and the activations of each batch are stored. At the end, we use the same average and max concatenated pooling trick that we use for computer vision models—but this time, we do not pool over CNN grid cells, but over RNN sequences.

For this `for` loop, we need to gather our data in batches, but each text needs to be treated separately, as they each have their own labels. However, it's very likely that those texts won't all be of the same length, which means we won't be able to put them all in the same array, as we did with the language model.

That's where padding is going to help: when grabbing a bunch of texts, we determine the one with the greatest length; then we fill the ones that are shorter with a special token called `xxpad`. To avoid extreme cases of having a text with 2,000 tokens in the same batch as a text with 10 tokens (so a lot of padding, and a lot of wasted computation), we alter the randomness by making sure texts of comparable size are put together. The texts will still be in a somewhat random order for the training set (for the validation set, we can simply sort them by order of length), but not completely so.

This is done automatically behind the scenes by the fastai library when creating our `DataLoaders`.

Tabular

Finally, let's take a look at `fastai.tabular` models. (We don't need to look at collaborative filtering separately, since we've already seen that these models are just tabular models or use the dot product approach, which we implemented earlier from scratch.)

Here is the `forward` method for `TabularModel`:

```
if self.n_emb != 0:
    x = [e(x_cat[:,i]) for i,e in enumerate(self.embeds)]
    x = torch.cat(x, 1)
    x = self.emb_drop(x)
```

```
if self.n_cont != 0:
    x_cont = self.bn_cont(x_cont)
    x = torch.cat([x, x_cont], 1) if self.n_emb != 0 else x_cont
return self.layers(x)
```

We won't show __init__ here, since it's not that interesting, but will look at each line of code in forward in turn. The first line is just testing whether there are any embeddings to deal with—we can skip this section if we have only continuous variables:

```
if self.n_emb != 0:
```

self.embeds contains the embedding matrices, so this gets the activations of each

```
x = [e(x_cat[:,i]) for i,e in enumerate(self.embeds)]
```

and concatenates them into a single tensor:

```
x = torch.cat(x, 1)
```

Then dropout is applied. You can pass embed_p to __init__ to change this value:

```
x = self.emb_drop(x)
```

Now we test whether there are any continuous variables to deal with:

```
if self.n_cont != 0:
```

They are passed through a batchnorm layer

```
x_cont = self.bn_cont(x_cont)
```

and concatenated with the embedding activations, if there were any:

```
x = torch.cat([x, x_cont], 1) if self.n_emb != 0 else x_cont
```

Finally, this is passed through the linear layers (each of which includes batchnorm, if use_bn is True, and dropout, if ps is set to some value or list of values):

```
return self.layers(x)
```

Congratulations! Now you know every single piece of the architectures used in the fastai library!

Conclusion

As you can see, the details of deep learning architectures need not scare you now. You can look inside the code of fastai and PyTorch and see just what is going on. More importantly, try to understand *why* it's going on. Take a look at the papers that are referenced in the code, and try to see how the code matches up to the algorithms that are described.

Now that we have investigated all of the pieces of a model and the data that is passed into it, we can consider what this means for practical deep learning. If you have unlimited data, unlimited memory, and unlimited time, then the advice is easy: train a huge model on all of your data for a really long time. But the reason that deep learning is not straightforward is that your data, memory, and time are typically limited. If you are running out of memory or time, the solution is to train a smaller model. If you are not able to train for long enough to overfit, you are not taking advantage of the capacity of your model.

So, step 1 is to get to the point where you can overfit. Then the question is how to reduce that overfitting. Figure 15-3 shows how we recommend prioritizing the steps from there.

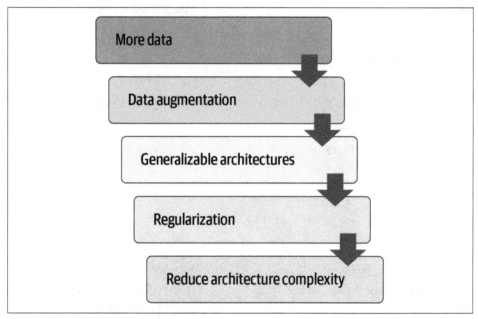

Figure 15-3. Steps to reducing overfitting

Many practitioners, when faced with an overfitting model, start at exactly the wrong end of this diagram. Their starting point is to use a smaller model or more regularization. Using a smaller model should be absolutely the last step you take, unless training your model is taking up too much time or memory. Reducing the size of your model reduces the ability of your model to learn subtle relationships in your data.

Instead, your first step should be to seek to *create more data*. That could involve adding more labels to data that you already have, finding additional tasks that your model could be asked to solve (or, to think of it another way, identifying different kinds of labels that you could model), or creating additional synthetic data by using more or different data augmentation techniques. Thanks to the development of Mixup and similar approaches, effective data augmentation is now available for nearly all kinds of data.

Once you've got as much data as you think you can reasonably get hold of, and are using it as effectively as possible by taking advantage of all the labels that you can find and doing all the augmentation that makes sense, if you are still overfitting, you should think about using more generalizable architectures. For instance, adding batch normalization may improve generalization.

If you are still overfitting after doing the best you can at using your data and tuning your architecture, you can take a look at regularization. Generally speaking, adding dropout to the last layer or two will do a good job of regularizing your model. However, as we learned from the story of the development of AWD-LSTM, adding dropout of different types throughout your model can often help even more. Generally speaking, a larger model with more regularization is more flexible, and can therefore be more accurate than a smaller model with less regularization.

Only after considering all of these options would we recommend that you try using a smaller version of your architecture.

Questionnaire

1. What is the head of a neural net?
2. What is the body of a neural net?
3. What is "cutting" a neural net? Why do we need to do this for transfer learning?
4. What is `model_meta`? Try printing it to see what's inside.
5. Read the source code for `create_head` and make sure you understand what each line does.
6. Look at the output of `create_head` and make sure you understand why each layer is there, and how the `create_head` source created it.
7. Figure out how to change the dropout, layer size, and number of layers created by `cnn_learner`, and see if you can find values that result in better accuracy from the pet recognizer.
8. What does `AdaptiveConcatPool2d` do?
9. What is nearest neighbor interpolation? How can it be used to upsample convolutional activations?
10. What is a transposed convolution? What is another name for it?
11. Create a conv layer with `transpose=True` and apply it to an image. Check the output shape.
12. Draw the U-Net architecture.
13. What is BPTT for Text Classification (BPT3C)?
14. How do we handle different length sequences in BPT3C?

15. Try to run each line of `TabularModel.forward` separately, one line per cell, in a notebook, and look at the input and output shapes at each step.

16. How is `self.layers` defined in `TabularModel`?

17. What are the five steps for preventing overfitting?

18. Why don't we reduce architecture complexity before trying other approaches to preventing overfitting?

Further Research

1. Write your own custom head and try training the pet recognizer with it. See if you can get a better result than fastai's default.

2. Try switching between `AdaptiveConcatPool2d` and `AdaptiveAvgPool2d` in a CNN head and see what difference it makes.

3. Write your own custom splitter to create a separate parameter group for every ResNet block, and a separate group for the stem. Try training with it, and see if it improves the pet recognizer.

4. Read the online chapter about generative image models, and create your own colorizer, super-resolution model, or style transfer model.

5. Create a custom head using nearest neighbor interpolation and use it to do segmentation on CamVid.

CHAPTER 16

The Training Process

You now know how to create state-of-the-art architectures for computer vision, natural language processing, tabular analysis, and collaborative filtering, and you know how to train them quickly. So we're done, right? Not quite yet. We still have to explore a little bit more of the training process.

We explained in Chapter 4 the basis of stochastic gradient descent: pass a mini-batch to the model, compare it to our target with the loss function, then compute the gradients of this loss function with regard to each weight before updating the weights with the formula:

```
new_weight = weight - lr * weight.grad
```

We implemented this from scratch in a training loop, and saw that PyTorch provides a simple `nn.SGD` class that does this calculation for each parameter for us. In this chapter, we will build some faster optimizers, using a flexible foundation. But that's not all we might want to change in the training process. For any tweak of the training loop, we will need a way to add some code to the basis of SGD. The fastai library has a system of callbacks to do this, and we will teach you all about it.

Let's start with standard SGD to get a baseline; then we will introduce the most commonly used optimizers.

Establishing a Baseline

First we'll create a baseline using plain SGD and compare it to fastai's default optimizer. We'll start by grabbing Imagenette with the same `get_data` we used in Chapter 14:

```
dls = get_data(URLs.IMAGENETTE_160, 160, 128)
```

We'll create a ResNet-34 without pretraining and pass along any arguments received:

```
def get_learner(**kwargs):
    return cnn_learner(dls, resnet34, pretrained=False,
                       metrics=accuracy, **kwargs).to_fp16()
```

Here's the default fastai optimizer, with the usual 3e-3 learning rate:

```
learn = get_learner()
learn.fit_one_cycle(3, 0.003)
```

epoch	train_loss	valid_loss	accuracy	time
0	2.571932	2.685040	0.322548	00:11
1	1.904674	1.852589	0.437452	00:11
2	1.586909	1.374908	0.594904	00:11

Now let's try plain SGD. We can pass `opt_func` (optimization function) to `cnn_learner` to get fastai to use any optimizer:

```
learn = get_learner(opt_func=SGD)
```

The first thing to look at is `lr_find`:

```
learn.lr_find()
```

```
(0.017378008365631102, 3.019951861915615e-07)
```

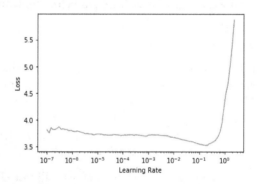

It looks like we'll need to use a higher learning rate than we normally use:

```
learn.fit_one_cycle(3, 0.03, moms=(0,0,0))
```

epoch	train_loss	valid_loss	accuracy	time
0	2.969412	2.214596	0.242038	00:09
1	2.442730	1.845950	0.362548	00:09
2	2.157159	1.741143	0.408917	00:09

Because accelerating SGD with momentum is such a good idea, fastai does this by default in `fit_one_cycle`, so we turn it off with `moms=(0,0,0)`. We'll be discussing momentum shortly.

Clearly, plain SGD isn't training as fast as we'd like. So let's learn some tricks to get accelerated training!

A Generic Optimizer

To build up our accelerated SGD tricks, we'll need to start with a nice flexible optimizer foundation. No library prior to fastai provided such a foundation, but during fastai's development, we realized that all the optimizer improvements we'd seen in the academic literature could be handled using *optimizer callbacks*. These are small pieces of code that we can compose, mix, and match in an optimizer to build the optimizer step. They are called by fastai's lightweight `Optimizer` class. These are the definitions in `Optimizer` of the two key methods that we've been using in this book:

```
def zero_grad(self):
    for p,*_ in self.all_params():
        p.grad.detach_()
        p.grad.zero_()

def step(self):
    for p,pg,state,hyper in self.all_params():
        for cb in self.cbs:
            state = _update(state, cb(p, **{**state, **hyper}))
        self.state[p] = state
```

As we saw when training an MNIST model from scratch, `zero_grad` just loops through the parameters of the model and sets the gradients to zero. It also calls `detach_`, which removes any history of gradient computation, since it won't be needed after `zero_grad`.

The more interesting method is `step`, which loops through the callbacks (`cbs`) and calls them to update the parameters (the `_update` function just calls `state.update` if there's anything returned by `cb`). As you can see, `Optimizer` doesn't do any SGD steps itself. Let's see how we can add SGD to `Optimizer`.

Here's an optimizer callback that does a single SGD step, by multiplying `-lr` by the gradients and adding that to the parameter (when `Tensor.add_` in PyTorch is passed two parameters, they are multiplied together before the addition):

```
def sgd_cb(p, lr, **kwargs): p.data.add_(-lr, p.grad.data)
```

We can pass this to `Optimizer` using the `cbs` parameter; we'll need to use `partial` since `Learner` will call this function to create our optimizer later:

```
opt_func = partial(Optimizer, cbs=[sgd_cb])
```

Let's see if this trains:

```
learn = get_learner(opt_func=opt_func)
learn.fit(3, 0.03)
```

epoch	train_loss	valid_loss	accuracy	time
0	2.730918	2.009971	0.332739	00:09
1	2.204893	1.747202	0.441529	00:09
2	1.875621	1.684515	0.445350	00:09

It's working! So that's how we create SGD from scratch in fastai. Now let's see what this "momentum" is.

Momentum

As described in Chapter 4, SGD can be thought of as standing at the top of a mountain and working your way down by taking a step in the direction of the steepest slope at each point in time. But what if we have a ball rolling down the mountain? It won't, at each given point, exactly follow the direction of the gradient, as it will have *momentum*. A ball with more momentum (for instance, a heavier ball) will skip over little bumps and holes, and be more likely to get to the bottom of a bumpy mountain. A ping pong ball, on the other hand, will get stuck in every little crevice.

So how can we bring this idea over to SGD? We can use a moving average, instead of only the current gradient, to make our step:

```
weight.avg = beta * weight.avg + (1-beta) * weight.grad
new_weight = weight - lr * weight.avg
```

Here `beta` is some number we choose that defines how much momentum to use. If `beta` is 0, the first equation becomes `weight.avg = weight.grad`, so we end up with plain SGD. But if it's a number close to 1, the main direction chosen is an average of the previous steps. (If you have done a bit of statistics, you may recognize in the first equation an *exponentially weighted moving average*, which is often used to denoise data and get the underlying tendency.)

Note that we are writing `weight.avg` to highlight the fact that we need to store the moving averages for each parameter of the model (they all their own independent moving averages).

Figure 16-1 shows an example of noisy data for a single parameter with the momentum curve plotted in red, and the gradients of the parameter plotted in blue. The gradients increase, then decrease, and the momentum does a good job of following the general trend without getting too influenced by noise.

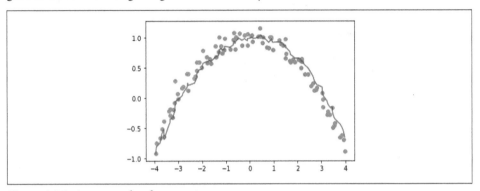

Figure 16-1. An example of momentum

It works particularly well if the loss function has narrow canyons we need to navigate: vanilla SGD would send us bouncing from one side to the other, while SGD with momentum will average those to roll smoothly down the side. The parameter `beta` determines the strength of the momentum we are using: with a small `beta`, we stay closer to the actual gradient values, whereas with a high `beta`, we will mostly go in the direction of the average of the gradients and it will take a while before any change in the gradients makes that trend move.

With a large `beta`, we might miss that the gradients have changed directions and roll over a small local minima. This is a desired side effect: intuitively, when we show a new input to our model, it will look like something in the training set but won't be *exactly* like it. It will correspond to a point in the loss function that is close to the minimum we ended up with at the end of training, but not exactly *at* that minimum. So, we would rather end up training in a wide minimum, where nearby points have approximately the same loss (or if you prefer, a point where the loss is as flat as possible). Figure 16-2 shows how the chart in Figure 16-1 varies as we change `beta`.

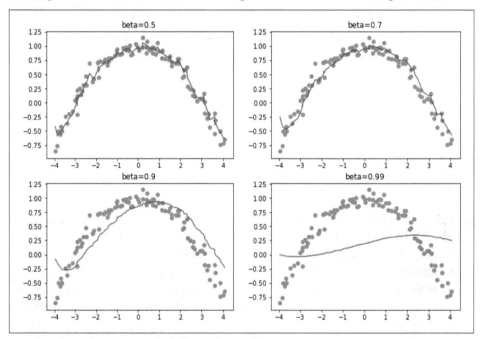

Figure 16-2. Momentum with different beta values

We can see in these examples that a `beta` that's too high results in the overall changes in gradient getting ignored. In SGD with momentum, a value of `beta` that is often used is 0.9.

`fit_one_cycle` by default starts with a `beta` of 0.95, gradually adjusts it to 0.85, and then gradually moves it back to 0.95 at the end of training. Let's see how our training goes with momentum added to plain SGD.

To add momentum to our optimizer, we'll first need to keep track of the moving average gradient, which we can do with another callback. When an optimizer callback returns a `dict`, it is used to update the state of the optimizer and is passed back to the optimizer on the next step. So this callback will keep track of the gradient averages in a parameter called `grad_avg`:

```
def average_grad(p, mom, grad_avg=None, **kwargs):
    if grad_avg is None: grad_avg = torch.zeros_like(p.grad.data)
    return {'grad_avg': grad_avg*mom + p.grad.data}
```

To use it, we just have to replace `p.grad.data` with `grad_avg` in our step function:

```
def momentum_step(p, lr, grad_avg, **kwargs): p.data.add_(-lr, grad_avg)

opt_func = partial(Optimizer, cbs=[average_grad,momentum_step], mom=0.9)
```

`Learner` will automatically schedule `mom` and `lr`, so `fit_one_cycle` will even work with our custom `Optimizer`:

```
learn = get_learner(opt_func=opt_func)
learn.fit_one_cycle(3, 0.03)
```

epoch	train_loss	valid_loss	accuracy	time
0	2.856000	2.493429	0.246115	00:10
1	2.504205	2.463813	0.348280	00:10
2	2.187387	1.755670	0.418853	00:10

```
learn.recorder.plot_sched()
```

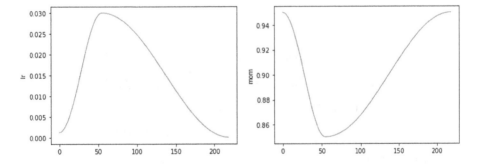

We're still not getting great results, so let's see what else we can do.

RMSProp

RMSProp is another variant of SGD introduced by Geoffrey Hinton in Lecture 6e of his Coursera class "Neural Networks for Machine Learning" (*https://oreil.ly/FVcIE*). The main difference from SGD is that it uses an adaptive learning rate: instead of using the same learning rate for every parameter, each parameter gets its own specific learning rate controlled by a global learning rate. That way, we can speed up training by giving a higher learning rate to the weights that need to change a lot, while the ones that are good enough get a lower learning rate.

How do we decide which parameters should have a high learning rate and which should not? We can look at the gradients to get an idea. If a parameter's gradients have been close to zero for a while, that parameter will need a higher learning rate because the loss is flat. On the other hand, if the gradients are all over the place, we should probably be careful and pick a low learning rate to avoid divergence. We can't just average the gradients to see if they're changing a lot, because the average of a large positive and a large negative number is close to zero. Instead, we can use the usual trick of either taking the absolute value or the squared values (and then taking the square root after the mean).

Once again, to determine the general tendency behind the noise, we will use a moving average—specifically, the moving average of the gradients squared. Then we will update the corresponding weight by using the current gradient (for the direction) divided by the square root of this moving average (that way, if it's low, the effective learning rate will be higher, and if it's high, the effective learning rate will be lower):

```
w.square_avg = alpha * w.square_avg + (1-alpha) * (w.grad ** 2)
new_w = w - lr * w.grad / math.sqrt(w.square_avg + eps)
```

The eps (*epsilon*) is added for numerical stability (usually set at 1e-8), and the default value for alpha is usually 0.99.

We can add this to Optimizer by doing much the same thing we did for avg_grad, but with an extra **2:

```
def average_sqr_grad(p, sqr_mom, sqr_avg=None, **kwargs):
    if sqr_avg is None: sqr_avg = torch.zeros_like(p.grad.data)
    return {'sqr_avg': sqr_mom*sqr_avg + (1-sqr_mom)*p.grad.data**2}
```

And we can define our step function and optimizer as before:

```
def rms_prop_step(p, lr, sqr_avg, eps, grad_avg=None, **kwargs):
    denom = sqr_avg.sqrt().add_(eps)
    p.data.addcdiv_(-lr, p.grad, denom)

opt_func = partial(Optimizer, cbs=[average_sqr_grad,rms_prop_step],
                   sqr_mom=0.99, eps=1e-7)
```

Let's try it out:

```
learn = get_learner(opt_func=opt_func)
learn.fit_one_cycle(3, 0.003)
```

epoch	train_loss	valid_loss	accuracy	time
0	2.766912	1.845900	0.402548	00:11
1	2.194586	1.510269	0.504459	00:11
2	1.869099	1.447939	0.544968	00:11

Much better! Now we just have to bring these ideas together, and we have Adam, fastai's default optimizer.

Adam

Adam mixes the ideas of SGD with momentum and RMSProp together: it uses the moving average of the gradients as a direction and divides by the square root of the moving average of the gradients squared to give an adaptive learning rate to each parameter.

There is one other difference in how Adam calculates moving averages. It takes the *unbiased* moving average, which is

```
w.avg = beta * w.avg + (1-beta) * w.grad
unbias_avg = w.avg / (1 - (beta**(i+1)))
```

if we are the i-th iteration (starting at 0 as Python does). This divisor of 1 - (beta**(i+1)) makes sure the unbiased average looks more like the gradients at the beginning (since beta < 1, the denominator is very quickly close to 1).

Putting everything together, our update step looks like this:

```
w.avg = beta1 * w.avg + (1-beta1) * w.grad
unbias_avg = w.avg / (1 - (beta1**(i+1)))
w.sqr_avg = beta2 * w.sqr_avg + (1-beta2) * (w.grad ** 2)
new_w = w - lr * unbias_avg / sqrt(w.sqr_avg + eps)
```

As for RMSProp, eps is usually set to 1e-8, and the default for (beta1,beta2) suggested by the literature is (0.9,0.999).

In fastai, Adam is the default optimizer we use since it allows faster training, but we've found that beta2=0.99 is better suited to the type of schedule we are using. beta1 is the momentum parameter, which we specify with the argument moms in our call to fit_one_cycle. As for eps, fastai uses a default of 1e-5. eps is not just useful for numerical stability. A higher eps limits the maximum value of the adjusted learning rate. To take an extreme example, if eps is 1, then the adjusted learning will never be higher than the base learning rate.

Rather than show all the code for this in the book, we'll let you look at the optimizer notebook in fastai's *https://oreil.ly/24_O[GitHub repository]* (browse the *_nbs* folder and search for the notebook called *optimizer*). You'll see all the code we've shown so far, along with Adam and other optimizers, and lots of examples and tests.

One thing that changes when we go from SGD to Adam is the way we apply weight decay, and it can have important consequences.

Decoupled Weight Decay

Weight decay, which we've discussed in Chapter 8, is equivalent to (in the case of vanilla SGD) updating the parameters with the following:

```
new_weight = weight - lr*weight.grad - lr*wd*weight
```

The last part of that formula explains the name of this technique: each weight is decayed by a factor of `lr * wd`.

The other name for weight decay is *L2 regularization*, which consists of adding the sum of all squared weights to the loss (multiplied by the weight decay). As we saw in Chapter 8, this can be directly expressed on the gradients:

```
weight.grad += wd*weight
```

For SGD, those two formulas are equivalent. However, this equivalence holds only for standard SGD because, as we've seen with momentum, RMSProp, or in Adam, the update has some additional formulas around the gradient.

Most libraries use the second formulation, but it was pointed out in "Decoupled Weight Decay Regularization" (*https://oreil.ly/w37Ac*) by Ilya Loshchilov and Frank Hutter that the first one is the only correct approach with the Adam optimizer or momentum, which is why fastai makes it its default.

Now you know everything that is hidden behind the line `learn.fit_one_cycle`!

Optimizers are only one part of the training process, however. When you need to change the training loop with fastai, you can't directly change the code inside the library. Instead, we have designed a system of callbacks to let you write any tweaks you like in independent blocks that you can then mix and match.

Callbacks

Sometimes you need to change how things work a little bit. In fact, we have already seen examples of this: Mixup, fp16 training, resetting the model after each epoch for training RNNs, and so forth. How do we go about making these kinds of tweaks to the training process?

We've seen the basic training loop, which, with the help of the `Optimizer` class, looks like this for a single epoch:

```
for xb,yb in dl:
    loss = loss_func(model(xb), yb)
    loss.backward()
    opt.step()
    opt.zero_grad()
```

Figure 16-3 shows how to picture that.

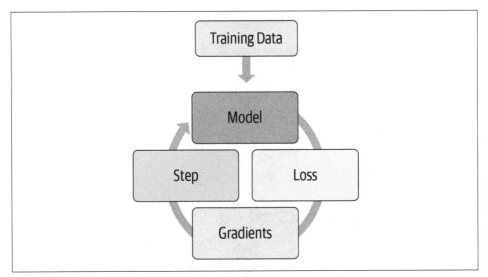

Figure 16-3. Basic training loop

The usual way for deep learning practitioners to customize the training loop is to make a copy of an existing training loop, and then insert the code necessary for their particular changes into it. This is how nearly all code that you find online will look. But it has serious problems.

It's not likely that some particular tweaked training loop is going to meet your particular needs. Hundreds of changes can be made to a training loop, which means there are billions and billions of possible permutations. You can't just copy one tweak from a training loop here, another from a training loop there, and expect them all to work together. Each will be based on different assumptions about the environment that it's working in, use different naming conventions, and expect the data to be in different formats.

We need a way to allow users to insert their own code at any part of the training loop, but in a consistent and well-defined way. Computer scientists have already come up with an elegant solution: the callback. A *callback* is a piece of code that you write and inject into another piece of code at a predefined point. In fact, callbacks have been used with deep learning training loops for years. The problem is that in previous libraries, it was possible to inject code in only a small subset of places where this may have been required—and, more importantly, callbacks were not able to do all the things they needed to do.

In order to be just as flexible as manually copying and pasting a training loop and directly inserting code into it, a callback must be able to read every possible piece of information available in the training loop, modify all of it as needed, and fully control when a batch, epoch, or even the whole training loop should be terminated. fastai is the first library to provide all of this functionality. It modifies the training loop so it looks like Figure 16-4.

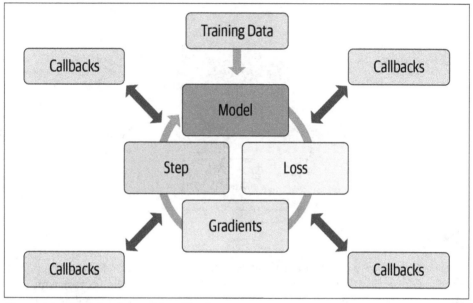

Figure 16-4. Training loop with callbacks

The effectiveness of this approach has been borne out over the last couple of years— by using the fastai callback system, we were able to implement every single new paper we tried and fulfill every user request for modifying the training loop. The training loop itself has not required modifications. Figure 16-5 shows just a few of the callbacks that have been added.

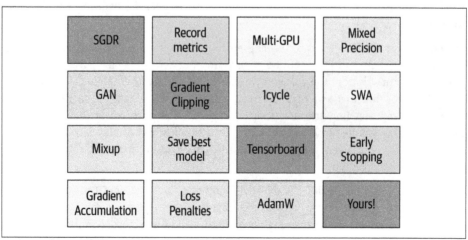

Figure 16-5. Some fastai callbacks

This is important because it means that whatever ideas we have in our heads, we can implement them. We need never dig into the source code of PyTorch or fastai and hack together a one-off system to try out our ideas. And when we do implement our own callbacks to develop our own ideas, we know that they will work together with all of the other functionality provided by fastai—so we will get progress bars, mixed-precision training, hyperparameter annealing, and so forth.

Another advantage is that it makes it easy to gradually remove or add functionality and perform ablation studies. You just need to adjust the list of callbacks you pass along to your fit function.

As an example, here is the fastai source code that is run for each batch of the training loop:

```
try:
    self._split(b);                                   self('begin_batch')
    self.pred = self.model(*self.xb);                 self('after_pred')
    self.loss = self.loss_func(self.pred, *self.yb);  self('after_loss')
    if not self.training: return
    self.loss.backward();                             self('after_backward')
    self.opt.step();                                  self('after_step')
    self.opt.zero_grad()
except CancelBatchException:                          self('after_cancel_batch')
finally:                                              self('after_batch')
```

The calls of the form self('...') are where the callbacks are called. As you see, this happens after every step. The callback will receive the entire state of training and can also modify it. For instance, the input data and target labels are in self.xb and self.yb, respectively; a callback can modify these to modify the data the training loop sees. It can also modify self.loss or even the gradients.

Let's see how this works in practice by writing a callback.

Creating a Callback

When you want to write your own callback, the full list of available events is as follows:

begin_fit
    Called before doing anything; ideal for initial setup.

begin_epoch
    Called at the beginning of each epoch; useful for any behavior you need to reset at each epoch.

begin_train
    Called at the beginning of the training part of an epoch.

begin_batch

Called at the beginning of each batch, just after drawing said batch. It can be used to do any setup necessary for the batch (like hyperparameter scheduling) or to change the input/target before it goes into the model (for instance, by applying Mixup).

after_pred

Called after computing the output of the model on the batch. It can be used to change that output before it's fed to the loss function.

after_loss

Called after the loss has been computed, but before the backward pass. It can be used to add a penalty to the loss (AR or TAR in RNN training, for instance).

after_backward

Called after the backward pass, but before the update of the parameters. It can be used to make changes to the gradients before said update (via gradient clipping, for instance).

after_step

Called after the step and before the gradients are zeroed.

after_batch

Called at the end of a batch, to perform any required cleanup before the next one.

after_train

Called at the end of the training phase of an epoch.

begin_validate

Called at the beginning of the validation phase of an epoch; useful for any setup needed specifically for validation.

after_validate

Called at the end of the validation part of an epoch.

after_epoch

Called at the end of an epoch, for any cleanup before the next one.

after_fit

Called at the end of training, for final cleanup.

The elements of this list are available as attributes of the special variable event, so you can just type event. and hit Tab in your notebook to see a list of all the options

Let's take a look at an example. Do you recall how in Chapter 12 we needed to ensure that our special reset method was called at the start of training and validation for each epoch? We used the `ModelResetter` callback provided by fastai to do this for us. But how does it work exactly? Here's the full source code for that class:

```
class ModelResetter(Callback):
    def begin_train(self):    self.model.reset()
    def begin_validate(self): self.model.reset()
```

Yes, that's actually it! It just does what we said in the preceding paragraph: after completing training or validation for an epoch, call a method named `reset`.

Callbacks are often "short and sweet" like this one. In fact, let's look at one more. Here's the fastai source for the callback that adds RNN regularization (AR and TAR):

```
class RNNRegularizer(Callback):
    def __init__(self, alpha=0., beta=0.): self.alpha,self.beta = alpha,beta

    def after_pred(self):
        self.raw_out,self.out = self.pred[1],self.pred[2]
        self.learn.pred = self.pred[0]

    def after_loss(self):
        if not self.training: return
        if self.alpha != 0.:
            self.learn.loss += self.alpha * self.out[-1].float().pow(2).mean()
        if self.beta != 0.:
            h = self.raw_out[-1]
            if len(h)>1:
                self.learn.loss += self.beta * (h[:,1:] - h[:,:-1]
                                               ).float().pow(2).mean()
```

Code It Yourself

Go back and reread "Activation Regularization and Temporal Activation Regularization" on page 397, and then take another look at the code here. Make sure you understand what it's doing and why.

In both of these examples, notice how we can access attributes of the training loop by directly checking `self.model` or `self.pred`. That's because a `Callback` will always try to get an attribute it doesn't have inside the `Learner` associated with it. These are shortcuts for `self.learn.model` or `self.learn.pred`. Note that they work for reading attributes, but not for writing them, which is why when `RNNRegularizer` changes the loss or the predictions, you see `self.learn.loss =` or `self.learn.pred =`.

When writing a callback, the following attributes of `Learner` are available:

`model`
    The model used for training/validation.

data

    The underlying `DataLoaders`.

loss_func

    The loss function used.

opt

    The optimizer used to update the model parameters.

opt_func

    The function used to create the optimizer.

cbs

    The list containing all the `Callbacks`.

dl

    The current `DataLoader` used for iteration.

x/xb

    The last input drawn from `self.dl` (potentially modified by callbacks). `xb` is always a tuple (potentially with one element), and `x` is detuplified. You can assign only to `xb`.

y/yb

    The last target drawn from `self.dl` (potentially modified by callbacks). `yb` is always a tuple (potentially with one element), and `y` is detuplified. You can assign only to `yb`.

pred

    The last predictions from `self.model` (potentially modified by callbacks).

loss

    The last computed loss (potentially modified by callbacks).

n_epoch

    The number of epochs in this training.

n_iter

    The number of iterations in the current `self.dl`.

epoch

    The current epoch index (from 0 to `n_epoch-1`).

iter

    The current iteration index in `self.dl` (from 0 to `n_iter-1`).

The following attributes are added by `TrainEvalCallback` and should be available unless you went out of your way to remove that callback:

`train_iter`
  The number of training iterations done since the beginning of this training

`pct_train`
  The percentage of training iterations completed (from 0 to 1)

`training`
  A flag to indicate whether we're in training mode

The following attribute is added by `Recorder` and should be available unless you went out of your way to remove that callback:

`smooth_loss`
  An exponentially averaged version of the training loss

Callbacks can also interrupt any part of the training loop by using a system of exceptions.

Callback Ordering and Exceptions

Sometimes callbacks need to be able to tell fastai to skip over a batch or an epoch, or stop training altogether. For instance, consider `TerminateOnNaNCallback`. This handy callback will automatically stop training anytime the loss becomes infinite or NaN (*not a number*). Here's the fastai source for this callback:

```
class TerminateOnNaNCallback(Callback):
    run_before=Recorder
    def after_batch(self):
        if torch.isinf(self.loss) or torch.isnan(self.loss):
            raise CancelFitException
```

The line `raise CancelFitException` tells the training loop to interrupt training at this point. The training loop catches this exception and does not run any further training or validation. The callback control flow exceptions available are as follows:

`CancelBatchException`
  Skip the rest of this batch and go to `after_batch`.

`CancelTrainException`
  Skip the rest of the training part of the epoch and go to `after_train`.

`CancelValidException`
  Skip the rest of the validation part of the epoch and go to `after_validate`.

`CancelEpochException`
  Skip the rest of this epoch and go to `after_epoch`.

`CancelFitException`
  Interrupt training and go to `after_fit`.

You can detect if one of those exceptions has occurred and add code that executes right after with the following events:

`after_cancel_batch`
  Reached immediately after a `CancelBatchException` before proceeding to `after_batch`

`after_cancel_train`
  Reached immediately after a `CancelTrainException` before proceeding to `after_train`

`after_cancel_valid`
  Reached immediately after a `CancelValidException` before proceeding to `after_valid`

`after_cancel_epoch`
  Reached immediately after a `CancelEpochException` before proceeding to `after_epoch`

`after_cancel_fit`
  Reached immediately after a `CancelFitException` before proceeding to `after_fit`

Sometimes callbacks need to be called in a particular order. For example, in the case of `TerminateOnNaNCallback`, it's important that `Recorder` runs its `after_batch` after this callback, to avoid registering an NaN loss. You can specify `run_before` (this callback must run before...) or `run_after` (this callback must run after...) in your callback to ensure the ordering that you need.

Conclusion

In this chapter, we took a close look at the training loop, exploring variants of SGD and why they can be more powerful. At the time of writing, developing new optimizers is an active area of research, so by the time you read this chapter, there may be an addendum on the book's website (*https://book.fast.ai*) that presents new variants. Be sure to check out how our general optimizer framework can help you implement new optimizers quickly.

We also examined the powerful callback system that allows you to customize every bit of the training loop by enabling you to inspect and modify any parameter you like between each step.

Questionnaire

1. What is the equation for a step of SGD, in math or code (as you prefer)?
2. What do we pass to `cnn_learner` to use a nondefault optimizer?
3. What are optimizer callbacks?
4. What does `zero_grad` do in an optimizer?
5. What does `step` do in an optimizer? How is it implemented in the general optimizer?
6. Rewrite `sgd_cb` to use the `+=` operator, instead of `add_`.
7. What is momentum? Write out the equation.
8. What's a physical analogy for momentum? How does it apply in our model training settings?
9. What does a bigger value for momentum do to the gradients?
10. What are the default values of momentum for 1cycle training?
11. What is RMSProp? Write out the equation.
12. What do the squared values of the gradients indicate?
13. How does Adam differ from momentum and RMSProp?
14. Write out the equation for Adam.
15. Calculate the values of `unbias_avg` and `w.avg` for a few batches of dummy values.
16. What's the impact of having a high `eps` in Adam?
17. Read through the optimizer notebook in fastai's repo and execute it.
18. In what situations do dynamic learning rate methods like Adam change the behavior of weight decay?
19. What are the four steps of a training loop?
20. Why is using callbacks better than writing a new training loop for each tweak you want to add?
21. What aspects of the design of fastai's callback system make it as flexible as copying and pasting bits of code?
22. How can you get the list of events available to you when writing a callback?
23. Write the `ModelResetter` callback (without peeking).

24. How can you access the necessary attributes of the training loop inside a callback? When can you use or not use the shortcuts that go with them?

25. How can a callback influence the control flow of the training loop?

26. Write the `TerminateOnNaN` callback (without peeking, if possible).

27. How do you make sure your callback runs after or before another callback?

Further Research

1. Look up the "Rectified Adam" paper, implement it using the general optimizer framework, and try it out. Search for other recent optimizers that work well in practice and pick one to implement.

2. Look at the mixed-precision callback inside the documentation (*https://docs.fast.ai*). Try to understand what each event and line of code does.

3. Implement your own version of the learning rate finder from scratch. Compare it with fastai's version.

4. Look at the source code of the callbacks that ship with fastai. See if you can find one that's similar to what you're looking to do, to get some inspiration.

Foundations of Deep Learning: Wrap Up

Congratulations—you have made it to the end of the "foundations of deep learning" section of the book! You now understand how all of fastai's applications and most important architectures are built, and the recommended ways to train them—and you have all the information you need to build these from scratch. While you probably won't need to create your own training loop or batchnorm layer, for instance, knowing what is going on behind the scenes is very helpful for debugging, profiling, and deploying your solutions.

Since you understand the foundations of fastai's applications now, be sure to spend some time digging through the source notebooks and running and experimenting with parts of them. This will give you a better idea of exactly how everything in fastai is developed.

In the next section, we will be looking even further under the covers: we'll explore how the actual forward and backward passes of a neural network are done, and we will see what tools are at our disposal to get better performance. We will then continue with a project that brings together all the material in the book, which we will use to build a tool for interpreting convolutional neural networks. Last but not least, we'll finish by building fastai's `Learner` class from scratch.

PART IV

Deep Learning from Scratch

CHAPTER 17

A Neural Net from the Foundations

This chapter begins a journey where we will dig deep into the internals of the models we used in the previous chapters. We will be covering many of the same things we've seen before, but this time around we'll be looking much more closely at the implementation details, and much less closely at the practical issues of how and why things are as they are.

We will build everything from scratch, using only basic indexing into a tensor. We'll write a neural net from the ground up, and then implement backpropagation manually so we know exactly what's happening in PyTorch when we call `loss.backward`. We'll also see how to extend PyTorch with custom *autograd* functions that allow us to specify our own forward and backward computations.

Building a Neural Net Layer from Scratch

Let's start by refreshing our understanding of how matrix multiplication is used in a basic neural network. Since we're building everything up from scratch, we'll use nothing but plain Python initially (except for indexing into PyTorch tensors), and then replace the plain Python with PyTorch functionality after we've seen how to create it.

Modeling a Neuron

A neuron receives a given number of inputs and has an internal weight for each of them. It sums those weighted inputs to produce an output and adds an inner bias. In math, this can be written as

$$out = \sum_{i=1}^{n} x_i w_i + b$$

if we name our inputs $(x_1, \cdots, x_n)$, our weights $(w_1, \cdots, w_n)$, and our bias b. In code this translates into the following:

```
output = sum([x*w for x,w in zip(inputs,weights)]) + bias
```

This output is then fed into a nonlinear function called an *activation function* before being sent to another neuron. In deep learning, the most common of these is the *rectified linear unit*, or *ReLU*, which, as we've seen, is a fancy way of saying this:

```
def relu(x): return x if x >= 0 else 0
```

A deep learning model is then built by stacking a lot of those neurons in successive layers. We create a first layer with a certain number of neurons (known as the *hidden size*) and link all the inputs to each of those neurons. Such a layer is often called a *fully connected layer* or a *dense layer* (for densely connected), or a *linear layer*.

It requires you to compute, for each input and each neuron with a given weight, the dot product:

```
sum([x*w for x,w in zip(input,weight)])
```

If you have done a little bit of linear algebra, you may remember that having a lot of those dot products happens when you do a *matrix multiplication*. More precisely, if our inputs are in a matrix x with a size of batch_size by n_inputs, and if we have grouped the weights of our neurons in a matrix w of size n_neurons by n_inputs (each neuron must have the same number of weights as it has inputs) as well as all the biases in a vector b of size n_neurons, then the output of this fully connected layer is

```
y = x @ w.t() + b
```

where @ represents the matrix product and w.t() is the transpose matrix of w. The output y is then of size batch_size by n_neurons, and in position (i,j) we have this (for the mathy folks out there):

$$y_{i,j} = \sum_{k=1}^{n} x_{i,k} w_{k,j} + b_j$$

Or in code:

```
y[i,j] = sum([a * b for a,b in zip(x[i,:],w[j,:])]) + b[j]
```

The transpose is necessary because in the mathematical definition of the matrix product m @ n, the coefficient (i,j) is as follows:

```
sum([a * b for a,b in zip(m[i,:],n[:,j])])
```

So the very basic operation we need is a matrix multiplication, as it's what is hidden in the core of a neural net.

Matrix Multiplication from Scratch

Let's write a function that computes the matrix product of two tensors, before we allow ourselves to use the PyTorch version of it. We will use only the indexing in PyTorch tensors:

```
import torch
from torch import tensor
```

We'll need three nested `for` loops: one for the row indices, one for the column indices, and one for the inner sum. `ac` and `ar` stand for number of columns of `a` and number of rows of `a`, respectively (the same convention is followed for `b`), and we make sure calculating the matrix product is possible by checking that `a` has as many columns as `b` has rows:

```
def matmul(a,b):
    ar,ac = a.shape # n_rows * n_cols
    br,bc = b.shape
    assert ac==br
    c = torch.zeros(ar, bc)
    for i in range(ar):
        for j in range(bc):
            for k in range(ac): c[i,j] += a[i,k] * b[k,j]
    return c
```

To test this out, we'll pretend (using random matrices) that we're working with a small batch of 5 MNIST images, flattened into 28*28 vectors, with a linear model to turn them into 10 activations:

```
m1 = torch.randn(5,28*28)
m2 = torch.randn(784,10)
```

Let's time our function, using the Jupyter "magic" command `%time`:

```
%time t1=matmul(m1, m2)
```

```
CPU times: user 1.15 s, sys: 4.09 ms, total: 1.15 s
Wall time: 1.15 s
```

And see how that compares to PyTorch's built-in `@`?

```
%timeit -n 20 t2=m1@m2
```

```
14 µs ± 8.95 µs per loop (mean ± std. dev. of 7 runs, 20 loops each)
```

As we can see, in Python three nested loops is a bad idea! Python is a slow language, and this isn't going to be efficient. We see here that PyTorch is around 100,000 times faster than Python—and that's before we even start using the GPU!

Where does this difference come from? PyTorch didn't write its matrix multiplication in Python, but rather in C++ to make it fast. In general, whenever we do computations on tensors, we will need to *vectorize* them so that we can take advantage of the speed of PyTorch, usually by using two techniques: elementwise arithmetic and broadcasting.

Elementwise Arithmetic

All the basic operators (+, -, *, /, >, <, ==) can be applied elementwise. That means if we write a+b for two tensors a and b that have the same shape, we will get a tensor composed of the sums of the elements of a and b:

```
a = tensor([10., 6, -4])
b = tensor([2., 8, 7])
a + b
```

```
tensor([12., 14.,  3.])
```

The Boolean operators will return an array of Booleans:

```
a < b
```

```
tensor([False,  True,  True])
```

If we want to know if every element of a is less than the corresponding element in b, or if two tensors are equal, we need to combine those elementwise operations with torch.all:

```
(a < b).all(), (a==b).all()
```

```
(tensor(False), tensor(False))
```

Reduction operations like all, sum, and mean return tensors with only one element, called *rank-0 tensors*. If you want to convert this to a plain Python Boolean or number, you need to call .item:

```
(a + b).mean().item()
```

```
9.666666984558105
```

The elementwise operations work on tensors of any rank, as long as they have the same shape:

```
m = tensor([[1., 2, 3], [4,5,6], [7,8,9]])
m*m
```

```
tensor([[ 1.,  4.,  9.],
        [16., 25., 36.],
        [49., 64., 81.]])
```

However, you can't perform elementwise operations on tensors that don't have the same shape (unless they are broadcastable, as discussed in the next section):

```
n = tensor([[1., 2, 3], [4,5,6]])
m*n
```

```
RuntimeError: The size of tensor a (3) must match the size of tensor b (2) at
dimension 0
```

With elementwise arithmetic, we can remove one of our three nested loops: we can multiply the tensors that correspond to the i-th row of a and the j-th column of b before summing all the elements, which will speed things up because the inner loop will now be executed by PyTorch at C speed.

To access one column or row, we can simply write a[i,:] or b[:,j]. The : means take everything in that dimension. We could restrict this and take only a slice of that dimension by passing a range, like 1:5, instead of just :. In that case, we would take the elements in columns 1 to 4 (the second number is noninclusive).

One simplification is that we can always omit a trailing colon, so a[i,:] can be abbreviated to a[i]. With all of that in mind, we can write a new version of our matrix multiplication:

```
def matmul(a,b):
    ar,ac = a.shape
    br,bc = b.shape
    assert ac==br
    c = torch.zeros(ar, bc)
    for i in range(ar):
        for j in range(bc): c[i,j] = (a[i] * b[:,j]).sum()
    return c

%timeit -n 20 t3 = matmul(m1,m2)

1.7 ms ± 88.1 µs per loop (mean ± std. dev. of 7 runs, 20 loops each)
```

We're already ~700 times faster, just by removing that inner for loop! And that's just the beginning—with broadcasting, we can remove another loop and get an even more important speedup.

Broadcasting

As we discussed in Chapter 4, *broadcasting* is a term introduced by the Numpy Library (*https://oreil.ly/nlV7Q*) that describes how tensors of different ranks are treated during arithmetic operations. For instance, it's obvious there is no way to add a 3×3 matrix with a 4×5 matrix, but what if we want to add one scalar (which can be represented as a 1×1 tensor) with a matrix? Or a vector of size 3 with a 3×4 matrix? In both cases, we can find a way to make sense of this operation.

Broadcasting gives specific rules to codify when shapes are compatible when trying to do an elementwise operation, and how the tensor of the smaller shape is expanded to match the tensor of the bigger shape. It's essential to master those rules if you want to be able to write code that executes quickly. In this section, we'll expand our previous treatment of broadcasting to understand these rules.

Broadcasting with a scalar

Broadcasting with a scalar is the easiest type of broadcasting. When we have a tensor a and a scalar, we just imagine a tensor of the same shape as a filled with that scalar and perform the operation:

```
a = tensor([10., 6, -4])
a > 0
```

```
tensor([ True,  True, False])
```

How are we able to do this comparison? 0 is being *broadcast* to have the same dimensions as a. Note that this is done without creating a tensor full of zeros in memory (that would be inefficient).

This is useful if you want to normalize your dataset by subtracting the mean (a scalar) from the entire dataset (a matrix) and dividing by the standard deviation (another scalar):

```
m = tensor([[1., 2, 3], [4,5,6], [7,8,9]])
(m - 5) / 2.73
```

```
tensor([[-1.4652, -1.0989, -0.7326],
        [-0.3663,  0.0000,  0.3663],
        [ 0.7326,  1.0989,  1.4652]])
```

What if you have different means for each row of the matrix? In that case, you will need to broadcast a vector to a matrix.

Broadcasting a vector to a matrix

We can broadcast a vector to a matrix as follows:

```
c = tensor([10.,20,30])
m = tensor([[1., 2, 3], [4,5,6], [7,8,9]])
m.shape,c.shape
```

```
(torch.Size([3, 3]), torch.Size([3]))
```

```
m + c
```

```
tensor([[11., 22., 33.],
        [14., 25., 36.],
        [17., 28., 39.]])
```

Here the elements of c are expanded to make three rows that match, making the operation possible. Again, PyTorch doesn't actually create three copies of c in memory. This is done by the expand_as method behind the scenes:

```
c.expand_as(m)
```

```
tensor([[10., 20., 30.],
        [10., 20., 30.],
        [10., 20., 30.]])
```

If we look at the corresponding tensor, we can ask for its `storage` property (which shows the actual contents of the memory used for the tensor) to check there is no useless data stored:

```
t = c.expand_as(m)
t.storage()
```

```
 10.0
 20.0
 30.0
[torch.FloatStorage of size 3]
```

Even though the tensor officially has nine elements, only three scalars are stored in memory. This is possible thanks to the clever trick of giving that dimension a *stride* of 0. on that dimension (which means that when PyTorch looks for the next row by adding the stride, it doesn't move):

```
t.stride(), t.shape
```

```
((0, 1), torch.Size([3, 3]))
```

Since m is of size 3×3, there are two ways to do broadcasting. The fact it was done on the last dimension is a convention that comes from the rules of broadcasting and has nothing to do with the way we ordered our tensors. If instead we do this, we get the same result:

```
c + m
```

```
tensor([[11., 22., 33.],
        [14., 25., 36.],
        [17., 28., 39.]])
```

In fact, it's only possible to broadcast a vector of size n with a matrix of size m by n:

```
c = tensor([10.,20,30])
m = tensor([[1., 2, 3], [4,5,6]])
c+m
```

```
tensor([[11., 22., 33.],
        [14., 25., 36.]])
```

This won't work:

```
c = tensor([10.,20])
m = tensor([[1., 2, 3], [4,5,6]])
c+m
```

```
RuntimeError: The size of tensor a (2) must match the size of tensor b (3) at
dimension 1
```

If we want to broadcast in the other dimension, we have to change the shape of our vector to make it a 3×1 matrix. This is done with the unsqueeze method in PyTorch:

```
c = tensor([10.,20,30])
m = tensor([[1., 2, 3], [4,5,6], [7,8,9]])
c = c.unsqueeze(1)
m.shape,c.shape
```

```
(torch.Size([3, 3]), torch.Size([3, 1]))
```

This time, c is expanded on the column side:

```
c+m
```

```
tensor([[11., 12., 13.],
        [24., 25., 26.],
        [37., 38., 39.]])
```

As before, only three scalars are stored in memory:

```
t = c.expand_as(m)
t.storage()
```

```
 10.0
 20.0
 30.0
[torch.FloatStorage of size 3]
```

And the expanded tensor has the right shape because the column dimension has a stride of 0:

```
t.stride(), t.shape
```

```
((1, 0), torch.Size([3, 3]))
```

With broadcasting, if we need to add dimensions, they are added by default at the beginning. When we were broadcasting before, PyTorch was executing c.unsqueeze(0) behind the scenes:

```
c = tensor([10.,20,30])
c.shape, c.unsqueeze(0).shape,c.unsqueeze(1).shape
```

```
(torch.Size([3]), torch.Size([1, 3]), torch.Size([3, 1]))
```

The unsqueeze command can be replaced by None indexing:

```
c.shape, c[None,:].shape,c[:,None].shape
```

```
(torch.Size([3]), torch.Size([1, 3]), torch.Size([3, 1]))
```

You can always omit trailing colons, and ... means all preceding dimensions:

```
c[None].shape,c[...,None].shape
```

```
(torch.Size([1, 3]), torch.Size([3, 1]))
```

With this, we can remove another `for` loop in our matrix multiplication function. Now, instead of multiplying `a[i]` with `b[:,j]`, we can multiply `a[i]` with the whole matrix b using broadcasting, and then sum the results:

```
def matmul(a,b):
    ar,ac = a.shape
    br,bc = b.shape
    assert ac==br
    c = torch.zeros(ar, bc)
    for i in range(ar):
#       c[i,j] = (a[i,:]          * b[:,j]).sum() # previous
        c[i]   = (a[i ].unsqueeze(-1) * b).sum(dim=0)
    return c

%timeit -n 20 t4 = matmul(m1,m2)

357 µs ± 7.2 µs per loop (mean ± std. dev. of 7 runs, 20 loops each)
```

We're now 3,700 times faster than our first implementation! Before we move on, let's discuss the rules of broadcasting in a little more detail.

Broadcasting rules

When operating on two tensors, PyTorch compares their shapes elementwise. It starts with the *trailing dimensions* and works its way backward, adding 1 when it meets empty dimensions. Two dimensions are *compatible* when one of the following is true:

- They are equal.
- One of them is 1, in which case that dimension is broadcast to make it the same as the other.

Arrays do not need to have the same number of dimensions. For example, if you have a 256×256×3 array of RGB values, and you want to scale each color in the image by a different value, you can multiply the image by a one-dimensional array with three values. Lining up the sizes of the trailing axes of these arrays according to the broadcast rules shows that they are compatible:

```
Image  (3d tensor): 256 x 256 x 3
Scale  (1d tensor):  (1)   (1)  3
Result (3d tensor): 256 x 256 x 3
```

However, a 2D tensor of size 256×256 isn't compatible with our image:

```
Image  (3d tensor): 256 x 256 x   3
Scale  (2d tensor):  (1)  256 x 256
Error
```

In our earlier examples with a 3×3 matrix and a vector of size 3, broadcasting was done on the rows:

```
Matrix (2d tensor):    3 x 3
Vector (1d tensor): (1)    3
Result (2d tensor):    3 x 3
```

As an exercise, try to determine what dimensions to add (and where) when you need to normalize a batch of images of size 64 x 3 x 256 x 256 with vectors of three elements (one for the mean and one for the standard deviation).

Another useful way of simplifying tensor manipulations is the use of Einstein summation convention.

Einstein Summation

Before using the PyTorch operation @ or `torch.matmul`, there is one last way we can implement matrix multiplication: *Einstein summation* (`einsum`). This is a compact representation for combining products and sums in a general way. We write an equation like this:

```
ik,kj -> ij
```

The lefthand side represents the operands dimensions, separated by commas. Here we have two tensors that each have two dimensions (i,k and k,j). The righthand side represents the result dimensions, so here we have a tensor with two dimensions i,j.

The rules of Einstein summation notation are as follows:

1. Repeated indices on the left side are implicitly summed over if they are not on the right side.
2. Each index can appear at most twice on the left side.
3. The unrepeated indices on the left side must appear on the right side.

So in our example, since k is repeated, we sum over that index. In the end, the formula represents the matrix obtained when we put in (i,j) the sum of all the coefficients (i,k) in the first tensor multiplied by the coefficients (k,j) in the second tensor... which is the matrix product!

Here is how we can code this in PyTorch:

```
def matmul(a,b): return torch.einsum('ik,kj->ij', a, b)
```

Einstein summation is a very practical way of expressing operations involving indexing and sum of products. Note that you can have one member on the lefthand side. For instance,

```
torch.einsum('ij->ji', a)
```

returns the transpose of the matrix a. You can also have three or more members:

```
torch.einsum('bi,ij,bj->b', x, y, z)
```

This will return a vector of size b, where the k-th coordinate is the sum of a[k,i] b[i,j] c[k,j]. This notation is particularly convenient when you have more dimensions because of batches. For example, if you have two batches of matrices and want to compute the matrix product per batch, you could do this:

```
torch.einsum('bik,bkj->b', x, y)
```

Let's go back to our new `matmul` implementation using `einsum` and look at its speed:

```
%timeit -n 20 t5 = matmul(m1,m2)
```

```
68.7 µs ± 4.06 µs per loop (mean ± std. dev. of 7 runs, 20 loops each)
```

As you can see, not only is it practical, but it's *very* fast. `einsum` is often the fastest way to do custom operations in PyTorch, without diving into C++ and CUDA. (But it's generally not as fast as carefully optimized CUDA code, as you see from the results in "Matrix Multiplication from Scratch" on page 495.)

Now that we know how to implement a matrix multiplication from scratch, we are ready to build our neural net—specifically, its forward and backward passes—using just matrix multiplication.

The Forward and Backward Passes

As we saw in Chapter 4, to train a model, we will need to compute all the gradients of a given loss with respect to its parameters, which is known as the *backward pass*. In a *forward pass*, where we compute the output of the model on a given input, based on the matrix products. As we define our first neural net, we will also delve into the problem of properly initializing the weights, which is crucial for making training start properly.

Defining and Initializing a Layer

We will take the example of a two-layer neural net first. As we've seen, one layer can be expressed as y = x @ w + b, with x our inputs, y our outputs, w the weights of the layer (which is of size number of inputs by number of neurons if we don't transpose as before), and b is the bias vector:

```
def lin(x, w, b): return x @ w + b
```

We can stack the second layer on top of the first, but since mathematically the composition of two linear operations is another linear operation, this makes sense only if we put something nonlinear in the middle, called an activation function. As mentioned at the start of this chapter, in deep learning applications the activation function most commonly used is a ReLU, which returns the maximum of x and 0.

We won't actually train our model in this chapter, so we'll use random tensors for our inputs and targets. Let's say our inputs are 200 vectors of size 100, which we group into one batch, and our targets are 200 random floats:

```
x = torch.randn(200, 100)
y = torch.randn(200)
```

For our two-layer model, we will need two weight matrices and two bias vectors. Let's say we have a hidden size of 50 and the output size is 1 (for one of our inputs, the corresponding output is one float in this toy example). We initialize the weights randomly and the bias at zero:

```
w1 = torch.randn(100,50)
b1 = torch.zeros(50)
w2 = torch.randn(50,1)
b2 = torch.zeros(1)
```

Then the result of our first layer is simply this:

```
l1 = lin(x, w1, b1)
l1.shape
```

```
torch.Size([200, 50])
```

Note that this formula works with our batch of inputs, and returns a batch of hidden state: l1 is a matrix of size 200 (our batch size) by 50 (our hidden size).

There is a problem with the way our model was initialized, however. To understand it, we need to look at the mean and standard deviation (std) of l1:

```
l1.mean(), l1.std()
```

```
(tensor(0.0019), tensor(10.1058))
```

The mean is close to zero, which is understandable since both our input and weight matrices have means close to zero. But the standard deviation, which represents how far away our activations go from the mean, went from 1 to 10. This is a really big problem because that's with just one layer. Modern neural nets can have hundreds of layers, so if each of them multiplies the scale of our activations by 10, we won't have numbers representable by a computer by the end of the last layer.

Indeed, if we make just 50 multiplications between x and random matrices of size 100×100, we'll have this:

```
x = torch.randn(200, 100)
for i in range(50): x = x @ torch.randn(100,100)
x[0:5,0:5]
```

```
tensor([[nan, nan, nan, nan, nan],
        [nan, nan, nan, nan, nan],
```

```
    [nan, nan, nan, nan, nan],
    [nan, nan, nan, nan, nan],
    [nan, nan, nan, nan, nan]])
```

The result is nans everywhere. So maybe the scale of our matrix was too big, and we need to have smaller weights? But if we use too small weights, we will have the opposite problem—the scale of our activations will go from 1 to 0.1, and after 50 layers we'll be left with zeros everywhere:

```
x = torch.randn(200, 100)
for i in range(50): x = x @ (torch.randn(100,100) * 0.01)
x[0:5,0:5]

tensor([[0., 0., 0., 0., 0.],
        [0., 0., 0., 0., 0.],
        [0., 0., 0., 0., 0.],
        [0., 0., 0., 0., 0.],
        [0., 0., 0., 0., 0.]])
```

So we have to scale our weight matrices exactly right so that the standard deviation of our activations stays at 1. We can compute the exact value to use mathematically, as illustrated by Xavier Glorot and Yoshua Bengio in "Understanding the Difficulty of Training Deep Feedforward Neural Networks" (*https://oreil.ly/9tiTC*). The right scale for a given layer is $1/\sqrt{n_{in}}$, where n_{in} represents the number of inputs.

In our case, if we have 100 inputs, we should scale our weight matrices by 0.1:

```
x = torch.randn(200, 100)
for i in range(50): x = x @ (torch.randn(100,100) * 0.1)
x[0:5,0:5]

tensor([[ 0.7554,  0.6167, -0.1757, -1.5662,  0.5644],
        [-0.1987,  0.6292,  0.3283, -1.1538,  0.5416],
        [ 0.6106,  0.2556, -0.0618, -0.9463,  0.4445],
        [ 0.4484,  0.7144,  0.1164, -0.8626,  0.4413],
        [ 0.3463,  0.5930,  0.3375, -0.9486,  0.5643]])
```

Finally, some numbers that are neither zeros nor nan! Notice how stable the scale of our activations is, even after those 50 fake layers:

```
x.std()

tensor(0.7042)
```

If you play a little bit with the value for scale, you'll notice that even a slight variation from 0.1 will get you either to very small or very large numbers, so initializing the weights properly is extremely important.

Let's go back to our neural net. Since we messed a bit with our inputs, we need to redefine them:

```
x = torch.randn(200, 100)
y = torch.randn(200)
```

And for our weights, we'll use the right scale, which is known as *Xavier initialization* (or *Glorot initialization*):

```
from math import sqrt
w1 = torch.randn(100,50) / sqrt(100)
b1 = torch.zeros(50)
w2 = torch.randn(50,1) / sqrt(50)
b2 = torch.zeros(1)
```

Now if we compute the result of the first layer, we can check that the mean and standard deviation are under control:

```
l1 = lin(x, w1, b1)
l1.mean(),l1.std()
```

```
(tensor(-0.0050), tensor(1.0000))
```

Very good. Now we need to go through a ReLU, so let's define one. A ReLU removes the negatives and replaces them with zeros, which is another way of saying it clamps our tensor at zero:

```
def relu(x): return x.clamp_min(0.)
```

We pass our activations through this:

```
l2 = relu(l1)
l2.mean(),l2.std()
```

```
(tensor(0.3961), tensor(0.5783))
```

And we're back to square one: the mean of our activations has gone to 0.4 (which is understandable since we removed the negatives), and the std went down to 0.58. So like before, after a few layers we will probably wind up with zeros:

```
x = torch.randn(200, 100)
for i in range(50): x = relu(x @ (torch.randn(100,100) * 0.1))
x[0:5,0:5]
```

```
tensor([[0.0000e+00, 1.9689e-08, 4.2820e-08, 0.0000e+00, 0.0000e+00],
        [0.0000e+00, 1.6701e-08, 4.3501e-08, 0.0000e+00, 0.0000e+00],
        [0.0000e+00, 1.0976e-08, 3.0411e-08, 0.0000e+00, 0.0000e+00],
        [0.0000e+00, 1.8457e-08, 4.9469e-08, 0.0000e+00, 0.0000e+00],
        [0.0000e+00, 1.9949e-08, 4.1643e-08, 0.0000e+00, 0.0000e+00]])
```

This means our initialization wasn't right. Why? At the time Glorot and Bengio wrote their article, the most popular activation in a neural net was the hyperbolic tangent (tanh, which is the one they used), and that initialization doesn't account for our ReLU. Fortunately, someone else has done the math for us and computed the right scale for us to use. In "Delving Deep into Rectifiers: Surpassing Human-Level Performance" (*https://oreil.ly/-_quA*) (which we've seen before—it's the article that introduced the ResNet), Kaiming He et al. show that we should use the following scale instead: $\sqrt{2/n_{in}}$, where n_{in} is the number of inputs of our model. Let's see what this gives us:

```
x = torch.randn(200, 100)
for i in range(50): x = relu(x @ (torch.randn(100,100) * sqrt(2/100)))
x[0:5,0:5]

tensor([[0.2871, 0.0000, 0.0000, 0.0000, 0.0026],
        [0.4546, 0.0000, 0.0000, 0.0000, 0.0015],
        [0.6178, 0.0000, 0.0000, 0.0180, 0.0079],
        [0.3333, 0.0000, 0.0000, 0.0545, 0.0000],
        [0.1940, 0.0000, 0.0000, 0.0000, 0.0096]])
```

That's better: our numbers aren't all zeroed this time. So let's go back to the definition of our neural net and use this initialization (which is named *Kaiming initialization* or *He initialization*):

```
x = torch.randn(200, 100)
y = torch.randn(200)

w1 = torch.randn(100,50) * sqrt(2 / 100)
b1 = torch.zeros(50)
w2 = torch.randn(50,1) * sqrt(2 / 50)
b2 = torch.zeros(1)
```

Let's look at the scale of our activations after going through the first linear layer and ReLU:

```
l1 = lin(x, w1, b1)
l2 = relu(l1)
l2.mean(), l2.std()

(tensor(0.5661), tensor(0.8339))
```

Much better! Now that our weights are properly initialized, we can define our whole model:

```
def model(x):
    l1 = lin(x, w1, b1)
    l2 = relu(l1)
    l3 = lin(l2, w2, b2)
    return l3
```

This is the forward pass. Now all that's left to do is to compare our output to the labels we have (random numbers, in this example) with a loss function. In this case, we will use the mean squared error. (It's a toy problem, and this is the easiest loss function to use for what is next, computing the gradients.)

The only subtlety is that our outputs and targets don't have exactly the same shape—after going though the model, we get an output like this:

```
out = model(x)
out.shape

torch.Size([200, 1])
```

To get rid of this trailing 1 dimension, we use the `squeeze` function:

```
def mse(output, targ): return (output.squeeze(-1) - targ).pow(2).mean()
```

And now we are ready to compute our loss:

```
loss = mse(out, y)
```

That's all for the forward pass—let's now look at the gradients.

Gradients and the Backward Pass

We've seen that PyTorch computes all the gradients we need with a magic call to `loss.backward`, but let's explore what's happening behind the scenes.

Now comes the part where we need to compute the gradients of the loss with respect to all the weights of our model, so all the floats in w1, b1, w2, and b2. For this, we will need a bit of math—specifically, the *chain rule*. This is the rule of calculus that guides how we can compute the derivative of a composed function:

$$(g \circ f)'(x) = g'(f(x))f'(x)$$

Jeremy Says

I find this notation hard to wrap my head around, so instead I like to think of it as follows: if y = g(u) and u=f(x), then dy/dx = dy/du * du/dx. The two notations mean the same thing, so use whatever works for you.

Our loss is a big composition of different functions: mean squared error (which is, in turn, the composition of a mean and a power of two), the second linear layer, a ReLU, and the first linear layer. For instance, if we want the gradients of the loss with respect to b2 and our loss is defined by the following:

```
loss = mse(out,y) = mse(lin(l2, w2, b2), y)
```

The chain rule tells us that we have this:

$$\frac{dloss}{db_2} = \frac{dloss}{dout} \times \frac{dout}{db_2} = \frac{d}{dout}mse(out, y) \times \frac{d}{db_2}lin(l_2, w_2, b_2)$$

To compute the gradients of the loss with respect to b_2, we first need the gradients of the loss with respect to our output *out*. It's the same if we want the gradients of the loss with respect to w_2. Then, to get the gradients of the loss with respect to b_1 or w_1, we will need the gradients of the loss with respect to l_1, which in turn requires the gradients of the loss with respect to l_2, which will need the gradients of the loss with respect to *out*.

So to compute all the gradients we need for the update, we need to begin from the output of the model and work our way *backward*, one layer after the other—which is why this step is known as *backpropagation*. We can automate it by having each function we implemented (relu, mse, lin) provide its backward step: that is, how to derive the gradients of the loss with respect to the input(s) from the gradients of the loss with respect to the output.

Here we populate those gradients in an attribute of each tensor, a bit like PyTorch does with .grad.

The first are the gradients of the loss with respect to the output of our model (which is the input of the loss function). We undo the squeeze we did in mse, and then we use the formula that gives us the derivative of x^2: $2x$. The derivative of the mean is just $1/n$, where n is the number of elements in our input:

```
def mse_grad(inp, targ):
    # grad of loss with respect to output of previous layer
    inp.g = 2. * (inp.squeeze() - targ).unsqueeze(-1) / inp.shape[0]
```

For the gradients of the ReLU and our linear layer, we use the gradients of the loss with respect to the output (in out.g) and apply the chain rule to compute the gradients of the loss with respect to the input (in inp.g). The chain rule tells us that inp.g = relu'(inp) * out.g. The derivative of relu is either 0 (when inputs are negative) or 1 (when inputs are positive), so this gives us the following:

```
def relu_grad(inp, out):
    # grad of relu with respect to input activations
    inp.g = (inp>0).float() * out.g
```

The scheme is the same to compute the gradients of the loss with respect to the inputs, weights, and bias in the linear layer:

```
def lin_grad(inp, out, w, b):
    # grad of matmul with respect to input
    inp.g = out.g @ w.t()
    w.g = inp.t() @ out.g
    b.g = out.g.sum(0)
```

We won't linger on the mathematical formulas that define them since they're not important for our purposes, but do check out Khan Academy's excellent calculus lessons if you're interested in this topic.

Once we have defined those functions, we can use them to write the backward pass. Since each gradient is automatically populated in the right tensor, we don't need to store the results of those _grad functions anywhere—we just need to execute them in the reverse order of the forward pass, to make sure that in each function out.g exists:

```
def forward_and_backward(inp, targ):
    # forward pass:
    l1 = inp @ w1 + b1
    l2 = relu(l1)
    out = l2 @ w2 + b2
    # we don't actually need the loss in backward!
    loss = mse(out, targ)

    # backward pass:
    mse_grad(out, targ)
    lin_grad(l2, out, w2, b2)
    relu_grad(l1, l2)
    lin_grad(inp, l1, w1, b1)
```

And now we can access the gradients of our model parameters in w1.g, b1.g, w2.g, and b2.g. We have successfully defined our model—now let's make it a bit more like a PyTorch module.

Refactoring the Model

The three functions we used have two associated functions: a forward pass and a backward pass. Instead of writing them separately, we can create a class to wrap them together. That class can also store the inputs and outputs for the backward pass. This way, we will just have to call `backward`:

```
class Relu():
    def __call__(self, inp):
        self.inp = inp
        self.out = inp.clamp_min(0.)
        return self.out

    def backward(self): self.inp.g = (self.inp>0).float() * self.out.g
```

`__call__` is a magic name in Python that will make our class callable. This is what will be executed when we type `y = Relu()(x)`. We can do the same for our linear layer and the MSE loss:

```
class Lin():
    def __init__(self, w, b): self.w,self.b = w,b

    def __call__(self, inp):
        self.inp = inp
        self.out = inp@self.w + self.b
        return self.out

    def backward(self):
        self.inp.g = self.out.g @ self.w.t()
        self.w.g = inp.t() @ self.out.g
        self.b.g = self.out.g.sum(0)

class Mse():
    def __call__(self, inp, targ):
        self.inp = inp
        self.targ = targ
        self.out = (inp.squeeze() - targ).pow(2).mean()
        return self.out

    def backward(self):
        x = (self.inp.squeeze()-self.targ).unsqueeze(-1)
        self.inp.g = 2.*x/self.targ.shape[0]
```

Then we can put everything in a model that we initiate with our tensors w1, b1, w2, and b2:

```
class Model():
    def __init__(self, w1, b1, w2, b2):
        self.layers = [Lin(w1,b1), Relu(), Lin(w2,b2)]
        self.loss = Mse()

    def __call__(self, x, targ):
        for l in self.layers: x = l(x)
        return self.loss(x, targ)

    def backward(self):
        self.loss.backward()
        for l in reversed(self.layers): l.backward()
```

What is nice about this refactoring and registering things as layers of our model is that the forward and backward passes are now really easy to write. If we want to instantiate our model, we just need to write this:

```
model = Model(w1, b1, w2, b2)
```

The forward pass can then be executed as follows:

```
loss = model(x, y)
```

And the backward pass with this:

```
model.backward()
```

Going to PyTorch

The Lin, Mse, and Relu classes we wrote have a lot in common, so we could make them all inherit from the same base class:

```
class LayerFunction():
    def __call__(self, *args):
        self.args = args
        self.out = self.forward(*args)
        return self.out

    def forward(self):  raise Exception('not implemented')
    def bwd(self):      raise Exception('not implemented')
    def backward(self): self.bwd(self.out, *self.args)
```

Then we just need to implement forward and bwd in each of our subclasses:

```
class Relu(LayerFunction):
    def forward(self, inp): return inp.clamp_min(0.)
    def bwd(self, out, inp): inp.g = (inp>0).float() * out.g
```

```
class Lin(LayerFunction):
    def __init__(self, w, b): self.w,self.b = w,b

    def forward(self, inp): return inp@self.w + self.b

    def bwd(self, out, inp):
        inp.g = out.g @ self.w.t()
        self.w.g = inp.t() @ out.g
        self.b.g = out.g.sum(0)

class Mse(LayerFunction):
    def forward (self, inp, targ): return (inp.squeeze() - targ).pow(2).mean()
    def bwd(self, out, inp, targ):
        inp.g = 2*(inp.squeeze()-targ).unsqueeze(-1) / targ.shape[0]
```

The rest of our model can be the same as before. This is getting closer and closer to what PyTorch does. Each basic function we need to differentiate is written as a `torch.autograd.Function` object that has a `forward` and a `backward` method. PyTorch will then keep track of any computation we do to be able to properly run the backward pass, unless we set the `requires_grad` attribute of our tensors to `False`.

Writing one of these is (almost) as easy as writing our original classes. The difference is that we choose what to save and what to put in a context variable (so that we make sure we don't save anything we don't need), and we return the gradients in the backward pass. It's rare to have to write your own `Function`, but if you ever need something exotic or want to mess with the gradients of a regular function, here is how to write one:

```
from torch.autograd import Function

class MyRelu(Function):
    @staticmethod
    def forward(ctx, i):
        result = i.clamp_min(0.)
        ctx.save_for_backward(i)
        return result

    @staticmethod
    def backward(ctx, grad_output):
        i, = ctx.saved_tensors
        return grad_output * (i>0).float()
```

The structure used to build a more complex model that takes advantage of those `Func`tions is a `torch.nn.Module`. This is the base structure for all models, and all the neural nets you have seen up until now inherited from that class. It mostly helps to register all the trainable parameters, which as we've seen can be used in the training loop.

To implement an `nn.Module` you just need to do the following:

1. Make sure the superclass `__init__` is called first when you initialize it.

2. Define any parameters of the model as attributes with `nn.Parameter`.

3. Define a `forward` function that returns the output of your model.

As an example, here is the linear layer from scratch:

```
import torch.nn as nn

class LinearLayer(nn.Module):
    def __init__(self, n_in, n_out):
        super().__init__()
        self.weight = nn.Parameter(torch.randn(n_out, n_in) * sqrt(2/n_in))
        self.bias = nn.Parameter(torch.zeros(n_out))

    def forward(self, x): return x @ self.weight.t() + self.bias
```

As you see, this class automatically keeps track of what parameters have been defined:

```
lin = LinearLayer(10,2)
p1,p2 = lin.parameters()
p1.shape,p2.shape

(torch.Size([2, 10]), torch.Size([2]))
```

It is thanks to this feature of `nn.Module` that we can just say `opt.step` and have an optimizer loop through the parameters and update each one.

Note that in PyTorch, the weights are stored as an `n_out x n_in` matrix, which is why we have the transpose in the forward pass.

By using the linear layer from PyTorch (which uses the Kaiming initialization as well), the model we have been building up during this chapter can be written like this:

```
class Model(nn.Module):
    def __init__(self, n_in, nh, n_out):
        super().__init__()
        self.layers = nn.Sequential(
            nn.Linear(n_in,nh), nn.ReLU(), nn.Linear(nh,n_out))
        self.loss = mse

    def forward(self, x, targ): return self.loss(self.layers(x).squeeze(), targ)
```

fastai provides its own variant of `Module` that is identical to `nn.Module`, but doesn't require you to call `super().__init__()` (it does that for you automatically):

```
class Model(Module):
    def __init__(self, n_in, nh, n_out):
        self.layers = nn.Sequential(
            nn.Linear(n_in,nh), nn.ReLU(), nn.Linear(nh,n_out))
        self.loss = mse

    def forward(self, x, targ): return self.loss(self.layers(x).squeeze(), targ)
```

In Chapter 19, we will start from such a model and see how to build a training loop from scratch and refactor it to what we've been using in previous chapters.

Conclusion

In this chapter, we explored the foundations of deep learning, beginning with matrix multiplication and moving on to implementing the forward and backward passes of a neural net from scratch. We then refactored our code to show how PyTorch works beneath the hood.

Here are a few things to remember:

- A neural net is basically a bunch of matrix multiplications with nonlinearities in between.
- Python is slow, so to write fast code, we have to vectorize it and take advantage of techniques such as elementwise arithmetic and broadcasting.
- Two tensors are broadcastable if the dimensions starting from the end and going backward match (if they are the same, or one of them is 1). To make tensors broadcastable, we may need to add dimensions of size 1 with `unsqueeze` or a `None` index.
- Properly initializing a neural net is crucial to get training started. Kaiming initialization should be used when we have ReLU nonlinearities.
- The backward pass is the chain rule applied multiple times, computing the gradients from the output of our model and going back, one layer at a time.
- When subclassing `nn.Module` (if not using fastai's `Module`), we have to call the superclass `__init__` method in our `__init__` method and we have to define a `forward` function that takes an input and returns the desired result.

Questionnaire

1. Write the Python code to implement a single neuron.
2. Write the Python code to implement ReLU.
3. Write the Python code for a dense layer in terms of matrix multiplication.
4. Write the Python code for a dense layer in plain Python (that is, with list comprehensions and functionality built into Python).
5. What is the "hidden size" of a layer?
6. What does the `t` method do in PyTorch?
7. Why is matrix multiplication written in plain Python very slow?
8. In `matmul`, why is `ac==br`?

9. In Jupyter Notebook, how do you measure the time taken for a single cell to execute?

10. What is elementwise arithmetic?

11. Write the PyTorch code to test whether every element of a is greater than the corresponding element of b.

12. What is a rank-0 tensor? How do you convert it to a plain Python data type?

13. What does this return, and why?

```
tensor([1,2]) + tensor([1])
```

14. What does this return, and why?

```
tensor([1,2]) + tensor([1,2,3])
```

15. How does elementwise arithmetic help us speed up `matmul`?

16. What are the broadcasting rules?

17. What is `expand_as`? Show an example of how it can be used to match the results of broadcasting.

18. How does `unsqueeze` help us to solve certain broadcasting problems?

19. How can we use indexing to do the same operation as `unsqueeze`?

20. How do we show the actual contents of the memory used for a tensor?

21. When adding a vector of size 3 to a matrix of size 3×3, are the elements of the vector added to each row or each column of the matrix? (Be sure to check your answer by running this code in a notebook.)

22. Do broadcasting and `expand_as` result in increased memory use? Why or why not?

23. Implement `matmul` using Einstein summation.

24. What does a repeated index letter represent on the lefthand side of `einsum`?

25. What are the three rules of Einstein summation notation? Why?

26. What are the forward pass and backward pass of a neural network?

27. Why do we need to store some of the activations calculated for intermediate layers in the forward pass?

28. What is the downside of having activations with a standard deviation too far away from 1?

29. How can weight initialization help avoid this problem?

30. What is the formula to initialize weights such that we get a standard deviation of 1 for a plain linear layer, and for a linear layer followed by ReLU?

31. Why do we sometimes have to use the `squeeze` method in loss functions?

32. What does the argument to the `squeeze` method do? Why might it be important to include this argument, even though PyTorch does not require it?

33. What is the chain rule? Show the equation in either of the two forms presented in this chapter.

34. Show how to calculate the gradients of `mse(lin(l2, w2, b2), y)` by using the chain rule.

35. What is the gradient of ReLU? Show it in math or code. (You shouldn't need to commit this to memory—try to figure it using your knowledge of the shape of the function.)

36. In what order do we need to call the `*_grad` functions in the backward pass? Why?

37. What is `__call__`?

38. What methods must we implement when writing a `torch.autograd.Function`?

39. Write `nn.Linear` from scratch and test that it works.

40. What is the difference between `nn.Module` and fastai's `Module`?

Further Research

1. Implement ReLU as a `torch.autograd.Function` and train a model with it.

2. If you are mathematically inclined, determine the gradients of a linear layer in mathematical notation. Map that to the implementation in this chapter.

3. Learn about the `unfold` method in PyTorch, and use it along with matrix multiplication to implement your own 2D convolution function. Then train a CNN that uses it.

4. Implement everything in this chapter by using NumPy instead of PyTorch.

CHAPTER 18

CNN Interpretation with CAM

Now that we know how to build up pretty much anything from scratch, let's use that knowledge to create entirely new (and very useful!) functionality: the *class activation map*. It gives us some insight into why a CNN made the predictions it did.

In the process, we'll learn about one handy feature of PyTorch we haven't seen before, the *hook*, and we'll apply many of the concepts introduced in the rest of the book. If you want to really test out your understanding of the material in this book, after you've finished this chapter, try putting it aside and re-creating the ideas here yourself from scratch (no peeking!).

CAM and Hooks

The *class activation map* (CAM) was introduced by Bolei Zhou et al. in "Learning Deep Features for Discriminative Localization" (*https://oreil.ly/5hik3*). It uses the output of the last convolutional layer (just before the average pooling layer) together with the predictions to give us a heatmap visualization of why the model made its decision. This is a useful tool for interpretation.

More precisely, at each position of our final convolutional layer, we have as many filters as in the last linear layer. We can therefore compute the dot product of those activations with the final weights to get, for each location on our feature map, the score of the feature that was used to make a decision.

We're going to need a way to get access to the activations inside the model while it's training. In PyTorch, this can be done with a *hook*. Hooks are PyTorch's equivalent of fastai's callbacks. However, rather than allowing you to inject code into the training loop like a fastai `Learner` callback, hooks allow you to inject code into the forward and backward calculations themselves. We can attach a hook to any layer of the model, and it will be executed when we compute the outputs (forward hook) or during backpropagation (backward hook). A forward hook is a function that takes three things—a module, its input, and its output—and it can perform any behavior you want. (fastai also provides a handy `HookCallback` that we won't cover here, but take a look at the fastai docs; it makes working with hooks a little easier.)

To illustrate, we'll use the same cats and dogs model we trained in Chapter 1:

```
path = untar_data(URLs.PETS)/'images'
def is_cat(x): return x[0].isupper()
dls = ImageDataLoaders.from_name_func(
    path, get_image_files(path), valid_pct=0.2, seed=21,
    label_func=is_cat, item_tfms=Resize(224))
learn = cnn_learner(dls, resnet34, metrics=error_rate)
learn.fine_tune(1)
```

epoch	train_loss	valid_loss	error_rate	time
0	0.141987	0.018823	0.007442	00:16

epoch	train_loss	valid_loss	error_rate	time
0	0.050934	0.015366	0.006766	00:21

To start, we'll grab a cat picture and a batch of data:

```
img = PILImage.create(image_cat())
x, = first(dls.test_dl([img]))
```

For CAM, we want to store the activations of the last convolutional layer. We put our hook function in a class so it has a state that we can access later, and just store a copy of the output:

```
class Hook():
    def hook_func(self, m, i, o): self.stored = o.detach().clone()
```

We can then instantiate a `Hook` and attach it to the layer we want, which is the last layer of the CNN body:

```
hook_output = Hook()
hook = learn.model[0].register_forward_hook(hook_output.hook_func)
```

Now we can grab a batch and feed it through our model:

```
with torch.no_grad(): output = learn.model.eval()(x)
```

And we can access our stored activations:

```
act = hook_output.stored[0]
```

Let's also double-check our predictions:

```
F.softmax(output, dim=-1)
```

```
tensor([[7.3566e-07, 1.0000e+00]], device='cuda:0')
```

We know 0 (for `False`) is "dog," because the classes are automatically sorted in fastai, but we can still double-check by looking at `dls.vocab`:

```
dls.vocab
```

```
(#2) [False,True]
```

So, our model is very confident this was a picture of a cat.

To do the dot product of our weight matrix (2 by number of activations) with the activations (batch size by rows by cols), we use a custom `einsum`:

```
act.shape
```

```
torch.Size([512, 7, 7])
```

```
cam_map = torch.einsum('ck,kij->cij', learn.model[1][-1].weight, act)
cam_map.shape
```

```
torch.Size([2, 7, 7])
```

For each image in our batch, and for each class, we get a 7×7 feature map that tells us where the activations were higher and where they were lower. This will let us see which areas of the pictures influenced the model's decision.

For instance, we can find out which areas made the model decide this animal was a cat (note that we need to `decode` the input x since it's been normalized by the `Data Loader`, and we need to cast to `TensorImage` since at the time this book is written, PyTorch does not maintain types when indexing—this may be fixed by the time you are reading this):

```
x_dec = TensorImage(dls.train.decode((x,))[0][0])
_,ax = plt.subplots()
x_dec.show(ctx=ax)
ax.imshow(cam_map[1].detach().cpu(), alpha=0.6, extent=(0,224,224,0),
          interpolation='bilinear', cmap='magma');
```

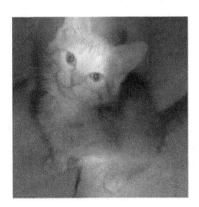

In this case, the areas in bright yellow correspond to high activations, and the areas in purple to low activations. In this case, we can see the head and the front paw were the two main areas that made the model decide it was a picture of a cat.

Once you're done with your hook, you should remove it as otherwise it might leak some memory:

```
hook.remove()
```

That's why it's usually a good idea to have the Hook class be a *context manager*, registering the hook when you enter it and removing it when you exit. A context manager is a Python construct that calls __enter__ when the object is created in a with clause, and __exit__ at the end of the with clause. For instance, this is how Python handles the with open(...) as f: construct that you'll often see for opening files without requiring an explicit close(f) at the end.

If we define Hook as follows

```
class Hook():
    def __init__(self, m):
        self.hook = m.register_forward_hook(self.hook_func)
    def hook_func(self, m, i, o): self.stored = o.detach().clone()
    def __enter__(self, *args): return self
    def __exit__(self, *args): self.hook.remove()
```

we can safely use it this way:

```
with Hook(learn.model[0]) as hook:
    with torch.no_grad(): output = learn.model.eval()(x.cuda())
    act = hook.stored
```

fastai provides this Hook class for you, as well as some other handy classes to make working with hooks easier.

This method is useful, but works for only the last layer. *Gradient CAM* is a variant that addresses this problem.

Gradient CAM

The method we just saw lets us compute only a heatmap with the last activations, since once we have our features, we have to multiply them by the last weight matrix. This won't work for inner layers in the network. A variant introduced in the 2016 paper "Grad-CAM: Why Did You Say That?" (*https://oreil.ly/4krXE*) by Ramprasaath R. Selvaraju et al. uses the gradients of the final activation for the desired class. If you remember a little bit about the backward pass, the gradients of the output of the last layer with respect to the input of that layer are equal to the layer weights, since it is a linear layer.

With deeper layers, we still want the gradients, but they won't just be equal to the weights anymore. We have to calculate them. The gradients of every layer are calculated for us by PyTorch during the backward pass, but they're not stored (except for tensors where `requires_grad` is `True`). We can, however, register a hook on the backward pass, which PyTorch will give the gradients to as a parameter, so we can store them there. For this, we will use a `HookBwd` class that works like `Hook`, but intercepts and stores gradients instead of activations:

```
class HookBwd():
    def __init__(self, m):
        self.hook = m.register_backward_hook(self.hook_func)
    def hook_func(self, m, gi, go): self.stored = go[0].detach().clone()
    def __enter__(self, *args): return self
    def __exit__(self, *args): self.hook.remove()
```

Then for the class index 1 (for `True`, which is "cat"), we intercept the features of the last convolutional layer, as before, and compute the gradients of the output activations of our class. We can't just call `output.backward`, because gradients make sense only with respect to a scalar (which is normally our loss), and `output` is a rank-2 tensor. But if we pick a single image (we'll use 0) and a single class (we'll use 1), we *can* calculate the gradients of any weight or activation we like, with respect to that single value, using `output[0,cls].backward`. Our hook intercepts the gradients that we'll use as weights:

```
cls = 1
with HookBwd(learn.model[0]) as hookg:
    with Hook(learn.model[0]) as hook:
        output = learn.model.eval()(x.cuda())
        act = hook.stored
    output[0,cls].backward()
    grad = hookg.stored
```

The weights for Grad-CAM are given by the average of our gradients across the feature map. Then it's exactly the same as before:

```
w = grad[0].mean(dim=[1,2], keepdim=True)
cam_map = (w * act[0]).sum(0)

_,ax = plt.subplots()
x_dec.show(ctx=ax)
ax.imshow(cam_map.detach().cpu(), alpha=0.6, extent=(0,224,224,0),
          interpolation='bilinear', cmap='magma');
```

The novelty with Grad-CAM is that we can use it on any layer. For example, here we use it on the output of the second-to-last ResNet group:

```
with HookBwd(learn.model[0][-2]) as hookg:
    with Hook(learn.model[0][-2]) as hook:
        output = learn.model.eval()(x.cuda())
        act = hook.stored
    output[0,cls].backward()
    grad = hookg.stored

w = grad[0].mean(dim=[1,2], keepdim=True)
cam_map = (w * act[0]).sum(0)
```

And we can now view the activation map for this layer:

```
_,ax = plt.subplots()
x_dec.show(ctx=ax)
ax.imshow(cam_map.detach().cpu(), alpha=0.6, extent=(0,224,224,0),
          interpolation='bilinear', cmap='magma');
```

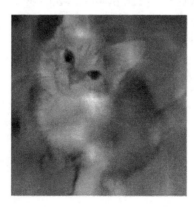

Conclusion

Model interpretation is an area of active research, and we just scraped the surface of what is possible in this brief chapter. Class activation maps give us insight into why a model predicted a certain result by showing the areas of the images that were most responsible for a given prediction. This can help us analyze false positives and figure out what kind of data is missing in our training to avoid them.

Questionnaire

1. What is a hook in PyTorch?
2. Which layer does CAM use the outputs of?
3. Why does CAM require a hook?
4. Look at the source code of the `ActivationStats` class and see how it uses hooks.
5. Write a hook that stores the activations of a given layer in a model (without peeking, if possible).
6. Why do we call `eval` before getting the activations? Why do we use `no_grad`?
7. Use `torch.einsum` to compute the "dog" or "cat" score of each of the locations in the last activation of the body of the model.
8. How do you check which order the categories are in (i.e., the correspondence of index→category)?
9. Why are we using `decode` when displaying the input image?
10. What is a context manager? What special methods need to be defined to create one?
11. Why can't we use plain CAM for the inner layers of a network?
12. Why do we need to register a hook on the backward pass in order to do Grad-CAM?
13. Why can't we call `output.backward` when `output` is a rank-2 tensor of output activations per image per class?

Further Research

1. Try removing `keepdim` and see what happens. Look up this parameter in the PyTorch docs. Why do we need it in this notebook?
2. Create a notebook like this one, but for NLP, and use it to find which words in a movie review are most significant in assessing the sentiment of a particular movie review.

CHAPTER 19

A fastai Learner from Scratch

This final chapter (other than the conclusion and the online chapters) is going to look a bit different. It contains far more code and far less prose than the previous chapters. We will introduce new Python keywords and libraries without discussing them. This chapter is meant to be the start of a significant research project for you. You see, we are going to implement many of the key pieces of the fastai and PyTorch APIs from scratch, building on nothing other than the components that we developed in Chapter 17! The key goal here is to end up with your own `Learner` class and some callbacks—enough to be able to train a model on Imagenette, including examples of each of the key techniques we've studied. On the way to building `Learner`, we will create our own versions of `Module`, `Parameter` and a parallel `DataLoader` so you'll have a very good idea of what those PyTorch classes do.

The end-of-chapter questionnaire is particularly important for this chapter. This is where we will be pointing you in the many interesting directions that you could take, using this chapter as your starting point. We suggest that you follow along with this chapter on your computer, and do lots of experiments, web searches, and whatever else you need to understand what's going on. You've built up the skills and expertise to do this in the rest of this book, so we think you are going to do great!

Let's begin by gathering (manually) some data.

Data

Have a look at the source to `untar_data` to see how it works. We'll use it here to access the 160-pixel version of Imagenette for use in this chapter:

```
path = untar_data(URLs.IMAGENETTE_160)
```

To access the image files, we can use get_image_files:

```
t = get_image_files(path)
t[0]
```

```
Path('/home/jhoward/.fastai/data/imagenette2-160/val/n03417042/n03417042_3752.JP
 > EG')
```

Or we could do the same thing using just Python's standard library, with glob:

```
from glob import glob
files = L(glob(f'{path}/**/*.JPEG', recursive=True)).map(Path)
files[0]
```

```
Path('/home/jhoward/.fastai/data/imagenette2-160/val/n03417042/n03417042_3752.JP
 > EG')
```

If you look at the source for get_image_files, you'll see it uses Python's os.walk; this is a faster and more flexible function than glob, so be sure to try it out.

We can open an image with the Python Imaging Library's Image class:

```
im = Image.open(files[0])
im
```

```
im_t = tensor(im)
im_t.shape
```

```
torch.Size([160, 213, 3])
```

That's going to be the basis of our independent variable. For our dependent variable, we can use Path.parent from pathlib. First we'll need our vocab

```
lbls = files.map(Self.parent.name()).unique(); lbls
```

```
(#10) ['n03417042','n03445777','n03888257','n03394916','n02979186','n03000684','
 > n03425413','n01440764','n03028079','n02102040']
```

and the reverse mapping, thanks to L.val2idx:

```
v2i = lbls.val2idx(); v2i
```

```
{'n03417042': 0,
 'n03445777': 1,
 'n03888257': 2,
 'n03394916': 3,
 'n02979186': 4,
```

```
        'n03000684': 5,
        'n03425413': 6,
        'n01440764': 7,
        'n03028079': 8,
        'n02102040': 9}
```

That's all the pieces we need to put together our `Dataset`.

Dataset

A `Dataset` in PyTorch can be anything that supports indexing (`__getitem__`) and `len`:

```
class Dataset:
    def __init__(self, fns): self.fns=fns
    def __len__(self): return len(self.fns)
    def __getitem__(self, i):
        im = Image.open(self.fns[i]).resize((64,64)).convert('RGB')
        y = v2i[self.fns[i].parent.name]
        return tensor(im).float()/255, tensor(y)
```

We need a list of training and validation filenames to pass to `Dataset.__init__`:

```
train_filt = L(o.parent.parent.name=='train' for o in files)
train,valid = files[train_filt],files[~train_filt]
len(train),len(valid)
```

```
(9469, 3925)
```

Now we can try it out:

```
train_ds,valid_ds = Dataset(train),Dataset(valid)
x,y = train_ds[0]
x.shape,y
```

```
(torch.Size([64, 64, 3]), tensor(0))
```

```
show_image(x, title=lbls[y]);
```

n03417042

As you see, our dataset is returning the independent and dependent variables as a tuple, which is just what we need. We'll need to be able to collate these into a mini-batch. Generally, this is done with `torch.stack`, which is what we'll use here:

```
def collate(idxs, ds):
    xb,yb = zip(*[ds[i] for i in idxs])
    return torch.stack(xb),torch.stack(yb)
```

Here's a mini-batch with two items, for testing our `collate`:

```
x,y = collate([1,2], train_ds)
x.shape,y
```

```
(torch.Size([2, 64, 64, 3]), tensor([0, 0]))
```

Now that we have a dataset and a collation function, we're ready to create `DataLoader`. We'll add two more things here: an optional `shuffle` for the training set, and a `ProcessPoolExecutor` to do our preprocessing in parallel. A parallel data loader is very important, because opening and decoding a JPEG image is a slow process. One CPU core is not enough to decode images fast enough to keep a modern GPU busy. Here's our `DataLoader` class:

```
class DataLoader:
    def __init__(self, ds, bs=128, shuffle=False, n_workers=1):
        self.ds,self.bs,self.shuffle,self.n_workers = ds,bs,shuffle,n_workers

    def __len__(self): return (len(self.ds)-1)//self.bs+1

    def __iter__(self):
        idxs = L.range(self.ds)
        if self.shuffle: idxs = idxs.shuffle()
        chunks = [idxs[n:n+self.bs] for n in range(0, len(self.ds), self.bs)]
        with ProcessPoolExecutor(self.n_workers) as ex:
            yield from ex.map(collate, chunks, ds=self.ds)
```

Let's try it out with our training and validation datasets:

```
n_workers = min(16, defaults.cpus)
train_dl = DataLoader(train_ds, bs=128, shuffle=True, n_workers=n_workers)
valid_dl = DataLoader(valid_ds, bs=256, shuffle=False, n_workers=n_workers)
xb,yb = first(train_dl)
xb.shape,yb.shape,len(train_dl)
```

```
(torch.Size([128, 64, 64, 3]), torch.Size([128]), 74)
```

This data loader is not much slower than PyTorch's, but it's far simpler. So if you're debugging a complex data loading process, don't be afraid to try doing things manually to help you see exactly what's going on.

For normalization, we'll need image statistics. Generally, it's fine to calculate these on a single training mini-batch, since precision isn't needed here:

```
stats = [xb.mean((0,1,2)),xb.std((0,1,2))]
stats
```

```
[tensor([0.4544, 0.4453, 0.4141]), tensor([0.2812, 0.2766, 0.2981])]
```

Our `Normalize` class just needs to store these stats and apply them (to see why the `to_device` is needed, try commenting it out, and see what happens later in this notebook):

```
class Normalize:
    def __init__(self, stats): self.stats=stats
    def __call__(self, x):
        if x.device != self.stats[0].device:
            self.stats = to_device(self.stats, x.device)
        return (x-self.stats[0])/self.stats[1]
```

We always like to test everything we build in a notebook, as soon as we build it:

```
norm = Normalize(stats)
def tfm_x(x): return norm(x).permute((0,3,1,2))
```

```
t = tfm_x(x)
t.mean((0,2,3)),t.std((0,2,3))
```

```
(tensor([0.3732, 0.4907, 0.5633]), tensor([1.0212, 1.0311, 1.0131]))
```

Here `tfm_x` isn't just applying `Normalize`, but is also permuting the axis order from NHWC to NCHW (see Chapter 13 if you need a reminder of what these acronyms refer to). PIL uses HWC axis order, which we can't use with PyTorch, hence the need for this `permute`.

That's all we need for the data for our model. So now we need the model itself!

Module and Parameter

To create a model, we'll need `Module`. To create `Module`, we'll need `Parameter`, so let's start there. Recall that in Chapter 8 we said that the `Parameter` class "doesn't add any functionality (other than automatically calling `requires_grad_` for us). It's used only as a 'marker' to show what to include in `parameters`." Here's a definition that does exactly that:

```
class Parameter(Tensor):
    def __new__(self, x): return Tensor._make_subclass(Parameter, x, True)
    def __init__(self, *args, **kwargs): self.requires_grad_()
```

The implementation here is a bit awkward: we have to define the special `__new__` Python method and use the internal PyTorch method `_make_subclass` because, at the time of writing, PyTorch doesn't otherwise work correctly with this kind of subclassing or provide an officially supported API to do this. This may have been fixed by the time you read this, so look on the book's website to see if there are updated details.

Our `Parameter` now behaves just like a tensor, as we wanted:

```
Parameter(tensor(3.))
```

```
tensor(3., requires_grad=True)
```

Now that we have this, we can define `Module`:

```
class Module:
    def __init__(self):
        self.hook,self.params,self.children,self._training = None,[],[],False

    def register_parameters(self, *ps): self.params += ps
    def register_modules   (self, *ms): self.children += ms

    @property
    def training(self): return self._training
    @training.setter
    def training(self,v):
        self._training = v
        for m in self.children: m.training=v

    def parameters(self):
        return self.params + sum([m.parameters() for m in self.children], [])

    def __setattr__(self,k,v):
        super().__setattr__(k,v)
        if isinstance(v,Parameter): self.register_parameters(v)
        if isinstance(v,Module):    self.register_modules(v)

    def __call__(self, *args, **kwargs):
        res = self.forward(*args, **kwargs)
        if self.hook is not None: self.hook(res, args)
        return res

    def cuda(self):
        for p in self.parameters(): p.data = p.data.cuda()
```

The key functionality is in the definition of `parameters`:

```
self.params + sum([m.parameters() for m in self.children], [])
```

This means that we can ask any `Module` for its parameters, and it will return them, including for all its child modules (recursively). But how does it know what its parameters are? It's thanks to implementing Python's special `__setattr__` method, which is called for us anytime Python sets an attribute on a class. Our implementation includes this line:

```
if isinstance(v,Parameter): self.register_parameters(v)
```

As you see, this is where we use our new `Parameter` class as a "marker"—anything of this class is added to our `params`.

Python's `__call__` allows us to define what happens when our object is treated as a function; we just call `forward` (which doesn't exist here, so it'll need to be added by subclasses). Afterward, we'll call a hook, if it's defined. Now you can see that PyTorch hooks aren't doing anything fancy at all—they're just calling any hooks have been registered.

Other than these pieces of functionality, our `Module` also provides `cuda` and `training` attributes, which we'll use shortly.

Now we can create our first `Module`, which is `ConvLayer`:

```
class ConvLayer(Module):
    def __init__(self, ni, nf, stride=1, bias=True, act=True):
        super().__init__()
        self.w = Parameter(torch.zeros(nf,ni,3,3))
        self.b = Parameter(torch.zeros(nf)) if bias else None
        self.act,self.stride = act,stride
        init = nn.init.kaiming_normal_ if act else nn.init.xavier_normal_
        init(self.w)

    def forward(self, x):
        x = F.conv2d(x, self.w, self.b, stride=self.stride, padding=1)
        if self.act: x = F.relu(x)
        return x
```

We're not implementing `F.conv2d` from scratch, since you should have already done that (using `unfold`) in the questionnaire in Chapter 17. Instead we're just creating a small class that wraps it up along with bias and weight initialization. Let's check that it works correctly with `Module.parameters`:

```
l = ConvLayer(3, 4)
len(l.parameters())
```

```
2
```

And that we can call it (which will result in `forward` being called):

```
xbt = tfm_x(xb)
r = l(xbt)
r.shape
```

```
torch.Size([128, 4, 64, 64])
```

In the same way, we can implement `Linear`:

```
class Linear(Module):
    def __init__(self, ni, nf):
        super().__init__()
        self.w = Parameter(torch.zeros(nf,ni))
        self.b = Parameter(torch.zeros(nf))
        nn.init.xavier_normal_(self.w)

    def forward(self, x): return x@self.w.t() + self.b
```

And test that it works:

```
l = Linear(4,2)
r = l(torch.ones(3,4))
r.shape
```

```
torch.Size([3, 2])
```

Let's also create a testing module to check that if we include multiple parameters as attributes, they are all correctly registered:

```
class T(Module):
    def __init__(self):
        super().__init__()
        self.c,self.l = ConvLayer(3,4),Linear(4,2)
```

Since we have a conv layer and a linear layer, each of which has weights and biases, we'd expect four parameters in total:

```
t = T()
len(t.parameters())
```

```
4
```

We should also find that calling cuda on this class puts all these parameters on the GPU:

```
t.cuda()
t.l.w.device
```

```
device(type='cuda', index=5)
```

We can now use those pieces to create a CNN.

Simple CNN

As we've seen, a `Sequential` class makes many architectures easier to implement, so let's make one:

```
class Sequential(Module):
    def __init__(self, *layers):
        super().__init__()
        self.layers = layers
        self.register_modules(*layers)

    def forward(self, x):
        for l in self.layers: x = l(x)
        return x
```

The `forward` method here just calls each layer in turn. Note that we have to use the `register_modules` method we defined in `Module`, since otherwise the contents of `layers` won't appear in `parameters`.

All the Code Is Here

Remember that we're not using any PyTorch functionality for modules here; we're defining everything ourselves. So if you're not sure what `register_modules` does, or why it's needed, have another look at our code for `Module` to see what we wrote!

We can create a simplified `AdaptivePool` that only handles pooling to a 1×1 output, and flattens it as well, by just using `mean`:

```
class AdaptivePool(Module):
    def forward(self, x): return x.mean((2,3))
```

That's enough for us to create a CNN!

```
def simple_cnn():
    return Sequential(
        ConvLayer(3 ,16 ,stride=2), #32
        ConvLayer(16,32 ,stride=2), #16
        ConvLayer(32,64 ,stride=2), # 8
        ConvLayer(64,128,stride=2), # 4
        AdaptivePool(),
        Linear(128, 10)
    )
```

Let's see if our parameters are all being registered correctly:

```
m = simple_cnn()
len(m.parameters())
```

```
10
```

Now we can try adding a hook. Note that we've left room for only one hook in `Module`; you could make it a list, or use something like `Pipeline` to run a few as a single function:

```
def print_stats(outp, inp): print (outp.mean().item(),outp.std().item())
for i in range(4): m.layers[i].hook = print_stats

r = m(xbt)
r.shape
```

```
0.5239089727401733 0.8776043057441711
0.43470510840415955 0.8347987532615662
0.4357188045978546 0.7621666193008423
0.46562111377716064 0.7416611313819885
torch.Size([128, 10])
```

We have data and model. Now we need a loss function.

Loss

We've already seen how to define "negative log likelihood":

```
def nll(input, target): return -input[range(target.shape[0]), target].mean()
```

Well actually, there's no log here, since we're using the same definition as PyTorch. That means we need to put the log together with softmax:

```
def log_softmax(x): return (x.exp()/(x.exp().sum(-1,keepdim=True))).log()

sm = log_softmax(r); sm[0][0]

tensor(-1.2790, grad_fn=<SelectBackward>)
```

Combining these gives us our cross-entropy loss:

```
loss = nll(sm, yb)
loss

tensor(2.5666, grad_fn=<NegBackward>)
```

Note that the formula

$$\log \left(\frac{a}{b} \right) = \log (a) - \log (b)$$

gives a simplification when we compute the log softmax, which was previously defined as `(x.exp()/(x.exp().sum(-1))).log()`:

```
def log_softmax(x): return x - x.exp().sum(-1,keepdim=True).log()
sm = log_softmax(r); sm[0][0]

tensor(-1.2790, grad_fn=<SelectBackward>)
```

Then, there is a more stable way to compute the log of the sum of exponentials, called the *LogSumExp* trick (*https://oreil.ly/9UB0b*). The idea is to use the following formula

$$\log \left(\sum_{j=1}^{n} e^{x_j} \right) = \log \left(e^{a} \sum_{j=1}^{n} e^{x_j - a} \right) = a + \log \left(\sum_{j=1}^{n} e^{x_j - a} \right)$$

where a is the maximum of x_j.

Here's the same thing in code:

```
x = torch.rand(5)
a = x.max()
x.exp().sum().log() == a + (x-a).exp().sum().log()

tensor(True)
```

We'll put that into a function

```
def logsumexp(x):
    m = x.max(-1)[0]
    return m + (x-m[:,None]).exp().sum(-1).log()
```

```
logsumexp(r)[0]
```

```
tensor(3.9784, grad_fn=<SelectBackward>)
```

so we can use it for our `log_softmax` function:

```
def log_softmax(x): return x - x.logsumexp(-1,keepdim=True)
```

Which gives the same result as before:

```
sm = log_softmax(r); sm[0][0]
```

```
tensor(-1.2790, grad_fn=<SelectBackward>)
```

We can use these to create `cross_entropy`:

```
def cross_entropy(preds, yb): return nll(log_softmax(preds), yb).mean()
```

Let's now combine all those pieces to create a `Learner`.

Learner

We have data, a model, and a loss function; we need only one more thing before we can fit a model, and that's an optimizer! Here's SGD:

```
class SGD:
    def __init__(self, params, lr, wd=0.): store_attr(self, 'params,lr,wd')
    def step(self):
        for p in self.params:
            p.data -= (p.grad.data + p.data*self.wd) * self.lr
            p.grad.data.zero_()
```

As we've seen in this book, life is easier with a `Learner`. The `Learner` needs to know our training and validation sets, which means we need `DataLoaders` to store them. We don't need any other functionality, just a place to store them and access them:

```
class DataLoaders:
    def __init__(self, *dls): self.train,self.valid = dls
```

```
dls = DataLoaders(train_dl,valid_dl)
```

Now we're ready to create our `Learner` class:

```
class Learner:
    def __init__(self, model, dls, loss_func, lr, cbs, opt_func=SGD):
        store_attr(self, 'model,dls,loss_func,lr,cbs,opt_func')
        for cb in cbs: cb.learner = self
```

```
def one_batch(self):
    self('before_batch')
    xb,yb = self.batch
    self.preds = self.model(xb)
    self.loss = self.loss_func(self.preds, yb)
    if self.model.training:
        self.loss.backward()
        self.opt.step()
    self('after_batch')

def one_epoch(self, train):
    self.model.training = train
    self('before_epoch')
    dl = self.dls.train if train else self.dls.valid
    for self.num,self.batch in enumerate(progress_bar(dl, leave=False)):
        self.one_batch()
    self('after_epoch')

def fit(self, n_epochs):
    self('before_fit')
    self.opt = self.opt_func(self.model.parameters(), self.lr)
    self.n_epochs = n_epochs
    try:
        for self.epoch in range(n_epochs):
            self.one_epoch(True)
            self.one_epoch(False)
    except CancelFitException: pass
    self('after_fit')

def __call__(self,name):
    for cb in self.cbs: getattr(cb,name,noop)()
```

This is the largest class we've created in the book, but each method is quite small, so by looking at each in turn, you should be able to follow what's going on.

The main method we'll be calling is fit. This loops with

```
for self.epoch in range(n_epochs)
```

and at each epoch calls self.one_epoch for each of train=True and then train=False. Then self.one_epoch calls self.one_batch for each batch in dls.train or dls.valid, as appropriate (after wrapping the DataLoader in fastprogress.progress_bar). Finally, self.one_batch follows the usual set of steps to fit one mini-batch that we've seen throughout this book.

Before and after each step, Learner calls self, which calls __call__ (which is standard Python functionality). __call__ uses getattr(cb,name) on each callback in self.cbs, which is a Python built-in function that returns the attribute (a method, in this case) with the requested name. So, for instance, self('before_fit') will call cb.before_fit() for each callback where that method is defined.

As you can see, `Learner` is really just using our standard training loop, except that it's also calling callbacks at appropriate times. So let's define some callbacks!

Callbacks

In `Learner.__init__` we have

```
for cb in cbs: cb.learner = self
```

In other words, every callback knows what learner it is used in. This is critical, since otherwise a callback can't get information from the learner, or change things in the learner. Because getting information from the learner is so common, we make that easier by defining `Callback` as a subclass of `GetAttr`, with a default attribute of `learner`:

```
class Callback(GetAttr): _default='learner'
```

`GetAttr` is a fastai class that implements Python's standard `__getattr__` and `__dir__` methods for you, so that anytime you try to access an attribute that doesn't exist, it passes the request along to whatever you have defined as `_default`.

For instance, we want to move all model parameters to the GPU automatically at the start of `fit`. We could do this by defining `before_fit` as `self.learner.model.cuda`; however, because `learner` is the default attribute, and we have `SetupLearnerCB` inherit from `Callback` (which inherits from `GetAttr`), we can remove the `.learner` and just call `self.model.cuda`:

```
class SetupLearnerCB(Callback):
    def before_batch(self):
        xb,yb = to_device(self.batch)
        self.learner.batch = tfm_x(xb),yb

    def before_fit(self): self.model.cuda()
```

In `SetupLearnerCB`, we also move each mini-batch to the GPU, by calling `to_device(self.batch)` (we could also have used the longer `to_device(self.learner.batch)`. Note, however, that in the line `self.learner.batch = tfm_x(xb),yb`, we can't remove `.learner`, because here we're *setting* the attribute, not getting it.

Before we try our `Learner`, let's create a callback to track and print progress. Otherwise, we won't really know if it's working properly:

```
class TrackResults(Callback):
    def before_epoch(self): self.accs,self.losses,self.ns = [],[],[]

    def after_epoch(self):
        n = sum(self.ns)
        print(self.epoch, self.model.training,
            sum(self.losses).item()/n, sum(self.accs).item()/n)
```

```
def after_batch(self):
    xb,yb = self.batch
    acc = (self.preds.argmax(dim=1)==yb).float().sum()
    self.accs.append(acc)
    n = len(xb)
    self.losses.append(self.loss*n)
    self.ns.append(n)
```

Now we're ready to use our `Learner` for the first time!

```
cbs = [SetupLearnerCB(),TrackResults()]
learn = Learner(simple_cnn(), dls, cross_entropy, lr=0.1, cbs=cbs)
learn.fit(1)
```

```
0 True 2.1275552130636814 0.2314922378287042
```

```
0 False 1.9942575636942674 0.2991082802547771
```

It's quite amazing to realize that we can implement all the key ideas from fastai's
`Learner` in so little code! Let's now add some learning rate scheduling.

Scheduling the Learning Rate

If we're going to get good results, we'll want an LR finder and 1cycle training. These
are both *annealing* callbacks—that is, they are gradually changing hyperparameters as
we train. Here's `LRFinder`:

```
class LRFinder(Callback):
    def before_fit(self):
        self.losses,self.lrs = [],[]
        self.learner.lr = 1e-6

    def before_batch(self):
        if not self.model.training: return
        self.opt.lr *= 1.2

    def after_batch(self):
        if not self.model.training: return
        if self.opt.lr>10 or torch.isnan(self.loss): raise CancelFitException
        self.losses.append(self.loss.item())
        self.lrs.append(self.opt.lr)
```

This shows how we're using `CancelFitException`, which is itself an empty class, used
only to signify the type of exception. You can see in `Learner` that this exception is
caught. (You should add and test `CancelBatchException`, `CancelEpochException`,
etc. yourself.) Let's try it out, by adding it to our list of callbacks:

```
lrfind = LRFinder()
learn = Learner(simple_cnn(), dls, cross_entropy, lr=0.1, cbs=cbs+[lrfind])
learn.fit(2)
```

```
0 True 2.6336045582954903 0.11014890695955222

0 False 2.230653363853503 0.18318471337579617
```

And take a look at the results:

```
plt.plot(lrfind.lrs[:-2],lrfind.losses[:-2])
plt.xscale('log')
```

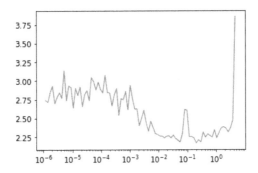

Now we can define our `OneCycle` training callback:

```
class OneCycle(Callback):
    def __init__(self, base_lr): self.base_lr = base_lr
    def before_fit(self): self.lrs = []

    def before_batch(self):
        if not self.model.training: return
        n = len(self.dls.train)
        bn = self.epoch*n + self.num
        mn = self.n_epochs*n
        pct = bn/mn
        pct_start,div_start = 0.25,10
        if pct<pct_start:
            pct /= pct_start
            lr = (1-pct)*self.base_lr/div_start + pct*self.base_lr
        else:
            pct = (pct-pct_start)/(1-pct_start)
            lr = (1-pct)*self.base_lr
        self.opt.lr = lr
        self.lrs.append(lr)
```

We'll try an LR of 0.1:

```
onecyc = OneCycle(0.1)
learn = Learner(simple_cnn(), dls, cross_entropy, lr=0.1, cbs=cbs+[onecyc])
```

Let's fit for a while and see how it looks (we won't show all the output in the book—try it in the notebook to see the results):

```
learn.fit(8)
```

Finally, we'll check that the learning rate followed the schedule we defined (as you see, we're not using cosine annealing here):

```
plt.plot(onecyc.lrs);
```

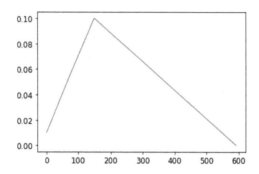

Conclusion

We have explored how the key concepts of the fastai library are implemented by re-implementing them in this chapter. Since it's mostly full of code, you should definitely try to experiment with it by looking at the corresponding notebook on the book's website. Now that you know how it's built, as a next step be sure to check out the intermediate and advanced tutorials in the fastai documentation to learn how to customize every bit of the library.

Questionnaire

Experiments

For the questions here that ask you to explain what a function or class is, you should also complete your own code experiments.

1. What is glob?
2. How do you open an image with the Python imaging library?
3. What does L.map do?
4. What does Self do?
5. What is L.val2idx?
6. What methods do you need to implement to create your own Dataset?
7. Why do we call convert when we open an image from Imagenette?

8. What does ~ do? How is it useful for splitting training and validation sets?

9. Does ~ work with the L or Tensor classes? How about NumPy arrays, Python lists, or Pandas DataFrames?

10. What is ProcessPoolExecutor?

11. How does L.range(self.ds) work?

12. What is __iter__?

13. What is first?

14. What is permute? Why is it needed?

15. What is a recursive function? How does it help us define the parameters method?

16. Write a recursive function that returns the first 20 items of the Fibonacci sequence.

17. What is super?

18. Why do subclasses of Module need to override forward instead of defining __call__?

19. In ConvLayer, why does init depend on act?

20. Why does Sequential need to call register_modules?

21. Write a hook that prints the shape of every layer's activations.

22. What is LogSumExp?

23. Why is log_softmax useful?

24. What is GetAttr? How is it helpful for callbacks?

25. Reimplement one of the callbacks in this chapter without inheriting from Callback or GetAttr.

26. What does Learner.__call__ do?

27. What is getattr? (Note the case difference from GetAttr!)

28. Why is there a try block in fit?

29. Why do we check for model.training in one_batch?

30. What is store_attr?

31. What is the purpose of TrackResults.before_epoch?

32. What does model.cuda do? How does it work?

33. Why do we need to check model.training in LRFinder and OneCycle?

34. Use cosine annealing in OneCycle.

Further Research

1. Write `resnet18` from scratch (refer to Chapter 14 as needed), and train it with the `Learner` in this chapter.

2. Implement a batchnorm layer from scratch and use it in your `resnet18`.

3. Write a Mixup callback for use in this chapter.

4. Add momentum to SGD.

5. Pick a few features that you're interested in from fastai (or any other library) and implement them with the objects created in this chapter.

6. Pick a research paper that's not yet implemented in fastai or PyTorch and do so with the objects you created in this chapter. Then:

   - Port the paper over to fastai.

   - Submit a pull request to fastai, or create your own extension module and release it.

   Hint: you may find it helpful to use `nbdev` (*https://nbdev.fast.ai*) to create and deploy your package.

CHAPTER 20

Concluding Thoughts

Congratulations! You've made it! If you have worked through all of the notebooks to this point, you have joined the small, but growing group of people who are able to harness the power of deep learning to solve real problems. You may not feel that way —in fact, you probably don't. We have seen again and again that students who complete the fast.ai courses dramatically underestimate their effectiveness as deep learning practitioners. We've also seen that these people are often underestimated by others with a classic academic background. So if you are to rise above your own expectations and the expectations of others, what you do next, after closing this book, is even more important than what you've done to get to this point.

The most important thing is to keep the momentum going. In fact, as you know from your study of optimizers, momentum is something that can build upon itself! So think about what you can do now to maintain and accelerate your deep learning journey. Figure 20-1 can give you a few ideas.

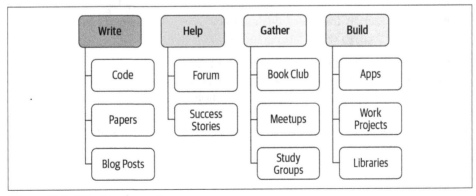

Figure 20-1. What to do next

We've talked a lot in this book about the value of writing, whether it be code or prose. But perhaps you haven't quite written as much as you had hoped so far. That's OK! Now is a great chance to turn that around. You have a lot to say at this point. Perhaps you have tried some experiments on a dataset that other people don't seem to have looked at in quite the same way. Tell the world about it! Or perhaps you are thinking about trying out some ideas that occurred to you while you were reading—now is a great time to turn those ideas into code.

If you'd like to share your ideas, one fairly low-key place to do so is the fast.ai forums (*https://forums.fast.ai*). You will find that the community there is very supportive and helpful, so please do drop by and let us know what you've been up to. Or see if you can answer a few questions for those folks who are earlier in their journey than you.

And if you do have some successes, big or small, in your deep learning journey, be sure to let us know! Posting about them on the forums is especially helpful, because learning about the successes of other students can be extremely motivating.

Perhaps the most important approach for many people to stay connected with their learning journey is to build a community around it. For instance, you could try to set up a small deep learning meetup in your local neighborhood, or a study group, or even offer to do a talk at a local meetup about what you've learned so far or some particular aspect that interested you. It's OK that you are not the world's leading expert just yet—the important thing to remember is that you now know about plenty of stuff that other people don't, so they are very likely to appreciate your perspective.

Another community event that many people find useful is a regular book club or paper reading club. You might find some in your neighborhood already, and if not, you could try to get one started. Even if there is just one other person doing it with you, it will help give you the support and encouragement to get going.

If you are not in a location where it's easy to get together with like-minded folks in person, drop by the forums, because people are always starting up virtual study groups. These generally involve a bunch of folks getting together over video chat once a week or so to discuss a deep learning topic.

Hopefully, by this point, you have a few little projects that you've put together and experiments that you've run. Our recommendation for your next step is to pick one of these and make it as good as you can. Really polish it up into the best piece of work that you can—something you are really proud of. This will force you to go much deeper into a topic, which will test your understanding and give you the opportunity to see what you can do when you put your mind to it.

Also, you may want to take a look at the fast.ai free online course (*https:// course.fast.ai*) that covers the same material as this book. Sometimes, seeing the same material in two ways can really help to crystallize the ideas. In fact, human learning researchers have found that one of the best ways to learn material is to see the same thing from different angles, described in different ways.

Your final mission, should you choose to accept it, is to take this book and give it to somebody you know—and get somebody else started on their own deep learning journey!

Creating a Blog

In Chapter 2, we suggested that you might want to try blogging as a way to help digest the information you're reading and practicing. But what if you don't have a blog already? Which platform should you use?

Unfortunately, when it comes to blogging, it seems like you have to make a difficult decision: either use a platform that makes it easy but subjects you and your readers to advertisements, paywalls, and fees, or spend hours setting up your own hosting service and weeks learning about all kinds of intricate details. Perhaps the biggest benefit to the "do-it-yourself" approach is that you really own your own posts, rather than being at the whim of a service provider and their decisions about how to monetize your content in the future.

It turns out, however, that you can have the best of both worlds!

Blogging with GitHub Pages

A great solution is to host your blog on a platform called GitHub Pages (*https:// pages.github.com*), which is free, has no ads or paywall, and makes your data available in a standard way such that you can at any time move your blog to another host. But all the approaches we've seen to using GitHub Pages have required knowledge of the command line and arcane tools that only software developers are likely to be familiar with. For instance, GitHub's own documentation (*https://oreil.ly/xemwJ*) on setting up a blog includes a long list of instructions that involve installing the Ruby programming language, using the `git` command-line tool, copying over version numbers, and more—17 steps in total!

To cut down on the hassle, we've created an easy approach that allows you to use an *entirely browser-based interface* for all your blogging needs. You will be up and running with your new blog within about five minutes. It doesn't cost anything, and you can easily add your own custom domain to it if you wish to. In this section, we'll explain how to do it, using a template we've created called `fast_template`. (NB: be sure to check the book's website (*https://book.fast.ai*) for the latest blog recommendations, since new tools are always coming out.)

Creating the Repository

You'll need an account on GitHub, so head over there now and create an account if you don't have one already. Normally, GitHub is used by software developers for writing code, and they use a sophisticated command-line tool to work with it—but we're going to show you an approach that doesn't use the command line at all!

To get started, point your browser to *https://github.com/fastai/fast_template/generate* (make sure you're logged in). This will allow you to create a place to store your blog, called a *repository*. You will see a screen like the one in Figure A-1. Note that you have to enter your repository name using the *exact* format shown here—that is, your GitHub username followed by `.github.io`.

Figure A-1. Creating your repository

Once you've entered that, and any description you like, click "Create repository from template." You have the choice to make the repository "private," but since you are creating a blog that you want other people to read, having the underlying files publicly available hopefully won't be a problem for you.

Now, let's set up your home page!

Setting Up Your Home Page

When readers arrive at your blog, the first thing that they will see is the content of a file called *index.md*. This is a Markdown (*https://oreil.ly/aVOhs*) file. Markdown is a powerful yet simple way of creating formatted text, such as bullet points, italics, hyperlinks, and so forth. It is very widely used, including for all the formatting in Jupyter notebooks, nearly every part of the GitHub site, and many other places all over the internet. To create Markdown text, you can just type in plain English and then add some special characters to add special behavior. For instance, if you type a * character before and after a word or phrase, that will put it in *italics*. Let's try it now.

To open the file, click its filename in GitHub. To edit it, click the pencil icon at the far righthand side of the screen, as shown in Figure A-2.

Figure A-2. Edit this file

You can add to, edit, or replace the text that you see. Click the "Preview changes" button (Figure A-3) to see what your Markdown text will look like in your blog. Lines that you have added or changed will appear with a green bar on the lefthand side.

Figure A-3. Preview changes to catch any mistakes

To save your changes, scroll to the bottom of the page and click "Commit changes," as shown in Figure A-4. On GitHub, to *commit* something means to save it to the Git-Hub server.

Figure A-4. Commit your changes to save them

Next, you should configure your blog's settings. To do so, click the file called *_config.yml* and then click the edit button as you did for the index file. Change the title, description, and GitHub username values (see Figure A-5). You need to leave the names before the colons in place, and type your new values in after the colon (and a space) on each line. You can also add to your email address and Twitter username if you wish, but note that these will appear on your public blog if you fill them in here.

```
1    # Welcome to Jekyll!
2    #
3    # This config file is meant for settings that affect your whole blog.
4    #
5    # If you need help with YAML syntax, here are some quick references for you:
6    # https://learn-the-web.algonquindesign.ca/topics/markdown-yaml-cheat-sheet/#yaml
7    # https://learnxinyminutes.com/docs/yaml/
8
9    title: Edit _config.yml to set your title!
10   description: This is where the description of your site will go. You should change it by editing the _config.yml file.
11   github_username: jph00
```

Figure A-5. Fill in the config file

After you're done, commit your changes just as you did with the index file; then wait a minute or so while GitHub processes your new blog. Point your web browser to *<username>.github.io* (replacing *<username>* with your GitHub username). You should see your blog, which will look something like Figure A-6.

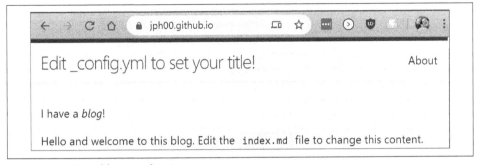

Figure A-6. Your blog is online!

Creating Posts

Now you're ready to create your first post. All your posts will go in the *_posts* folder. Click that now, and then click the "Create file" button. You need to be careful to name your file using the format *<year>-<month>-<day>-<name>.md*, as shown in Figure A-7, where *<year>* is a four-digit number, and *<month>* and *<day>* are two-digit numbers. *<name>* can be anything you want that will help you remember what this post was about. The *.md* extension is for Markdown documents.

Figure A-7. Naming your posts

You can then type the contents of your first post. The only rule is that the first line of your post must be a Markdown heading. This is created by putting # at the start of a line, as seen in Figure A-8 (that creates a level-1 heading, which you should just use once at the start of your document; you can create level-2 headings using ##, level 3 with ###, and so forth).

Figure A-8. Markdown syntax for a title

As before, you can click the Preview button to see how your Markdown formatting will look (Figure A-9).

Figure A-9. What the previous Markdown syntax will look like on your blog

And you will need to click the "Commit new file" button to save it to GitHub, as shown in Figure A-10.

Figure A-10. Commit your changes to save them

Have a look at your blog home page again, and you will see that this post has now appeared—Figure A-11 shows the result with the sample post we just added. Remember that you will need to wait a minute or so for GitHub to process the request before the file shows up.

Figure A-11. Your first post is live!

You may have noticed that we provided a sample blog post, which you can go ahead and delete now. Go to your _posts_ folder, as before, and click _2020-01-14-welcome.md_. Then click the trash icon on the far right, as shown in Figure A-12.

Figure A-12. Delete the sample blog post

In GitHub, nothing actually changes until you commit—including when you delete a file! So, after you click the trash icon, scroll down to the bottom of the page and commit your changes.

You can include images in your posts by adding a line of Markdown like the following:

```
![Image description](images/filename.jpg)
```

For this to work, you will need to put the image inside your _images_ folder. To do this, click the _images_ folder, and then click the "Upload files" button (Figure A-13).

Figure A-13. Upload a file from your computer

Now let's see how to do all of this directly from your computer.

Synchronizing GitHub and Your Computer

There are lots of reasons you might want to copy your blog content from GitHub to your computer—you might want to be able to read or edit your posts offline, or maybe you'd like a backup in case something happens to your GitHub repository.

GitHub does more than just let you copy your repository to your computer; it lets you _synchronize_ it with your computer. That means you can make changes on GitHub, and they'll copy over to your computer; and you can make changes on your computer, and they'll copy over to GitHub. You can even let other people access and modify your blog, and their changes and your changes will be automatically combined the next time you sync.

To make this work, you have to install an application called GitHub Desktop (*https://desktop.github.com*) on your computer. It runs on Mac, Windows, and Linux. Follow the directions to install it, and when you run, it'll ask you to log in to GitHub and select the repository to sync. Click "Clone a repository from the Internet," as shown in Figure A-14.

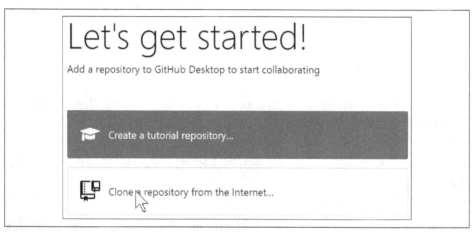

Figure A-14. Clone your repository on GitHub Desktop

Once GitHub has finished syncing your repo, you'll be able to click "View the files of your repository in Explorer" (or Finder), as shown in Figure A-15, and you'll see the local copy of your blog! Try editing one of the files on your computer. Then return to GitHub Desktop, and you'll see the Sync button is waiting for you to press it. When you click it, your changes will be copied over to GitHub, where you'll see them reflected on the website.

Figure A-15. Viewing your files locally

If you haven't used `git` before, GitHub Desktop is a great way to get started. As you'll discover, it's a fundamental tool used by most data scientists. Another tool that we hope you now love is Jupyter Notebook—and there's a way to write your blog directly with that too!

Jupyter for Blogging

You can also write blog posts using Jupyter notebooks. Your Markdown cells, code cells, and all the outputs will appear in your exported blog post. The best way to do this may have changed by the time you are reading this book, so check out the book's website (*https://book.fast.ai*) for the latest information. As we write this, the easiest way to create a blog from notebooks is to use `fastpages` (*http://fastpages.fast.ai*), a more advanced version of `fast_template`.

To blog with a notebook, just pop it in the *_notebooks* folder in your blog repo, and it will appear in your list of blog posts. When you write your notebook, write whatever you want your audience to see. Since most writing platforms make it hard to include code and outputs, many of us are in the habit of including fewer real examples than we should. This is a great way to instead get into the habit of including lots of examples as you write.

Often, you'll want to hide boilerplate such as import statements. You can add `#hide` to the top of any cell to make it not show up in output. Jupyter displays the result of the last line of a cell, so there's no need to include `print`. (Including extra code that isn't needed means there's more cognitive overhead for the reader; so don't include code that you don't really need!)

Data Project Checklist

There's a lot more to creating useful data projects than just training an accurate model! When Jeremy used to do consulting, he'd always seek to understand an organization's context for developing data projects based on the following considerations, summarized in Figure B-1:

Strategy
> What is the organization trying to do (*objective*), and what can it change to do it better (*levers*)?

Data
> Is the organization capturing the necessary data and making it available?

Analytics
> What kinds of insights would be useful to the organization?

Implementation
> What organizational capabilities are available?

Maintenance
> What systems are in place to track changes in the operational environment?

Constraints
> What constraints need to be considered in each of the preceding areas?

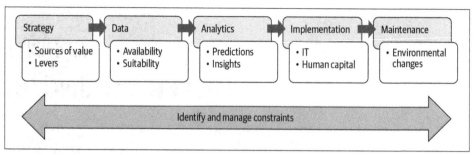

Figure B-1. The analytics value chain

He developed a questionnaire that he had clients fill out before a project started, and then throughout the project he'd help them refine their answers. This questionnaire is based on decades of projects across many industries, including agriculture, mining, banking, brewing, telecoms, retail, and more.

Before we go through the analytics value chain, the first part of the questionnaire has to do with the most important employees for your data project: data scientists.

Data Scientists

Data scientists should have a clear path to becoming senior executives, and there should also be hiring plans in place to bring data experts directly into senior executive roles. In a data-driven organization, data scientists should be among the highest-paid employees. Systems should be in place to allow data scientists throughout the organization to collaborate and learn from each other.

- What data science skills are currently in the organization?
- How are data scientists being recruited?
- How are people with data science skills being identified within the organization?
- What skills are being looked for? How are they being judged? How were those skills selected as being important?
- What data science consulting is being used? In which situations is data science outsourced? How is this work transferred to the organization?
- How much are data scientists being paid? Who do they report to? How are their skills kept current?
- What is the career path for data scientists?
- How many executives have strong data analysis expertise?
- How is work for data scientists selected and allocated?
- What software and hardware do data scientists have access to?

Strategy

All data projects should be based on solving strategically important problems. Therefore, an understanding of business strategy must come first.

- What are the five most important strategic issues at the organization today?
- What data is available to help deal with these issues?
- Is a data-driven approach being used for these issues? Are data scientists working on these?
- What are the profit drivers that the organization can most strongly impact? (See Figure B-2.)

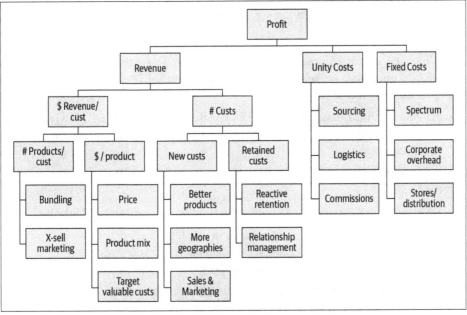

Figure B-2. Factors that may be important profit drivers at an organization

- For each of those key profit drivers identified, what are the specific actions and decisions that the organization can take that might influence that driver, including both operational actions (e.g., call customer) and strategic decisions (e.g., release new product)?
- For each of the most important actions and decisions, what data might be available (either within the organization, or from a vendor, or that could be collected in the future) that may help to optimize the outcome?

- Based on the preceding analysis, what are the biggest opportunities for data-driven analysis within the organization?
- For each opportunity:
  — What value driver is it designed to influence?
  — What specific actions or decisions will it drive?
  — How will these actions and decisions be connected to the project's results?
  — What is the estimated ROI of the project?
  — What time constraints and deadlines, if any, may impact it?

Data

Without data, we can't train models! Data also needs to be available, integrated, and verifiable.

- What data platforms does the organization have? These may include data marts, OLAP cubes, data warehouses, Hadoop clusters, OLTP systems, departmental spreadsheets, and so forth.
- Provide any information that has been collated that provides an overview of data availability at the organization, and current work and future plans for building data platforms.
- What tools and processes are available to move data between systems and formats?
- How are the data sources accessed by different groups of users and admins?
- What data access tools (e.g., database clients, OLAP clients, in-house software, SAS) are available to the organization's data scientists and sysadmins? How many people use each tool, and what are their positions in the organization?
- How are users informed of new systems, changes to systems, new and changed data elements, and so forth? Provide examples.
- How are decisions made regarding data access restrictions? How are requests to access secured data managed? By whom? Based on what criteria? How long is the average time to respond? What percentage of requests are accepted? How is this tracked?
- How does the organization decide when to collect additional data or purchase external data? Provide examples.
- What data has been used so far to analyze recent data-driven projects? What has been found to be most useful? What was not useful? How was this judged?
- What additional internal data may provide insights useful for data-driven decision making for proposed projects? What about external data?

- What are the possible constraints or challenges in accessing or incorporating this data?

- What changes to data collection, coding, integration, etc. have occurred in the last two years that may have impacted the interpretation or availability of the collected data?

Analytics

Data scientists need to be able to access up-to-date tools appropriate for their own particular needs. New tools should be regularly assessed to see if they offer a significant improvement over current approaches.

- What analytics tools are used at the organization and by whom? How are they selected, configured, and maintained?

- What is the process to get additional analytical tools set up on a client machine? What is the average time to complete this? What percentage of requests are accepted?

- How are analytical systems built by external consultants transferred to the organization? Are external contractors asked to restrict the systems used to ensure that the results conform to internal infrastructure?

- In what situations has cloud processing been used? What are the plans for using the cloud?

- In what situations have external experts been used for specialist analytics? How has this been managed? How have the experts been identified and selected?

- What analytics tools have been tried for recent projects?

- What worked, and what didn't? Why?

- Provide any outputs that are available from work done to date for these projects.

- How have the results of this analysis been judged? What metrics? Compared to what benchmarks? How do you know whether a model is "good enough"?

- In what situations does the organization use visualization, versus tabular reporting, versus predictive modeling (and similar machine learning tools)? For more advanced modeling approaches, how are the models calibrated and tested? Provide examples.

Implementation

IT constraints are often the downfall of data projects. Consider them up front!

- Provide some examples of past data-driven projects that have had successful and unsuccessful implementations, and provide details on the IT integration and human capital challenges and how they were faced.

- How is the validity of analytical models confirmed prior to implementation? How are they benchmarked?

- How are the performance requirements defined for analytical project implementations (in terms of speed and accuracy)?

- For the proposed projects, provide information about the following:
  - What IT systems will be used to support the data-driven decisions and actions
  - How this IT integration will be done
  - What alternatives are available that may require less IT integration
  - What jobs will be impacted by the data-driven approaches
  - How these staff will be trained, monitored, and supported
  - What implementation challenges may occur
  - Which stakeholders will be needed to ensure implementation success, and how they might perceive these projects and their potential impact on them

Maintenance

Unless you track your models carefully, you may find them leading you to disaster.

- How are analytical systems built by third parties maintained? When are they transferred to internal teams?

- How are the effectiveness of models tracked? When does the organization decide to rebuild models?

- How are data changes communicated internally, and how are they managed?

- How do data scientists work with software engineers to ensure that algorithms are correctly implemented?

- When are test cases developed, and how are they maintained?

- When is refactoring performed on code? How is the correctness and performance of models maintained and validated during refactoring?

- How are maintenance and support requirements logged? How are these logs used?

Constraints

For each project being considered, enumerate potential constraints that may impact the success of the project.

- Will IT systems need to be modified or developed to use the results of the project? Are there simpler implementations that could avoid substantial IT changes? If so, how would using a simplified implementation result in a significant reduction in impact?
- What regulatory constraints exist on data collection, analysis, or implementation? Have the relevant legislation and precedents been examined recently? What workarounds might exist?
- What organizational constraints exist, including in culture, skills, or structure?
- What management constraints are there?
- Have there been any past analytics projects that may impact how the organization views data-driven approaches?

Index

objectives via Drivetrain Approach, 64
occupations and gender, 112, 113
OCR (see numerical digit classifier)
one-hot encoding
    definition, 225
    embedding categorical variables, 259-265,
        297
        multiple columns for variable levels, 297
    entity embedding contrasted, 278
    label smoothing, 249
    look-up index as one-hot-encoded vector,
        259
    multi-label classifier, 225, 227
online advertisement bias, 112
online applications (see web applications)
online resources (see web resources)
optical character recognition (see numerical
    digit classifier)
optimization
    Adam as default, 479
    creating an optimizer, 174-180
    generic optimizer, 473
    gradient descent, 162, 182
    layers and, 180
    module parameters, 265
    nonlinearity added, 176
    numerical digit classifier, 170-180
    pet breeds image classifier, 194-203
    stochastic gradient descent, 170-180
ordinal columns in tabular data, 286
out-of-domain data, 60
    image classifier in production, 87
out-of-memory error, 214
outputs
    cells containing executable code, 16, 44
    forward hook for custom behavior, 519
    image, 18
    results of last execution, 44
    table, 17
    text, 18
    web display Output widget, 81
overfitting
    avoid only when occurring, 30
    definition, 40
    importance of, 30, 468
    layers and, 30
    learning rate finder, 205
    model memorizing training set, 29
    reducing, 468

    regularizing RNNs against, 394
    retrain from scratch, 213
    training versus validation loss, 212
    validation set, 49
        hyperparameter picked by, 231
    weight decay against, 264
O'Neill, Cathy, 115

P

padding a convolution, 411
Pandas library
    DataFrame
        color-code image values, 136
        DataLoaders object from, 222-226
        multi-label CSV file, 220
    dataset viewing, 286
    fastai TabularPandas class, 290, 318
    get_dummies for categorical variables, 297
    NumPy needed, 283
    tabular data processing, 283, 318
    tutorial, 222
papers (see research papers)
Papert, Seymour, 6
Parallel Distributed Processing (PDP) book
    (Rumelhart, McClelland, and PDP Research
    Group), 6
parameters
    architecture requiring many, 32
    calling module calls forward method, 261
    deeper models and, 180
    definition, 40, 181
    derivative of a function, 153
    exporting models, 78
    hyperparameters, 49
        random forest insensitivity, 299
        validation set picking threshold, 231
    importance of, 32
    loss function selected by fastai, 194
    machine learning concepts, 21, 24
    more accuracy from more parameters, 213
    neural networks beyond understanding, 88
    Parameter class, 266
        building Learner class from scratch,
           531-534
Parr, Terence, 294
partial function to bind arguments, 229
PASCAL multi-label dataset, 220
path to dataset
    ls method, 79, 135, 186

Path object returned, 27
PDP Research Group, 6
Pearl, Judea, 310
pedophiles and YouTube, 103
Perceptrons book (Minsky and Papert), 6
performance of model as loss, 24, 40
Perkins, David, 9
person's face center in image (see key point
    model)
pet breeds image classifier (see image classifier
    models)
pet images dataset, 17, 28, 186, 364
pickle system for save method, 292
PIL images, 135
Pipeline class, 359
Pitts, Walter, 5
pixels
    image basics, 133-136
    pixel count
        image sizes same, 71, 189
        pretrained models, 28
        size tradeoffs, 28
        sizing difficulties, 73
        tensor shape, 139
    pixel similarity, 137-142
plain text data approach, 283
PointBlock, 233
policy's role in ethics, 123-126
    rights and policy, 125
positive feedback loop, 26
precision of numbers and training, 214
predictions
    activations transformed into, 195
    bagging, 298-323
    button for web application, 82
    definition, 24
    dependent variable for, 287
    hypothetical world of, 310
    independent variable, 24, 71
    inference instead of training, 79
    inference with image classifier, 79
    as machine learning limitation, 25
    metric measuring quality, 31
    model changing system behavior, 89
    model overconfidence, 212
    movie recommendation system, 46
    overfitting and, 30
    predictive modeling competitions, 51
    predictive policing algorithm, 89

random forest confidence, 302
sales from stores, 278
    (see also tabular data)
softmax sum of 1 requirement, 227
stroke prediction, 62, 112
viewing, 195
prerequisite for book, xx
presizing, 189
pretrained models
    accuracy from, 31
    convolutional neural network parameter, 31
    definition, 31, 40
    discriminative learning rates, 210
    fine-tuning first model, 17
    first model, 17
    freezing, 207
    last layer and, 31, 207
    NLP English language, 330
    normalization of data, 242
        statistics distributed with model, 242
    pixel count required, 28
    recommendation system rarity, 47
    self-supervised learning for, 329
    tabular model rarity, 46
    transfer learning, 32, 162
        freezing, 207
    Wikipedia for pretraining NLP, 329
privacy
    deployed apps, 85
    regulation needed, 124
    rights and policy, 125
probabilistic matrix factorization, 271
process end-to-end
    actionable outcomes via Drivetrain
        Approach, 63
    applicability of deep learning to problem, 60
    begin in known areas, 59, 129
        (see also beginning)
    capabilities and contraints of deep learning,
        57
    data availability, 58
    data biases, 68
    data cleaning, 77
    data gathering, 65-68
    DataLoaders, 70-72
        customization, 70
    deployment
        app from notebook, 82
        Binder free app hosting, 84

source code of function displayed, 335
special tokens, 334
spec_add_spaces, 335
Splunk.com fraud detection, 38
spreadsheet data for models, 45
starting (see beginning)
stem in convolutional neural network, 452, 460
stochastic gradient descent (SGD)
    about, 23, 148-153, 471
    backward, 155
    building Learner class from scratch, 537
    calculating gradients, 153-155
    cyclical momentum, 431
    example end-to-end, 157-162
    mini-batches, 170
    momentum, 474-477
    multilayered neural networks learned with,
        282
    optimization of numerical digit classifier,
        170-180
    SGD class, 175, 471-474
    stepping with learning rate, 156-157
    summarizing, 162
store sales predictions
    embedding distance and store distance, 280
stride-1 convolutions, 412
stride-2 convolutions, 411
    increasing number of features, 419
stroke prediction, 62, 112
subword tokenization, 336
summary method
    debugging image dataset, 192
    debugging tabular dataset, 226
    debugging text dataset, 342
Suresh, Harini, 105
Sweeney, Latanya, 95
symbolic computation library, 510
SymPy library and calculus, 510
Syntactic Structures book (Chomsky), 188
Szegedy, Christian, 250, 435

T

Tabular classes, 322
tabular data for models
    about, 45, 277
    advice for modeling, 325
    architecture, 466
    categorical embeddings, 277
    current state of, 62

as data type, 186
    dataset for deep dive, 284
        data leakage, 310
        date handling, 289
        examining data, 285
        neural network model, 318
        ordinal columns, 286
        overfitting, 295
        TabularPandas class, 290, 318
    decision trees as first approach, 283
        about, 282, 287
        bagging, 298-323
        displaying tree, 292-295
        libraries for, 283
        metric, 287, 295, 301
        training, 288-296
    deep learning not best starting point, 282
    entity embedding, 278
    model interpretation, 302
        data leakage, 310
        feature importances, 303
        partial dependence, 308
        removing low-importance variables, 305
        removing redundant features, 306
        tree interpreter, 312
        tree variance for prediction confidence,
            302
    multi-label classification, 220-222
    neural network model, 318
    ordinal columns, 286
    predicting sales from stores, 278
    pretrained model rarity, 46
    recommendation systems as, 62
TabularPandas class, 290
TabularProc, 290
tech industry and gender, 121
temporal activation regularization, 397
tensor core support by GPUs, 214
tensors
    about, 143
    all images in directory, 137
    APIs, 144
    broadcasting, 147, 147
    color image as rank-3 tensor, 423
    column selected, 144
    creating a tensor, 144
    definition, 181
    displaying as images, 138
    elementwise arithmetic, 496

About the Authors

Jeremy Howard is an entrepreneur, business strategist, developer, and educator. Jeremy is a founding researcher at fast.ai, a research institute dedicated to making deep learning more accessible. He is also a Distinguished Research Scientist at the University of San Francisco, a faculty member at Singularity University, and a Young Global Leader with the World Economic Forum.

Jeremy's most recent startup, Enlitic, was the first company to apply deep learning to medicine, and was selected as one of the world's top 50 smartest companies by MIT Tech Review in both 2015 and 2016. Jeremy was previously president and chief scientist at the data science platform Kaggle, where he was the top-ranked participant in international machine learning competitions for two years running. He was the founding CEO of two successful Australian startups (FastMail and Optimal Decisions Group, purchased by Lexis-Nexis). Before that, he spent eight years in management consulting, at McKinsey & Co and AT Kearney. Jeremy has invested in, mentored, and advised many startups, and contributed to many open source projects.

In addition to being a regular guest on Australia's highest-rated breakfast news program, he has given a popular talk on TED.com and produced a number of data science and web development tutorials and discussions.

Sylvain Gugger is a research engineer at HuggingFace. He was previously a research scientist at fast.ai, with a focus on making deep learning more accessible by designing and improving techniques that allow models to train fast on limited resources.

Prior to this, he taught computer science and mathematics in a CPGE program in France for seven years. The CPGE are highly selective classes taken by handpicked students after finishing high school to prepare them for the competitive exam to enter the country's top engineering and business schools. Sylvain has also written several books covering the entire curriculum he was teaching, published at Éditions Dunod.

Sylvain is an alumnus of the École Normale Supérieure (Paris, France), where he studied mathematics, and has a master's degree in mathematics from the University of Paris XI (Orsay, France).

Acknowledgments

We'd particularly like to highlight the amazing work of Alexis Gallagher and Rachel Thomas. Alexis was far more than a technical editor. His influence is felt in every chapter, and he wrote many of the most insightful and compelling explanations in this book. He also provided deep insight into the design of the fastai library, especially the data block API. Rachel provided most of the material for Chapter 3, and also provided input on ethics issues throughout the book.

Thank you to the fast.ai community, including the thirty thousand members of *forums.fast.ai*, the five hundred contributors to the fastai library, and the hundreds of thousands of *course.fast.ai* students. Special thanks to fastai contributors who have gone the extra mile, including Zachary Muller, Radek Osmulski, Andrew Shaw, Stas Bekman, Lucas Vasquez, and Boris Dayma. And also to those researchers who have used fastai for groundbreaking research, such as Sebastian Ruder, Piotr Czapla, Marcin Kardas, Julian Eisenschlos, Nils Strodthoff, Patrick Wagner, Markus Wenzel, Wojciech Samek, Paul Maragakis, Hunter Nisonoff, Brian Cole, and David E. Shaw. Thank you also to Hamel Hussain, who has created some of the most inspiring projects with fastai, and has been the driving force behind the `fastpages` blogging platform. And huge thanks to Chris Lattner, for his inspiration in bringing ideas from Swift and his enormous knowledge of programming language design to our many discussions, which greatly influenced the design of fastai.

Thank you to all the folks at O'Reilly for their work to make this book far better than we could have imagined, including Rebecca Novak, who ensured that all the notebooks for the book would be freely available, and that the book would be published in full color; Rachel Head, whose comments improved every part of the book; and Melissa Potter, who helped ensure that the process kept moving forward.

Thank you to all our technical reviewers—an extraordinary group of people who gave insightful and thoughtful feedback: Aurélien Géron, the author of one of the best machine learning books we've ever read, who was generous enough to help us make our book better too; Joe Spisak, PyTorch product manager; Miguel De Icaza, the legend behind Gnome, Xamarian, and much more; Ross Wightman, creator of our favorite PyTorch model zoo; Radek Osmulski, one of the most brilliant fast.ai alumni we've had the pleasure of getting to know; Dmytro Mishkin, cofounder of the Kornia project and author of some of our favorite deep learning papers; Fred Monroe, who has helped us with so many projects; and Andrew Shaw, director at WAMRI and creator of the wonderful *musicautobot.com*.

Special thanks to Soumith Chintala and Adam Paszke for creating PyTorch, and the whole PyTorch team for making it such a joy to use. And of course, thank you to our families for all their support and patience throughout this big project.

Colophon

The animal on the cover of *Deep Learning for Coders with fastai and PyTorch* is a boarfish (*Capros aper*), the only known member of its genus. Mostly found in eastern Atlantic waters, this fish inhabits an area that spans from Norway to as far south as Senegal, including the Aegean and Mediterranean seas. Boarfish can be found at depths ranging from 130–1,968 feet in the pelagic zone: the section of the open sea that is neither close to the sea floor nor the shore and home to the largest aquatic habitat on Earth.

The boarfish is small and reddish-orange in coloration, with large eyes and a protractile mouth. Its body is compressed, deep, and rhombic, shaped as wide as it is high. Boarfish typically measure 5 inches long, but as a sexually dimorphic species, the females are larger; the record length stands at 11 inches. Although vulnerable to prey due to their size, these shoaling fish travel in groups, allowing them enhanced defense against predators as well as making it easier for them to mate and find food. Its closest relatives are the shortspine boarfish (*Antigonia combatia*), a native to tropical and sub-tropical waters and the deepbody boarfish (*Antigonia capros*), found in the neighboring western Atlantic waters.

While the current conservation status of the boarfish is of "Least Concern," many of the animals on O'Reilly covers are endangered; all of them are important to the world.

The cover illustration is by Karen Montgomery, based on a black and white engraving from *Johnson's Natural History*. The cover fonts are Gilroy Semibold and Guardian Sans. The text font is Adobe Minion Pro; the heading font is Adobe Myriad Condensed; and the code font is Dalton Maag's Ubuntu Mono.

O'REILLY®

There's much more where this came from.

Experience books, videos, live online training courses, and more from O'Reilly and our 200+ partners—all in one place.

Learn more at oreilly.com/online-learning

Printed in the USA
CPSIA information can be obtained
at www.ICGtesting.com
JSHW051643180324
59436JS00013B/201